MORE GREAT TALES OF
CRIME & DETECTION

Short Stories featuring
the World's Most Famous Detectives

MORE GREAT TALES OF CRIME & DETECTION

Short Stories featuring the World's Most Famous Detectives

Edited by
PETER HAINING

CHARTWELL
BOOKS, INC.

Published by Chartwell Books
a division of Book Sales, Inc
114 Northfield Avenue, Raritan Center
Edison, New Jersey 08818

This edition produced for sale in the U.S.A.,
its territories and dependencies only

First published in Great Britain in 1994 by Orion
An imprint of Orion Books Ltd
Orion House, 5 Upper St Martin's Lane, London WC2H 9EA

Typeset by Deltatype Ltd, Ellesmere Port, Cheshire
Printed in Great Britain by Clays Ltd, St Ives plc

Contents

Contents

Contents

In Memory of
JACK WARNER
Dixon of Dock Green
– my first Cop on the Box

Introduction

It has been said – though by whom no one is quite sure – that police work is ninety-nine per cent boredom and one per cent terror. This being so, why should television serials about the men and women who tackle crime be amongst the most popular and longest-running programmes on TV all over the world? What, for example, compelled as many as nineteen million viewers in Britain in January 1993 to tune in to the final episode about the introverted Inspector Morse, while somewhere in excess of sixteen million people still continue to watch *Taggart* ten years after the dour Scottish policeman made his debut? There are plenty of other instances of this public fascination with the custodians of the law – series which feature the likes of P.D. James's Dalgleish, Ruth Rendell's Wexford and Lynda La Plante's Jane Tennison to name but three – all attracting audiences in excess of the magical ten million figure. While even old series that now enjoy cult status such as *The Untouchables, The Sweeney, Columbo, Kojak, Cagney and Lacey* and a number of others are all drawing substantial followings on satellite and cable TV.

Nor can it be argued that this is a new phenomenon. Series about those who seek to maintain law and order – the Crimebusters – have been a part of television since its inception half a century ago. Indeed, even before the first policemen made their appearances on the flickering, black and white programmes offered by the new medium, their predecessors had already been favourites on the radio and in the movies for years.

If there *is* an explanation for this continuing fascination, then I believe it has nothing to do with the psychology of crime, a morbid fascination with violence and death, or even the vicarious thrill of watching from the safety of the armchair while good attempts to overcome evil. It is simply that the police series on television offers a narrative puzzle that challenges the viewer. Nor does it have much to do with time or place: whether the setting is period (*Inspector Alleyn*) or contemporary (*The Bill*) the appeal is still the same: whodunnit and, possibly, why?

As drama, the crime series is in the unique position of being able to tell any story, encompassing human life at every level of society. It is also true that despite a certain amount of evidence to the contrary, the public at large still retains its abiding belief in policemen who are decent, truthful and perceived to have a bit of character about them. And most people, it seems to me, like stories about crime on TV because they provide a sense of certainty which is not available in real life.

Those who provide us with this sort of entertainment, whether it is in print, broadcast on the radio, or on the screen, learned these facts years ago. The first true story of detection – or 'ratiocination' as it was called – Edgar Allan Poe's *The Murders in the Rue Morgue*, which he wrote in 1841, may have only been around for a little over a century, but the chord it struck found such a universal appeal and has been so effectively translated into the other mediums, that it is now impossible to imagine a world without the fictional crime fighter. As Colin Dexter, the highly successful creator of *Morse*, reflected in an interview a short while ago: 'Law and order is a big issue, people are worried about a crime-ridden society. Part of the appeal of crime literature and TV is that the wrong is always righted.'

In my previous collection of crime short stories based on television series, I concentrated very much on the detectives, both the amateurs and the professionals, British, American and even some from Europe and further afield. In this new anthology the focus has been shifted to the men and women of the police forces who have proved to be equally popular with viewers since the day the first TV sets arrived in the nation's living rooms. Cops on the box have, in fact, been as much a part of the history and development of television as news programmes, outside broadcasts and drama productions in general. Only the names and the methods of the crimebusters have changed.

Even before the outbreak of the Second World War when the BBC had just opened the world's first television service – it was then only available to a few thousand viewers living in the immediate vicinity of its headquarters, Alexandra Palace – one of its first major drama presentations was an adaptation of a crime story by Edgar Wallace, at the time probably the biggest selling thriller writer in the world. After the war, when TV was launched in America, too, a mixture of programmes featuring policemen from literature or else especially created for the medium, were soon providing regular entertainment for the public. The tradition which they began in the days when TV screens were little bigger than this book, when the pictures were in black and white and all the transmissions were live, has never seriously been under threat. There have been changes of emphasis over the years, of course, with the polite enquiry of the classic whodunnit giving way to hard-nosed and gritty realism. And if the typical contemporary American police series still does seem to favour a high-speed car chase and shoot-out, in Britain the cerebral policeman who unravels the crime by a mixture of intuition and painstaking enquiry now holds the greatest appeal.

To represent this remarkable half a century of crimebusters on TV, I have assembled a collection of stories featuring the most popular characters whose careers together span the whole era of television. Some of their names will be instantly familiar, others are perhaps less well-known – but all have contributed to the evolution of the genre, as the introductions to the stories will, I hope, make clear. The facts behind the making of these series and the stars who appeared in them are often every bit as intriguing as the stories themselves! At least I have certainly had a great deal of pleasure just 'getting the facts, Ma'am,' if I can paraphrase one of the early favourites, Sergeant Joe Friday of *Dragnet*.

I have found it particularly interesting to discover during my researches that the earliest cops on the box were normally to be found in secondary roles. In two of the very first series, for example, the BBC's *The Ringer* and the American-made *Boston Blackie*, the police officers worked in uneasy alliance with reformed criminals who operated on the very edge of the law. They were followed by lawmen who were more often than not the bewildered benefactors of the activities of gentlemen rogues such as *The Lone Wolf* and *The Falcon*. A third group were even aided by some of those who made their living by courtesy of the law like the publisher of mysteries, Jerry North, and the lawyer, John J.Malone. It was these characters who inevitably took pride of place in the billing until the advent of Sergeant Joe Friday and Britain's Fabian of the Yard who opened a new era of crime-on-TV which is still being written today.

It is also quite clear to me now that memories of many of these crimebusters have long survived the passing of their series. History shows that for a number of them there were plans they should go out with a bang – perhaps the kind of a dramatic death that Sir Arthur

Conan Doyle devised for Sherlock Holmes, sending him plunging over the Reichenbach Falls locked in mortal combat with Professor Moriarty, apparently never to be seen again. A similar fate was even discussed for Inspector Morse: he was to find true love at last and then get himself killed. But just as Conan Doyle was forced to bow to public demand and bring Holmes back from the dead, so Morse was spared this final indignity. With television continuing to look for more stories to satisfy the unceasing demands of the armchair detectives, who is to say that was not a good decision? For can *anyone* be really sure that such an exceptional policeman might not be called upon, Holmes-like, to return once again . . .

PETER HAINING,
February 1994

The Kidnapping of Inspector Mander

BY EDGAR WALLACE

The actor with the distinction of having been the first cop on the box was the tall and gentlemanly Harold Warrender who played Chief Inspector Bliss in the September 1939 BBC adaptation of Edgar Wallace's famous story, The Ringer about a reformed criminal and master of disguise, Arthur Milton, who frequents the underworld and helps the police to 'get their man'. Warrender, who had appeared on the radio (most frequently as a quiz master!) and in several films including I Spy (1933) and Mimi (1935), portrayed the Chief Inspector as an immaculately dressed, archetypal Scotland Yard man who normally went by the book, but had come to appreciate the value of the shadowy figure known as The Ringer in fighting crime in London and was not above accepting his assistance. The same could not be said for his assistant, the self-opinionated Inspector Mander (played by Gordon Harker, familiar for his roles in films as Cockney crooks or policemen) whose irritating manner not only annoyed his superior officer but even The Ringer, whose capabilities he was always denigrating. Playing The Ringer was Franklyn Dyall, a popular star of stage and screen who had made his debut in silent movies in 1916 and had actually appeared in one of the earlier screen versions of the story made in 1931 where he played Meister, the villain. For the TV adaptation – which drew on a number of the other short stories Edgar Wallace had written about The Ringer – Dyall doubled as Arthur Milton; with Judy Kelly as his beautiful wife, Cora Ann, who is often drawn into her husband's crime crusades. It was not only a landmark TV production, but one which its limited audience was actually lucky to have seen at all . . .

Although Edgar Wallace (1875–1932) had died a few years earlier, he was still widely regarded as the 'King of Thrillers' at the time of the broadcast. Indeed, the enormous debts which he had left behind at his death had, remarkably, been paid off in a matter of a few years by a vigorous reprinting of his most popular books. And even with the storm clouds of war starting to gather over the nation as Hitler became an increasing threat to peace in Europe, Wallace was still the man to provide hundreds of thousands with popular escapist reading. It was therefore, perhaps no surprise that the embryo medium of television should have turned to his works as the basis for the very first crime serial – especially as a considerable number of his books had already been adapted for radio and film. Nor that the choice of story to dramatise should have been the perennially popular, The Ringer.

Wallace's series of tales about Milton, the man who bends the law to his own purposes, had begun in 1925 with The Gaunt Stranger, which became an instant bestseller. A year later it had been adapted by Wallace himself for a very successful run on the London stage; while two years later, British Lion Pictures brought the story to the cinema starring Leslie Faber. In subsequent years, The Ringer was to become the most frequently filmed of all its author's books, and then finally made its debut on TV in September 1939 when it was introduced to the small circle of television viewers able to receive the service just days before the outbreak of the Second World War. It was, in fact, to prove the last major television drama production by the BBC prior to the closing down of the service for the duration of the war.

The production was transmitted live at a time of great uncertainty when there was already a public debate about whether entertainment should be allowed on the screen at all. 'Should the motto of entertainment in time of crisis be business as usual?' The Times asked in a leader, 'Or should entertainment be sacrificed to give short courses in first aid, instruction in fire fighting, the handling of incendiary bombs and the like?'. It is therefore perhaps not surprising to learn that the production values left much to be desired. As Grace Wyndham Goldie, the first television critic of the Listener, *commented in the only review of the transmission still extant: 'On the stage, an actor can react to his surroundings – but the television camera brought the actors near to us and showed us their reactions without showing us simultaneously the surroundings they were reacting to. So though we knew when one of them was afraid, the sense of his fear was not communicated to us and the expression of it was bound to appear overdone. Television still has much to learn from the stage.' (The medium has, however, undoubtedly learned the appeal of Edgar Wallace's fiction, for subsequently his books have provided the inspiration for a number of one-off productions as well as series such as the thirty-nine half-hour episodes of* The Four Just Men *begun in 1959, and the hour-long* Edgar Wallace Mystery Theatre *produced in the mid- sixties.)*

It was to be six years, in fact, before BBC TV would begin transmitting again, but memories of The Ringer *certainly remained with those viewers who had watched the unfolding drama on those grim September evenings. As a reminder of the production, I have chosen to open this collection not with one of* The Ringer *and Chief Inspector Bliss's more traditional alliances in bringing to justice criminals, jewel thieves, embezzlers or even a murderer, but an unusual tale focusing on Bliss's uneasy relationship with Mander, and* The Ringer's *exasperated threat to put the tiresome Inspector 'where he belongs'. In the light of how the relationships between so many of the police officers in later TV series have proved such a key element in their success, this story written by Edgar Wallace over sixty years ago can be seen very much as a forerunner of that whole tradition . . .*

GOVERNMENT DEPARTMENTS KEEP a sharp eye on post-prandial oratory. They do not like their servants, high or low, to talk shop in their leisure hours. Certainly they strongly discount anything that has the appearance of being criticism of superiors; and Inspector Mander overstepped the bounds when, at a police banquet, and in the course of proposing such an innocuous toast as 'The Ladies', he made a reference to The Ringer.

'People sometimes criticise us because notorious criminals remain at large,' he said. (The quotation is from the *Outer London News and Suburban Record*.) 'I am not so sure that we have done all we might have done, or that the right methods have been employed to bring him under arrest. This man is not only a menace to society, but a mark of reproach against our administration.'

If Chief Inspector Bliss had not disliked him so intensely, he would have broken Inspector Mander. It was the knowledge that he actively loathed this cocksure officer that induced him to excuse his error. Nevertheless, Inspector Mander stepped upon the carpet before a very high official and spent a most uncomfortable ten minutes, during which he did most of the listening.

It was three days after the publication of Mander's speech in a weekly newspaper that Bliss received a letter from The Ringer.

I am rather tired of Mander, and I think I will put him where he belongs. Fools rather terrify me because they have the assistance of Providence – which is distinctly unfair.

You may tell Mr Mander from me that before the end of the week has passed I shall get him.

Bliss sent for his subordinate.

'Read this,' he said.

Mander read and forced a smile, but the superintendent knew that he was none too happy.

'He has never threatened you before, has he?' asked Bliss.

Mander laughed, but there was no real mirth in it.

'That kind of bunk doesn't scare me,' he said. 'I've been threatened by –'

'By The Ringer?' asked Bliss maliciously, enjoying the officer's discomfiture.

Mander moved uneasily in his chair.

'Well, no, not by The Ringer, but – er – I don't take very much notice of that.'

And then he brightened visibly.

'You can see, chief, that this fellow's scared of me, and –'

'Excuse me a moment while I laugh,' said Bliss sardonically. 'Scared of you! What job are you on now?'

Mr Mander was dealing with a case of car-stealing. He had got on the track of a fairly important organisation which, if it did not actually steal, certainly played the part of a receiver. Bliss listened and nodded.

'You ought to be safe,' he said. 'You've got Sergeant Crampton working with you; he's a pretty intelligent man.'

Mander winced.

'The Duke of Kyle –' he began, and the nose of Mr Bliss wrinkled.

'The Duke of Kyle is a great authority on the breeding of pigs and nothing else – oh, yes, I read his letter in the *Monitor*, praising your speech. That nearly got you hung. But he's no authority on The Ringer.'

The Duke of Kyle was one of those peers who had very little occupation in life other than the breeding of pigs and the inditing of letters to newspapers. He had written his unqualified approval of Mr Mander's speech, and had, moreover, suggested fantastical and not even novel methods for bringing The Ringer to justice. Bliss had read and had feared for his Grace.

*

That night Mander was at Notting Dale Police Station, pursuing his inquiries, and was coming down the steps when a beautiful limousine drew up at the door and a lady in evening dress stepped down. She was fair-haired and very beautiful; her hands sparkled with diamonds; from her ears hung two glittering stones.

'Can you tell me where I can find Inspector Mander?' she asked, and Mander, susceptible to feminine charms, lifted his hat. 'You're he? Mr Bliss said I should find you here.'

'Is anything wrong, madam?'

The lady nodded; she seemed a little breathless, considerably agitated.

'It is about my car,' she said, lowering her voice, 'a coupé. It was stolen this afternoon while I was shopping in Bond Street. Somebody enticed the chauffeur away . . . It isn't the loss of the car. I wonder if I could speak to you alone? Could you come back to Berkeley Square with me?'

Mander gave instructions to his men and followed the lady into the luxurious, delicately perfumed interior. She was silent for a while.

'It isn't the loss of the car,' she said again, 'but I foolishly left my handbag in the pocket. There are letters there – it's very difficult to tell you this – that I – I wish to recover. I can speak to you confidentially?'

'Certainly, madam,' said Mander.

His proximity to such a fragrant, lovely being was a little intoxicating.

'The Duke and I are not on very good terms, but there has never been a question of – divorce. These letters will make a tremendous difference to me. Is it true that such things can be recovered through the – the underworld?'

Mander smiled.

'They say so in books, and it has happened in real life,' he said, 'but it has never been my experience.'

If Inspector Mander had been a little more experienced he would have returned a different answer.

'They're compromising letters, I suppose?'

'Compromising? Yes – well, I suppose they are. They're from a boy – my cousin. Oh, dear, oh, dear!' She wrung her hands in despair.

'I'll try to get them for your Grace,' said Mander gallantly.

He did not know which duchess this was. His acquaintance with the peerage was slight and sketchy, and the only member he knew was an impoverished lord who occasionally found himself on the verge of prosecution.

She opened a little flap in the car before her and took out a jewelled cigarette case – in that half-light the diamond monogram sparkled brilliantly.

'Do smoke.'

He took a cigarette and politely offered her a light to the cigarette she put between her red lips. There was a little microphone attachment at the side of the car, and she pressed a button. Mander saw the chauffeur bend his head towards the earpiece.

'Drive round the park for a little while before you go to Berkeley Square,' she commanded.

In the light of his match Mander had seen the ducal coronet and a 'K'. The Duchess of –? Kyle, of course!

'The trouble with Bertie is that he's very indiscreet,' she said. 'He writes letters . . .'

Mander, who had settled himself more comfortably in the corner of the car, most unaccountably fell asleep at this juncture.

The ringing of the telephone bell brought Bliss from his bed and into the cold room where the instrument was. Detectives are human, and they never quite get accustomed to being wakened at half-past three in the morning.

'Mander? What do I know about Mander? Why? Ring him up, my dear man,' he said testily.

'He's not in his house, sir. We haven't seen him since he went away with the lady.'

Bliss was instantly wide awake.

'Which lady?'

The man at the other end of the phone told him of the car that called at Notting Dale.

'It's the Duke of Kyle's car,' said that same Sergeant Crampton in whose intelligence Bliss had expressed his unbounded faith. 'We found it abandoned on Hampstead Heath. It had been stolen from his Grace's garage.'

'Have you searched it?'

'Yes, sir. We found rather an important clue – a lady's card, with a few words scribbled in pencil.'

'Bring the car round and pick me up,' said Bliss, and was waiting in the street before the police tender came in sight.

By the light of the headlamps he examined the card. In a woman's hand was written:

The Leek. First left, first right. – Stillman.

'Now, look at this, sir,' said the sergeant.

He switched on the lights inside the car, which was upholstered in fawn. The tiny carpet on the floor was of the same colour, but near the left-hand door was a large red patch, and on the padded upholstery on the near side of the car a larger patch level with a man's head.

'It's blood,' said the sergeant. 'I saw him go off, and that's the seat he occupied.'

The local inspector of police was present at the examination.

'What is The Leek? Is there such a place near here?'

The inspector shook his head.

'No, but Stillman is the name of a house agent. He lives in Shardeloes Road. I've sent one of my men to wake him. He ought to be up by now: will you come round?'

They drove round to Shardeloes Road and found a sleepy, middle-aged man.

'The Leek is a cottage – I always call it The Leek; that was the former name of it. It's an empty house on the edge of the heath.'

He took the card, examined it, and nodded.

'That's right. A lady asked to see it and I gave her the directions. That's the handwriting of my clerk.'

'Have you the keys of this place?'

'Yes, at my office. If you wait, I'll dress.'

They waited while he dressed, accompanied him to his office in the steep hill street, and, crossing the heath, dipped into a depression. The road ran for some distance through an avenue of trees, at the end of which were three or four houses. Mr Stillman stopped the car at the first of these, and the detectives jumped out.

It was a gloomy-looking little house with a forecourt behind the high wall. They passed into the garden through a wicket gate, and Sergeant Crampton, using his lamp, led the way. Presently he stopped.

'Look at this,' he said.

On the stone flags were certain red stains, which were still wet. A little farther along were others. When they reached the door they found it half open.

Bliss went ahead with Crampton into the musty-smelling house, his lamp searching the walls carefully. There was blood on the floor, blood on the walls; the trail led him upward to the front room.

Here the evidence of tragedy was almost complete. There were bloodstains everywhere, but if there was no sign of the body there was evidence of a struggle, for one of the walls was spattered red, and near the door he found the sanguinary print of a gloved hand.

He made a careful scrutiny of every room, but apparently only the front room had been visited by Mander and his captor.

At four o'clock they were coming out of the house, when a car drove up and a man stepped out. Crampton went to interview him, and returned with the information that it was the Duke of Kyle's secretary.

'I had to telegraph to his Grace about the car being stolen,' he said. 'His Grace is very much upset. The Ringer visited him last night.'

'Where?' asked Bliss quickly.

'At Clane Farm – it is near Sevenoaks. His lordship has a large pig-breeding establishment there,' said this middle-aged gentleman.

Apparently the Duke had been retiring for the night, when somebody had tapped on the window of his study; he had drawn up the window and seen a strange and, to him, a terrifying face.

'He was armed,' said the secretary, his voice quaking. 'He made the most terrible threats to his Grace. He said he was bringing a Mr Mander to stay with him that night, and that they would both be found in the same condition in the morning.'

'Did he notify the police?' asked Bliss.

'No, sir.' The secretary shook his head. 'His Grace is a very courageous man. It was very curious that I should have been getting on to him at the moment that he was trying to get into communication with me. He told me he was sitting up all night, and that he would be heavily armed.'

Bliss noted down the exact location of the pig farm.

'Can you get on to his Grace and tell him that we're coming down almost immediately?' he asked. 'I want to make an examination of this road.'

After Mr Whistle – for such was his peculiar name – had departed the detective began a systematic search for further clues.

The path outside was of gravel, and, although there were stains which had the appearance of blood, they were not sufficiently definite or informative to help very much. Fifty yards along the road, however, Bliss made a discovery. It was a large piece of bloodstained satin, rolled up and thrown on one side. From here the evidences of tragedy were clear to the naked eye. They followed the track of the tell-tale spots across the heath until they came to the edge of a pond, where they had ceased.

Bliss observed that the pond was within easy walking distance of the place where the car had been found, and this puzzled him. If Mander had been killed, why had not the body been immediately disposed of? Why had it been taken to the house?

This was not the only thing that puzzled him. The detectives probed into the water with their sticks, but at the place where the track ceased the water was deep. Bliss gave instructions that the pond was to be dragged, but did not wait to see the result.

Ten minutes later the police car was speeding across Westminster Bridge on its southward journey.

Daylight broke before they reached Clane Farm. It was rather a difficult place to locate, and Bliss regretted that he had not brought the secretary with him. They found it at last and saw that there were strange activities, for in the narrow lane they met three men beating the hedges and obviously searching for something. Bliss stopped the car and was addressed by the red-faced leader:

'Are you the police?' he demanded. 'That's quick work. I only telephoned you a quarter of an hour ago.'

'I'm from Scotland Yard,' said Bliss. 'What's the trouble?'

'Trouble?' roared the man, going red in the face. 'Pride of Kent's been stolen. He couldn't have got out of his pen—'

'Who's Pride of Kent?'

'The finest hog in the country,' said the man. 'He's taken every first prize, and I wouldn't have lost him for a thousand pounds. When his Grace hears about it there's going to be trouble.'

'When was he lost?'

'Last night. He was in his sty, and he couldn't have got out by himself,' said the man. 'One of these villagers must have come up and stolen him. If we catch him there's going to be trouble. I wouldn't be surprised if he'd been killed. You found blood, didn't you, Harry?'

'Yes, sir, I found blood,' said the man he addressed. 'It were near the old building.'

'Where is his Grace?' asked Bliss.

The man stared at him.

'His Grace? Why, he's in Scotland.'

The eyes of Mr Bliss opened.

'In Scotland? Are you sure?'

'Yes, I'm sure,' said the man impatiently. 'I had a letter from his Grace yesterday. At least, not from his Grace, but from his secretary, Miss Erford.'

Superintendent Bliss did not so much as wince.

'Is there a Mr Whistle?'

The man had never heard of Mr Whistle.

Bliss regretted even more that he had not brought the 'secretary' with him, though he had no doubt that that gentleman would have found a very excellent excuse for remaining in London.

'There are lots of people who didn't like Pride of Kent,' the man proceeded. 'Some of these pigmen had a grudge against him because he was a bit savage; but he was the best hog in the county, and I don't know what his Grace will say if I can't find him.'

'Where was this pig kept?' asked Bliss.

The Pride of Kent lived in a handsome mansion which many of his Grace's tenants might have envied. It was a low building, before which was an ample yard, where the joy of the piggery could rest at his well-fed ease. A steel grating was unfastened and the pigman explained just how impossible it was for anybody but an educated porker to let himself out.

'My theory is that it happened last night,' said the man. 'There was a van seen in the lane—'

'What is this?' said Bliss, and, stooping, picked up a round tin. It was half-filled with a brown, treacly substance. 'Have you seen this before?'

The foreman shook his head. There was a small label on the tin, a wafer of paper, and on this was written the word 'Poison'.

'The Ringer is about the most thoughtful man I have ever met with,' said Bliss bitterly, for he recognised the queer 'n' that Henry Arthur Milton invariably made. 'We'll have that for analysis,' he said. 'I suppose the Pride of Kent was rather fond of sweet things? I thought so. This looks to me like golden syrup – and something else! I can well understand why he didn't put up a squeak.'

The pigman did not see the grim jest.

'What is that over there?' asked Bliss. He pointed to a range of buildings, each with its little front forecourt.

'We keep the young pigs there. They are his last litter,' said the pigman proudly. 'You won't find a better lot in Kent or anywhere else.'

The forecourts were filled with little porkers, all engaged at that moment in their morning meal. At the second pen Mr Bliss paused. In one corner was a round felt hat sadly battered and slightly gnawed.

'I think I'd like to go in here,' said Bliss, and stepped in among the terrified little pigs, who scampered in all directions save one – this was significant. They did not go into the dark little house where they slept at night. One or two did approach the entrance, but turned and fled instantly.

Bliss stooped low and passed through the door. The man who sat propped up in one corner bound hand and foot and scientifically gagged stared pathetically into the eyes of his chief.

'Come in here,' called Bliss, and the two detectives who were with him followed.

It took them some little time to unfasten his bonds, but presently Mr Mander staggered out into the light and was stimulated with brandy.

He had nothing to say; he could only babble about a beautiful lady, and somebody who carried him on his back. His most distinct recollection was facing the tiny eyes of a dozen little pigs, who resented his intrusion into their sleeping quarters.

'Queer, isn't it?' said Bliss absently. 'He said he'd put you where you belonged. I won't be so uncomplimentary as to say that he did.'

'This woman was one of the prettiest—'

'I have met Cora Ann Milton before, but I didn't know she was in England,' said Bliss; 'and I don't suppose she is this morning.'

One of the servants of the house came hurrying towards him.

'There's a telephone message for you, sir—'

Bliss waved him aside.

'I know all about it. They've found the body of the Pride of Kent in the pond at Hampstead. I know exactly where the bloodstains came from. I'm pretty sure I know where that unfortunate hog was killed.'

Boston Blackie's Mary

BY JACK BOYLE

America's first cop on the box did not materialise until some years after the end of the Second World War, in January 1949 to be precise, when Inspector Webb (played by Boris Aplon) hosted the weekly, thirty-minute series on ABC, Stand By For Crime, in which a whodunnit was acted out and viewers were invited to phone in their suggestions as to who had been the murderer before the Inspector revealed all. The success of this programme encouraged ABC to devise Photocrime *in the autumn of 1949 which, although produced in association with* Look *magazine, lasted for just thirteen weeks. Probably the series' most memorable feature was the breezy star with the unlikely name Inspector Hannibal Cobb, played by Chuck Webster. Two years later, the rival network, CBS, were rather luckier with* Racket Squad, *another thirty-minute weekly series in which Captain John Braddock (Reed Hadley) of the New York City Police headed a special squad of officers dedicated to catching con-men and fraudsters. The series was produced by Hal Roach jnr, son of the famous Hollywood comedy film maker.*

Then, in a curious parallel to what had occurred earlier across the Atlantic in England, the first really successful series co-starring a policeman was also based on the work of a very popular writer of thrillers and featured a character who operated on both sides of the law. The character's name was Boston Blackie and, like The Ringer, he had graduated to television from films and the radio. Following a career in crime, Blackie has turned to helping the law, in particular Inspector Faraday, a man who somehow never quite believes that Blackie has been rehabilitated and will one day return to his old ways. Although Blackie was originally a highly motivated and rather serious figure, in the later films and on television he became much more light-hearted and dapper. Notwithstanding this, the series ran very successfully for fifty-eight episodes spread over two years. What has remained quite unchanged is the fact that both Blackie and his creator were truly extraordinary men.

Jack Boyle (1889–1930) had started his working life as a newspaper reporter in San Francisco and was even editor for a while before his life suddenly fell apart. He plunged into opium addiction and was, for a time, a strong-arm bandit to pay for his habit. Finally arrested, it was while he was serving time as a convict that he turned to writing again and this, he later admitted, saved him from going back into a life of crime. On his release, Jack began to contribute to several of the top-selling magazines of the day and also created Boston Blackie whose adventures appeared in Argosy, Cosmopolitan *and* Redbook. *The success of this crook-turned-crimebuster not only made Boyle financially secure, but brought him more work writing film scripts. Despite his achievements in the movies, however, it is for Boston Blackie that he is remembered today – and how much of his own life he put into the character may be judged from the following comments in an introduction to his only full-length novel,* Boston Blackie, *published in 1919: 'To the police and the world, he is a professional crook, a skilled and daring safecracker, an incorrigible criminal made doubly dangerous by intellect. But to me Blackie is something more – a man with more than a spark of the Divine Spirit that lies hidden somewhere in the heart of even the worst of men. University graduate, scholar and gentleman, the Blackie I know is a man of many inconsistencies and a strangely twisted code of morals.'*

Despite his name, Blackie actually has nothing to do with Boston and lives in San Francisco with Mary, his 'best loved pal and confidante'. He does not regard himself as a criminal, but rather a man at war with a corrupt society. The popularity of Boyle's stories saw Boston Blackie make his debut on the screen in the silent movies Boston Blackie's Little Pal *(1918) and* Blackie's Redemption *(1919), in both of which he was played by Bert Lytell. In 1922, Lionel Barrymore took over the role and made him a more debonair and wily character in* The Face in the Fog. *In the string of movies which followed he was played by David Powell, William Russell, Forrest Stanley, Raymond Glenn and, lastly, Chester Morris who, in fourteen pictures made between 1941 and 1949, transformed him into an almost mirror-image of* The Ringer, *operating on the edge of the law and often in uneasy collusion with Inspector Faraday (played by Richard Lane). Blackie was also for some years the star of a weekly* *radio show and then in 1951 made his television debut played by Kent Taylor with Lois Collier as Mary and Frank Orth as Inspector Faraday. Perhaps due to the character's reputation, the Boston Blackie series was allocated a high budget for its time (each of the thirty-minute episodes cost over $21,000), yet it was considered suitable only for adult viewing and was transmitted at 10.30 p.m. just before the last news programme of the evening. Nonetheless, the words with which Blackie was introduced every week, 'Friend to those who have no friends; enemy to those who make him an enemy,' became a national catch-phrase. The ex-crook with a heart of gold who was then living in Los Angeles was undoubtedly somewhat removed from the original rough-hewn model, and to those who may only have ever seen him on television, here is one of the best of Jack Boyle's original but now rare stories from which the legend of Boston Blackie sprang . . .*

THE GREAT JUTE-MILL of the San Gregorio penitentiary was called by the board of prison commissioners 'a marvel of industrial efficiency'. The thousand stripe-clad men who worked there – hopeless, revengeful bits of human flotsam wrecked on the sea of life by their own or society's blunders – called the mill 'the T.B. factory' – 'T.B.' of course meaning 'tuberculosis'. Both were right.

The mill was in full operation. Hundreds of shuttles clanged swiftly back and forth across the loom-warps with a nerve-racking, deafening din. The jute-dust rose and fell, swelled and billowed, covering the floor, the walls, the looms and the men who worked before them. Blue-clad guards armed with heavy canes lounged and loitered through the long aisles between the machines that were turning out so rapidly hundreds of thousands of grain sacks, destined some day to carry the State's harvest to the four corners of a bread-hungry world.

To the eye, everything in the mill was as usual. Every convict was in his place, feverishly busy, for each man's task was one hundred pounds of sackcloth a day, and none was ignorant of what happened in 'Punishment Hall' to any who checked in short by even a single yard. Outwardly nothing seemed amiss, and yet the guards were restless and uneasy. They gripped their canes and vainly sought this new, invisible menace that all felt but none could either place or name.

Instinctively they glanced through the windows to the top of the wall outside, where gun-guards paced with loaded rifles. The tension steadily increased as the morning dragged slowly away. Guards stopped each other, paused, talked, shook their heads perplexedly and moved on, doubly watchful. Something was wrong: but what?

If they could have read the brain of one man – a convict whose face as he bent over his loom bore the stamp of power, imagination, and the ability to command men – they would have known. They would have seen certain carefully chosen striped figures pause momentarily as they passed among the weavers delivering 'cobs' for the shuttles. They would have guessed the message these men left – a message that would have been drowned in the roar of the machinery had it been shouted instead of spoken in the silent lip-language of the prison.

The word went out through the mill in ever-widening circles, leaving always in its wake new hope, new hatred and desperate determination. Those who received it first passed it on to others near them – others chosen after long study by the convict leader; for a single traitor could wreck the great scheme and bring upon all concerned punishment of a kind that the outside world sometimes reads about but seldom believes.

Trusted lieutenants, always approached on legitimate errands, reported back to their leader the acceptance of his plans by the hundred men selected for specific tasks in the first great *coup*. Each had been given detailed instructions and knew precisely what was required of him. Each, tense, alert and inspired by the desperate determination of their leader, awaited the signal which was to precipitate what all knew was truly a life-and-death struggle, with all the cards against them.

A convict with a knife-scar across his cheek and sinister eyes agleam with excitement approached the loom at which worked the one man in the secret whose face betrayed nothing unusual. The convict emptied a can of 'cobs' and spoke, though his lips made no perceptible movement.

'Everythin' sittin' pretty, Blackie,' he said. 'Everybody knows wa't's doin' and w'at to do. Nobody backed out. Give the high-sign any old time you're ready, an' there'll be more mess round this old T.B. factory than she's ever seen.'

Boston Blackie, the leader, looked quickly into the eyes of his lieutenant.

'You told them all there's to be no killing?' he questioned with anxiety, for none knew better than he that bloodshed and murder ride hand in hand, usually, with the sudden mastery by serfs about to be unleashed.

'Told 'em all w'at you said, word fer word,' replied the man; 'though I don't get this no-blood scheme myself. Give'em a taste of w'at they give us, fer mine. But I done what you told me. Let 'er go, w'en you're ready!'

Boston Blackie, university graduate, student, safe-blower and international crook – a man honoured in the underworld and feared by police from Maine to California – looked up and glanced around the mill. Covert eyes from a hundred looms were watching him with eager expectancy. The guards, sensing the culmination of the danger all had been seeking, involuntarily turned toward Blackie's too, and reading his eyes, started toward him on a run.

Instantly Boston Blackie leaped to the top of his loom, high above the sea of faces beneath him, and flung up both arms, the signal of revolt.

One convict seized the whistle-cord of the mill siren, and out over the peaceful California valley beyond the grey prison walls there echoed for miles the shrill scream of the whistle. Another convict threw off the power that turned the mill machinery. The looms stopped. The deafening noise within the mill ceased as if by magic.

The guards rushing toward Blackie with clubs aloft, were seized and disarmed in a second by squads of five convicts who acted with military precision and understanding. Ropes appeared suddenly from beneath striped blouses, and the blue-coated captives were bound, hands behind their backs. Two squads of ten ran through the mill armed with heavy wooden shuttles seized from looms, and herded to the rear scores of their fellows who, because of doubtful loyalty, had not been entrusted with the secret.

The guards' phones connecting with the executive offices from the prison were jerked from the walls, though there was none left free to use them. The great steel doors of the mill were flung shut and bars dropped into place on the inside, making them impregnable to anything less than artillery.

In three minutes the convicts were in complete control of the mill, barred from outside assault by steel doors and brick walls.

The gun-guards on the walls surrounding the mill-yard turned their rifles toward its walls but they held their fire, for there was no living thing at which to shoot.

Calmly, with arms folded, Boston Blackie still stood on his loom watching the quick, complete fruition of the plans that had cost him many sleepless hours on his hard cell-house bunk.

Of all the officers in the San Gregorio prison, Captain Denison, head of the mill-guards, was hated most. He was hated for his favouritism to pet 'snitches' – informers who bought trivial privileges at usurer's cost to their fellows. He was despised for his cowardice, for he was a coward and the convicts instinctively recognised it. When he was found hiding behind a pile of rubbish in a dark corner of the mill and dragged, none too gently, into the circle of captive guards, a growl of satisfaction, wolfish in its hoarse, inarticulate menace, swelled through the throng that confronted him. What Captain Denison saw as he turned his ashen face toward them would have cowed a far braver man than he – and he fell on his knees and begged piteously for his life.

Boldness might have saved him; cowardice doomed him. As he sank to his knees mumbling inarticulate pleas, a convict with a wooden bludgeon in his hand leaped to his side and seized him by the throat.

'We've got you now, damn you,' cried the volunteer executioner, called 'Turkey' Burch because of the vivid-hued neck beneath his evil face. 'Denison, if you've got a God, which I doubt, talk to Him now as you never will till you meet Him face to face. Pray, you dog, pray! Do you remember the night you sent me to the strait-jacket to please one of your rotten snitches? I told you when you laughed at my groans that some day I'd get you. Well, that day has come.'

Burch stooped toward his victim, his lips curling back over his teeth hideously.

'In just sixty seconds,' he snarled, 'this club is going to put you where you've put many a one of us – underground.'

The prostrate mill-captain tried to speak, but choked back his words. The convict's grip on his throat tightened like a vice. A roar of approval came from the stripe-clad mob. Someone leaped forward and kicked the kneeling form. Burch raised his club, swinging it about his head for the death-blow. 'Stop!'

The sharp command was spoken with authority. Involuntarily Burch hesitated and turned.

Boston Blackie sprang from his vantage-point on the loom and snatched the club from Burch's hand. He flung it on the floor and roughly shouldered his fellow-convict from the man he had saved.

'I said no blood, and that goes as it lays, Turkey,' he said quietly but with finality.

The convicts, being human – erringly human, but still human – screamed their protest as Blackie's intervention saved the man all hated with the deep hatred of real justification. Turkey Burch, encouraged by the savage protest from his mates, caught up his club.

'Get out of my way, Blackie,' he cried. 'That skunk on the floor has to die, and not even you are going to save him.'

'Listen,' said Blackie when the howl of approbation that followed his threat died down: 'He's going out of this mill without a scratch. I planned and started this revolt, and I'm going to finish it my own way.'

Burch was a leader among the men scarcely second in influence to Blackie himself. The blow Blackie had intercepted would have been compensation, to his inflamed mind, for years of grievances and many long hours of physical torture. He caught up his club again.

Boston Blackie seized an iron bar from a man beside him.

'All right,' he said, standing aside from the kneeling Captain Denison. 'Croak him whenever you're ready, Turkey, but when you kill him, I kill you. It's your move.'

The two convicts faced each other, Blackie alert and determined, Burch sullen and in doubt. For the first time the crowd behind was stilled. Thirty tense seconds passed, in which life and death hung on balanced scales.

'Why don't you do something?' Blackie said to Burch with a smile. Then he threw his iron bar to the floor. 'Boys,' he continued, turning to the crowd, 'I hate that thing on the floor there that's wearing a captain's uniform more than any of you. I didn't stop Burch from croaking him because he doesn't deserve it. I stopped him because if there is one drop of guard's blood shed here today, we convicts must lose this strike. If we keep our heads, we win. Now it's up to you. If you want to pay for that coward's blood with your own, Denison dies. But if he does, I quit you here and now. If you say so, he goes unharmed and we'll finish this business as we began it – right.'

He turned unarmed to Burch, standing irresolute with his club.

'You're the first to vote, Turkey. What's the verdict?' he asked.

Burch hesitated in sudden uncertainty. Denison cowered on the floor with chattering teeth. Then the convict tossed aside his club and stepped away from his prisoner.

'You've run this business so far, Blackie,' he said slowly, 'and I guess it's up to us to let you finish it in your own way. If you say the dog must go free, free he goes, say I.'

There was a chorus of approval from the convict mob.

'Fine,' said Blackie. 'I knew you boys had sense if I only gave you a chance to use it. Now we've work to do. The first thing is to boot our dear Captain out those doors, and I nominate Turkey Burch to do it.'

Action always pleases a mob. Joyous approval greeted the suggestion. Denison was dragged to the doors. They were unbarred, and then, propelled by Turkey Burch's square-toed brogan, Captain

Denison shot through and into the yard, where he was under the protecting rifles of the guards on the walls. One after another the captives were treated similarly.

'Take this message to Deputy Warden Sherwood,' said Blackie as the last of the bound bluecoats stood ready to be kicked past the doors. 'Tell him we control this mill. Tell him all this gun-guards and Gatling guns can't touch us in here. Tell him that unless within one hour he releases from Punishment Hall the ten men he sent there yesterday for protesting against the rotten food, we're going to tear down his five-million-dollar mill. We're going to wait just one hour, tell him, for his answer. Now go.'

The man shot out. The doors were banged shut and barred behind him, while the mill resounded with the joyous shouts and songs of the convicts, hugging each other in the unrestrained abandonment what followed the first victory any of them had ever known over discipline.

Deputy Warden Martin Sherwood, disciplinarian and real head of the prison management, sat in his office gripping an unlighted cigar between his lips. The screaming siren had warned him of trouble in the mill. Wall-guards reporting over a dozen phones had told him all they knew – that the men had seized the mill and barred its doors against attack and were ejecting guards one by one.

'Any of them hurt?' Sherwood inquired.

'Apparently not, sir,' the subordinate answered. 'Their hands are tied, but they don't seem to be harmed. Captain Denison is out and on his way up to you.'

'If Denison is out and unharmed, nobody needs a doctor,' Sherwood said with a glint his eyes that just missed being disappointment. 'If they had spilled any blood, his would have been first. Strange! Twenty men at the mercy of a thousand uncaged wolves, and nobody dead, eh? I wouldn't have believed it possible, and I thought I knew cons.'

He turned and saw a nervous assistant buckling on a revolver.

'Take off that gun and get it outside the gates quick,' he commanded. 'Don't leave even a bean-shooter inside these walls. This is no ordinary riot. There's headwork behind this. It looks as if we might be in real trouble.'

Deputy Warden Sherwood reached into his desk, struck a match and lighted his cigar. When Martin Sherwood lighted tobacco, he was pleased. The whole prison knew this habit. Among the convicts the sight of the deputy warden smoking invariably sent a silently spoken warning from lip to lip.

'The old man's smoking. Be careful. Some one's going to hang in the sack (strait-jacket) tonight,' they would say, and the prediction was seldom unfulfilled.

It was true that Martin Sherwood took grim, silent delight in inflicting punishment. He hated and despised convicts and took pleasure in making them cringe and beg under the iron rod of his discipline. Somewhere well back in his ancestry was a cross of Indian blood – a cross that revealed itself in coarse, coal-black hair, in teeth so white and strong and perfect they were all but repulsive, and lastly in the cruelties of Punishment Hall – cruelties that made San Gregorio known as 'the toughest stir in the country.'

There was a reason for this strange twist in the character of a man absolutely fearless and otherwise fair. Years before, he had brought a bride to his home just outside the prison walls. She was pretty and young and weak – just the sort of girl the attraction of opposites would send to a man like Martin Sherwood. There were a few months of happiness during which Sherwood sometimes was seen to smile even among the convicts.

Then came the crash. A convict employed as a servant in the deputy's home completed his sentence and was released. With him went the Deputy's wife, leaving behind a note that none but the deserted husband ever saw. He never revealed by word or look the wound that festered in his heart, but from that day he was a man as unfeeling as iron – a man who hated convicts and rejoiced in their hatred of him. Punishment Hall, when he could use its tortures with justice, became his instrument of revenge.

This perhaps explains why Martin Sherwood sat in his office calmly smoking a cigar when Captain Denison, white and shaken, rushed in and tumbled into a chair. His superior read in a glance the story of the scene in the mill.

'They might as well have killed you in the mill as to send you here to die of fright in my office,' the Deputy said with such biting sarcasm that Denison, terror-stricken as he was, flushed.

A few quick, incisive questions brought out the facts about the revolt. 'Deputy, there is serious trouble ahead,' Denison warned in conclusion. 'These cons have a leader they obey like a regiment of soldiers. He is –'

'Boston Blackie, of course,' interrupted Sherwood. 'There isn't a man down there who could have planned and executed a plot like this but Blackie. I should have known better than to put him where he could come in contact with the men.'

The guard who had been given the convict leader's ultimatum to the deputy warden rushed in.

'He says he wants the men out of Punishment Hall and your promise of better food from now on, or he'll tear the mill down in an hour,' the man reported.

The Deputy Warden tossed away his cigar and stepped out into the courtyard, bright with a thousand blossoms of the California spring.

'Sends an ultimatum to me, does he?' he repeated softly to himself. 'He's a man with real nerve and brains. There is no way for me to reach the men while they're inside the mill. I must get them out and up here in this yard where the Gatlings and rifle-guards will have a chance. And then I'll break Mr Boston Blackie and the rest of them in the jacket – one by one.'

His eyes gleamed as he thought. He turned to the men in his office.

'I'm going down to the mill,' he said. 'Have a Gatling gun ready in each of the four towers that cover this yard – ready but out of sight, do you understand?'

'Down to the mill?' cried Denison in amazement. 'Deputy, you don't realise the spirit of that mob. You won't live five minutes. They will murder you as surely as you put yourself in their power. Don't go.'

'If I am not back in half an hour, your prediction will have been fulfilled,' Sherwood said. He took his pocket-knife and a roll of bills from his pocket and locked them in his desk. 'If I am not back in half an hour, Denison, call the Warden at his club in San Francisco, tell him what has happened and that they got me. Say my last word was for him to call on the Governor for a regiment of militia as quickly as he can get it here. But for the next half-hour do nothing except get your nerve back – if you can.'

Sherwood pulled a straw from a whisk-broom on his desk, stuck in between his teeth, from which his lips curled back until the abnormally long incisors were revealed, and started for the mill-yard as calmly as though he were going to a luncheon.

White-faced guards at the last gate tried to stay him. The uproar from within the mill was deafening. Songs, curses and cries of frenzied exultation came from behind the steel-barred doors.

'Open the gates,' commanded Sherwood. 'Lock them behind me and don't reopen them again even if you think it's to save my life.'

Still holding the straw clenched between his teeth, the Deputy crossed the yard, neither hurrying nor hesitating. Nothing in his face or demeanor gave the slightest indication that he knew he was delivering himself, unarmed, into the power of a thousand crazy men, every one of whom had reason to hate him with that sort of undying hatred that grows from wrongs unavenged and long suppressed.

Sherwood hammered on the door with his fist. The clamour inside suddenly died.

'Open the door, boys,' he commanded. 'I'm coming in to talk to you. I'm alone and unarmed.'

The man on guard at the door raised the iron wicket and looked out.

'It's the Deputy,' he whispered. He's alone, too. Once we get him inside!' The man sank his teeth into his lip until blood streamed across his chin. Primeval savagery, hidden only skin-deep in any man, reverts to the surface hideously among such men in such an hour.

With hands trembling with eagerness, the convict unbarred the door, and Martin Sherwood stepped quickly in and faced the mob.

For five seconds that seemed an hour there was dead silence. It was broken by an inarticulate, inhuman, menacing roar of rage that rose to a scream as the men realised the completeness of their power over the man who to them was the living embodiment of the law which denied them everything that makes live liveable.

A man in the rear of the mob thrust aside his fellows, rushed at the Deputy and spat in his face. As calmly as though he were in his own office, Sherwood drew out his handkerchief and wiped his cheek, but never for an instant did his eyes waver from the inflamed ones of the men he faced. His teeth, whiter and more animal-like than ever, it seemed, gleamed like a wolf's fangs as he chewed at the straw between them.

'I'll remember that, Kelly, the next time I get you in the jacket,' he said slowly to the man who had spat upon him. The convict laughed, but pressed backward, cowed against his will by the fearless assurance of his antagonist.

Boston Blackie was in the rear of the mill when the sudden silence warned him of new developments at the front door. Forcing his way through the crowd, he was within ten feet of the Deputy Warden before he saw him. The striped leader's face paled as he recognised Sherwood – paled with fear not of him but for him. If the official were killed, as there was every probability he would be, he knew it meant the gallows for himself and a score of the men behind him. He had risked everything on his ability to prevent bloodshed. The lives of all of them depended on the safety of the hated autocrat who stood before him calmly chewing a broom-straw in the midst of hundreds of men hungering for his life.

Blackie caught the Deputy Warden by the shoulder and turned him toward the door.

'Go,' he said. 'Get out before they kill you.'

Sherwood threw off his hand.

'You may be able to command this convict rabble, Blackie,' he said in a voice perfectly audible in the new silence which had fallen on the mob, 'but you can't command me. I came to talk to these men, and I'm going to do it.'

From somewhere in the rear came a metal weight which missed Sherwood's head by inches and crashed against the door behind him. The screaming blood-cry rose again. One struck at the Deputy's head with a shuttle, but Blackie, quicker in eye and hand, hit first and laid the man senseless at his feet. Then he jumped to the top of the loom.

'Men, if you want to hang,' he cried, his voice rising even above the bedlam about him, 'I'll go along with you, if you'll listen to me first.'

The outcry died down for a moment, and Blackie talked to them. He made no pleas, asked no favours. He told them their situation and his plan to attain the ends for which they had revolted – the release of the prisoners in Punishment Hall and better food for themselves. He pointed out the futility of the hope of escape, ringed about as they were by Gatling guns and rifles in a score of watchtowers, even if they could force the walls as one suggested. Gradually, by sheer force of mind, he dominated the crowd; and when at last he called on them to follow him to the end, their cheer was that of soldiers to a recognised leader.

All through this harangue Sherwood stood listening, his face as unexpressive as the walls behind him.

'Deputy,' said Blackie, turning to him, 'we have been told you said you would keep the men in Punishment Hall in the strait-jacket until they die, if necessary, to find out who smuggled out the letter complaining about the rotten food. Is that true?'

'It is,' said Sherwood, who never lied.

'We make three demands, then,' said Blackie: 'first, the release of all the men undergoing punishment; second, your promise that no man concerned in this revolt shall be punished; third, your guarantee that henceforth we get the food for which the State pays but which the commissary-captain steals.'

'And if I refuse, what then?' asked Sherwood.

'At noon we will destroy the mill.'

'Boys,' said the Deputy, 'I have listened to your spokesman. You know I can't grant your demands without consulting the Warden, who is in San Francisco. I will do this, however. I will declare a half-holiday. It is almost dinner-time. Come over to the upper yard, have your dinner as usual and we'll all watch a ball-game in the afternoon. Before night I will give you your answer.'

With the thought of the Gatling guns and rifles that covered the upper yard in his mind, Sherwood smiled grimly. The men cheered and made a rush in the direction of the doors, thinking the victory won.

'Wait,' cried Blackie, barring the way with uplifted arms. 'Nobody is going to stir out of this mill until you, Mr Sherwood, have given us a definite promise all our demands are granted. You would like enough to get us into the upper yard away from these protecting walls and where we couldn't do a dollar's worth of damage, but we're not going. When the men in Punishment Hall are free and you, who have never been known to lie, have told us we'll be fed right and no one harmed or punished now or in the future for this morning's work, we'll go into the upper yard – not before.'

'Boys,' said the Deputy, still hoping to urge the man into the trap, 'do as I suggest. Why should you let this man' – contemptuously indicating Blackie – 'order you around. He's only a con like yourselves. Come on up to the yard, and I'll issue an extra ration of tobacco all round. Are you going to go along with me or stay here with him?'

'We'll stay,' answered Blackie for the men. 'It's no use, Deputy; the game doesn't work this time.'

A shout from the men proved Sherwood's defeat. He wasn't a man to delay or lament over a beaten hand.

'You're quite a general, Blackie,' said the Deputy slowly, a flicker of admiration in his eyes. 'I'll give you an answer in fifteen minutes. But' – he looked straight into Boston Blackie's eyes with steely determination – 'don't think you are always going to have all the cards as you have today. The next time you and I clash, I'm going to break you like this.'

He jerked the straw from his mouth and twisted it apart; then he walked out of the mill.

A quarter of an hour later ten pain-racked prisoners from the punishment chambers were welcomed back to the mill with an outburst of exaltation such as San Gregorio Penitentiary had never seen. With them came the Deputy Warden's acceptance of Boston Blackie's terms. The men rioted joyously in an abandonment of happiness. In the midst of the turbulent jollification a half-witted, one-armed boy nicknamed 'the Squirrel' climbed to the top of a loom, drew out his one treasure, a mouth-organ, and tried to express his joy in the one way he knew – and his dismal interpretation of 'The Star Spangled Banner' floated out over the crowd.

'Cut out the bum music,' cried a burly convict to whom the spirit of the hour had given a wanton impulse to command. 'Where d'you figger in this, you nutty Squirrel?'

The boy's eyes filled with tears, and his notes faltered and died in the middle of a bar.

Boston Blackie, always sensitive to the feelings of others, stopped the lad as he slunk from his perch on the loom and lifted him back.

'Go ahead. Play, little Squirrel,' he said encouragingly. 'Your music is as good as a band. Go to it. You're one of us, you know, and we're all happy.'

Intuitively Blackie had salved the wound caused by the gibe. Radiant now, the Squirrel pressed his mouth-organ to his lips and played on and on with a light in his dull eyes that made Blackie mutter: 'Poor kid! A pardon wouldn't make him any happier.'

And the convicts, only one degree less childish than the Squirrel, celebrated and sang in their cells that night until at last they settled into silence and care-free sleep. No thought of a tomorrow disturbed them: but Boston Blackie, quiet and wakeful, lay on his cell bunk anxiously probing the future. In his mind he still saw the broken bits of Martin Sherwood's broom-straw fluttering to the mill floor and heard his threat:

'The next time you and I clash, I'm going to break you like this.'

Mary Dawson – Boston Blackie's Mary she was, to his world and hers – was a prison widow who never missed visiting day at the San Gregorio Penitentiary. Twice each month she crossed the bay from San Francisco to the prison. Twice each month, with others like herself beside her, she rode from the station to the prison-gates in the rickety old stage and waited in the reception room a-quiver with impatience and longing for the first glimpse of the man she loved. When he came, when he caught her in his arms and kissed her, looking into her face with eyes that answered the love in hers, then for a pitifully short half-hour both forgot prisons and the law and separations and were happy.

Boston Blackie and his Mary reckoned time from visiting-day to visiting-day. Those half-hours together, separated though they were by thirteen long blank days, made life endurable. Neither ever spoke of the long years that must elapse before Blackie would walk out through the gates and go home a free man with Mary. Blackie reckoned them at night in his cell, and Mary checked them off each day on a calendar in her rooms, but when they were together, they let no evil thoughts mar their happiness.

Ever since the strike, Blackie had been apprehensive and watchful. Deputy Warden Sherwood had made no attempt to punish any of the men concerned in the revolt. He was not a man to break his word, but when any of the men involved in it transgressed a prison rule, even in a trifling matter, the punishment that followed proved that Sherwood neither forgave nor forgot.

On a bright Saturday afternoon Blackie was impatiently pacing the yard, awaiting the summons to the reception room and Mary. It came at last, and he hurried through the gates, pass in hand. She was waiting for him and sprang to his side, hands outstretched and trembling with eagerness, in her fear of losing even one second of their thirty precious minutes. Their kiss was interrupted by the gruff voice of Ellis, the reception-room guard.

'Wait a minute there, Blackie,' he commanded. 'Who is this woman?'

'Who is she?' repeated the convict in blank amazement. 'Why she is Mary, my wife. You surely know her well enough. She has been here every visiting-day.'

'I know she has managed to slip in here on visiting-days,' Ellis said. 'But what I ask you is, who and what is she? We're told she's an ex-con herself. If so, she can't visit you. The rules don't permit it.'

The man turned to Mary.

'Isn't this your picture?' he asked sneeringly as he handed her a photograph of a woman with a prison number pinned across the breast.

It was Mary's picture. Years before, Mary Dawson, daughter of Dayton Tom, a professional crook, had been sent to the penitentiary because she declined to clear herself at the expense of her father's pals. She was not and never had been anything worse than Boston Blackie's Mary, but now her past had suddenly risen up to deprive her of the single treasure that life held – her half-hour visits with Blackie.

'It's my photograph,' she said in a voice choked with anguish, for she knew prison rules too well not to realise what that admission meant. 'But Mr Ellis, please, please don't bar me because of that. I'm not a thief. I never was. I did time – yes; but I wasn't guilty. For God's sake, don't take our visits away from us. They're – they're – all we – have.' The girl's voice was broken by her sobs.

'Of course you weren't guilty! That's what they all say,' the guard answered. 'You better beat it, woman, while you've got a chance. You're lucky the Deputy don't put the city dicks (detectives) on to you. There's a bunch of them over here today, too.'

Boston Blackie, white as a marble image, glared into the guard's face with eyes that narrowed dangerously. The man's reference to the Deputy made everything clear. This was Martin Sherwood's revenge for the mill revolt.

'Did the Deputy tell you to bar Mary from visiting me?' he demanded of the guard.

'What's that to you?' the man answered with pointed insolence. 'I don't want her here, and she's barred – that's all. She's got nerve to come here anyway among decent women, the –'

The word never left his lips. Boston Blackie's blow caught him on the chin, and Ellis sprawled across the room and toppled to the floor. In a second Blackie was upon him again, grasping his throat in a frenzy of savagery.

The whole reception room was in an uproar. Women screamed; convicts shouted encouragement. Blackie's vice-grip was strangling the all-but-unconscious guard. Mary's voice, pleading with him frantically, restored the convict to sanity.

'Don't kill him! Don't kill him!' she begged. 'For your sake and mine, let him go, dear. Think what it means to us both!'

Slowly Blackie's grip loosened. He dropped the man and took Mary in his arms.

'Good-bye, dear one,' he said. 'I've tried to get by here without trouble, but Sherwood won't let me. From now on I've just one purpose. I'm going to beat this place. I'm going to escape. Watch and wait for me; it may be a month; it may be a year – but some day I'll come.'

Guards summoned by the uproar rushed in, and one struck Blackie over the head with a club, laying him bleeding and senseless.

Blackie, still unconscious, was carried inside the gates and to the Deputy's office, where Sherwood was informed that Boston Blackie had committed the most heinous of prison crimes; he had struck an officer.

'Take him to Punishment Hall and leave him there for tonight. Don't give him punishment of any kind. I'll attend to him in the morning,' the Deputy ordered.

As the guards carried Boston Blackie across the yard toward the punishment chamber, Martin Sherwood took a match from his desk and lighted the cigar he had been chewing.

Boston Blackie lay on the floor in Punishment Hall trussed up in the strait-jacket as tightly as two able-bodied guards could draw the ropes. Great beads of perspiration stood on his forehead. A thin trickle of blood showed on his chin, beneath where his clenched teeth bit into the flesh. The man's eyes betrayed the torture he was suffering, but no sound came from his lips.

Martin Sherwood stood above him, looking down at the helpless form in the canvas sack. He was smoking.

A prison strait-jacket hanging on a wall is nothing alarming to the eye, but in operation it is an instrument of most fiendish torture. The victim stands upright, arms straight down before him and hands on the front of each leg. The jacket itself is a heavy canvas contrivance that extends from the neck to the knees with eyelets in the back in which ropes make it possible to clinch it to any degree desired, as a woman's corset can be tightened. When the jacket is adjusted over the arms and body, the man is laid face downward on the floor and guards tighten the jacket by placing a foot on the small of the convict's back and drawing in the ropes with their full strength.

Fully tightened, the jacket shuts off blood circulation throughout the body almost completely. For the first five minutes, oppressed breathing is the only inconvenience felt. Then the stagnating of the blood commences to cause the most excruciating torture – a thousand pains as if white-hot needles are being passed through the flesh run through the body. The feet and limbs swell and turn black. Irresistible weights seem to be crushing the brain.

Four hours in the jacket made one convict a paralytic for life. Some men have endured it for a half or three-quarters of an hour without crying out, but only a few.

Boston Blackie had been in the jacket for an hour and five minutes, and as yet Martin Sherwood had waited in vain for groans or pleas for release.

The prison physician stood by, looking on anxiously. One man had died after the jacket had been used on him in San Gregorio, and the newspapers made quite a fuss about it. The doctor didn't want a repetition of that trouble, and yet he knew the man on the floor had been under punishment fully twenty minutes too long. Still the Deputy gave no indication to release him.

Five minutes passed. Blackie's face was a ghastly purple. Blood oozed from his nostrils. He rolled aimlessly to and fro on the floor, but his lips still were clenched, and no sound came from them.

'He's had enough – more than enough, Deputy,' he urged. 'Hadn't we better call it off?'

'Never till he begs,' said Sherwood, biting off his cigar in the middle and tossing it away. Perspiration stood out on his brow too.

Five more minutes passed, and the form on the floor, too horrible now to be described, ceased to roll and toss. The doctor stooped over him quickly.

'He's out,' he announced. 'You've got to quit now, Sherwood. A few more minutes are likely to kill him, and anyway he's unconscious and you're not doing any good.'

'Release him,' said the Deputy Warden curtly. 'Take him over to the hospital and bring him around. We'll try it again tomorrow.'

Hours later Boston Blackie, slowly and painfully, came back into what seemed a blurred and hideous world.

'He didn't break me,' he said over and over to himself. 'I've beaten him again. I'll do it just once more, too. Nobody has ever escaped from this place since Martin Sherwood has been deputy, but I will.'

The relieved doctor gave Blackie a drink that sent him off into an uneasy slumber in which he was climbing an interminable ladder to a garden from which Mary stretched down her arms to him, but when he seized her hands the fingers shrivelled into cigars, and her face changed to Martin Sherwood's whose white teeth bit into his flesh until he clenched his lips to keep from crying out.

'When Blackie gets out of the hospital, put him in charge of the lawn in front of my office,' said Sherwood to the assignment captain the following morning. 'I have decided not to give him any more of the jacket.'

The captain wonderingly obeyed. It was the first time he had ever known the Deputy to deviate from his inflexible rule that a convict once sent to the jacket stayed until he begged for mercy.

Martin Sherwood, from within his office, stood fixedly studying Boston Blackie, who was spraying the courtyard lawn with a hose. The convict was more like a skeleton than a living man. His striped coat hung sack-like across his emaciated shoulders. His cheek-bones seemed about to burst through the crinkled, parchment-like skin that covered them. His eyes were dull, deep-set and haggard, his movements slow and languid like a confirmed invalid's.

'He's ill, without a doubt,' mused the Deputy Warden. 'The doctor's evidently right about the stomach trouble. No man could counterfeit his appearance; and yet –' Sherwood's brow was wrinkled with perplexity as he studied the convict. 'Everything may be as it seems. If he were any man but Boston Blackie, I should be wasting my time thinking about it. But because he is Boston Blackie, I'm puzzled. It's three months since I barred his wife from the prison and gave him the jacket – three months in which he has been docile as a lamb, though I know such a man must have murder in his heart every time he lays eyes on me. Why this calm?'

The perplexed furrow in the Deputy's brow deepened. For ten minutes he stood studying Blackie without making a movement or a sound.

'One of two things is true,' the Deputy concluded. 'Either he is just a common con after all and I did break him in the jacket, or else he's getting ready to cover my king with the ace of trumps. Suppose his plan, whatever it is, requires him to sleep in the hospital.' He'd have to be sick to get there, of course – really sick, too.'

Just then Boston Blackie, unconscious of the Deputy's scrutiny, turned toward him, and the sunlight fell full on his emaciated face.

'God, he looks like a corpse now,' was Sherwood's thought. 'It's impossible that this sickness is a trick, and yet nothing is impossible to a man who can stand the jacket without a murmur. I'm going to play safe. I'm going to move him out of the hospital, though there isn't a surer place to keep a man inside the walls, as far as I can see. I'll move him, anyway. If he tries to get back there again, I'll know I'm right.'

Sherwood turned to his clerk.

'Phone to the doctor to come over,' he said.

The physician protested strongly against the Deputy Warden's order to transfer Boston Blackie from his cell in the hospital to one of the dormitories in the cell-house. 'The man's nothing but a living corpse now, Deputy,' he argued. 'He has a stomach complaint I haven't been able to diagnose. He isn't likely to live another three months. He hasn't eaten a thing but hard crusts of bread for weeks. Let him die in the hospital.'

'Move him over to C Dormitory tomorrow morning,' Sherwood commanded with finality. 'I'm going to put him in with Tennessee Red, who'll keep me informed of what he does nights. I've got a hunch, Doctor, that Mr Boston Blackie is framing another surprise party for us. I'll find some excuse to move Red's present cell-mate out by tomorrow morning.'

The doctor went back to the hospital shaking his head at the strange vagaries of his superior concerning Boston Blackie. He sent his runner, the half-witted, one-armed boy Blackie had protected on the day of the strike, for the turnkey.

'The Deputy has ordered Boston Blackie out of the hospital,' he said when the messenger returned with the officer. 'He thinks Blackie is framing something. I told him the man won't do anything worse than die, but he's set on moving him and so we'll have to do it. Looks to me as if Blackie's sort of on the old man's nerves since the affair of the jacket. I never knew him to worry so much about any man in the prison. He's going to put him in with Tennessee Red, his chief stool-pigeon, and see what he can find out. The Deputy won't have Red's cell-partner out until tomorrow, so don't say anything to Blackie tonight.'

The officers separated. The Squirrel climbed back on his stool and looked out through the barred windows to the lawn, where he could see Boston Blackie laboriously dragging his hose across the grass. There was new grief in the Squirrel's dull eyes. He had heard what the doctor had told the turnkey. They were going to take Blackie away from the hospital dormitory – Blackie, who gave the Squirrel tobacco and the inside of a loaf of bread each night – Blackie, who always protected him when the other men teased him – Blackie, his friend. The boy's eyes filled with tears. Blackie was the only one who liked to hear the Squirrel play his mouth-organ, and now they were going to take him away. But Blackie was smart. The doctor had said 'not until tomorrow'. Maybe if the Squirrel told Blackie at dinner-time what he had heard, Blackie would find some way to make them let him stay in the hospital. Slowly the ideas filtered through the haze that clouded the dull brain.

Boston Blackie was sitting in his dormitory cell slowly chewing the crust of a half-loaf of bread, from which he had hollowed out the soft inner portion that his tortured stomach couldn't digest, when the Squirrel slipped by the turnkey and dodged silently into the cell. The boy laid his finger on his lips as Blackie started to speak.

'They mustn't know I'm here,' he said. 'I heard what the doctor told the screw (turnkey). 'They're going to take you away, out of the hospital.'

Boston Blackie's loaf fell to the floor.

'When, little Squirrel, when?' he whispered hoarsely, gripping the boy by the shoulder. A great fear showed in the convict's eyes.

'Tomorrow, when the Deputy gets a place ready for you with Tennessee Red,' the boy answered.

'Thank God, I've one more night. One night must be enough.' Blackie, scarcely aware that he was voicing his mind, sank back in relief so intense it left his whole body dripping with perspiration. A new danger occurred to him.

'What else did the doctor say, little Squirrel?' he asked.

'He said the Deputy thinks you are framing something, but it isn't so because you're going to die in three months. Are you going to die in three months, Blackie?'

'No, not in three months, little Squirrel,' answered Blackie, and then softly to himself he added, '– but maybe tonight.' He turned again to the boy, his mind swiftly grappling with the details of the task before him, which must be done now in a single night.

'Will you play your mouth-organ for me tonight, Squirrel?' he asked. 'Will you play it *all* the time from lock-up until the lights go out? All the time, Squirrel, and loud so I can hear it plain. Here's a sack of tobacco for you. You won't forget? All the time, and loud.'

'Yes, all the time and loud,' the boy repeated, dog-like devotion in his eyes.

Boston Blackie mopped a forehead dripping with cold perspiration. All his hopes of freedom depended on a half-witted boy and his mouth-organ.

Boston Blackie's mind that afternoon was a jumble of torturing doubts, painstaking calculation and unflinching resolution. The Deputy Warden's intuition had not misled him. Blackie had planned an escape, and his every act for weeks had been done with that sole purpose in view. His plan required that he sleep in the hospital dormitory used for the tuberculosis patients and others unfit for cell-houses, but not bedridden. To accomplish this he diluted prison laundry soap, strong with lye, and drank it day after day until it ruined his stomach and left him unable to digest any food but hard-baked crusts of bread. The lye had caused him excruciating anguish, but in ten days it accomplished its purpose. Blackie had been ordered to the hospital dormitory to be put on a diet and given treatment for his puzzling stomach trouble. He had been there two months and was still using the lye to prevent the possibility of being turned back to his old quarters. He had wrecked his physique, but each night saw him a step nearer his goal.

He wasn't ready to make his bid for freedom, but the Deputy with uncanny divination had given him no choice. He must make the attempt that night or never.

First he took a spade and laboriously began to dig around the rose-bushes that flanked the lawn. No one saw him uncover a rudely improvised saw made with his hoe-file from a steel knife stolen from the kitchen. The saw and a tobacco sack containing a five-dollar bill were quickly hidden in his blouse. The bill had come from Mary in the cover of a book sent to him according to instructions delivered by a discharged convict.

Next he asked permission to air his blankets on the clothes line in the lower yard. The toolhouse in which his garden implements were kept was near by. From beneath its floor he took the treasures that had cost him the hardest work and greatest risk – a civilian pair of trousers, a blue shirt and a mackinaw coat made from a blanket, and cap. It had taken him one full month to steal them from the tailor-shop where the clothes of the new arrivals were kept after they received their prison stripes. The trousers Blackie put on under his striped ones, pinning up the legs well out of sight. When his blankets went back to his cell, the coat, shirt, and cap were hidden in them.

A half-hour before lock-up time Blackie rolled up his garden hose and carried it to the toolhouse. Once within its doors and alone, he cut off six feet of the hose and wound it around his body, tying it securely in place. Next from a pile of rubbish he unearthed a single rubber glove which he had filched one day from the dispensary. He had tried in vain to get its mate. Two hundred feet of heavy twine from the mill completed the list of his preparations.

It would have puzzled even a man as shrewd as Martin Sherwood to determine how Boston Blackie planned to escape from San Gregorio Penitentiary with the motley array of contraband he had gathered together. The hospital dormitory where he celled was on the top floor of a detached building that stood alone in the yard, fully a hundred feet from the wall that surrounded the prison. It was conceivably possible for a man with even such a makeshift saw as Blackie's to cut the bars of his window and escape his cell, but freedom from his cell was a long step from real freedom. There still remained the thirty-foot wall to be scaled – a wall guarded on top by a gun-guard in a watchtower, and patrolled at the bottom all night by other armed guards.

At five o'clock Boston Blackie and the other hospital inmates were locked in their cells for the night. Thereafter, twice each hour, a guard was scheduled to pass and inspect the cells. At five minutes past five the Squirrel, faithful to his promise, began to play on his mouth-organ.

And as the boy played, Blackie chipped away the soap and lamp-black with which he had plugged a half-sawn window-bar and cut at it with his pitifully inadequate saw in frantic haste. The noise of the mouth-organ drowned the gentle rasping of the saw, a vitally necessary precaution.

A mirror hung on the wall near the door warned Blackie of the approach of the guard each time he made his rounds. Hour after hour the Squirrel played, and hour after hour Blackie sawed. He had spent a month and a half sawing through the first bar and halfway through the second. Tonight in four hours he must complete the task, for at nine o'clock 'lights out' would sound throughout the prison, and silence would settle over the dormitory, making further work on the bar impossible.

The saw-blade cut into his hands and tore his finger-tips. His arms were numb with pain. The singsong rasping seemed like a voice crying out a warning to the guards. The saw grew hot, and again and again he had to cool it in the water-bucket. Often it seemed as if he couldn't drive his tortured muscles another second, but he conjured into his mind a picture of Martin Sherwood's face with the teeth gleaming in a white line as he bent over a form in a strait-jacket. Sheer will-power kept the saw moving then, and so slowly it was almost imperceptible; but surely, nevertheless, it bit through the steel that seemed a living thing bent on binding Blackie to years of prison slavery and punishment.

At last it was done! With fifteen precious minutes to spare, the saw grated through the outer rim of rust and left the bar severed. With two bars cut and bent outward, Blackie knew he could squeeze his body through the window to the wide ledge outside and four stories above the guarded courtyard below. He swept the glistening filings into his water-bucket, hid the saw, worn now smooth as a knife, and tumbled into his bunk a quivering wreck.

The prison-bell tolled out nine; the lights winked out; and silence settled over the dormitory.

At one o'clock Blackie waited for the guard to pass, and then, with a half-hour at his disposal, slipped out of his convict clothes and fashioned them into a dummy which he covered with blankets to resemble a sleeping man.

He dressed in his civilian clothes, with his six-foot length of hose coiled about his body. He tucked his one glove carefully into his breast beside the ball of twine. Then he pulled out one of the heavy legs of his stool and tied it across his back. His preparations were complete. He took another stool-leg, and, using it as a lever, bent the severed bars straight out. A moment later he stood outside on the window ledge.

Below him the wall fell away sheer for four stories. Six feet above his head the rain-gutter marked the level of the flat roof. So far, Blackie had followed in the footsteps of other men who had tried to escape. But the others, once free from their cells, had gone down, each to be shot to death as he lurked in the courtyard vainly seeking a means to cross the towering wall that barred him in.

Instead of going down, Blackie went up. He took off his shoes and hung them about his neck. With fingers and toes clutching the bricks that jutted out a few inches around the window coping, he climbed slowly and with infinite caution. A single slip, the slightest mis-step, and Martin Sherwood would smile and light a cigar in the morning when they carried his body in.

Inch by inch Blackie raised himself, pressing his body close to the wall to keep from overbalancing. For the first time he realised his physical weakness. His arms were like dead things, and unresponsive to the iron will that commanded them. Again and again, in the agony of forcing his wasted muscles to obedience, he thought of releasing his clutch and falling to a quick death – relief! But always, in the wake of that thought, Martin Sherwood's face danced before his eyes, and the cruel satisfaction of the Deputy nerved Blackie to climb on.

At last his groping, bloody fingers clutched the edge of the roof-gutter. He faced the last crucial task. He must now swing his feet clear and raise himself to the roof by his arms alone – no great feat for a well man but, to the ill and exhausted convict, one that taxed even his iron resolution to the last atom of its resource.

Somehow he did it and lay at last safe on the roof, blinking back at the stars, which hung so low it seemed he could reach up and touch them. He lay still, thoughtlessly content, until the chiming prison-bell forced on his wandering mind the realisation that a precious half-hour was gone, leaving him still inside the walls that barred the road to Mary.

Blackie rose and crept silently to the edge of the roof nearest the wall. He was high above that stone barricade from which he was separated by a full hundred feet of space. Nothing, apparently, spanned that impassable gap, and yet when one looked again, something did span it – two glistening copper wires that ran down from the roof at a sharp angle to a pole outside the wall above which they hung a full twenty feet. They were uninsulated, live wires which fed the prison machinery and lighting system with a current that was death to whatever touched them – yet they were the key to Boston Blackie's plan of escape.

Carefully he unwound the length of rubber hose from about his body. Carefully he laid the insulating rubber over the strands of shining metal. With infinite pain he bound and rebound the stool-leg to the dangling length of rubber that hung beneath them. The result was a crazily insecure trapeze which swung under wires the touch of which was fatal.

Then Boston Blackie pulled out his ball of jute twine and attached it to a brick chimney, the only thing upright and secure in sight. He glanced toward the wall far beneath him, where a sleepy guard dozed in his tower; then Blackie unhesitatingly seated himself on the bar of his improvised trapeze. With his back toward the wall, he swung clear of the roof and began to slide down the wires, regulating his speed with the cord on the chimney.

The light wires swayed and sagged but supported his weight. Yard by yard he let himself down. Half the perilous journey through the air was accomplished, and he was directly over the wall, when the chimney cord that kept him from shooting madly backward down the incline, suddenly snapped. The hose trapeze shot downward at headlong speed. Instinctively Boston Blackie reached up with both hands to seize the wires and check his fall.

Even as he reached, realisation of the certain death they carried flashed through his brain. He stayed one hand within inches of the wires. With the other – the one covered with his single rubber glove – he caught one of the wires and gradually checked his fall. Slowly he slid over the wall and down toward the pole outside the prison enclosure. When its shadow warned him he had almost reached it, he stopped himself and, turning his head, studied the network of wires with deep caution. Seeing no way of avoiding their death-dealing touch if he tried to work his way through them and clamber down the pole, he slipped from his seat on the trapeze, hung by his hands for the fraction of a second and dropped.

The fall jarred him from head to foot but left him crouching by the light-pole – uninjured and outside the walls.

For five minutes he lay motionless, watching for any sign of alarm from the walls. None came; he was free.

Slowly and on his stomach, Indian-fashion, Blackie worked his way out from San Gregorio and across the sweet-smelling fields that led toward the world of free men. When the last watchtower was behind him, he rose to his feet and raised his arms toward the blinking and kindly stars in a fervent but unspoken prayer of thanksgiving. He had done the impossible. He had escaped from the hitherto unbeatable prison ruled by Martin Sherwood.

Just as the morning bell was rousing the sleepy cell-houses at San Gregorio to another weary day of serfdom, a gaunt wraith of a man climbed a rear stairway to a tiny apartment on Laguna Street, San Francisco. The early morning fog added to his ghost-like appearance as he softly rapped at the bedroom window with the knock that is the open sesame of the underworld. The woman sleeping within awoke instantly with a start, but lay quiet, fearing she still dreamed, for in her dream she had been with Boston Blackie, her husband.

Again she heard the soft rap at the window. She sprang to the sash, looked out and threw it open, seizing in her arms the scarecrow of a man who stood there and dragging him inside.

'Mary!' he cried.

'Blackie!' she answered.

All the endearments of all the languages of the world accentuated a hundredfold were in the two words.

'God in heaven, I thank you,' she whispered, falling to her knees with Blackie's stained and haggard face clasped to her breast.

'Boston Blackie is missing from his cell in the hospital, sir. He sawed two window-bars and got out during the night. He left his clothes rolled into a dummy on his bunk, and the night-guard didn't discover it until the morning a moment ago. But he can't be far away. He couldn't have got over the wall and must be hidden somewhere about the prison, the night-captain thinks. He has ordered the whole force out to make a search.'

The hospital turnkey saluted the Deputy Warden and stood awaiting his orders. There was no surprise in Martin Sherwood's eyes, and no excitement in his manner.

'And so he's gone,' he said. 'His convict suit in his bunk, you say?' The guard nodded.

'Tell the captain he needn't bother to search the prison yard or buildings. He's wasting his time,' Sherwood continued. 'Blackie has five to seven hours' start at least, and he's miles away from here now.'

'But he can't be. He must be inside the walls. He couldn't have got over them,' protested the guard.

'He's over the walls, safe enough,' Sherwood returned with conviction. 'Boston Blackie isn't a man to saw his way out of a cell and then hide in a dark corner of the prison and wait for us to find him. He's gone, without a doubt.'

The Deputy pulled his phone toward him and called the chief of police of San Francisco at his home.

'Boston Blackie, the safe-blower, has escaped,' he said when a sleepy voice answered him over the wire. 'What? It's the first time, yes, but there has to be a first time for everything, you know, particularly when you are dealing with a man like Blackie. Now, Chief, he's bound to go straight to Mary Dawson, a woman who is living somewhere in your town. I wish you would put your best men out quick to locate her. It ought to be easy, for every crook in town knows them both, and somebody will be sure to tell where she is living. You haven't a second to spare, for both she and Blackie will drop out of sight before night so completely we never will find them. We'll offer five hundred dollars reward for Blackie. Sure! All right. I'll be over.'

Martin Sherwood hung up the phone and turned to the work before him with something akin to pleasureable anticipation on his face. Like all truly strong men he found satisfaction in a battle with a worthy foeman.

Meanwhile, in Mary Dawson's Laguna Street apartment, Boston Blackie was no less alert than Martin Sherwood.

'Does anyone know of this address?' he asked the woman who sat on his knee stroking his hair and running gentle, loving fingers sadly over the deep lines left in his haggard face by pain and illness.

'I moved only a month ago when you sent me word,' she said. 'Scarcely anyone knows. I met Diamond Frank and Stella last week, and they were up here to dinner.'

'We must get away from here at once,' Blackie said. 'We've got to disappear so completely it will be humanly impossibly to trace us. One overlooked clue – the slightest in the world – will lead the Deputy Warden to us. He's no ordinary copper. It's a hundred to one he has half the detectives in the town out hunting this flat now, for he knows, of course, that I'd go to you. But, little sweetheart, I'll promise you this: whether he finds us or not, he'll never take Boston Blackie back to San Gregorio. Have you any guns?'

Mary nodded, shuddering, and began to throw clothes into a trunk.

'Never mind packing the trunk, Mary,' Blackie corrected. 'Just throw together what you can get into a couple of suitcases, dear. We'll leave everything else behind. We're not going to use any transfer-men in this move, little woman.'

Mary sighed as she obeyed without question. Little feminine trinkets are dear to a woman, and she hated to leave them, but Blackie's word was the only law she knew.

There was nothing to distinguish the man and woman carrying suitcases, who took a street-car near Mary's apartment and crossed to the other side of the city, from scores of other passengers who travelled with them – except the man's emaciation. They rented a room in a modest lodging-house on the edge of a good residence district.

'Mary,' said Blackie the moment they were alone, 'there's work for you to do quickly. We're safe here until tonight, but no longer. Go downtown to Levy's theatrical costuming shop. Tell them you're playing a grandmother's part in an amateur play and get a complete old woman's outfit – white wig, clothes, shoes, everything. Get a cheap hat and a working-girl's hand-me-down, too. You're too well dressed not to attract attention where we're going. Draw every dollar we have in the bank just as soon as possible, for every moment you are on the street is a danger. You better bring me something to eat, too – just a loaf of bread, for I ruined my stomach with lye to get into the prison hospital, and I can't eat anything but crusts. Above everything, be careful no one recognises you and tails you out here. Every copper in town must be looking for us by this time.'

He drew two revolvers from the suitcase, looked carefully to their loads and laid them on the bed.

'I'm going to sleep while you're gone. I didn't get much rest last night,' he said, smiling happily.

*

At noon that day, while Boston Blackie lay sleeping in the crosstown lodging-house, the police located Mary Dawson's Laguna Street apartment. Diamond Frank had casually mentioned the address to another crook, who happened to mention it to a bartender who was a stool-pigeon; and so, deviously but surely, it finally reached head-quarters.

The chief of police called in a dozen of his best men, armed them and sent them out in two autos.

'Take no chances with him. boys,' the chief warned. 'When he's lying dead in a morgue, it might be safe to walk in on him, but I wouldn't gamble on it then unless I had seen him killed. He's a bad one. Take care of yourselves.'

The chief's men did so to the very best of their ability. They put officers with drawn guns at every door and window – outside. When everything was ready and not even a mouse could have escaped from the house without being riddled by a dozen bullets, the captain in charge of the expedition asked who would volunteer to enter the apartment and arrest the escaped convict. The policemen shifted uneasily on their feet and glanced expectantly at each other, but no one spoke. Someone had an inspiration.

'Let's send the landlady to the door with a phoney letter,' he suggested. 'When the girl comes to the door, we'll grab her and bust in on Blackie before he knows were in the joint.

The plan was adopted. The landlady knocked on the door, with four brawny men behind her ready to seize whoever opened it. There was no response. Repeated knocks were equally fruitless. Finally the landlady took a passkey, and opened the door.

'Gone,' chorused the detectives as they saw the empty rooms.

'The girl's out somewhere probably to meet him. Then they'll come back here, both of 'em,' the captain declared. 'They haven't blowed. Look at the trunks and clothes. Now we'll get 'em dead to rights. We'll just plant inside here and cover them when they come back.'

But the guards in Mary's flat stayed there three days ready to pounce on the man – who never came. Meanwhile Sherwood started a canvass of every hotel and lodging-house in the city. On the third day a detective brought in the information that a landlady, when shown Blackie's picture, identified it as that of a man who came with his wife and rented a room on the morning of the escape. They had two suit-cases. The woman went out and came back with some packages. The next morning when she went to collect her rent for the second day, the couple had gone. That was all the landlady could tell.

'I thought so,' Sherwood mused when the news was phoned to him.

'He's hidden somewhere he thinks is perfectly secure. Every exit from the city is guarded, but that's pretty much wasted effort, for Boston Blackie, if I know him, won't stir from his place of refuge for weeks, maybe months. The man who finds him now will have real reason to compliment himself. And,' he added with unalterable determination, 'I'm going to be that man.'

Sherwood turned the management of the prison over to a subordinate and spent his time directing the investigation of the hundreds of clues the reward brought to the police. But all proved futile. Fewer and fewer clues came in. A newer sensation crowded stories of the hunt for Boston Blackie from the first pages of the newspapers. The police frankly were beaten. Only Martin Sherwood kept at the task.

Sherwood puzzled and pondered for days without finding the clue he sought. Every detail of the escaped convict's appearance as he last saw him on the prison lawn was graven photographically into his brain. He remembered the emaciated face, the too-brilliant eyes, the shrunken shoulders from which the flesh had fallen away during his illness in the hospital.

'The doctor said that illness was real,' he pondered. 'Stomach trouble, he said, and he's not a man to be fooled. Blackie was really sick, without a doubt, and yet that sickness couldn't have been mere chance. He hadn't eaten anything but outer crusts of bread for weeks. Even the night he escaped he left the inside of a loaf in his cell. Ah! The inside of a loaf – and he always did that – always threw away the inside of bread loaves because he couldn't digest them.'

Martin Sherwood sprang to his feet more nearly excited than he had been in years.

'It's a long chance,' he said to himself. 'But it is a chance. He'll be more than human if he has thought of that too.'

The Deputy Warden ordered his car and drove out to the city incinerator where the garbage wagons of the city consigned their ill-smelling burdens to a cleansing flame. Sherwood explained to the superintendent.

'Tell every garbage-collector in the city,' he said, 'that I'll pay the man who finds the hollowed-out insides of loaves of bread in a garbage can one hundred dollars for the address from which the can was filled.'

'In three days, Mary, just three short days, we'll sail together through the Golden Gate. You and I will be together with a new world ahead, and Martin Sherwood behind, nursing the bitterness of defeat!'

Mary, with a better, sweeter happiness in her eyes than Boston Blackie had ever seen there, clung to him as he spoke. They were in the two small rooms – kitchen and bedroom – in which they had lain securely hidden during the ten days which had elapsed since Blackie's flight from prison. Their landlady, who scrubbed office-building floors at night to support herself, lived alone in the floor below. The house was an attic cottage with a garden, in San Francisco's sunny Mission. Boston Blackie and his Mary sat hand in hand planning a future without a flaw – a future as rosy-hued as the girl's cheeks. The realisation of their hopes was very near now. In three days the *Colon* sailed for Central American ports. Their passage was paid. The hunt for Blackie had died down. Once aboard the steamer and out of the harbour, a matter of little risk now, they would be safe and free and unafraid.

So they sat and planned in happy whispers – for caution still bade them be low-voiced while their landlady was in the house – while just below them, low-voiced and cautious too, Martin Sherwood questioned the landlady.

'I have no roomers but a Miss Collins and her mother, who is an invalid, poor soul. They have the two rooms in the attic,' she was telling the Deputy. 'The girl is learning shorthand and don't go out much. The old lady is crippled with rheumatism and can't leave the rooms. Oh, they are nice, quiet, respectable people, sir.'

Sherwood was deeply puzzled. From the garbage-can behind this house had come a half-dozen loaves of bread in three days, with the crusts – and only the crusts – eaten off. He had come to the house after painstaking preparation, feeling that Boston Blackie and victory were in his grasp. The landlady's story of a girl who studied shorthand, and an invalid mother, found no place in his theory of what he would find there, and yet it was evident the woman spoke the truth.

'What does the girl look like? What is the colour of her hair?' he asked.

'Red, sir – a beautiful red like a polished copper kettle.'

Mary's hair was coal black. For the first time Martin Sherwood's confidence was shaken.

'When did they come here?' he asked.

'Why, let me see,' the woman reckoned on her fingers. 'It was a week ago Thursday, sir, in the evening. They saw my advertisement in the paper, and came just before I went to work – which is nine o'clock, sir.'

Blackie had escaped early on the morning of the day she mentioned. On that Thursday night he and Mary had disappeared from the lodging-house which was their first place of refuge. The date and hour of their arrival decided Sherwood. He would have a look at this redhaired girl and her invalid mother.

'I would like to go up and see them for a moment,' he told the woman. 'I'm an officer.' He showed his star. 'Oh, no, nothing wrong at all. I just want to see them. I like to keep track of people in the district.'

'Certainly, sir. I'll call Miss Collins and –'

'No, no – that isn't necessary,' hastily interrupted Sherwood. 'I'll just step upstairs and knock.'

Though he tried to step lightly, as Sherwood's tread sounded on the uncarpeted stairway there was a sudden shuffling of feet on the floor above. He smiled, for that augured well, and he felt for the gun slung inside his coat. Then he rapped.

Muffled sounds came from behind the door. A chair squeaked as it was pushed across the floor. A few seconds of silence, and then, plain and unmistakable, came the sound of a woman sobbing hysterically. Sherwood tried the door, found it locked, and knocked again peremptorily.

The door suddenly was flung wide open, and in a flood of light from within a woman faced him – a woman with a wealth of bronze hair that should have been black, a woman with tears on cheeks that were as bloodless as death, a woman whom he instantly recognised as Boston Blackie's Mary.

Martin Sherwood sprang inside with drawn revolver ready to answer the stream of lead he expected from some corner of the room. None came. Instead he saw a woman, white-haired and evidently feeble, sitting beside a bed with bowed head while her body shook with convulsive sobs. On the bed, covered with a sheet that was drawn up over the face, lay a silent, motionless form that told its own story.

Sudden disappointment gripped Martin Sherwood's heart. Had the man he had rated so highly cheated him of his long-coveted triumph only by the coward's expedient of suicide?

'Where's Boston Blackie?' he demanded, his gun still covering the room.

Mary pointed silently to the still figure on the bed.

'Dead!' exclaimed the Deputy Warden. 'When? How?'

'An hour ago,' she sobbed. 'You starved him to death in your prison.' She dropped to her knees. 'God have mercy on us now!' she prayed.

Sherwood strode to the bed. beside which the aged woman still sat sobbing, and leaning over, lifted the sheet. As he did so, his gun for the first time failed to cover all the room. Beneath the sheet, instead of the face he expected, he saw a roll of blankets carefully moulded and tied into the semblance of a human form. Before he could turn, cold steel was pressed against the base of his brain.

'Drop that gun, Sherwood,' said Boston Blackie's voice from behind him. 'Drop it quick. Raise it one inch, and you'll be as dead as you thought I was.'

Sherwood hesitated as a full realisation of the new situation flashed through his mind; then he smiled as he thought of the posse he had thrown around the house and let his revolver slip through his fingers to the bed. Here was a worthy antagonist – a bit too worthy, as the cards lay just then! But the deal was far from done.

'Pick up his gun, Mary, and lay it on the table in the corner well out of the Deputy's way,' directed Blackie. 'Then see if he has another. I don't care to move the muzzle of my gun from his neck just yet. Now,' he continued. 'slip off these skirts. I'm not overly well used to them, even though I've worn them for ten days, and if Mr Sherwood should forget the company he's in and get suddenly reckless, they might be in my way.'

'Now turn around, Sherwood, and face the music,' ordered Blackie a moment later.

The Deputy Warden turned and faced the convict behind whom lay a discarded white wig and an old woman's garments. He met his captor's eyes without a tremor, and smiled.

'Well done, Blackie, I must admit,' he said. 'But I should have known when you didn't shoot as I came in, things weren't as they seemed.

'I didn't expect you. Sherwood.' Blackie replied, 'but as you see, I made preparations to receive you in case you came.'

The convict's face grew pale and suddenly grave. His grip on the gun levelled at the Deputy's gun tightened.

'You understand, Sherwood, I've got to kill you,' he said then.

'As matters stand, naturally it wouldn't surprise me,' the Deputy answered. His voice was absolutely calm and unshaken, his eyes without the remotest trace of fear.

'If you have anything to say or do or think, be quick,' said the convict.

'I haven't – thank you.'

The men stared into each other's eyes, the silence broken only by Mary's sobs.

'I hate to kill a man as brave as you in cold blood,' said Boston Blackie slowly. 'You're a brave man, Sherwood, even when you don't hold all the cards in the game as you do inside your prison. I hate to kill you, but I've got to. I can't tie and gag you. You'd get free before we could get away from the city. I can't risk that.'

'Naturally not,' said Sherwood.

'I couldn't trust your promise not to bother me, in a life-or-death matter like this, if I let you go alive,' continued Blackie with troubled eyes.

'I wouldn't give it if you did.' There was no hesitation in the answer.

'Well, then.' The gun that covered the Deputy Warden's head swayed downward until the muzzle covered his heart. 'Are you ready?'

'Any time,' said Sherwood.

The hammer rose under the pressure of the convict's finger on the trigger. Mary Dawson, crying hysterically now, turned away her face and covered her ears.

'Do you want to go, Mary, before I – I do what I must do?' asked Blackie, realising what the scene with its inevitable end must mean to the girl. 'It would be better for you to go, dear.'

'No, no,' she cried. 'I want to share with you all blame for what you do. I won't go until you do.'

Sherwood turned his eyes curiously on the woman. Sherwood knew what he would have risked for such a woman and such love.

Boston Blackie's face was strangely grey. The hammer of the revolver rose, hesitated, fell – then rose again. The Deputy, his gaze returning from the woman's face, looked into the gun unflinchingly and in silence. Another pause freighted with that sort of tension that crumbles the strongest; then slowly the convict let the muzzle of his weapon drop below the heart of the man he faced.

'Sherwood,' he said in a voice that broke between his words, 'I hate you as I hate no living man, but I can't kill you as you stand before me unarmed and helpless. I'm going to give you a chance for your life.' He stepped backward and picked up the Deputy Warden's revolver. He pushed a table between himself and the man he couldn't kill. He laid the revolvers side by side on it, one pointing toward him, the other toward Sherwood. The clock on the mantel showed three minutes of the hour.

'Sherwood,' he said, 'in three minutes the clock will strike. I'm exactly as far from the guns as you. On the first stroke of the clock we'll reach together for them – and the quickest hand wins.'

Martin Sherwood studied Boston Blackie's face with something in his eyes no other man had ever seen there. He glanced toward the guns on the table. It was true he was exactly as near them as the convict. Nothing prevented him from reaching them and firing at the first touch of his finger on the trigger. Blackie deliberately had surrendered his irresistible advantage to give him, Martin Sherwood, his prison-torturer, an even chance for life. For the first time the Deputy's eyes were unsteady and his voice throaty and shaken.

'I won't bargain with you, Blackie,' he said.

'You're afraid to risk an even break?'

'You know I'm not,' Sherwood answered, his gaze turning once more to the woman who stood by the door, staring panic-stricken. It was plain that the issue to be decided in that room was life or death to her as well as to the men.

Boston Blackie reached for his gun, hoping the Deputy Warden would do likewise and end, in one quick exchange of shots, the strain he knew was breaking his nerve. Sherwood let Blackie recover his weapon without moving a muscle. Once more the convict's revolver rose till it covered Martin Sherwood's heart. They stood again as they had been, the Deputy at the mercy of the escaped prisoner.

Seconds passed, then minutes, without a word or motion on either side of the table over which the triangular tragedy was being settled not at all as any of those concerned had planned. The strain was unbearable. The muscles of the convict's throat twitched. His face was drawn and distorted.

'Pick up that gun and defend yourself,' he cried.

'No!' shouted Sherwood, the calm which his mighty will had until then sustained snapping like an overtightened violin-string.

'You want to make me feel like a murderer,' cried Blackie in anguish. 'Why didn't I give you bullet for bullet when you came in the door? I could have killed you then. Now I can't unless you'll fight. Once more I ask you, will you take an even break?'

'No,' cried Sherwood again.

With a great cry – the cry of a strong man broken and beaten – Boston Blackie threw his gun upon the floor.

'You win, Sherwood,' he sobbed, losing self-control completely for the first time in a life of daily hazards. 'You've beaten me.'

He staggered drunkenly toward Mary and folded her in his arms.

'I tried to force myself to pull the trigger by thinking of the life we hoped for together, dear, but I couldn't do it,' he moaned brokenly. 'I'll go back with him now. Everything is over.'

'I'm glad you didn't, dear,' she cried, clinging to him. 'It would have been murder. I don't want you to do that, even to save our happiness. But I'll wait for you, dear one, wait till your time is done and you come back to me again.'

*

Boston Blackie straightened his shoulders and turning to Sherwood, held out his wrists for the handcuffs.

'Come, come,' he urged. 'For God's sake don't prolong this. Don't stand there gloating. Take me away.'

Martin Sherwood, with something strangely new transfiguring the face Boston Blackie knew and hated, reached to the table and took up his gun slowly. Just as slowly he dropped it into his pocket. He looked into the two grief-racked faces before him, long and silently.

'I'm sorry I disturbed you folks,' he said quietly at last. 'I came here looking for an escaped convict named Boston Blackie. I have found only you, Miss Collins, and your mother. I'm sorry my misinformation has subjected you both to annoyance. The police officers who are outside – 'The Deputy Warden opened a crack in the window-curtain and pointed out to them dim shapes in the darkness – 'and who surround this house, will be withdrawn at once. Had Boston Blackie been in this room, and had he by some mischance killed me, his shot would have brought a dozen men armed with sawn-off shotguns. Escape for him was absolutely impossible. I saw to that before I entered here alone to capture him. But it has all been a blunder. The man I wanted to take back to prison is not here, and I can only hope my apology will be accepted.'

Blackie stared at him with blazing, unbelieving eyes. From Mary came a cry in which all the pent-up anguish of the lifetime that had been lived in the last half-hour found sudden relief.

'Good night, folks,' said Martin Sherwood, offering Boston Blackie his hand. The convict caught it in his own, and the men looked into each other's eyes for a second. Then the Deputy Warden went out and closed the door behind him.

Mary sprang into Blackie's arms, and they dropped together into a chair, dazed with a happiness greater than either had ever known.

'He is a man,' said Blackie. 'He is a man even though he's a copper.'

Martin Sherwood let himself out of the house and beckoned the cordon of police to him as he looked back at the windows of the attic rooms and spoke softly to himself.

'He is a man,' he said. 'He is a man, even though he is a convict.'

It was the greatest praise and the greatest concession either had ever made to another man.

A Man Called Falcon

BY MICHAEL ARLEN

The success of Boston Blackie *not surprisingly prompted the rival American TV networks to find their own crime series. CBS took another old favourite of the movies,* The Lone Wolf, *aka the reformed gentleman jewel thief Michael Lanyard, and starred the suave Hollywood leading man Louis Hayward in the title role. As his name implied,* The Lone Wolf *operated on his own and his liaisons with the law were few and far between. This was not the case with ABC's* The Adventures of The Falcon, *another character who had also been a movie favourite for a decade and now enjoyed a new lease of life on television from 1954. Created originally as a tough guy in a short story written by the bestselling English novelist Michael Arlen (1895–1956) in which he came to the aid of Chief Inspector Poss of Scotland Yard,* The Falcon – *real name Gay Stanhope Falcon – had in the intervening years on the screen become something of a handsome charmer who only took on difficult assignments for beautiful clients. This was rather at variance with Arlen's story in which The Falcon had been met unceremoniously breaking into a woman's bedroom in order to burglarise her safe!*

The first movie, entitled The Gay Falcon, *had been produced by RKO in 1941 with the smooth English actor George Sanders in the leading role. Four films later, Sanders, fearful of getting typecast, became the first (and only) American series detective to die on screen: allowing his 'brother', played by Tom Conway, to take over as The Falcon. (Coincidentally, Sanders and Conway were also brothers in real life.) Conway proved rather less inhibited about typecasting than Sanders and subsequently played the role ten times before handing over to John Calvert for three final appearances in the late forties.*

Interestingly, in 1945, Leslie Charteris, creator of The Saint, filed a complaint alleging unfair competition against RKO who were then not only making The Falcon pictures, but also those featuring The Saint – with George Sanders the star of both! Charteris maintained that the two characters were identical and The Falcon was nothing but a plagiarism of The Saint. The film company who were, in fact, paying Michael Arlen considerably less for the use of his character than Charteris, took a simple way out of what could have been a lengthy and costly action – they dropped The Saint.

When ABC producer Bernard Schubert masterminded The Falcon's return to the small screen in 1954 he set out to restore something of his original character by casting Charles McGraw, a veteran Hollywood tough-guy character actor, as the hard-edged, gravel-voiced hero. However, Schubert did feel compelled to change his hero's name to the more overtly masculine Mike Waring, and to dispense altogether with Chief Inspector Poss – substituting Douglas Fowley as Captain Allen, a wary police collaborator. In all a total of thirty-nine black and white, half-hour episodes of The Adventures of The Falcon were screened during the next two years, often being transmitted in certain areas of America at the same time as The Lone Wolf. In those days before videos, one can only imagine the frustration that must have been felt by those who enjoyed both series!

A Man Called Falcon (which has also been published as Gay Falcon) was originally written by Michael Arlen in 1940 and subsequently provided the basis not only for the movies but also a radio series (which ran on Mutual from 1945) and the TV series. What follows is therefore the only piece of fiction he ever wrote about the legendary Falcon . . .

NOW OF THIS man who called himself Gay Falcon many tales are told, and this is one of them.

It is told how, late one night not long ago, a pretty lady awoke to find a man in her bedroom, and how this outrage on her privacy started a train of most peculiar events which finally ended in as sensational a murder as you could wish to see.

But let us take one thing at a time.

Her dreamless sleep so rudely shattered, the pretty lady blinked in the sudden light which the intruder, behaving in a manner quite unsuitable in a decent burglar, had switched on.

'What is it?' she cried. 'What do you want?'

She was surprised, not frightened. It took more than a man to frighten this pretty lady, as many a man had found. Flinging her bedjacket about her shoulders, her famous blue eyes, now so entirely devoid of the desire to please that photographers would have recognised her only with difficulty, regarded the stranger with surprise and contempt. But such treatment appeared only to nourish his disagreeable assurance.

'Lady, be good,' he said. 'Don't ring. Don't telephone.'

It should be pointed out that the tall intruder must indeed have lacked all sensibility, for even when addressing the lady he did not remove his hat, which was of weathered felt, the colour of rain on Piccadilly, and worn at an angle over his left eye which might have been called debonair anywhere but in a lady's bedroom.

'You are easy to look at,' he said thoughtfully, 'even without the makeup. Easy on the eye.'

While these compliments were vulgar and ill-timed, they were deserved in full measure. The lady made a very pretty picture. Her bedjacket matched her bedspread, which was of white satin fringed with white ermine, while everything about her – hair, eyes, features, complexion – was of the very best and most attractive quality obtainable for women over twenty-five but under thirty.

But this lady's beauty can need no description when it is revealed that her name was Mrs Temple, Diana Temple, of London, Paris, and New York one of the ten or maybe ten thousand best-dressed women in the world, excluding China and the Solomon Islands.

Of the fellow Temple, her husband, nothing can be said since nothing is known, apart from the fact that he had a brother. Once upon a time this brother had run away to sea, while Temple had married Diana, and neither was ever heard of again.

But the rude intruder made no attempt to conceal the fact that Diana Temple was no more to him than just another woman. As she swiftly stretched out a hand to her bedside table, he more swiftly put the telephone and bell-push out of her reach.

'Lady, be calm,' he said. 'This is the one occasion when Diana Temple is not going to do what she likes with a man. I don't want to get tough with you – so be good, my pretty.'

Her lovely eyes widened with frank curiosity as she stared up at the man's dark, saturnine face. He was tall, his clothes were as you like it for an old suit casually worn, his face was long and lean and dark, and his eyes were deep, hard shadows.

'You are a strange burglar, I think,' she said, 'and somehow –'

'Somehow?' he said, and flicked off his hat.

'Why,' she cried. 'I've met you before!'

'Yes,' he said. 'We slept together through Lady Taura's dinner party two weeks ago.'

'We danced together, too,' she said. 'I remember – Gay Falcon. Your name is Gay Falcon!'

'I have others equally improbable.'

'Tell me frankly, Mr Falcon – do you enjoy being such a contemptible beast?'

'I enjoy the company of a woman of courage, Mrs Temple. It relieves me that you take so lightly the fact that you are going to be robbed.'

When she smiled you saw at once why men who were prudent with their wives pressed pearls and diamonds on Diana Temple.

'But,' she smiled, 'I am not going to be robbed. How silly of you to be so recognisable, Mr Falcon. You *can* rob me, of course. But you will be arrested tomorrow.'

'We shall see,' said the man who called himself Gay Falcon. 'Don't you remember something else about Lady Taura's party apart from the fact that we danced together?'

'Dear me,' she said, staring, 'her emerald! Of course – her lovely emerald, which was found to be missing next morning.' She measured the man with a cold and detached curiosity which might have mortified a less assured scoundrel. 'You are a clever thief, Mr Falcon.'

'It was nice work, certainly. Of course, the stone is not worth the sum Lady Taura will collect from the insurance in due course – but still, it was nice work.'

'I'm glad you are pleased, Mr Falcon. It must be pleasant to make such a success of one's chosen profession.'

'I haven't said I stole it, Mrs Temple.'

The saturnine stranger unsmilingly surveyed the spacious bedroom.

Mrs Temple lost nothing of her poise when she saw that the thief's eyes had come to rest on her dressing-table. There, on a small tray of crimson velvet, like bright fruit fallen from the trees of an ambitious maiden's dreams, lay the necklace of rubies and bracelets of rubies and clips of rubies she had worn at dinner.

'You won't really mind my taking those,' he said, 'since they are so well insured.'

'Since you know so much, Mr Falcon, you will know that the insurance cannot repay me for their romantic and sentimental value.'

The man glanced at her with a queer cold smile, and Mrs Temple felt really uneasy for the first time. 'In that case,' he said, 'I won't take them. Observe my big heart.'

She heard herself, and with infinite surprise, laughing unsteadily.

'Then you must go away empty-handed, Mr Falcon, for everything else is at my bank.'

The tall man's eyes had come to rest on the only picture in the austere room. This was a small Italian primitive, the colour still bright on the cracked wood, of the Virgin Mary with the Child, and it was let into the wall just beside the bed behind the bedside table.

And as the man approached the primitive set into the wall, Mrs Temple, the calm and remote Mrs Temple, stared at him with suddenly uncontrollable terror.

'Oh, no!' she whispered. 'No – please!'

'I fancy,' he said, reaching out a hand past the telephone to the lower right corner of the primitive, 'I fancy, Mrs Temple, that you won't tell the police about what I am going to do now.'

She fought him with all her strength. Quite silently, but for bitter little sighs of feminine despair, her lovely features distorted with fear, she beat her arms frantically against him in a vain attempt to prevent him from opening the little secret safe in the wall.

But when she had done all she could, she regained her practised dignity. She did not look to see what he was taking from the secret safe. She lay very still and stared up at the ceiling with wide open eyes that seemed to be counting some ghosts that walked there.

He looked back at her from the door and was about to say something. Then he saw how she lay still and looked to be counting ghosts that walked across the ceiling and he went out without a word.

She was the most frightened woman he had ever seen, and it was interesting to wonder why, since it was not of him that she was so frightened.

On the following morning, the activities of the man who called himself Gay Falcon were surprising in a simple burglar.

Passing through the imposing doors of a very large new building on Pall Mall, known to all the world as the headquarters of Universal & Allied Assurance, he was immediately taken up to the handsome boardroom. It was just one minute after noon.

Nine gentlemen appeared to have been awaiting his entrance. Of these, a few were directors of Universal & Allied, while others represented important firms of underwriters and assessors. The sulky features of the ninth gentleman were recognisable to readers of popular newspapers as being those of Chief Inspector Poss of Scotland Yard. As he sat on the board-table, he made no secret of the fact that he disapproved strongly of his present situation and was quite un-prepared to change his mind in the near future.

The man called Falcon had with him a small but evidently well-filled leather satchel. He slid this with an expert shove down the length of the long table to the handsome grey-haired gentleman who sat at its head.

'There you are, Mr Hammersley. In the last few years, your people and other underwriters have paid out close to a hundred thousand pounds in claims on the lost or stolen jewellery represented by that little lot.'

It was only Chief Inspector Poss who examined the jewellery with any degree of close attention. The others merely glanced at it, some with inexpert eyes, while their interest was centred on the tall lean figure of Falcon.

'If that is the case,' said Mr Hammersley, 'as it very probably is, your commission of five per cent will come to five thousand pounds, which is very nice money, Mr Falcon.'

'When you hired me, Mr Hammersley, did you think you were hiring a nursemaid?'

'Oh, we are not complaining,' said a large smiling, ruddy man.

'Thank you very much,' said Gay Falcon. It was obvious that he was not a man who would have succeeded in politics, where charm of manner is said to be an advantage.

'And now,' said the smiling, ruddy man, 'perhaps we can hear how you have managed to succeed so quickly where the police have so consistently failed.'

Falcon's hard, unsmiling eyes flicked over the Chief Inspector, who, bent over the table, was still examining the jewellery. Then his gaze went back to the large ruddy man with the twinkling blue eyes. This was Mr Harvey Morgan, always known as 'Chappie' Morgan, a very successful financier and popular sportsman. It was apparent from Falcon's expression that he thought more amiably of Chappie Morgan than of his associates.

'Well, what's your story?' said handsome Mr Hammersley sharply.

'My father was a dentist in Leicester and my mother died when I was a child. Shortly afterward I decided to leave home and become an engine-driver, but owing to –'

'We asked you, Mr Falcon, for your story about this recovered jewellery.'

Chappie Morgan gave a loud bark of laughter.

'Listen Hammersley,' said the man called Falcon, 'you people hired me because the police failed to justify reasonable suspicions that underwriters were being cleverly robbed. I have confirmed your suspicions and returned part of the jewellery. I am not a policeman. I am not a storyteller. I am a man who makes a living by keeping his mouth shut. The money due me should be paid into my account at Barclays Bank, Piccadilly branch.'

Chief Inspector Poss looked across the table very steadily. 'That won't do, Falcon.'

'Mister Falcon, Chief Inspector. What won't do?'

'Gentlemen,' said the Chief Inspector to the board, 'I told you a month ago that it was highly irregular to give a free hand in this matter to a man like this Falcon –'

'Mr Flatfoot,' said Gay Falcon, 'one more crack from you and I'll give the whole story to the newspapers, then you and your efficient detectives will be looking for jobs as film extras.'

'Better be a good boy, Poss,' grinned Chappie Morgan.

'I am not easily frightened, gentlemen. But now you will appreciate why I warned you against engaging *Mister* Falcon. This stuff is stolen jewellery, some of it very famous jewellery. And we know for a fact that not one little bit of it has passed through the hands of any fence in England. You are taking a grave risk, gentlemen. If we don't hear from this man Falcon how he has managed to succeed where the police have failed, you share with him the risk of being charged with aiding and abetting a receiver of stolen jewellery.'

'Quit kidding,' said Falcon. 'It's their property, isn't it, since they've paid all claims on it? Try arresting them for receiving back their own property and see how you like it.'

'But *you* can be charged, *Mister* Falcon, for all sorts of mis-demeanours, I make no doubt. Now behave yourself and help the police by telling me how you recovered this property.'

'Brains,' said Falcon. 'Naughty boy, where are yours?'

The Chief Inspector's grim face had reddened and he was about to retort in a manner unworthy of the high traditions of Scotland Yard when Mr Hammersley intervened with practised authority.

'I'm afraid, Chief Inspector, that while we must agree with you that Mr Falcon's attitude is highly irregular, we cannot encourage you to take any action against him. It was with your knowledge that we engaged him to recover this jewellery, which the police had failed to find for two years.'

'And now,' said Chappie Morgan, 'Scotland Yard is angry because Falcon won't give away his little secret.'

'The law,' said Chief Inspector Poss, with commendable restraint, 'does not acknowledge secrets in respect of other people's stolen property. This man Falcon's position requires investigation.' He picked up a jewel from amongst the heap on the table. 'Now here is the famous Taura emerald, which Lady Taura reported as stolen or missing two weeks ago –'

'Insured at nine thousand pounds,' said someone.

'Yes. And here it is, recovered. But how? It was stolen at or after a ball given by Lady Taura. And you were there, *Mister* Falcon.'

'Does the fact that I dance better than you do, Chief Inspector, mean that I'm a criminal? Now let me tell you all something. These insurance claims for lost and stolen jewellery from society people over the last two years and more have been part of a very clever racket. I want to find out who is behind this racket. When I do, I'll maybe talk. In fact I promise to talk. Good day to you, gentlemen. Good day, Chief Inspector.'

'You're asking for trouble, Falcon. Remember, there's an unsolved murder somewhere behind these thefts – that of Stella Bowman last year. I warn you again, Falcon.'

'It's years and years, Chief Inspector, since I burst out crying because a policeman didn't like me.'

Now it is on record that no well-known beauty can long survive the rigorous life of being a well-known beauty day in and day out if she does not acquire the courageous gift of being able to 'put off' engagements at more or less the last minute. Mrs X regrets that she is unable to dine because she has a headache and is going to bed with a boiled egg. Mrs X regrets that she cannot lunch today because her doctor has forbidden her to go out.

They always sound like lies. They usually are lies, but people are eager to forgive lies who will find the truth intolerable. For while it is true that people do not like to be put off, it is also true that those people who are by nature liable to be put off invariably live to fight another day for yet another engagement with the same inconsiderate guest.

Therefore Mrs Temple had little hesitation, that very afternoon, in telephoning to Lady Soda's house and regretting that she could not dine that evening with Sir Theodore and Lady Soda owing to this and that.

The fact that she was dining with the man who called himself Gay Falcon, who had telephoned that afternoon in the most casual manner imaginable, was nobody's business but her own. Anyway, Mrs Temple knew, for she was a student of worldliness in all its nasty little niceties, that Sir Theodore and Lady Soda would inevitably invite her again.

She met Mr Falcon at a small restaurant near Jermyn Street which had recently become well known to thinking men of the wealthier sort for its serious attitude in matters of importance. As always, she wore her slender cool beauty with that faint air of detached amusement which is the natural gift of women born to enchant others but never to deceive themselves.

Mr Falcon had taken care they should not be overheard by engaging a corner table. The black-and-white effect of his dinner-jacket emphasised his dark saturnine face and deep eyes and greying hair. It also became apparent to a close observer that he knew how to laugh at many things.

She said: 'Dear me, for an ugly man you are really quite good-looking.'

'Just wait,' he said, 'till you get the lowdown on my kind heart as well, and then you will wonder where I've been all your life. I haven't ordered any dinner, since you never know what a pretty woman will eat, if at all. Have some melon. Have some caviar. Have a steak and onions. Have some grouse. Diana Temple, you are a very pretty woman. Have what you like.'

'How nice it is,' she said, over dinner, 'to be with someone with whom I don't have to pretend anything. Dear me, I am a thief. I am a bad woman. Now you know about me – what about you? What are you? Who are you?'

'And why,' he smiled darkly, 'did I do to you what I did last night?'

'Yes, why?'

'Diana, I'm a man who has done many things. I've been a soldier, a gambler, a secret agent, an aeroplane salesman, a white hunter, a purser, a husband, a co-respondent, a war-correspondent, a long- distance swimmer, a professional dancer, a good salmon-fisherman. I have no rheumatism, no patience, and no money. For further information apply to Scotland Yard for free booklet on the man called Gay Falcon.'

'No money? Then how do you make a living?'

'By engaging in dangerous enterprise – and I've not been killed – yet.'

'But *I* am not a dangerous enterprise, Mr Falcon. Why did you engage yourself in my business?'

'Mrs Temple, some more grouse?'

'No, thank you, Mr Falcon.'

'Then just one more potato? What is one more potato to a figure like yours? Have I told you that I was once married to a woman in New York with a figure just like yours, but she –'

She said, 'Mr Falcon, why did you, who engage in dangerous enterprises, pick on me?'

Over the rim of his wine glass, his sardonic eyes, now unsmiling, regarded her fair face intently. Her gaze did not waver, but that meant little to a man who knew from experience that liars and thieves and killers can look you straighter in the eyes than many an honest man.

'Then I shall ask you a question, too,' he said. 'Why were you so infernally frightened last night?'

'Frightened?' She smiled with a wavering uncertainty that made her beauty poignant. 'But isn't it natural – when a strange man bursts into a woman's –'

'You were not,' he pointed out, 'frightened of me.'

Her eyes fell slowly, and she seemed to be counting the little bright bubbles in her wineglass.

'There is someone in your life, Diana Temple, of whom you are very frightened. For you love life, and you are frightened for your life. And it is because I am out to find and catch that someone that this is a dangerous enterprise.'

Very still, her eyes gave and absorbed, she said nothing. Then she shivered a very little. She did not look at him.

'I don't want,' she whispered to the last bursting bubble in her glass, 'to die.'

'It would be a pity, I agree. Let me tell you a story, Mrs Temple. There are a number of wealthy and respectable women in this world who are now and then in need of hard cash. Perhaps they have lost too much at racing or at cards or owe their brokers more than they can pay. Perhaps husbands or trustees simply will not pay up again.

'They are not women who would willingly do anything criminal. Looking around for money, they see only their jewellery. They think of selling a ring or bracelet, but if they try to sell to a well-known jeweller they fear their husbands will find out or their credit will be damaged, and from an obscure merchant they can hope only for a very poor bargain.

'There is the insurance. Fine jewels belonging to individuals are invariably insured at their replaceable value and not at what you or I could sell them for at second-hand. Therefore, they will get very much more from the insurance than from selling the stuff, even if they knew how.

'But the very fact that insurance companies can exist and thrive is due to something fundamental in human nature – that the vast majority of people are honest, that a small number would be faintly dishonest if not frightened of the law, while only a very small percentage are really dishonest.

'So the respectable women I speak of would not dream of cheating the underwriters by throwing a ruby into a lake, while some would like to but daren't for fear of breaking down when answering the searching questions of practised investigators.

'Then one day along comes the answer to their troubles. Let us say that a Mrs de Courcy Fish, well known to readers of unimportant papers as an important person, owes her bookmaker a thousand quid. She daren't tell her old man because he is hard up himself and she has promised never to gamble again. Her bookmaker is getting nasty, like in the storybooks. And then one day a voice on the telephone tells her just what to do to raise the wind.

'"Mrs de Snooks Fish," says the voice, "don't worry about your debts. Yes, I know all about you. All you have to do is to claim the fifteen hundred insurance on that ruby ring you have lost."

'"My ruby!" she cries. "But I haven't lost it. I've never lost anything."

'"Oh yes, you have, madam. You have lost your ruby tomorrow night at Delsarto's, where you and your husband have supper so often after the theatre. You were sitting – tomorrow night – at your usual table, and somehow owing to a slight scratch on your finger your ring was bothering you. So you put it, or you thought you did, beside your plate and – really very stupidly – forgot it there for a few minutes while you got up to dance. Or if your husband didn't want to dance tomorrow night, you went to powder your nose. Anyway, some ten minutes or so after you got back, you missed the ring. But being uncertain whether you really had taken it off or whether it had dropped off your finger while dancing and so on and forget this talk and I am so sorry you have lost your ruby tomorrow night and good day to you, madam."

'That, Mrs Temple, is more or less how this insurance racket started. One clever thing about it was that the people who put in claims for lost or stolen jewellery had never or very seldom lost anything before, and so were and are rated as first-class risks. And another clever thing was that the women concerned really did delude themselves that they really had lost or mislaid or dropped the stuff, as indeed they had, in one way.

'That is my story, Diana – and your story, too.'

Watching her, he did not help her light her cigarette. Carefully, she blew out the match, and for a long minute stared at its burnt tip.

She said: 'How did you find me out?'

'I have been interested in you for some time. I wondered how you had enough money to live and dress as you do, since your husband disappeared years ago.'

'My uncle –' she said.

'My uncle my eye, beautiful. Then I watched you at Lady Taura's party. She has a large income, but I happen to know she has to pay her broker five thousand pounds soon or be sold out of her American securities. She had her emerald at dinner. She had it at midnight. She did *not* have it after she had gone into the library for a gossip with the Home Secretary – though she didn't seem to notice her loss until the next morning. Well, a hostess has much on her mind. But I saw the emerald, and left it where it had apparently slipped from her finger between the cushions of the sofa on which she had been chatting with the Home Secretary – and on which, later on, you were flirting with that young ass, Chubby Wimpole.'

She looked at him steadily.

'You win,' she said. 'What are you going to do? Why haven't you told the police already?'

'Because you are only a frightened minnow, beautiful. What good will it do to put you behind bars? I want to catch the shark. And so I shall catch him, or know why.'

She was intent on crushing out her half-smoked cigarette.

'Don't!' she whispered. 'Leave him alone.' Suddenly, never looking at him, she spoke very quickly. 'Yes, I am frightened. He's a killer. Leave him alone, Mr Falcon. I warn you. He doesn't know yet – I dare *not* tell him – that you've taken the stuff from me. He's retiring from business next week. Then he comes to collect my lot – it's less than half of what there is in all – and starts on his travels, a retired and rich business man, to South America. Leave him alone, Gay Falcon. There's only one life.'

'What about yours? What shall you do?'

She smiled faintly. 'Diana Temple,' she said, 'has taken a suite at the Ritz in Paris as from tomorrow. Perhaps you will dine with me there very soon, Mr Falcon? Yes, I'm running away – from fear, crime, everything.' Her fingers, diving quickly into her vanity-bag, as quickly slipped a small packet of tissue-paper into his hand. 'You missed this last night. Put it among your collection. Then you have done all you were hired to do and can take a holiday.'

Shielded by the tablecloth, he examined the clip in his palm – a magnificent square emerald set in baguette diamonds.

'Lost or stolen,' he said, 'two nights ago at the Avalons' dance in

Belgrave Square. I see. Thank you, Mrs Temple.' He tossed the tissue-paper on the table, and slipped the clip into his pocket. 'Now go home, beautiful. And I hope you mean what you say about running away. I don't like your friend, and if he should think the police are after you and that you might talk, then it will be a poor lookout for your dressmakers.'

Her clear wide eyes, still poignant with hidden fear, regarded him thoughtfully. 'Why don't you,' she said slowly, as though each word was an ordeal, 'try to force his name out of me?'

'Because I've guessed it. Because I don't want you to be bumped off before you dine with me again – I'm particular about women, and I prefer them alive. Because I want better evidence than my guess or your word. Because it's bedtime. Good night, Diana.'

She almost snatched up her bag and, as though she couldn't trust herself to say another word, left him very quickly. Had she glanced back from the restaurant door, she would have surprised a look of queer anxiety on his usually saturnine face. The man called Gay Falcon had never in his life made a secret of the fact that he wished pretty women well, no matter what they might wish for him.

Not ten minutes later, he let himself into his flat in St James's Square nearby. He showed no surprise at finding two visitors comfortably awaiting him in the sitting room. One of them was Chief Inspector Poss and the other was a beefy type whom even a blind thief would instantly have recognised as a detective.

'We rang the bell,' said Poss innocently, 'but as nobody answered and the door was ajar, we just came in to wait for you. This is Detective Sergeant Daisy, but his name does him an injustice.

Gay Falcon, still standing, looked slowly round, glanced into his bedroom, then looked at the Chief Inspector with a smile in his deep hard eyes which would have done credit to a tiger suddenly confronted by a man with a niblick.

'You've got some cheek, Poss,' he said amiably enough. 'I'm sorry you've had your search for nothing.'

'Not quite nothing,' said the Chief Inspector with satisfaction. 'You'll have to explain these in due course.' He took three passports from an inside pocket and held them up. 'Three passports, one for a man of independent means called Gay Stanhope Falcon, one for a soldier called Colonel Rock, who looks quite a bit like you, and one for a journalist with an address in Paris called Spencer Pott, who would be your twin brother but for his moustache. You will have to explain these, *Mister* Gay Stanhope Falcon.'

Detective Sergeant Daisy appeared to have formed a high opinion of his superior's sense of humour and Falcon had to wait for his rugged laughter to die down before he said, 'You'll have to do your own explaining tomorrow morning, Chief Inspector, when you get a telephone call, as I fancy you will, from General Icelin. But don't let me interfere with your evening out. What do you want?'

The Chief Inspector was looking at him thoughtfully.

'Do you know, Falcon, I shan't be a bit surprised to find that you are or have been military intelligence. You've got that nasty look back in your eyes which one associates with MI. I'll give these passports back at one word from the right quarter, don't worry about that. What *is* worrying me is your attitude about this jewellery affair. Look here, Falcon, I'd much rather have you working with me than against me or on your own.'

Falcon, his hands in his pockets, looked unsmilingly from one to the other of the two burly detectives.

'You didn't break into my flat to hand me a bouquet, Poss. What brought you here? A telephone message – about an hour ago?'

Both the Chief Inspector and his subordinate started with surprise.

'We'll go into that later, Falcon. Now listen, and take it easy. We've got to search you. You can refuse – then you come along with us and we'll search you all according to law. But it will be simpler if you allow us to search you here.'

Falcon's eyes went to the telephone for a quick second. Then he said: 'Go ahead, but be quick. You and I are going to be busy tonight.'

The two detectives, with Falcon's help, were quickly finished, finding nothing more than any man's usual belongings.

Poss sighed. 'It was too good to be true. We received information to the effect that you would have in your possession the emerald and diamond clip stolen at Lady Avalon's dance the other night.'

Falcon looked deadly serious. He snapped, 'If you had found it, what would you have had to do?'

The Chief Inspector stared, puzzled by Falcon's expression. 'As far as anyone would know – anyone who might not know that we *might* be on your side – we would have to hold you pending full inquiries. You'd be charged first, of course.' He added sharply, 'What's up, Falcon? What's on your mind?'

Falcon said, 'Wait a minute.' Pacing up and down, he appeared to come to a conclusion, and stood facing the Chief Inspector.

'Poss, the man who tried to frame me tonight didn't think the charge would stick – he's too clever for that. But he *did* think it would keep me quiet for a few days – so that he could get clear of the country. He's frightened. And he's dangerous.'

'You mean,' Poss said, 'that these insurance thefts are tied to –'

'They're tied to murder. You were reminding me this morning of that pretty Mrs Bowman who was found strangled in her flat one night last year. She was going to give certain information about stolen jewellery to Scotland Yard the next day, wasn't she?'

Poss said, 'Apart from just one blurred fingerprint on a tumbler, we didn't get within a thousand miles of whoever killed Stella Bowman.'

Falcon said, 'Get this. If you do exactly as I say for the next hour or two, you'll put handcuffs on the owner of that finger print, the brain behind the insurance racket, and the killer of another pretty woman like the well-known Mrs Bowman.'

The Chief Inspector reddened. 'Another? What's this, Falcon? Who is it?'

'Take it easy, Poss. This murder won't come off. Now will you do as I say?'

The Chief Inspector, glancing at his subordinate, said, 'Go ahead, Falcon. You'll back me up, Daisy? We can but try. This chap Falcon knows a hell of a sight more about this than we do – perhaps more than is good for him. It certainly would be nice to get that Bowman strangler.'

They sat in watchful silence while Falcon dialled a number. When he heard Diana Temple's voice, he said: 'Listen, beautiful, your little ploy didn't come off.'

She gave a little shivering gasp.

'I know,' he said softly, 'I know how frightened you are. Listen –'

'But if,' she gasped, 'he finds out that the police aren't holding you and that you've given them my name and they're going to question me, he will come and –'

'The police are here with me, after searching me without success. You should have told me at dinner that he'd instructed you to frame me. Then I could have taken steps to see to your safety. But it's not too late now, if you'll do what you are told.'

'But – but what *did* you do with the clip?'

'You'll find it at the bottom of your bag, where I slipped it back. I trust nobody, sweetheart. Now, for your own safety, will you follow my instructions to the letter?'

'Yes – oh, yes! I can't face him when he finds you really are after him.'

'You will have to face him, Diana, because he will come to see you very soon. He has a key, of course? I'm going to let him know in the next few minutes that the police are to question you in the morning.'

'But you mustn't – you can't! You're telling him to kill me, like he did –'

'Be calm, lady. You'll be better protected than Stella Bowman. Now do as you're told. Go to bed immediately.'

'Yes? And?'

'That's all. Just go to bed. And wait. Just wait. Read a nice thriller, if you like.'

She laughed unsteadily. 'I thought better – of you – than to make fun of my fears.'

'Don't worry – I'm going to cure you of your fears for ever. Trust in me, beautiful.'

He snapped down the receiver and turned to the Chief Inspector, who was glaring at him. 'You're risking a woman's life, Falcon – even though she is an accomplice.'

'One moment, Poss. If you're going to arrest this woman –and you've no idea who she is yet – I go no further with this business. This girl is dining with me in Paris the day after tomorrow, and I simply won't have my evening messed up, and that's flat.'

'One thing at a time, Falcon. All right, don't fly off the handle. Now, how are you going to let the big man know we're after this dame?'

'*You* are going to let him know, Poss. It is now eleven. Mr Harvey Morgan, known as Chappie, is at his desirable residence in Grosvenor Street nearby giving a men's dinner. Ring him up right now and tell him, just as a matter of interest, that you were given some bogus information about that man Falcon tonight, that you've searched him without success for stolen property, that Falcon has promised to work with you and has given you the name of a lady whom you're going to question first thing in the morning, and that you're ringing him up just to tell him and other directors of Universal & Allied that you'll have some interesting information to give them at noon tomorrow. Snap to it, Chief Inspector.'

'Holy smoke!' said Poss. 'Chappie Morgan, is it! This is going to make the headlines all right. Chappie Morgan! I always wondered where he really came from.'

'Last year,' said Detective Sergeant Daisy with relish, 'I made a nice little bit on a horse of his at Gatwick. The bookmakers are going to take a day off when Chappie hangs. It's said he's won packets and –'

'That's enough of your low gossip, Daisy,' said the Chief Inspector severely. 'Now, Falcon, this Mr Harvey Morgan is an important man. You really mean me to ring him up and –?'

Gay Falcon showed his teeth in a grin which lacked even the pretence of amiability. 'You must introduce me to your mother, Poss, so I can ask her if you were bumped on the head when you were a child. Now get busy, man, before that dinner party breaks up.'

When the Chief Inspector had spoken his piece to Harvey Morgan, he turned a jaundiced eye on Gay Falcon.

'If his reactions to that rigmarole,' he said bitterly, 'weren't those of an innocent man, I'll – I'll disguise myself as a police woman.'

'What did he say?' said Falcon.

'First, he chuckled himself silly, and then –'

'I've known a laughing murderer,' said Sergeant Daisy. 'He had some kind of gland trouble and –'

'You shut up,' said the Chief Inspector violently. 'And then, when I tell Chappie that juicy bit about the important information I'm going to give them at noon tomorrow, he says he always knew Gay Falcon was a clever chap with a mind so crooked that he could see round corners, and he congratulates us all.'

'Right!' said Falcon briskly. 'Now, Poss, if you can be serious for a moment, put on that awful bowler of yours and follow me. Either of you got a gun?'

'No, we haven't. We're policemen, not gentlemen detectives.'

'Okay. Sailors can't swim, either.'

Falcon snatched an automatic from a drawer and was slipping it into his pocket when Poss said, 'I'll have that, mister. You've a licence, I suppose?'

'Oh, no,' said Falcon savagely. 'Mussolini himself gave it to me to use as a toothpick whenever I felt extra peaceful after meals.'

Mrs Temple's apartment was on the fourth floor of one of those handsome new blocks of flats which try very hard to look like imposing homes for rich people and succeed in looking like hospitals for rich people being treated for loneliness.

The bedroom window of each flat gave out on to a small balcony. This was not strictly a balcony but in the nature of a decoration, and therefore it was a somewhat tight fit for the substantial figures of the two detectives and Gay Falcon.

Mrs Temple, whose maid slept in the domestic quarters, had let them in and passed them through her bedroom to the hideout on the balcony. She had tried to smile at Falcon, but she had confessed to wishing he had thought of trying some other method of catching his shark.

Chief Inspector Poss, squeezed into a corner of the balcony, was not in the best of tempers. For one thing, it was a chilly night, and for another, he didn't like being on balconies.

'We'd look darn silly,' he said sourly, 'if this thing gave way and we fell into the square like a ton of Juliets in trousers.'

'We're only doing our duty sir,' said Daisy, who was enjoying himself.

The bedroom window was ajar so that they could hear anything that passed in the room. The thick curtains were not drawn, but the white net across the windows was sufficient to make the visibility poor. Still, the watchers on the tiny balcony could see everything in outline, and they could hear the slightest sound. Mrs Temple was in bed, her eyes on a book.

'I don't like this,' said the Chief Inspector. 'Suppose he pulls a gun on her before we can stop him?'

'It would be tough luck on her, wouldn't it?' said Falcon. 'She certainly makes a pretty picture.'

Suddenly the bedroom door was seen to open noiselessly. The watchers stood rigid, Poss with the automatic in his hand. A man came in, a tall bulky shape. Mrs Temple, unaware, still had her eyes on her book.

'Well, Diana?'

The start of surprise with which she put down the book was, considering how frightened she must be, a pretty piece of acting.

'Harry! What is it – why have you come tonight, when you said –?'

He came toward the bed and his face became clearer to the watchers on the balcony. Chief Inspector Poss turned startled eyes on Falcon.

'Diana,' the man said conversationally, 'I'm afraid I have bad news for you. But in a way it's your own fault for not having managed to frame Falcon and give me time to get away.'

'But I tried to, darling, only he must have suspected and –'

'I know, I know. Luck is good or bad. It's bad now, Diana –' for you. Falcon has been very clever. It was that fool Morgan who insisted on engaging him for this investigation, and now he knows a sight too much. I was dining with Chappie tonight when the police rang him up to say that they're going to question you in the morning, and I fear, Diana, that I can't risk that. Of course, a wife can't give evidence against her husband, but she can – if she hates going to prison as much as you do – give the police a lot of very dangerous information.'

Detective Sergeant Daisy, more pop-eyed than ever, stared at Poss and whispered, 'Lumme, 'Arry Temple in the flesh! I 'ad my suspicions of 'im ten years ago, just before he vanished, and then he was as bald as my palm.'

Temple was sitting on the side of his wife's bed now. They could not see her expression. They could only see that she stiffened against the pillows behind her.

'Harry,' she whispered, 'you can't – you can't! Not to *me!*

'I don't want to, Diana, but how can I help myself? With the jewellery I've got tucked away and my American investments, I can still live my life out in Mexico. And I've always told you I wouldn't be taken – and if, at the worst, I've got to be, I'd rather hang than rot in prison. But I fancy I can get away tonight, in Chappie's aeroplane from Heston. I'm really sorry, Diana, because I've loved you for ten years, and you've been a darned helpful wife, but I can't trust you when you're questioned tomorrow, and –'

'But they will get you anyway,' she whispered frantically. Probably all the airports are watched. I told Falcon your name and that you killed Stella Bowman –'

As she said that name, Temple's expression, hitherto queerly normal and almost affectionate, hardened into such savage contempt that she screamed.

'You double-crossing vixen,' he said very quietly, and as she screamed again, his bulk obliterated all but her fair, hysterical face and his hands dug deep into her throat.

As the watchers on the balcony burst into the room, Harry Temple, his gloved hands still savaging his wife's throat, gave a thick, sobbing gasp. His handsome face stared at them with a look of idiotic surprise, and then he leapt frantically toward the door.

Poss and Daisy had no difficulty in holding him while Gay Falcon, his eyes darting about the room, stood by the bed patting Mrs Temple's clutching hand. Trying to smile up at him thankfully, her breath came in bruised, hysterical sobs.

Temple, held by the detectives, seemed to collapse.

'Henry Edward Hammersley,' Poss began in his official voice, 'or Henry Edward Temple, I am going to charge you with the attempted murder of your wife. There will be other charges. You will accompany me to Vine Street and –'

Harry Temple turned blindly toward the bed and, his blurred eyes accusing his wife, made some thick incoherent sounds even as a violent spasm made him sag helpless in the detectives' arms. Poss and Daisy got him to a chair. Poss reddened with temper.

'Daisy, ring a doctor quick. He's poisoned himself somehow.'

Mrs Temple, sobbing uncontrollably, suddenly clung tight to Gay Falcon's arm.

'I won't,' Poss said savagely, 'ever hear the end of this if he gets away with it – right under my nose. But how could I have stopped him?'

'You couldn't help it,' Falcon said. 'I'll back you up.'

'Please, *please*,' Diana Temple sobbed, 'don't let him – die – in here! *Please* – I can't bear any more! He always said he'd poison himself if –'

Poss was busy searching the unconscious man's pockets.

Falcon pointed to a tiny rubber bulb and some remnants of smashed glass on the floor between the bed and the chair on which Temple lay.

'That's how he did it, Poss – a hypodermic. We crushed it under our feet as he dropped it. You don't have to tell me it smells of bitter almonds – they always do.'

Poss, carefully putting the remnants of the hypodermic into a handkerchief, said soothingly: 'All right, Mrs Temple, we'll do our best. Falcon, give me a hand while Daisy is telephoning and we'll get Temple out into the hall.'

'I can't,' said Gay Falcon, smiling tenderly at Mrs Temple's lovely, distracted face. 'This lady is in no state to be left alone even for a moment – and I guess she needs a doctor a deal more than Harry Temple does by now.'

Poss looked at him with disgust, but just then Sergeant Daisy came back and between them they heaved Temple's inert bulk out of the room.

Falcon at once sat on the bed, and while she clung to him with terror that would not be soothed he ran the fingers of one hand protectively through her soft hair.

'Thank God,' she whispered, 'you were here, Gay Falcon! Where would I be now but for you? Oh, I can't bear to think of –'

Poss re-entered the room and looked at them, particularly at Falcon, with severe disapproval.

'Mrs Temple,' he said sternly, 'I regret to have to tell you that your husband has cheated the law. I shall have to take a brief statement from you now, while a full statement can be taken in the morning in the presence of your lawyer. Mr Falcon, will you be so good as to leave the lady alone for just one minute so that she can give me her undivided attention?'

Still clinging to Falcon's arm, Diana Temple was obviously on the verge of an hysterical collapse.

'I simply can't talk now,' she pleaded frantically. 'Gay, please tell him – make him leave it all till –'

Poss said: 'I sympathise, Mrs Temple, but a couple of minutes will suffice. From what we overheard we can establish that the dead man was the brain behind the insurance thefts and also the murderer of

Stella Bowman. Further, we were ourselves witnesses of as clear a case of attempted murder as –'

'Attempted?' said Gay Falcon, still caressing Mrs Temple's hair. 'Why attempted, Poss? Henry Edward Temple was very thoroughly murdered – right under our noses – by his loving wife.'

As she tried to wrench herself away, he held her to him more tightly, in what was now a grotesque parody of affection. She said not a word, her breath coming in thick gasps, then suddenly she threw her head back and started screaming.

Falcon let her fall back on to the bed. She went on screaming, contorting her body frantically beneath the bedclothes. Daisy ran in, pop-eyed.

'Let her yell,' Falcon said. 'She's an expert on hysterics. Restrain your pity, Daisy – she had darn little for Stella Bowman when she strangled her.'

Poss said: 'But look here, we found the smashed hypodermic with which he –'

Falcon held out a pocket handkerchief, on which lay another small hypodermic, unbroken, half full.

'She had two – I was looking for this under the pillow while you and she thought I was flirting with her. It was almost undetectable murder, given the circumstances. A clear case of a thief and murder – so we were expected to think – poisoning himself to escape the law. But what actually happened was that as Temple made a grab at her, she chucked one hypodermic on to the floor, pretty certain it would be trodden underfoot, and then, just as we came in, jabbed him in the thigh with the other. You'll find her fingerprints on this.'

Diana Temple, her lovely eyes dilated, lay staring at Gay Falcon.

'You beast!' she whispered. 'You sneaky, filthy Romeo! But you can't prove I killed Stella Bowman!'

Falcon regarded her absently. 'You should watch your words, Mrs Temple – they will be used against you.'

Once outside in the hall, Poss said: 'How did you get on to her?'

'Not till almost the last minute, Poss. Though I have been married to two pretty women and thought I was hard-boiled, she had me on a string all right. She had me just where she wanted me, believing that she was being victimised by Hammerseley or Morgan, I wasn't quite certain which. It was always obvious that an insurance man was behind this racket.

'And then, at almost the very last minute, she made a mistake. Remember, she told Temple quite *unnecessarily* that she had told *me* who he was and that he had killed Stella Bowman. Then I knew that she was goading him into trying to kill her, and I wondered why. Remember, she did not accuse him of having killed Mrs Bowman, all she said was that she had told me so –

'So that we, listening, could pin the charge on him, and also, when he made a grab at her, so that she could get a good chance of putting him away? All right, that can stick. You can kill in self-defence – but not with poison, and not when you *know* detectives are there to protect you. But why did she have to put Temple away?

'Because if he escaped, she would always be frightened of him and he might interfere with her life as the beautifully dressed and frantically fashionable Diana Temple – and being one of the best-dressed women in the world has been the money motive behind her crimes. Because, again, if he was arrested he would have given us proofs that she was not only the brains behind the insurance racket but also the killer of Stella Bowman.

'But I fancy she was right there – you will never convict her of that crime. Temple's death will be quite enough to go on with. An unpleasant character. But she *will* look swell in the box, all in black.'

The Man Who Swallowed A Horse

BY CRAIG RICE

Although The Amazing Mr Malone *ran for only one season on ABC from September 1951 to March 1952 it is fondly remembered by older viewers as the first crime series to feature a wise-cracking relationship between a Chicago lawyer and a police Captain. John J Malone, the lawyer with a taste for beautiful women and a thirst for strong drink, had a wonderful foil in Captain Daniel Von Flanagan of the homicide squad which had originated in print, transferred successfully to the cinema, and then made it to TV – though not with the success it had enjoyed in the other two media. What both readers and viewers found fascinating about Malone was that although he treated his practice with seeming irresponsibility, he could inspire great loyalty from the police and his clients and was never happier than when he was sharing a drink (or four) with them at Joe the Angel's City Hall Bar. He had an effortless line of small talk and a cynical sense of humour which was always available to help Captain Von Flanagan solve the hardest cases – cases which made for good viewing because of their frequent surprise endings. Malone also has the distinction of being the very first in the line of television lawyers who would reach their apogee in* Perry Mason.

The little Chicago lawyer made his debut in 1939 in the novel, Eight Faces at Three *by Craig Rice (1908–57), a woman whose own life has its elements of mystery. Five books later came* Having A Wonderful Crime *(1943) which inspired the first Malone movie with Pat O'Brien in the title role and George Zucco as Captain Von Flanagan. Brian Donlevy and Robert Armstrong filled the same roles in two further movies and a long-running radio series was also aired from 1947. Edward Peterson produced* The Amazing Mr Malone *for ABC and* cast Lee Tracy as Malone and George Murphy as his friend from the homicide department. The series included a number of the much-loved features from Craig Rice's original stories – in particular Joe Angel's bar and Malone's office with his 'Personal File' where he always kept a bottle of rye for 'emergencies' – as well as the sort of beautiful girls to whom the lawyer was invariably attracted. These roles provided opportunities for a number of pretty young actresses who would later go on to appear in major Hollywood movies. All in all, The Amazing Mr Malone *deserved a better fate than the one to which it was condemned by poor ratings.*

Craig Rice, the creator of Malone, had been born Georgiana Ann Randolph in Chicago, and apparently spent her early life working in the city on radio and in public relations. For a number of years she tried unsuccessfully to write novels, poetry and music, but it was not until her first story of John J Malone, which she published under a pen-name, that she enjoyed some hard-won success. Despite going on to write a number of other highly successful thrillers and several film scripts for Hollywood (including two for The Falcon*), Craig Rice kept her private life very much to herself, and little is known about the rest of her life – including how many times she was married. Records indicate she was certainly wed four times, and may even have had three other husbands! She also refused to explain the origin of her pseudonym, and it has only recently been established that she ghosted two thrillers for the famous burlesque dancer, Gypsy Rose Lee –* The Strip-Tease Murders *(1941) and* Mother Finds A Body *(1943). There is, however, no mystery about her success with the stories of John J Malone and* The Man Who Swallowed A Horse *inspired a humorous exchange between the lawyer and Captain Von Flanagan in one of the early episodes. It serves as a reminder of the best elements in the series.*

'THE MAN WAS killed.,' John J Malone, the famous criminal lawyer, said, 'in a particularly vicious manner. Mr Duck was scared to death by his psychiatrist.'

'Nonsense,' Homicide Captain von Flanagan growled. He paused. They looked at the late Mr Duck, who had just been moved from the operating room. 'Where is Dr Nash, anyway?'

'He's lying down,' the white-faced nurse said. 'The shock –' she gulped. 'Of course we knew Mr Duck had a bad heart, but no one thought – it was really just a harmless little joke. I mean, it was meant to be one.'

She added, 'Mrs Duck is in the doctor's office with him.'

The little attorney and von Flanagan took a last glance at the dead Mr Duck. He had been a portly man with a broad face that had once been red and thick-veined. A small incision had been made in his abdomen, hardly more than a scratch.

'He just suddenly gasped and died,' the nurse said. Her eyes narrowed. 'Dr Nash and Mrs Duck are great friends.'

Malone looked her over. A pretty little thing she was, with reddish gold hair and a sweet mouth.

'Let's go into the office,' von Flanagan said. 'Malone, how did you get into this?'

'Mr Duck was my client,' Malone said. 'He told me he was going to this psychiatrist his wife recommended. For an operation. Because he'd swallowed a horse.'

'Malone,' the police officer said sharply, 'you've been drinking.'

'Mr Duck was positive he'd swallowed a horse,' the little counsellor-at-law said stubbornly. He added reminiscently, 'I remember once when you thought you had a mouse in your mouth.'

Von Flanagan growled and pushed open the door to the office. Dr Nash was supine on the couch, his handsome face pale. Mrs Duck sat beside him, holding his hand.

She jumped up, startled, and cried out, 'It wasn't anyone's fault.'

The doctor said, 'Mr Duck was convinced he had swallowed a horse. We decided to practise a harmless little deception. We put him under anaesthesia, made a slight incision, and before he came to, we led a horse into the operating room. Hardly conventional procedure, but – well, I explained to him we'd operated and extracted the horse, and he would be as good as new. Mr Duck took one look at the horse and – just died.'

'It was murder,' Malone said. 'You knew about his heart – you knew the slightest shock would kill him. And if I'm not mistaken, you and the charming Mrs Duck have plans for the future.'

'Prove it,' Mrs Duck said angrily.

'I can,' Malone said. 'He told me all about it in a letter . . . all about his ailment and the planned operation. What he didn't know about was the gimmick you had in mind. That was what murdered him.'

Later, sitting in Joe the Angel's City Hall Bar, von Flanagan growled, 'I still think you made it all up.'

'Naturally,' Malone said, signalling for two more gins. 'But it scared

Dr Nash, who isn't such a stable character, into breaking down and telling you the truth. A signed confession, no less. And you pay for the next drink.'

'If he changes his mind,' the police officer said gloomily, 'it's going to be hell selling this story to a jury.' He scowled into his glass. 'Tell me the truth, Malone, or you pay for the next drink.'

'Mr Duck really did think he'd swallowed a horse,' Malone told him. 'He really did have a fixation. And he did think that the operation was going to make him as good as new.'

'But why did he drop dead the minute he looked at the horse?' von Flanagan demanded.

'Because,' Malone said patiently, 'the horse in the operating room was a white horse. The horse Mr Duck thought he'd swallowed was a black one.'

The Stranger in Church

BY JACK WEBB

Just a week before Christmas 1951 – on 16 December, to be precise – television and crime-on-TV history was made when the first episode of Dragnet, *featuring the cases of Sergeant Joe Friday of the Los Angeles Police Department, was screened by NBC. In the next seven years, two hundred and sixty-three black and white, thirty-minute episodes of the series were shown, earning the show the reputation of being arguably the most successful police series ever. Certainly, over forty years later* Dragnet *(which was also known as* Badge 714, *after Sergeant Friday's police number) is still fondly remembered by those old enough to have watched it in both America and Britain (where it was transmitted by ITV from September 1955) and a younger generation who now avidly collect the video tapes of the show which have recently become available. It was, quite simply, as Leslie Halliwell wrote in his* Television Companion, *'a revolutionary cop show recording the minutiae of investigation, conversation and characterisation in stretches of apparently flat but hypnotic dialogue.' And not only did the creator-star, Jack Webb (1920–82), become a cult figure with viewers, but his catch-phrases, 'My name's Friday – I'm a cop'; 'All we want is the facts, ma'am' and 'Book him on a 358', became a part of everyday conversation on both sides of the Atlantic. The legend was further enhanced when the series went over to colour in 1967 for another ninety-eight episodes, and, after Jack Webb's death, the memory lived on in a movie starring Dan Aykroyd followed by yet another series in 1989 (shown in Britain as* The Big Dragnet) *but now featuring two younger police officers, Sergeant Vic Daniels (Jeffrey Osterhage) and Detective Carl Molina (Bernard White).*

The success of Dragnet *was undoubtedly largely due to the dedication and perseverance of Jack Webb, a character actor and occasional short story writer, who got the idea in 1948 while taking part in a documentary movie about police work called* He Walked By Night. *Webb realised how inaccurately police work was usually depicted in the media and devised a format in which the everyday details of crimebusting were to be shown without glamour or sensationalism. He even picked the title from a piece of dialogue he had spoken in the 1948 movie. Initially, Webb could only interest radio in the idea, but the show rapidly attracted a huge audience and in 1951 the creator-producer-director took the idea to NBC. The reception he got there was lukewarm, he revealed later, although the network did agree to give the show a four-week trial run. The rest, as they say, is history.*

Authenticity was Jack Webb's keyword from the very start of the series and he based every episode on real cases researched in the archives of the Los Angeles Police Department. Later, he explained both the concept and where his character's name had come from: 'I wanted Friday to be a steady, plodding kind of cop; the sort the public never really understands or appreciates or even hears about. The image of the 50,000 honest, decent, home-loving guys who do their work without the help of a bottle or a gun in their hand. I chose the name Friday because I wanted a name that had no connotations – he could be English, Jewish, Greek or anything. He could be all men to all people in their living rooms.' Initially, Friday's partner was Sergeant Ben Romero, but tragically after just three episodes, the actor playing the role, Barton Yarborough (who had also appeared in the radio series), died of a heart attack. He was replaced by Barney Phillips as Sergeant Ed Jacobs, who would in turn be superseded by Herb Ellis, Ben Alexander and, finally, Harry Morgan when the series went into colour. (Interestingly, the co-star of the very first episode was a certain Raymond Burr whose role as a maniac with a bomb was a far cry from the lawyer named Perry Mason who would later make him famous.)

The indefatigable Webb never missed an episode and was rarely out of shot despite all his many off-screen commitments, not least of them as the narrator. The realistic feel of the series was also underlined by the evocative signature tune and an announcer's voice declaring, 'Ladies and gentlemen, the story you are about to see is true – only the names have been changed to protect the innocent.' Jack Webb became so thoroughly identified with his role that he rarely acted again when the series finished, turning instead to producing other TV series and writing. Although he never wrote a specific short story featuring Joe Friday, officers modelled on him can be found in one or two of his tales

– such as The Stranger in Church. *As Friday himself might have said,*
'Only the name has been changed . . .'

THE FIRST TIME Father Shanley saw the blonde, he shared the
experience with every male parishioner over the age of fourteen
and under seventy. It was true that her black dress was smart, and that
the black bit of lace with little bows all caught like fish in a net was
quite the proper hat for one of the more fashionable parishes, but she
did not belong in St Anne's. Not among the Marquezes, the
Gonzalezes, the Alejandros and the Cervantes. Moreover, even
though she sat quietly through the early Mass, she was that sort of
woman who made the mere fact of her sex a most disturbing element.

The second time he saw the blonde, she was dead – remarkably and
brutally dead. Nor was there any question of what the murder weapon
had been. The splinters of the tall, dark Scotch bottle were strewn on
the cheap carpet from wall to wall and the reek of expensive whisky
filled the shabby room.

It was after midnight when Sergeant Golden reached the parish house
beside the church of St Anne.

At nine o'clock, when Father had phoned Homicide from the dead
woman's apartment, Sammy Golden had been down on South Center
on a case of little interest to anyone excepting the medical examiner.

Lieutenant Adams had gone out on the priest's urgent call. He had
been preceded by Officers Gault and Savage, whose radio car had been
in the Royal Heights area. The initial inquiry had been completed.

Now, Sammy had come to St Anne's because he was a friend, and
also because Dan Adams had not been satisfied with Father's story.

Adams had said, 'You know I don't doubt Father, Sammy, but . . .
it's just, well . . .' He had paused and run distracted hands through his
short-cropped red hair. 'Hell, look at the facts. Forget it's Shanley for a
minute. He says he's seen the girl once, in his church last Sunday, that
when he spoke to her after the service, she didn't even answer him, yet
when she called tonight, she knew all about him, refused to see him at
the parish house in the morning and insisted that he come to the Vista
del Sur Apartments right away.'

'Why?'

'Yeah, why?' Dan grinned briefly. 'From the way Father spoke, I had the feeling that he didn't like the sound of it at all, that he actually was quite upset at going to *that woman's* apartment alone, and would have gotten out of it if she hadn't said that she had been told he was the one man she could trust, that if she ever needed him he would come.'

'Told by who?' Sammy demanded.

'Whom,' said Adams. 'You go find out.'

So he had, and the light was on over the front door. Golden climbed from his car and opened the gate under the arbour over-burdened with pale pink roses.

Father Shanley was at the door before he could ring. 'Come in, Sammy. Come in.'

Sammy followed him into the house. 'I'm sorry I was out when you called. I was attending a wake down on South Center. Dan Adams filled me in when he got back. I came as soon as I could.'

'Then you've talked to Dan. Good. Heaven knows I've been over the details often enough tonight. I've got some coffee ready. You go on into the study. Are you still on duty?'

'Officially,' Sammy said carefully, 'the night watch ended twenty minutes ago. So far as I know, nobody's paying me any overtime.'

'Good, I'll bring a little brandy, then. I wouldn't admit it to anyone but you, Sammy, but this has been a night and I could use a drop of something.' Father paused with his hand against the kitchen door. 'Yes, Sammy, I sure could!'

Sergeant Golden went on down the hall past the dining room and into the familiar surroundings of the study where he spent so many, many hours and where talk hadn't always been a crime. He wore a puzzled frown. It was nearly ten years now since he and Father had clashed and then joined forces, and he had never seen his friend so nervous. Sure, he had been through a shocking experience, but the shock of violent death was nothing new to Joseph Shanley.

The opposite door swung open to the pressure of Father's toe and he came in bearing a tray in both hands. He carried a coffeepot, cups, saucers, a bottle of Christian Brothers, two small snifters and paper napkins on the tray. Sammy helped him arrange things on the small table beside the big chair.

Sammy straightened up, shoving his hands into his pockets. 'All right, Father, what is it? Let's get rid of it.'

Father Shanley set the pot down carefully and met the detective's glance steadily. 'You heard how she was killed?'

'Whisky bottle.'

'That's right. Dan tell you that the bottle hadn't been emptied?' Sammy waited.

The priest handed him a drink. 'Upstairs in my closet,' he said soberly, 'is one of my black suit coats, stained across the lapels and rather damp. It smells strongly of whisky.'

'What in the devil —'

'Precisely my own thoughts,' Father agreed. 'Incidentally,' he added dryly, 'it's not the coat I was wearing when I paid my call.'

Sammy tasted his brandy, felt the warmth of it on his tongue and then finished it off quickly. The priest reached for the bottle. Golden shook his head. 'Maybe I needed one, too.'

Shanley said quietly, 'It's rather frightening, isn't it? That they knew when I found the girl I'd report her death. That they knew when I found the coat I'd report it rather than clean it or otherwise dispose of it — either of which would have been relatively simple. Being sure of these things when I was the only witness to my own actions.'

'Don't let it spook you,' Sammy said. 'It may be our one break.'

'Break?'

'The fellow knows you. Chances are, you know him.' He grinned without humour. 'Also, Father, he doesn't like you very much.'

'No, Sammy,' the pain was clear in Father's glance. 'Not that, not *murder* because of hatred of me!'

It was nine o'clock the following morning when the big man left the Carlton Plaza and walked ten blocks to Center Street. He turned south into the Latin-American district a few blocks above skid row. In the foyer of theatre the billboards advertised *Cuatro contra el imperio* and *Dos diabolitos en aduros* and with his back to the girl in the tiny cubicle of the box office, he removed his tie and slipped it in his jacket pocket. Then he unbuttoned the two top buttons of his shirt and ran his hand roughly through his grey-flecked hair. These small actions, plus the fact he had not shaved, were enough to put him on Center Street without attracting undue attention.

On down the street, he paused before a hole in the wall called La Fiesta. But there were only two young men at the bar, so he walked on until he came to El Charro. Here, there were quite a number along the shabby bar. The big man went in. He paid for his first beer with a twenty-dollar bill. He left the change carelessly on the damp wood before him. A great many glances evidenced more interest in his money than he did.

He was on his second beer when the husky voice inquired, 'You like to buy Lupe a little drink, *si*?'

'Why not?'

Her brassy hair had dark roots. There was a gold cap on one front tooth and her smile was enormous. She more than covered the stool beside him.

The bartender glanced at them sourly.

'Bring Lupe a drink,' the big man said.

'Sure, Joe,' Lupe agreed. 'I gotta friend. What's your name, friend?' Her left hand rested on his knee. 'Whisky and soda, Joe.'

The friendship prospered through five whiskys and soda.

'Fren',' Lupe said, her soft body rocking, 'good fren' with no name. You wanna good time, good fren'?'

The man let his gaze wander the joint. Joe was at the far end emptying a case of beer into the cooler under the back bar. The stools on either side of them were empty. He leaned closer. 'You want to earn twenty bucks, Lupe?'

'Twenty bucks, *por Dios!*'

'Good. Now listen to me, Lupe.' He lowered his voice to a harsh whisper. 'I'm going to make a phone call and you're going to do the talking. Okay?'

'Okay . . .'

It was a little after noon when Captain Bill Cantrell and Sergeant Golden climbed from the official sedan at the curb in front of the parish house. Father Shanley laid down the shears with which he was trimming the flamboyant pillar of Gladiator roses beside the small front porch and then peeled off his gloves.

'Captain Cantrell, Sammy, I'm delighted to see you.' The priest's smile was genuine.

'Are you, Father?' Cantrell growled. He threw the remnants of a tattered cigar at a rosebush. 'Mind if we come in?'

His face sobering, Joseph Shanley swung open the gate. 'Sammy's told you about the coat?'

'Yeah,' Cantrell admitted. 'Funny thing, that coat.'

'I don't find it so,' Father said gravely. 'I expect you would like to have it.'

The captain from Homicide nodded. He didn't look any happier about it than Sammy did, and Sammy hadn't even spoken. Bill Cantrell said, 'This isn't easy for us, Father. We have a search warrant. Would you like us to serve it?'

The priest's strong, tanned hands gripped the top of the fence. 'Please,' he said quietly, 'would you mind telling me what this is all about?'

'Father,' Sammy began, 'this is –'

'I'll do the talking,' Cantrell said abruptly. He returned to Shanley. 'We have received some information. In it certain allegations were made. If you would like to be represented by an attorney, we'll permit you to call one.'

'But, why?'

'Then we may make the search?'

The priest nodded without speaking. As they started up the front steps, he said, 'One favour. It might benefit all of us if I were to find an errand for Mrs Mulvaney outside the house before you go to work.'

The priest returned to the front hall. 'I've convinced her that the Fuertes need her pepper-pot soup more than I do. They've all had a virus this last week. And after that, she's going to do some shopping to replace the soup and she's been wanting new curtains for the kitchen windows. So, if we could start upstairs while she's putting on her bonnet, that should give you ample time . . .'

They began their search in the priest's sparse, almost Spartan bedroom, beneath the still, watching eyes on the dusty gold crucifix.

Father Shanley never forgot Sergeant Golden's expression as he turned from the bottom dresser drawer, his hands coming up from the bleached Navy suntans that were now the priest's old work clothes. In his grasp was a pair of flimsy nylons.

'Well, Father?' It was Cantrell who spoke, not Golden.

Joseph Shanley came out of the shock slowly. 'Her legs were bare,' he said with a hollow detachment. 'I remember because the door was open and the light was on and I could see her calves and ankles and feet and those new shoes with the clean, clean soles. So, of course, I hurried in. What else could I do? She was on the floor, you see. Not at all in a proper position and, of course, I could smell the liquor.'

'Sammy,' Father said, 'Sammy . . .'

Before Golden could reply, Cantrell caught his arm and squeezed. Sammy looked down at the stockings in his hand. The Captain's bloodshot eyes never left the priest.

Father spoke quickly, a sudden, bitter anger rising in his voice. 'Good heavens, you two don't think . . .'

'Sometimes we have to,' Captain Cantrell said soberly. 'You'd better come downtown with me for awhile, Father.'

'Is this an arrest?'

'I didn't say that.' He turned his glance to Sammy, rubbing the back of his neck. 'You stay here, Sergeant. I'm going to have a team from the lab comb the place. Somebody might have been careless. After they arrive, you can beat it home. Report as regularly for the night watch.'

*

Sammy had watched them go and felt like Judas. An involuntary Judas, sure, but then, what Judas is not? And even if he had not carried the story of Father's liquor-spattered coat to headquarters, the phone call this morning would have done the job. It had been an anonymous call, but not a crank one, a call from an exceedingly nervous woman with a Spanish accent who insisted that she has seen *a priest* hurrying from the Vista del Sur Apartments where the 'mystery blonde' had been killed *at eight-thirty*.

It had been nine when Father had called Homicide to report the murder and, according to Shanley, eight-thirty when the blonde had called him to come to her.

So, somebody was lying. Sammy backed up and started over; so the woman was a liar. Why? Last night he had suggested that someone did not like Father. True as that might be, it was not half enough by far. Because you had to go back to the beginning and start with a blonde. A handsome blonde, a sexy blonde, an expensive blonde who had moved into a cheap apartment in a neighbourhood where she didn't belong, who attended a church where she didn't fit and who had died most violently only last night.

According to her driver's licence, she was Sally M. Cox, five foot four inches tall, weighed one hundred and thirty pounds and lived at the Vista del Sur address. Inasmuch as she had moved to that address less than three weeks ago, the driver's licence was brand new. It said exactly what she wanted it to say and no more. There was no previous record of the State of California's having issued a driver's permit to one Sally M Cox. She had a checking account at the Royal Heights branch of the Bank of Southern California. She had made an initial deposit of three thousand dollars in cash. The currency had been in old bills of varying denominations. There had been nothing irregular about it except that the amount was startling in Royal Heights.

Insofar as anyone could determine, Sally Cox had been born three weeks ago, when she had made a bank deposit, rented a furnished apartment and taken a driver's test. She had lived a short life and there was little evidence that it had been happy.

When the Crime Lab crew arrived, Sammy left.

He walked down to Ney and caught a bus into town. It wasn't like Cantrell to leave any of his men without transportation. But nobody had been like nobody this morning. Or last night, for that matter.

Off the bus, he headed for the garage under the big white police department building and then changed his mind. It wasn't much farther to the morgue.

'Cox,' he said, 'Sally M Cox.'

The attendant led the way. It was cold in the morgue. Quiet.

'Don't often get a looker,' he said. He pulled back the covering from her head and shoulders. 'Right pretty,' he said, 'if you forget what was done to her. A few years ago, I bet she was something terrific.'

Sammy glanced at the attendant, coming out of his study of the face before him. 'What did you say?'

'I just said that a few years ago . . .'

'Where's your phone?'

'Back there on the desk where you came in.'

Sammy swung away from the man and headed out.

'Put her away?' the attendant shouted after him.

'You stay put,' Golden said over his shoulder. 'Both of you,' he added rather needlessly.

'Jack York'll be right down,' the detective said when he returned. York was the best artist on the force.

'You on to something, Sergeant?' the attendant asked.

'I don't know,' Sammy said honestly.

'You think the priest had anything to do with it?'

Golden's right hand flashed out and caught a fistful of shirt front. His eyes were bleak. 'Where did you hear anything like that?'

'Say, who do you think . . .' The man's voice trailed off, suddenly frightened.

'I asked you a question.'

'I don't know nothin', just what the night man told me when I come on.'

Sammy let go of the shirt. 'Your friend's got a lousy mouth.'

'Sure, Sergeant, sure. Say, I just remember, you and that priest . . .'

'That's right,' Sammy agreed quietly, 'me and *that* priest.'

Officer York arrived with pencils and pad. Sammy grinned crookedly. 'You bring some imagination, Jack?'

'What's on your mind?'

Sergeant Golden nodded at Sally Cox. 'Can you do her face as though she were twenty pounds lighter, seven or eight years younger and wearing her hair loose to her shoulders?'

York frowned and studied the full, sensuous, sleeping expression. Then, rapidly, he went to work. Before he was half-way through, Sammy sighed. Then his expression grew thoughtful. In twenty minutes, the sketch was complete.

The police artist held it up for inspection. 'Somebody you know, if I may ask?'

'Sari Angel,' Sammy said softly. 'The Naked Angel.' He stared down at the mortal remains on the table. *Good afternoon*, he thought; *good afternoon and good-bye* ... There was a certain justice in her final violence.

Sammy took the picture from York. 'You can put her to bed,' he said to the attendant.

The two officers left together.

'Naked Angel,' York said.

'A stripper once. Sensational. Also the girlfriend of a guy named Gerald Dempsy. He had his wife killed because of her. Father Shanley brought him back from Mexico single-handed. We sent him up ...' Sammy paused, frowning.

'I don't get it,' York said.

'Neither do I,' Golden admitted.

Captain William Cantrell made the call to Folsom Prison from his office.

Gerald Dempsy had been released five weeks ago after serving seven years and nine months. He had been a model prisoner. He had corresponded with a Sara Engel while he was there and a woman who had identified herself as the same had visited him a number of times during the last two years.

'That would be after she stopped being the Angel,' Sammy said.

Cantrell nodded, his burned-out eyes watching the sergeant.

Sammy switched from the girl then and came back to Dempsy. 'And he did hate Father,' he said. 'He had more reason to than any other human being.'

'But he wouldn't kill *her*,' Cantrell growled.

'Eight years of hating,' Sammy said grimly, 'is a hell of a long time.'

'No proof.' Cantrell threw his cigar at a basket in the corner.

'We'll get it.'

'How?'

'Find Dempsy.'

'Sure.' The Captain's voice was sour. 'In a week, a month, a year. He's a smart boy. He's not broke. He'll be a thousand miles from here.'

'He wasn't when he made that phone call this morning.'

'That was a Mexican woman.'

'Sure,' Sammy said, 'she did the talking. But Sally Cox was created to frame Father, to disgrace him.'

Cantrell slapped his hands hard on the desk before him. His voice was rough. 'You did a good job identifying the Angel – I'll give you that. And we'll get an all-points out on Dempsy – I'll give you that, too. But we've got a murderer to find, not a two-bit lousy frame. Now you take the night off and go on home. You've done a day's work and I'll put somebody in to handle your spot on the night watch.'

Sammy's nails bit into the palms of his hands. He relaxed them with an effort. 'Where's Father, Bill?'

'Down the hall having a talk with Dan and Ed Haggerty – a long talk.'

Silently, Sergeant Golden turned to walk from the room.

'And you leave 'em alone,' Cantrell shouted.

'Sure,' Sammy said, 'sure, Bill.'

He knew what Cantrell had said with never saying a word about it. Identifying the Angel and proving Dempsy was loose hadn't helped Father. If Dempsy had murdered his girl friend, it had to be proved. And if it were not . . . *Booze on the priest's coat, torn nylon stockings hidden in a drawer* . . .

He got off the elevator opposite RECORDS.

He signed for two photos from the Dempsy file.

He started with the Biltmore Hotel. Dempsy had always lived high. Dempsy had money. Dempsy had been a tipper.

After the Biltmore, he hit the Statler.

It was seven-thirty in the evening when he walked into the Carlton Plaza. There was no Dempsy on the register. The registration clerk wasn't 'very good about faces'. The bell captain started to shake his head, and then hesitated.

'Seven, eight years older,' Sammy said quickly. 'Probably has put on weight. None of the tan that's in these shots. Been in prison.'

The man nodded abruptly. 'I'm not certain,' he said. He didn't mean it. They started through the bellhops.

The third bellhop said, 'That would be nine eighteen, sir. I took his bags up myself.'

The hotel detective's name was Grierson. They rode up together.

Outside nine eighteen Grierson glanced up and down the hall and then slipped a snub-nosed .38 from a shoulder holster into his right jacket pocket. He used his left hand to insert the pass key into the lock. The door opened silently.

A single lamp was burning beside the easy chair. Newspapers were scattered around it. The big man on the bed had an arm cocked across his face. He was not aware of them until they were in the room with the door closed behind them.

'All right, Dempsy,' Sammy said.

The big man swung his legs from the bed and sat up. When the light hit the planes of his face, his cheeks were shining. He stared at the two men with swollen eyes.

Lord, Sammy thought, *he's been crying like a baby*. It wasn't the victory Sammy'd expected. It was somehow shameful, somehow embarrassing. There was a framed photograph on the chest of drawers. The slim blonde girl in it looked like an angel. It had been taken many years ago.

Grierson broke the strange charade. 'This your man?'

'This is the man,' Sammy repeated. He crossed the room to the phone. Cantrell was still in his office.

'I've picked up Dempsy,' Sergeant Golden said. 'We're in room nine eighteen at the Carlton Plaza.' His own voice sounded hollow.

Eight-thirty, nine-thirty, ten-thirty. Gerald Dempsy talked. All the hatred Sammy had guessed came spilling out. A nursed hatred, a nurtured hatred, all aimed at one man. It had coiled and grown through the prison years, it had blossomed with the invention of Sally Cox. Two individuals getting even for the wasted years. For the years Father Joseph Shanley had lost them when he captured Dempsy. Sari Angel and Gerald Dempsy, planning, scheming, thinking, forming an antichrist out of a man most considered nearly a saint.

But it hadn't worked, Dempsy said, hadn't worked, because Sari Angel was dead.

And he wept again.

It was a closed-door session. The captain and the sergeant together in Cantrell's office.

'The man's a psychopath,' Sammy said viciously.

'Is he?' Cantrell rubbed at the corners of his burning eyes.

'You don't believe him, Bill?'

'Somebody killed the Angel.'

'Dempsy.'

'You sure he did, Sammy?' Cantrell worked the cellophane wrapper off a cigar.

'God,' Sammy said, 'I don't know.'

'We've sent Shanley home,' Cantrell said, his rough voice almost gentle. 'I think you'd better go and pay him another call.'

'Me!' Sammy raised a tortured glance. 'I've crucified him already.'

'Sure,' Cantrell agreed. 'I can send Prouty and Mendez. We have to talk to him again.'

'I'll go.'

'Dan Adams better go with you.'

'Alone,' Sammy said. He took a deep breath. 'It's better that way.'

'Yeah,' Bill said. He watched Sergeant Golden walk to the door. It was a damned long walk. The truth was hard to come by sometimes.

Golden took his own car. He drove out West Ney in the backwash of the big east-west freeway through the dirty shirt tails of the city.

I could use a drink, Sammy thought. He kept driving.

The Chino Poblano was just three blocks from the parish house.

Sammy parked in front of the joint. *After tonight,* he thought, *I'm going to get drunk and stay drunk*. It would be better than thinking. Anything would.

It was an old bar, shiny from a thousand damp cloths, worm-eaten with the marks of careless cigarettes. The light inside was dusty and the electric fan made a quiet music. The men spoke mostly in the gentle cadence of their native tongue and even at this late hour there was a table of dominoes. Sammy ordered a double shot with a water chaser.

The bartender brought his drink. Sammy paid.

'It is the *rubia*,' the bartender said. 'That is why you are here, Sergeant?'

'I'm here for a drink,' Sammy said. He tried to remember the man's name, but he had met so many of Father's people. *Father's people* – the phrase was like an open wound.

The bartender scowled. 'Even dead, such a one makes trouble. I could have told you that from the first time I saw her.'

'In church?'

The man thumped his forefinger on the bar. 'In here. Upon the same stool as the one you occupy. Before God!' The domino players had turned their heads and were watching.

'Here?' Sammy repeated. He tried to stop the excitement curling inside him.

'*Pues,* and why not?' The bartender shrugged. 'It is the nearest place.'

'Alone?'

'That I will give her. She came alone. She left alone. In this place, that is not an easy thing. I speak in confidence, Sergeant, because you are a friend of *el padre*.'

'About the woman,' Sammy snapped.

'*Si*,' said the bartender, '*muy guapa*, that one. She was not unfriendly, you understand. But she could handle men. All fire and ice. And when it was cold, Sergeant' – he grinned – 'it was very, very cold. Even such a pig as Miguel could see that.'

'Miguel?'

'Miguel Milpas. A fool. A chaser. Big in the stomach, bigger in the head. A big trouble in here. A bad drunk.'

Sammy leaned forward. 'This Milpas, where would I find him?'

The bartender called to the domino players, '¿*Dónde está la casa de Miguel?*'

There was a quick flutter of consideration in Spanish.

'Around the corner on Mercado,' the bartender translated. 'Fourth house on the right.'

'Thanks.' Sammy left his drink unfinished.

In a poor district, Mercado was the poorest street. Dark, leaning houses, broken fences. Sammy went up the walk and on to a warped and sagging porch. He knocked. He pounded. In the house next door, a child began to cry. Across the street, a window went up.

The door before him swung open. 'Wha' do you wan'?' A big shadow in the greater shadow behind it.

'Are you Miguel Milpas?'

'Who wan's to know?'

'I'm a police officer. I want –'

The door slammed toward him. Sammy met it with his shoulder. The man was running through the house. The detective stumbled after him, following the clatter of footsteps. Then the footsteps stopped and he heard the squeal of wood against wood as when a badly fitted drawer is pulled.

It came from the left and Sammy crouched as he moved down a dark, narrow hall toward the dark room at the end. The shot exploded over his head.

From the memory of the flash, he dived for Miguel. His head smashed into the gross barrel of Miguel's belly.

Sammy got up first. He lit a match, caught the gleam of the nickel-plated pistol and kicked it across the room before he found the finger switch on the old brass fixture. The light showed a fat, ugly drunk, holding his stomach and moaning.

Golden stood over him. 'Get up, Milpas.'

'¡*Por Dios!* I am broken in two.'

Sammy grabbed a handful of hair and pulled the man's head up and back. 'The blonde woman, Sally Cox, last night!'

Miguel groaned.

'The blonde woman!' Sammy repeated.

'I did not mean to. She open the door when I knock. She is angry to see me. She grab a bottle, a wild cat, *gata, gatada!*' He closed his eyes and tried to rock forward. Golden let go of the man and stepped back.

'Well, now, if that isn't a picture!'

Sammy swung toward the door. Lieutenant Adams leaned against the frame, a broad grin on his freckled face. 'Bill thought somebody should tag along and pick up your stitches.'

'You heard?' Sammy demanded.

'I heard.'

Golden felt his own grin growing. 'Well, what are we waiting for?'

Adams jerked a thumb at the man on the floor. 'For him to get well,' he said.

It was late the next afternoon when Sammy finally reached the parish house of St Anne's. He had had ten hours' sleep, a shave, a shower, and a quart of beer to celebrate rejoining the human race.

Father Joseph Shanley took him into the study with an arm about his shoulders. The priest had heard enough to know that he was clear of the tall cloud, but he had not heard the details.

'Miguel Milpas,' Father shook his head. 'One of my failures . . .'

'A big trouble,' Sammy quoted the bartender, 'a bad drunk.'

'Nevertheless . . .' the priest said.

'You were darned lucky we found him. Maybe you were even lucky he did it. Dempsy and the Angel were out to get you and get you good. The night before last you were bound for an assignation. After you arrived at the apartment you were to be doused with liquor, and she was going to run from the apartment, her clothes torn, screaming at the top of her lungs. A lot of people would have seen you. Then Dempsy was to have picked her up and they would have vanished into the night. One phone call, and the police would have found an apartment abandoned by a terror-stricken woman, witnesses and you wandering around smelling of whisky.'

Father shuddered.

'He almost made it at that. Because even with Sari dead, he had enough hatred left to improvise.'

'That poor man . . .' Joseph Shanley stared at Sammy Golden. 'What will you people do to him?'

'Not much, actually. Aside from entering the parish house, it's hard to put a finger on anything he did that's strictly illegal.'

The detective shrugged. 'One thing I can tell you, though, we'll put the fear of God in him where you're concerned.'

A ghost of a smile touched the corners of Father's eyes. 'Isn't that a little outside of your bailiwick, Sergeant?'

'You go to . . .' Sammy began and stopped. There was too little logic in the last word, and besides, they had been there only last night.

The Traffic in Damnation

BY ROBERT FABIAN

The year 1954 also saw the debut of the first police series on British TV when crime programmes made their long delayed return to the screen almost fifteen years after the landmark production of The Ringer. The man responsible for introducing viewers on this side of the Atlantic to what had been keeping families glued to their sets in America was Donald Wilson, a writer, script-editor and later producer at the BBC, whose career would be crowned when he won a BAFTA award in 1967 for the famous period series, The Forsyte Saga. Wilson was a fan of crime and mystery fiction, and in 1954 devised The Six Proud Walkers which Leslie Halliwell has described as 'the BBC's first adult cliffhanger series ... in which a gentlemanly detective inspector narrated stories of crime the audience were invited to solve before the denouement'. The series was shown live, each episode lasting for thirty minutes. Audience response to The Six Proud Walkers was good (indeed the format was revived ten years later by Douglas Allen), and led directly to the launching on 13 November of the BBC's first post-war detective series, Fabian of the Yard. The weekly, pre-filmed half-hour stories were semi-fictional re-creations of police cases, all recounted by the unorthodox Inspector Robert Fabian of Scotland Yard. Such was the popularity of the grainy episodes – partly filmed on location – and the terse manner of the Inspector, that the series made the real Fabian a household name and the actor who played him, Bruce Seton, a cult figure. Bob Fabian had, in fact, seen life in the raw in London during his long career at the Yard and knew many of the criminal figures intimately – a fact which enabled him to supply the series with its authentic atmosphere and dialogue. Seton, for his part, was a veteran character actor who had appeared in films since the

thirties and starred in a number of classic crime stories including Sweeney Todd *(1936) and* King of the Underworld *(1952), both starring the old master of melodrama, Tod Slaughter. Three years before Fabian, Seton had also played Detective Sergeant John Flint in a radio series,* Flint of the Flying Squad, *created by Alan Stranks as a more serious alternative to the ligh-hearted tales of the beat policeman* PC 49.

Fabian of the Yard *was not only a popular success, but was able to show the use of scientific techniques in police work as well as the painstaking methods that were required to bring criminals to justice. It was as much a trail-blazer in its way as* Dragnet *had been in America. (Despite its undoubtedly strongly British flavour,* Fabian of the Yard *was transmitted in America in 1956 by CBS where it was re-titled* Patrol Car.) *Apart from inspiring the series, Robert Fabian (1906–1978) was an accomplished writer and after his retirement wrote* Fabian of the Yard *(1952) and* London After Dark *(1954) which were used in the TV series. Although the majority of episodes featured more traditional crimes such as robbery, kidnapping and even the occasional murder, it also made excursions into the areas of gang violence, prostitution and drugs which Fabian had seen at first hand while Chief of the Vice Squad. These were dangerous subjects for television to tackle in the fifties and if the vice may have been a little stylised to save the feelings of impressionable viewers, it nevertheless provided a glimpse into the London underworld which the average person knew nothing about. A particularly powerful episode dealt with drug-taking among the young and was based on the following story by Robert Fabian. In certain respects (though not the prices or some of the prejudices) it is still this same appalling trade that today provides storylines for the successors to* Fabian of the Yard . . .

THE FIRST DRUG trafficker I ever met was Eddie the Villain, and I shall never forget him because it also happened to be my first week on duty as a policeman. I was a uniformed constable, with the white-and-blue armlet on my left wrist to indicate to the world that I was on my beat and not entitled to smoke, gossip or loiter. A police officer old enough to be my father was showing me around. He was due to retire in a few months, and all that mixed-up backyard of Soho, which had been his life for so many years, was just about to become mine, in his place.

We walked down Lisle Street, and my companion paused, drawing me into the shadows, as a tall, slim negro came out of a house. He was superbly well dressed – perhaps somewhat over-dressed – in a tightly tailored black overcoat with velvet collar, homburg hat, and cigar in his big teeth. He glanced alertly up and down the street, but did not see us. A white girl was with him – a pretty, delicate little creature, but rather dishevelled and forlorn, I thought.

'Who is it?' I asked, when they had gone. The old policeman said solemnly: 'That, son, was Eddie Manning – called Eddie the Villain. And take my advice, son, if it means pinching that fellow, never go alone. If you get an urge to talk to him, don't. If he wants to give you a cigarette, refuse it. Never take a drink from him, never go to his place if you want information. Scrub him out of your life – he's the worst man in London.'

I was only a beginner in the Metropolitan Police, and did not wish to seem to be teaching my elders and betters their business, but this did seem to be a very negative approach to crime for a police officer.

'Surely,' I said, 'he wants dealing with?'

My companion nodded. 'He surely does,' he said, 'but as I've only got a few months to do for my twenty-five years and my pension, I'll leave that to you!'

As I was thinking this one over, he added: 'Now remember what I told you, son, and try nothing rash with that fellow. He'll try to dope you, bribe you, trap you. I know two decent youngsters who fell foul of him, and they both simply disappeared. Some well-known men and women have died at his place under drugs or some other diabolical practice.'

I did a great deal more thinking about Eddie the Villain in the next couple of years, and discovered a few things about him, although I did not go out of my way either to avoid him or to get in his path. I did not want to make the mistake of taking on a full-scale villain like Eddie Manning before I knew a great deal more about the rules of the game we were both playing on opposite sides. I found that he was from Jamaica and had been in England about ten years, working quite honestly at first in a munitions factory, and then taking a job as jazz drummer with a travelling dance-band. It was here, presumably, that he picked up the threads of drug-trafficking, and was to discover that he had a diabolical genius for it.

He had an elaborately furnished flat in Lisle Street, that was frequented by white girls who seemed willing to do anything for him and his friends, but that was nothing the police could put a finger on, although we strongly suspected that Eddie was giving dope-parties in various parts of London, and injections of cocaine at 10s. per time, also gaming parties with fixed cards and roulette wheels that were fitted with electrically operated brake-shoes, to stop on any number or colour that best favoured the bank. It was not my job in those days to catch him, and in any case he was a difficult one to get red-handed. He had his own team of strong-arm villains – both white and coloured boys who were usually full of drugs – and kept a profitable sideline in protecting prostitutes. Eddie was undoubtedly a villain!

Then I picked up the rumour that – as with so many of his kind – he was beginning to fancy himself too much, and had become careless. I passed on this hint to the proper quarters – I was still in uniform – and the next thing was that detectives arrested Eddie and found opium, an opium pipe and capsules of cocaine in his possession. In the court it was also stated that a man had died at Eddie's flat from an overdose of heroin, believed to have been supplied by Manning; also a young girl had died from cocaine poisoning, and had neither admitted nor denied that the drug was obtained from Manning.

He received three years' penal servitude, and that took a good deal of the shine out of him. When he came out he opened a little club, and by this time I was a fully experienced detective officer, and he had no terrors for me. I used to call around at his premises regularly to administer a little frightening powder, as we call it. He never fancied me, and would always roll his big white eyeballs sulkily whenever he saw me coming down the steps of his cellar club. I am glad to say that it was as a direct result of information that I picked up and passed on to my immediate superiors that Eddie got his final prison sentence, in 1929. I had heard the whisper that he had gone into the business of receiving stolen property, after he had been chased out of the drug racket. It was something of a come-down for his type, but, when the moment was right, I dropped my whisper and Eddie's abode was raided. It was found to contain luggage worth £400 that had been stolen from the then Mr Duff Cooper and further stolen property worth over £1,500.

This flat was in St Ann's Court, Wardour Street, and when he went to prison that finished his nasty little cellar club in Berwick Street, which was always filled with prostitutes and coloured boys. Manning's first prison sentence, by the way, was sixteen months for shooting a man in the street, in Cambridge Circus.

Unfortunately the end of Eddie Manning did not put an effective finish to the drug traffic in London. It has, with the passing of years, veered considerably from cocaine and opium to marijuana cigarettes, and to the use of such drunks as pethidine and morphine. But it still goes on, and the victims are – as always – found to be most numerous among the ranks of jazz-crazy youngsters. There is, I believe, some scientific foundation for the claim that marijuana addiction can help a musician, for this drug has some effect upon that part of the brain which responds to rhythmical vibrations, and it is as a result of this that the cult of 'reefer' smoking has been so closely bound up with jive musicians and coloured men. It is easy enough to grow – there was a time when drug traffickers were discovered to be growing marijuana upon desolate bomb-sites around Liverpool. It is the chopped leaves and seeds of the hemp plant (*Cannabis indica*) and it will grow anywhere that a dandelion or nettle will grow. You can find it in canary seed.

It is, however, a great compliment to the fine police work of Britain that it is such a rarity to find the reefer plant being cultivated here. The drug traffickers find it more practical to smuggle it in from the African coastal ports, or from the West Indies, often by way of the oil tankers.

Britain, by the way, has a better record in the battle against dope than any other country in the world. We have nothing to be sensationally alarmed about in this country, but there is no denying that it does go on to a very undesirable extent. I had it brought home to me dramatically the other day, when I took a taxi and found it belonged to one of my friends. Jim the taxi-driver plies around Soho and Leicester Square, and we are frequently meeting each other on our various rounds. He knows London fully as well as I do. And he thinks he knows all the answers. But there is one answer, I found, that old Jim doesn't know. It is the problem of his own daughter, Shirley.

As I paid him, I asked: 'How's that pretty daughter of yours, Jim? You didn't show me her photo this trip.'

He went suddenly white. 'Shirley's OK,' he said hesitantly, then – 'Mr Fabian, could I ask you some advice?' He put his crumpled glove on the meter-flag, and followed me into a café.

As we stirred coffee, Jim told me about nineteen-year-old Shirley. She was a drug addict.

'We didn't suspect at first, Mr Fabian. All I knew was that as soon as I got home for my tea, we'd have a blazing row. Usually about her stopping out late. She'd rush up to her poky little bedroom and stay there, sulking. Wouldn't come out. Her mum and me tried to listen to the radio, but we knew what we were really listening for – the sound of our Shirley sneaking downstairs, and the click of the front-door latch as she went out!'

The match-flame he was sucking into his pipe, trembled. 'I've never yet struck her,' he said. 'But no daughter of mine is going to stop out until dawn – hanging around these filthy cafés and dance halls . . . or worse places, for all I know!

'What can I do, Mr Fabian? Is it too late to help her?'

There was nothing Jim could do. In my twenty-eight years among London's night life, I have known many drug addicts. Few have ever been cured.

When Shirley stepped, shivering with cold and nerves, into London's night streets, it was not to seek pleasure. She needed drugs. Whatever the price, it had to be paid. Wherever the drug-peddler sold his stuff, she had to go. She couldn't bargain. He had only to sit there, smiling, and wait . . .

There are far too many girls like her in London's night-life today. Spotted at a dance by some schemer who covets her fresh youthfulness, tempted with a habit-forming drug – as a cigarette – candy – a fruit drink – a pinch of snuff 'to pep you up!' Within a few months, she cannot remain in her respectable home. She must follow her evil supplier into his underworld. They are truly the damned souls of London. And nearly all of them are under twenty-one.

Chelsea, in the districts around the King's Road and Old Church Street, is London's headquarters of the cocaine, morphine, pethidine addicts.

Chelsea drug addicts! You wouldn't think them glamorous if you could see them, as I have. That pale, dull young man in frayed grey suit and duffle coat, who is not enjoying his beer. The middle-aged woman, with dyed hair streaky with grey. She wears black corduroy trousers and a purple utility box-jacket. Her drink, too, is beer. It stays almost untasted.

They don't come to enjoy a drink, nor each other's company. They gather to listen greedily for the whisper of a fellow addict – 'I've found a new doctor who . . .' There are ninety-two doctors who are known drug addicts. Five of them are women.

Yes, those are the Chelsea drug addicts. No sparkling artists who loll on silken couches and dream beautifully of paradise. All the Chelsea addicts I know are pale, drawn, indifferent. Usually they have dandruff and watering eyes. Cocaine, morphine, pethidine, are hard to get. Their lives are not much fun. But let them get a youngster in their clutches, and they will poison him – or her – without a qualm. It makes them feel less lonely and doomed.

They are the forlorn remnants of those Bright Young Things – remember them? – who filled the newspapers of twenty-five years ago.

Pink champagne, it was in those days, and caffeine pills and glucose injections, to give 'pep' – and then . . . cocaine. Today, in London, only these few shivering drug addicts remain, as the ghosts of Mayfair's gay yesterday.

I have tried cocaine. It was given me by a man who would have liked nothing better than to get the Chief of the Flying Squad in his power as a dope addict.

I had a slight cold. 'Here, try this, Bob,' he said. 'It's a new menthol snuff – clears your head wonderfully.'

I took a pinch on my thumbnail, and sniffed. There was a sudden freezing sensation in my nose. My face went numb. Then I found myself laughing too loudly, talking too much . . . I had enough sense to go home.

Next morning was one of shivering nausea and acute misery of mind. I lay and dreamed about that glittering white powder. I wanted it like a thirsty man wants water, like a drowning man wants a gasp of air.

I did not often carry a grudge in my police work. But within a week I had him in gaol, where he could not supply anybody – even me – with the stuff.

Most of London's black-market drugs – heroin, cocaine, morphine, pethidine – come these days from stolen medical supplies, forged prescriptions. The drugs that the smugglers concentrate upon are opium and marijuana. In five years, the number of prosecutions for marijuana has increased by 2,100 per cent.

Marijuana is easier to get than morphine. The dried leaf can be sold to drug-peddlers for £50 a pound. You don't need to smoke it. It can be made into candy, chewed like gum, mixed with canned fruit-juice for drinking. The effect is the same. There is not much taste. That's why youth is so vulnerable to it. They don't even need to know they're having it!

Jive musicians still use it persistently. From marijuana addicts, come the bobby-sox terms, like: 'It sends me . . . in the groove . . . hep (those in the know) . . . squares (not in the know) . . . out of this world . . . higher than a kite . . .'.

Where jive is, youth is. And there, too, is marijuana. It is the drug of America, just as opium is the drug of China. And today, along the Charing Cross Road, where America is worshipped, marijuana claims its victims. Young gangsters use it to get courage. Girls are betrayed by it. It is the easiest, newest weapon of the West End ponce.

Every pound of marijuana can make one thousand cigarettes. They sell for 7s. 6d. each . . . Once you are an addict, the drug-peddler may want payment more precious than three halfcrowns.

When police raided a private dance hall, The Club Eleven, on 15 April last year, they found Shirley among two hundred and fifty persons, aged between seventeen and thirty. All were searched. Ten white boys and one negro had packets of marijuana and cocaine. Three were American sailors.

Flung on the dance-hall floor when the raid began, were twenty-three packets of marijuana, handfuls of marijuana cigarettes, a packet of cocaine, a small, sticky wad of prepared opium, and an empty morphine ampoule.

Shirley, giggling stupidly, did not seem to be aware that her ear-lobe was dinted by human teeth-marks, and running with blood. She was bandaged, taken home in a police car. It was two a.m. Next day, Shirley wept and made many promises . . .

Ten weeks later, when the Paramount Dance Hall in the Tottenham Court Road was raided, Shirley was again discovered. This time with coloured men. Eight men were arrested – one so drug-crazed that he attacked the police. The marijuana smoker gets mad criminal courage. Give him a gun, and he will shoot.

Shirley did not, this time, give her parents' address. She didn't live there, now. She was living with a swarthy taciturn man of bad breath and worse record. She was chained to him, tighter than ever was medieval slave-girl, by bangles of the dope hunger. It was her nineteenth birthday that week.

Both Club Eleven and Paramount Dance Hall have been closed by the police. But, a few months ago, when twenty-five police officers raided the A to Z Dance Club in Gerrard Street, Shirley was there again!

Blame Shirley? Well, let's go to the case of a wealthy young London medical student whom I arrested for obtaining drugs by forgery. He promised to take a cure, and went to an expensive private sanatorium. Gently, he was 'tapered off' from the drug habit. His daily doses grew less. This was his case record:

3rd day: Patient restless, cannot sleep, vomits at food. Complains of cold, although given six blankets.

4th day: Eyes, nose, mouth, watering ceaselessly. Complains of pains. Given sedative but cannot endure contact with bed. Tried to sleep on floor, and received severe abrasions on knees and elbows, from writhing during night.

6th day: Still vomits at sight of food. Alternately sweating, then clammy. Vomiting and diarrhoea. Rising blood pressure, dilated pupils. Yawns and sneezes constantly.

8th day: Complains of aching muscles, burning stomach, severe headache, says 'eyeballs hurt as if about to burst' . . .

This patient stayed six months at the sanatorium. He was employed in the open air, given good food, cigarettes, sedatives. Three months after his discharge, he was again in the hands of the police – for stealing drugs from a doctor's car. What chance do you think a young girl has against a habit that grips you like that?

If you smoke heavily, drink regularly, 'can't face the day without a cup of tea' – be glad nobody gave you a marijuana cigarette or pinch of cocaine to sniff when you were in your foolish, adventurous teens. You possess exactly the same weaknesses as any drug addict.

The hell of dope addicts is that, to get their supplies, they *must* go to the underworld. A boy must steal – a girl must learn to pay in sickening ways – for the handful of dried leaves, the pinch of white numbing powder, the chunk of deadly brown gum, without which their bodies writhe and brains bleed.

A sensitive, cultured negro, who had failed his exams due to marijuana addiction, and landed in Wormwood Scrubs for theft, told me: 'I smoke marijuana because it makes me feel less black.'

With that, one can sympathise. But Shirley had started using drugs 'because it helped me jive better'. Poor Shirley!

PC *Crawford's First Pinch*

BY TED WILLIS

In 1955 two of the most famous television crime series of all time were launched: the American Highway Patrol, *starring the fast-talking Broderick Crawford as Chief Dan Matthews, and his virtual antithesis,* Dixon of Dock Green, *with Jack Warner as the archetypal calm and patient British bobby. Despite being produced very cheaply,* Highway Patrol *succeeded because of Crawford's magnetism on the screen as he relentlessly tracked down criminals and then, after receiving the latest piece of information over his patrol car radio, would mutter the immortal words. 'Ten-four'.*

George Dixon, by contrast, stood quietly in the shade of a blue police lamp or behind the desk of Dock Green Police Station and coped with every eventuality from lost pets to murder. The solid and dependable George had actually been created by Ted Willis in the 1950 film, The Blue Lamp, *during which he was brutally shot and killed. Five years later, the character was still haunting Willis when he was asked by the BBC to create a new series to augment the popularity of* Fabian of the Yard. *What could be more natural than to contrast the high-flying Fabian with a stolid man on the beat – and so George Dixon was revived to star in a series that would ultimately run to three hundred and sixty-seven episodes (transposing from black and white into colour in the process) and last for twenty-one years until Jack Warner reached the age of eighty and his character had become a British institution. In the early episodes, the stories tended to feature domestic incidents, but as the series' popularity grew with audiences of over fourteen million, Dixon was promoted to a desk sergeant and the main action was the preseve of the CID and his son-in-law, Detective Sergeant Andy Crawford, played by Peter Byrne. What never changed* was Dixon's opening salute to the camera and his words uttered with a sniff, 'Evenin' all.' Among the other perennial characters were George's daughter, Mary Crawford (first played by Billie Whitelaw and then Jeannette Hutchinson), Desk Sergeant Flint (Arthur Rigby) and PC Lauderdale (Geoffrey Adams). Jack Warner went to great pains to make Dixon authentic, and so identified with the role that when he died in 1981 Scotland Yard itself paid tribute to him as 'a gentleman who served both us and the public so well'.

Edward Henry 'Ted' Willis (1918–), the creator of Dixon, had been a novelist and short story writer before becoming famous almost overnight through this series. By his own admission, though, he had been worried when asked to write the initial six episodes that the idea of a non-violent series of 'Stories of a London Policeman' (as the programme was sub-titled) could be sustained. To aid him with the writing, he researched the police at work in Paddington Green and modelled Dixon on a real policeman he had once met at Leman Street Station in the East End of London. He also appeared in the Police Gazette for anecdotes from policemen themselves and received over a thousand replies. For this reason, he was to say years later, it was possible to root the stories in reality and 'give them the flavour of truth rather than fiction'. Just how real people believed the characters were was demonstrated when Willis contrived the 'death' of a popular character, PC Bob Penny, because the actor Anthony Parker wanted to go back to working in the theatre. The BBC received thousands of letters of protest, as did Jack Warner and Willis himself. 'One of mine contained simply the single word, "Murderer!" scrawled in lipstick on a half sheet of paper,' he said. The task of providing the scripts for the long-running series eventually had to be shared with other writers, but all of them sought to maintain the special interaction between the characters that made Dixon of Dock Green not just another TV series to its viewers but a part of their lives. At the very heart of this was undoubtedly the relationship between George Dixon and Andy Crawford, and it therefore seems appropriate to reprint here the very first story that introduced the two men and set the scene for what was to be for many years the longest-running TV series in the world. Though the image of the police world of which they were a part may have changed dramatically in the intervening period of time, the fame of the progamme itself endures as brightly as ever.

YOU'LL FIND DOCK Green east of the Tower, within earshot of Bow Bells and hard by Old Father Thames. A zestful, colourful slice of east London, and home town and stamping-ground of a policeman called George Dixon.

At the time of this first story Dixon was still a police constable, an old sweat who wanted nothing more fancy on his uniform than his number-flash, 706. A tall man, clean-featured, well set up. This day, a sweltering July day some years back, he was assembling with eight other constables for early-turn parade.

The parade was taken by a towering, barrel-chested station sergeant called Flint, a graduate of the old school and the terror of the nick. Flint bawled 'Fall in' and read out the registration numbers of stolen cars. The men noted them down then were told what beat they'd be working and briefed as to what had been or might be happening.

Flint called the last man. '706!'

'Sergeant.' Dixon came to attention.

'Eight beat. Watch out for heavy lorries parking on the pavement in Dock Lane and street photographers in the High Road. There was a fire at East Orient wharf last night – check the premises are secure. You'll be taking a new man round with you, so report to me after parade.'

'Sergeant.'

Flint lowered his clipboard, surveyed the line of men. 'Right. Produce appointments.' Truncheon, whistle and the police wallet containing the notebooks were held up for inspection. 'Atten-shun!' barked Flint. 'Right turn, quick march!'

The new man was in the station office, holding his helmet rather self-consciously and talking to PC 'Tub' Barrell, behind the counter. Flint introduced Dixon. The newcomer's name was Andy Crawford and he was a dark-haired, good-looking youngster in his mid-twenties. He was fresh from his thirteen weeks' training course at Peel House and Dixon guessed he still had some illusions. They shook hands, the new man put on his helmet and they set out for Eight beat.

As they walked through quiet 6 a.m. streets, occasionally pausing to check premises, Dixon gave a run-down on the nick. Dock Green was a sub-divisional station in the charge of a superintendent, known to the men as 'Father'. There were three inspectors, three station sergeants, nine sergeants, twenty-five constables and one cadet. The distaff side was represented by one policewoman sergeant and two WPCs. The CID had a detective inspector, two sergeants and three detective constables. Conditions at Dock Green nick were pretty good and Dixon had served there since he'd joined the Force.

Gradually the streets came alive. In the hot and busy High Road a street photographer was snapping away, blatantly breaking the law, and Dixon sent him packing. A busker was reminded he had to keep moving at a quarter-mile an hour. The drivers of illegally parked cars were warned and sent on their way.

'You'll find all sorts in this manor,' said Dixon, as they moved on towards the Central Library. 'Cockneys, mostly, but there's a whole lot of newcomers.'

His young companion nodded. Since they'd left the station he'd seen black faces, brown faces, yellow faces, blue-eyed and snub-nosed faces from across the Irish Sea. 'I guess that one's home-grown, though.' He indicated a fetching young piece in white linen shorts and shirt-blouse, padlocking her bicycle outside the library.

'Wise kid,' said Dixon, approving the padlocking, 'though it don't always stop the hooks.' He'd learned that Andy Crawford had his sights on the CID, and told him he could get his hand in by helping to nail the local bike-thieves, who were becoming a bit of a pain.

The Dock Lane pavements were clear of lorries and they continued towards the river. They checked the charred and blackened premises known as the East Orient wharf, walked through a square of once elegant Georgian houses. 'Sea-captains' houses, one time,' Dixon said. 'Split up into flats, now.' They walked past yelling high-spirited children in a school playground, passed a clutter of dockside cranes, went down a street of warehouses. 'Sniff,' said Dixon, and Andy duly sniffed. 'Spices, tea, tobacco, a bit of a whiff from the soap-factory and the tang of the good old river.'

'Quite a place, the Green,' said Andy. Dixon gave a confirmatory nod.

When they returned for their mid-morning break Flint was on the telephone, Tub Barrell was explaining something to a turbaned Sikh and standing by the counter was the girl in the white linen shorts. Dixon took off his helmet, smoothed his straight fair hair and went over. The girl seemed upset about something and he learned she'd had her bicycle stolen.

'I locked it, too!' she exclaimed, angry as well as upset, and threw a padlock and short length of chain on the counter.

'I know, miss. It's a bloomin' epidemic.'

Flint rang off and took the details. Ladies' Special Speedster, gold flashes on mudguards and front forks. 'Frame number?' The girl fished a slip of paper from her handbag and gave the number. Flint completed his notes, said the police would do what they could, the girl collected her padlock but left the useless chain and went off to catch a bus.

Andy was examining the chain. ''Scuse me, Sergeant,' he said tentatively, and held up the exhibit. 'This chain's been cut.'

'Has it, now,' said Flint, and took the chain.

'With blunt cutters, too,' said the unsuspecting Andy, and pointed with an efficient forefinger.

'With cutters, eh? Well, I never.'

'Whoever did it had a couple of goes before he got through the chain. You can see the marks.'

'Well, well,' said Flint, apparently deeply impressed. The Sikh passed on his way out and he seemed impressed, too. 'Look, lads,' said Flint, showing the chain to the others. 'Real CID stuff.'

'Clever bit of observation,' said Tub Barrell solemnly, and Andy visibly preened.

'Find a pair of blunt cutters and we've got the thief, eh?' said Flint, eyeing his new recruit.

'Matter of fact,' put in Dixon, 'I've a pair of blunt wire-cutters in the shed at home. I'm probably the bloke we're looking for.'

Andy's enthusiasm dimmed. 'Only trying to help,' he said, shortly.

'Don't be touchy, Crawford,' snapped Flint. 'Leg-pulls are all part of your training.' He turned to record the bike-theft in the occurrence book. 'Hop off and get your break.'

Downstairs in the busy canteen Andy shared a table with George Dixon and Danny Matthews, a young detective constable. They talked of the spate of bike-thefts and Matthews said if things didn't get a jerk on the DI would have them all on the big red rug. The thefts weren't the crime of the century but they took time away from the more important jobs. Andy mentioned the wire-cutters incident and said at least it proved that the bike-snatch wasn't off the cuff.

'Dead right,' said Matthews. 'Somewhere in a back-street shed there's a hook giving the bikes a quick respray and flogging 'em to types who don't ask awkward questions.'

'I'd like to nab him,' said Andy.

'You do that, mate.'

Matthews finished his coffee and went off. Dixon filled an old briar pipe and asked if Andy played snooker. Andy said he did. Dixon took him into the station's recreation-room and they knocked the balls about for the rest of their break and then went back on patrol.

They re-did the same ground, Dixon ringing in at prescribed intervals from the police-pillars then still in use. Once a light flashed on a pillar and they were detailed to man a crossing where the traffic-lights had failed. Or rather Dixon manned and Andy watched. It looked easy, the way the big-framed, calmly efficient policeman did it, but Andy knew that if he himself were out there he'd bring east London to a grinding halt.

While he waited on the pavement he kept a sharp eye open for possible bike-thieves, but bike-wise the Green was quiet. A relief came out for the traffic-crossing and they resumed their patrol. They approached the Star of India public-house and Dixon mentioned there was often trouble at the Star, especially at weekends. As they reached the pub Danny Matthews came out of the public bar and Andy gave him a nod of greeting. The nod was completely ignored and Matthews passed on without a second glance.

'Black mark,' said Dixon, as they walked on. 'The CID keep anonymous. If a hook saw you give the glad hand he'd have him on the grapevine before you could say Dan the Dick.'

Andy thanked him and logged it. He knew that CID men are allowed to drink on duty because much of their time is spent with 'noses' or informants, and he wondered to Dixon what the DC's present chore might concern. 'Anything from petty larceny to homicide,' said Dixon. 'The job's interesting because they never know what'll come up. That applies to the uniform branch, too,' he stressed. 'It's not all pavement-bashing, by a long chalk.'

It was coming up to 2 p.m. and they returned to the nick and signed off. They'd meet in the parade-room at 5.45 a.m. next day. They were on 'George' and 'Andy' terms now and the young PC would go round with the senior man for the rest of the three weeks' stint.

When Andy had gone Flint asked Dixon what he thought. 'He'll do,' said Dixon. 'He asks questions, uses his eyes, is keen to get on.'

'They all are, at the start,' said Flint. He'd handed over to his relief station sergeant and was changing into his civvy jacket preparatory to going home. 'By the way, I've seen Father. He asked me to have a word.'

'What about, Sarge?'

'About you.'

Sunday of that week was rest-day for Dixon and Andy and the young man was invited along to tea. Dixon, a widower, lived in a small rented house, one of a terrace, with a pint-sized garden in front and a larger plot at the rear. Dixon's daughter Mary kept house for him and it was Mary who answered Andy's ring.

'Hullo' she smiled.

'Hullo.' What a pip, thought Andy. She was a year or two younger than he, with intelligent grey-blue eyes, an aureole of chestnut curls and an up-curving, generous mouth. Great, he said to himself, and entered the house.

Dixon's burly figure was clad in cardigan and slacks and while Mary put the kettle on Andy was invited to inspect the back garden. The young man dutifully admired the summer blooms near the back door and the lettuces and other greenstuff in what Dixon called his market garden. For good measure the older man took his guest into the tool-shed and showed him the pair of blunt wire-cutters.

. They sat down to a lavish high tea. Andy hadn't been faced with such a repast since he'd left home and come to London, and he said so.

'Where are you staying?' Mary asked. 'The police section-house?'

'No. In digs.'

'Don't they feed you?'

'You need the CID to find the meat.'

Mary gave her father a glance but said nothing. After tea Dixon went out to make sure the black-fly weren't attacking his runner beans and Andy rolled up his shirt-sleeves and joined Mary at the kitchen sink. They talked about the bike-thefts, of which there'd been more, but there was an undercurrent of strong mutual attraction beneath the casual chat and for a time the bike-thefts seemed of less importance.

After an evening of police and Dock Green shop Andy left with an invite to return for a meal on Tuesday. He walked back to his digs through the sultry summer dusk thinking not of bikes but Mary Dixon.

The following day one of the sergeants was off sick and Dixon took his place as 'acting Jack', buckling on to his arm a cloth band bearing two stripes. Andy stayed in the station-office with him and Flint and had a taste of the never-ending stream of callers. There were people whose cars had been stolen, aliens registering a change of address or occupation, a man reporting his wife missing, a child found wandering, motorists asked to produce driving licences or insurance or MOT certificates, a woman complaining about her neighbour – a whole representative Dock Green gaggle. In the intervals between callers Dixon did paper-work and Tub Barrell performed his one-finger act on the office typewriter. CID men came to the counter and flipped through the occurrence book. Arrested persons were brought in and people 'helping the police with their inquiries'.

Andy kept the correspondence register, helped flag the crime and accident maps, did the filing, ran messages. At suitable intervals the reserve PC would look in the station office to say there was a message from 'T' division, and they'd take turns for a quick cuppa in the reserve-room. There was always something doing and for Andy the sign-off seemed to come an hour before its time.

On Tuesday they were back on patrol. At the early morning shift-change Flint reported there'd been more bike-thefts and the patrolmen were told brusquely to get some action. On patrol Andy looked about him with such zeal that Dixon said he'd wear his eyes out before they got back for their break. 'And anyhow, you don't know what you're looking at, yet.'

They were walking through the Dock Lane street market, with the traders busily preparing their stalls. 'I'm looking for a bloke getting ready to nick a bike,' Andy said.

'Bit early for that – hooks don't like getting up early. I meant you don't know this manor, so you can't tell what's usual from what's not. When you're genned up a bit you'll find you'll watch, as well as look, and you'll be getting somewhere.'

As they turned into the High Road an elderly woman came up and asked the way to the Town Hall. While Dixon directed her Andy glanced about him. People were going to work, children were on their way to school, the massive weekday traffic build-up had begun. Nothing special to Dock Green here – it was happening all over London.

But there *was* something. A boy with a bike. A smart new lady's cycle, with gold flashes on the front forks.

Andy called to Dixon he was going after the bike and darted across the High Road. The boy had pedalled down a side street and as Andy rounded a corner he saw him dismount and wheel the bike through ramshackle wooden gates. Andy was through the gates and into the yard before the boy had got his clips off.

'Just a minute, son.'

The youth looked up. 'I ain't your son,' he said, cocky. He picked up an empty sack lying by some old iron scrap and laid it over the bike.

'Take it off.'

'Why?'

'I want to see that bike.'

'Why?'

Andy put his toe under the sack and tossed it to one side. 'What are you hiding it for?'

'I'm not. It's a new bike, and I don't want it mucked up.'

'Is it yours, then?'

The youth grinned cheekily. 'No.'

Footsteps were heard outside and Dixon's tall figure swung into the yard. Andy turned. 'This bike, George. It's a girl's.'

'Well, so it is!' said the youth, mocking.

'No lip,' said Dixon. 'Where's your Dad?'

A door opened at the rear of the yard and a middle-aged man came over. He was stocky, red-haired and wore a greasy waistcoat over a collarless shirt. 'So it's the law, is it?' he frowned. 'What's the trouble?' The words were English, the accent strictly Emerald Isle.

'It's this young copper, Dad,' said the youth. 'He says I've knocked off our Hilda's bike.'

'Know anything about it, Ned?' asked Dixon.

'Listen,' the man said, scowling, 'bike-snatching's not my line, you know that.'

'We can't tell with you, though, can we?' said Dixon drily.

'I know what you're getting at, but that bike belongs to my daughter.' He began to roll a cigarette.

'Can we see her?' asked Andy.

'She's out.'

'When will she be back?'

The man seemed to be concentrating on his cigarette. 'She's . . . sort of away for the time being.'

The youth smothered a laugh. His father reached out and cuffed him. 'Get in the house,' he ordered. As the youth went by he cuffed him again. He scraped a match on the wall and lit up. 'That bike, now. It was got honest.'

'When can we see your daughter?' Dixon asked.

'You can't – so belt up.'

'Have you a receipt for the bike?'

'Somewhere. Dunno where, though.'

He would say no more about the bike. Dixon told Andy the man was Ned Cooney and while the young policeman looked for the frame number Dixon took Cooney to one side. 'Your girl. She OK?'

'I wouldn't know. She's gone missing.'

'She's seventeen, eighteen, isn't she?'

'Old enough to please herself.' He spat a shred of tobacco from his lip. He gave Dixon a morose, suspicious glance, frowned across at Andy.

The young PC stuffed his notebook into his breast pocket and came over. Cooney followed the two policemen to the gates. 'Look, Ned,' said Dixon, 'if your girl's really gone missing –'

'Good-day, copper,' said Cooney, and the gates were closed with a definitive jolt.

Over steak and chips at Dixon's that evening Andy mentioned he'd compared the bike-numbers and they didn't fit, after all. 'But I still don't believe Cooney's story.'

'I do,' said Dixon. 'Cooney's no mug. He knows we can check.'

'Mm,' said Andy, noncommittal. He knew George Dixon was essentially a warm-hearted character and liked to believe the best of everyone, but he might be wrong about Cooney.

'What's up?' asked Mary, sensing his disappointment. 'You should be glad Ned Cooney told the truth.'

'I was hoping we'd got a lead on the bike-thieves.'

'He lives with it,' smiled Dixon. 'It's his first big case.'

'Don't knock the guest,' said Mary, and rose to fetch the dessert. 'Anyway, I'm glad it's not Cooney,' she said as she went out. 'We need him for Saturday.'

Andy looked at Dixon and the older man explained there was a church jumble sale on Saturday at St Michael's Hall. 'Cooney's laid on to collect the old tots. Mary's roped me in, and if you don't watch it she'll nab you, too.'

While Dixon went down to the off-licence the young man joined Mary in the kitchen. As Mary washed up and he wiped she asked how he'd got on with her father. He said it was an education, walking the beat with George Dixon.

'It should be,' she smiled, 'he's been at it long enough.'

'Yes. Funny, really.'

Mary asked what was funny and learned Andy was puzzled as to why Dixon hadn't been made up to sergeant. The girl explained that her mother had died when Mary was eleven and that Dixon had had his hands full bringing his daughter up.

'I wasn't an easy kid to rear, believe me,' Mary smiled. 'Dad didn't have much time left to study for exams.' There was also the fact that Dixon liked his job and wanted to stick to it. Still, it seemed the Super had said that a man with Dixon's knowledge of the manor would be of more use in the station office than on the beat, and Dixon had been asked to think it over.

'He's not too keen,' said Mary. 'He doesn't mind "acting Jack" occasionally but he doesn't want sergeant. He's happier on the beat.'

Dixon returned from the off-licence and they talked over drinks for an hour or so then Andy pushed off. He'd been duly booked for jumble-duty on Saturday, then he was to have tea at the Dixons' and take Mary to the flicks. As he walked back to his digs he felt almost one of the family.

In Queen Street next day they were sent for by the manager of the supermarket to deal with a pair of shoplifters, and the following morning Andy went to the magistrates' court, where Dixon gave evidence. After the court they found some youths fooling suspiciously with some parked cars and Dixon ticked them off and said next time they'd have their collars felt. They dealt with a drunk at the Hope and Anchor, checked for persons missing, attended a traffic accident, brought in a stray dog, saw school-children across a busy road, told the time. There was no joy on the bike-thieves, though the occasional bike was still being nicked, and Andy continued to hope.

On Saturday afternoon he hurried back to his digs, changed into sports coat and slacks, had a quick meal then hared off to St Michael's church hall. Trestle tables had been arranged around the hall to form a three-sided rectangle and each table was piled high with an assortment of jumble – unwanted clothing and household stuff, many bargains, much junk. Other tables had been put together to form a makeshift canteen and Mary was busy there with the Dixons' neighbour, Jennie Wren, dishing out tea and cakes.

Half Dock Green seemed to be milling about. Mary's face was flushed with the heat, one or two damp curls had fallen over her forehead and she was laughing at something said by Jennie Wren. Andy thought she looked gorgeous and pushed his way purposefully through the horde of jumble-seekers.

'Hi,' said Mary, and beamed a welcome. She poured tea from a large brown pot, passed the cup to Andy and told him he could relieve Tom Wren on the door. 'Tuppence admission, and make sure no one sneaks in. When they've all gone you can help us tidy up and stack the tables. You with me?'

'You have a powerful friend.'

Andy drank his tea then went to relieve Tom Wren. Within an hour the crowd thinned out and by the time Dixon arrived the hall was empty save for the helpers, stacking the unsold jumble.

'Ned Cooney's outside,' Dixon told Andy. He said hullo to the others, took off his old sports coat and carried some jumble to the waiting van.

Andy went down the path with another bundle as Ned Cooney came up. 'Afternoon,' said the young man but the Irishman gave him a surly look and pushed by into the hall. 'I don't think he likes me,' grinned Andy.

'We're nobody's pin-up,' said Dixon, 'and he thinks you think he's somehow mixed up with those bikes.'

'Good set-up, anyway.' Andy stuffed jumble into the van. 'A junk-yard, an old van roaming around . . .'

'Forget it,' said Dixon, as they went up the path.

'I don't necessarily think he nicked 'em. I just don't write him off yet, that's all.'

'You're a CID natural.' Compliment, or reproof? Andy wasn't sure.

The last pile of old tots was loaded, Cooney left fifteen shillings for the funds and went out to his van. As he climbed into the driving-seat Dixon came up, putting on his jacket. 'Heard from your daughter?' Cooney ignored him, started the engine. 'Well, have you?'

'No.' He engaged gear.

'You still don't know where she is, what's happened to her?'

'No.'

'You think she might be in some trouble?' Cooney scowled, released the handbrake. 'Look, if you want us to do anything –'

'You've done enough, don't you think?' growled the man. 'Six months, you got me.'

'That was your fault.'

'Yeah, maybe.' Cooney let in the clutch and drove off.

Dixon gazed after the van. Cooney was normally a cheerful character, but this business of his daughter had soured him. The man wasn't a mug and he wasn't a villain, either – obviously he was worried about his daughter, but he refused to turn to the police.

Dixon turned back for the hall. Fair enough. Let him play it his own way.

After their visit to the local flicks Andy and Mary walked not too quickly back through the lamp-lit streets. To Andy, even in the harsh sodium street lighting Mary still looked gorgeous. They turned in at Dixon's gate, walked up the little path to the front door.

Mary took her key from her handbag. 'You'll come in for supper?'

'Thanks, no.'

She was surprised. 'Why not?'

'There's supper at the digs,' he lied. The fact was that in the house there'd be bright lights, a third person, a change of mood. He smiled. 'Good flicks, weren't they. Great day, altogether.'

'Smashing,' she said, and meant it.

Andy was loath to go. A light breeze from the river brought the smell of privet. A plane tree outside the Dixons' gate partly screened the glare of the street lamp and Mary's upturned face was lit by a dappled light. Andy wanted very much to kiss her but was unsure of the reception, so he funked it and they shook hands.

'See you in the week?' he asked. She nodded, smiling. 'Tuesday?' She said yes, and kissed him.

They said goodnight and kissed again. Andy went out of the gate and walked away with an orchestra playing. He turned at the street corner and looked back across the line of tiny sodium-lit front gardens. Mary was still there. She raised her hand to wave and the orchestra played on.

Police work quietens down on Sundays and the day began with little more than a routine patrol through half-empty, litter-strewn streets. The bike-thefts had eased up and anyhow it was believed the CID had a useful lead. Dixon told Andy that on the way home from his allotment the previous evening he'd run into Ned Cooney. Hard luck, said Andy, but Dixon said no, it was useful. 'We had a pint and a jaw. You can forget about those bikes – he's staying clean. And he's got problems.'

Andy heard that Cooney's wife had walked out on him a year or two back and that his daughter Hilda had been keeping the home going. The girl was huffed by her father's crime-prone lifestyle and when Cooney came home from his last spell inside they'd had a blazing row and she'd packed her bags.

He'd found she'd been running around with some smart alec in a flash car. He was anxious about his daughter and wanted to get her back and make amends. When a one-time hook tried to make a go of it Dixon was willing to give a hand, but the girl wasn't technically missing and there wasn't much the police could do. Dixon had said he'd ask around.

The patrol continued. Dock Green was waking up from its Sunday morning lie-in. Some people were going to church, others were off for a day's outing. At twelve the pubs opened and the whelk-stalls began to appear. The open-air market in Dock Lane was even bigger on Sunday mornings and as they walked down the Lane it seemed like a major extension of yesterday's jumble sale. You could buy shirts, suits, ties, dresses, household goods, puppies, song-birds, patent medicines, flash jewellery – you named it, the Lane would flog it. The traders bawled, the crowds milled about, dogs barked, it was a homespun Cockney bedlam. It was also a right place for 'whizzers' – pick-pockets – Dixon said, and you kept your eyes on the people, not on the stalls.

As they left the street market Dixon said he had a soft spot for the

Lane, for it was there he'd met Kate, his wife. Kate, a spirited young eighteen-year-old, had worked for a catering firm and she'd been driving the firm's van through Dock Lane one afternoon on her way to the Town Hall. The van had clipped a greengrocer's stall – or the stall had clipped the van, no one was sure which – and Dixon, a young copper fresh on the beat, had arrived to find a traffic snarl-up and Kate having a row with the stall-holder.

He'd got mixed up in the row himself, but things were sorted out and that evening, on duty at the Town Hall reception, he'd met Kate again. 'We took it from there,' smiled Dixon, reflectively. 'What began as a good old ding-dong ended with wedding bells.'

Andy learned that one reason for Dixon's interest in finding Hilda Cooney was that she reminded him very much of the girl he married, also he knew from his own experience the tough time Ned Cooney must have had after his wife had gone. 'And now the girl's gone,' he said, 'and it's tougher still.'

Dixon rang in from a police pillar and they were told to look for a 'jimmer', a Peeping Tom, who'd been bothering the houses backing on to Riverside Park. They didn't find the jimmer, but on their way back past the Star of India a punch-up started in the public bar and they were called in to sort things out. As they returned to the station Danny Matthews passed them in a CID car, and this time Andy didn't nod. 'You're learning,' said Dixon.

They signed off. Flint asked Dixon if he'd thought any more about the promotion idea and Dixon said he had, but hadn't decided. Dixon went home, and Andy went back to his digs and changed into casuals. The landlady served a rather frugal Sunday dinner and told him her son was coming back from the merchant navy and they could do with Andy's room. No hurry, and she'd help him get new digs. Andy wasn't heart-broken.

He went out, found a call-box and put through a call to his parents. All was well at home and he told them the nick was great. He left the call-box and found he was at a loose end. He thought of calling on the Dixons but didn't want to wear his welcome out. He didn't want to appear too eager with Mary, either.

He bought a paper outside the tube station, then left Dock Green and walked west past St Paul's and down Ludgate Hill. He admired the distinctive helmets of the City police and noted that all the constables seemed about seven feet tall. He left the City police at Temple Bar and went through the Strand to Trafalgar Square. He was still at a loose end. There was some kind of protest meeting going on in the Square but he didn't want that involvement right now and thought he'd try the National Gallery and get some culture. He got the culture all right but he also got just his own company – everyone seemed to be with someone.

He left the Gallery and found the protest had got a bit lively. Police were dispersing the crowd and an injured PC was being helped to an ambulance. There was a shout of 'Fascist stooge'. Andy hung around for a bit then left the Square and walked through St James's Park. There were mostly couples, young and old, there also. He had tea at the Strand Corner House and found he was the only loner.

London was a great city, a great lonely city. Some weekday evenings he'd spent in the station's recreation-room, but Sunday was different, and you could see too much of the nick. Next Sunday he'd try and spend with Mary. On this one he'd go to the flicks.

When they came up from their break next morning Matthews was in the station office with a man in his early forties. Matthews went into the CID room and Flint told Dixon to take the man through for charging. Andy asked if the charge was about bike-thefts but Flint said the man was a 'come-on', the front man of a con-gang, and that the bike-lead had snapped off short.

'You'd better come and watch,' said Flint. Tub Barrell was left in the office. Flint collected his papers and they went to the charge-room. 'All right, turn your pockets out,' barked Flint and languidly the man complied. Dixon checked his belongings and Flint made out the list.

One of the belongings was an envelope a little larger than postcard size, containing a number of pin-ups. 'Time you grew up,' said Dixon. He looked at a photograph and frowned. 'Where'd you get this?'

'Don't really know, old boy.'

Dixon turned the card over. On the back was stamped a phone number. 'Make a note,' Dixon told Andy. Andy wrote down the number, Dixon put Hilda Cooney's photograph back in the envelope and went on with his checking. Matthews came in with the charge-sheet and the man was formally charged.

Dixon checked the phone number with the GPO switch-board and was given the address of a photographer's studio in south-west London. When he and Andy resumed patrol they looked in at Cooney's junk-yard. The boy told them his father was out and Dixon said he'd call that evening.

As they assembled for parade next morning Dixon told Andy that Cooney was going over to the studio that afternoon and had asked if Dixon would go with him – Cooney was quickish with his fists and needed someone to damp his ardour, especially if his daughter was around. Mary expected Andy for tea and if Dixon hadn't returned they were to go ahead without him.

Dixon had other news. Mary and he had talked over Andy's digs situation and if Andy cared to take it he could have the Dixons' spare room. 'What d'you think, Andy?'

'George, call me "lodger".'

Dixon was out when Andy called and Mary took the young man up to see his room. It was a pleasant little back bedroom, spotlessly clean and furnished in a simple pre-war style. It looked out on the garden, and over the huddle of roofs and chimney-pots Andy could glimpse the massive dome of St Paul's, dominating even the tower blocks in the City, as he hoped it always would.

'I do an office job till four,' said Mary. 'I get the shopping and do most of the meals, but on early turn you'll have to leave the house at half-past five, and I do not – repeat not get your early breakfast.'

'I'll get my breakfast, George's, and creep into your tent with a cuppa.'

'Watch it, buster.'

They agreed terms and went downstairs. At that same moment Dixon, wearing everyday clothes, was standing in the stuffy little basement room decked out as a photographic studio. He'd been received by a snazzily dressed young man, ceaselessly chewing gum, and was waiting for a model whose professional name was Diane but whom Dixon knew as Hilda Cooney.

The door opened and the girl came in. She was a raven-haired Irish colleen, her face heavy with make-up, an ankle-length dressing-gown wrapped loosely about her.

Dixon was standing in the shadows by the spotlight. The girl threw him a casual half-contemptuous glance and began to take off her gown. 'You needn't bother, Hilda,' said Dixon, and stepped forward.

The girl swung round. 'Mr Dixon!' She stared, astonished, disbelieving. 'What's the big idea?'

'Business. Your Dad's business, really – but I'm in it with him.' The girl frowned, perplexed, uneasy, then turned quickly on impulse and opened the door. 'Sit down,' said Dixon.

'You get lost!'

'Sit down!' There was a note of command in Dixon's voice and though the girl hesitated, she moved to the divan and sat there. She looked up, frowning defiantly, and Dixon was reminded sharply of the spirited look in Kate's eyes when he'd happened upon that snarl-up so long ago in Dock Lane.

He switched off the spotlight, pulled up the blind and let sunlight filter in from the street above. He glanced round the tawdry little room. 'Why're you doing this, Hilda?'

The girl didn't answer at once, then, 'It's a job, isn't it?' she said.

'Aren't there other jobs?'

'I've got a father – remember?'

'What does that mean?'

It meant quite a lot, she told him. Sooner or later, with every previous job she'd had they'd found out about Ned Cooney. There'd been a subtle change in their attitude and she'd been encouraged to leave. A friend had got her a job with this studio, where it didn't matter about her father and where she'd get training to be a proper professional model.

Dixon told her she could find less crummy set-ups than this one and that her father wanted her back. She said he could tell that to the dicky-birds. 'It's true,' he affirmed. 'Your leaving home shook him rigid. I think if you went back you'd find him a different man.'

The doorbell shrilled while they were talking and they heard footsteps and then the sound of men's voices. The girl glanced at the door, wondering. 'That's my Dad.' The voices grew suddenly angry and she stood up in some alarm. The room door burst open and Ned Cooney strode in, followed by the irate gum-chewer.

'I asked you to wait in the van,' said Dixon, annoyed.

'Sorry, I had to see her.'

Cooney turned to his daughter but the young man grabbed his arm and told him to push off or he'd get the law. 'The law's over there,' said Cooney, grimly, slapping the arm away.

'Eh?' asked the young man, startled.

'Come on, sonny,' said Dixon, 'they want to talk.'

'You get out, both of you!' blustered the gum-chewer. He grabbed Cooney's arm again. The Irishman wrenched himself free, grasped the young man by the front of his sporty waistcoat and sent him staggering back against the spotlight. The spot collapsed with a crash and he went down with it. He scrambled up and threw himself fiercely at the older man. Hilda Cooney cried out, afraid for her father. Dixon interposed his big frame between the two struggling men and forced them apart. They stood there, breathing hard and for once the young man's jaws had stopped moving.

Dixon took his arm. 'I told you,' he said. 'They want to talk.' This time the young man complied.

Dixon glanced back as they left the room. Ned Cooney and his daughter stood some distance apart, looking self-consciously at each other, not speaking. Cooney essayed a tentative smile. 'Hullo, love,' he said, quietly. Hilda stared back at him, then her face puckered miserably and tears cleaved a path through her make-up. Dixon closed the door.

He returned home at half-past six and tucked straight into his meal, for he was helping at a boys' club that evening while Andy and Mary went up west to a show. He told them Hilda Cooney had been winkled out of the sleazy studio set-up and driven back home. He didn't know how things would work out, but the signs were favourable.

Dixon went off to the boys' club, Andy and Mary made for Dock Green tube. This time on their return Andy came in to supper and he walked back to his digs with the orchestra playing Love's Old Sweet Song.

The week passed mainly without incident, save for another two bike-thefts. On Saturday Andy moved his things into the back bedroom then helped Mary with the weekend shopping. When they came back Cooney's old van was driving away from the house. In the living room Dixon was gazing thoughtfully at a slip of paper. He looked at Andy. 'You have it,' he said, and passed it over.

The paper had a Dock Green address on it. 'So what, George?'

'Worth checking,' said Dixon. 'A back-street workshop. It might be linked with those bikes.'

'From Ned Cooney?' asked Mary, unpacking the shopping bags.

'Yep. He's not keen on being a nose but he don't like kids' bikes pinched, either.' He nodded at the paper. 'His way of saying "Thanks".'

Andy was about to put the paper in his wallet, then he paused. 'But this is your lead – not mine.'

'It's yours. If you hadn't chased after that bike and ended up in Cooney's junk-yard all this wouldn't have happened. Start checking, Andy. If you find anything, report to the sarge and the CID.'

Over the weekend Andy checked and duly reported. On Monday he returned to the workshop with DC Matthews and together they made the arrest. It was a weird feeling, booking the man – he wasn't much older than Andy himself – but it meant one hook less in the Green.

'Bright boy,' said Mary, as she set the table for supper. 'Be chief superintendent in no time, ordering Dad about.'

'He'll be ordering me,' Andy told her. 'He'll soon be sergeant.'

'Not on your Nellie,' said Dixon.

That night it was some time before Andy dropped off to sleep. He stretched out in his bed, listening to the night-sounds from the Green, thinking things over. Here he was in these terrific digs, virtually a second home. In the adjoining bedroom was a policeman colleague, rock-solid, genial, a man he'd known for two short weeks but who seemed a life-long friend. Across the landing in the remaining bedroom was the daughter of the house, a girl whom one day he knew he'd ask to marry.

He thought of his job. He'd started off with some illusions, but most had been shed on the way. As Dixon had said, the police were nobody's pin-up and the job had problems and difficulties. But they didn't affect George Dixon's attitude. It was a good job, a vital job, a career, and right now Andy didn't wish for any other.

Another week with George and he'd finish his induction and be out on his own . . .

The soft sound of a tug's siren drifted in from the river. Somewhere a church clock chimed. A distant train rattled across a road-bridge.

Great place, the Green. Andy turned on his side, closed his eyes, and drifted off to sleep.

A Little Push From Cappy Fleers

BY GILBERT RALSTON

Naked City *which hit American television screens at the end of September 1958 is another milestone cop series which is still remembered – and reshown – because of its uniqueness, the quality of its scripts and acting, and because of the number of TV firsts it achieved during its five-year run which started with half-hour episodes and then expanded to ninety-nine stories each lasting an hour. It was, quite simply, one of the all-time great crimebuster series: the first to be shot primarily on location; the first to hire guest stars; and the first to use ordinary men and women as extras.* Naked City *was ostensibly about the cases of a veteran Detective Lieutenant and his young assistant – but more impressive than any characters was the 'naked city' itself, which producer Herbert B. Leonard lost no opportunity to show in panoramic shots and sweeping camera views of the crowded streets and towering skyscraper blocks. It set the dramas in their actual environment and was certainly the earliest crime show to emphasise this factor in a way that is now commonplace. Indeed, the narrator's final words at the end of each episode perfectly underlined the concept: 'There are eight million stories in the* Naked City *– this has been one of them.'*

The series had been created by the writer-producer Sterling Silliphant based on the very successful 1948 movie of the same title in which both police and criminals had been shown to have their good and bad sides. When Naked City *began, James Franciscus played young Detective Jim Halloran with John McIntire as his mentor, Detective Lieutenant Dan Muldoon. Despite – or perhaps because of – the instant success of the series, McIntire announced that he was leaving at the end of the first season and his 'death' was facilitated by his patrol car crashing into a petrol lorry during a chase sequence. McIntire's case is cited in television history as the first instance where a star who wished to give up a role had to be killed off to ensure continuity. Although Franciscus remained with the series throughout its duration, he had two further partners, the ageing Lieutenant Mike Parker (Horace McMahon) and young Detective Adam Flint (Paul Burke). The list of guest stars who appeared in* Naked City *reads like a Who's Who of Hollywood: Gene Hackman, Leslie Nielsen, Peter Fonda, Walter Matthau, Robert Duvall, George C. Scott, Robert Redford, Martin Sheen, William Shatner and Dustin Hoffman who actually made two appearances. The roster of scriptwriters was equally impressive: Charles Beaumont, Gene Roddenberry, Howard Rodman, Gilbert Ralston and W.R. Burnett who would shortly after have his own series,* The Asphalt Jungle. *But even star actors and writers were not all that* Naked City *offered its viewers: the episodes had some of the strangest titles ever seen on TV outside comedy shows: 'The Well Dressed Termite', 'If Any Are Frozen, Warm Them', 'The King of Venus Will Take Care of You', 'Howard Running Bear Is a Turtle' are just typical of many more. Not a few of the bizarrest were the handiwork of Gilbert Ralston (1928–), a novelist, short story writer and TV scriptwriter, whose sardonic sense of humour and interest in crime, resulted in his being one of the most prolific contributors to* Naked City. *Among his best remembered episodes are 'Vengeance Is a Wheel', 'The Sweet Smiling Face of Truth' and 'A Kettle of Precious Fish'. His story* A Little Push From Cappy Fleers *was the inspiration for the episode, 'A Very Cautious Boy' which starred another young actor who, twenty years later, would become a household name in another hugely successful police series,* Columbo *–Peter Falk.*

IT WASN'T LONG after Pop died and the bank took the place back, when I hitched a ride on a truck to New Orleans to get some construction work, or maybe ship out on one of those Gulf freighters. I hung around for a while but couldn't find anything unless I had a union card, which I didn't. So I thought I'd go to California and pick fruit, or maybe get in the movies. Billy Jo Cartright, a fellow I met, went with me. We hitched rides as far as San Antonio, then Billy went to work for his uncle, who grew cotton. The uncle said I could stay too, but I kind of had California in my head, so I said no thanks and went on. I had sort of a plan if I couldn't find anything to do in Los Angeles, so after I saw the lines of fellows in front of the employment places, I went to the dime store and bought a hammer and nails and a can of paint, and made a shoeshine box. I spent three dollars for some polish and a couple of brushes and went looking for a building, out on the bus all the way to the Sunset Strip, which I had heard about. Out by La Cienega there was a long row of the kind of buildings I wanted, two-storey, with maybe twenty offices, and no doormen. I went to the rental agent and asked him if I could go around the offices and shine shoes. He talked to me for a while; then said okay, so I began in the upstairs corner office. That's how I met Mr Danny Froken.

He had a big place, with some girls at desks in the outside room. One of the girls looked up at me. 'I'm the shoeshine boy,' I said.

'Just a minute,' she said, and pressed a thing on her desk. 'Mr Froken, want your shoes shined? The boy's here.' Then she told me to go in. There were actors' pictures on the wall and a big desk at the end of the room with a little man at it, looking at some papers. I went over by him and sat down on the shoeshine box. He didn't look up, just stuck his foot out. I remember the shoes because they were small, like a boy's, and hardly needed a shine at all. When I was through, he stuck a hand in a pocket and gave me fifty cents. He looked kind of surprised when I gave it back to him.

'You're my first customer,' I said. 'This one's free.'

He had a funny face, all tight and wrinkled and very serious. He looked at me for a moment. I got sort of uncomfortable, then he smiled.

'What's your name?' he said.

'Cappy,' I said. 'Cappy Fleers.'

'That's an odd name.'

'Not where I come from, Mr Froken,' I told him.

'Where's that?'

'Seneca, West Virginia.'

'You're a long way from home, Cappy.'

'Yes, sir,' I said.

'Thanks for the shine.'

'You're welcome, Mr Froken.' I started out.

'Cappy.'

I turned back.

'Come every day at ten o'clock.' He smiled again as I went out. I went through that building like a field of wheat and the next one to it in the afternoon. Made enough to pay my room and had two dollars left for food.

Everything went fine after that. Pretty soon I had a whole string of offices to go to and everybody knew me by name. Mr Froken was the best to me. Every day, when I did his shoes, we'd talk a little. He was interested in the way I lived in Seneca and would ask me questions.

About two weeks after I started the shoeshine business, Miss Faulkner, the lady on the desk outside his office, stopped me when I started to go in.

'Hold it a minute, Cappy,' she said. 'Mr Froken's got a houseful.'

I waited while she pressed the key on her desk.

'Cappy's here, Mr Froken,' she said. 'All right to send him in?'

Mr Froken said it was okay.

The office was full of people, sitting around on chairs, all talking at once. They were arguing about a movie script, two fellows in the corner pretty excited. Over in the other corner I saw Ray Prestwick, the big actor. He just sat there big as life, listening and smoking a cigarette while I did Mr Froken's shoes. When I finished, Mr Froken said, 'This is Cappy Fleers. If you two could write as well as he can shine shoes, we wouldn't be here.' Everybody laughed.

'Go ahead, Cappy. Shine 'em up,' Mr Froken said.

I did the writers' first, while they got back into their fight, mostly with each other. I never heard such an argument. Finally I got to Mr Prestwick. He had some nice brown shoes on, English leather. I got a big charge out of doing his shoes. He paid for them all. It was a funny feeling, getting paid by a big star, even for a shoeshine.

'Thank you, Mr Prestwick,' I said, and headed for the door.

Mr Prestwick called after me. 'Hey, Cappy,' he said. 'You know anything about yard work?'

'I know some farming,' I told him.

'This is not exactly farming,' he said. 'Mowing, and things like that.'

'If it grows, I guess it wouldn't be strange to me,' I said.

'I need a man on my place. Want a job?'

'Who'll do Mr Froken's shoes?' I asked him. Everybody laughed, even Mr Froken. I felt kind of bad that he thought it was funny. He smiled at me again, with that nice sort of look, so it was all right.

'Take the job, Cappy,' he said. 'I'll send 'em over.'

Next thing I knew I was in the outside office with an address on a piece of paper in my hand. I sat for a long time in the cafeteria on the corner, thinking about it, and Mr Froken, and how things happened.

The address worried me some when I looked at the map. It was way up in a place called Laurel Hills, in the mountains back of Hollywood, without any bus. I figured I'd have to get some kind of car to get there. to work each day, but with only $73.00 in the box in my room I didn't see how I could work it. I thought about it some when I went back to finish off with my customers.

The next day was Saturday and I was supposed to go to Mr Prestwick's house in the morning. I got up early and took the bus way out on the Sunset, where Laurel Street cut in. Then I walked the rest of the way. They lived on top of a hill on a street without any sidewalks, all full of houses that looked like castles. I opened the gate and went into the yard. They had a lot of it, all green and big trees and plants around, everything wet and cool-looking, sprinklers going, up near a big stone house. There was a lady over at the side. She had a pair of shears in her hand for cutting flowers and an armful of them already cut.

'Hello –' she said. 'Cappy?'

I said I was. She was the prettiest little thing, dark-haired, with her face all lit up with the flowers.

'Ray said you'd be coming up today. Come in, and we'll talk.' She led the way into the kitchen. It was the biggest one I ever saw, all white tile and machinery. She sat me down at the table and gave me a cup of coffee.

'Mr Prestwick will be back soon. Was it a hard walk?' I knew then that she had seen me coming up the street.

'No, ma'am,' I said. 'I was watching the pretty day.'

'So was I,' she said. 'That's how I saw you.'

'Yes, ma'am,' I said.

'Come on out. I'll show you around.'

We went outside again, and walked around the grounds. Everything looked pretty good except some of the trees needed pruning back and the oleander bushes on one side were choking for space. The grass was nice and healthy, with the spring of good turf under it.

'We just got this place,' she said. 'The old owner took the gardener away with him. That's why we need you.'

'I've never done this kind of work before, ma'am. I hope I'll satisfy.'

'Mr Froken told me you were a farm boy. If we get stuck, we'll get a book.'

'Mr Froken?' I said. 'You know him, ma'am?'

'Mr Froken is my husband's agent. He's a good friend. That's how we heard about you.'

'I'll bet that's why Mr Froken used to ask me about Seneca. And all those other things.'

Then she took me back to the pool. There was a shed there with enough mowers and edgers and seeders and things to open a store.

'I think you'll find everything you'll need here, Cappy. If there's anything else, just let me know.'

'We could put in a stand of alfalfa with this, ma'am.' I told her. She laughed like a little girl.

'Your room's over the garage,' she said.

I must have looked surprised.

'Didn't he tell you?' she said. 'Mr Prestwick expected you to stay here. We're away a lot. We want a hand on the place.'

I just listened, marvelling at the way things happened.

After we looked around a little more, she showed me my room. There was a bed and a dresser and two chairs, even a television in the corner. It even had its own bathroom.

'I'll try to keep it neat, ma'am,' I said.

She looked at me for a moment, a funny expression in her eyes.

'You do that, Cappy,' she said finally. 'You do that.'

I moved my stuff in the next day, after church, and started on the yard. I had an itch to prune those trees and was up in one of them when Mr Prestwick came out. I climbed down, and said good morning.

'Everything all right, Cappy?' he said.

I said everything was just fine.

'You'll find lunch in the kitchen at one o'clock,' he said. 'The cook's name is Rosa. Stay on her good side. She's a terror.'

I didn't have any trouble with her. She was a fat Italian lady who really set a table. I didn't talk much to her at first, just stayed polite and enjoyed the food, which seemed to please her. After a few days we got to be pretty good friends, and sometimes when the Prestwicks were out we used to talk and she would tell me about the Old Country and how she lived in Italy when she was a girl. We were both farm raised so I guess that helped.

It took a while to get the yard and house the way I liked it, all clipped and roomy with the flowers healthy and bright. I put in a new piece of grass in the back and made a little sitting place like a rock garden back of the pool. It was a pretty place, looking out over the tops of the hills. Mrs Emma, that's what Rosa told me to call Mrs Prestwick, liked to sit there when she read a book.

It was a strange time. I didn't have a car, except Mr Prestwick said I could borrow one when I had an errand or something I wanted to do, but, even so, at first I didn't leave the place much. Once in a while, Mrs Emma would talk to me when I was in the yard, or Mr Prestwick would ask for something, and I would get it for him in the car. Then I started driving Rosa around when she wanted to go somewhere, or taking Mr Prestwick to the studio when he was working. He didn't like driving and I did, so that made it nice. I'll say one thing. That yard *shone*. Even my Pop would have liked it.

Time sort of slipped by. Then one day I was clipping the hedge and turned around and Mr Froken was standing there. He held out a hand to me, that little smile of his on his face again.

'I forgot to send the shoes, Cappy,' he said.

'Mr Froken,' I said. 'Am I glad to see you!'

'You're doing a fine job, Cappy,' Mr Froken said. 'The Prestwicks couldn't do without you.'

Somehow, hearing him tell it was better than anything I heard in my life. I couldn't stop smiling. Like a fool, I couldn't say much.

'I hope you're happy here.'

'It's a wonderful place,' I said.

He turned to go into the house.

'Mr Froken,' I said.

'Yes?'

'Thank you,' I said.

'That's all right, Cappy,' he said. 'An active agent has to look after the welfare of his clients.'

I picked a big bunch of flowers and put them in his car.

Just before Christmas was a big and exciting time at the house, all kinds of people coming and going, Mr Froken in and out, Rosa and I so busy we didn't have time to think about anything, which was just as well for me. Christmas used to be pretty good at our house, even after Ma died and there was only Pop and me. When I thought about it, I got pretty low, so it was better to be busy.

Christmas Day was another high time. The house was full of people, we had some extra help in to serve, and I took care of the cars and helped with the drinks, except for Mr Prestwick, who only drank coffee. Rosa and I started at six in the morning to get ready, so when the last of the people left we were pretty tired, sitting in the kitchen with coffee when Mr Prestwick came out. He said Merry Christmas to us both and gave us each a hundred-dollar cheque. Old Rosa gave him an Italian hug and I shook hands. Then I went to my room. On the dresser was a little Christmas tree, all covered with spangles. Under it was a package. I opened it. It was a wallet, the most beautiful leather I ever saw. Across the front of it was my name in golden letters, 'Cappy Fleers' – in *gold letters*. I just looked at it and at the card. It was from Mrs Emma, who wrote 'Love from the Prestwicks' on it. Next to it was a scarf from Rosa. I sat on the bed, holding the presents in my hands for a long time. Then I noticed something else. On the dresser was another box. In it was a watch, a gold watch, with a gold band on it. My name was on that too, on the back. It said 'Cappy Fleers with the affection and admiration of Danny Froken.' Well, I was overcome.

After that, Mrs Emma decided that I'd better go to school nights, two or three times a week, so I did, the Adult Education course at the high school. I enjoyed it, especially the English. I read a lot of books. Mrs Emma used to pick some new ones up for me when she went shopping, then when I saw her in the yard she'd talk with me about them.

I met a girl at the school. Mrs Emma devilled me a little about it, till I asked Norma – that was her name – to go to the movies with me. She wasn't a very pretty girl but I liked her a lot. She was kind of quiet, like Mrs Emma, and fun to be with. We had some good times together.

All this time, I took care of the house and yard, and drove Mr Prestwick to and from his work. I used to drive him down in the morning and go and get him in the afternoon. The fellows on the gate at the studio got to know me, and used to wave me right in when I drove up, and let me park the car right outside the studio door where Mr Prestwick was working. Sometimes I'd go in and watch the picture being made, and once in a while Mr Froken would be there and he'd smile that funny smile of his and I'd look at the time where he could see me, so that he could see that I was wearing his watch. It was a little game with us. Mr Froken was getting old. Each time I saw him he seemed to shrink a little. You could almost see the bones under the skin of his face, he was so thin. I talked to Mrs Emma about it. She said that Mr Froken wasn't very well. She said maybe the layers were peeling off a little so that the kindness and integrity were beginning to show through. Mrs Emma worried me, she was so sad. Not only about that, but about the trouble that began with Mr Prestwick.

I guess actors are different in the way they think about things. Mr Prestwick was always nice to me so I had no complaint, but it was different somehow. Maybe down underneath he cared, but I always thought he kind of saw himself in a place or situation, then did what he thought he was supposed to do. Anyway, he wasn't like the others. They always said exactly what they meant. Mr Prestwick said what he was *supposed* to mean. That's a big difference. Anyway, when he won that Oscar, things began to change. Mr Prestwick was busier than ever and the next thing we knew he was playing in that war picture with Kitty Lamson, and was a real big star again. He went away to Mexico to do the location shooting for three weeks and when he came back he was different. That's when he bought me the uniform and cap to wear when I took him in the car. I didn't mind, but I heard Mrs Emma fussing about it to him. Anyway, I wore it and took him to the studio first time I had it on. They were making the interior shots of the war picture and I figured I'd arrive a little early that afternoon so I could watch some of the scenes. I came back at five o'clock, and didn't see Mr Prestwick anywhere. I knocked on the door of his dressing room at five-thirty. That's the first time I ever saw him with a drink. He told me to go back to the car and wait for him. When I turned at the door of the studio, I saw Miss Lamson come out of the dressing room with him. By the time they got to the car, I was waiting with the door open. He put her in and gave me an address at the beach in Malibu. Every once in a while as I drove them, I watched her in the rearview mirror. She had an actress face, very beautiful, black hair and big red lips. She laughed a lot and made jokes all the way to her house. When we got there, he got out and took her to the door. She said something and he laughed and went in. When he came back he was pretty drunk, didn't say much, just rode home in the back seat of the car. That was the first thing I noticed. Two days later he phoned and asked Rosa to tell me to get a bag packed for him so that he could go away for two days' location. I brought the bag to the studio and left it in his room. On my way out I saw Al Morgan, the assistant director. I asked him where the location was they were going to. He said that it was on the beach at the other side of San Diego. He told me that the company would be there Monday and Tuesday. This was only *Friday*. That was the second thing. I worked on the lawn that afternoon, thinking about it.

Wednesday, when Mr Prestwick had a day off, Mr Froken came. Mrs Emma was out and Rosa was shopping, so I went into the house to see if they needed coffee or anything. They were in Mr Prestwick's den and I could hear him yelling all the way out in the hall. So I didn't go in, and I didn't listen. After a while Mr Froken came out, got in his car and drove away. I never saw him look like that before – worried and sad and nervous. That was the third thing.

Next day I saw Mrs Emma in the little garden place I fixed up for her. She was sitting in her chair all alone. I went to see if she wanted anything. She told me that Mr Prestwick had another week's location to do and would I please ask Rosa to pack his bag and take it down to the studio. When I looked back at her, her face was all twisted up and tears were running down it. She just sat there, crying. I went to get the bag, my stomach all tight and knotted up.

This time when I went to the studio dressing room, Mr Prestwick was in it. He called me in and looked at me, hard.

'Cappy,' he said. 'I want you to do something for me.'

'Yes, sir,' I said.

'I am going to stay at the Malibu Beach house for a few days. I want you to call for me there, each morning.'

I said I would.

'And I want you to keep it to yourself. Man-to-man. Okay?'

I started to speak, then didn't.

'Yes, sir,' I said.

When I got to the studio door again, I felt like I might throw up. When I looked up, Mr Froken was standing there.

'Mr Froken,' I said. 'What am I going to do?'

He looked at me for a long time. 'Nothing, Cappy.' I guess I must have looked funny. He put a hand on my shoulder. 'This is not your trouble,' he said. 'It's mine – and Mrs Emma's. Do one thing for me?'

'Yes, sir,' I said.

'If he starts to drink, call me. Sometimes he can't stop.' Then he went on while I got into the car.

Everything was terrible after that. Mr Prestwick was living down at Kitty Lamson's house and didn't come home at all. Mrs Emma looked sick and thin, and wouldn't eat, even when Rosa tried to make her. Rosa looked at me most of the time like I was some kind of a traitor. I brought things down to Mr Prestwick when he asked me and drove him to work until the picture was finished. Even then he stayed away. All the time Mrs Emma got thinner and thinner. Then the papers began to write about it, every day some dirty little thing. Reporters called Mrs Emma. It was a rotten time. Then the phone call came for me. I took it in the kitchen. It was that Kitty Lamson. She was sort of whispering, but very serious.

'Cappy,' she said. 'This is Miss Lamson. Better get down here. Mr Prestwick needs you right away.'

I didn't like the way her voice sounded, so I ran to the car and drove out of the yard without telling anyone. When I got to the beach house, Miss Lamson let me in. She was sort of laughing and sly in spite of being very pretty, and I could see that she had drunk a lot. She could barely walk, and just pointed inside. I went into the living room looking for Mr Prestwick, then on to the porch. The house was way up on a cliff, over the ocean, on the Palisades, and had a big cement porch all across the back, with a stairway going to the beach, crisscrossing right down the cliff. All the rooms faced on the porch and when I turned back I could see Mr Prestwick in the one next to the living room. He was on a chair, his head down and hanging. I ran in. She was there behind me, giggly and horrible.

'Take him home, Cappy,' she said. 'He's a mess. A real mess.' Then she laughed. Mr Prestwick looked sort of grey and his breath was making funny noises. I grabbed him up and laid him on the sofa. Then I ran to the phone and called Mr Froken. He got right on the phone and said to hold everything till he got there. Miss Lamson had gone into the other room. I could hear her in there playing some loud music on the phonograph. I took Mr Prestwick's tie off and washed his face. His hands were cold. I rubbed them. I was still working on him when Mr Froken came. He took a look at him, with his face sort of hard and set. 'Let him sleep a little, Cappy,' he said. 'Then we'll put him in a hospital. I know a place.' We went out to the other room. She was still there, still with the crazy music on the phonograph. She was dancing, whirling around and around without her shoes on. Mr Froken crossed over to the phonograph and shut it off. She stopped like a cat, still laughing. Mr Froken just stood there, his hands shaking.

'You filth!' he said.

She just stood there looking at him, then she slapped his face. He stood, without moving. Then she spat, right in his face. I grabbed her and put her down on a chair. Mr Froken took his handkerchief out and wiped his face. He let the handkerchief slip to the floor and walked away from her out on the porch. I watched her for a minute. I was afraid to leave her. Then she got up and began to dance again, wild, round and round the room. I looked out at Mr Froken. He was way out by the stairway, down to the beach. She was running the whole length of the room, back and forth, under her breath humming music. When she ran out on the porch I ran between her and Mr Froken. Then I saw him. He was all bent over and holding on to the top of the stair rail. He looked up at me

'Cappy –' he said. 'Cappy.' Then he fell. I ran for the rail. He was maybe twenty steps down, all crumpled up. I went to him. I held him in my arms. Mr Froken was dead. I wished it was me. I loved Mr Froken.

After a while I carried him back up the stairs. He was light, like a little boy. She was standing there her hand on her mouth. I went by her and put Mr Froken down on the sofa in the living room. I called on the telephone for the ambulance, then just stood there, looking at Mr Froken. The ambulance came, and two fellows from the Police Department a little later. They took Mr Froken away. Miss Lamson sat in a chair, not saying a word, just kind of shaking her head while the policemen looked around the room. They asked me who the man was in the other room and who I was. I told them. They were making notes, sort of slow about it. Then they talked to her. She sat in the chair, quiet. It was wonderful how she had changed, hardly drunk at all. She told them he fell down the stairs and that she didn't see it. She said I saw it all. Then they turned to me.

'Tell us about it, Mr Fleers.' It was the old quiet one who asked.

I sat in the chair, not saying anything for a moment, then I looked right at him.

'She pushed him,' I said. 'She hit him, then she pushed him when he was by the stairs. She was drunk. She hit him, then she pushed him.'

'Liar,' she screamed at me.

'I'll swear to it,' I said.

Suddenly she was at me, clawing and scratching and screaming dirty things. They pulled her off. 'That's what she did to him,' I said. 'She was so drunk she can't remember.'

After, when they took her away, I took Mr Prestwick home. Mrs Emma put him to bed. Then I went down to the police station and wrote down what I had said. They said I'd have to come back when the trial came up. I said I would, and they took down a lot of other things I told them. It wasn't really a lie. About the pushing, I mean. She did push him. She pushed us all, Mr Prestwick, Mr Froken, Mrs Emma, Rosa, me – the whole family. I just pushed back a little.

Things are getting back to normal now. I can't tell you what's happened to Miss Lamson. I feel so bad about Mr Froken, I don't even read the papers about it, and her trial hasn't come up yet. I'll bet you one thing. I'll bet she won't get off. Not after what I wrote down at the police station.

The Flushing of Al Capone

BY ELIOT NESS

The Untouchables, *which followed* Naked City *on to the* ABC *network a year later, is also considered a landmark production in television crime history – though not altogether for the best reasons. It was, in fact, much criticised at the time for its excessive violence; by Italian-American groups for giving all the gangsters Italian names; and even by the estate of Al Capone who sued the producers for one million dollars for using his name and likeness without permission. Yet this said, Leslie Halliwell has maintained that the stories about an elite squad of Chicago crimebusters who tracked down the gangster and criminals of the Prohibition Era were certainly well made but, 'now seem rather tame'. Nevertheless, he wrote in 1987, 'Its music (by Wilbur Hatch and Nelson Riddle), its commentary (by the famous American newspaper columnist, Walter Winchell) and its stars all helped to keep the world tuned in for four seasons, and of all TV series it has had the best re-run life.' The series was based on the real-life exploits of Eliot Ness, a treasury department official, who broke the power of Al Capone in Chicago in 1931. Ness, played by the dour veteran actor Robert Stack, has since been described as the most feared TV crime fighter of all time, and certainly he and his men burst into the living rooms of viewers every week with all guns blazing. Apart from the ever-present members of* The Untouchables *team (played by Jerry Paris, Nick Georgiade, Abel Fernandez, Steve London, Anthony George and Paul Picerni), with Neville Brand as Al Capone, the show attracted an impressive list of guest stars including Lee Marvin, Charles Bronson, Robert Redford, Jack Klugman, Richard Conte, Jack Lord and Telly Savalas, who made three appearances over a decade ahead of his starring role as Kojak.*

Eliot Ness (1903–57) was only twenty-six years old when he and his hand-picked, tightly knit group moved into the frightened city of Chicago to take on Al Capone's brutal empire of bootleggers and gangsters. They found themselves enmeshed in a web of corruption and faced by a hail of bullets, assassination attempts and bombs as they battled to uphold the laws of prohibition. Afterwards, Ness wrote an account of his work which was first made into a two-part TV special, The Scarface Mob, *broadcast in April 1959, and then developed into the series of hour-long black and white episodes by producer Quinn Martin. Inevitably, the stories soon used up the facts of Eliot's career and began to draw on the legends of other famous US criminals. The show also took liberties with* The Untouchables' *use of guns – in real life they rarely used them – and it was when the number of shoot-outs per episode became excessive that complaints were received by ABC. As youngsters were known to represent a considerable percentage of the audience, the decision was taken to play down the violence, while Robert Stack's Ness was made into a more sympathetic and less grim and unsmiling character. At the end of each episode a statement also provided the information that the stories had been fictionalised. Notwithstanding these changes,* The Untouchables *continued as a ratings winner until May 1963 – and shortly afterwards crossed the Atlantic to be screened by ITV from 1966 to 1969 where it enjoyed similar success. In 1987, the fame of Eliot Ness and his men was underlined still further when a full-length movie of the story was made starring Kevin Costner, with Sean Connery playing one of his team and Robert De Niro as Capone. Here, though, as a reminder of how the legend of* The Untouchables *began, is Eliot Ness's own account . . .*

WE HAD BEEN in the brewery-busting business almost six months when the prison gates swung open at Holmesburg, Pennsylvania, and Al Capone walked out a free man on the morning of 17 March 1930.

There was wild excitement in Chicago as the public and the underworld awaited the homecoming of the scarfaced chieftain who ruled the city with an iron fist in a glove of steel.

Speculation was rife as to what he was going to do, how the gangs of Chicago would react to his return and what sort of reception was being planned by the city and federal governments. The newspapers devoted lurid black headlines to the story.

Chicago officials had been making eye-catching statements as the time drew near for Capone's release. The law promised he would be given a hot reception.

'We'll clap him in jail as soon as he sets foot in the city,' boasted one high police figure.

Captain John Stege, head of the Chicago detective bureau, posted twenty-five men in the vicinity of Capone's home on Prairie Avenue. Their instructions were to take the chubby-faced gang overlord into custody as soon as he arrived, but they waited four days and nights without avail.

'Scarface Al' had apparently disappeared into thin air after being met at the prison by a 'royal' entourage that whisked him out of sight. Since there was no indictment against him, however, the police obviously weren't too anxious to locate him.

But we knew immediately where he was, thanks to the wire tap on the Montmartre.

When word came that Capone had disappeared, I laid siege to the headset in our rented basement apartment.

One of the first orders of business among the mob when he returned, I knew, would be the extermination of the Eliot Ness squad which had become a thorn in Al's pasty white side. The orders, I was fairly certain, would filter through brother Ralph's telephone.

On 18 March, the day after Capone's release, I was at the headset when the buzzer sounded and an urgent voice demanded:

'Is Ralph there?'

'On the phone,' was the reply.

'Listen, Ralph,' the voice pleaded frantically. 'We're up in Room 718 in the Western and Al is really getting out of hand. He's in terrible shape. Will you come up, please? You're the only one who can handle him when he gets like this. We've sent for a lot of towels.'

'Okay,' Ralph replied. 'I'll be up a little later. Just take care of things the best you can right now.'

Without question, Al Capone, celebrating his release from prison not wisely but much too well, was drunk and almost out of control up in Room 718 at the Western Hotel. I didn't know what the towels were for, whether to wet him down or clean him up, but it was obvious that Ralph wasn't worried.

About fifteen minutes after that call, the buzzer sounded again.

'Ralph,' said the caller, 'this is Jake Lingle. Where's Al? I've been looking all over for him and nobody seems to know where he is.'

Ralph pretended ignorance.

'I don't know where he is, either, Jake,' he hedged. 'I haven't heard a word from him since he got out.'

Lingle, a Chicago *Tribune* police reporter, sounded agitated and I marvelled at his effrontery.

'Jesus, Ralph, this makes it very bad for me. I'm supposed to have my finger on these things, y'know. It makes it very embarrassing with my paper. Now get this, I want you to call me the minute you hear from him. Tell him I want to see him right away.'

'All right,' Ralph replied. 'I will.'

Within an hour, Lingle called Ralph again.

'Ralph?'

'Yes.'

'This is Jake again. Have you heard from Al yet?'

'No. Not yet.'

Lingle's voice became aggressively indignant.

'Listen, you guys ain't giving me the runaround, are you? Just remember, I wouldn't do that if I was you.'

Ralph's voice became a bit warmer and friendlier.

'Now, Jake, you know I wouldn't do that. It's just that I haven't heard from Al. What else can I tell you?'

'Okay, okay,' Lingle growled. 'Just remember to tell him that I want to talk to him right away.'

The phone banged down and I wondered what reason Lingle had to play it so high and mighty with the Capones.

Four days after his return from prison, Capone finished up his celebration. Defying the law to pin anything on him, he walked blithely into police headquarters accompanied by his lawyer.

'I hear you want me,' Capone challenged.

No one did, as it developed, and 'Scarface Al' returned in triumph to his headquarters at the Lexington Hotel, where he occupied the three top floors.

It was an ironic demonstration of the power of this man who had started out as a hard-fisted roughneck addicted to red neckties, gaudy shirts and flashy jewellery.

His fortune was estimated at $50,000,000. He rode around in a $30,000 automobile which, with its body armour of steel plate and bulletproof windows, weighed seven tons. He owned an estate in Florida worth $500,000, and on one meaty finger he wore an eleven-carat diamond which had cost $50,000. Capone never carried less than $50,000 in cash, scattering $25 tips to hat-check girls and $100 gratuities to waiters. He was known around the gambling spots as 'a sucker for the ponies'.

But those who took him for a 'sucker' elsewhere usually wound up dead. Acquiring the poise which comes with power, Capone had become even more dangerous: together with his ruthlessness, he had the quality of a great businessman. Under that patent leather hair he had sound judgment, diplomatic shrewdness and the diamond-hard nerves of a gambler, all balanced by cold common sense.

He had always been a fighter, this man who scorned the law, but even more deadly was the fact that he held with the Sicilian tradition of secret murder. Catching an enemy off guard was the cornerstone of his strategy. Rarely did hate actuate him; when it did, however, those who had incurred his wrath were marked for death.

We weren't going to be caught off guard if I could help it. To prepare for an emergency, I decided to make a survey of the area around his Lexington headquarters.

Taking Lahart with me, I had Basile drive us around the block several times while we charted the exits, parking areas and alleyways.

As we swung past the main entrance, a hoodlum named Frank Foster, alias Frankie Frost, who acted as a liaison man between Capone and 'Bugs' Moran, swaggered out of the lobby. We were almost face to face through the car window for a fleeting second, and from his startled expression I knew that he had recognised me.

Looking back, I saw him stare after us for a moment, then hurry across the street and leap into a parked car facing in the opposite direction.

'Swing it around fast, Frank,' I tapped Basile on the shoulder, 'and follow the black sedan just pulling out behind the bread truck.'

Foster swung left at the first intersection, and we could see him peering back. Then his car shot forward in an effort to lose us.

'Get him, Frank,' I urged. 'Swing him into the curb.'

The chase covered two miles as we raced block after block through crowded city streets, the speedometer flicking past sixty miles an hour. Careening around corners, weaving between cars, ignoring traffic lights and scattering pedestrians with a blaring horn, we missed disaster several times by a matter of inches.

Basile, hunched over the wheel with cold concentration, finally drew abreast of Foster's sedan. The gangster threw us a wide-eyed stare as we shot ahead of him and then, with a quick wrench of the wheel accompanied by a shrieking of rubber and a squealing of brakes, we slewed in front to force the sedan to the curb.

Lahart and I leaped from the car before it had stopped rolling.

Sprinting back as Marty raced to the other side of Foster's car, I wrenched open the door. Foster shrank back as I pushed my revolver into his face. Reaching in, I grabbed a handful of coat, dragged him out of the car and slammed him up against the side of the sedan.

'Make one move and you'll wish you hadn't,' I said.

But Foster, a swarthy, hard-faced man of about five feet eight inches, wasn't ready to act as tough as he looked. He was shaking as his hands shot meekly into the air. Jamming my pistol into his midriff, I searched him quickly.

From a hand-tooled shoulder holster under the left armpit of his dapper pin-striped suit, I lifted a snub-nosed .38 Colt revolver exactly like the one I had pointed at his diamond-studded belt buckle.

Strangely enough, I noted as the excitement of the chase ebbed and I looked around to take my bearings, we had brought him to heel right in front of the Transportation Building where our offices were located.

'Now we'll go up to my office and talk awhile,' I told Foster, putting away my gun and pocketing his. 'And don't get any funny ideas about making a break for it.'

Foster marched docilely between us, but once assured that he wasn't going to receive rough physical treatment, remained firmly silent when we questioned him about Capone and the rackets.

'I don't have to say nothin',' he repeated over and over, so after a fruitless half-hour we turned him in on a gun-carrying charge.

There had been frequent gang murders in the few months preceding 'Scarface Al's' return. A serious breach was threatening to disrupt the 'peace treaty' Capone had negotiated at Atlantic City. Meanwhile, the Secret Six had established the nation's first large-scale crime detection laboratory at Northwestern University.

I had met Major Calvin Goddard, the ballistics expert in charge of the laboratory, and on a hunch I decided to drive out to Evanston and show him the gun I had taken from Foster.

Goddard's big body was hunched over a microscope as I walked into a laboratory crammed with steel files and numerous glass-fronted cases. His dark hair was rumpled and a shoulder holster was pushed around to the centre of his back so it wouldn't interfere with his arms as he worked.

The major was never without a gun, even in the privacy of his laboratory on the quiet Northwestern campus. There was a tremendous amount of damning material stored in those bulging files, and so bold were the gangsters who infested Chicago that even this serene spot wasn't completely safe from an invasion aimed at the destruction of evidence.

Peering at me through thick-rimmed glasses, the major waved his recognition, his deep voice hearty as he said:

'Be with you in a second, Eliot.'

He straightened up and shook hands with a hard, firm grip.

'Just ran a test on a bullet fired from a gun we picked up and found out it's the same gun used in a killing on the South Side a couple of months ago,' he told me in the manner of a proud parent recounting a child's cute saying.

Reaching into my topcoat pocket, I pulled out the gun I had taken from Foster and handed it to him.

'Major, I'm not quite certain just how this ballistics business works, but I thought maybe you'd like to look at this gun I picked up from a punk named Frank Foster.'

Goddard took it, examined it and checked to make certain it was loaded.

'Come here,' he directed. 'I'll show you exactly how it works.'

Moving to a large wastebasket solidly packed with cotton waste, he fired into the wadding. The sound of the shot reverberated through the room like summer thunder. He was digging into the waste for the expended bullet when a uniformed guard poked his head through the doorway and made a quick inspection of the room.

'It's okay, George. Just running a test,' Goddard grunted.

The guard flicked his hand in a semi-salute and withdrew.

'We take our precautions,' the major said, jerking his head toward the door. 'Now, look, here's the way this thing works.'

He placed the bullet under his microscope and adjusted the lens.

'Take a look through there and you'll see lines along the side of the bullet which were left by the rifling of the pistol barrel.' I peered into the microscope and saw these long scratches. 'Every pistol's rifling varies somewhat so that by comparing two bullets you can tell whether or not they were shot from the same weapon,' he added.

He then went on to explain how a bullet taken from a body could be compared with a test bullet from a gun taken from a suspect to determine whether the pistol carried by the suspect had fired the killing shot.

When I was ready to leave, Goddard picked up the bullet he had fired from the Foster gun and dropped it into an envelope. His voice sounded eager.

'I'll check this against some of the bullets in our unsolved file. But whether I can match it or not, I'll keep this one on file in case this gun ever pops up again.'

I dropped the Foster gun into my topcoat pocket, drove back to my office in the Transportation Building and locked the revolver in one of the drawers of the steel filing cabinets where we kept our own records.

I could see already that the return of Capone was having a marked influence on us. We were so few against so many, and the arrogant theatrics of 'Scarface Al's' homecoming boasted to the world that he had lost little, if any, of his murderous power. It made you feel like a sitting duck in a shooting gallery.

Immediately following the gangster chief's homecoming, I put increased pressure on my men to uncover several more breweries. They didn't need my prodding, but perhaps I was over-eager to show Capone that times and types had changed.

With the unbeatable tactics we had now developed into a science, we cost him another two hundred and fifty thousand dollars in beer, equipment and trucks by wiping out two more breweries. We also took five men into custody, which meant that the bail bond fees were mounting into staggering totals, too. But the next two raids uncovered nothing but dry holes, with obvious indications that the breweries had been hastily moved.

'I can't understand it,' I told Lahart as we tried to figure out how the mob could have known in advance about our raids.

Pondering the question, I found myself looking intently at the telephone. Suddenly it occurred to me that if we could tap their phones, wasn't it possible that they could have tapped ours?

Going downstairs to a public booth, I called Harrison at the telephone company and asked him to run a thorough check on my line.

It was exactly as I suspected.

He called back later to say that he had cleared our lines and would run a check each week.

A telephone company investigation showed that several telephone workers had recently left their jobs and 'gone over to the syndicate for bigger money,' he told me. He had also learned, from a friend of one of those who had left, that the syndicate employed a crew of union electricians to assist their telephone experts.

'But we're on to them now, and we'll make certain that you aren't bothered any more,' he promised.

Yet, a few weeks later two more raids proved futile. A check showed that our telephones were clear of taps.

I was puzzling over this newest problem when the 'Kid' strutted into my office, and from his manner I knew that he had something out of the ordinary on his mind. As he settled into a chair and went through the usual routine of adjusting his sharply creased trousers, the telephone rang.

'Boss,' Basile informed me from the outer office, 'I just thought you'd like to know the Kid's got another new car. It's a big splashy job that must of set him back a chunk.'

'Fine,' I replied. 'Thanks.'

Turning to the 'Kid' I said: 'Let's see how much money you have in that getaway fund.'

He protested momentarily and then, realising that I was adamant, pulled out the Postal Savings deposit book. It showed a five-hundred-dollar balance and no recent withdrawals of any large amount.

'They're treating you fairly well, huh?' I asked him.

'Can't kick,' he answered expansively.

The young man's blitheness never failed to stagger me. He was sitting astride a powder keg, playing both ends against the middle and yet he seemed not to be aware that he lived in a dream world which might turn suddenly into a nightmare. My voice was gruff as I held his eyes with mine.

'Today I want some information. And I want straight answers.'

He recognised the uncompromising tone and shifted uncomfortably in his chair.

'We've made a couple of raids lately,' I snapped. 'When we got there the places had been cleaned out, lock, stock and barrel. What I want to know is, how come? Where are they getting their information?'

An injured look came into his eyes; he shook his head vigorously from side to side.

'Search me. Honest to God, Mr Ness, I don't know where they got the information. But I can tell you one thing.'

'What's that?'

'Well, since the boss man got back, the word has gone out that anybody who finds out that you are watching a certain brewery and tips off the mob gets a fast five-hundred-dollar reward,' he said. 'That means a lot of people must be looking at you whenever your guys leave this office.'

It made sense. In the two most recent instances someone had probably recognised one of our men and relayed the information to the mob.

Fidgeting in his chair, the 'Kid' coughed nervously. I knew that something important was on his mind.

'Okay, what is it?' I demanded.

He reached into his inside coat pocket and pulled out a plain envelope.

'Mr Ness,' he began uneasily, 'I don't want you to get mad at me. I told them it wouldn't do any good but they told me to try it anyhow. So I gotta try.'

Jerking upright, he slid the envelope on to the desk in front of me and then retreated hastily into his chair. I folded back the unsealed flap and came out with two crackling, brand new notes.

Each one was a thousand-dollar bill.

Momentarily hypnotised, I sat there staring down at the first thousand-dollar bills I had ever seen. From a distance I heard the 'Kid' saying:

'They said that if you'll take it easy, you'll get the same amount – two thousand dollars – each and every week.'

I could feel the anger rising in my chest and reached out to take a vice-like grip on my throat. My jaws locked so tightly that my teeth ached; the fingers holding the bills started to shake and I knew, as I jammed the bills back into the envelope and looked up at the 'Kid,' that my face was a distorted mask. He pushed back in his chair as I rose from my chair and held his arms out in front of him like a man warding off a blow.

'Don't hit me, Mr Ness,' he choked. 'I didn't mean to do this but they made me. Honest they did. I told them it wasn't any use trying.'

Fighting to get hold of myself, I walked around the desk and stood in front of him. Slowly I reached down, pulled him up out of the chair and, opening his jacket, stuffed the envelope back into his inner pocket. My voice sounded strange.

'Listen – and listen carefully,' I told him. 'I want you to take this envelope back to them and tell them that Eliot Ness can't be bought – not for two thousand a week, ten thousand or a hundred thousand. Not for all the money they'll ever lay their scummy hands on.'

The 'Kid' started backing toward the door.

'Tell them they'll never understand it,' I growled, almost to myself.

White-faced, the 'Kid' had the door half open when I stopped him. He flinched as I walked toward him.

'Get this straight,' I glared. 'Make damned sure that that money gets back to the person who gave it to you. I mean *all* of it. Because if I ever find out that you kept it, so help me God I'll break you into tiny pieces with my bare hands.'

Gulping audibly, the 'Kid' held up his right hand like a man taking an oath.

'I swear it, Mr Ness. I swear it.'

With that, the door banged behind him. The flood of anger was receding now, and I turned back to my desk.

With the 'boss man' back, the first step was bribery. What next?

That night my car was stolen again. I wondered, as I called Betty and broke another date and took a taxi home, whether it would be found this time or whether it would disappear as completely as Marty's had.

Next morning the indignant Basile popped in to tell me that it had been found abandoned on the South Side.

'Only one thing, boss,' he fumed. 'The bastards who took it also took the front wheels off of it. I had to get it towed into the garage.'

Nuisance retaliation! They still hadn't given up their hopes of diminishing the efficiency of my outfit through bribery. This was clear later that morning when Lahart and Seager burst into my office. Marty was volubly incredulous.

'Chief,' he gasped, 'those monkeys tried to buy us off.'

I listened with interest as he told me how he and Seager had been tracking a load of barrels from the cleaning plant at 38th and Shields.

'Sam's driving down the street about two blocks behind the load, and as far as we can tell there isn't a convoy with the barrel truck this time,' Marty was saying. 'All of a sudden – zoom, there's the Ford coupé right beside us and one of the pearl grey hats flips something into our car. It sails right past Sam's nose and lands right in my lap.'

Sam bit the end off a cigar and his head disappeared behind a bluish cloud of smoke as he lit up while Marty continued breathlessly.

'Well, I thought for a second maybe we were on the receiving end of a pineapple. But what am I holding but a roll of bills big enough to choke a horse!'

Marty chuckled.

'Sam takes one look, sees what it is and says: "Watch me catch 'em. Then you can give them a lateral pass." So off we go, and while he's running down that souped-up Ford I make a quick count and as near as I can estimate – because of the way we're bouncing along – there has to be two thousand bucks in that roll.'

Nodding, I asked Marty: 'Did you catch them?'

'I'll say,' he laughed. 'Sam came up so close beside them we'll both need a new paint job. Then I pitched a pass that would have made Frank Carideo of Notre Dame look like a substitute. It hit the monkey who was driving right in the eye – and he almost wrecked both of us.'

A new surge of confidence swept through me as I heard Marty's story. These two men earned the sum total of twenty-eight hundred dollars a year. They had been tempted with the better part of a year's salary, yet had scorned a bribe which probably would have been impossible to trace. My voice was gruff.

'At the risk of being awfully corny, I want you guys to know that I'm pretty damned proud of you.'

'What the hell, Eliot,' Sam said. 'We want to beat 'em, not join 'em.'

'I've got to admit one thing,' Marty interrupted kiddingly. 'I had to make three or four swings before I got off that pass. Those bills just didn't seem to want to leave Pappa's hand.'

'Bunk,' Sam grunted. 'You hit that guy on the first peg, and you were so mad I thought you were going right through the window after him.'

I told them of the offer which had been made to me through the 'Kid,' the anger rising in me again as I related the details. Marty let loose a reflective whistle.

'Boy, what they tossed us was just carfare, huh?'

'No,' I replied. 'They know that's big money to people like us. They just can't understand that some people won't be bought. But sooner or later the idea will simmer through their thick skulls and then, in all probability, they'll try some rough stuff. But it sure is nice to know that my guys can't be bought.'

'You can tell the world!' Marty cracked.

His words rang in my ears insistently.

Why not? I thought. Why not do just that? – and 'tell the world' – and 'Scarface Al' Capone – that Eliot Ness and his men couldn't be bought. The idea kept bouncing around inside my head as Marty and Sam filled me in on their progress in trying to locate another brewery.

'That's exactly what we're going to do,' I declared.

'What's that?' Sam asked.

'Tell the world, just as Marty suggested. I'm going to make a few calls and then I'm going to take you two to lunch – on the government – to make up in a very minor way for that two thousand dollars you tossed away this morning. Then we're coming back here and "tell the world."'

They both looked puzzled. But they got the drift as I leafed through the telephone book and began to call the newspapers and newsreel outfits.

'This is going to ruin my social life in places like the Montmartre,' Marty chuckled as I called the *Tribune* and, having attained some notoriety as a 'gangbuster', was swiftly put through to the city desk.

'But you'll be a big hero,' I joked.

Completing my calls, in which I informed each newspaper and motion-picture company that I was having a 'sensational' press conference at two o'clock that afternoon, I took my two men to lunch.

'And,' I told them in the elevator, 'you can have all you can eat – as long as you take the thirty-five-cent blue-plate special.'

There was little conversation as we ate, each busy with his own thoughts. I began to study these two vastly different men – the gusty, irrepressible Lahart and the stolid, unemotional Seager. Why, I wondered, were they in this? In my case, it was a heterogeneous mixture, a passion for police work, a dislike of seeing people abused and, basically, the thrill of action.

'Sam,' I finally asked Seager as he waded through a chunk of apple pie, 'what made you come into this thing?'

He chewed reflectively for several seconds, his square jaw working steadily, and then laid aside his fork.

'Police work is about all I've ever known, Eliot. I couldn't take that tour of duty in the death house any more. I had to get outside where I could move around and see people who still had some sort of hope. Then this came along and, well, it's quite an experience.'

He prodded a piece of crust with his fork and then looked me right in the eye.

'Maybe it'll surprise you, Eliot, but I've always wanted a chicken farm. Now I've seen just about all the trouble I want. If I get through this one – or I guess I should say "when" – I think I'll settle for that farm.'

I was surprised, because I had never pictured Sam as the country type. Yet I was even more astonished when Lahart chimed in solemnly:

'Damned if I know what my reasons were, except that the job in the post office was driving me crazy and I wanted some kicks. But let me tell you, Sam, that farm idea sounds pretty good. Imagine, nothing to worry about but whether the hens are layin'.'

It's getting to all of us, I thought as we left the restaurant. It isn't facing danger that cuts you up inside. It's the waiting and the not knowing what's coming.

When we returned to the office, Basile was shrugging off the questions of more than a dozen reporters and cameramen. Flashbulbs began to pop as we walked in and, raising my hands to quiet them, I told them there would be plenty of time for everything.

'First, let's go into my office and I'll give you the story. Then you can take all the pictures you want.'

When they were settled, and while the newsreels were setting up their cameras, I told them of the attempted briberies. I related in detail how an emissary of Capone's had tried to buy me off for two thousand dollars a week and how Marty and Sam had thrown back their flying bribe.

Pencils scribbled rapidly, and there was a rush for telephones. Flashlight bulbs popped incessantly and the story had to be repeated for the motion-picture cameras.

It was a long, wearisome process but well worth the effort. Possibly it wasn't too important for the world to know that we couldn't be bought, but I did want Al Capone and every gangster in the city to realise that there were still a few law enforcement agents who couldn't be swerved from their duty.

As the last group was leaving, I heard one of the men say:

'Those guys are dead pigeons.'

Pigeons, I thought grimly, who will take a lot of killing. At the very outset I had chosen my men with an eye toward their ability to take care of themselves under almost any conditions. These men were not hoodlums who had all their courage in their trigger finger. They were alert, fearless and extremely fit and capable. They trusted nobody except themselves, and we had long since devised a system of working in pairs. They would be hard to cut down, I knew.

Meanwhile, defiance of the type we had exhibited was unheard of in a racket-infested city where opposition was so consistently bought off or killed off. Our revelation of the bribes was a sensation. The story was splashed across front pages from coast to coast.

One story opened:

Eliot Ness and his young agents have proved to Al Capone that they are untouchable.

A caption writer adopted it for another paper and over our pictures rode the bold, black words:

'THE UNTOUCHABLES'

The wire service picked up the phrase and the words swept across the nation.

So were born 'The Untouchables'.

Dressing-Up

BY W. R. BURNETT

With the ever-growing popularity of crime series on television it was only going to be a matter of time before an American producer would decide to adapt the highly influential work of the novelist and screenwriter W.R. Burnett, whose book Little Caesar *(1929) is today regarded as one of the first, and best, authentic, native American crime novels. Nor does Burnett's influence end there, for as Chris Steinbrunner and Otto Penzler have written* in their Encyclopedia of Mystery and Detection, *'His books and screenplays have had an important impact on the crime film – some of the cinematic milestones in this genre are attributable to him.' Especially, in fact,* Little Caesar, *made in 1930, with Edward G. Robinson as Rico the small-time crook who ruthlessly gains control of the underworld: the role that made him a star and initiated a whole cycle of gangster movies;* Scarface *(1932) in which Paul Muni played a vicious bootlegger who kills all those who cross him; and* The Asphalt Jungle *(1950) about criminal low-life, which John Huston directed with Sterling Hayden, Louis Calhern, Sam Jaffe and Marilyn Monroe. Such, indeed, was the success and influence of this film that it has been remade twice, in 1958 and 1972, and parodied three times as* Badlanders *(1958),* Cairo *(1963) and* Cool Breeze *(1972).*

Appropriately, therefore, it was The Asphalt Jungle *that finally brought Burnett's tough and authentic crime writing to American television screens when ABC launched a series of hour-long episodes in the spring of 1961. Although the series was still full of the same kind of villains that Burnett wrote about so well, the main focus was shifted to the activities of a Deputy Police Commissioner, Matthew Gower (played by the splendid Hollywood character actor, Jack Warden) who was determined to break the power of the criminal rings in his city. Aiding him was a special squad of undercover agents led by Captain Gus Honochek (Arch Johnson) and Sergeant Danny Keller (Bill Smith) who spent many episodes living amongst their quarry. Particularly powerful episodes such as 'The Last Way Out', 'The Kidnap', 'The Nine-Twenty Hero' and 'Dark Night' captured the essence of Burnett's gritty prose and were brilliantly underscored by the great Duke Ellington's musical soundtrack.*

William Riley Burnett (1899–1983) wanted to be a writer from his childhood in Springfield, Ohio, but had no luck selling any of his early novels, short stories or plays until he moved to Chicago and there, immersed in the uneasy days of the Roaring Twenties, wrote Little Caesar. *The adaptation of this for the screen less than a year later inspired Burnett to produce more crime novels as well as to write for films and television where he subsequently enjoyed great success. The same year that* Little Caesar *was published, he also wrote a short story, 'Dressing-Up', which appeared in the August issue of the prestigious* Harper's *magazine. The following year it won the O. Henry Memorial Award for the best short story. Thirty years on, in 1961, it also formed the basis for what many people believe to have been the best episode of* The Asphalt Jungle, *'The Sniper', which co-starred Jack Klugman as the small-time gangster, Blue. It is reprinted here as a tribute to Burnett's extraordinary talent and to the TV series in which it featured.*

WHEN THE STORE manager saw Blue and his girl, Birdy, coming in the front door, he turned to Al, one of the clerks, and said:

'Look at this, Al. The stockyards're moving down town.'

Al laughed, then he put on his best professional manner, clasped his hands in front of his stomach, inclined his head slightly, and walked up to Blue.

'What can I do for you, sir?'

Blue was short and stocky. His legs were thin, his waist small, but his shoulders were wide enough for a man six feet tall. His face was red and beefy, and his cheekbones were so prominent that they stuck out of his face. He looked up at Al.

'I'm buying an outfit, see,' he said. 'I'm gonna shed these rags and climb into something slick.'

'Yes, sir,' said Al. 'How about one of our new spring models?'

'He wants a grey suit,' said Birdy, adjusting her new fur neckpiece.

'Double-breasted,' said Blue.

'Yes, sir,' said Al.

'But first I want some silk underwear,' said Blue. 'I'm dressing from the hide out.'

The store manager came over and smiled.

'Take good care of this young man, won't you, Mr Johnson?'

'Yes, sir,' said Al.

'Warm, isn't it?' the store manager said to Birdy.

'Yeah, ain't it?' said Birdy, taking off her neckpiece and dangling it over her arm like the women in the advertisements.

The store manager walked to the back of the shop and talked to the cashier:

'There's a boy that's got a big hunk of money all of a sudden,' he said, 'and he's gonna lose it the same way.'

'Yeah?' said the cashier. 'Well, I wish my rich uncle that I haven't got would die. Take a look at that neckpiece his girl's wearing. He didn't get that for five dollars.'

Al spread out the silk underwear on the counter, and Blue looked through it. Birdy held up a lavender shirt.

'Here you are, Blue. Here's what you ought to get.'

'Say . . .!' said Blue.

'Yes, sir,' said Al; 'we're selling lots of that. Just had an order for a dozen suits from Mr Hibschmann out in Lake Forest.'

'That's where the swells come from,' said Birdy.

Blue looked at the lavender shirt and the lavender shorts and said: 'All right. I'll take a dozen.'

Al glanced up from his order book, caught the manager's eye, and winked. The manager came up to Blue, put his hand on his shoulder and said:

'My dear sir, since you seem to know real stuff when you see it, I'll let you in on something. We got a new shipment of cravats that we have only just begun to unpack. But if you'd like to look at them, I'll send down to the stockroom for them.'

'Sure,' said Blue.

'Thanks awfully,' said Birdy.

'It's our very best stock. Handmade cravats of the best material obtainable.'

'We want the best, don't we, Blue?' said Birdy.

'Sure,' said Blue.

While the manager sent for the cravats, Blue bought a dozen silk shirts, some collars, a solid gold collar pin, some onyx cuff links, a set of military brushes, and two dozen pairs of socks. Al bent over his order book and wrote in the items swiftly, computing the possible amount of this windfall. In a few minutes a stock boy brought up the neckties and stood with his mouth open while Blue selected a dozen of the most expensive ties. The manager noticed him.

'Just leave the rest of the stock, please,' he said, then he turned his back to Blue and hissed, 'Get out of here!'

The stock boy went back to the basement, and the manager turned back to Blue, smiling.

'Those cravats retail at four dollars apiece,' he said, 'but because you're giving us such a nice order, I'll let you have them for three fifty.'

'OK,' said Blue.

'Them sure are swell ties, Blue,' said Birdy, putting her arm through his. 'Won't we be lit up though?'

'Sure,' said Blue.

When the accessories had been selected, Blue began to try on the suits Al brought him. Blue strode up and down in front of the big triple mirror, puffed out his chest, struck attitudes, and studied his profile, which he had never seen before except in one Bertillon picture. Al stayed at his elbow, offering suggestions, helping him with the set of a coat, telling him how wonderful he looked; and the manager stayed in the background, occasionally making a remark to Birdy whom he addressed as 'Madam.'

Blue, after a long consultation with Birdy, selected two of the most expensive suits: a blue serge single-breasted and a grey double-breasted. Then he bought a grey felt hat at twelve dollars, a small sailor at eight, and a panama at eighteen.

'Well,' said Blue, 'I guess you guys got about as much of my jack as you're gonna get.'

'How about shoes?' Al put in.

'By God, I forgot,' said Blue. 'Hey, Birdy, I forgot shoes. Ain't that good? Look at this suitcase!'

He held up his foot. He was wearing big tan brogans, and there was a hole in the sole which went clear through the sock to the skin.

'Put your foot down, Blue,' said Birdy. 'Where you think you're at?'

Blue bought a pair of tan oxfords, a pair of black oxfords, and a pair of white and tan sport shoes.

'Now we're done,' said Blue. 'I guess I ought to look pretty Boul' Mich' now.'

Al totalled up the bill. Birdy and the manager had a long conversation about the weather; and Blue stood before the triple mirror studying his profile.

Al hesitated before he told Blue the amount of the bill. He called for the manager to OK it, then he said:

'Cash or charge, sir?'

Blue took out his billfold which was stuffed with big bills.

'Cash,' he said, 'how much?'

'Four hundred and sixty-five dollars,' said Al.

Blue gave him five one-hundred-dollar bills.

'Now,' said Blue, 'I want you to get that grey suit fixed up right away so's I can put it on. I'm gonna dress from the hide out, and you guys can throw my old duds in the sewer.'

'Yes, sir,' said Al. 'I'll get our tailor right away. We got a dressing room on the second floor.'

The cashier rang up the sale and gave the change to the manager.

'Are you going away for the summer?' asked the manager as he handed Blue his change.

'Yeah,' said Blue; 'me and the girl friend are gonna see New York. It'll be our first trip.'

'That'll be nice,' said the manager. 'Are you in business for yourself?'

Blue glanced at Birdy, and she shook her head slightly.

'I'm in the oil business,' said Blue. 'I got some wells. I'm from Oklahoma.'

'That's interesting,' said the manager.

When they were leaving the café Blue took out his billfold and gave the doorman a five-dollar bill. The doorman's eyes popped but he managed to bow and smile.

'Yes, sir, yes, sir,' he said. 'Do you want a cab?'

'Yeah,' said Blue, hanging on to Birdy who was drunker than he was.

'Yeah, you're damn right we want a cab,' said Birdy. 'Do we look like the kind of people that walk?'

'That's right,' said Blue.

'Yes, sir,' said the doorman, and he went out into the middle of the street and blew his whistle.

Before the taxi came a small sedan drew up at the curb across the street, and two men got out.

'There he is,' said one of them, pointing at Blue.

'Hello, Guido,' shouted Blue. 'Look at me. Ain't I Boul' Mich'?'

Guido ran across the street, took Blue by the arm, shook him several times and said:

'You got to sober up, keed! Get it! You got to sober up. Somebody spilled something, see? Me and Bud's taking it on the lam. Saint Louie won't look bad to us.'

'Yellow,' said Blue.

'Sure,' said Guido; 'but I got a stake and I'm gonna spend some of it before I get bumped. Somebody wised Mike's boys up. They're looking for Pascal right now.'

'What the hell!' said Blue, laughing. 'Look at me, Guido. Ain't I Boul' Mich'? I got silk underwear under this suit. Look at Birdy.'

'Look at me,' said Birdy; 'ain't I Boul' Mich'?'

'Say,' said Guido, 'you better ditch that tommy and put in with us. We got room in the heap.'

'Not me,' said Blue. 'I ain't scairt of Mike Bova. I'll bump him next.'

'All right,' said Guido; 'you'll have a swell funeral.'

'Guido,' called the other man, 'let that bum go.'

'So long, Blue,' said Guido.

'So long,' said Blue.

'Bye, bye, Guido,' said Birdy.

Guido crossed the street, got into the driver's seat, slammed the door, and the sedan moved off. The taxi was waiting, and the doorman helped Birdy and Blue into it.

'Good-night, sir,' said the doorman.

Birdy was lying on the lounge flat on her back with her hands under her head and an empty drinking glass sitting upright on her stomach. Blue, in his shirtsleeves, his collar wilted and his tie untied, was sitting at the table reading a crumpled newspaper. There were three-inch headlines.

BOVA'S LIEUTENANT KILLED
SHOT DOWN AS HE LEFT
HIS OFFICE BY GUNMEN

'You hear me!' said Blue. 'Funniest thing ever pulled. There I was waiting in a room across the street trying to read a magazine, and Pascal was sitting with his head against the wall sleeping. "Christ," I says, "there's Pete now." He was coming out of his office. We wasn't looking for him for two hours yet. So I jist set there. Hell, I couldn't move, see, 'cause he come sudden, see, and I was figuring he wouldn't be out for two hours yet. "Pascal," I says, "there's Pete now." But

Pascal he jist opens his eyes like a fish and don't say nothing. Pete he stops and looks right up at the window where I'm sitting, see, and I wonder does this guy know something. Hell, I couldn't move. I wasn't ready, see? Well, so Pascal he slips and falls over and hits his head. This makes me laugh but still I couldn't move my trigger finger. Pete he holds out his hand like he's looking for rain, then I let him have it. I don't know. It was funny. I jist let him have it without knowing it, see, and before, I couldn't pull that trigger when I wanted to. When the old Thompson starts to bark, Pascal gets up and yells, 'What you smoking for, you bum? It ain't time yet.' Then he looks out the window and there's Pete on the sidewalk dead as yesterday's newspaper and an old woman is pointing up at us. We ditch the gun and beat it down the back stairs. That's all there was to it. There wasn't nobody in the alley, see, so we jist walked along slow, and pretty soon we come to a drugstore and went in to get some cigs 'cause we smoked all ours waiting for that guy to come out.'

'Pour me a little drink, honey,' said Birdy.

Blue got up, took a big flask out of his hip pocket, and poured Birdy another drink. Then he sat down, took out his billfold and extracted a couple of railroad tickets.

'Look at them, old kid,' he said. 'When we ride, we ride. Twentieth Century to New York. That's us, kid; and won't we give 'em a treat over in Brooklyn! Say, them Easterners think we're still shooting Indians. Hell, Chi makes that place look like a YMCA. Yeah, I used to know Ruby Welch, and he was big stuff from Brooklyn; but what did he do when Guido started gunning for him? He got himself put in the can as a vag. Yeah, we ought to go big over in New York, kid. What they need over there is guts. We can give 'em that, kid. When somebody needs somebody for the No. 1 caper, Blue's the guy for the job. I was born with a rod in my cradle and I'm the best there is. Yeah, when the Big Boy wanted Pete bumped who did he call on first? Old Blue, yes, sir, old Blue.'

Blue got up, turned on the gramophone, and started to dance with a chair.

'Hey,' he said, 'come on, let's dance, Birdy. We're big shots now, Birdy; let's dance. Look at me! If I had my coat on I'd look like the Prince of Wales. Boul' Mich', kid; that's us; Boul' Mich'. We'll knock their eyes out on Fifth Avenue, kid; yes, sir. Let's dance.'

'I'm getting sick,' said Birdy.

Blue went over and looked down at her. Her face was pale and drawn; there were blue circles under her eyes.

'Getting sick, Birdy?'

'Yeah. I can't stand it like I used to when I was with The Madam. Put me to bed, honey.'

Blue picked Birdy up and carried her into the bedroom. Birdy began to hiccup.

'Gimme glass of water,' she said.

'You don't want water,' Blue said; 'you want a nice big slug.'

'No, gimme glass of water.'

She lay down on the bed and, before Blue could bring her a glass of water, she was asleep. He stood looking down at her, then he went back into the living room, took a long pull at his flask, and picked up the crumpled newspaper. But he had read the account of the killing of Big Pete so many times that he knew it by heart. He sat staring at the paper, then he threw it on the floor and sat rolling a cigarette between his palms.

It had begun to get light. He heard a milk wagon passing the house. He got up and went over to the window. The houses were still dark, and far off down the street a string of lighted elevated cars ran along the horizon, but the sky was grey and in the east some of the clouds were turning yellow. It was quiet. Blue began to notice how quiet it was.

'Birdy,' he called.

But he heard her snoring, and turned back to the table.

The telephone rang, but when he answered it there was nobody on the line.

'What's the idea?' he said.

He sat down at the table, took out his billfold and counted his money, then he took out the railroad tickets and read everything printed on them. Again he noticed how quiet it was. He got up, put away his billfold, and went into the bedroom. Birdy was sleeping with her mouth open, flat on her back, with her arms spread out. Blue lay down beside her and tried to sleep, but he turned from side to side, and finally gave it up.

'I don't feel like sleeping,' he thought. 'I'm all het up about going East on The Century. Here I am, old Blue, riding The Century dressed up like John Barrymore and with a swell frail. Yeah, that's me. Boul' Mich' Blue.'

He got up, put on his coat, and began to pose in front of the living room mirror.

'Boul' Mich' Blue,' he said.

Finally he sat down at the table and laid out a game of solitaire; but he had so many bad breaks with the cards that he began to cheat and then lost interest in the game.

'I know,' he said, 'what I need is food.'

He got up and went to the refrigerator, but there wasn't anything in it except a few pieces of cold meat.

'Hell!' he said, 'I guess I'll have to go down to Charley's.'

He put on his new soft hat, but hesitated. If they was looking for Pascal, they was looking for him, too. Right now there wasn't nobody on the streets and it was a good time to bump a guy.

'Hell!' he said, buttoning his coat, 'I got a streak of luck. It'll hold. Boul' Mich' Blue'll be on The Century to-morrow. Yeah bo! I ain't scairt of no Mike Bova.'

When Blue came out of the apartment house the sun was just coming up. The alleys and areaways were still dark, but there was a pale yellow radiance in the streets. There was no one about; no sign of life. Not even a parked car.

'Hell!' said Blue; 'safe as a tank-town.'

A window across the street was raised, and Blue ducked without meaning to; but a fat woman put her head out of the window and stared into the street.

There was nobody in Charley's, not even a waiter. Behind the counter the big nickel coffee urns were sending up steam. Blue took out a fifty-cent piece and flung it on the counter. Wing, the counterman, looked in from the kitchen.

'Come on, Wing,' said Blue, 'snap it up.'

'Didn't know you, kid,' said Wing. 'Ain't you dressed up, though? Must've struck it.'

'I sure did,' said Blue. 'Give me a combination and some muddy water.'

'Muddy water, hell,' said Wing. 'I jist made that Java.'

Blue leaned on the counter and stared at himself in the mirror, while Wing went back to make his sandwich.

'Hey, Wing,' Blue shouted, 'did you know I was going East on The Century?'

'Are, hunh?' Wing shouted back. 'You're on the big time now, ain't you, kid?'

'That's the word,' said Blue.

Blue turned to look out into the street. He saw a man passing, and stared at him. The man was small and had a slouch hat pulled down over his face. Blue thought he recognised him and slid his gun out of the holster under his armpit and put it in his coat pocket. The man passed without looking in.

'I got the jumps,' said Blue. 'It's that rotten gin.'

Wing came in with the sandwich, drew Blue a cup of coffee, then leaned his elbows on the counter and watched Blue eat.

'Well,' said Wing, 'I see where they got Big Pete.'

'Yeah,' said Blue.

'I knew they was gonna,' said Wing. 'I got inside dope.'

'Yeah?' said Blue.

'It was coming to him.'

'Yeah.'

Blue finished his sandwich, lighted a cigarette, and sipped his coffee. It was broad daylight now, and trucks had begun to pass the restaurant.

'Going East, are you, kid?' said Wing.

'Yeah,' said Blue. 'I got in on a big cut and I don't have to worry none for some time. I jist took my dame down and dressed her up this afternoon. Is she hot? Me, I got silk underwear on.'

He unbuttoned his shirt and showed Wing his lavender underwear.

'You're sure a dressed-up boy,' said Wing. 'I bet you paid ten bucks for that hat you got on.'

'Twelve,' said Blue. 'It was the best they had. I paid eighteen for a panama. You like this suit?'

'It's red hot,' said Wing; then with a twinge of envy, 'if I wasn't going straight maybe I could wear rags like that.'

'How long's your parole got to run yet?'

'Plenty long. And I got the dicks down on me. They thought I'd stool for 'em in this ward. But that ain't my way.'

'Why don't you make a break for Canada?'

'Yeah,' said Wing, 'and get jerked back to stir.'

Blue finished his coffee, paid his check, and gave Wing a dollar bill. Wing turned the bill over and over.

'Say,' he said, 'give me another buck and I'll put you on to something hot at Arlington.'

Blue laughed and tossed Wing a silver dollar.

'Never mind the tip,' he said. 'I know lots of better ways to lose my dough. Why don't you lay off the ponies, Wing? You can't beat that racket.'

'I got the itch,' said Wing.

Blue looked into the mirror and adjusted his hat to the proper angle.

'Well,' he said, 'I'm leaving you. I'll send you a postcard from the Big Burg, Wing.'

But Blue noticed that Wing had begun to get nervous; his face was twitching.

'Blue,' said Wing, 'for Christ's sake watch your step. I'm telling you straight, kid. One of Mike's boys was in here buzzing me about you jist 'fore she began to get light. I'm telling you straight, kid. It ain't my fight and I wasn't gonna peep. But you're a right guy, Blue.'

Blue rubbed his hand over his face, then he said:

'It was The Wolf. I seen him go past.'

'Yeah,' said Wing.

'Jesus!' said Blue, 'which way'd I better go?'

'I'd put you upstairs . . .' Wing began.

'No use,' said Blue. 'The Wolf seen me.'

Wing drew himself a cup of coffee and drank it at a gulp.

'If they knew I'd peeped they'd bump me sure,' said Wing.

Blue stood staring at the counter, then he pulled his hat down over his eyes, and slipped his right hand into the pocket where the gun was.

'Well,' he said, 'the alley's no good. It's blind my way. The side street won't get me no place. So all I got's the front way. Hell!' he went on, puffing out his chest, 'I got a streak of luck, Wing. It'll hold.'

Wing drew himself another cup of coffee.

'Here's hoping,' he said.

Blue went to the door and, putting his head out a little way, looked up and down. The street was deserted except for a truck which was coming toward him slowly. It was a Standard Oil truck.

'Wing,' he said, 'has any of Mike's boys got a hide-out anywhere around here?'

'Don't know of none.'

'Well,' said Blue, 'here I go.'

'So long,' said Wing.

Blue stepped out of the restaurant, threw his shoulders back, and began to walk slowly toward Birdy's apartment. The Standard Oil truck passed him and went on. The street was quiet. At the end of the street he saw an elevated on its way toward the Loop.

'I wish I was on that baby,' he said. But the nearer he got to the apartment the surer he became that his luck would hold. Hell! it was the first break he'd had since he and Guido hijacked that big Detroit shipment. He had tickets on The Century. When a guy has tickets on The Century he uses them. And that wasn't all. He was a big shot now; the Big Boy had promised him a bonus; he had on silk underwear.

'Hell!' said Blue, 'it ain't in the cards.'

Across from Birdy's apartment he saw the same fat woman leaning out of the window. When he looked up she drew her head in hastily. Blue made a dash for the door, but across the street a Thompson gun began to spit. Blue stumbled, dropped his gun, and ran blindly out into the middle of the street; then he turned and ran blindly back toward the house. An iron fence caught him just below the belt and he doubled over it. Across the street a window was slammed.

Mobile Commandos

BY TROY KENNEDY MARTIN

The realistic, no-holds-barred depiction of the police in a TV series finally arrived in Britain in 1960 when the BBC launched Z-Cars with the cantankerous Chief Inspector Charlie Barlow, his understated assistant, Detective Sergeant John Watt, and the team of young police constables who drove patrol cars around a fictionalised area of Liverpool called Newtown. The programme, which was to last for six hundred and sixty-seven episodes (a mixture of twice-a-week twenty-five-minute transmissions or single fifty-minute broadcasts, initially in black and white and later colour) was born at the start of the Swinging Sixties and survived until almost the dawn of the Technological Eighties. It undoubtedly revolutionised the image of the British police – as well as drawing fierce complaints from the Force itself, some of whose members thought it was demeaning to the status of officers. Yet within weeks, Z-Cars had become essential viewing, and with the passing years has proved to be one of the single biggest influences on all subsequent crime series. It made household names of its stars, too: Stratford Johns as the bad-tempered Barlow; Frank Windsor as the kindly Watt; not to mention Joseph Brady (Jock Weir), Brian Blessed ('Fancy' Smith), James Ellis (Bert Lynch), Jeremy Kemp (Bob Steele) and Colin Welland (David Graham) as the 'mobile commandos' in Z Victor One and Z Victor Two forever trying to keep on top of the crimes being committed in the high-rise blocks and industrial estates of Newtown and the adjacent Seaport. The stories became famous for portraying both the police and criminals warts and all, and there were occasions when the villains got away and crime did pay. Although the series was sometimes hampered by having to use studio sets to depict conversations taking place in apparently speeding vehicles, it was not

above using bad language and occasional violence to sustain its gritty realism. These elements undoubtedly later contributed to the Chief Constable of Lancashire withdrawing his co-operation for location shooting – but this did little to affect the enormous appeal of the programme to viewers of all ages. The series' wailing theme tune by Johnny Keating also became one of the most instantly recognisable on television for a generation.

Z-Cars was a particular triumph for its creator, Troy Kennedy Martin (1932–), the son of a Glaswegian-Irishman, who had struggled to make his way as a scriptwriter until the fateful day he happened to be lying in bed with mumps and amused himself by listening in to police messages on his radio. 'I got a vastly different impression of the police than that given on Dixon of Dock Green,*' he said later, 'so I decided to write a series about what their lives were* really *like.' Despite the success of* Z-Cars, *Troy left before the first year was out – 'because there was so much politicking,' he later told the* Sunday Times *– but has since won awards for his later TV work such as* Reilly, Ace of Spies *and* Edge of Darkness. *Other writers who continued the saga have included a number of now-famous names like John Hopkins, Allan Prior, Robert Barr and Alan Plater, all of whom added further layers to its hallmarks of authentic dialogue and believable situations. Here, though, the man who initiated a new era in realism in television crime series, recounts how the Z-Cars team was born . . .*

I

ON A SPRING morning in 1960, just about dawn, PC Reg Farrow was blown to bits with a sawn-off shotgun outside Freeman's Toothpaste factory on the Industrial Estate.

Reg Farrow left three children orphaned and his second wife a widow, while the maniac that had done for him left nothing but his dabs all over the cashier's box of the works canteen. He got away with £4 of tea money and a two-hour start before the hunt was on.

The Industrial Estate is that scattering of factories surrounded by barbed wire which lies north of Newtown's big flats, and the noise of the shotgun startled all the nightwatchmen along the West Estate road. Old, underpaid and living in dreams of pools, horses and dogs, they were blasted through by the noise as if it had been the draught of death itself. Frightened, they phoned each other to check that what they heard was what they heard. Then, this confirmed, they all phoned the police station at once, jamming the lines and confusing Percy Twentyman, who was unfortunate enough to be duty sergeant on that particular scale.

Percy, a short streak of profanity, dark like a Liverpool Spaniard with a smarmy smile and a way with women, got the gist of what was up (sound of an explosion near the West Gate) put the boot in Ian Sweet, the young constable dozing at the duty desk, and disappeared with him into the blackness of Newtown's night in the area car, an ancient Hillman which made as much noise as Twentyman did himself.

Ten minutes later they were at the West Gate, braking to a halt while the old nightwatchmen clustered around them like witches on a Scottish heath.

'Like the sound of a ruddy cannon' – the first said, frightened.

'Where was it?' Percy asked them.

'Along there.' The frightened fellow pointed down the road towards Freeman's.

'That's right,' the others said. 'It's the truth, along there.'

'A shotgun, I'd know a shotgun anywhere,' said Grandpa Maddigan. 'Someone's shot a shotgun.'

'Where's Reg Farrow?' young PC Sweet asked them, sticking his head out of the car. 'He's not been round yet, has he?'

'He's been round all right,' said the nightwatchmen. 'Had some tea with me,' the frightened one said.

'He had something a bit stronger with me,' Grandpa Maddigan said. 'Say, where is Reg Farrow?' Grandpa suddenly was frightened. 'It was a shotgun I heard and where's Reg Farrow?' he shouted at Percy. 'Where is he?' As if Reg was somewhere in the boot of the Hillman and Percy was hiding him.

'How the hell should I know,' said Percy, but suddenly he did know, know it like putting his hand in a deep freeze at the greengrocers. 'Fan out behind me,' Percy said, getting out of the car. 'Fan out and we'll make a search, all down the road.' He said it quietly, quickly.

'But what about our works then,' the frightened ones said.

'To hell with your works!' Percy said. 'Let's go, and no holding back neither.'

He started to move down the centre of the road, but the old men were too frightened to follow. He stopped and wheeled angrily.

'Don't stand there like dummies out of Lewis's.' The words echoed across the estate. 'Sweet, get behind them and put the boot up anyone who doesn't move. Earn your pay!' he shouted.

'Yes, Sergeant,' Sweet said, wondering what was up; secretly knowing what was up, but not because of intuition like Percy, but because sooner or later he knew he was going to meet it sweet or sour, the way a woman knows that tonight's the night and she can't get out of it.

'Keep well out, keep the whole area covered,' Percy shouted, and Sweet found himself walking down the road. They fanned out in front of him, dark figures in the dawn. Five old figures of a Greek chorus with Percy Twentyman of Liverpool fame walking ahead of them on the crown of the road, and PC Sweet, scarcely out of being a cadet, bringing up the rear.

On either side the factories loomed up on them. Dark towering menageries of steel which produced Britain's wealth in these the boom years, and gave the people of this Newtown money to save, to buy, to eat, to court, to bear children, to get drunk, beat their wives, have holidays in Blackpool or keep the boys at the sixth form of the Grammar, or send money home to grandparents in Ireland, bet on pools or to buy a plot in the graveyard for themselves when they die, or to put a shilling in the plate of a Sunday Church or a pound up the stocking of a whore. These, the big factories, did not make the people of Newtown what they were, but they gave them the opportunity to become what they wanted to become.

The seven crossed under the high tension cables and heard the singing of their wires. They wheeled slowly down the bending road, watching and seeing nothing but dark shapes and hearing the clinker dying in the boilers, the drum of the oil pipes, the splash from the gutterings.

They passed the machine shops which lay rain-sodden and quiet, filled with black, silent machines. They walked with queer echoes through the empty goods yard. They made seven distorted shadows against the deserted loading bays.

But too soon they stood at the gates of Freeman's. They halted, looking at what was left of Reg; the body swaying in the barbed wire like a lump of venison; the wire croaking under its weight in the wind: the wheel of his bike still tinkling and swinging where it lay in the mud.

The old men made funny noises in their throats. Sweet suddenly knew the strangeness of death in the shape of Reg who had signed the book before him an hour ago. He could not understand. He thought of religious instruction taught ten years back by a nun. He stayed rooted to the ground.

Percy Twentyman was not a religious man. He opened the gates, picked up a rusty iron bar lying in the grass and went in to kill whoever had done it to our Reg. But the maniac was gone. And there was nothing Percy could do but come out, raise the alarm, and go back to break the ghastly news to Reg's second wife. And to fill in that first form for the widows' and orphans' fund.

Chief Inspector Charlie Barlow stood freezing by Reg Farrow's open grave. He was cold, angry, fed up and wet – although to look at him you wouldn't think it. Around him the crowd was breaking up with the reluctance of pub customers on a fine Friday night, although the wind was sweeping the cemetery with long, low squalls of rain; although the band had stopped playing; although the Mayor had got into his car and was being shook hands with by the Superintendent and all the other county officials before being driven off.

'You 'aven't caught him 'ave you Charlie,' the Mayor had said to Barlow at the graveside.

'No sir, we 'aven't, but we will,' Barlow had said to him, knowing well the maniac was in Manchester, and if and when he'd be picked up he'd be booked elsewhere.

'Well, keep at it, Charlie,' the Mayor had said. 'Mr Farrow was well known in the district; yes, well known and liked.' The Mayor had looked around at the band, the reporters, the dignitaries and representatives of trade unions and Co-operatives and clubs and sporting organisations and the lone huddle of Reg's family, who stood quite still in the rain being almost embraced with Percy Twentyman's long kind arms.

'Yes, well known and liked,' the Mayor had said, like the stupid fat beggar he was. 'Keep at it Charlie.'

Barlow watched the big Austin Princess sink under the weight of the man as he got in, still shaking hands with officials. Then it was moving through the puddles, slowly nudging its way past members of the Co-op band who were making for the pub over the hill, where along with other mourners they'd steam the wet from their clothes and hold a thirsty lunch hour wake. No one knew Reg Farrow, or what he was like. Barlow thought bitterly of his loss of his dead friend. They come because he was a policeman, Barlow thought; that was all. But he supposed on second thoughts that that was enough, so he forgave the Mayor for his pompous, awkward words.

Mrs Farrow came towards him with Percy. The children held on to Ian Sweet. Because of the strangeness of it all the children were crying. So was PC Sweet. He kissed Mrs Farrow as she passed by. She clutched at Barlow desperately, hungry for the kindness. She wouldn't be all alone in her grief, he thought; a few of them knew Reg. He let her hold and bury her face in his chest. Emotion didn't frighten Barlow because under his skin of dourness he was a passionate man.

'It's all right Doris. I know how you feel, love,' he said, stroking her, 'Me and Reg joined the force together didn't we? Way back in '34.'

'I wasn't born then,' she said sobbing.

'Aye, we was young,' Barlow said. 'Ourselves we was young.' Twentyman was on the other side of her, making signs it was time to get her out of the rain and back to her kitchen and a cup of tea. 'Are you taking her home Percy?' Barlow said.

'When we've got the family together, sir,' Sergeant Twentyman said, taking her gently from Barlow.

'Where's John Watt then, Percy – any news?'

'Well, he's still with the Manchester police seeing as if the maniac's done a bunk that way,' Percy said.

'Aye,' Barlow said. 'Likely he has. I'll be up here all day in case I'm wanted by anyone at the office.'

'Yes, sir,' Sergeant Twentyman said, not ever knowing the ways of the CID, or why a detective would stand in the rain at the graveyard on the day of the funeral – except to pay his respects.

'Thank you Mr Barlow,' Doris Farrow kept saying for no reason at all. She kept coming back to his arms, and Barlow let her lie there as long as she wanted although he was thinking of new things now which were connected, he felt, with Reg's death.

Detective Chief Superintendent Robins' Ford Zephyr belted past the old Saxon church just as the Austin Princess of Newtown's Mayor whooshed out of the cemetery. Robins banged on the brakes and missed ramming the big black official car by the thickness of a coat of paint. A look of disappointment crossed the faces of those who watched this, as if having spent the morning at the funeral, nothing would have been better for them to see than a right good crash before lunch.

The Mayor's chauffeur, protesting, was half out of the car indeed, ready to bluff it out, knowing His Worship could use himself in a fight, chain and all. Then he stopped, seeing who it was behind the wheel of the Ford.

Robins stayed stone-faced and coldly watched the chauffeur clamber back into the Princess. Then, with a courtesy which he did not feel, Robins reversed the Ford, and waited for the Princess to pass him, which it did without a word from either of its occupants.

A minute later, Robins had his car parked in the churchyard and was trudging through the gates of the cemetery, making his way past the last of the mourners drifting home towards their dinner.

For a town of fifty thousand people, Robins thought, the cemetery was small. But no one, he reasoned, had had time to die in Newtown. Except people like Reg Farrow he supposed, and kids run over by motorcars, and the odd Irishman who fell off a crane. Mind you, the crime rate was high, Robins reminded himself. But it was a new town, Newtown was. Fifty thousand odd people jerked out of the warm, big buildings of the old cities and stuck into a bright intelligent life planned on the drawing board and not quite modified for people of this plane. Robins could understand why the crime rate was high.

He trudged over the eight acres of pasture (the scheduled expansion of the cemetery over the next twenty years) to the trim little corner, where the gravestones of the old village, long since swallowed up by the semi-detacheds, slumped under the willow trees. He passed the war memorial, briefly taking off his hat to that older generation who lost out at Gallipolli and on the Somme; then he was walking between Edwardian seraphs and 1930s urns to where Reg Farrow's grave lay heavy with wreaths, the smell of wet upturned soil and the scent of flowers all about it. He halted just short of the grave as he saw Mrs Farrow taking her leave of Charlie Barlow. Percy Twentyman saw him, and looked at him as if to say: 'Do you want a word with the widow, sir?' And Robins shook his head. He had written a letter – she'd seen enough senior officials for one week, he thought.

He watched Percy take her away from Barlow, up the path towards the church to rejoin her kids. Percy fancies her, he thought, as he watched the brusque but gentle way the ex-Liverpool sergeant helped her up the path. Doesn't do any harm at a time like this, he thought, for a late husband's friend to fancy his widow. He moved over to join Barlow.

'Charlie.'

'Hallo sir, I thought you'd get here.' Barlow kept the surprise out of his voice as he always did with Robins.

'Been in Manchester.'

'Oh, aye.'

They stood facing each other. Both over six foot. Both around fourteen stone, both big men, slightly pot belly with the amount of ale they'd supped. But both fit, although Robins smoked too much and Barlow ate too much.

They didn't like each other. But somehow this did not matter. Neither had time to think about it. Robins was the best CID boss the county had ever had; Barlow knew that and Robins knew Barlow was his best divisional chief.

'Been in Manchester,' Robins repeated. 'This maniac's in Manchester. It's seven to two –'

'Might backtrack, sir,' Barlow said. 'Might come back this way if he knows you're after him in the city.'

'Not a chance in hell,' Robins said, 'not a snowball's chance in hell fire!'

'Well, I'm thinking of staying round here for the rest of the day,' Barlow said stubbornly. 'Just in case.'

'In this weather?' Robins scoffed, then spat and banged his pockets for a cigarette. Barlow stood his ground.

'He might come back from Manchester. I've known murderers come to the grave of their victims like dogs to a smell.'

'You're daft Charlie Barlow,' Robins said. 'Dying of pneumonia. We'll be laying you down there along with Reg Farrow.' He pointed at the plot next to the grave. 'It's seven to two he's run to Manchester. He's a barmpot. He killed a policeman. He's run to a big city; he'll shoot someone else out of fright and he'll be knocked off.'

'Well if he's in Manchester,' Barlow said mildly, 'I've nowt to do but stay here, in case he comes back.'

'Comes back?' Robins said.

'Comes back!' Barlow said. 'Remember the Salisbury nutcase caught at the grave?'

'It's your division,' Robins said, 'but, it's you that's off your nut, Charlie.'

They were silent. Barlow moved back against an old statue of the angel Gabriel and fished for his cigarettes. He lit one, and watched Robins critically paying his last respects to old Reg; wondering whether Robins was thinking of Reg as a case to be solved, or as an old lost friend. After all, they'd joined the force in the same year – Robins, him, and Reg.

1934 was it? When the cotton was being twisted like a hangman's noose round the neck of the Lancashire worker, the three of them as cadets were escorting the strikers through the black towns; the miners were walking on London, and the depression was a great bellow of pain in the sky. And he, Charles Barlow, and Detective Chief Superintendent Robins, and the dead Reg Farrow would never forget it.

Yes, they'd never forget that they and many like them had voted in the Labour Government in '45, and went on voting for it long after the youngsters with the money had turned towards the Tories. They would never forget that hunger – and the luck that they were over six feet tall. These were the two facts that had shaped their lives; that had got them into the county force, when the rest of the men in the county were starving. For thirty years the force had fed, clothed and clobbered them; had worked them night and day, but now, had turned to them as their leaders in the angry sixties, in a boom time, when nobody knew what the hell the future would be.

Robins had been promoted Chief of the CID; he, Barlow, had survived to become head of tough, new Victor Division. Only old Reg hadn't made it; a horny old PC with a taste for the hard stuff, and a naughty hand with the women. He'd been a demon for work on a bicycle, and he'd been blasted to pieces by some nutcase out of Freemans. Only old Reg hadn't survived, Barlow thought, and he hoped that some stirrings of conscience were stirring in Robins' lousy soul as he stood at the grave there scratching his head.

Robins jammed his hat on and came back to where Barlow sheltered in the lee of the angel Gabriel. He took a cigarette from his subordinate and said 'ta'.

'They stood there silently for five minutes; the urge to speak growing on Barlow as he got more wet and the water got to trickling down the three rolls of flesh that were his chin. Soon they were inside the collar of his drip-dry shirt and mixing with the sweat of his body.

'But Robins stood thinking, saying nothing.

'Reg needn't have died,' Barlow said eventually with an effort to appear logical.

'What do you mean needn't?' It seemed Robins knew the argument was coming.

'If I'd had a crime patrol!' Barlow said firmly circling the grave.

'Look Charlie, crime patrols don't work! We've tried it on other divisions.'

'Why not on ours? We've a new divison, with new problems. If we'd had a crime patrol.' But Barlow was cut short.

'They don't work!' Robins shouted. 'They don't work! They don't ruddy well work!'

'Reg on his bicycle – what chance did he have against a nutcase with a shotgun?' Barlow was circling Reg's grave now, as if trying to raise from the dead to aid him in his argument.

'An ordinary PC on the beat has the same chance as Reg. An ordinary PC doing his duty –'

'This isn't the ruddy Stone Age, sir,' Barlow shouted, losing his temper.

And then Robins lost his temper. Three nights of a murder-hunt and the pain of Reg's death, left him tired and angry. 'Men have tried to reorganise the British police before now, Charlie Barlow, and where did it get them! New brooms sweep it clean every bloody year, with new ideas, new schemes, new men. Where does it get them? Into a swamp of misfortune.' His hand was banging chunks out of Gabriel's feet. 'It's the old things, tried by experience, that save us from catastrophe every time we fall into it, you know that.'

But Barlow wasn't listening. 'If we'd have had two crime cars with two tough PCs inside of them, roaming the town, wireless controlled, mobile bloody commandos, Reg'd be alive today!' Barlow nearly fell into Reg's grave, so excited did he get.

'Don't point the death of Reg Farrow at me,' Robins shouted back. 'Don't use a dead man to further your ambitions; to build up your own divisional empire bigger and bigger, Charlie Barlow. Don't use Reg Farrow as an excuse to get hold of fast cars and more men, and make a ruddy little Napoleon of yourself.'

'You know that's not why I'm asking,' Barlow retorted. 'If Reg Farrow was in a car –'

'Shut it Charlie! I'm warning you! I'm warning you!' It was an order. There was silence about the grave. Barlow sat down on a gravestone, oblivious of the wet soaking through the seat of his raincoat.

'I'm staying here till you find Reg's murderer,' he said to Robins. 'The only place he's likely to come back to is here, so if you don't catch him, I'll wait for him here.'

Robins looked at him and his voice was quieter. 'You'll die of bloody pneumonia Charlie, and where'll that get us. I'll just 'ave lost a good man!' He wheeled and left the graveside.

'Aye, you've lost one already,' Barlow shouted after him. 'We joined together didn't we, Reg, you and me.'

Robins turned and slowly came back towards him. Slowly he spoke to Barlow. 'We've tried crime cars in three or four divisions. They didn't work.'

'They'll work in Victor division – my division,' Barlow said. 'They'll have to work.'

'They need the cream of the young uniformed constables – what uniformed superintendent is going to hand over his best men to us – us in the CID?'

'I can get the best young men in Victor division to work for me,' Barlow said, 'and I can get permission from my Super to do it. Newtown's an open and wide division. We get all the old problems, but now need new ways to deal with them.'

'They need to be looked after, wet-nursed, cared for, by a seasoned detective-sergeant,' Robins went on. 'And there isn't one sergeant in your division who'd volunteer to do double duty in a bloody awful job like this.'

'There's my Sergeant Watt,' Barlow said. 'He'd be keen. My John Watt!'

'He's Divisional Crime Prevention Officer is your John Watt.'

'He'd volunteer like a shot, would John Watt.'

Robins looked at Barlow. 'I'll speak to Assistant Chief Constable about it.'

He left the graveyard and this time he did not look back.

Barlow watched him go. He dropped his rain-sodden cigarette and paced about the grave. Was Robins right, and he, Charlie Barlow, wrong? Was Reg's death an excuse for him to build up his own empire? Or was the dream of a crime patrol something that could become a reality?

They said at HQ that uniformed PCs working in cars for the CID was daft. They said at HQ that uniformed men and plainclothes detectives got on like chalk and cheese. Could a crew of not-quite-uniformed PCs, not-quite-CID detectives, in fact not quite one thing nor t'other, but a bastard form of commando and not anybody's responsibility but at everyone's beck and call, not quite paid any more, but working night and bloody day; could such a crew exist and come down like the wrath of God on Newtown's tearaways and cut the crime rate?

Barlow looked down on Reg's grave. He, Charlie and Robins had started off from the same beginnings. He and Robins had become big detectives and had lost track of Reg over the years. And now Reg was dead.

He knew that Reg's murderer would be caught and he didn't want to avenge Reg. But he wanted to do something for him. In these days of the sixties, Barlow thought, they needed new men, with tough methods, to come into the force. Something new, Barlow thought, to help the beatmen like Reg. Crime cars, Barlow thought. What we're going to have before the year is out in this division, is cars with anti-crime commandos in them. He looked down at the grave. Commandos! That would've made old Reg laugh, Barlow thought.

He moved up the hill to a place where he got the best view of the grave, and sat down at the bottom of a tree and huddled into himself against the rain, waiting and watching, and thinking of his new patrol and how it could be made to work. How it would spread over the country and over every force in the country. How he, Barlow, would be promoted to Chief Constable and soon get a Knighthood and become not a little Napoleon, but the biggest bloody Napoleon in the police force since Lord Trenchard. In this way he passed the wet afternoon.

Watt braked his Anglia at the edge of the grave. The night was black as pitch. He left his headlamps on and got out, switching off the engine. The rain was gone, but the night was still wet with its memory. There was a cold wind. Watt moved to the grave and picked up a wreath. In rain-blurred ink it said: 'To PC Reginald Farrow from Newtown UDC.' Watt laid it gently down again and picked up another. 'To PC Farrow,' Watt read out, 'shot down in execution of his duty. Newtown Co-operative Society.' He stared at the wreath-strewn grave for a second, and dropped the flowers into the black pit that was Reg Farrow's resting place. He stood a moment longer in contemplation, the wind in his face and blowing at his dirty mac.

'John! It's you!' Barlow was behind him coming out of the dark like a ghost.

'Aye,' Watt said. 'I was looking for you, sir.'

Barlow pulled him towards the shelter of a sepulchre. 'Give us a ciggy, John,' he said. 'I ran out about four, and I've had nowt to eat nor drink, and I'm fair starved with the wind. Fair starved! I must have been out here twelve hours or so.'

'They caught him,' Watts said.

Barlow was surprised. 'Caught him? The one that killed Reg?'

'Aye, in Manchester. With shotgun dabs an' all,' Watt said.

'When?' Barlow asked.

'Matter of an hour ago. I met Mr Robins at the station. He gave me this note to give you, sir.'

Watt passed the note to Barlow who took out his reading glasses, polished the wet off them and crouched by the headlamps to see what Robins had to say to him.

While he was doing this, Watt scrutinised the grave.

'How did it go at the funeral?'

'A big turn-out.'

'I'm sorry I wasn't here —'

'None of you was here,' Barlow said. 'You were out hunting his killer. If we weren't understaffed, you would have been here!'

'Well, he was caught in Manchester!' Watt said.

Barlow swore.

'You had the band had you?' Watt tried to visualise the burial.

'Yes the tuba went flat with the rain!'

'But it was right fair,' Watt insisted.

'Aye. It was a good send off for Reg.' Barlow paused. He had Robins' note open and was reading it, hardly believing what it said. FIND A SERGEANT AND FOUR YOUNG COMMANDOS AND I'LL GET YOU TWO CARS, OFFICIAL PERMISSION AND MONEY TO RUN A PATROL ON ONE MONTH'S TRIAL. I THINK IT'S DAFT, BUT I'LL DO IT FOR REG. JUST ONCE. COME AND SEE ME TOMORROW ABOUT IT. Thus the note ended. It was signed Robins.

'Aye.' Barlow got up satisfied. 'Reg had a right fair send off. Who was the killer?'

'Like you said. A barmpot from the Pool,' Watt said looking at more wreaths. 'Name of Barr. Headquarters have been on with a message. He's coughed. It's enough to top him.'

'Aye, if it's him, he'll be topped all right,' Barlow said looking at Reg's grave. There was silence except for the water soaking into the ground.

'They've got the trick cyclists on to him,' Watt said eventually.

'They always do when a policeman is murdered,' Barlow said.

'Still, if he's a nutcase they won't top him.'

'Aye, that's the law.' Barlow seemed to shake himself free of his thoughts. 'Aye, well that's that, if they've caught him.'

'Can I give you a lift back, sir?'

'Aye, you can do that John,' Barlow said.

They walked slowly to the Anglia, but before they got into it they took one long last look at the grave. Then they got in and the car drove away.

Watt drove fast through the wet night. It was getting on for twelve, and he'd been up, like his boss, all day and all the previous night. He wanted sleep fast.

'It's not an Alfa-ruddy-Romeo you're driving!' Barlow said to him. 'And you're not Stirling Moss, John Watt.'

'Sorry, sir,' Watt said patiently, braking to a steady fifty. He had forgotten for one moment that his boss was the worst second-seat driver in the north of England. He sensed Barlow's eyes glued nakedly to the green glow of the speedometer and he spoke to take his mind off the trip.

'So the funeral was right fair,' he asked him.

Barlow was watching the speedometer. 'There was a big turn-out.'

'The rain didn't spoil it?'

'No.'

'Well, they caught him,' Watt said.

'Aye, in Manchester. Thirty's the speed limit, John Watt.'

Watt went into third. 'If we had a crime patrol like you always say in Newtown, when the burglar alarm went at factory, it would have been two tough commandos that tearaway met, and not old Reg on his bicycle.' He went on making the kind of conversation he knew Barlow liked.

'You're not the only one who said we need crime cars.

The Boss said so in this note,' Barlow said, waving Robins' message in front of Watt's nose.

'What!!?' Watt said. The car swerved.

'I said the Boss is writing we need a couple of crime cars,' Barlow said. 'Are you driving this car John Watt or is there a fairy doing it for you under the bonnet?'

'Oh, aye,' Watt said suspiciously. 'What's Mr Robins say in the note?'

'They got that fund going for Doris Farrow – it's got twelve hundred pounds in it,' Watt said eventually.

'That's not bad,' Barlow said.

'It's only been a day and a half.' He paused. 'What did the Boss say in that note?'

'Never mind,' Barlow said. 'You still pigging it alone in your house!' he added.

'Aye,' Watt said, puzzled.

'Wife not come back?' Barlow asked.

'Nay, and she won't,' Watt said.

'You should have married a woman who understood CID work,' Barlow said.

'It didn't suit her.'

'What?' Barlow looked up.

'My work,' Watt said. 'It didn't suit her.'

'Aye,' Barlow said.

'She won't come back – she's not that sort,' Watt said, ticking off the weeks.

'With her mother, is she?' Barlow asked innocently.

'No – gone to London.'

'Nay!' said Barlow.

Watt looked up. 'She won't come back – not from London!'

Barlow paused. *Now*, he thought. 'I asked, because I'm telling you something,' he said slowly.

'I thought so, sir.' *Now* he's going to ask me to do something, Watt thought.

'What the Boss said at the funeral was that this division needs two crime patrols, working twenty-four hours a day, manned by the hardest and brightest lads we can lay our hands on. And you're going to be in charge of them.'

Barlow closed his eyes in terror, as in the wet Watt braked the car, shrieking to a halt.

'Me?' he said astonished, switching off the engine.

'Aye, you John,' Barlow said, opening his eyes.

'Look sir, I'm Crime Prevention Officer for this division.' Watt was hissing like a killer. 'Remember? I work twenty-four hours a day as it is.'

'You won't be the first feller who has to squeeze forty-eight hours work into a twenty-four-hour day. Me, for example,' Barlow said comfortably.

Watt's eyes were blazing with rage. 'You've got it all worked out.'

'And with no wife you've got more time to spend on crime patrols,' Barlow explained logically.

'I said you'd got it all worked out,' Watt shouted.

There was a long silence which Barlow broke. 'You said yourself that Reggie would be alive if –'

'All right. All right. All right,' Watt said. 'I'll do it.' He started the car. Barlow sighed with relief. 'That's better. I told the Boss you'd volunteer like a shot. Keen feller is John Watt, I said.'

'Aye,' Watt said bitterly, 'I suppose you want me picking the crews.'

'Yes,' said Barlow. 'By lunchtime tomorrow. We're going to see the Chief at County HQ.'

'You've got it all worked out haven't you?'

'Drive more careful John Watt, we've a big day in the morning,' Barlow said, having, as always, the last word.

2

By the following morning the rain was gone, brushed over the Pennines by an early wind. By midday, the sun was out, and spread all over Lancashire. It brought out with it the kids who turned the streets into a fiesta of laughing and crying and fighting and dancing, while over the walls and through the windows and out of the doors their mothers talked about the goings on in the buildings.

Of all the towns in the county, the sun seemed to shine its hardest over Newtown, and under its influence the clear morning air was splintered by the shouts and cries of ten thousand children and the scolding talk of their mothers. And right bang in the middle of this

Tower of Babel, at what was known as The Centre, where four roads starred themselves out, dividing the town neatly into four sections (North Vale, South Vale, East Vale, and West Vale), lay the police station.

The Office, Barlow called it. Home, John Watt called it. The Stir, Clink, Bog, Nick, depending on what you are, and where you come from. The people of Newtown, coming from far and wide, and rich in character, had many other names for it if asked, which they weren't, except by students on sociological surveys from the universities of the south.

By one o'clock, Barlow was out at the door slapping his belly in the heat of the sun, thinking about a game of golf for tomorrow, Sunday, and wondering what Robins would have to say at Headquarters that afternoon.

Watt's Anglia arrived amidst a host of dancing three-year-old juvenile delinquents, who would hardly let it into the station.

Barlow, taking pity, strode out and sent them running like a school of fish frightened by a plunging stone.

Inside the car, he and Watt exchanged a good morning and a course was set firmly on the forty-mile route to the County Headquarters, via two pleasant pubs which always had a welcome for the Chief Inspector. Whatever the outcome of the talk, Barlow thought, at least they'd get a good lunch out of it.

Hardly were they gone than Twentyman was out sniffing the air. To one side of the police station is the fire station, and on this day its gaunt red engines had been brought out into the sun where they seemed to drowse like dragons, all bright and fierce in their paint and brass trimmings. And there, under the dark side of one of them, where its pump and ladders cast a shadow not over long but adequate for its purpose, lay Police Constable Fancy Smith, of Leigh, taking a crafty kip after his lunchtime pint; well clear he thought of Sergeant Twentyman's sharp eyes.

Fancy, so called for the Italian cut of his civilian gear, his combed hair and his way with women, weighed round on sixteen stone for his twenty-three years, and was celebrated for the way he could roll on the toughest tearaway and squash him to death. Apart from his weight, he had a sharp Lancashire tongue which he used to all manner of folk, be they Teds or the bosses, and he was sometimes liked by neither. But at the moment his tongue was hanging out useless, for his mouth, open like the Mersey Tunnel was emitting snores of great loudness, an uncommon noise, which once heard can never be forgotten.

It was the noise of his snores in fact that led Twentyman swiftly across the tarmac that adjoined the police station to the fire park until he stood above the sleeping figure.

'Get up you whore,' he said. 'Get up and find me Jock Weir, you lazy, sleeping cod of a man.'

'I'm off duty, Sergeant,' Fancy said, talking and still trying to stay asleep, a difficult thing to do.

'Off duty!!' said the Sergeant. 'Off duty!! In my patch you are never off duty you lazy, filthy insubordinate –'

'And Jock Weir,' Fancy said, turning on his side, 'is off duty too. Both our scales start tonight at ten.'

'Off duty!' Twentyman said. 'What do you think you are, a policeman or something in fancy dress?'

'I'm wearing me uniform in case there's a national emergency,' Fancy said. 'But short of it,' Fancy continued, 'I'm staying here in the sun, and Jock Weir is playing Rugby League against the City. Our scales start at ten. And two to ten we're off duty.'

'Right,' Twentyman said, retreating furious. 'Right – I'll have to get someone that's on duty, won't I?'

'Aye,' Fancy said. 'You will. Get Lynch or Bob Steele, they're always lazing about.'

Twentyman walked back to the station. He turned and shouted, his voice carrying across the tarmac. 'How you can talk of laziness Fancy Smith when you're lying there in the sun like a day tripper at Blackpool.'

'Aye,' said Fancy stretching himself luxuriously. 'I know me rights – we folk from Leigh don't let anyone push us around. We know our rights in Leigh.'

Twentyman banged into the station. 'Steele!' he shouted. Steele, who was creeping out by the back door. froze.

'Yes, Sergeant Twentyman,' Bob Steele said. His scarred tough face was inscrutable.

'Are you sneaking out the back way?' Twentyman came round and looked at him.

'I've just come in,' Steele said, 'and I'm *going* out. I'm not *sneaking* out, it's me dinner hour.'

'Steele,' Twentyman said, 'you're on duty.'

'I'm on two till ten,' Steele said, 'and it's not yet two – so I'm off duty.'

Twentyman's face went purple.

'Why not get hold of Lynch?' Steele said quickly. 'He's the feller you need.'

'You're right!' Twentyman said appeased. 'I want the crossroads to the race-course watched this tea-time – and Lynch can do it,' he said satisfied, 'I knew I'd find the right man. You tell him.'

'I don't know where Lynch is,' Steele said.

'You're a copper aren't you, find him,' Twentyman said, picking up the telephone.

'I don't know where he is, and Janey'll kill me if I'm late for me dinner. Can't you –'

'You find Lynch before two, wherever he is!' Twentyman used his tough voice. 'That's an order you cheeky young. . .'

Steele got out quickly. 'If I see him I'll let him know you want him. Ta-ra, Sarge,' he said, his voice coming floating back to the Sergeant. But the phone in Twentyman's hands attracted his attention before he could call him back.

'Fire station,' the distorted voice said through the phone. 'Newtown Fire Station.'

'Hullo Jim, this is Percy,' Twentyman said. 'Are you having a turn-out this afternoon?'

'Aye, Percy, in about half an hour. It's a practice alarm.'

'Good, Jim. Will you ring me just before you're about to go?' Twentyman said sweetly.

'Why?' Jim said.

'There's one of my men kipping underneath your No. 2 turntable engine. No! Don't get him out Jim,' Twentyman went on quickly. 'I just want you to go ahead with the turn-out and find out what happens when a man like my Fancy Smith wakes up to find the world ringing like an alarm bell, and five fire engines charging at him like summat out of a horror comic.'

'But he might get kilt,' Jim said protesting.

'Never!' Twentyman said. 'Fancy kilt? You're joking!'

Bob Steele came up the road at speed, his face shining with sweat, his big boots still shining with the morning's polish and the baggy bottoms of his pants flapping in the breeze. The whole morning he'd been in court where he'd withstood the cross-questioning of one Mick Doolan, an Irish lawyer, whose client, young Maddigan, had flattened a bus conductor the previous Saturday night. Young Maddigan was now on his way to jail; Mick Doolan was being besieged by angry Maddigans in the Court Tavern; and Bob was hurrying home to Janey, his wife, for his dinner. Despite the thirst on him, which would have warped the enamel of a statue of St Joseph, Bob was needing his dinner. He was determined to be home on time, what with Janey still simmering over the argument last night, and Lynch, off duty, no doubt hanging around her after his food.

That quick look into the station had been a mistake Bob now knew, for it put him on the horns of a ruddy dilemma. If Lynch was not at Bob Steele's house, eating his, Bob Steele's meal, he'd have to go back and tell Sergeant Twentyman that he couldn't find Lynch. And Twentyman then would have him on ruddy point duty outside of the racecourse all afternoon instead. What kind of a job was that, Bob thought, for any man or beast?

On the other hand, Bob reasoned, if Lynch was at his house eating his meal and chatting up his wife then he, Steele, would have missed his dinner and run home for nowt. In that case he could have had a pint or two outside the court. What's more, he knew that conniving, bog-trotting Irishman from Belfast, Herbert Lynch, would have been filling Janey full of lies about who was responsible for the booze-up on Sunday night when both of them had got back in Simpson's grocery van the worse for wear.

Bob swore. It was six of one, half a dozen of another, he thought. You can't win every time, especially against Lynch. But he quickened his pace.

Janey Steele had a black eye. She was a pretty girl of twenty-five years and looked good even over a kitchen stove. She had a good body, good legs and a quick smile, when she could use it, which wasn't often, with her husband and Lynch always up to their surreptitious beer-drinking, gambling, on-the-town ways. That just got her down. As she fried up more chips for a hungry Lynch, she wondered when Bob would be home from court; whether he'd have stopped off for a drink on the way; and whether he knew that her mother with her middle-class fusspot ideas was coming over to visit them for tea. She walked into the living room where Lynch sat at the table eating Bob's meal, and drinking Bob's ale.

'Very tasty Janey,' Lynch said. 'Have you a drop more sauce?' He looked up at her, a dark Irishman of thirty or so with mocking eyes, a thin face and a lean body.

'There was a half bottle in that, Lynch,' Janey said, 'before you started ruining it with sauce. What can you taste but sauce?'

Lynch changed the subject hastily. 'Let's have a look at your eye, love. Aye, it's a shiner!'

'It's all right,' Janey said stiffly. 'Get on with your eating and don't mention it before Bob, it's a sore point.'

'It's a sore eye – you're married to a barbarian,' Lynch said.

'It was an accident,' Janey said.

'Don't give me none of that,' Lynch said, eating his last chip. 'An accident, I ask you. How did it happen?'

Janey went into the kitchen. 'You're a prying Irish policeman,' she shouted back at him.

'How did it happen, Janey?' Lynch followed her into the kitchen.

'He came in late for his dinner last Sunday, and he promised he'd be early.'

'Now Janey,' Lynch said, taking a pear out of the open tin with his fingers.

'So I went for him with the hotpot and he tried to stop me. That's all,' she said simply, taking the tin away from Lynch's thieving hands.

'Now Janey,' Lynch said reprovingly. She turned on him with a saucepan high in her hand.

'And if it was you who'd come through that door, I would have killed you, Lynch. It's you with your drinking and habits learned in the Pool that kept him from his dinner,' she shouted.

Lynch's face went all innocent. 'Me? Me? All we had was a quiet drink and an argument,' he said indignantly.

Bob Steele entered the garden of what was known as a police dwelling. If he's not here, Bob reasoned, I'll get Fancy Smith to tell Sergeant Twentyman I couldn't find him. He turned the key in the lock. If he is here, he thought, I'll hit him, so help me God, I'll hit him.

He walked into the living room. An empty plate, an empty mug, two empty tins of ale and an empty sauce bottle littered the empty table by his empty seat. Lynch's head was poked round the corner from the kitchen.

'Lynch!' Steele shouted. 'Janey!'

'She's a good cook, Janey is,' Lynch said, trying to find at all cost one friend in the house.

Steele pointed a finger at him. 'I married her to cook for me – not the rest of the Newtown Police Force,' he stopped, and then with vengeance said, 'Twentyman's after you for point duty.'

Lynch groaned and swore as Janey entered the room. She saw her tall husband looking very sternly his twenty-eight years and fourteen stone of raw muscle.

'Janey, where's me dinner?' Steele said, his pockmarked face and grey eyes cold and angry.

'He's et it,' she said and stalked out.

'He's et it?' Steele repeated. 'Et it?'

Lynch smiled glassily, 'Your dinner happened to be getting cold so I saw it off, Bob.'

'You saw it off! Just like that!' Steele said, taking off his coat slowly. 'You et it. Without thinking of me coming out of court after all me talking! You et me dinner.' The enormity of it was slowly growing like a great storm in his belly.

Janey entered again with a pie and two chips on the plate. 'Here's your dinner, Bob Steele. Eat it and shut it,' she said.

'Where's all the ruddy chips?' Steele said exploding.

'I'm frying more chips,' she said.

'He's et all the chips?' pointing at Lynch, almost gibbering.

'Bob Steele, you'd begrudge a teetotaller a drink of water,' Lynch said. The pity, the concern in his voice fooled Steele for one moment into thinking it was Lynch who was the victim of this argument. But he silently counted ten then clenched his fist and moved towards him as Janey burst in with extra chips.

'Here's your chips, and you shouldn't be having them,' she said, plonking them on the table and saving Lynch from a just and proper beating.

'And why not?' Steele said, forgetting Lynch, and sitting down reaching for the vinegar.

'Because you're getting fat,' Janey said.

'Fat?' Steele was staggered.

'And you sup too much ale.' Janey heaped on the indignities. 'And you bet on horses.'

'You're not married to a monk,' Steele said.

'Will you shut it up, both of you,' Lynch said reproachfully, 'arguing away.'

'You didn't even kiss me good morning, Bob,' Janey shouted, looking for some kind of offensive weapon.

'With Lynch eating my dinner,' Steele said. 'And after last night's row.'

'Bob Steele!' Janey said. 'You go on like a record!'

She ran out of the room and slammed the door. Steele lowered himself silently and thoughtfully into his chair, picked up a chip and wondered how a man in his position, hungry, unfed, almost cuckolded, and reasonable, could come into his house and cause so much anger against himself.

Lynch came over timorously and poured himself a mug of tea – to the top. He heaped in about six spoons of sugar and half a bottle of milk. What was left of the tea in the pot, a tiny trickle, he poured earnestly into Bob's mug. Bob looked at him, wondering just how far Lynch could go before committing suicide. Lynch looked away at the wall where it was stained.

'Is that the stain the hotpot made?' Lynch asked.

'What do you know about that hotpot?' Steele said, with his mouth full of hot chips.

'It's the sort of stain a hotpot would make if thrown by an angry wife,' Lynch said, critically, looking at the wall as if deducing it all.

'Well, look at broken chair where a very frightened husband threw himself to avoid being blinded for life,' Steele said, pointing at the chair in the corner.

'You shouldn't have hit her,' Lynch said. 'Bit her with love, but not hit her.'

'Stop acting like God Almighty, Lynch,' Steele said.

'And get to your cross-road at race-course. Twentyman's orders. Go on, get going.'

Lynch got up, hitched up his trousers. 'Aye – Twentyman. He's the devil incarnate. Janey!' he shouted. 'I'm off!'

She came out of the kitchen sullenly. ''Bye Herbert,' she said.

'If you want to leave him,' Lynch said, 'you know where you can stay.'

'Get to your cross-roads,' Steele growled, 'and with luck someone might run over you.'

'Ta-ra,' Lynch said. He took the last chips off Steele's plate, ate them, and left the room. The front door banged, and Steele went into the bathroom. He pulled from under the bath a bottle of ale which he'd stuck there, well clear of Lynch's thirsty hands. Janey followed him in as he unscrewed the bottle.

'I don't know why you feed him,' Steele said.

'You sup ale with him,' she said.

'I don't see why I have to pay for his food and his ale,' he said. 'He'll be after you next.'

'Not if you love me,' she said. He took no notice. She turned to the kitchen, disappointed. He followed her quietly, creeping up on her as she slowly reached the sink. He caught her, and she shrieked out.

'Married three years and you fall for the same trick every time,' he said. 'You're a barmpot.' He kissed her black eye. They held each other roughly and talked spasmodically.

'I love you so much,' she said. 'Bob, so much, so much, it frightens me. Supposing anything should happen?'

'It's a rough area – they don't like police, nor policemen's wives about here,' Steele whispered.

'I'm just afraid for you,' she said. 'Reggie Farrow for instance.'

'You can get killed walking across the road these days,' Steele said, kissing her.

'You all say that,' she said. 'All of you.'

'It'll be all right, once these new estates settle down.' He kissed her – 'once' –

'You all say once this, and once that happens it'll be all right. By that you'll be dead and who will care.'

'I'm sorry about that eye,' he said, changing the subject.

She giggled. 'It's done me good with the neighbours. I get some respect along this street now, better than a stretch in Strangeways.' She giggled like a schoolgirl, tried to get a look at it in her reflection on the window glass.

He kissed her and forced her, in a way she knew and liked, towards the hall and up towards their bedroom.

'Bob – you will look after yourself, won't you? You will. You won't let what happened to Reggie Farrow happen to –'

'I'll look after myself,' he said. 'One day I'm going to become Detective Chief Superintendent of all the county.'

Then he pulled her laughing up the stairs.

3

Watt's Anglia stopped outside of the headquarters of the County Constabulary.

'You've got the names of the four fellers that you want fixed firmly in your mind?' Barlow asked John Watt.

'Aye,' Watt said shortly. 'You know, sir, I still feel I've been taken for a ride on this job –'

'You swore on your word of honour last night in the pouring wet rain, John Watt,' Barlow said earnestly, 'in fact on poor Reg Farrow's grave.'

'It was in this car,' John Watt said. 'Not in front of Reg's grave.'

'All right John, in this car, I concede the point,' Barlow said. 'You did not actually swear in front of Reg Farrow's open grave. But it was just like swearing in front of an open grave of a dear lost friend, John,' he went on, as Watt tried to get out of the car and away from Barlow, whose persuasive mood he knew. 'John, you must keep your word on this, or you'll he haunted till the day you leave the force.'

'Aye – by you,' John Watt said. 'You'd never let me forget it, would you?'

'And don't lose your temper with Mr Robins, John, or he might cancel the whole project.'

Watt grunted. Barlow got out of the car comfortably sober, and on the whole well-disposed towards life, in a way that can only be got by an hour spent downing a few pints during Saturday lunch time at a country pub.

Robins strode across the car park towards them. *He* was not so well disposed towards life. In fact, he was not at all disposed towards anything.

'I've spent the lunchtime talking to the Assistant Chief Constable about furthering your bloody ambitions on this crime car patrol,' he told Barlow. 'Come into the club and let's get a drink before they close.' He wheeled and strode ahead without waiting for them. 'I've had nowt to eat nor drink since last night,' he said. They caught up with him fast. He had to be humoured.

'Sir!' A police cadet was running alongside them.

'What is it, son?' Robins said curtly.

'There's been a break-in on the premises of Midland Aviation. They've arrested a feller.'

'The crime car could've gone to that, sir, if you were using them,' Barlow said. Robins gave him a look that could have felled an archbishop.

'Midland Aviation. All security work isn't it?' Robins said.

'Yes it is, sir,' the cadet said, getting out of breath keeping up with Robins' rapid strides.

'Send a Special Branch man down to find out what it's all about son. OK?'

'Aye sir.' The cadet spun off, and ran for the wireless room.

The three detectives reached the low-lying building of the club. 'In you get, John Watt,' Robins said. 'And order for us pints and chasers of whisky. I'll pay.'

'Aye, sir,' John Watt said, knowing Mr Robins had something to say to Barlow. He shut the door behind them. Barlow and Robins stayed outside in the sun, watching the police cars cavorting on the skid pan, belting down the hundred-yard straight; putting on their brakes and taking the skid broadside on; correcting on the throttle and coming off the other end straight.

'They'll get no training, your boys,' Robins said, with gloomy satisfaction.

'They won't will they? No driving instruction up here?' Barlow said.

'Not this first month.'

'So you think it'll last longer than a month?'

'It's an experiment.' Robins looked at Barlow.

'An experiment which I hope works, Charlie. I just hope it does, for your sake and mine, because I've gone out on a limb to give you this chance. You don't know what they're saying in there.' Robins' arm embraced the whole of County Headquarters. 'Uniformed police careering round in cars like summat out of a Hollywood film, they're saying. The next thing you'll be wanting, they say, is to arm them with machine guns.'

'No, sir, I just want me two cars,' Barlow said. 'That's all.'

'That's all! !' Robins said. 'Let's have a drink and see your John Watt – he is keen to do it, is he?'

'Like a shot, he volunteered, sir – all my lads are keen, sir.'

'Good. Good,' Robins said. 'Because if he and they aren't, the idea falls thro'.'

He entered the bar and Barlow followed him, saying a silent prayer that his tough sergeant would not antagonise the Boss and kill the whole thing stone dead before it had even got started.

The bar was empty. It was Saturday and all the men except for duty officers were at home, watching football or racing or sleeping off their lunches or even working. John Watt had the drinks waiting for them, lonely, on the counter. They each took their pint, raised it, said 'cheers', and took a decent draught.

'Pint drinking in the dinner hour,' Robins said, 'is not a polite way to behave, but today's special in't it Charlie?'

'It is, sir.'

'And any road I don't care fer jokers who pretend they're not pint drinkers and then put away two half instead,' said Robins, draining the glass.

'Sepulchres,' Barlow said. 'Of an indeterminate white. They do that sort of trick.'

'Will they top this fellow you caught in Manchester, sir?' John Watt changed the conversation with subtle flattery unusual for him.

'Would you like another, sir?' Barlow said.

'Yes, just one,' Robins said, 'And a sandwich. A lunch that's all liquid does more harm than good, I'd say.'

Barlow made the order. Robins turned on John Watt and looked at him almost for the first time; looked at the slightly grizzled fair hair of the tough small blue-eyed sergeant of thirty-eight, whose wife had left him and who was a bit of a dark horse in the force.

'They won't top him,' Robins said, noting the intelligent lonely eyes of the man.

'Is he a barmpot?' Barlow said over his shoulder at the bar.

'Medical history as long as your arm,' Robins said. 'Still it's had one good effect.'

'Aye, the new crime cars,' Barlow said.

'You're taking over i/c crime patrol,' Robins told Watt rather than asked him.

'So I believe, sir,' Watt said.

Robins pushed his finger into Watt's chest. 'Get keen young lads with a knack for catching thieves. That's what we want.' He spoke like a Pope interpreting the words of God.

'Aye!' Watt said, noncommittal.

Robins drained his glass. 'I don't care what they look like, but get 'em hard. They're soft, that's what's the trouble with the young generation. They're soft, aren't they Charlie, soft.'

'Aye,' Barlow said. 'Stick most of them in warm water, and they'd ruddy well dissolve.'

Watt stiffened. 'There are some good lads amongst them, sir.'

'Ruddy soft lot,' Robins said, chasing the pint with a double scotch.

'I said they're not all soft,' Watt said. Then he realised he'd spoken too loudly for a sergeant. Robins was not a man used to being contradicted.

'Well, who have you got?' Robins said softly. 'Name young men you don't think are just jelly babies.'

'Go on tell him, John,' Barlow said, praying silently the same old prayer; that Watt wasn't going to explode the scheme before it was even started. To get hold of Robins on an empty stomach – Barlow cursed silently – this was the height of bad luck.

'Name your men, Sergeant Watt,' Robins said abruptly, in his eyes the contempt of a man who dares a challenge to his authority.

'Tell him John,' Barlow said quietly.

There was a silence. Watt looked up slowly. 'Herbert Lynch,' Watt said.

Even Barlow was thunderstruck by Watt's choice.

'Lynch?' Robins said, the wind taken out of his sails. 'He's not a copper – he's a con man!'

'He can use himself,' Watt said stubbornly. He tapped his glass on the bar. 'I've seen him. He can use himself.'

'Lynch?' Robins said, still amazed.

'He can use himself,' Watt said.

'I said for a crime car crew, not a ruddy circus. He's all talk and ladies, is Lynch.'

'I said he can use himself,' Watt said, banging his glass. 'He's a good man. And.' Watt added, 'he can catch thieves.'

There was silence. 'All right,' Robins said slowly, 'so you choose Lynch. Put a reliable man with him will you.'

'Steele,' Watt said.

'Steele?' Robins tried to remember. 'Him that's new at Newtown? Don't think I know him.'

'Him with the pretty wife, Janey,' Barlow said.

'Aye,' Watt said. 'Very attractive wife.'

'Well keep Lynch away from her, that's all I say,' Robins said.

'Steele can look after his own!' Watt said shortly. 'That's why I'd put him with Lynch.'

'All right.' Robins swallowed his second whisky. 'If you put those together it might work. But only a barmpot would do it.'

Watt was silent.

'What about the second car then?' Robins said.

'Smith, sir,' Watt said.

'Which Smith?'

'Fancy Smith,' Watt said.

'Him from Leigh,' Barlow said encouragingly. 'Him that thinks Leigh is the centre of the earth.'

'You pick 'em don't you,' Robins said bitterly. 'I fight all morning, miss me dinner hour for your new crime patrols – and look at the men you pick. Lynch, new boy Steele, Fancy Smith!'

Watt was silent.

'Fancy Smith's not a copper,' Robins said eventually. 'He's a Ted in copper's uniform.'

'He's from Leigh, and he can use himself,' Watt said, imitating Fancy's famous pugilistic pose.

'He can dress himself too, can't he,' Robins said. 'He wears those Eyetalian clothes, off duty, doesn't he?'

'Well he's from Leigh – it's in Lancashire,' Watt said.

'Well he looks as if he comes from ruddy Rome,' Robins said. 'You pick 'em, don't you.'

'Aye,' Watt said.

'Who would you put with him John?' Barlow said, hoping that Watt would pick on one feller who would be favourites with the Boss.

'Jock Weir. Him that plays Rugby League for Wigan.'

'Aye,' Barlow said smoothly. 'That's a good choice John.'

'He's hard all right,' Robins conceded.

'He's fast with a ball. There's no doubt on it, sir,' Barlow said.

'Is he bright?' Robins asked.

'He's all right in a bundle,' Watt said.

'Is he bright I said?' Robins looked irritable.

'Brighter than he looks,' Watt said. 'And he can use himself.'

'Use himself! I know it's important John Watt,' Robins said, 'but can you think of any qualities these fellers have, apart from their ability to look after themselves in a barney?'

Before Watt could argue their glasses were whipped away. 'Time gentlemen please,' the steward said, and Robins' attention for the while was diverted from the matter in hand, for in matter of fact there was still two minutes of drinking time left, and all three from long, long experience knew it.

Jock Weir, subject of three senior detectives' valuable conversation over lunchtime ale, pushed his way through a fighting crowd outside of the city stand at the Borough Park. Jock hated himself, hated the crowd, hated the match that was to start in twenty minutes and wondered why he played football at all.

It was the third round in cup, and he felt sick. He pushed on visualising the omelette and buttermilk that was floating around inside of him, and which was all he could stomach before any important match. He thrust his way through miners and cotton workers shouting for tickets; past school boys hunting autographs. He hammered on the locked door by the training rooms knowing he was going to throw up with excitement.

The door was opened and Jock pushed past Doc Rafferty who had opened it, and made for the downstairs lavatory as screaming fans were forced back and out by the old man. Cursing, the Doc locked the door and hurried back to the lav where Jock knelt on the floor vomiting. The Doc reached his side and patted his back making soothing noises. Stevenson, the opposing centre, passed by and stopped, watching Jock without pity.

'You'll be in there again before the day is out,' Stevenson said pleasantly, 'because I am going to put a boot through your stomach.'

'Set off, Stevenson,' the Doc said. 'One more word like that and I'll have you reported.' Stevenson moved towards the Borough changing room, but he came back.

'You watch it, you bluebottle,' he said. 'You can't have me booked for playing a rough game, not even if I kill you.'

Then he left as the old doc slammed the lavatory door.

Jock continued to cough. 'Psychological warfare,' Doc said patting him on the back. 'That's all he's talking.'

'Where's he playing?' Jock said, wiping the sick off his mouth, and standing unsteadily.

'The Borough have moved him into the centre, Jock,' the Doc said.

'Aye,' Jock said feeling for the door, 'I'm playing in the centre.'

'Their plan is –' said Doc, his seventy-year-old wiry body supporting the sick Scot, '– the plan of the Borough is to blow a hole in the middle.'

'I'm in the middle,' Jock said, walking down the drab green and brown corridor that smelled of Ellerman's and mud.

'Then they plan to go through the middle.'

'Aye, that's what they're planning,' the Doc said seriously.

'I'll take Stevenson with me when I go, I'll kick his crutch in; he'll never bed another woman if I can help it,' Jock said.

'Aye, that's right, lad, you stop 'm, lad.'

Jock was crying as he reached the dressing room; crying himself into the deadly passionate football player which had made him the star of the city's Rugby League team and its only unpaid professional.

'I'll knacker him for life,' Jock shouted, as he undressed with the rest of the team helping him into his kit.

'That's right, you nail him,' the captain said.

Outside in the pub across the road called The British Sportsman, the honest British punters were laying evens on Jock being carried off the field before half time.

Watt and Barlow followed Robins into the information room; Sally Clarkson and Katy Hoskins, blonde and brunette, were on duty breathing a kind of rhythm into the flashing lights on the large map that covered two sides of the room.

It always fascinated John Watt to see the hundred or so lights flicking on and off on the map; and know that somewhere in the county one of the hundred cars on active duty would be speeding down a road being guided by Katy or Sally to an accident, an illness or a fight.

'It's quiet,' Robins said.

'It's the sunshine, sir. Thieves don't work this weather,' Barlow said.

'Wait till tonight, the drunks who won't want to come home. With the full moon, we'll have more calls tonight than we've had any Saturday,' Katy said.

'If it's dry, it's the drunks and domestics,' said Sally plugging in a car-to-car call.

'And if it's wet,' said Katy, 'it's the drivers killing each other on the roads.'

'You can't win can you,' said Watt.

'If you've got crime cars you can,' said Barlow cheerfully.

'What we need are ex-para Rugby players, like Jock Weir from Malaya,' Watt said, going through the incident charts. 'Look at the number of these fights last Friday night.'

'Lancashire's not a jungle, you know, Sergeant,' Robins said.

'There's parts of it – is as near as I'd come to one, sir,' Watt said. 'Newtown on a Friday night, sir. Seaport when the whalers come in, and the streets are awash wi' ale and then sometimes the whole ruddy division's a mix up. It's this rebuilding and rehousing of all these new factories,' he gestured at the map. 'And Newtown's only a part of the county.'

'Do you hear that, Charlie? Do you hear what he's saying?' Robins said, walking up and under the huge winking map which towered over him. 'It's pioneering lad, that's what it is. Newtown's new with new roads, new factories. Some folk expect 'em to walk off blue prints just like that. And the people to settle in just like that. It's pioneering that's what it is. And that means problems.'

'It's a jungle, sir, if I may say so,' Watt said curtly, as if dismissing it.

Robins was more curious than angry at Watt's bitterness. 'You're a bit of a puritan, Sergeant Watt, aren't you. Where are you from?'

'Lancaster, sir,' Watt said.

'You young lads,' Robins said gently. 'You're not broad-minded – there's nowt wrong with Lancashire, lad, that's not human nature.'

There was silence, except for Sally and Katy giving out the afternoon messages to the cars.

'All right,' Robins said, dismissing them. 'Get your crews and start catching the villains – catching them mind you, not chasing 'em.'

'Yes sir,' Watt said.

'Bye Charlie.' Robins shook Barlow's hand. 'Good luck Sergeant Watt, and remember – there's nowt wrong with Lancashire, but human nature.'

'Yes sir,' Watt repeated.

'Katy,' Robins said. 'Tell me offhand. Any radio prefix been made available for Mr Barlow's experimental cars?'

'Yes sir,' Katy said. 'They'll be using the letter Z. It's all we've got free.'

'Hear that Charlie?' Robins said. 'The letter Z is yours.'

'Z cars.' Barlow let it roll round on his tongue. 'I think it might stick, what do you think John?'

Watt shrugged. 'It could, sir.'

'Z cars,' Barlow said again. 'Goodbye, sir, and thank you.'

'Don't forget Charlie,' Robins said. 'One month.'

'Z Cars,' Barlow said pleased.

'And catch the beggars, don't just chase 'em!' Robins shouted after them. But Watt and Barlow were gone.

'Anything more from that feller arrested on the premises of Midland Aviation,' Robins asked Katy.

'Yes,' she said, without a slight glimmer of a smile. 'He's turned out to be their managing director – otherwise the county's very quiet.'

What's A Ghoul Like You Doing In A Place Like This?

BY PETER LESLIE

The Avengers, *which made its debut on Britain's ABC network in January 1961, has subsequently proved to be as influential in the history of crime-on-TV as the BBC's Z-Cars. Interestingly, too, this one hundred and sixty-one-episode-long cult series now perhaps best remembered for the exotic, leather-clad female assistants who accompanied the dandified crimebuster John Steed (played by Patrick Macnee) had actually evolved from a very traditional 'cops and robbers' series called* Police Surgeon *shown in 1960. Although* Police Surgeon *had not been a ratings winner, letters from viewers indicated that the young star, Ian Hendry, was very popular and it became the task of ABC's head of drama, Sydney Newman, to find a new series for him. Newman, who would later mastermind* Doctor Who *for the BBC, decided to turn Hendry into a man with a mission who would outwit murderers, criminals and other law-breakers with a mixture of bravery and tongue-in-cheek wit. To help Dr David Keel — as Hendry's character was known — Newman introduced a rather shadowy undercover agent named Steed, and in casting the urbane Patrick Macnee in the part took what was to prove arguably the most crucial step in the creation of a legend. As* The Avengers, *the two men were an instant hit — but at the end of the first season Hendry indicated that he did not want to continue. So Macnee became the central character instead, complete with a bowler, furled umbrella and a female aide in the curvaceous shape of Honor Blackman, whose leather outfits and judo skill made her an instant focus of viewer and media attention. Male members of the audience in particular had never seen anything quite like her before!*

Two years later, when The Avengers *was just about to be transmitted in colour, Honor Blackman decided to give up her role, and was replaced by Diana Rigg as the luscious Emma Peel. She, too, left the series in 1969 after a very successful partnership with Macnee, and opened the way for his third partner, Linda Thorson, playing the sexy and exuberant Tara King. The last episode to feature this pair, appropriately entitled 'Getaway', was shown in September 1969, but the story did not end there. For in 1976, Albert Fennell and Brian Clemens, who had been key figures in the writing of the old series, created* The New Avengers *in which Macnee once again set out in his own inimitable style to bring law-breakers to justice – now aided by two assistants, Joanna Lumley (some years ahead of her* Absolutely Fabulous *success) and Gareth Hunt. Unfortunately, the series did not have quite the originality as its predecessor and lasted for just twenty-six episodes. Notwithstanding this, the legend of* The Avengers *was already assured and the status it enjoys has diminished very little from that day to this.*

A number of writers who contributed to The Avengers *have subsequently made major contributions to other popular TV series, including Brian Clemens, Dennis Spooner, James Mitchell, Robert Banks Stewart, Philip Levene, Jeremy Burnham and Terry Nation, famous for his creation of the Daleks for* Doctor Who. *It was one of Jeremy Burnham's episodes, 'You'll Catch Your Death', set at eerie Walsingham House and starring Patrick Macnee, Linda Thorson and Patrick Newell as their superior, Mother, which inspired this short story by Peter Leslie, written in 1969. Peter, a veteran writer of film and TV tie-in paperback books, had earlier written two Avenger novels in conjunction with Patrick Macnee,* Deadline *(1965) and* Dead Duck *(1965). His story serves as a reminder of another series which has been imitated but never equalled . . .*

THE SIGHTSEEING BUS crawled slowly through a network of London streets, a glittering giant shining with polished chromium and clear-view glass.

There were only three passengers, for the bus was actually no more than a front. It was the temporary mobile headquarters of Mother, who sat in one of the rear seats, directly behind John Steed and Tara King.

'Tell me, Steed,' said Mother. 'Do you believe in ghosts?'

'Not really, Mother. Why?'

There was a short pause. 'I have a job in mind for you and Miss King. It concerns going down to Batley Abbey, Sir Hubert Corringham's place.'

'Aha! Reputedly the most haunted house in England,' smiled Steed. 'What's Sir Hubert's problem?'

'He doesn't know he's got one,' said Mother. 'Our chaps have uncovered what appears to be a kidnap plot. The other side want Sir Hubert, you know. He has a mind crammed with research secrets involving the work he does. No use throwing a scare into him by warning him, though. You know how neurotic he's reputed to be . . . terrible temper, flies into passions at the slightest thing, and so on. No, he needs to be looked after, and that's where you come in.'

'Won't he guess something's up when two bodyguards appear out of nowhere to dog his every footstep?' said Steed with a lift of one eyebrow. Mother's tongue clucked irritably.

'It's not going to be like that at all, Steed. Sir Hubert is giving a grand party and ball down at Batley Abbey this Saturday. One of these ridiculous fancy-dress bal-masque affairs. Our tip-off says that the kidnap attempt's to be made during the ball. How, and by whom, I have no idea. But you and Miss King will be there to keep your eyes open and see that nothing happens to Sir Hubert.'

Steed looked a trifle pained. 'In – er – fancy dress, Mother . . ?'

'Naturally. In fancy dress!'

'I must say,' said Tara as she sat beside Steed in the big Rolls-Royce, speeding through the countryside north-east of London, 'you don't actually look very different from usual.'

Steed grinned. 'A ruffled shirt . . . suit rather long in the jacket. A trifle more curl to the brim of the old bowler. Quite a comforting inspiration of mine to dress as an Edwardian dandy.'

Tara looked vaguely envious. It was all very well for Steed, but she'd had to rig out like the sort of Edwardian lady that someone like Steed might be squiring. 'These ridiculous whalebone corsets are positively killing me,' she grumbled. 'And the high button boots aren't exactly the last word in comfort.'

'You look absolutely charming,' said Steed with a feeble attempt at reassurance. Tara didn't reply.

The car turned off the Newmarket Road and threaded its way into the lonely fen country. Already, dusk was falling, and the shock-headed trees sighed mournfully in the wind that rippled the dull water of bottomless dykes. Tara shivered and drew the heavy car-coat more tightly around her shoulders.

'It's certainly eerie enough around here, Steed! How much farther to the Abbey?'

'Only a couple of miles. You'll see the lights of it across the marshes soon.'

Sure enough, way across the expanse of whispering reeds, half-shrouded by low-lying mist, they saw it. A towering heap of restored medieval masonry, the lower windows all alight and dancing with yellow fire in the uncertain gloom. Steed turned the Rolls down the side road that led to the Abbey and pulled up in a car park already packed with vehicles of every description. Vehicles that had only one thing in common . . . a four-figure value.

Tara thought oddly that the presence of these reassuringly opulent cars did nothing to dispel the chilly, almost forbidding atmosphere of the Abbey. Somewhere out in the misty fens, a sheep coughed, and all at once she remembered a half-forgotten phrase she'd read in a book long ago. Likening the cough of an unseen animal to a man with his throat cut. She shivered again, and hurried after Steed into the shelter of the towering, arched doorway.

The scene within the Abbey was little short of fantastic. The very garishness of it drove all the disturbing thoughts out of Tara's mind in an instant. The Great Hall itself was lofty and vaulted, and it had been lit for the occasion with flaring sconces that threw great, living shadows over the grouped displays of arms on the walls and up into the recesses of the roof. At the far end, stone-flagged staircases, curling round and up to a balustraded minstrels' gallery, from which huge oak doors led off to the rest of the ancient building. But the Hall itself was packed with guests. Guests in every conceivable costume from the over-popular harlequin, through soldiers, sheiks, sultans and Satans. Through witches, ladies-in-waiting, queens and courtesans. Robin Hood, Sir Francis Drake, Lord Nelson, Napoleon. The variety was endless.

'Where's our friend Sir Hubert?' whispered Tara.

Steed waited until a liveried footman had passed, handing them each a glass of champagne. Then he pointed discreetly to a tall, lean figure dressed from head-to-foot in a close-fitting garb of doublet and hose. All in black, and with a black hood over his face cut with slits for mouth and eyes. At his belt, a dagger, and balanced in one hand, a heavy and very genuine executioner's axe.

'That one,' said Steed. 'Quite honestly, I wouldn't fancy trying a kidnap attempt. One swing from that axe, and you just wouldn't be bothering any more.'

'What's our plan of action, Steed? We can't just hang about waiting for something to happen, can we?'

Steed shook his head. 'Certainly not. First of all, I want you to keep your eye on Sir Hubert, and see if you can make a head-count of the guests. Everyone seems to be standing still and chatting in groups at the moment. In the meantime, I'm going to slip out and collar the guest list.'

Tara began counting . . . no easy job. And Steed made his way unobtrusively to the large antechamber between the Hall and the main doors.

'Everyone arrived?' He asked the question amiably of one of Sir Hubert's servants, an elderly man who was dressed for the occasion in the chain-mail garb of an ancient door-keeper.

'Yes indeed, sir.'

Steed smiled, pretended to take a look around the ancient walls, and 'accidentally' bumped a suit of armour standing just inside the doors. His champagne glass slipped from his hand and shattered on the flagged floor.

'Goodness! I'm most awfully sorry. . .'

But the door-keeper brushed Steed's apologies aside. 'Not to worry, sir. I'll just run and fetch a cloth. One of the footmen will soon give you a fresh glass.'

As soon as the man was out of the way, Steed leaned over for the typed guest-list hanging beside the servant's chair, and ran his eye rapidly down it. Swiftly, he totalled the numbers and found they came to one hundred and twenty. He just had time to double-check before shuffling footsteps heralded the return of the old man, and he hastily replaced the list on its hook.

With another flow of apologies, he sidled back into the hall and rejoined Tara. 'Well?'

'One hundred and twenty, Steed.'

'Sure?'

'Absolutely.'

Steed made a face. 'That's a confounded nuisance. I'd hoped there'd be a gate-crasher . . . someone well-masked, perhaps. Someone who'd come in through a window. But it seems that the kidnap attempt's going to be made by one of Sir Hubert's legitimate guests. In other words, someone he knows is a traitor.'

'Is that really likely?' Tara looked extremely dubious.

'No, it isn't. But there doesn't seem to be any other answer. The only people here apart from guests are his servants, and they've all got impeccable records. They've got to have, since their boss is a research scientist.'

Tara pursed her lips. 'Suppose our kidnapper had waylaid one of the guests and pinched his costume? He could have got in that way, without upsetting the numbers present.'

'That's a thought. . . .' But Steed was cut off as Tara gripped his arm suddenly. 'Look, Steed. Sir Hubert's going upstairs.

The figure of the black executioner was striding rapidly up the stone steps to the minstrels' gallery, and immediately, Steed began to push his way through the thick press of people. 'Mustn't let him out of our sight,' he whispered to Tara, following close behind him.

They reached the gallery in time to see one of the heavy doors leading from it slam closed. Cautiously, Steed stepped towards it and turned the handle.

An empty corridor yawned at him. A corridor that stretched away through islands of darkness between guttering sconces with doors leading off it in both directions.

'Where on earth's he gone?' Tara mouthed the words almost silently. She realised shiveringly that she would have whispered even if there had been no need. The sinister atmosphere of the place seemed to demand it.

'Heaven knows!' Steed gripped his umbrella in clenched fists. Was that something moving, way down in the darkness of the far corridor? No . . . nothing but a figment of the chilling mist that seeped through every crack in window and wall.

'What was that?' Tara's voice cracked on the last word, and Steed felt her fingernails digging into his arm. 'I heard something . . . like a groan . . .'

'For goodness' sake don't start letting your imagination run away with you, Tara.' Steed sounded oddly irritable. It wasn't like him, but there definitely was something in this Abbey. Something intangible and oppressive.

'No . . . listen! There it is again!' Tara was convinced. 'From one or another of these rooms leading off. . . .'

Then, with startling abruptness, a door right beside them opened wide, and the black executioner stepped out so swiftly that he almost fell over them where they were standing.

The axe dropped to the floor, and Steed and Tara stood momentarily transfixed.

Sir Hubert stooped, retrieved the axe, and said, amiably: 'I say, were you looking for something?'

Steed recovered his composure. 'Er – actually, just doing a bit of sightseeing. Looking for the ghosts, and all that. Rather impertinent of us, I'm afraid, Sir Hubert.'

The man smiled. They could just see his lips through the lower slit in his mask. 'Not at all, not at all dear boy. Place is literally teeming with ghosts, of course. Seen 'em myself many a time. Grey lady, and all that. And a cavalier. Really traditional stuff. But come along now – you'll have to admit that no self-respecting phantom would go roaming around the place with all the jollity that's going on below!' He took both Steed and Tara by the arms and urged them back towards the minstrels' gallery. 'Come and have some more refreshment. Are you enjoying yourselves? So glad you were able to come . . .'

They reached the Hall again, and Sir Hubert left them. Tara found another glass in her hand and sipped it gratefully.

'Phew, that quite put the wind up me. He appeared so jolly suddenly!'

'Got a bit of a start myself,' admitted Steed. 'But he didn't.'

'Who? Sir Hubert?'

'Exactly. And remember what Mother said about him? Neurotic . . . always flying off the handle at the slightest thing?'

'What are you getting at, Steed?'

'Just this. I've never seen anyone calmer than our black executioner friend. And what's more, he treated us just like guests he'd actually invited, not like the planted bodyguards that we actually are. Fine – so Mother pulled strings and really *had* us invited, but Sir Hubert wouldn't normally be so amiable to guests he didn't know personally.'

'So you mean . . .'

'I mean that the person under that mask *isn't* Sir Hubert Corringham!'

'What are we going to do about it, Steed?'

Tara looked at him round-eyed. He thought, inconsequentially, that the expression went rather well with her Edwardian clothes.

'Get him on his own and try and make him betray himself,' said Steed.

'And then put on the pressure and see what's been done with the real Sir Hubert.'

'Let's work on the assumption that our man didn't like us mooching about upstairs, and shepherded us down again deliberately,' said Steed. 'This way, Tara.' The pair of them made idly for the stairs and began to climb. 'He's noticed,' whispered Tara.

At the top, they walked quickly along the gallery and through the same studded door that gave on to the gloomy grey corridor. Instantly, Steed pushed open the doorway through which the black executioner had appeared, but a swift glance inside revealed nothing but an empty, stone-floored room with a massive dead fireplace and uncurtained, lead-lattice windows. The room smelled of long neglect.

'Wonder what the dickens he was doing in here . . ?'

'Never mind . . . he's coming up the stairs to the gallery!'

Steed took Tara's hand and hurried her along the corridor. The murkiness seemed to close around them, pulling at their clothes with sad, thread-like fingers.

'Where are we going, Steed?'

'Only into the shadows. I don't want him to see us immediately.'

They stopped, and waited. It could only have been seconds, but somehow it seemed like hours. And in the dead silence that they kept, Tara felt her blood freeze as a distinct and shuddering groan came from somewhere in the darkness close by!

'You *must* have heard that, Steed!'

His fingers squeezed her hand. He just had time to whisper: 'From one of the rooms right beside us. Wouldn't mind betting it's the real Sir Hubert.' And then the door at the far end of the corridor opened, and the figure in black came through. For a moment, he was silhouetted against the light from below . . . a sinister, thin figure, with the heavy axe trailed beside him. And then the door boomed closed, and the light from a suddenly flaring sconce picked the eyes behind the hood out in startling red.

As Steed had expected, the executioner made for the door of the empty room and opened it. The moment his back was turned to them, Steed launched himself cat-footed down the ten yards of corridor, his right hand outstretched ready to seize the axe.

But in the split second before he reached his quarry, there came again that sobbing groan, and the man obeyed a natural reflex to turn.

If there had been any doubt in Steed's mind about the man's identity, it was gone now. The eyes blazed with sudden fury, and the axe swung swiftly and dextrously aloft.

'You interfering snooper. . .'

The blade hissed down and bit chunks from the floor where, an instant before, Steed had been standing. But he launched himself sideways in a desperate dive that sent him slithering into the empty room, and his feet, lashing together in an expert scissors, plucked the black-clad ankles and sent the man staggering with windmilling arms.

Now Tara rushed forward, and forgetting the restrictions of her long skirt, snatched at the hood on the man's head.

The man fell, but gathered himself in an instant, to spring at Steed anew, this time with the dagger whipped from his belt and pointing professionally upwards. Steed's bowler came off in one deftly

controlled movement, and the lunging knife met the steel reinforce-
ment of the hat's crown with a nerve-jangling impact. The singing
blade dropped to the floor. Then the crown of the hat came up at the
point of the man's out-thrust jaw, and he went cartwheeling back to
sprawl full length over Tara.

Steed jumped after him, but Tara, encumbered by the voluminous
clothes she wore, caught her heel as she tried to get up. Steed cannoned
into her and slipped, off balance, almost on top of the executioner.

And then another door in the passage opened, and a quiet, sibilant
voice with just a trace of a foreign accent, said: 'Stop. That is enough.'

The newcomer was small and dapper, and Steed had no difficulty in
recognising an Eastern-pattern automatic held rigidly in one fist.

The gun beckoned impatiently. 'In here, please. Quickly now. You
too, Saunders.'

Steed and Tara, warily keeping their hands well in view, preceded
the panting executioner into another of the cheerless rooms of that old
abbey. In there, just as Steed had guessed, was the real Sir Hubert
Corringham, tied hand and foot, a white bandage around his head
through which blood had seeped and darkened.

The man with the gun introduced himself as the big door closed on
his captives.

'I am Miroff. And you . . .' he looked appraisingly at Steed's clothes
'. . . are undoubtedly Steed.'

Steed said, calmly: 'Quite a neat little plan you had worked, Miroff.
Someone to impersonate Sir Hubert while you got him away. Too bad
we had to tumble to your game.'

'Annoying, but no more,' said Miroff smoothly. 'You can hardly
imagine you can do me any harm now, Steed. A helicopter is coming to
pick us up shortly.' He glanced at his watch. 'In fifteen minutes. The
revellers will not hear its engines over the noise they are making.'

'And us?' Tara looked at Miroff uncertainly.

'Oh, have no fear. I do not approve of undue violence, even though I
did have to knock Sir Hubert over the head. When Saunders and I
leave here with Sir Hubert, you will merely be left tied up and locked
in.'

Swiftly, Saunders, who had played his part as the black executioner,
lashed Steed's and Tara's hands behind their backs, linked them
together at the wrists, and adroitly gagged them. Then, with expert
ease, he picked up the unconscious Sir Hubert and slung him across his
back like a sack of potatoes. Miroff followed him out of the room, and
Steed and Tara heard a heavy key grate in the lock.

Instantly, Steed went to work. His umbrella lay on the floor where it had been flung in the struggle, he brought his right heel crashing down on the handle, and the tip burst apart, flattened out. The bottom edges of it were jagged where they'd split away from the wood . . .

It took longer to slide gently down and pick up the small sharp fragment than it did for Steed to work the edge of it against Tara's bonds and cut them through. But then they were both free, and tearing the gags from their mouths.

'How on earth are we going to get out?'

Tara stared at the barred windows frantically. 'We can shout ourselves blue in the face, but nobody's going to hear us below!'

Steed grinned rather ruefully, and glanced down with a sigh at his immaculate suit. Then he said: 'I'll turn my back while you loosen those awful whalebones of yours, Tara. I'm afraid we've got rather an unpleasant climb ahead of us.'

'A climb?'

'Up the chimney. You know what they're like in these ancient places. Wide enough to get a horse and cart up, and set with rungs so that the sweeps could skip up and down 'em with no trouble.'

Tara shuddered, but Steed was right. It was the only way. Moments later, they were scrambling together up the vast flue, powdered with the fine grey dust of centuries. Pitch blackness surrounded them, and there was silence save for the sounds of their efforts. Yet there seemed to be a whispering alongside them . . . a ghostly presence that might have been the wind playing in the chimney stacks above, might have been long-forgotten voices full of warning and foreboding.

The thought drove Tara on, though the climb couldn't have been more difficult in the long skirt. Then, far above, she fancied she saw a lighter patch of grey . . . the winking of a star. At last the blessed fresh air, and the dust-grimed pair clambered out on to the roof of the Abbey.

The whole flat panorama of the lonely fens stretched away on all sides, the thin fingers of the dykeside willows thrusting upwards through the thin trails of rolling mist.

'I can't see any sign of them.' Tara was whispering again.

'We couldn't have a better vantage point,' said Steed grimly.

Close to the chimney stacks, and crouched low so they wouldn't be visible against the starry skyline, Steed and Tara kept quiet and shivered.

And then, faint and far off, the distant rhythmic throbbing of an aerial engine, growing stronger second by second.

Tara clutched at his sleeve. 'Look! Down there!'

From a small clump of willows not twenty yards from the house, two figures detached themselves from the inky shadows and began to wade through the shifting mist. One of them had something bulky over his shoulder.

'That's them,' gritted Steed. He saw Miroff stop, and flash a torch briefly. Five stabbing flashes.

Cautiously, Steed grasped Tara's hand and the two of them began to slither down the age-old slates of the sloping part of the Abbey roof.

It was those very slates that spelled disaster. Time-worn and loose, one of them gave way and slid as Steed's heel came down on it, and he fell heavily on his back, dragging Tara with him.

The two bodies came hurtling off the edge of the roof and into empty space within a positive shower of slates.

Neither expected to survive the fall, but they say the fen dykes are bottomless in the hours of darkness, and the one they plunged into was deep enough to save them having anything more than the breath knocked out of them.

Beyond, as Steed spluttered and choked and half-pushed Tara to safety, the helicopter made its touch-down, and Miroff and Saunders broke into a flat run towards it.

Winded as they were, Steed and Tara were powerless to stop them; they could only watch as the two men flung their captive into the helicopter and jumped aboard after him. The noise of the rotors began to rise in pitch . . .

And then it happened. So startlingly that Steed and Tara found themselves rooted to the spot as though by some invisible force.

The horseman, in flowing cavalier costume, seemed to come from one corner of the Abbey . . . charging straight at the helicopter with sword clear of scabbard, waving defiantly in the air.

The pilot must have seen him . . . reacted with sudden shock to swing the lifting machine to one side. The whirling rotor blades scythed sickeningly through the spiked branches of a willow, jammed and screamed to a halt . . . and the helicopter fell on its nose into a dyke, the perspex of the cabin canopy shattering under the impact.

Tara heard Steed bellowing beside her as they broke into a run. 'What a stroke of luck! Some crazy character from the party choosing to go galloping around the countryside at just that moment!'

They reached the helicopter and found there was no work for them there. Already limp and unconscious, Sir Hubert Corringham had suffered nothing in the crash. He lay prone on the dyke bank. The others had not been so lucky. The pilot was groaning with pain and both Miroff and Saunders were unconscious.

Steed rubbed his hands together and looked around. 'No sign of our unknown helper, Tara. Did you see where he went?'

'No . . . I didn't. One moment he was there, and the next, he seemed to have just disappeared. I say, Steed . . .' Tara's voice was suddenly very small. 'Do you remember hoofbeats? *I* don't . . .'

It was twenty-four hours later, and Sir Hubert Corringham, well recovered, had just told Steed and Tara something about the Abbey and his ancestors who had made it their home over the centuries. Steed had asked him, in fact. Because after a check of the guests, it had been definitely proved that nobody had chosen to wear a style of fancy dress anything like a cavalier.

'The sixth baronet,' said Sir Hubert, 'died here trying to protect his sons from a squadron of Oliver Cromwell's cavalry. It's said that his ghost haunts the Abbey, though I've never seen it myself. But it's said that he appears whenever a member of the Corringham family is faced with peril . . .'

Tara looked at Steed and bit her lip. 'What are you going to say next time Mother asks you if you believe in ghosts . . .?'

Sadie When She Died

BY ED MCBAIN

The year 1961 also brought another first for cops on television: the first series to feature life in and around a police station, a genre subsequently exploited so successfully in Hill Street Blues *and the more recent* NYPD Blue. *The original NBC series,* 87th Precinct, *came to the small screen with an enviable pedigree, however, being based on the bestselling novels by Ed McBain which have been described by critics as 'the finest series of police procedurals ever written'. Begun in 1956 with* Cop Hater, *the stories are all set in a Precinct that McBain insists is not located in New York, although the mythical island of Isola is undoubtedly Manhattan. The squad of policemen whom he introduced in that first novel, and who have subsequently appeared in forty-five more, are an unforgettable bunch: Detective Steve Carella, with his beautiful deaf-mute wife, Teddy; the indomitable Lieutenant Peter Byrnes; Detective Meyer Meyer, weighed down by his father's sense of humour in giving his son the same forename and surname; and Detective Bert Kling, the youngest member of the group.*

*Two of Ed McBain's novels about the squad had, in fact, already been successfully adapted for the cinema before NBC producer Hubbell Robinson masterminded the transition to television (*Cop Hater *with Robert Loggia as Carella (1958) and* The Mugger *(1959) with Kent Smith). The result was even better with the New York Times later calling* 87th Precinct *'one of the classiest cop shows of the 1960s'. The combination of policemen at work juxtapositioned with the highs and lows of their personal lives gave the stories an added dimension and made the people themselves both believable and interesting. Robert Lansing portrayed Detective Steve Carella as a likable if somewhat moody man, often at his best in scenes with his wife,* *brilliantly played by Gena Rowlands. Also popular with viewers were Norman Fell (as Meyer), Ron Harper (Kling) and Gregory Walcott (as Detective Roger Havilland). Filmed largely on location in Manhattan, the fifty-minute black and white episodes became compulsory weekly viewing and were made even more atmospheric by Morton Stevens' powerful theme tune. 87th Precinct was also transmitted successfully on the ITV network during 1962.*

Ed McBain (aka Evan Hunter (1926 –) was born in New York and got firsthand experience of the tough city streets while working as a teacher. From his experiences of violence and racial tension he wrote The Blackboard Jungle *(1954) which became an immediate bestseller – and later a film with Bill Hailey's 'Rock Around the Clock' as the theme tune and allegedly the spark of teenage riots in cinemas on both sides of the Atlantic. The success of the book also freed Hunter to write. Although he has subsequently enjoyed considerable success as a mainstream novelist, it is the crime novels written as McBain which are undoubtedly the most popular. All have been widely admired for their insight into police procedures as well as their vivid portrayal of the mixture of brutality and slapstick which makes up a large part of the everyday lives of officers in rough neighbourhoods. For years, McBain regularly used to go out with police squads in order to keep himself up to date with what was happening in the force. Until, that is, the day he found himself in an alley with two policemen who were chasing an armed robber. 'They pulled out their guns and there were shots going everywhere,' he recalls. 'It suddenly occurred to me that there were three guns on the scene and I was the only one who hadn't got one!' Such real life dramas notwithstanding, it was undoubtedly McBain's ability to bring together all the facets of police work in his stories which in turn helped make the TV show popular and so influential on later 'precinct' series like* Hill Street Blues. Sadie When She Died, *one of his rare short stories about Carella and his men, is typical of the quality of the material that was used in this highly regarded – and still much missed – sixties crime landmark.*

'I'M VERY GLAD she's dead,' the man said.

He wore a homburg, muffler, overcoat, and gloves. He stood near the night table, a tall man with a narrow face, and a well-groomed grey moustache that matched the greying hair at his temples. His eyes were clear and blue and distinctly free of pain or grief.

Detective Steve Carella wasn't sure he had heard the man correctly. 'Sir,' Carella said, 'I'm sure I don't have to tell you –'

'That's right,' the man said, 'you don't have to tell me. It happens I'm a criminal lawyer and am well aware of my rights. My wife was no good, and I'm delighted someone killed her.'

Carella opened his pad. This was not what a bereaved husband was supposed to say when his wife lay disembowelled on the bedroom floor in a pool of her own blood.

'Your name is Gerald Fletcher.'

'That's correct.'

'Your wife's name, Mr Fletcher?'

'Sarah. Sarah Fletcher.'

'Want to tell me what happened?'

'I got home about fifteen minutes ago. I called to my wife from the front door, and got no answer. I came into the bedroom and found her dead on the floor. I immediately called the police.'

'Was the room in this condition when you came in?'

'It was.'

'Touch anything?'

'Nothing. I haven't moved from this spot since I placed the call.'

'Anybody in here when you came in?'

'Not a soul. Except my wife, of course.'

'Is that your suitcase in the entrance hallway?'

'It is. I was on the coast for three days. An associate of mine needed advice on a brief he was preparing. What's your name?'

'Carella. Detective Steve Carella.'

'I'll remember that.'

While the police photographer was doing his macabre little jig around the body to make sure the lady looked good in the rushes, or as good as any lady *can* look in her condition, a laboratory assistant named Marshall Davies was in the kitchen of the apartment, waiting for the medical examiner to pronounce the lady dead, at which time Davies would go into the bedroom and with delicate care remove the knife protruding from the blood and slime of the lady, in an attempt to salvage some good latent prints from the handle of the murder weapon.

Davies was a new technician, but an observant one, and he noticed that the kitchen window was wide open, not exactly usual on a December night when the temperature outside hovered at twelve degrees. Leaning over the sink, he further noticed that the window opened on to a fire escape on the rear of the building. He could not resist speculating that perhaps someone had climbed up the fire escape and then into the kitchen.

Since there was a big muddy footprint in the kitchen sink, another one on the floor near the sink, and several others fading as they travelled across the waxed kitchen floor to the living room, Davies surmised that he was on to something hot. Wasn't it possible that an intruder *had* climbed over the window sill, into the sink, and walked across the room, bearing the switchblade knife that had later been pulled viciously across the lady's abdomen from left to right? If the ME ever got through with the damn body, the boys of the 87th would be half-way home, thanks to Marshall Davies. He felt pretty good.

The three points of the triangle were Detective Lieutenant Byrnes, and Detectives Meyer Meyer and Steve Carella. Fletcher sat in a chair, still wearing homburg, muffler, overcoat and gloves as if he expected to be called outdoors at any moment. The interrogation was being conducted in a windowless cubicle labelled Interrogation Room.

The cops standing in their loose triangle around Gerald Fletcher were amazed but not too terribly amused by his brutal frankness.

'I hated her guts,' he said.

'Mr Fletcher,' Lieutenant Byrnes said, 'I *still* feel I must warn you that a woman has been murdered –'

'Yes. My dear, wonderful wife,' Fletcher said sarcastically.

'. . . which is a serious crime . . .' Byrnes felt tongue-tied in Fletcher's presence. Bullet-headed, hair turning from iron-grey to ice-white, blue-eyed, built like a compact line-backer, Byrnes looked to his colleagues for support. Both Meyer and Carella were watching their shoelaces.

'You have warned me repeatedly,' Fletcher said. 'I can't imagine why. My wife is dead – someone killed her – but it was not I.'

'Well, it's nice to have your assurance of that, Mr Fletcher, but this alone doesn't necessarily still our doubts,' Carella said, hearing the words and wondering where the hell they were coming from. He was, he realised, trying to impress Fletcher. He continued, 'How do we know it *wasn't* you who stabbed her?'

'To begin with,' Fletcher said, 'there were signs of forcible entry in the kitchen and hasty departure in the bedroom; witness the wide-open window in the aforementioned room and the shattered window in the latter. The drawers in the dining-room sideboard were open –'

'You're very observant,' Meyer said suddenly. 'Did you notice all this in the four minutes it took you to enter the apartment and call the police?'

'It's my *job* to be observant,' Fletcher said. 'But to answer your question, no. I noticed all this *after* I had spoken to Detective Carella here.'

Wearily, Byrnes dismissed Fletcher who then left the room.

'What do you think?' Byrnes said.

'I think he did it,' Carella said.

'Even with all those signs of a burglary?'

'*Especially* with those signs. He could have come home, found his wife stabbed – but not fatally – and finished her off by yanking the knife across her belly. Fletcher had four minutes, when all he needed was maybe four seconds.'

'It's possible,' Meyer said.

'Or maybe I just don't like the guy,' Carella said.

'Let's see what the lab comes up with,' Byrnes said.

The laboratory came up with good fingerprints on the kitchen window sash and on the silver drawer of the dining-room sideboard. There were good prints on some of the pieces of silver scattered on the floor near the smashed bedroom window. Most important, there were good prints on the handle of the switchblade knife. The prints matched; they had all been left by the same person.

Gerald Fletcher graciously allowed the police to take *his* fingerprints, which were then compared with those Marshall Davies had sent over from the police laboratory. The fingerprints on the window sash, the drawer, the silverware, and the knife did not match Gerald Fletcher's.

Which didn't mean a damn thing if he had been wearing his gloves when he'd finished her off.

On Monday morning, in the second-floor rear apartment of 721 Silvermine Oval, a chalked outline on the bedroom floor was the only evidence that a woman had lain there in death the night before. Carella sidestepped the outline and looked out the shattered window at the narrow alleyway below. There was a distance of perhaps twelve feet between this building and the one across from it.

Conceivably, the intruder could have leaped across the shaftway, but this would have required premeditation and calculation. The more probable likelihood was that the intruder had fallen to the pavement below.

'That's quite a long drop,' Detective Bert Kling said, peering over Carella's shoulder.

'How far do you figure?' Carella asked.

'Thirty feet. At least.'

'Got to break a leg taking a fall like that. You think he went through the window head first?'

'How else?'

'He might have broken the glass out first, then gone through,' Carella suggested.

'If he was about to go to all that trouble, why didn't he just *open* the damn thing?'

'Well, let's take a look,' Carella said.

They examined the latch and the sash. Kling grabbed both handles on the window frame and pulled up on them. 'Stuck.'

'Probably painted shut,' Carella said.

'Maybe he *did* try to open it. Maybe he smashed it only when he realised it was stuck.'

'Yeah,' Carella said. 'And in a big hurry, too. Fletcher was opening the front door, maybe already in the apartment by then.'

'The guy probably had a bag or something with him, to put the loot in. He must have taken a wild swing with the bag when he realised the window was stuck, and maybe some of the stuff fell out, which would explain the silverware on the floor. Then he probably climbed through the hole and dropped down feet first. In fact, what he could've done, Steve, was drop the bag down first, and *then* climbed out and hung from the sill before he jumped, to make it a shorter distance.'

'I don't know if he had all that much time, Bert. He must have heard that front door opening, and Fletcher coming in and calling to his wife. Otherwise, he'd have taken his good, sweet time and gone out the kitchen window and down the fire escape, the way he'd come in.'

Kling nodded reflectively. 'Let's take a look at that alley,' Carella said.

In the alleyway outside, Carella and Kling studied the concrete pavement, and then looked up at the shattered second-floor window of the Fletcher apartment.

'Where do you suppose he'd have landed?' Kling said.

'Right about where we're standing.' Carella looked at the ground. 'I don't know, Bert. A guy drops twenty feet to a concrete pavement, doesn't break anything, gets up, dusts himself off, and runs the fifty-yard dash, right?' Carella shook his head. 'My guess is he stayed right where he was to catch his breath, giving Fletcher time to look out the window, which would be the natural thing to do, but which Fletcher didn't.'

'He was anxious to call the police.'

'I still think he did it.'

'Steve, be reasonable. If a guy's fingerprints are on the handle of a knife, and the knife is still in the victim –'

'*And* if the victim's husband realises what a sweet set up he's stumbled into, wife lying on the floor with a knife in her, place broken into and burglarised, why *not* finish the job and hope the burglar will be blamed?'

'Sure,' Kling said. 'Prove it.'

'I can't,' Carella said. 'Not until we catch the burglar.'

While Carella and Kling went through the tedious routine of retracing the burglar's footsteps, Marshall Davies called the 87th Precinct and got Detective Meyer.

'I think I've got some fairly interesting information about the suspect,' Davies said. 'He left latent fingerprints all over the apartment and footprints in the kitchen. A very good one in the sink, when he climbed in through the window, and some middling-fair ones tracking across the kitchen floor to the dining room. I got some excellent pictures and some good blow-ups of the heel.'

'Good,' Meyer said.

'But more important,' Davies went on, 'I got a good walking picture from the footprints on the floor. If a man is walking slowly, the distance between his footprints is usually about twenty-seven inches. Forty for running, thirty-five for fast walking. These were thirty-two inches. So we have a man's usual gait, moving quickly, but not in a desperate hurry, with the walking line normal and not broken.'

'What does that mean?'

'Well, a walking line should normally run along the inner edge of a man's heel prints. Incidentally, the size and type of shoe and angle of the foot clearly indicate that this *was* a man.'

'OK, fine,' Meyer said. He did not thus far consider Davies' information valuable nor even terribly important.

'Anyway, none of this is valuable nor even terribly important,' Davies said, 'until we consider the rest of the data. The bedroom window was smashed, and the Homicide men were speculating that the suspect had jumped through the window into the alley below. I went down to get some meaningful pictures, and got some pictures of where he must have landed – on both feet, incidentally – and I got another walking picture and direction line. He moved toward the basement door and into the basement. But the important thing is that our man is injured, and I think badly.'

'How do you know?' Meyer asked.

'The walking picture downstairs is entirely different from the one in the kitchen. When he got downstairs he was leaning heavily on the left leg and dragging the right. I would suggest that whoever's handling the case put out a physicians' bulletin. If this guy hasn't got a broken leg, I'll eat the pictures I took.'

A girl in a green coat was waiting in the apartment lobby when Carella and Kling came back in, still retracing footsteps, or trying to. The girl said, 'Excuse me, are you the detectives?'

'Yes,' Carella said.

'The super told me you were in the building,' the girl said. 'You're investigating the Fletcher murder, aren't you?' She was quite soft spoken.

'How can we help you, miss?' Carella asked.

'I saw somebody in the basement last night, with blood on his clothes.'

Carella glanced at Kling and immediately said, 'What time was this?'

'About a quarter to eleven,' the girl said.

'What were you doing in the basement?'

The girl looked surprised.

'That's where the washing machines are. I'm sorry, my name is Selma Bernstein. I live here in the building.'

'Tell us what happened, will you?' Carella said.

'I was sitting by the machine, watching the clothes tumble, which is simply *fascinating*, you know, when the door leading to the backyard opened – the door to the alley. This man came down the stairs, and I don't even think he saw me. He went straight for the stairs at the other end, the ones that go up into the street. I never saw him before last night.'

'Can you describe him?' Carella asked.

'Sure. He was about twenty-one or twenty-two, your height and weight, well, maybe a little bit shorter, five ten or eleven, brown hair.'

Kling was already writing. The man was white, wore dark trousers, high-topped sneakers, and a poplin jacket with blood on the right sleeve and on the front. He carried a small red bag, 'like one of those bags the airlines give you'.

Selma didn't know if he had any scars. 'He went by in pretty much of a hurry, considering he was dragging his right leg. I think he was hurt pretty badly.'

What they had in mind, of course, was identification from a mug shot, but the IS reported that none of the fingerprints in their file matched the ones found in the apartment. So the detectives figured it was going to be a tough one, and they sent out a bulletin to all of the city's doctors just to prove it.

Just to prove that cops can be as wrong as anyone else, it turned out to be a nice easy one after all.

The call came from a physician in Riverhead at 4:37 that afternoon, just as Carella was ready to go home.

'This is Dr Mendelsohn,' he said. 'I have your bulletin here, and I want to report treating a man early this morning who fits your description – a Ralph Corwin of 894 Woodside in Riverhead. He had a bad ankle sprain.'

'Thank you, Dr Mendelsohn,' Carella said.

Carella pulled the Riverhead directory from the top drawer of his desk and quickly flipped to the Cs. He did not expect to find a listing for Ralph Corwin. A man would have to be a rank amateur to burglarise an apartment without wearing gloves, then stab a woman to death, and then give his name when seeking treatment for an injury sustained in escaping from the murder apartment.

Ralph Corwin was apparently a rank amateur. His name was in the phone book, and he'd given the doctor his correct address.

Carella and Kling kicked in the door without warning, fanning into the room, guns drawn. The man on the bed was wearing only undershorts. His right ankle was taped.

'Are you Ralph Corwin?' Carella asked.

'Yes,' the man said. His face was drawn, the eyes in pain.

'Get dressed, Corwin. We want to ask you some questions.'

'There's nothing to ask,' he said and turned his head into the pillow. 'I killed her.'

Ralph Corwin made his confession in the presence of two detectives of the 87th, a police stenographer, an assistant district attorney, and a lawyer appointed by the Legal Aid Society.

Corwin was the burglar. He'd entered 721 Silvermine Oval on Sunday night, 12 December, down the steps from the street where the garbage cans were. He went through the basement, up the steps at the other end, into the backyard, and climbed the fire escape, all at about ten o'clock in the evening. Corwin entered the Fletcher apartment because it was the first one he saw without lights. He figured there was nobody home. The kitchen window was open a tiny crack; Corwin squeezed his fingers under the bottom and opened it all the way. He was pretty desperate at the time because he was a junkie in need of cash. He swore that he'd never done anything like this before.

The man from the DA's office was conducting the Q and A and asked Corwin if he hadn't been afraid of fingerprints, not wearing gloves. Corwin figured that was done only in the movies, and anyway, he said, he didn't own gloves.

Corwin used a tiny flashlight to guide him as he stepped into the sink and down to the floor. He made his way to the dining room, emptied the drawer of silverware into his airline bag. Then he looked for the bedroom, scouting for watches and rings, whatever he could take in the way of jewellery. 'I'm not a pro,' he said. 'I was just hung up real bad and needed some bread to tide me over.'

Now came the important part. The DA's assistant asked Corwin what happened in the bedroom.

A. There was a lady in bed. This was only like close to ten-thirty, you don't expect nobody to be asleep so early.

Q. But there was a woman in bed.

A. Yeah. She turned on the light the minute I stepped in the room.

Q. What did you do?

A. I had a knife in my pocket. I pulled it out to scare her. It was almost comical. She looks at me and says, 'What are you doing here?'

Q. Did you say anything to her?

A. I told her to keep quiet, that I wasn't going to hurt her. But she got out of bed and I saw she was reaching for the phone. That's got to be crazy, right? A guy is standing there in your bedroom with a knife in his hand, so she reaches for the phone.

Q. What did you do?

A. I grabbed her hand before she could get it. I pulled her off the bed, away from the phone, you know? And I told her again that nobody was going to hurt her, that I was getting out of there right away, to just please calm down.

Q. What happened next?

A. She started to scream. I told her to stop. I was beginning to panic. I mean she was really yelling.

Q. Did she stop?

A. No.

Q. What did you do?

A. I stabbed her.

Q. Where did you stab her?

A. I don't know. It was a reflex. She was yelling. I was afraid the whole building would come down. I just . . . I just stuck the knife in her. I was very scared. I stabbed her in the belly. Someplace in the belly.

Q. How many times did you stab her?

A. Once. She . . . she backed away from me. I'll never forget the look on her face. And she . . . she fell on the floor.

Q. Would you look at this photograph, please?

A. Oh, no . . .

Q. Is that the woman you stabbed?

A. Oh, no . . . I didn't think . . . Oh, no!

A moment after he stabbed Sarah Fletcher, Corwin heard the door opening and someone coming in. The man yelled, 'Sarah, it's me, I'm home.' Corwin ran past Sarah's body on the floor and tried to open the window, but it was stuck. He smashed it with his airline bag, threw the bag out first to save the swag because, no matter what, he knew he'd need another fix, and he climbed through the broken window, cutting his hand on a piece of glass. He hung from the sill, and finally let go, dropping to the ground. He tried to get up, and fell down again. His ankle was killing him, his hand bleeding. He stayed in the alley nearly fifteen minutes, then finally escaped via the route Selma Bernstein had described to Carella and Kling. He took the train to Riverhead and got to Dr Mendelsohn at about nine in the morning. He read of Sarah Fletcher's murder in the newspaper on the way back from the doctor.

On Tuesday, 14 December, which was the first of Carella's two days off that week, he received a call at home from Gerald Fletcher. Fletcher told the puzzled Carella that he'd gotten his number from a friend in the DA's office, complimented Carella and the boys of the 87th on their snappy detective work, and invited Carella to lunch at the Golden Lion at one o'clock. Carella wasn't happy about interrupting his Christmas shopping, but this was an unusual opportunity, and he accepted.

Most policemen in the city for which Carella worked did not eat very often in restaurants like the Golden Lion. Carella had never been inside. A look at the menu posted on the window outside would have frightened him out of six months' pay. The place was a faithful replica of the dining room of an English coach house, circa 1627: huge oaken beams, immaculate white cloths, heavy silver.

Gerald Fletcher's table was in a secluded corner of the restaurant. He rose as Carella approached, extended his hand, and said, 'Glad you could make it. Sit down, won't you?'

Carella shook Fletcher's hand, and then sat. He felt extremely uncomfortable, but he couldn't tell whether his discomfort was caused by the room or by the man with whom he was dining.

'Would you care for a drink?' Fletcher asked.

'Well, are you having one?' Carella asked.

'Yes, I am.'

'I'll have a scotch and soda,' Carella said. He was not used to drinking at lunch.

Fletcher signalled the waiter and ordered the drinks, making his another whisky sour.

When the drinks came, Fletcher raised his glass. 'Here's to a conviction,' he said.

Carella lifted his own glass. 'I don't expect there'll be any trouble,' he said. 'It looks airtight to me.'

Both men drank. Fletcher dabbed his lips with a napkin and said, 'You never can tell these days. I hope you're right, though.' He sipped at the drink. 'I must admit I feel a certain amount of sympathy for him.'

'Do you?'

'Yes. If he's an addict, he's automatically entitled to pity. And when one considers that the woman he murdered was just nothing but a —'

'Mr Fletcher . . .'

'Gerry, please. And I know: it isn't very kind of me to malign the dead. I'm afraid you didn't know my wife, though, Mr Carella. May I call you Steve?'

'Sure.'

'My enmity might be a bit more understandable if you had. Still, I shall take your advice. She's dead, and no longer capable of hurting me, so why be bitter. Shall we order, Steve?'

Fletcher suggested that Carella try either the trout *au meunière* or the beef and kidney pie, both of which were excellent. Carella ordered prime ribs, medium rare, and a mug of beer.

As the men ate and talked, something began happening, or at least Carella *thought* something was happening; he might never be quite sure. The conversation with Fletcher seemed on the surface to be routine chatter, but rushing through this inane, polite discussion was an undercurrent that caused excitement, fear, and apprehension. As they spoke, Carella knew with renewed certainty that Gerald Fletcher had killed his wife. Without ever being told so, he knew it. *This* was why Fletcher had called this morning; *this* was why Fletcher had invited him to lunch; *this* was why he prattled on endlessly while every contradictory move of his body signalled on an almost extrasensory level that he *knew* Carella suspected him of murder, and was here to *tell* Carella (*without* telling him) that, 'Yes, you stupid cop, I killed my wife. However much the evidence may point to another man, however many confessions you get, I killed her and I'm glad I killed her. And there isn't a damn thing you can do about it.'

Ralph Corwin was being held before trial in the city's oldest prison, known to law enforcers and lawbreakers alike as Calcutta. Neither Corwin's lawyer nor the district attorney's office felt that allowing Carella to talk to the prisoner would be harmful to the case.

Corwin was expecting him. 'What did you want to see me about?'

'I wanted to ask you some questions.'

'My lawyer says I'm not supposed to add anything to what I already said. I don't even *like* that guy.'

'Why don't you ask for another lawyer? Ask one of the officers here to call the Legal Aid Society. Or simply tell him. I'm sure he'd have no objection to dropping out.'

Corwin shrugged. 'I don't want to hurt his feelings. He's a little cockroach, but what the hell.'

'You've got a lot at stake here, Corwin.'

'But I killed her, so what does it matter *who* the lawyer is? You got it all in black and white.'

'You feel like answering some questions?' Carella said.

'I feel like dropping dead, is what I feel like. Cold turkey's never good, and it's worse when you can't yell.'

'If you'd rather I came back another time . . .'

'No, no, go ahead. What do you want to know?'

'I want to know exactly how you stabbed Sarah Fletcher.'

'How do you *think* you stab somebody? You stick a knife in her.'

'Where?'

'In the belly.'

'Left-hand side of the body?'

'Yeah. I guess so.'

'Where was the knife when she fell?'

'I don't know what you mean.'

'Was the knife on the *right*-hand side of her body or the *left*?'

'I don't know. That was when I heard the front door opening and all I could think of was getting out of there.'

'When you stabbed her, did she *twist* away from you?'

'No, she backed away, straight back, as if she couldn't believe what I done, and . . . and just wanted to get *away* from me.'

'And then she fell?'

'Yes. She . . . her knees sort of gave way and she grabbed for her belly, and her hands sort of – it was terrible – they just . . . they were grabbing *air*, you know? And she fell.'

'In what position?'

'On her side.'

'*Which* side?'

'I could still see the knife, so it must've been the opposite side. The side opposite from where I stabbed her.'

'One last question, Ralph. Was she dead when you went through that window?'

'I don't know. She was bleeding and . . . she was very quiet. I . . . guess she was dead. I don't know. I guess so.'

Among Sarah Fletcher's personal effects that were considered of interest to the police before they arrested Ralph Corwin was an address book found in the dead woman's handbag on the bedroom dresser. In the Thursday afternoon stillness of the squad room, Carella examined the book.

There was nothing terribly fascinating about the alphabetical listings. Sarah Fletcher had possessed a good handwriting, and most of the listings were obviously married couples (Chuck and Nancy Benton, Harold and Marie Spander, and so on), some were girl-friends, local merchants, hairdresser, dentist, doctors, restaurants in town or across the river. A thoroughly uninspiring address book – until Carella came to a page at the end of the book, with the printed word MEMORANDA at its top.

Under the word, there were five names, addresses, and telephone numbers written in Sarah's meticulous hand. They were all men's names, obviously entered at different times because some were in pencil and others in ink. The parenthetical initials following each entry were all noted in felt marking pens of various colours:

Andrew Hart, 1120 Hall Avenue, 622–8400 (PB&G) (TG)

Michael Thornton, 371 South Lindner, 881–9371 (TS)

Lou Kantor, 434 North 16 Street, FR 7–2346 (TPC) (TG)

Sal Decotto, 831 Grover Avenue, FR 5–3287 (F) (TG)

Richard Fenner, 110 Henderson, 593–6648 (QR) (TG)

If there was one thing Carella loved, it was a code. He loved a code almost as much as he loved German measles. He flipped through the phone book, and the address for Andrew Hart matched the one in Sarah's handwriting. He found an address for Michael Thornton. It, too, was identical to the one in her book. He kept turning pages in the directory, checking names and addresses. He verified all five.

At a little past eight the next morning, Carella got going on them. He called Andrew Hart at the number listed in Sarah's address book. Hart answered, and was not happy. 'I'm in the middle of shaving,' he said. 'I've got to leave for the office in a little while. What's this about?'

'We're investigating a homicide, Mr Hart.'

'A *what*? A homicide? Who's been killed?'

'A woman named Sarah Fletcher.'

'I don't know anyone named Sarah Fletcher,' he said.

'She seems to have known you, Mr Hart.'

'Sarah *who*? Fletcher, did you say?' Hart's annoyance increased.

'That's right.'

'I don't know anybody by that name. Who says she knew me? I never heard of her in my life.'

'Your name's in her address book.'

'*My* name? That's impossible.'

Nevertheless, Hart agreed to see Carella and Meyer at the office of Hart and Widderman, 480 Reed Street, sixth floor, at ten o'clock that morning.

At ten, Meyer and Carella parked the car and went into the building at 480 Reed, and up the elevator to the sixth floor. Hart and Widderman manufactured watchbands. A huge advertising display near the receptionist's desk in the lobby proudly proclaimed 'H&W Beats the Band!' and then backed the slogan with more discreet copy that explained how Hart and Widderman had solved the difficult engineering problems of the expansion watch bracelet.

'Mr Hart, please,' Carella said.

'Who's calling?' the receptionist asked. She sounded as if she were chewing gum, even though she was not.

'Detectives Carella and Meyer.'

'Just a minute, please,' she said, and lifted her phone, pushing a button in the base. 'Mr Hart,' she said, 'there are some cops here to see you.' She listened for a moment and then said, 'Yes, sir.' She replaced the receiver on its cradle, gestured toward the inside corridor with a nod of her golden tresses, said, 'Go right in, please. Door at the end of the hall,' and then went back to her magazine.

The grey skies had apparently infected Andrew Hart. 'You didn't have to broadcast to the world that the police department was here,' he said immediately.

'We merely announced ourselves,' Carella said.

'Well, OK, now you're here,' Hart said, 'let's get it over with.' He was a big man in his middle fifties, with iron-grey hair and black-rimmed eyeglasses. 'I told you I don't know Sarah Fletcher and I don't.'

'Here's her book, Mr Hart,' Carella said. 'That's your name, isn't it?'

'Yeah,' Hart said, and shook his head. 'But how it got there is beyond me.'

'Is it possible she's someone you met at a party, someone you exchanged numbers with?'

'No.'

'Are you married, Mr Hart?'

'No.'

'We've got a picture of Mrs Fletcher. I wonder –'

'Don't go showing me any pictures of a corpse,' Hart said.

'This was taken when she was still very much alive, Mr Hart.'

Meyer handed Carella a manilla envelope. He opened the flap and removed from the envelope a framed picture of Sarah Fletcher, which he handed to Hart. Hart looked at the photograph, and then immediately looked up at Carella.

'What is this?' he said. He looked at the photograph again, shook his head, and said, 'Somebody killed her, huh?'

'Yes, somebody did,' Carella answered. 'Did you know her?'

'I knew her.'

'I thought you said you didn't.'

'I didn't know Sarah Fletcher, if that's who you think she was. But I knew *this* broad, all right.'

'Who'd *you* think she was?' Meyer asked.

'Just who she told me she was. Sadie Collins. She introduced herself as Sadie Collins, and that's who I knew her as. Sadie Collins.'

'Where was this, Mr Hart? Where'd you meet her?'

'A singles bar. The city's full of them.'

'Would you remember when?'

'At least a year ago.'

'Ever go out with her?'

'I used to see her once or twice a week.'

'When did you stop seeing her?'

'Last summer.'

'Did you know she was married?'

'Who, Sadie? You're kidding.'

'She never told you she was married?'

'Never.'

Meyer asked, 'When you were going out, where'd you pick her up? At her apartment?'

'No. She used to come to my place.'

'Where'd you call her when you wanted to reach her?'

'I didn't. She used to call me.'

'Where'd you go, Mr Hart? When you went out?'

'We didn't go out too much.'

'What *did* you do?'

'She used to come to my place. The truth is, we never went out. She didn't want to go out much.'

'Didn't you think that was strange?'

'No,' Hart shrugged. 'I figured she liked to stay home.'

'Why'd you stop seeing her, Mr Hart?'

'I met somebody else. A nice girl. I'm very serious about her.'

'Was there something wrong with Sadie?'

'No, no. She was a beautiful woman, beautiful.'

'Then why would you be ashamed –'

'Ashamed? Who said anything about being ashamed?'

'I gathered you wouldn't want your girlfriend –'

'Listen, what *is* this? I stopped seeing Sadie six months ago. I wouldn't even talk to her on the phone after that. If the crazy babe got herself killed –'

'Crazy?'

Hart suddenly wiped his hand over his face, wet his lips and walked behind his desk. 'I don't think I have anything more to say to you gentlemen.'

'What did you mean by crazy?' Carella asked.

'Good day, gentlemen,' Hart said.

Carella went to see Lieutenant Byrnes. In the lieutenant's corner office, Byrnes and Carella sat down over coffee. Byrnes frowned at Carella's request.

'Oh, come on, Pete!' Carella said. 'If Fletcher *did* it –'

'That's only *your* allegation. Suppose he *didn't* do it, and suppose *you* do something to screw up the DA's case?'

'Like what?'

'I don't know like what. The way things are going these days, if you spit on the sidewalk, that's enough to get a case thrown out of court.'

'Fletcher hated his wife,' Carella said calmly.

'Lots of men hate their wives. Half the men in this city hate their wives.'

'But her little fling gives Fletcher a good reason for . . . Look, Pete, he had a motive; he had the opportunity, a golden one, in fact; and he had the means – another man's knife sticking in Sarah's belly. What more do you want?'

'Proof. There's a funny little system we've got here – it requires proof before we can arrest a man and charge him with murder.'

'Right. And all I'm asking is the opportunity to *try* for it.'

'Sure, by putting a tail on Fletcher. Suppose he sues the city?'

'Yes or no, Pete? I want permission to conduct a round-the-clock surveillance of Gerald Fletcher, starting Sunday morning. Yes or no?'

'I must be out of my mind,' Byrnes said, and sighed.

Michael Thornton lived in an apartment building several blocks from the Quarter, close enough to absorb some of its artistic flavour, distant enough to escape its high rents. A blond man in his apartment, Paul Wendling, told Kling and Meyer that Mike was in his jewellery shop.

In the shop, Thornton was wearing a blue work smock, but the contours of the garment did nothing to hide his powerful build. His eyes were blue, his hair black. A small scar showed white in the thick eyebrow over his left eye.

'We understand you're working,' Meyer said. 'Sorry to break in on you this way.'

'That's OK,' Thornton said. 'What's up?'

'You know a woman named Sarah Fletcher?'

'No,' Thornton said.

'You know a woman named Sadie Collins?'

Thornton hesitated. 'Yes,' he said.

'What was your relationship with her?' Kling asked.

Thornton shrugged. 'Why? Is she in trouble?'

'When's the last time you saw her?'

'You didn't answer my question,' Thornton said.

'Well, you didn't answer ours either,' Meyer said, and smiled. 'What was your relationship with her, and when did you see her last?'

'I met her in July, in a joint called The Saloon, right around the corner. It's a bar, but they also serve sandwiches and soup. It gets a big crowd on weekends, singles, a couple of odd ones for spice – but not a gay bar. I saw her last in August, a brief, hot thing, and then goodbye.'

'Did you realise she was married?' Kling said.

'No. Is she?'

'Yes,' Meyer said. Neither of the detectives had yet informed Thornton that the lady in question was now unfortunately deceased. They were saving that for last, like dessert.

'Gee, I didn't know she was married.' Thornton seemed truly surprised. 'Otherwise, nothing would've happened.'

'What *did* happen?'

'I bought her a few drinks and then I took her home with me. Later, I put her in a cab.'

'When did you see her next?'

'The following day. It was goofy. She called me in the morning, said she was on her way downtown. I was still in bed. I said, 'So come on down, baby.' And she did. *Believe* me, she did.'

'Did you see her again after that?' Kling asked.

'Two or three times a week.'

'Where'd you go?'

'To my pad on South Lindner.'

'Never went any place but there?'

'Never.'

'Why'd you quit seeing her?'

'I went out of town for a while. When I got back, I just didn't hear from her again. She never gave me her number, and she wasn't in the directory, so I couldn't reach her.'

'What do you make of this?' Kling asked, handing Thornton the address book.

Thornton studied it and said, 'Yes, what about it? She wrote this down the night we met – we were in bed, and she asked my address.'

'Did she write those initials at the same time, the ones in parentheses under your phone number?'

'I didn't actually see the page itself, I only saw her writing in the book.'

'Got any idea what the initials mean?'

'None at all.' Suddenly he looked thoughtful. 'She *was* kind of special, I have to admit it.' He grinned. 'She'll call again, I'm sure of it.'

'I wouldn't count on it,' Meyer said. 'She's dead.'

His face did not crumble or express grief or shock. The only thing it expressed was sudden anger. 'The stupid . . .' Thornton said. 'That's all she ever was, a stupid, crazy . . .'

On Sunday morning, Carella was ready to become a surveillant, but Gerald Fletcher was nowhere in sight. A call to his apartment from a nearby phone booth revealed that he was not in his digs. He parked in front of Fletcher's apartment building until five p.m. when he was relieved by Detective Arthur Brown. Carella went home to read his son's latest note to Santa Claus, had dinner with his family, and was settling down in the living room with a novel he had bought a week ago and not yet cracked, when the telephone rang.

'Hello?' Carella said into the mouthpiece.

'Hello, Steve? This is Gerry. Gerry Fletcher.'

Carella almost dropped the receiver. 'How are you?'

'Fine, thanks. I was away for the weekend, just got back a little while ago, in fact. Frankly I find this apartment depressing as hell. I was wondering if you'd like to join me for a drink.'

'Well,' Carella said. 'It's Sunday night, and it's late . . .'

'Nonsense, it's only eight o'clock. We'll do a little old-fashioned pub crawling.'

It suddenly occurred to Carella that Gerald Fletcher had already had a few drinks before placing his call. It further occurred to him that if he played this *too* cozily, Fletcher might rescind his generous offer.

'Okay. I'll see you at eight-thirty, provided I can square it with my wife.'

'Good,' Fletcher said. 'See you.'

Paddy's Bar and Grill was on the Stem, adjacent to the city's theatre district. Carella and Fletcher got there at about nine o'clock while the place was still relatively quiet. The action began a little later, Fletcher explained.

Fletcher lifted his glass in a silent toast. 'What kind of person would you say comes to a place like this?'

'I would say we've got a nice lower-middle-class clientele bent on making contact with members of the opposite sex.'

'What would you say if I told you the blonde in the clinging jersey is a working prostitute?'

Carella looked at the woman. 'I don't think I'd believe you. She's a bit old for the young competition, and she's not *selling* anything. She's waiting for one of those two or three older guys to make their move. Hookers don't wait, Gerry. *Is* she a working prostitute?'

'I haven't the faintest idea,' Fletcher said. 'I was merely trying to indicate that appearances can sometimes be misleading. Drink up, there are a few more places I'd like to show you.'

He knew Fletcher well enough by now to realise that the man was trying to tell him something. At lunch last Tuesday, Fletcher had transmitted a message and a challenge: *I killed my wife, what can you do about it?* Tonight, in a similar manner, he was attempting to indicate something else, but Carella could not fathom exactly what.

Fanny's was only twenty blocks away from Paddy's Bar and Grill, but as far removed from it as the moon. Whereas the first bar seemed to cater to a quiet crowd peacefully pursuing its romantic inclinations, Fanny's was noisy and raucous, jammed to the rafters with men and women of all ages wearing plastic hippie gear purchased in head shops up and down Jackson Avenue.

Fletcher lifted his glass. 'I hope you don't mind if I drink myself into a stupor,' he said. 'Merely pour me into the car at the end of the night.' Fletcher drank. 'I don't usually consume this much alcohol, but I'm very troubled about that boy.'

'What boy?' Carella asked.

'Ralph Corwin,' Fletcher said. 'I understand he's having some difficulty with his lawyer and, well, I'd like to help him somehow.'

'*Help* him?'

'Yes. Do you think the DA's office would consider it strange if I suggested a good defence lawyer for the boy?'

'I think they might consider it passing strange, yes.'

'Do I detect a note of sarcasm in your voice?'

'Not at all.'

Fletcher squired Carella from Fanny's to, in geographical order, The Purple Chairs and Quigley's Rest. Each place was rougher, in its way, than the last. The Purple Chairs catered to a brazenly gay crowd, and Quigley's Rest was a dive, where Fletcher's liquor caught up with him, and the evening ended suddenly in a brawl. Carella was shaken by the experience, and still couldn't piece out Fletcher's reasons.

Carella received a further shock when he continued to pursue Sarah Fletcher's address book. Lou Kantor was simply the third name in a now wearying list of Sarah's bedmates, until she turned out to be a tough and striking woman. She confirmed Carella's suspicions immediately.

'I only knew her a short while,' she said. 'I met her in September, I believe. Saw her three or four times after that.'

'Where'd you meet her?'

'In a bar called The Purple Chairs. That's right,' she added quickly. 'That's what I am.'

'Nobody asked,' Carella said. 'What about Sadie Collins?'

'Spell it out, Officer, I'm not going to help you. I don't like being hassled.'

'Nobody's hassling you, Miss Kantor. You practise your religion and I'll practise mine. We're here to talk about a dead woman.'

'Then talk about her, spit it out. What do you want to know? Was she straight? Everybody's straight until they're *not* straight any more, isn't that right? She was willing to learn. I taught her.'

'Did you know she was married?'

'She told me. So what? Broke down in tears one night, and spent the rest of the night crying. I knew she was married.'

'What'd she say about her husband?'

'Nothing that surprised me. She said he had another woman. Said he ran off to see her every weekend, told little Sadie he had out-of-town business. *Every* weekend, can you imagine that?'

'What do you make of this?' Carella said, and handed her Sarah's address book, opened to the MEMORANDA page.

'I don't know any of these people,' Lou said.

'The initials under your name,' Carella said. 'TPC and then TG. Got any ideas?'

'Well, the TPC is obvious, isn't it? I met her at The Purple Chairs. What else could it mean?'

Carella suddenly felt very stupid. 'Of course. What else could it mean?' He took back the book. 'I'm finished,' he said. 'Thank you very much.'

'I miss her,' Lou said suddenly. 'She was a wild one.'

Cracking a code is like learning to roller-skate; once you know how to do it, it's easy. With a little help from Gerald Fletcher, who had provided a guided tour the night before, and a lot of help from Lou Kantor, who had generously provided the key, Carella was able to crack the code wide open – well, almost. Last night, he'd gone with Fletcher to Paddy's Bar and Grill, or PB&G under Andrew Hart's name; Fanny's, F under Sal Decotto; The Purple Chairs, Lou Kantor's TPC; and Quigley's Rest, QR for Richard Fenner on the list. Probably because of the fight, he hadn't taken Carella to The Saloon, TS under Michael Thornton's name – the place where Thornton had admitted first meeting Sarah.

Except, what the hell did TG mean, under all the names but Thornton's?'

By Carella's own modest estimate, he had been in more bars in the past twenty-four hours than he had in the past twenty-four years. He decided, nevertheless, to hit The Saloon that night.

The Saloon was just that. A cigarette-scarred bar behind which ran a mottled, flaking mirror; wooden booths with patched, fake leather seat cushions; bowls of pretzels and potato chips; jukebox gurgling; steamy bodies.

'They come in here,' the bartender said, 'at all hours of the night. Take yourself. You're here to meet a girl, am I right?'

'There *was* someone I was hoping to see. A girl named Sadie Collins. Do you know her?'

'Yeah. She used to come in a lot, but I ain't seen her in months. What do you want to fool around with her for?'

'Why? What's the matter with her?'

'You want to know something?' the bartender said. 'I thought she was a hooker at first. Aggressive. You know what that word means? Aggressive? She used to come dressed down to here and up to there, ready for action, selling everything she had, you understand? She'd come in here, pick out a guy she wanted, and go after him like the world was gonna end at midnight. And always the same type. Big guys. You wouldn't stand a chance with her, not that you ain't big, don't misunderstand me. But Sadie liked them gigantic, and mean. You know something?'

'What?'

'I'm glad she don't come in here any more. There was something about her – like she was compulsive. You know what that word means, compulsive?'

Tuesday afternoon, Arthur Brown handed in his surveillance report on Gerald Fletcher. Much of it was not at all illuminating. From 4.55 p.m. to 8.45 p.m. Fletcher had driven home, and then to 812 North Crane and parked. The report *did* become somewhat illuminating when, at 8.46 p.m., Fletcher emerged from the building with a redheaded woman wearing a black fur coat over a green dress. They went to Rudolph's restaurant, ate, and drove back to 812 Crane, arrived at 10.35 p.m. and went inside. Arthur Brown had checked the lobby mailboxes, which showed eight apartments on the eleventh floor, which was where the elevator indicator had stopped. Brown went outside to wait again, and Fletcher emerged alone at 11.40 p.m. and drove home. Detective O'Brien relieved Detective Brown at 12.15 a.m.

Byrnes said, 'This woman could be important.'

'That's just what I think,' Brown answered.

Carella had not yet spoken to either Sal Decotto or Richard Fenner, the two remaining people listed in Sarah's book, but saw no reason to pursue that trail any further. If the place listings in her book had been chronological, she'd gone from bad to worse in her search for partners.

Why? To give it back to her husband in spades? Carella tossed Sarah's little black book into the manilla folder bearing the various reports on the case, and turned his attention to the information Artie Brown had brought in last night. The redheaded woman's presence might be important, but Carella was still puzzling over Fletcher's behaviour. Sarah's blatant infidelity provided Fletcher with a strong motive, so why take Carella to his wife's unhappy haunts, why *show* Carella that he had good and sufficient reason to kill her? Furthermore, why the offer to get a good defence attorney for the boy who had already been indicted for the slaying?

Sometimes Carella wondered who was doing what to whom.

At five o'clock that evening, Carella relieved Detective Hal Willis outside Fletcher's office building downtown, and then followed Fletcher to a department store in midtown Isola. Carella was wearing a false moustache stuck to his upper lip, a wig with hair longer than his own and of a different colour, and a pair of sunglasses.

In the department store, he tracked Fletcher to the Intimate Apparel department. Carella walked into the next aisle, pausing to look at women's robes and kimonos, keeping one eye on Fletcher, who was in conversation with the lingerie salesgirl.

'May I help you, sir?' a voice said, and Carella turned to find a stocky woman at his elbow, with grey hair, black-rimmed spectacles, wearing army shoes and a black dress. Her suspicious smile accused him of being a junkie shoplifter or worse.

'Thank you, no,' Carella said. 'I'm just looking.'

Fletcher made his selections from the gossamer undergarments that the salesgirl had spread out on the counter, pointing first to one garment, then to another. The salesgirl wrote up the order and Fletcher reached into his wallet to give her either cash or a credit card; it was difficult to tell from an aisle away. He chatted with the girl a moment longer, and then walked off toward the elevator bank.

'Are you *sure* I can't assist you?' the woman in the army shoes said, and Carella answered, 'I'm positive,' and moved swiftly toward the lingerie counter. Fletcher had left the counter without a package in his arms, which meant he was *sending* his purchases. The salesgirl was gathering up Fletcher's selections and looked up when Carella reached the counter.

'Yes, sir,' she said. 'May I help you?'

Carella opened his wallet and produced his shield. 'Police officer,' he said. 'I'm interested in the order you just wrote up.'

The girl was perhaps nineteen years old, a college girl working in the store during the Christmas rush. Speechlessly, she studied the shield, eyes bugging.

'Are these items being sent?' Carella asked.

'Yes, *sir*,' the girl said. Her eyes were still wide. She wet her lips and stood up a little straighter, prepared to be a perfect witness.

'Can you tell me where?' Carella asked.

'Yes, *sir*,' she said, and turned the sales slip toward him. 'He wanted them wrapped separately, but they're all going to the same address. Miss Arlene Orton, 812 North Crane Street, right here in the city, and I'd guess it's a swell –'

'Thank you very much,' Carella said.

It felt like Christmas Day already.

The man who picked the lock on Arlene Orton's front door, ten minutes after she left her apartment on Wednesday morning, was better at it than any burglar in the city, and he happened to work for the Police Department. It took the technician longer to set up his equipment, but the telephone was the easiest of his jobs. The tap would become operative when the telephone company supplied the police with a list of so-called bridging points that located the pairs and cables for Arlene Orton's phone. The monitoring equipment would be hooked into these and whenever a call went out of or came into the apartment, a recorder would automatically tape both ends of the conversation. In addition, whenever a call was made from the apartment, a dial indicator would ink out a series of dots that signified the number being called.

The technician placed his bug in the bookcase on the opposite side of the room. The bug was a small FM transmitter with a battery-powered mike that needed to be changed every twenty-four hours. The technician would have preferred running his own wires, but he dared not ask the building superintendent for an empty closet or workroom in which to hide his listener. A blabbermouth superintendent can kill an investigation more quickly than a squad of gangland goons.

In the rear of a panel truck parked at the kerb some twelve feet south of the entrance to 812 North Crane, Steve Carella sat behind the recording equipment that was locked into the frequency of the bug. He sat hopefully, with a tuna sandwich and a bottle of beer, prepared to hear and record any sounds that emanated from Arlene's apartment.

At the bridging point seven blocks away and thirty minutes later, Arthur Brown sat behind equipment that was hooked into the telephone mike, and waited for Arlene Orton's phone to ring. He was in radio contact with Carella.

The first call came at 12.17 p.m. The equipment tripped in automatically and the spools of tape began recording the conversation, while Brown simultaneously monitored it through his headphone.

'Hello?'

'Hello, Arlene?'

'Yes, who's this?'

'Nan.'

'Nan? You sound so different. Do you have a cold or something?'

'Every year at this time. Just before the holidays. Arlene, I'm terribly rushed, I'll make this short. Do you know Beth's dress size?'

The conversation went on in that vein, and Arlene Orton spoke to three more girlfriends in succession. She then called the local supermarket to order the week's groceries. She had a fine voice, deep and forceful, punctuated every so often (when she was talking to her girlfriends) with a delightful giggle.

At four p.m., the telephone in Arlene's apartment rang again.
'Hello?'
'Arlene, this is Gerry.'
'Hello, darling.'
'I'm leaving here a little early. I thought I'd come right over.'
'Good.'
'I'll be there in, oh, half an hour, forty minutes.'
'Hurry.'

Brown radioed Carella at once. Carella thanked him, and sat back to wait.

On Thursday morning, two days before Christmas, Carella sat at his desk in the squad room and looked over the transcripts of the five reels from the night before. The reel that interested him most was the second one. The conversation on that reel had at one point changed abruptly in tone and content. Carella thought he knew why, but he wanted to confirm his suspicion.

Fletcher: I meant after the *holidays*, not the trial.

Miss Orton: I may be able to get away, I'm not sure. I'll have to check with my shrink.

Fletcher: What's he got to do with it?

Miss Orton: Well, I have to pay whether I'm there or not, you know.

Fletcher: Is he taking a vacation?

Miss Orton: I'll ask him.

Fletcher: Yes, ask him. Because I'd really like to get away.

Miss Orton: Ummm. When do you think the case (inaudible).

Fletcher: In March sometime. No sooner than that. He's got a new lawyer, you know.

Miss Orton: What does that mean, a new lawyer?

Fletcher: Nothing. He'll be convicted anyway.

Miss Orton: (Inaudible).

Fletcher: Because the trial's going to take a lot out of me.

Miss Orton: How soon after the trial . . .

Fletcher: I don't know.

Miss Orton: She's dead, Gerry, I don't see . . .

Fletcher: Yes, but . . .

Miss Orton: I don't see why we have to wait, do you?

Fletcher: Have you read this?

Miss Orton: No, not yet. Gerry, I think we ought to set a date now. A provisional date, depending on when the trial is. Gerry?

Fletcher: Mmmm?

Miss Orton: Do you think it'll be a terribly long, drawn-out trial?

Fletcher: What?

Miss Orton: Gerry?

Fletcher: Yes?

Miss Orton: Where are you?

Fletcher: I was just looking over some of these books.

Miss Orton: Do you think you can tear yourself away?

Fletcher: Forgive me, darling,

Miss Orton: If the trial starts in March, and we planned on April for it . . .

Fletcher: Unless they come up with something unexpected, of course.

Miss Orton: Like what?

Fletcher: Oh, I don't know. They've got some pretty sharp people investigating this case.

Miss Orton: What's there to investigate?

Fletcher: There's always the possibility he didn't do it.

Miss Orton: (Inaudible) a signed confession?

Fletcher: One of the cops thinks I killed her.

Miss Orton: You're not serious. Who?

Fletcher: A detective named Carella. He probably knows about us by now. He's a very thorough cop. I have a great deal of admiration for him. I wonder if he realises that.

Miss Orton: Where'd he even get such an idea?

Fletcher: Well, I told him I hated her.

Miss Orton: What? Gerry, why the hell did you do that?

Fletcher: He'd have found out anyway. He probably knows by now that Sarah was sleeping around with half the men in this city. And he probably knows I knew it, too.

Miss Orton: Who cares what he found out? Corwin's already confessed.

Fletcher: I can understand his reasoning. I'm just not sure he can understand mine.

Miss Orton: Some reasoning. If you were going to kill her, you'd have done it ages ago, when she refused to sign the separation papers. So let him investigate, who cares? Wishing your wife dead isn't the same thing as killing her. Tell that to Detective Copolla.

Fletcher: Carella. (Laughs). I'll tell him, darling.

According to the technician who had wired the Orton apartment, the living room bug was in the bookcase on the wall opposite the bar. Carella was interested in the tape from the time Fletcher had asked Arlene about a book – 'Have you read this?' – and then seemed preoccupied. It was Carella's guess that Fletcher had discovered the bookcase bug. What interested Carella more, however, was what Fletcher had said after he knew the place was wired. Certain of an audience now, Fletcher had:

(1) Suggested the possibility that Corwin was not guilty.

(2) Flatly stated that a cop named Carella suspected him.

(3) Expressed admiration for Carella, while wondering if Carella was aware of it.

(4) Speculated that Carella had already doped out the purpose of the bar-crawling last Sunday night, was cognizant of Sarah's promiscuity, and knew Fletcher was aware of it.

(5) Made a little joke about 'telling' Carella.

Carella felt as eerie as he had when lunching with Fletcher and later when drinking with him. Now he'd spoken, through the bug, directly to Carella. But what was he trying to say? And why?

Carella wanted very much to hear what Fletcher would say when he *didn't* know he was being overheard. He asked Lieutenant Byrnes for permission to request a court order to put a bug in Fletcher's automobile. Byrnes granted permission, and the court issued the order.

Fletcher made a date with Arlene Orton to go to The Chandeliers across the river, and the bug was installed in Fletcher's 1972 car. If Fletcher left the city, the effective range of the transmitter on the open road would be about a quarter of a mile. The listener-pursuer had his work cut out for him.

By ten minutes to ten that night, Carella was drowsy and discouraged. On the way out to The Chandeliers, Fletcher and Arlene had not once mentioned Sarah nor the plans for their impending marriage. Carella was anxious to put them both to bed and get home to his family. When they finally came out of the restaurant and began walking toward Fletcher's automobile, Carella actually uttered an audible, 'At *last*,' and started his car.

They proceeded east on Route 701, heading for the bridge, and said nothing. Carella thought at first that something was wrong with the equipment, then finally Arlene spoke and Carella knew just what had happened. The pair had argued in the restaurant, and Arlene had been smouldering until this moment.

'Maybe you don't want to marry me at all,' she shouted.

'That's ridiculous,' Fletcher said.

'Then why won't you set a date?'

'I have set a date.'

'You haven't set a date. All you've done is say *after the trial. When,* after the trial? Maybe this whole damn thing has been a stall. Maybe you *never* planned to marry me.'

'You know that isn't true, Arlene.'

'How do I know there really *were* separation papers?'

'There were. I told you there were.'

'Then why wouldn't she sign them?'

'Because she loved me.'

'If she loved you, then why did she do those horrible things?'

'To make me pay, I think.'

'Is that why she showed you her little black book?'

'Yes, to make me pay.'

'No. Because she was a slut.'

'I guess. I guess that's what she became.'

'Putting a little TG in her book every time she told you about a new one. *Told Gerry,* and marked a little TG in her book.'

'Yes, to make me pay.'

'A slut. You should have gone after her with detectives. Gotten pictures, threatened her, forced her to sign –'

'No, I couldn't have done that. It would have ruined me, Arl.'

'Your precious career.'

'Yes, my precious career.'

They both fell silent again. They were approaching the bridge now. Carella tried to stay close behind them, but on occasion the distance between the two cars lengthened and he lost some words in the conversation.

'She wouldn't sign the papers and I . . . adultery because . . . have come out.'.

'And I thought . . .'

'I did everything I possibly could.'

'Yes, Gerry, but now she's dead. So what's your excuse now?'

'I'm suspected of having *killed* her, damn it!'

Fletcher was making a left turn, off the highway. Carella stepped on the accelerator, not wanting to lose voice contact now.

'What difference does that make?' Arlene asked.

'None at all, I'm sure,' Fletcher said. 'I'm sure you wouldn't mind at all being married to a convicted murderer.'

'What are you talking about?'

'I'm talking about the possibility . . . Never mind.'

'Let me hear it.'

'All right, Arlene. I'm talking about the possibility of someone accusing me of the murder. And of my having to stand trial for it.'

'That's the most paranoid –'

'It's not paranoid.'

'Then what is it? They've caught the murderer, they –'

'I'm only saying suppose. How could we get married if I killed her, if someone says I killed her?'

'No one has said that, Gerry.'

'Well, *if* someone should.'

Silence. Carella was dangerously close to Fletcher's car now, and risking discovery.

Carella held his breath and stayed glued to the car ahead.

'Gerry, I don't understand this,' Arlene said, her voice low.

'Someone could make a good case for it.'

'Why would anyone do that? They know that Corwin –'

'They could say I came into the apartment and . . . They could say she was still alive when I came into the apartment. They could say the knife was still in her and I . . . I came in and found her that way and . . . finished her off.'

'Why would you do that?'

'To end it.'

'You wouldn't kill anyone, Gerry.'

'No.'

'Then why are you even suggesting such a terrible thing?'

'If she wanted it . . . If someone accused me . . . If someone said I'd done it . . . that I'd finished the job, pulled the knife across her belly, they could claim she *asked* me to do it.'

'What are you saying, Gerry?'

'I'm trying to explain that Sarah might have –'

'Gerry, I don't think I want to know.'

'I'm only trying to tell you –'

'No, I don't want to know. Please, Gerry, you're frightening me.'

'*Listen* to me, damn it! I'm trying to explain what *might* have happened. Is that so hard to accept? That she might have *asked* me to kill her?'

'Gerry, please, I –'

'I *wanted* to call the hospital, I was *ready* to call the hospital, don't you think I could *see* she wasn't fatally stabbed?'

'Gerry, please.'

'She begged me to kill her, Arlene, she begged me to end it for her, she . . . Damn it, can't *either* of you understand that? I tried to show him, I took him to all the places, I thought he was a man who'd understand. Is it that difficult?'

'Oh, my God, *did* you kill her? *Did* you kill Sarah?'

'No. Not Sarah. Only the woman she'd become, the slut I'd forced her to become. She was Sadie, you see, when I killed her – when she died.'

'Oh, my God,' Arlene said, and Carella nodded in weary acceptance.

Carella felt neither elated nor triumphant. As he followed Fletcher's car into the kerb in front of Arlene's building, he experienced only a familiar nagging sense of repetition and despair. Fletcher was coming out of his car now, walking around to the kerb side, opening the door for Arlene, who took his hand and stepped on to the sidewalk, weeping. Carella intercepted them before they reached the front door of the building.

Quietly, he charged Fletcher with the murder of his wife, and made the arrest without resistance.

Fletcher did not seem at all surprised.

So it was finished, or at least Carella thought it was.

In the silence of his living room, the telephone rang at a quarter past one.

He caught the phone on the third ring.

'Hello?'

'Steve,' Lieutenant Byrnes said. 'I just got a call from Calcutta. Ralph Corwin hanged himself in his cell, just after midnight. Must have done it while we were still taking Fletcher's confession in the squad room.'

Carella was silent.

'Steve?' Byrnes said.

'Yeah, Pete.'

'Nothing,' Byrnes said, and hung up.

Carella stood with the dead phone in his hands for several seconds and then replaced it on the hook. He looked into the living room, where the lights of the tree glowed warmly, and thought of a despairing junkie in a prison cell, who had taken his own life without ever having known he had not taken the life of another.

It was Christmas day.
Sometimes none of it made any sense at all.

Man in the Dark

BY ROY HUGGINS

The Fugitive *is only one of several highly successful TV crime shows that were devised by Roy Huggins (1914–) during his long association with American television. In 1958, for instance, he created the 'hip' detective series,* 77 Sunset Strip, *featuring two private eyes, Stu Bailey (played by Efrem Zimbalist jnr) and Jeff Spencer (Roger Smith) who operated on the famous Hollywood street and took on cases for a string of glamorous showbiz people. The real star of the show, however, was a character named Lloyd Kookson III – 'Kookie' to his friends – played by Edd Byrnes whose laid-back attitude to life and vocabulary of 'jive-talk' made him an idol with teenage viewers across the nation – who, in turn, imitated his language and copied his habit of constantly combing his hair! After* The Fugitive, *Huggins also created* Run For Your Life *with Ben Gazzara as a man given two years to live who throws himself into a series of adventures (conversely, the show lasted for three!) and* The Outsider *(1968) starring Darren McGavin as 'loner' sleuth, David Ross, operating from a derelict building in Los Angeles. A fourth series,* The Rockford Files, *featured a similarly furtive private eye, Jim Rockford, played by James Garner, who had survived five years of wrongful imprisonment and set himself up as a crime investigator in a trailer parked on a Los Angeles beach. This, too, was also a long-running success, from 1974 to 1980. But* The Fugitive, *which Huggins launched in September 1963, not only won an Emmy in 1965 for Outstanding Drama Series, and has recently been turned into a full-length movie starring Harrison Ford, remains his favourite. It is deservedly acknowledged as one of the* classic *television drama serials.*

Roy Huggins' fascination with loners developed during his own youth. Born in Portland, Oregon, he graduated from school with, he says 'the distinction of being voted the sloppiest kid', and then 'bummed around for several years'. He was briefly an industrial engineer before discovering his true métier as a writer and, ultimately, as a producer of films and television series. The Fugitive, which ABC began transmitting in September 1963, rapidly earned cult status as for one hundred and twenty episodes the hero Dr Richard Kimble (David Janssen), who had been wrongly accused of murdering his wife, kept one step ahead of the law in the person of Lieutenant Philip Gerard (Barry Morse) as he crisscrossed America in a variety of identities searching for an elusive one-armed man, Fred Johnson (Bill Risch), he knew had actually committed the killing. The final confrontation of the three characters was so eagerly awaited in August 1967 that the film had to be stored in great secrecy and then shown simultaneously all over the world on 29 August 1967, not surprisingly attracting record viewing figures. The legend of The Fugitive has long outlived the end of the series, however, and memories were revived for vast numbers of viewers when it was turned into a movie in 1993 with Tommy Lee Jones as the wise-cracking Lieutenant Gerard, very nearly stealing the picture from Harrison Ford, not forgetting a spectacular train crash that is already famous. Huggins had actually evolved the whole idea for the series from the following story, Man in the Dark which he wrote during his engineering days for Fantastic magazine in the autumn of 1952. Neither he – nor the readers of that long defunct magazine – could have had the slightest idea of the remarkable chain of events it would begin . . .

S HE CALLED ME at four-ten. 'Hi, Poopsie.'
   I scowled at her picture in the leather frame on my desk. 'For Chrisakes, Donna, will you lay off that 'Poopsie stuff? It's bad enough in the bedroom, but this is over the phone and in broad daylight.'

She laughed. 'It kind of slipped out. You know I'd never say it where anyone else could hear. Would I, Poopsie?'

'What's all that noise?'

'The man's here fixing the vacuum. Hey, we eating home tonight, or out? Or are you in another deadline dilemma?'

'No dilemma. Might as well –'

'Can't hear you, Clay.'

I could hardly hear *her*. I raised my voice. 'Tell the guy to turn that goddam thing off. I started to say we might as well eat out and then take in that picture at the Paramount. Okay?'

'All right. What time'll you get home?'

'Hour – hour'n a half.'

The vacuum cleaner buzz died out just as she said, '´Bye now,' and the two words sounded loud and unnatural. I put back the receiver and took off my hat and sat down behind the desk. We were doing a radio adaptation of *Echo of a Scream* that coming Saturday and I was just back from a very unsatisfactory rehearsal. When things don't go right, it's the producer who gets it in the neck, and mine was still sensitive from the previous week. I kept a small office in a building at Las Palmas and Yucca, instead of using the room allotted me at NBS. Some producers do that, since you can accomplish a lot more without a secretary breathing down your neck and the actors dropping in for gin rummy or a recital of their love life.

The telephone rang. A man's voice, deep and solemn, said, 'Is this Hillside 7–8691?'

'That's right,' I said.

'Like to speak to Mr Clay Kane.'

'I'm Clay Kane. Who's this?'

'The name's Lindstrom, Mr Kane. Sergeant Lindstrom, out of the sheriff's office, Hollywood sub-station.'

'What's on your mind, Sergeant?'

'We got a car here, Mr Kane,' the deep slow voice went on. 'Dark blue '51 Chevrolet, two-door, licence 2W78–40. Registered to Mrs Donna Kane, 7722 Fountain Avenue, Los Angeles.'

I could feel my forehead wrinkling into a scowl. 'That's my wife's car. What do you mean: you "got" it?'

'Well, now, I'm afraid I got some bad news for you, Mr Kane.' The voice went from solemn to grave. 'Seems your wife's car went off the road up near the Stone Canyon Reservoir. I don't know if you know it or not, but there's some pretty bad hills up –'

'I know the section,' I said. 'Who was in the car?'

'. . . Just your wife, Mr Kane.'

My reaction was a mixture of annoyance and mild anger. 'Not *my* wife, Sergeant. I spoke to her on the phone not five minutes ago. She's at home. Either somebody stole the car or, more likely, she loaned it to one of her friends. How bad is it?'

There was a pause at the other end. When the voice spoke again, the solemnity was still there, but now a vague thread of suspicion was running through it.

'The car burned, Mr Kane. The driver was still in it.'

'That's terrible,' I said. 'When did it happen?'

'We don't know exactly. That's pretty deserted country. Another car went by after it happened, spotted the wreck and called us. We figure it happened around two-thirty.'

'Not my wife,' I said again. 'You want to call her, she can tell you who borrowed the car. Unless, like I say, somebody swiped it. You mean you found no identification at all?'

'. . . Hold on a minute, Mr Kane.'

There followed the indistinct mumble you get when a hand is held over the receiver at the other end of the wire. I waited, doodling on a scratch pad, wondering vaguely if my car insurance would cover this kind of situation. Donna had never loaned the car before, at least not to my knowledge.

The sergeant came back. 'Hate to trouble you, Mr Kane, but I expect you better get out here. You got transportation, or would you want one of our men to pick you up?'

This would just about kill our plans for the evening. I tried reasoning with him. 'Look here, Officer, I don't want to sound cold-blooded about this, but what can I do out there? If the car was stolen, there's nothing I can tell you. If Mrs Kane let somebody use it, she can tell you who it was over the phone. Far as the car's concerned, my insurance company'll take care of that.'

The deep slow voice turned a little hard. 'Afraid it's not that simple. We're going to have to insist on this, Mr Kane. Take Stone Canyon until you come to Fontenelle Way, half a mile or so south of Mulholland Drive. The accident happened about halfway between those two points. I'll have one of the boys keep an eye out for you. Shouldn't take you more'n an hour at the most.'

I gave it another try. 'You must've found *some* identification, Sergeant. Something that –'

He cut in sharply. 'Yeah, we found something. Your wife's handbag. Maybe she loaned it along with the car.'

A dry click meant I was alone on the wire. I hung up slowly and sat there staring at the wall calendar. That handbag bothered me. If Donna had loaned the Chevvy to someone, she wouldn't have gone off and left the bag. And if she'd left it on the seat while visiting or shopping, she would have discovered the theft of the car and told me long before this.

There was one sure way of bypassing all this guesswork. I picked up the receiver again and dialled the apartment.

After the twelfth ring I broke the connection. Southern California in August is as warm as anybody would want, but I was beginning to get chilly along the backbone. She could be at the corner grocery or at the Feldmans' across the hall, but I would have liked it a lot better if she had been in the apartment and answered my call.

It seemed I had a trip ahead of me. Stone Canyon Road came in between Beverly Glen Boulevard and Sepulveda, north of Sunset. That was out past Beverly Hills and the whole district was made up of hills and canyons, with widely scattered homes clinging to the slopes. A car could go off almost any one of the twisting roads through there and not be noticed for a lot longer than two hours. It was the right place for privacy, if privacy was what you were looking for.

The thing to do, I decided, was to stop at the apartment first. It was on the way, so I wouldn't lose much time, and I could take Donna along with me. Getting an explanation direct from her ought to satisfy the cops, and we could still get in a couple of drinks and a fast dinner, and make that première.

I covered the typewriter, put on my hat, locked up and went down to the parking lot. It was a little past four-twenty.

II

It was a five-minute trip to the apartment building where Donna and I had been living since our marriage seven months before. I waited while a fat woman in red slacks and a purple and burnt-orange blouse pulled a yellow Buick away from the kerb, banging a fender or two in the process, then parked and got out on to the walk.

It had started to cool off a little, the way it does in this part of the country along toward late afternoon. A slow breeze rustled the dusty fronds of palm trees lining the parkways along Fountain Avenue. A thin pattern of traffic moved past and the few pedestrians in sight had the look of belonging there.

I crossed to the building entrance and went in. The small foyer was deserted and the mail box for 2C, our apartment, was empty. I unlocked the inner door and climbed the carpeted stairs to the second floor and walked slowly down the dimly lighted corridor.

Strains of a radio newscast filtered through the closed door of the apartment across from 2C. Ruth Feldman was home. She might have word, if I needed it. I hoped I wouldn't need it. There was the faint scent of jasmine on the air.

I unlocked the door to my apartment and went in and said, loudly: 'Hey, Donna. It's your ever-lovin'.'

All that came back was silence. Quite a lot of it. I closed the door and leaned against it and heard my heart thumping away. The white metal Venetian blinds at the living room windows overlooking the street were lowered but not turned and there was a pattern of sunlight on the maroon carpeting. Our tank-type vacuum cleaner was on the floor in front of the fireplace, its hose tracing a lazy S along the rug like a grey python, the cord plugged into a wall socket.

The silence was beginning to rub against my nerves. I went into the bedroom. The blind was closed and I switched on one of the red-shaded lamps on Donna's dressing table. Nobody there. The double bed was made up, with her blue silk robe across the foot and her slippers with the powder blue pompons under the trailing edge of the pale yellow spread.

My face in the vanity's triple mirrors had that strained look. I turned off the light and walked out of there and on into the bathroom, then the kitchen and breakfast nook. I knew all the time Donna wouldn't be in any of them; I had known it from the moment that first wave of silence answered me.

But I looked anyway . . .

She might have left a note for me, I thought. I returned to the bedroom and looked on the night stand next to the telephone. No note. Just the day's mail: two bills, unopened; a business envelope from my agent, unopened, and a letter from Donna's mother out in Omaha, opened and thrust carelessly back into the envelope.

The mail's being there added up to one thing at least: Donna had been in the apartment after three o'clock that afternoon. What with all this economy wave at the Post Offices around the country, we were getting one delivery a day and that not before the middle of the afternoon. The phone call, the vacuum sweeper, the mail on the nightstand: they were enough to prove that my wife was around somewhere. Out for a lipstick, more than likely, or a carton of Fatimas, or to get a bet down on a horse.

I left the apartment and crossed the hall and rang the bell to 2D. The news clicked off in the middle of the day's baseball scores and after a moment the door opened and Ruth Feldman was standing there.

'Oh. Clay.' She was a black-haired little thing, with not enough colour from being indoors too much, and a pair of brown eyes that, in a prettier face, would have made her something to moon over on long winter evenings. 'I *thought* it was too early for Ralph; he won't be home for two hours yet.'

'I'm looking for Donna,' I said. 'You seen her?'

She leaned negligently against the door edge and moved her lashes at me. The blouse she was wearing was cut much too low. 'No-o-o. Not since this morning anyway. She came in about eleven for coffee and a cigarette. Stayed maybe half an hour, I guess it was.'

'Did she say anything about her plans for the day? You know: whether she was going to see anybody special, something like that?'

She lifted a shoulder. 'Hunhuh. She did say something about her agent wanting her to have lunch with this producer – what's his name? – who does the Snow Soap television show. They're casting for a new musical and she thinks that's why this lunch. But I suppose you know about that. You like to come in for a drink?'

I told her no and thanked her and she pouted her lips at me. I could come in early any afternoon and drink her liquour and give her a roll in the hay, no questions asked, no obligations and no recriminations. Not just because it was me, either. It was there for anyone who was friendly, no stranger and had clean fingernails. You find at least one like her in any apartment house, where the husband falls asleep on the couch every night over a newspaper or the television set.

I asked her to keep an eye out for Donna and tell her I had to run out to Stone Canyon on some urgent and unexpected business and that I'd call in the first chance I got. She gave me a big smile and an up-from-under stare and closed the door very gently.

I lighted a cigarette and went back to the apartment to leave a note for Donna next to the telephone. Then I took a last look around and walked down one flight to the street, got into the car and headed for Stone Canyon.

III

It was a quarter past five by the time I got out there. There was an especially nasty curve in the road just to the north of Yestone, and off on the left shoulder where the bend was sharpest three department cars were drawn up in a bunch. A uniformed man was taking a smoke behind the wheel of the lead car; he looked up sharply as I made a U-turn and stopped behind the last car.

By the time I had cut off the motor and opened the door, he was standing there scowling at me. 'Where d'ya think you're goin', Mac?'

'Sergeant Lindstrom telephoned me,' I said, getting out on to the sparse sun-baked growth they call grass in California.

He ran the ball of a thumb lightly along one cheek and eyed me stonily from under the stiff brim of his campaign hat. 'Your name Kane?'

'That's it.'

He took the thumb off his face and used it to point. 'Down there. They're waitin' for you. Better take a deep breath, Mac. You won't like what they show you.'

I didn't say anything. I went past him and on around the department car. The ground fell away in what almost amounted to a forty-five-degree slope, and a hundred yards down the slope was level ground. Down there a knot of men were standing near the scorched ruins of what had been an automobile. It could have been Donna's Chevvy or it could have been any other light job. From its condition and across the distance I couldn't tell.

It took some time and a good deal of care for me to work my way to the valley floor without breaking my neck. There were patches of scarred earth spaced out in a reasonably straight line all the way down the incline where the car had hit and bounced and hit again, over and over. Splinters of broken glass lay scattered about, and about halfway along was a twisted bumper and a section of grillwork. There was a good deal of brush around and it came in handy for hanging on while I found footholds. It was a tough place to get down, but the car at the bottom hadn't had any trouble making it.

A tall, slender, quiet-faced man in grey slacks and a matching sports shirt buttoned at the neck but without a tie was waiting for me. He nodded briefly and looked at me out of light blue eyes under thick dark brows.

'Are you Clay Kane?' It was a soft, pleasant voice, not a cop's voice at all.

I nodded, looking past him at the pile of twisted metal. The four men near it were looking my way, their faces empty of expression.

The quiet-faced man said, 'I'm Chief Deputy Martell, out of Hollywood. They tell me it's your wife's car, but that your wife wasn't using it. Has she told you yet who was?'

'Not yet; no. She was out when I called the apartment, although I'd spoken to her only a few minutes before.'

'Any idea where she might be?'

I shrugged. 'Several, but I didn't have a chance to do any checking. The sergeant said you were in a hurry.'

'I see. . . . I think I'll ask you to take a quick glance at the body we took out of the car. It probably won't do much good, but you never know. I'd better warn you: it won't be pleasant.'

'That's all right,' I said. 'I spent some time in the Pacific during the war. We opened up pill boxes with flame throwers.'

'That should help.' He turned and moved off, skirting the wreckage, and I followed. A small khaki tarpaulin was spread out on the ground, bulged in the centre where it covered an oblong object. Not a very big object. I began to catch the acrid-sweetish odour of burned meat, mixed with the faint biting scent of gasoline.

Martell bent and took hold of a corner of the tarpaulin. He said flatly, 'Do the best you can, Mr Kane,' and flipped back the heavy canvas.

It looked like nothing human. Except for the contours of legs and arms, it could have been a side of beef hauled out of a burning barn. Where the face had been was a smear of splintered and charred bone that bore no resemblance to a face. No hair, no clothing except for the remains of a woman's shoe still clinging to the left foot; only blackened, flame-gnawed flesh and bones. And over it all the stench of a charnel house.

I backed away abruptly and clamped down on my teeth, fighting back a wave of nausea. Martell allowed the canvas to fall back into place. 'Sorry, Mr Kane. We can't overlook any chances.'

'It's all right,' I mumbled.

'You couldn't identify . . . her?'

I shuddered. 'Christ, no! Nobody could!'

'Let's have a look at the car.'

I circled the wreck twice. It had stopped right side up, the tyres flat, the hood ripped to shreds, the engine shoved halfway into the front seat. The steering wheel was snapped off and the dashboard appeared to have been worked over with a sledge hammer. Flames had eaten away the upholstery and blackened the entire interior.

It was Donna's car; no doubt about that. The licence plates showed the right number and a couple of rust spots on the right rear fender were as I remembered them. I said as much to Chief Deputy Martell and he nodded briefly and went over to say something I couldn't hear to the four men.

He came back to me after a minute or two. 'I've a few questions. Nothing more for you down here. Let's go back upstairs.'

He was holding something in one hand. It was a woman's bag: blue suede, small, with a gold clasp shaped like a question mark. I recognised it and my mouth felt a little dry.

It was a job getting up the steep slope. The red loam was dry and crumbled under my feet. The sun was still high enough to be hot on my back and my hands were sticky with ooze from the sagebrush.

Martell was waiting for me when I reached the road. I sat down on the front bumper of one of the department cars and shook the loose dirt out of my shoes, wiped most of the sage ooze off my palms and brushed the knees of my trousers. The man in the green khaki uniform was still behind the wheel of the lead car but he wasn't smoking now.

I followed the sheriff into the front seat of a black and white Mercury with a buggy whip aerial at the rear bumper and a radio phone on the dash. He lit up a small yellow cigar in violation of a fire hazard signboard across the road from us. He dropped the match into the dashboard ashtray and leaned back in the seat and bounced the suede bag lightly on one of his broad palms.

IV

He said, 'One of the boys found this in a clump of sage halfway down the slope. You ever see it before?'

'My wife has one like it.'

He cocked an eye at me. 'Not like it, Mr Kane. This is hers. Personal effects, identification cards, all that. No doubt at all.'

'. . . Okay.'

'And that's your wife's car?'

'Yeah.'

'But you say it's not your wife who was in it?'

'No question about it,' I said firmly.

'When did you see her last?'

'Around nine-thirty this morning.'

'But you talked to her later, I understand.'

'That's right.'

'What time?'

'A few minutes past four this afternoon.'

He puffed out some blue smoke. 'Sure it was your wife?'

'If I wouldn't know, who would?'

His strong face was thoughtful, his blue eyes distant. 'Mrs Kane's a singer, I understand.'

'That's right,' I told him. 'Uses her maiden name: Donna Collins.'

He smiled suddenly, showing good teeth. 'Oh, sure. The missus and I heard her on the "Dancing in Velvet" programme last week. She's good – and a mighty lovely young woman, Mr Kane.'

I muttered something polite. He put some cigar ash into the tray and leaned back again and said, 'They must pay her pretty good, being a radio star.'

'Not a star,' I explained patiently. 'Just a singer. It pays well, of course – but nothing like the top names pull down. However, Donna's well fixed in her own right; her father died a while back and left her what amounts to quite a bit of money. . . . Look, Sheriff, what's the point of keeping me here? I don't know who the dead woman is, but since she was using my wife's car, the one to talk to is Mrs Kane. She's bound to be home by this time; why not ride into town with me and ask her?'

He was still holding the handbag. He put it down on the seat between us and looked off toward the blue haze that marked the foothills south of Burbank. 'Your wife's not home, Mr Kane,' he said very quietly.

A vague feeling of alarm stirred within me. 'How do you know that?' I demanded.

He gestured at the two-way radio. 'The office is calling your apartment at ten-minute intervals. As soon as Mrs Kane answers her phone, I'm to get word. I haven't got it yet.'

I said harshly, 'What am I supposed to do – sit here until they call you?'

He sighed a little and turned sideways on the seat far enough to cross his legs. The light blue of his eyes was frosted over now, and his jaw was a grim line.

'I'm going to have to talk to you like a Dutch uncle, Mr Kane. As you saw, we've got a dead woman down there as the result of what, to all intents and purposes, was an unfortunate accident. Everything points to the victim's being your wife except for two things, one of them your insistence that you spoke to her on the phone nearly two hours *after* the accident. That leaves us wondering – and with any one of several answers. One is that you're lying; that you didn't speak to her at all. If that's the right answer, we can't figure out the reason behind it. Two: your wife loaned a friend the car. Three: somebody lifted it from where it was parked. Four: you drove up here with her, knocked her in the head and let the car roll over the edge.'

'Of all the goddam –!'

He held up a hand, cutting me off. 'Let's take 'em one at a time. I can't see any reason, even if you murdered her, why you'd say your wife telephoned you afterwards. So until and unless something turns up to show us why you'd lie about it, I'll have to believe she did make that call. As for her loaning the car, that could very well have happened, only it doesn't explain why she's missing now. This business of the car's being stolen doesn't hold up, because the key was still in the ignition and in this case.'

He took a folded handkerchief from the side pocket of his coat and opened it. A badly scorched leather case came to light, containing the ignition and trunk keys. The rest of the hooks were empty. I sat there staring at it, feeling my insides slowly and painfully contracting.

'Recognise it?' Martell asked softly.

I nodded numbly. 'It's Donna's.'

He picked up the handbag with his free hand and thrust it at me. 'Take a look through it.'

Still numb, I released the clasp and pawed through the contents. A small green-leather wallet containing seventy or eighty dollars and the usual identification cards, one of them with my office, address and phone number. Lipstick, compact, mirror, comb, two initialled handkerchiefs, a few hairpins. The French enamel cigarette case and matching lighter I'd given her on her twenty-fifth birthday three months ago. Less than a dollar in change.

That was all. Nothing else. I shoved the stuff back in the bag and closed the clasp with stiff fingers and sat there looking dully at Martell.

He was refolding the handkerchief around the key case. He returned it to his pocket carefully, took the cigar out of his mouth and inspected the glowing tip.

'Your wife wear any jewellery, Mr Kane?' he asked casually.

I nodded. 'A wristwatch. Her wedding and engagement rings.'

'We didn't find them. No jewellery at all.'

'You wouldn't,' I said. 'Whoever that is down there, she's not Donna Kane.'

He sat there and looked out through the windshield and appeared to be thinking. He wore no hat and there was a stong sprinkling of grey in his hair and a bald spot about the size of a silver dollar at the crown. There was a network of fine wrinkles at the corners of his eyes, as there so often is in men who spend a great deal of time in the sun. He looked calm and confident and competent and not at all heroic.

Presently he said, 'That phone call. No doubt at all that it was your wife?'

'None.'

'Recognised her voice, eh?'

I frowned. 'Not so much that. It was more what she said. You know, certain expressions nobody else'd use. Pet name – you know.'

His lips quirked and I felt my cheeks burn. He said, 'Near as you can remember, tell me about that call. If she sounded nervous or upset – the works.'

I put it all together for him, forgetting nothing. Then I went on about stopping off at the apartment, what I'd found there and what Ruth Feldman had said. Martell didn't interrupt, only sat there drawing on his cigar and soaking it all in.

After I was finished, he didn't move or say anything for what seemed a long time. Then he leaned forward and ground out the stub of the cigar and put a hand in the coat pocket next to me and brought out one of those flapped bags women use for formal dress, about the size of a business envelope and with an appliquéd design worked into it. Wordlessly he turned back the flap and let a square gold compact and matching lipstick holder slide out into the other hand.

'Ever see these before, Kane?'

I took them from him. His expression was impossible to read. There was nothing unusual about the lipstick tube, but the compact had a circle of brilliants in one corner and the initials H.W. in the circle.

I handed them back. 'New to me, Sheriff.'

He was watching me closely. 'Think a minute. This can be important. Either you or your wife know a woman with the initials H.W.?'

'. . . Not that I . . . Helen? Helen ! Sure; Helen Wainhope! Dave Wainhope's wife.' I frowned. 'I don't get it, Sheriff.'

He said slowly, 'We found this bag a few feet from the wreck. Any idea how it might have gotten there?'

'Not that I can think of.'

'How well do you know these Wainhopes?'

'About as well as you get to know anybody. Dave is business manager for some pretty prominent radio people. A producer, couple of directors, seven or eight actors that I know of.'

'You mean he's an agent?'

'Not that. These are people who make big money but can't seem to hang on to it. Dave collects their cheques, puts 'em on an allowance, pays their bills and invests the rest. Any number of men in that line around town.'

'How long have you known them?'

'Dave and Helen? Two-three years. Shortly after I got out here. As a matter of fact, he introduced me to Donna. She's one of his clients.'

'The four of you go out together?'

'Now and then; sure.'

'In your wife's car?'

'. . . I see what you're getting at. You figure Helen might have left her bag there. Not a chance, Sheriff. We always used Dave's Cadillac. Helen has a Pontiac convertible.'

'When did you see them last?'

'Well, I don't know about Donna, but I had lunch with Dave . . . let's see . . . day before yesterday. He has an office in the Taft Building.'

'Where do they live?'

'Over on one of those little roads off Beverly Glen. Not far from here, come to think about it.'

With slow care he pushed the compact and lipstick back in the folder and dropped it into the pocket it had come out of. 'Taft Building, hunh?' he murmured. 'Think he's there now?'

I looked at my strapwatch. Four minutes till six. 'I doubt it, Sheriff. He should be home by this time.'

'You know the exact address?'

'Well, it's on Angola, overlooking the southern tip of the Reservoir. A good-sized redwood ranch house on the hill there. It's the only house within a couple miles. You can't miss it.'

He leaned past me and swung open the door. 'Go on home, Kane. Soon as your wife shows up, call the station and leave word for me. I may call you later.'

'What about her car?'

He smiled without humour. 'Nobody's going to swipe it. Notify your insurance agent in the morning. But I still want to talk to Mrs Kane.'

I slid out and walked back to my car. As I started the motor, the black and white Mercury made a tight turn on screaming tyres and headed north. I pulled back on to the road and tipped a hand at the deputy. He glared at me over the cigarette he was lighting.

I drove much too fast all the way back to Hollywood.

V

She wasn't there.

I snapped the switch that lighted the end-table lamps flanking the couch and walked over to the window and stood there for a few minutes, staring down into Fountain Avenue. At seven o'clock it was still light outside. A small girl on roller skates scooted by, her sun-bleached hair flying. A tall thin number in a pale-blue sports coat and dark glasses got leisurely out of a green convertible with a wolf tail tied to the radiator emblem and sauntered into the apartment building across the street.

A formless fear was beginning to rise within me. I knew now that it had been born at four-thirty when I stopped off on my way to Stone Canyon and found the apartment empty. Seeing the charred body an hour later had strengthened that fear, even though I knew the dead woman couldn't be Donna. Now that I had come home and found the place deserted, the fear was crawling into my throat, closing it to the point where breathing seemed a conscious effort.

Where was Donna?

I lighted a cigarette and began to pace the floor. Let's use a little logic on this, Kane. You used to be a top detective-story writer; let's see you go to work on this the way one of your private eyes would operate.

All right, we've got a missing woman to find. To complicate matters, the missing woman's car was found earlier in the day with a dead woman at the wheel. Impossible to identify her, but we know it's not the one we're after because *that* one called her husband *after* the accident.

Now, since your wife's obviously alive, Mr Kane, she's missing for one of two reasons: either she can't come home or she doesn't want to. 'Can't' would mean she's being held against her will; we've nothing to indicate *that*. That leaves the possibility of her not wanting to come home. What reason would a woman have for staying away from her husband? The more likely one would be that she was either sore at him for something or had left him for another man.

I said a short ugly word and threw my cigarette savagely into the fireplace. Donna would never pull a stunt like that! Hell, we'd only been married a few months and still as much in love as the day the knot was tied.

Yeah? How do you know? A lot of guys kid themselves into thinking the same thing, then wake up one morning and find the milkman has taken over. Or they find some hot love letters tied in blue ribbon and shoved under the mattress.

I stopped short. It was an idea. Not love letters, of course; but there might be something among her personal files that could furnish a lead. It was about as faint a possibility as they come, but at least it would give me something to do.

The big bottom drawer of her desk in the bedroom was locked. I remembered that she carried the key in the same case with those to the apartment and the car, so I used the fireplace poker to force the lock. Donna would raise hell about that when she got home, but I wasn't going to worry about that now.

There was a big manilla folder inside, crammed with letters, tax returns, receipted bills, bank books and miscellaneous papers, I dumped them out and began to paw through the collection. A lot of the stuff had come from Dave Wainhope's office, and there were at least a dozen letters signed by him explaining why he was sending her such-and-such.

The phone rang suddenly. I damned near knocked the chair over getting to it. It was Chief Deputy Martell.

'Mrs Kane show up?'

'Not yet. No.'

He must have caught the disappointment in my voice. It was there to catch. He said, 'That's funny . . . Anyway, the body we found in that car wasn't her.'

'I told you that. Who was it?'

'This Helen Wainhope. We brought the remains into the Georgia Street Hospital and her husband made the ID about fifteen minutes ago.'

I shivered, remembering. 'How could he?'

'There was enough left of one of her shoes. That and the compact did the trick.'

'He tell you why she was driving my wife's car?'

Martell hesitated. 'Not exactly. He said the two women had a date in town for today. He didn't know what time, but Mrs Wainhope's car was on the fritz, so the theory is that your wife drove out there and picked her up.'

'News to me,' I said.

He hesitated again. '. . . Any bad blood between your wife and . . . and Mrs Wainhope?'

'That's a hell of a question!'

'You want to answer it?' he said quietly.

You bet I do! They got along fine!'

'If you say so.' His voice was mild. 'I just don't like this coincidence of Mrs Kane's being missing at the same time her car goes off a cliff with a friend in it.'

'I don't care about that. I want my wife back.'

He sighed. 'Okay. Give me a description and I'll get out an all-points on her.'

I described Donna to him at length and he took it all down and said he'd be in touch with me later. I put back the receiver and went into the living room to make myself a drink. I hadn't eaten a thing since one o'clock that afternoon, but I was too tightened up with worry to be at all hungry.

Time crawled by. I finished my drink while standing at the window, put together a second and took it back into the bedroom and started through the papers from Donna's desk. At 8.15 the phone rang.

'Clay? This is Dave – Dave Wainhope.' His voice was flat and not very steady.

I said, 'Hello, Dave. Sorry to hear about Helen.' It sounded pretty lame, but it was the best I could do at the time.

'You know about it then?'

'Certainly I know about it. It was Donna's car, remember?'

'Of course, Clay.' He sounded very tired. 'I guess I'm not thinking too clearly. I called you about something else.'

'Yeah?'

'Look, Clay, it's none of my business, I suppose. But what's wrong between you and Donna?'

I felt my jaw sag a little. 'Who said anything was wrong?'

'All I know is, she was acting awfully strange. She wanted all the ready cash I had on hand, no explanation, no –'

My fingers were biting into the receiver. 'Wait a minute!' I shouted. 'Dave, listen to me! You *saw* Donna?'

'That's what I'm trying to tell you. She –'

'When?'

'. . . Why, not ten minutes ago. She –'

'Where? Where was she? Where did you see her?'

'Right here. At my office.' He was beginning to get excited himself. 'I stopped by on my way from the Georgia –'

I cut him off. 'Christ, Dave, I've been going nuts! I've been looking for her since four-thirty this afternoon. What'd she say? What kind of trouble is she in?'

'I don't know. She wouldn't tell me anything – just wanted money quick. No cheques. I thought maybe you and she had had a fight or something. I had around nine hundred in the safe; I gave it all to her and she beat –'

I shook the receiver savagely. 'But she must have said *something*! She wouldn't just leave without . . . you know . . .'

'She said she sent you a letter earlier in the day.'

I dropped down on the desk chair. My hands were shaking and my mouth was dry. 'A letter,' I said dully. 'A letter. Not in person, not even a phone call. Just a letter.'

By this time Dave was making comforting sounds. 'I'm sure it's nothing serious, Clay. You know how women are. The letter'll probably tell you where she is and you can talk her out of it.'

I thanked him and hung up and sat there and stared at my thumb. For some reason I felt even more depressed than before. I couldn't understand why Donna wouldn't have turned to me if she was in trouble. That was always a big thing with us: all difficulties had to be shared . . .

I went into the kitchen and made myself a couple of cold salami sandwiches and washed them down with another highball. At nine-twenty I telephoned the Hollywood sub-station to let Martell know what Dave Wainhope had told me. Whoever answered said the chief deputy was out and to call back in an hour. I tried to leave a message on what it was about, but was told again to call back and got myself hung up on.

About ten minutes later the buzzer from downstairs sounded. I pushed the button and was standing in the hall door when a young fellow in a postman's grey uniform showed up with a special-delivery letter. I signed for it and closed the door and leaned there and ripped open the envelope.

A single sheet of dime-store paper containing a few neatly typed lines and signed in ink in Donna's usual scrawl.

> *Clay darling:*
>
> *I'm terribly sorry, but something that happened a long time ago has come back to plague me and I have to get away for a few days. Please don't try to find me, I'll be all right as long as you trust me.*
>
> *You know I love you so much that I won't remain away a day longer than I have to. Please don't worry, darling, I'll explain everything the moment I get back.*
>
> *All my love,*
>
> > *Donna*

And that was that. Nothing that I could get my teeth into; no leads, nothing to cut away even a small part of my burden of concern. I walked into the bedroom with no spring in my step and dropped the letter on the desk and reached for the phone. But there was no point to that. Martell wouldn't be back at the station yet.

Maybe I had missed something. Maybe the envelope was a clue? A clue to what? I looked at it. Carefully. The postmark was Hollywood. That meant it had gone through the branch at Wilcox and Selma. At five-twelve that afternoon. At five-twelve I was just about pulling up behind those department cars out on Stone Canyon Road. She would have had to mail it at the post office instead of a drop box for me to get it four hours later.

No return address, front or back, as was to be expected. Just a cheap envelope, the kind you pick up at Woolworth's or Kress'. My name and the address neatly typed. The 'e' key was twisted very slightly to the right and the 't' was tilted just far enough to be noticeable if you looked at it long enough.

I let the envelope drift out of my fingers and stood there staring down at Donna's letter. My eyes wandered to the other papers next to it . . .

I said, 'Jesus Christ!' You could spend the next ten years in church and never say it more devoutly than I did at that moment. My eyes were locked to one of the letters David Wainhope had written to Donna – and in its typewritten lines two individual characters stood out like bright and shining beacons: a tilted 't' and a twisted 'e'!

VI

It took some time – I don't know how much – before I was able to do any straight-line thinking. The fact that those two letters had come out of the same typewriter opened up so many possible paths to the truth behind Donna's disappearance that – well, I was like the mule standing between two stacks of hay.

Finally I simply turned away and walked into the living room and poured a good half inch of bonded bourbon into a glass and drank it down like water after an aspirin. I damned near strangled on the stuff; and by the time I stopped gasping for air and wiping the tears out of my eyes, I was ready to do some thinking.

Back at the desk again, I sat down and picked up the two sheets of paper. A careful comparison removed the last lingering doubt that they had come out of the same machine. Other points began to fall into place: the fact that the typing in Donna's letter had been done by a professional. You can always tell by the even impression of the letters, instead of the dark-light-erasure-strike-over touch you find in an amateur job. And I knew that Donna had never used a typewriter in her life!

All right, what did it mean? On the surface, simply that somebody had typed the letter for Donna, and at Dave Wainhope's office. It had to be his office, for he would hardly write business letters at home – and besides I was pretty sure Dave was strictly a pen-and-pencil man himself.

Now what? Well, since it was typed in Dave's office, but not by Dave or Donna, it would indicate Dave's secretary had done the work. Does that hold up? It's got to hold up, friend; no one else works in that office but Dave and his secretary.

Let's kind of dig into that a little. Let's say that Donna dropped in on Dave earlier in the afternoon, upset about something. Let's say that Dave is out, so Donna dictates a note to me and the secretary types it out. Very simple . . . But is it?

No.

And here's why. Here are the holes: first, the note is on dime-store paper, sent in a dime-store envelope. Dave wouldn't have that kind of stationery in his office – not a big-front guy like Dave. Okay, stretch it all the way out; say that Donna had brought her own paper and had the girl use it. You still can't tell me Dave's secretary wouldn't have told her boss about it when he got back to the office. And if she told *him*, he would certainly have told *me* during our phone conversation.

But none of those points compares with the biggest flaw of them all: why would Donna have *any*one type the letter for her when a handwritten note would do just as well – especially on a very private and personal matter like telling your husband you're in trouble?

I got up and walked down the room and lighted a cigarette and looked out the window without seeing anything. A small voice in the back of my mind said, 'If all this brain work of yours is right, you know what it adds up to, don't you, pal?'

I knew. Sure, I knew. It meant that Donna Kane was a threat to somebody. It meant that she was being held somewhere; that she had been forced to sign a note to keep me from reporting her disappearance to the cops until whoever was responsible could make a getaway.

It sounded like a bad movie and I tried hard to make myself believe that's all it was. But the more I dug into it, the more I went over the results of my reasoning, the more evident it became that there was no other explanation.

You do only one thing in a case like that. I picked up the phone and called Martell again. He was still out. I took a stab at telling the desk sergeant, or whoever it was at the other end, what was going on. But it sounded so complex and confused, even to me, that he finally stopped me. 'Look, neighbour, call back in about fifteen-twenty minutes. Martell's the man you want to talk to.' He hung up before I could give him an argument.

His advice was good and I intended to take it. Amateur detectives usually end up with both feet stuck in their oesophagus. This was a police job. My part in it was to let them know what I'd found out, then get out of their way.

That secretary would know. She was in this up to the hilt. I had seen her a few times: a dark-haired girl, quite pretty, a little on the small side but built right. Big blue eyes; I remembered that. Quiet. A little shy, if I remembered right. What was her name? Nora. Nora something. Campbell? Kenton? No. Kemper? That was it: Nora Kemper.

I found her listed in the Central District phone book. In the 300 block on North Hobart, a few doors below Beverly Boulevard. I knew the section. Mostly apartment houses along there. Nothing fancy, but a long way from being a slum. The right neighbourhood for private secretaries. As I remembered, she had been married but was now divorced.

I looked at my watch. Less than five minutes since I'd called the sheriff's office. I thought of Donna tied and gagged and stuck away in, say, the trunk of some car. It was more than I could take.

I was on my way out the door when I thought of something else. I went back into the bedroom and dug under a pile of sports shirts in the bottom dresser drawer and took out the gun I'd picked up in San Francisco the year before. It was a Smith & Wesson .38, the model they called the Terrier. I made sure it was loaded, shoved it under the waistband of my slacks in the approved pulp-magazine style and left the apartment.

VII

It was a quiet street, bordered with tall palms, not much in the way of street lights. Both kerbs were lined with cars and I had to park half a block down and across the way from the number I wanted.

I got out and walked slowly back through the darkness. I was a little jittery, but that was to be expected. Radio music drifted from a bungalow court and a woman laughed thinly. A couple passed me, arm in arm, the man in an army officer's uniform. I didn't see anyone else around.

The number I was after belonged to a good-sized apartment building, three floors and three separate entrances. Five stone steps, flanked by a wrought-iron balustrade, up to the front door. A couple of squat Italian cypresses in front of the landing.

There was no one in the foyer. In the light from a yellow bulb in a ceiling fixture I could make out the names above the bell buttons. Nora Kemper's apartment was 205. Automatically I reached for the button, then hesitated. There was no inner door to block off the stairs. Why not go right on up and knock on her door? No warning, no chance for her to think up answers before I asked the questions.

I walked up the carpeted steps to the second floor and on down the hall. It was very quiet. Soft light from overhead fixtures glinted on pale green walls and dark green doors. At the far end of the hall a large window looked out on the night sky.

Number 205 was well down the corridor. No light showed under the edge of the door. I pushed a thumb against a small pearl button set flush in the jamb and heard a single flatted bell note.

Nothing happened. No answering steps, no questioning voice. A telephone rang twice in one of the other apartments and a car horn sounded from the street below.

I tried the bell again, with the same result. Now what? Force the door? No sense to that, and besides illegal entry was against the law. I wouldn't know how to go about it anyway.

She would have to come home eventually. Thing to do was stake out somewhere and wait for her to show up. If she didn't arrive within the next half hour, say, then I would hunt up a phone and call Martell.

I went back to the stairs and was on the point of descending to the first floor when I heard the street door close and light steps against the tile flooring down there. It could be Nora Kemper. Moving silently, I took the steps to the third floor and stood close to the wall where the light failed to reach.

A woman came quickly up the steps to the second floor. From where I stood I couldn't see her face clearly, but her build and the colour of her hair were right. She was wearing a light coat and carrying a white drawstring bag, and she was in a hurry. She turned in the right direction, and the moment she was out of sight I raced back to the second floor.

It was Nora Kemper, all right. She was standing in front of the door to 205 and digging into her bag for the key. I had a picture of her getting inside and closing the door and refusing to let me in.

I said, 'Hold it a minute, Miss Kemper.'

She jerked her head up and around, startled. I moved toward her slowly. When the light reached my face, she gasped and made a frantic jab into the bag, yanked out her keys and tried hurriedly to get one of them into the lock.

I couldn't afford to have that door between us. I brought the gun out and said sharply, 'Stay right there. I want to talk to you.'

The hand holding the keys dropped limply to her side. She began to back away, retreating toward the dead end of the corridor. Her face gleamed whitely, set in a frozen mask of fear.

She stopped only when she could go no farther. Her back pressed hard against the wall next to the window, her eyes rolled, showing the whites.

Her voice came out in a ragged whisper. 'Wha-what do you want?'

I said, 'You know me, Miss Kemper. You know who I am. What are you afraid of?'

Her eyes wavered, dropped to the .38 in my hand. 'The gun. I –'

'Hunh-uh,' I said. 'You were scared stiff before I brought it out. Recognising me is what scared you. Why?'

Her lips shook. Against the pallor of her skin they looked almost black. 'I don't know what . . . Don't stand . . . Please. Let me go.'

She tried to squeeze past me. I reached out and grabbed her by one arm. She gasped and jerked away – and her open handbag fell to the floor, spilling the contents.

She started after them, but I was there ahead of her. I had seen something – something that shook me like a solid right to the jaw.

Three of them, close together on the carpet. I scooped them up and straightened and jerked Nora Kemper around to face me. I shoved my open hand in front of her eyes, letting her see what was in it.

'Keys!' I said hoarsely. 'Take a good look, lady! They came out of your purse. The keys to my apartment, my mailbox. *My wife's keys!*'

A small breeze would have knocked her down. I took a long look at her stricken expression, then I put a hand on her shoulder and pushed her ahead of me down the hall. I didn't have to tell her what I wanted: she unlocked the door and we went in.

When the lights were on, she sank down on the couch. I stood over her, still holding the gun. My face must have told her what was going on behind it, for she began to shake uncontrollably.

I said, 'I'm a man in the dark, Miss Kemper. I'm scared, and when I get scared I get mad. If you don't want a mouth full of busted teeth, tell me one thing: *where is my wife?*'

She had sense enough to believe me. She gasped and drew back. 'He didn't tell me,' she wailed. 'I only did what he told me to do, Mr Kane.'

'What *who* told you?'

'David. Mr Wainhope.'

I breathed in and out. 'You wrote that letter?'

'. . . Yes.'

'Did you see my wife sign it?'

She wet her lips. 'She wasn't there. David signed it. There are samples of her signature at the office. He copied from one of them.'

I hadn't thought of that. 'What's behind all this?'

'I – I don't know.' She couldn't take her eyes off the gun. 'Really I don't, Mr Kane.'

'You know a hell of a lot more than I do,' I growled. 'Start at the beginning and give it to me. All of it.'

She pushed a wick of black hair off her forehead. Some of the colour was beginning to seep back into her cheeks, but her eyes were still clouded with fear.

'When I got back to the office from lunch this afternoon,' she said, 'David was out. He called me a little after three and told me to meet him at the corner of Fountain and Courtney. I was to take the Hollywood street car instead of a cab and wait for him there.'

'Did he say why?'

'No. He sounded nervous, upset. I was there within fifteen minutes, but he didn't show up until almost a quarter to four.'

'Go on,' I said when she hesitated.

'Well, we went into an apartment building on Fountain. Dave took out some keys and used one of them to take mail out of a box with your name on it. Then he unlocked the inner door and we went up to your apartment. He had the key to it, too. He gave me the keys and we went into the bedroom. He told me to call you and what to say. Before that, though, he hunted up the vacuum cleaner and started it going. Then I talked to you on the phone.'

I stared at her. 'You did fine. The cleaner kept me from realising it wasn't Donna's voice, and I suppose at one time or another Helen must've found out Donna called me "Poopsie" and told Dave about it. Big laugh! What happened after that?'

Her hands were clenched in her lap, whitening the knuckles. Her small breasts rose and fell under quick shallow breathing. Fear had taken most of the beauty out of her face.

'Dave opened one of the letters he had brought upstairs,' she said tonelessly, 'and left it next to the phone. We went back downstairs and drove back to the office. On the way Dave stopped off and bought some cheap stationery. I used some of it to write that letter. He told me to mail it at the post office right away, then he walked out. I haven't seen him since.'

'Secretaries like you,' I said sourly, 'must take some finding. Whatever the boss says goes. You don't find 'em like that around the broadcasting studios.'

Her head swung up sharply. 'I happen to love Dave . . . and he loves me. We're going to be married – now that he's free.'

My face ached from keeping my expression unchanged. 'How nice for both of you. Only he's got a wife, remember?'

She looked at me soberly. 'Didn't you know about that?'

'About what?'

'Helen Wainhope. She was killed in an automobile accident this afternoon.'

'When did you hear that?'

'David told me when he called in around three o'clock.'

I let my eyes drift to the gun in my hand. There was no point in flashing it around any longer. I slid it into one of my coat pockets and fished a cigarette out and used a green and gold table lighter to get it going. I said, 'And all this hocus-pocus about signing my wife's name to a phoney letter, calling me on the phone and pretending to be her – all this on the same day Dave Wainhope's wife dies – and you don't even work up a healthy curiosity? I find that hard to believe, Miss Kemper. You must have known he was into something way over his head.'

'I love David,' she said simply.

I blew out some smoke. 'Love isn't good for a girl like you. Leave it alone. It makes you stupid. Good night, Miss Kemper.'

She didn't move. A tear began to trace a jagged curve along her left cheek. I left her sitting there and went over to the door and out, closing it softly behind me.

VIII

At eleven o'clock at night there's not much traffic on Sunset, especially when you get out past the bright two-mile stretch of the Strip with its Technicolour neons, its plush nightclubs crowded with columnists and casting-couch starlets and vacationing Iowans, its modernistic stucco buildings with agents' names in stylised lettering across the fronts. I drove by them and dropped on down into Beverly Hills where most of the homes were dark at this hour, through Brentwood where a lot of stars hide out in big estates behind hedges and burglar alarms, and finally all that was behind me and I turned off Sunset on to Beverly Glen Boulevard and followed the climbing curves up into the foothills to the north.

The pattern was beginning to form. Dave Wainhope had known his wife was dead long before Sheriff Martell drove out to break the news to him. I saw that as meaning one thing: he must have had a hand in that 'accident' on Stone Canyon Road. He could have driven out there with Helen, then let the car roll over the lip of the canyon with her in it. The motive was an old, old one: in love with another woman and his wife in the way.

That left only Donna's disappearance to account for. In a loose way I had that figured out too. She might have arrived at Dave's home at the wrong time. I saw her walking in and seeing too much and getting herself bound and gagged and tucked away somewhere while Dave finished the job. Why he had used Donna's car to stage the accident was something I couldn't fit in for sure, although Sheriff Martell had mentioned that Helen's car hadn't been working.

It added up – and in the way it added up was the proof that Donna was still alive. Even with the certainty that Dave Wainhope had coldbloodedly sent his wife plunging to a horrible death, I was equally sure he had not harmed Donna. Otherwise the obvious move would have been to place her in the car with Helen and drop them both over the edge. A nice clean job, no witnesses, no complications. Two friends on their way into town, a second of carelessness in negotiating a dangerous curve – and the funeral will be held Tuesday!

The more I thought of it, the more trouble I was having in fitting Dave Wainhope into the role of murderer at all. He was on the short side, thick in the waistline, balding, and with the round guileless face you find on some infants. As far as I knew he had never done anything more violent in his life than refuse to tip a waiter.

None of that proved anything, of course. If murders were committed only by people who looked the part, there would be a lot more pinochle played in Homicide Bureaux.

I turned off Beverly Glen at one of the narrow unpaved roads well up into the hills and began to zigzag across the countryside. The dank smell of the distant sea drifted in through the open windows, bringing with it the too sweet odour of sage blossoms. The only sounds were the quiet purr of the motor and the rattle of loose stones against the underside of the fenders.

Then suddenly I was out in the open, with Stone Canyon Reservoir below me behind a border of scrub oak and manzanita and the sheen of moonlight on water. On my left, higher up, bulked a dark sharp-angled building of wood and stone and glass among flowering shrubs and bushes and more of the scrub oak. I followed a gravelled driveway around a sweeping half-circle and pulled up alongside the porch.

I cut off the motor and sat there. Water gurgled in the radiator. With the headlights off, the night closed in on me. A bird said something in its sleep and there was a brief rustling among the bushes.

The house stood big and silent. Not a light showed. I put my hand into my pocket next to the gun and got out on to the gravel. It crunched under my shoes on my way to the porch. I went up eight steps and across the flagstones and turned the big brass door-knob.

Locked. I hadn't expected it not to be. I shrugged and put a finger against the bell and heard a strident buzz inside that seemed to rock the building.

No lights came on. I waited a minute or two, then tried again, holding the button down for what seemed a long time. All it did was use up some of the battery.

Now what? I tried to imagine David Wainhope crouched among the portières with his hands full of guns, but it wouldn't come off. The more obvious answer would be the right one: he simply wasn't home.

I wondered if he would be coming home at all. By now he might be halfway to Mexico, with a bundle of his clients' cash in the back seat and no intention of setting foot in the States ever again. He would have to get away before somebody found Donna Kane and turned her loose to tell what had actually happened. I had a sharp picture of her trussed up and shoved under one of the beds. It was all I needed.

I walked over to one of the porch windows and tried it. It was fastened on the inside. I took out my gun and tapped the butt hard against the glass. It shattered with a sound like the breaking up of an ice jam. I reached through and turned the catch and slid the frame up far enough for me to step over the sill.

Nobody else around. I moved through the blackness until I found an arched doorway and a light switch on the wall next to that.

I was in a living room which ran the full length of the house. Modern furniture scattered tastefully about. Sponge-rubber easy chairs in pastel shades. An enormous wood-burning fireplace. Framed Greenwich Village smears grouped on one wall. A shiny black baby grand with a tasselled gold scarf across it and a picture in a leather frame of Helen Wainhope. Everything looked neat and orderly and recently dusted.

I walked on down the room and through another archway into a dining room. Beyond it was a hall into the back of the house, with three bedrooms, one of them huge, the others ordinary in size with a connecting bath. I went through all of them. The closets had nothing in them but clothing. There was nothing under the beds, not even a little honest dirt. Everything had a place and everything was in its place.

The kitchen was white and large, with all the latest gadgets. Off it was a service porch, with a refrigerator, a deep freeze big enough to hold a body (but without one in it), and a washing machine. The house was heated with gas, with a central unit under the house. No basement.

Donna was still missing.

I left the lights on and went outside and around the corner of the house to the three-car garage. The foldback doors were closed and locked, but a side entrance wasn't. One car inside: a grey Pontiac convertible I recognised as Helen's. Nobody in it and the trunk was locked. I gave the lid a half-hearted rap and said, 'Donna? Are you in there?'

No answer. No wild drumming of heels, no threshing about. No sound at all except the blood rushing through my veins and I probably imagined that.

Right then I knew I was licked. He had hidden her somewhere else or he had taken her with him. That last made no sense at all, but then he probably wasn't thinking sensibly.

Nothing left but to call the sheriff and let him know how much I'd learned and how little I'd found. I should have done that long before this. I went back to the house to hunt up the telephone. I remembered seeing it on a nightstand in one of the bedrooms and I walked slowly back along the hall to learn which one.

Halfway down I spotted a narrow door I had missed the first time. I opened it and a light went on automatically. A utility closet, fairly deep, shelves loaded with luggage and blankets, a couple of electric heaters stored away for use on the long winter nights. And that was all.

I was on the point of leaving when I noticed that a sizeable portion of the flooring was actually a removable trapdoor. I bent down and tugged it loose and slid it to one side, revealing a cement-lined recess about five feet deep and a good eight feet square. Stone steps, four of them, very steep, went down into it. In there was the central gas furnace and a network of flat pipes extending in all directions. The only illumination came from the small naked bulb over my head and at first I could see nothing beyond the unit itself.

My eyes began to get used to the dimness. Something else was down there on the cement next to the furnace. Something dark and shapeless. . . A pale oval seemed to swell and float up toward me.

'Donna!' I croaked. 'My good God, it's Donna!'

I half fell down the stone steps and lifted the lifeless body into my arms. Getting back up those steps and along the hall to the nearest bedroom is something I would never remember.

And then she was on the bed and I was staring down at her. My heart seemed to leap once and shudder to a full stop and a wordless cry tore at my throat.

The girl on the bed was Helen Wainhope!

IX

I once heard it said that a man's life is made up of many small deaths, the least of them being the final one. I stood there looking at the dead woman, remembering the charred ruins of another body beside a twisted heap of blackened metal, and in that moment a part of me stumbled and fell and whimpered and died.

The telephone was there, waiting. I looked at it for a long time. Then I took a slow uneven breath and shook my head to clear it and picked up the receiver.

'Put it down, Clay.'

I turned slowly. He was standing in the doorway, holding a gun down low, his round face drawn and haggard.

I said, 'You killed her, you son of a bitch.'

He wet his lips nervously. 'Put it down, Clay. I can't let you call the police.'

It didn't matter. Not really. Nothing mattered any more except that he was standing where I could reach him. I let the receiver drop back into place. 'Like something left in the oven too long,' I said. 'That's how I have to remember her.'

I started toward him. Not fast. I was in no hurry. The longer it lasted, the more I would like it.

He brought the gun up sharply. 'Don't make me shoot you. Stay right there. Please, Clay.'

I stopped. It took more than I had to walk into the muzzle of a gun. You have to be crazy, I guess, and I wasn't that crazy.

He began to talk, his tongue racing, the words spilling out. 'I didn't kill Donna, Clay. It was an accident. You've got to believe that, Clay! I liked her; I always liked Donna. You know that.'

I could feel my lips twisting into a crooked line. 'Sure. You always liked Donna. You always liked me, too. Put down the gun, Dave.'

He wasn't listening. A muscle twitched high up on his left cheek. 'You've got to understand how it happened, Clay. It was quick like a nightmare. I want you to know about it, to understand that I didn't intend . . .'

There was a gun in my pocket. I thought of it and I nodded. 'I'm listening, Dave.'

His eyes flicked to the body on the bed, then back to me. They were tired eyes, a little wild, the whites bloodshot. 'Not in here.' he said. He moved to one side. 'Go into the living room. Ahead of me. Don't do anything . . . foolish.'

I went past him and on along the hall. He was close behind me, but not close enough. In the silence I could hear him breathing.

I sat down on a sponge-rubber chair without arms. I said, 'I'd like a cigarette, Dave. You know, to steady my nerves. I'm very nervous right now. You know how it is. I'll just put my hand in my pocket and take one out. Will that be all right with you?'

He said, 'Go ahead,' not caring, not even really listening.

Very slowly I let my hand slide into the side pocket of my coat. His gun went on pointing at me. The muzzle looked as big as the Second Street tunnel. My fingers brushed against the grip of the .38. A knuckle touched the trigger guard and the chill feel was like an electric shock. His gun went on staring at me.

My hand came out again. Empty. I breathed a shallow breath and took a cigarette and my matches from behind my display handkerchief. My forehead was wet. Whatever heroes had, I didn't have it. I struck a match and lighted the cigarette and blew out a long plume of smoke. My hand wasn't shaking as much as I had expected.

'Tell me about it,' I said.

He perched on the edge of the couch across from me, a little round man in a painful blue suit, white shirt, grey tie and brown pointed shoes. He had never been one to go in for casual dress like everyone else in Southern California. Lamplight glistened along his scalp below the receding hairline and the muscle in his cheek twanged spasmodically.

'You knew Helen,' he said in a kind of far-away voice. 'She was a wonderful woman. We were married twelve years, Clay. I must have been crazy. But I'm not making much sense, am I?' He tried to smile but it broke on him.

I blew out some more smoke and said nothing. He looked at the gun as though he had never seen it before, but he kept on pointing it at me.

'About eight months ago,' he continued, 'I made some bad investments with my own money. I tried to get it back by other investments, this time with Donna's money. It was very foolish of me. I lost that, too.'

He shook his head with slow regret. 'It was quite a large sum, Clay. But I wasn't greatly worried. Things would break right before long and I could put it back. And then Helen found out about it . . .

'She loved me, Clay. But she wouldn't stand for my dipping into

Donna's money. She said unless I made good the shortage immediately she would tell Donna. If anything like that got out it would ruin me. I promised I would do it within two or three weeks.'

He stopped there and the room was silent. A breeze came in at the open window and rustled the drapes.

'Then,' David Wainhope said, 'something else happened, something that ruined everything. This isn't easy for me to say, but . . . well, I was having an . . . affair with my secretary. Miss Kemper. A lovely girl. You met her.'

'Yes,' I said. 'I met her.'

'I thought we were being very – well, careful. But Helen is – was a smart woman, Clay. She suspected something and she hired a private detective. I had no idea, of course . . .

'Today, Helen called me at the office. I was alone; Miss Kemper was at lunch. Helen seemed very upset; she told me to get home immediately if I knew what was good for me. That's the way she put it: "if you know what's good for you!"'

I said, 'Uh-*hunh*!' and went on looking at the gun.

'Naturally, I went home at once. When I got here, Donna was just getting out of her car in front. Helen's convertible was also in the driveway, so I put my car in the garage and came into the living room. I was terribly upset, feeling that Helen was going to tell Donna about the money.

'They were standing over there, in front of the fireplace. Helen was furious; I had never seen her quite so furious before. She told me she was going to tell Donna everything. I pleaded with her not to. Donna, of course, didn't know what was going on.

'Helen told her about the shortage, Clay. Right there in front of me. Donna took it better than I'd hoped. She said she would have to get someone else to look after her affairs but that she didn't intend to press charges against me. That was when Helen really lost her temper.

'She said she was going to sue me for divorce and name Miss Kemper; that she had hired a private detective and he had given her a report that same morning. She started to tell me all the things the detective had told her. Right in front of Donna. I shouted for her to stop but she went right on. I couldn't stand it, Clay. I picked up the poker and I hit her. Just once, on the head. I didn't know what I was doing. It – it was like a reflex. She died on the floor at my feet.'

I said, 'What am I supposed to do – feel sorry for you?'

He looked at me woodenly. I might as well have spoken to the wall. 'Donna was terribly frightened. I think she screamed, then she turned and ran out of the house. I heard her car start before I realised she would tell them I killed Helen.

'I ran out, shouting for her to wait, to listen to me. But she was already turning into the road. My car was in the garage, so I jumped into Helen's and went after her. I wasn't going to do anything to her, Clay; I just wanted her to understand that I hadn't meant to kill Helen, that it only happened that way.

'By the time we reached that curve on Stone Canyon I was close behind her. She was driving too fast and the car skidded on the turn and went over. I could hear it. All the way down I heard it. I'll never get that sound out of my mind.'

I shivered and closed my eyes. There was no emotion in me any more – only a numbness that would never really go away.

His unsteady voice went on and on. 'She must have died instantly. The whole front of her face . . . My mind began to work fast. If I could make the police think it was my wife who had died in the accident, then I could hide Helen's body and nobody would know. That way Donna would be the one missing and they'd ask you questions, not me.

'The wreckage was saturated with gasoline. I – I threw a match into it. The fire couldn't hurt her, Clay. She was already dead. I swear it. Then I went up to the car and looked through it for something of Helen's I could leave near the scene.

'I came back here,' he went on tonelessly, 'and hid Helen's body. And all the time thoughts kept spinning through my head. Nobody must doubt that it was Helen in that car. If I could just convince you that Donna was not only alive *after* the accident, but that she had gone away . . .

'It came to me almost at once. I don't know from where. Maybe when staying alive depends on quick thinking, another part of your mind takes over. Miss Kemper would have to help me –'

I waved a hand, stopping him. 'I know all about that. She told me. And for Christ's sake stop calling her Miss Kemper! You've been sleeping with her – remember?'

He was staring at me.' She told you? Why? I was sure –'

'You made a mistake,' I said. 'That note you signed Donna's name to was typed on the office machine. When I found that out I called on your Miss Kemper. She told me enough to get me started on the right track.'

The gun was very steady in his hand now. Hollows deepened under his cheeks. 'You – you told the police?'

'Certainly.'

He shook his head. 'No. You didn't tell them. They would be here now if you had.' He stood up slowly, with a kind of quiet agony. 'I'm sorry, Clay.'

My throat began to tighten. 'The hell with being sorry. I know. I'm the only one left. The only one who can put you in that gas chamber out at San Quentin. Now you make it number three.'

His face seemed strangely at peace. 'I've told you what happened. I wanted you to hear it from me, exactly the way it happened. I wanted you to know I couldn't deliberately kill anyone.'

He turned the gun around and reached out and laid it in my hand. He said, 'I suppose you had better call the police now.'

I looked stupidly down at the gun and then back at him. He had forgotten me. He settled back on the couch and put his hands gently down on his knees and stared past me at the night sky beyond the windows.

I wanted to feel sorry for him. But I couldn't. It was too soon. Maybe some day I would be able to.

After a while I got up and went into the bedroom and put through the call.

Footprints

BY JEFFERY FARNOL

Jasper Shrig, the Cockney, pipe-smoking Bow Street Runner was the first historical detective – apart from Sherlock Holmes who had made his debut as early as 1937 on American television (see my earlier anthology, The Television Detectives' Omnibus*) – to appear on BBC TV, in May 1964. The Bow Street Runners, the first police force in England who had been set up in the middle of the lawless eighteenth century and were named after the location of their London head- quarters, had been rarely featured in crime fiction until the series of novels featuring Shrig written by Jeffery Farnol (1878–1952) began to appear in the twenties. Farnol, who was then already famous for his romantic tales of high adventure, had been born in Aston but spent almost ten years in America as a theatre scene-painter before returning home in 1910. Exchanging his brush for a pen, he then scored a tremendous popular success with his very first novel,* The Broad Highway*, published that same year. He followed this with a string of roistering tales, all with period settings, including* The Amateur Gentleman *(1913),* Black Bartlemy's Treasure *(1920) and* Peregrine's Progress *(1922). Jasper Shrig, who was allegedly based on a real Bow Street Runner, made his debut in* The Loring Mystery *(1925) and continued to display his own peculiar and original methods of detection in* The Jade of Destiny *(1936) and* Murder By Nail *(1942) as well as several short stories. He was certainly not an obvious choice for television, but made his debut in the series* Detective *which was introduced by Rupert Davies, in his already famous guise as Maigret. (Interestingly, Alan Dobie, who would later become familiar to viewers as another period police officer, Peter Lovesey's Victorian Detective Sergeant Cribb of the newly formed Criminal Investigation*

Department, in Cribb *(Granada, 1980–3), appeared briefly in the series as an archaeological sleuth.)*

Jasper Shrig was portrayed on the screen by Patrick Troughton, the veteran character actor who is perhaps best remembered for his role as the jaunty second Doctor Who. *(The producer of* Shrig, *Verity Lambert, had also earlier been in charge of* Doctor Who *which might well explain the excellent casting.) Despite a strong audience reaction, however, Troughton refused to repeat the role in a second series made in 1968, and the part was taken over by Colin Blakely, who presented Shrig as a rather more self-effacing though none the less doggedly persistent Runner. The colourful fifty-minute episodes were also enthusiastically received by the press, Robert Ottaway of the* Daily Sketch, *for instance, reporting that they were 'put across with gusto and zest – the chief joy derived from Colin Blakley as the Bow Street Runner who chased his villains without any of that confusing ambiguity about right and wrong – he knew a black heart when he sniffed one.'*

James Thomas of the Daily Express *also declared that 'Detectives have had it easy all these years compared to the old-fashioned operators like Jasper Shrig, in whose peculiar, bizarre world of crime detection there were no screaming sirens, no guns, nothing but a kind of high melodrama.' Nevertheless Thomas believed here was an off-beat law enforcement officer viewers would enjoy seeing again. Jeffery Farnol himself had sadly not lived long enough to enjoy this acclaim for a character for whom he always nursed a soft spot. The story of* Footprints *is an archetypal Jasper Shrig case and a reminder of a unique character who, as the* Express *said, deserves another revival.*

Mr JASPER SHRIG, of Bow Street, leaning back on the great cushioned settle, stretched sturdy legs to the cheery fire and, having lighted his pipe, sipped his glass of the famous 'One and Only' with a relish that brought a smile to his companion's comely visage.

'Pretty cosy, Jarsper, I think?'

'There ain't,' sighed Mr Shrig, glancing round about the trim, comfortable kitchen, 'a cosier place in London, say England, say the uniwerse than this here old "Gun" – thanks to you, Corporal Dick. You've only got an 'ook for an 'and but you're so 'andy wi' that 'ook, so oncommon 'andy that there ain't no vord for it, so, Dick – your werry good 'ealth, pal!'

Corporal Richard Roe, late of the Grenadiers, flushed and being a man somewhat slow of speech, muttered:

'Thankee, comrade,' and thereafter sat gazing at the bright fire and caressing his neatly trimmed right whisker with the gleaming steel hook that did duty for the hand lost at Waterloo.

'On sich con-wiwial occasions as this here,' murmured Mr Shrig, also gazing at the fire, 'when I'm as you might say luxooriating in a pipe, a glass and the best o' pals and comrades, my mind nat'rally runs to corpses, Dick.'

'Lord!' exclaimed the Corporal, somewhat surprised, 'why so, Jarsper?'

'Because, Dick, in spite o' Windictiveness in the shape o' bludgeons, knives, bullets, flat-irons and a occasional chimbley-pot, I'm werry far from being a corpse – yet. For vitch I'm dooly thankful. Now talkin' o' corpses, Dick –'

'But, Jarsper – I ain't.'

'No, but you will, for I am, d'ye see. Now folks as have been "took off" by wiolence or as you might say The Act, wictims o' Murder, Dick – vith a capital M, – said parties don't generally make pretty corpses, not as a rule – no.'

'Which,' said the Corporal, shaking his comely head, 'can't 'ardly be expected, Jarsper.'

'But,' continued Mr Shrig, sucking at his pipe with very evident enjoyment, 'contrairywise I 'ave never see an 'andsomer, cleaner, neater ca-daver than Sir W. Glendale made, – so smiling, so peaceful, – and mind ye, Dick, with a knife, a ordinary butcher's knife druv clean into 'is buzzum – up to the werry grip, or as you might say 'andle. Smiling he was, Dick, as if 'e 'ad been "took off" in the werry middle of a bee-ootiful dream . . . a dream – stop a bit!' exclaimed Mr Shrig and sat up, his eyes suddenly alert and very keen. 'A . . . dream!' he repeated.

'You said that afore, Jarsper – twice.'

''Twas the face of a man . . . as died . . . in his sleep . . . fast asleep!' mused Mr Shrig. 'Now why should a man sleep . . . so werry sound? You'll mind the case I think – eh, Dick?'

'For sure, Jarsper, the misfortunate gentleman was murdered about a year ago.'

'A year?' mused Mr Shrig, pausing with toddy glass at his grim, clean-shaven lips. 'Say nine months, say ten – stop a bit till I take a peep at my little reader.' Setting down his glass he drew from the bosom of his neat, brass-buttoned coat, a small, much worn notebook whose close written pages he thumbed slowly over, murmuring hoarsely: 'D E F G . . . Griggs . . . Goreham, Grant, – and 'ere we are – Glendale . . . Sir William . . . Baronet . . . Murdered . . . June one . . . Sitting at desk . . . Murderer – wanting!'

'Ay,' nodded the Corporal, leaning forward to touch the cheery fire with caressing poker, ''tis one o' them crimes as was never found out.'

'And, Dick, your memory sarved you true – for the Act was commit – eggsaxetly a year ago this here werry night!'

'And I suppose it never will be found out now, eh, Jarsper?'

'Why since you axes me so p'inted, Dick, I answers you, ready and prompt – oo knows? Hows'ever I'm a-vaiting werry patient.'

'Ay, but wot for?'

'Another chance p'raps . . . dewelopments!'

'Jarsper, I don't quite twig you.'

'Dick, I didn't expect as you would. Lookee now, – there's murderers vich, – if not took and "topped" or as you might say, scragged, – as gets that owdacious, – well, Murder grows quite an 'abit wi' 'em and – wot's that?'

'Eh?' said the Corporal, starting. 'I didn't hear anything.'

'Sounded like a dog whining somewheres,' murmured Mr Shrig, glancing vaguely about. 'There 'tis again!'

'You've got such precious sharp listeners, Jarsper,' said the Corporal, heaving his gigantic person lightly afoot as Mr Shrig rose, and together they crossed the snug kitchen and, opening the door, peered along the narrow, dim-lit passage beyond. Suddenly, as they stood thus mute and hearkening, from without the door at the end of this passage came a low, wailing cry, very desolate and evil to hear.

'That's no dog, Jarsper!' muttered the Corporal. 'Somebody's ill or hurt, – that's a child's voice or a woman's.'

'No, Dick, that's the woice o' fear . . . terror, Dick – lad. Now, stand by, pal.' So saying, Mr Shrig advanced towards that dim and narrow door, but the big Corporal, reaching forth a long arm, set him gently though firmly aside.

'Let me, comrade!' said he, motioning towards the door with his gleaming hook. 'Halt, Jarsper, there's too much viciousness laying in wait for you, so let me.' Then soundlessly he unbarred the door, drew it suddenly wide and – with a slithering rustle a vague shape swayed in and lay motionless at the Corporal's feet.

'A woman, Jarsper!' said he in hushed voice, stooping above this vague shape.

'Oh? Dead, Dick?'

'Looks that way, Jarsper.'

'Then in wi' her – so! Now shut the door – quick! Lock it, pal, and likewise bar it and shoot the bolts!'

II

'Lord love us, Jarsper!' whispered the Corporal, ruffling his short curly hair with glittering hook, and staring at the lovely form, outstretched upon the wide settle. 'Lord love us, here's a rum go!'

'Vich, Dick, you never said truer vord!' whispered Mr Shrig, staring also. 'For no go vas ever rummer, pal! . . . A tip-top svell by the looks o' her, a reg'lar heavy-toddling nob-ess, Dick!'

'Anyway, Jarsper, she ain't dead, thank God!'

'No, Dick, she's only swounding, vich females is apt to do now an' then, sich being their natur', d'ye see.'

'Which makes a man thankful as he never married, comrade.'

'Amen!' muttered Mr Shrig, fervently.

'But what's to do now, Jarsper? What's the correct evolution? How to bring the lady round, comrade?'

'Cold vater applied out'ardly is reckoned pretty good, Dick, but sperrits took innardly is better, I fancy. So get the rum, pal, or brandy – vichever comes 'andiest – stop a bit, this'll do!' And reaching his own glass of the 'One and Only,' Mr Shrig knelt beside the swooning girl whose face showed so pale beneath its heavy braids and coquettish ringlets of glossy, black hair, and tenderly raising this lovely head, he set the toddy to her lips, – but, even then, she shuddered violently and opening great, fearful eyes, recoiled so suddenly that the toddy-glass went flying.

'Dead!' she cried in awful, gasping voice, then checking the outcry upon her lips with visible effort she stared from Mr Shrig upon his knees, to the towering, soldierly figure of Corporal Richard Roe, and wringing her slim, gloveless hands, spoke in quick, breathless fashion:

'I want . . . who . . . which is Jasper Shrig, the Bow Street officer? I . . . I want Mr Shrig, of Bow Street –'

'Mam,' answered Mr Shrig gently, 'that werry identical same is now a-speaking.'

'Yes,' she cried, leaning towards him with a strange eagerness 'Yes . . . I see you are, now! You . . . oh you surely must remember me?'

'Ay . . . by Goles . . . I surely . . . do!' nodded Mr Shrig.

'I am Adela Glendale . . . a year ago I was . . . suspected of . . . of –'

'Not by me, leddy, never by me, mam.'

'No, no, you believed in me then, thank God! You were my good friend – then! But tonight. . . . Oh, Mr Shrig – dear Jasper Shrig,' she cried, and reaching out she clutched at him with both trembling hands in frantic appeal.

'You believed in me then, you were kind to me then, you stood between me and shameful horror a year ago. . . . Oh, be kind to me now, believe in me now . . . for tonight . . . it has happened again . . . horrible! Oh God help me, it has happened again!'

'Eh? . . . Murder?' questioned Mr Shrig in hoarse whisper.

'Yes – yes . . . and the house full of guests! . . . But he's dead . . . Uncle Gregory is dead – horrible! See – look at me!' And with swift, wild gesture she threw open the long mantle that shrouded her loveliness and showed white satin gown – its bosom and shoulder blotched with hideous stain. 'Look! Look!' she gasped, staring down at these dreadful evidences with shuddering horror. 'His blood . . . I'm foul of it . . . dear Uncle Gregory!'

Mr Shrig surveyed these ghastly smears with eyes very bright and keen, his lips pursed as if about to whistle though no sound came; then, drawing the cloak about her, he set himself to soothe and comfort her, and he did it with voice and touch so unexpectedly kind and gentle that Corporal Dick, smoothing neat whisker with his hook, stared for very wonder.

'And now,' said Mr Shrig when their visitor seemed more composed, 'now, Miss Adele, mam, 'spose you tell us all as you know.'

'But what; what can I tell you?' she answered with a gesture of helplessness. 'I only know that Uncle Gregory . . . dear Uncle Gregory is . . . horribly dead. Oh, Mr Shrig, I shall never forget the awful –'

'There, there, my dear!' said Mr. Shrig patting the quivering hand that clasped his so eagerly. 'But you mentioned summat about guests.'

'Yes, there were people to dinner, five or six. But –'

'Oo invited them?'

'My half-cousin, Roger. . . . But, oh, when I think of how uncle –'

'Any strangers among 'em, – these guests, Miss Adele?'

'No, they were family friends. . . . But Uncle Gregory had not been very well today and so soon as dinner was over, he excused himself and went to his room.'

'Upstairs to bed, mam?'

'Not upstairs, he sleeps on the ground floor at the back of the house, looking on to the garden.'

'And 'e vas ill today, you tell me? Sick, eh?'

'Oh, no no, it was only a touch of gout.'

'Gout, eh? Now did 'e say anything to you afore 'e went to his room?'

'Yes, he told me he felt very drowsy and could hardly keep his eyes open.'

'But gout, mam, don't make a man drowsy. Had Sir Gregory drank much wine at dinner?'

'Very little.'

'And yet,' murmured Mr Shrig, staring down at the slender hand he was still patting gently, 'and yet – so werry sleepy! Did he say anything more as you can call to mind now?'

'He ordered the butler to take his coffee to the bedroom, and told me he would come back later if the drowsiness passed off . . . And those were his last words, Mr Shrig, the very last words I shall ever hear him speak.'

'And now, mam, tell me o' poor Mr Roger, your cousin.'

'Half-cousin, Mr Shrig!' she corrected hastily. 'Roger was poor Uncle William's step-son.'

'Bit of an inwalid, ain't 'e?'

'Roger is a paralytic, he can't walk and uses a wheeled chair, – but surely you remember this, Mr Shrig; you seemed to fancy his society very much a year ago . . . when –'

'A year ago this werry night, Miss Adele, mam!' said Mr Shrig with ponderous nod. 'And a parrylitick . . . to . . . be . . . sure! Instead o' legs – veels, and at his age too, poor, unfort'nate young genleman!'

'Roger is older than you think, older than he looks . . . sometimes I think he never was young, and sometimes –' Here she shuddered violently again and clasped the strong hand she held, fast between her own. 'Oh, Mr Shrig,' she gasped, what . . . what can I do . . .? Uncle Gregory . . . I left him . . . sitting there in his great elbow-chair beside the fire . . . so still and dreadful! Oh tell me . . . what . . . what must I do –?'

'First,' answered Mr Shrig gently, 'you must give me your other little daddle – that's to say, your 'and, mam, my dear – so! Now . . . steady and easy it is . . . tell me just 'ow you found him.'

'As soon as I could leave the company I stole away' . . . I knocked softly on his door . . . I went in . . . The room was dark except for the fire but I . . . could see him . . . sitting in his great chair. I thought him dozing so I crept up to settle him more cosily and . . . to kiss him. I slipped my arm about him. I . . . I kissed his white head . . . so lightly and . . . Ah, God he slipped . . . sideways and . . . I saw –!'

'Dick,' murmured Mr Shrig, clasping ready arm about that horror-shaken form, 'the brandy!'

'No! no!' she gasped, 'I'm not going to . . . swoon. Only help me, Mr Jasper, be my friend for I . . . I'm afraid . . . terribly afraid! I was the last to speak with him, the last to see him alive –'

'No, Miss Adele, mam, the last to see 'im alive vas the man as killed him.'

'Oh . . . friend!' she murmured. 'My good, kind Jasper Shrig,' and viewing him through tears of gratitude, bowed her head against the shoulder of the neat, brass-buttoned coat and with face thus hidden, spoke again, her voice ineffably tender: 'But I'm afraid for – another also, Mr Shrig.'

'Ay, to be sure!' nodded Mr Shrig, 'Oo is 'e, Miss Adele, mam?'

'John!' she murmured, 'Mr Winton, – you remember him? He was Uncle Gregory's secretary. But, oh, Mr Shrig, three days ago they quarrelled! That is, uncle was very angry with poor John and – discharged him because . . . John had dared to fall in love with me.'

'Humph! And do you love said Mr John, mam?'

'With all my poor heart. So you see, if you are my friend and believe in me, you must be his friend too, for the danger threatening me, threatens him also . . . there is a dreadful shadow over us.'

'But then, mam, a shadder's only a shadder – even if it do go on veels.'

'Oh, Mr Shrig!'

'And 'ave you seen Mr John since day of discharge?'

Here she was silent, staring down great-eyed at her fingers that twined and clasped each other so nervously, until at last Mr Shrig laid his large firm hand upon them and questioned her again:

'Miss Adele – mam, if Shrig, o' Bow Street, bap-tismal name, Jarsper, is to aid you and said Mr John you must say eggsackly 'ow and also vhereabouts you see him this night.'

'I . . . I thought I saw him . . . in the garden,' she whispered.

'Didn't speak to 'im, then?'

'No, I was too distraught . . . sick with horror, I could only think of –' The faltering voice stopped suddenly as came a loud, imperious knocking on the outer door.

'Now oo in the vide uniwerse –'

'That must be John, now!' she cried, looking up with eyes bright and joyous, 'I hope, I pray it is.'

'But 'ow should he come to the "Gun," if you didn't tell 'im as you –'

'Oh, I bade Mary, my old nurse, tell him I'd run off to you . . . and oh, please see if it is indeed John.'

So, at a nod from Mr Shrig away strode the Corporal forthwith. Voices in the passage, a hurry of footsteps and in came a tall young man who, with no eyes and never a thought for anything on earth but the lovely creature who rose in such eager welcome, dropped his hat, was across the kitchen and had her in his arms, all in as many moments.

'My dear,' he murmured, 'oh, my dear, why did you run away? What new horror is this?'

'John, tell me, tell me – why were you in the garden tonight?'

'Dear heart, for word with you. Roger wrote me he'd contrive us a meeting, like the good, generous friend I'm sure he is –'

'Oh, John,' she wailed, clasping him as if to protect, 'how blind, how blind you are!'

'And, Mr Vinton, sir,' murmured Mr Shrig, pointing sinewy finger, 'your fob as was – ain't!' The young gentleman started, turned, clapped hand to fob pocket and glanced from the speaker to Adele with expression of sudden dismay.

'Gone!' he exclaimed. 'The seal you gave me, dear heart.'

'Ay, 'tis gone sure enough, sir,' nodded Mr Shrig. 'The question is: how? and likevise vheer? And now, seeing as none on us ain't likely to – tell, vot I says is – Corporal Dick, send out for a coach.'

'I've a hackney-carriage waiting,' said John, holding out his hand, 'for, by heaven, Mr Shrig, I'm heartily glad to have you with us at this dreadful time!'

'Then, sir,' answered Mr Shrig reaching for his hat and knobbly stick, 'all I axes is as you'll be guided by me, – both on you. If I says go, you'll go, – if I says stay, you stay and – wicy-wersa. And so, Corporal Dick, clap on your castor and come along o' Jarsper.'

III

Pallid faces, voices that whispered awfully and became awfully hushed when Mr Shrig, opening the door of the fatal room, passed in, beckoning Corporal Dick to follow.

'Dick,' said he, softly, 'shut the door and lock it.'

A stately chamber whose luxurious comfort was rendered cosier by the bright fire that flickered on the hearth with soft, cheery murmur; and before this fire a great, cushioned chair from which was thrust a limp arm that dangled helplessly, with a drooping hand whose long, curving fingers seemed to grope at the deep carpet.

'So, there it is, pal!' quoth Mr Shrig briskly. 'Let's see vot it's got to tell us,' and crossing to the chair he stooped to peer down at that which sprawled so grotesquely among its cushions.

'Dick,' said he at last, and so suddenly that the Corporal started, 'light them candles, will ee?'

'Candles, Jarsper?' inquired the Corporal, glancing vaguely about.

'Right afore ye, Dick, on the mantel-shelf.'

Having lit these candles at the fire, this big Corporal, who had faced unmoved the horrors of Waterloo, blenched at the thing in the chair which death had smitten in such gruesome fashion amid the comfort of this luxurious room.

'Oh – ecod, Jarsper!' he whispered.

'Ay,' nodded Mr Shrig, bending yet closer, "e's pretty considerable dead, I never see a deader, no! And yet, in spite o' the gore, 'e looks werry surprising peaceful . . . werry remarkably so! . . . Killed by a downward stab above the collarbone, lookee, – in the properest place for it . . .

A knife or, say a dagger and same – wanished . . . Eh, where are ye, Dick?'

'Comrade,' exclaimed the Corporal in sudden excitement, 'will ye step over here to the winder?'

'Eh . . . the vinder?' murmured Mr Shrig, his keen gaze roving from the figure in the chair to the gleaming moisture beneath it, to those helpless fingers and the shining object they seemed to grasp at, to the small table nearby with open book, the box of cigars, the delicate Sèvres cup and saucer. 'Eh . . . the vinder? Why so, Dick?'

'It's . . . open, Jarsper!'

'Oh?' murmured Mr Shrig, his roving gaze fixed at last. 'Is it? Look thereabouts and y'may see summat of a dagger, pal, or say, a knife.'

'Why, Jarsper . . . Lord love me, here it is!'

'Werry good, bring it over and let's take a peep at it. . . . Ah, a ordinary butcher's knife, eh, Dick? Vally about a bob – say, eighteen pence. Has it been viped?'

'No, comrade, it's blooded to the grip.'

'That cup and saucer now?' mused Mr Shrig.

'Half full o' coffee . . . vot's that got to tell us?' Saying which, he took up the dainty cup, sniffed at it, tasted its contents and stood beaming down at the fire, his rosy face more benevolent than usual. Then from one of his many pockets he drew a small phial into which he decanted a little of the coffee very carefully, whistling softly beneath his breath the while.

'What now, Jarsper?'

'Why, Dick, I'll tell ye, pat and plain, there's coffee in this world of all sorts, this, that and t'other and this is that. And, Dick, old pal, the only thing as flummoxes me now is veels.'

'Wheels?' repeated the Corporal. 'Jarsper, I don't twig.'

'Vell, no, Dick, no, it aren't to be expected. But you've noticed so werry much already, come and take another peep at our ca-daver. Now, vot d'ye see, pal?'

'Very remarkable bloody, Jarsper.'

'True! And vot more?'

'The pore old gentleman 'ad begun to smoke a cigar, – there it lays now, agin the fender.'

'Eh, cigar?' exclaimed Mr Shrig, starting. 'Now, dog bite me, if I 'adn't missed that. There 'tis sure enough and there . . . by Goles . . . there's the ash – look, Dicky lad, look – vot d'ye make o' that, now?'

'Why, Jarsper, I makes it no more than – ash.'

'Ay, so it is, Dick and werry good ash, too! Blow my dicky if I don't think it's the best bit of ash as ever I see!' Here, indeed, Mr Shrig became so extremely attracted by this small pile of fallen cigar-ash that he plumped down upon his knees before it, much as if in adoration thereof, and was still lost in contemplation of it when the Corporal uttered a sharp exclamation, and grasping his companion by the shoulder pointed with gleaming hook:

'Lord, comrade – oh, Jarsper!' said he in groaning voice. 'See – yonder! There's evidence to hang any man, – look there!' And he pointed to that small, shining object that twinkled just beneath the grasping fingers of that dangling, dead hand. 'Mr John's . . . Mr Winton's seal!' he whispered.

'Oh ar!' murmured Mr Shrig, his gaze roving back to the cigar-ash, 'I've been avondering 'ow it got there, ever since I see it, Dick, so eggsackly under corpse's daddle.'

'Why, Jarsper, he must ha' snatched it, accidental-like, in his struggle for life and, being dead, Lord love ye, Dick!' exclaimed Mr Shrig beaming up affectionately into the Corporal's troubled face. 'Now I never thought o' that. You're getting as 'andy with your 'ead as your 'ook! Deceased being alive, snatched it and, being dead, naterally drops it. Good! So now s'pose you picks it up and we takes a peep at it.'

'It's his'n, Jarsper, and no mistake!' sighed the Corporal. 'See, here's a J and a W and here, round the edge: "To John from Adele". So, God help the poor, sweet creatur, I says!'

'Amen, Dick, vith all my heart. So the case is pretty clear, eh?'

'A precious sight too clear, comrade.'

'Couldn't be plainer, eh pal?'

'No how, comrade.'

'Then, Dick lad, the vord is – march! No – stop a bit, – the vinder! Open? Yes. And wery easy to climb. But this here bolt now . . . this latch . . . pretty solid – von't do! But that hook o' yourn's soldier, I reckon, and you're precious strong, Dick, so – wrench it off.'

'Eh? Break it, Jarsper?'

'Ar! Off with it, pal! Ha – so, and off she comes! By Goles, you're stronger than I thought.'

'Ay, but Jarsper, why –'

'Hist, mum's the vord, Dick – so march it is and – lively, pal.'

IV

In the hall they were stayed by one who goggled at Mr Shrig from pale, plump face, bowed, rubbed nervous hands and spoke in quavering voice:

'A dreadful business, sirs, – oh a terrible –'

'Werry true!' nodded Mr Shrig. 'You're the butler, ain't you? Is your master about, I mean your noo master?'

'Mr Roger is . . . is in the library, sir; he desires a word with you, this way, if you please.' Leading them across wide hall the butler rapped softly at a door, opened it and ushered them into the presence of him who sat facing them from behind a large desk whereon lay books and papers all very orderly; and a strangely imposing, very handsome presence, this was, – immaculate as to clothes and linen, – a compelling face, with large eyes dreamily watchful beneath lofty, pale brow shaded by thick-clustering silky locks, a high-bridged nose, a thin-lipped, sensitive mouth.

For a long moment after the door had closed, Mr Roger Glendale sat there utterly still, viewing Mr Shrig with those dreamy yet watchful eyes, while Mr Shrig, silent also, stared back at Mr Roger's so luxuriant, silky hair, his pointed chin, his cravat, the snowy ruffles at his bosom, his modish, close-fitting coat that accentuated broad shoulders and slim waist. Thus they gazed upon each other, alike silent and motionless, until at last Corporal Dick stirred uneasily and, glancing from one intent face to the other, coughed gently behind his hook.

'So, Shrig, we meet again?' said Mr Roger, sighing gently and shaking his head. 'Our last meeting was –'

'A year ago this werry night, sir!'

'A strange coincidence, Shrig, and a very terrible one. By heaven, there seems to be some curse upon this house, some horrible fate that dogs us Glendales!'

'Werry much so indeed, sir!' nodded Mr Shrig, and his voice sounded so hearty as to be almost jovial.

'And 'ow do you find yourself these days, Mr Roger, pretty bobbish I 'opes, sir?'

Mr Roger blenched, throwing up a white, well cared for hand:

'An odious, a detestable word, Shrig!' he expostulated.

'Vich, sir?'

'Bobbish'! A hideous word and most inappropriate as regards myself for' – the sleepy eyes glared suddenly, the pale cheek flushed, the delicate fingers became a knotted fist – 'I am the same breathing Impotence! The same useless, helpless Thing, Shrig!'

'I shouldn't eggsackly call ye "useless," sir, nor go so fur as to name ye "'elpless", not me – no!'

'Then you'd be a fool, for I'm a log! I'm Death-in-life, a living corpse, live brain in dead body – look at me!' And suddenly, as by some unseen agency, he was whirled smoothly about . . . glided swiftly out from behind the desk and sat before them lolling in his wheeled chair. 'Look at me!' he repeated. 'Thus must I sit impotent, helpless while others enjoy, others snatch the sweets of life . . . I – I must watch . . . a poor, helpless futility!'

'And yet,' demurred Mr Shrig, 'you're astonishin' spry with your fambles, sir, your 'ands, Mr Roger, or as you might say, your daddles, sir!'

Mr Roger glanced at the white, shapely hands in question, flicked their fingers delicately and wheeled himself back behind the desk.

'Well, Shrig, my cousin, Miss Adele, forestalled me in summoning you, it seems, but you have seen . . . you have looked into this new horror that has smitten us Glendales?'

'Vith both peepers, sir!'

'Well, speak out, man! Have you discovered any trace of the assassin? Formed any conclusions?'

'Oceans, sir!' nodded Mr Shrig. 'The ass-assin is as good as took! Ye see the fax is all too plain, sir! First, – the open vinder. Second, – by said vinder, the fatal vepping – 'ere it is!' and from capacious pocket he drew an ugly bundle and unwinding its stained folds, laid the knife before his questioner.

'Very horrid!' said Mr Roger in hushed accents, viewing the dreadful thing with a very evident disgust, 'Anything more, Shrig?'

'Sir, me and my comrade, Corporal Richard Roe, found all as was to be found – this! Number Three! A clincher!' And beside that murderous knife he laid the gold seal, beholding which Mr Roger started in sudden agitation, took it up, stared at it and dropping it upon the desk, covered his eyes with his two hands.

'Aha, you reckernize it, eh, sir?' said Mr Shrig, thrusting it back into his pocket, and wrapping up the knife again. 'Yes, I see as you know it, eh, Mr Roger?'

'Beyond all doubt . . . to my sorrow! And you found it . . . near . . . the body?'

'Beneath its werry fingers, sir, looked as if it had fell out of its dyin' grasp. Pretty con-clusive, I think. And now, sir, 'aving dooly noted and brought along everything in the natur' of ewidence, I'll be toddling – no, stop a bit, – the cup!'

'Cup, Shrig? Pray what cup?'

'The coffee-cup used by deceased.'

'Why trouble to take that?'

'Well,' answered Mr Shrig dubiously, 'I don't 'ardly know, except for the fact as 'twere used by deceased aforesaid and might come in as evidence.'

'How so, Shrig? Evidence of what?'

'Well,' answered Mr Shrig, more dubiously than ever, 'I don't 'ardly know that either, but I'd better take it along. Ye see, sir, there's some coffee in it as they might like to examine.'

'But my poor uncle was stabbed, not poisoned.'

'No more 'e wasn't!' nodded Mr Shrig. 'And I ought to get my report in – sharp. And then again if said cup should be wanted I can fetch it tomorrow.'

'You locked the door, Shrig?'

'Seeing as the key vas a-missing, I did not, sir, but I've took all as is needful and vot I've left ain't agoing to run avay, no – 'twill stay nice an' quiet till the undertaker –'

'Good night!' said Mr Roger, ringing the bell at his elbow.

'Sir, good night!' answered Mr Shrig, and turning at the opening of the door, he and Corporal Dick followed the pallid butler who presently let them out into a pitch black night.

'Nice and dark!' said Mr Shrig, clapping on his hat.

'Very, sir.'

'Are you a butler as bleeves in ghosts?'

'No, sir . . . leastways –'

'Because I never see a more promising night for 'em. So if you should 'ear anything in the murdered corpse's room – woices, say, rappings, footsteps or groans, my adwice is – don't pay no manner o' 'eed.'

'No, no, sir, I won't indeed, I –'

'And don't go taking no liberties with the poor, old gent's slaughtered and stiffening remains, or as you might say, carkiss!'

'No . . . no! Oh my soul . . . not me, sir, I –'

'Then good night. And see as you locks an' bolts the door!' Even as he spoke, the stout oak closed behind them with the immediate sound of lock, chain and bolt, whereupon Mr Shrig became endued with a sudden fierce energy:

'Now, Dick – at the double!'

'Eh, but, Jarsper, what . . . where?'

'Run!' hissed Mr Shrig, and seizing his companion's arm, he broke into a heavy, though silent, trot . . . In among shadowy trees, across smooth dim lawns, along winding paths to a terrace whence a row of windows glinted down at them; which he counted in breathless whisper:

'Number five should be it. . . . And Number five she is! After me, pal!' And speaking, he opened this fifth window and clambered through with surprising agility.

'Eh – back again?' whispered the Corporal, glancing at the great chair before the dying fire. 'What now, comrade?'

'The bed, Dick, it's big enough to hide us both, and – sharp's the vord!' The heavy curtains of the huge, sombre four-poster rustled and were still, a cinder fell tinkling to the hearth and then came the Corporal's hoarse whisper:

'What are we waiting for, Jarsper?'

'The murderer.'

'Lord!' . . . A distant clock chimed the hour, then the Corporal whispered again:

'Must we wait long, comra –'

'P'raps – but I think not.'

'But who is he, Jas –'

'A desprit willain . . . dangerous, pal! But you've got your 'ook and I've got my barker.' Here was the sharp click of a cocked pistol.

'But, Jarsper, I don't –'

'Hist, pal! Votever you hear, votever you see, don't speak and don't stir 'til I give the vord. And now – listen!'

Silence, for the great house was very still; the clock chimed the quarter, the dying fire chinked, this room of death grew slowly darker; the clock chimed the half-hour . . . A faint, faint rattle at the door and into the room crept a sound of soft movement, with another sound very strange to hear – a crunching rustle that stole across the carpet towards the hearth; a moving, shapeless blot against the feeble fire-glow, a faint tinkle of china and then a voice sudden and harsh and loud:

'In the King's name!' A leap of quick feet, a whirl of sudden movement, a flurry of desperate strife, an inhuman laugh of chuckling triumph, and then Mr Shrig's gasping voice:

'Ecod, Dick, he's done us! Catch that arm . . . no good! I'm diddled again, by Goles, I am! Get the candles agoing – sharp!'

'Lord love us!' gasped Corporal Dick, the lighted candle wavering in his grasp, 'Mr Roger!'

'Ay – but look – look at 'im!'

Roger Glendale lolled in his wheeled chair, his eyes fixed upon the speaker in awful glare, his lips up-curling from white teeth . . . and from those writhen lips issued a wheezing chuckle.

'Right, Shrig . . . you were right . . . I'm not . . . not so helpless . . . as I seemed. . . . I was Master of Life . . . and Death. I'm . . . master still! I'm . . . away, Shrig, away. . . . And so . . . Good night!' The proud head swayed aslant, drooped forward, – the shapely hands fluttered and were still, and Corporal Dick, setting down the candle, wiped moist brow, staring with horrified eyes.

'Love us all!' he whispered. 'Dead – eh?'

'As any nail, Dick! Pizen, d'ye see. He was too quick for Jarsper and strong as any bull.'

'Comrade, how . . . how did ye know him for the killer?'

''Twas very simple, Dick – in that bit o' cigar ash as you p'inted out to me, I see the track of a veel, his footprints, so to speak, and – there ye are, pal!'

'Why, then . . . what now, comrade?'

'Now, Dick, get back to them as is a-vaiting so werry patient in the coach and tell 'em as Jasper says the shadder, being only a shadder, is wanished out o' their lives and the sun is rose and a-shining for 'em and so – let all be revelry and j'y!'

Dover Does Some Spadework

BY JOYCE PORTER

If Jasper Shrig was an unlikely candidate for TV fame as a crimebuster, Chief Inspector Wilfred Dover was even more so. 'The fictional detective one hates to love,' is how Ellery Queen has described the inspector, noting further that: 'the snarling, scowling, glaring, growling, grumbling, grunting, groaning, sneering, scoffing man from Scotland Yard may be a sloppy sleuth (clothingwise) and an invidious investigator (personalitywise), but as a detective he's – no question about it – one of a kind and no one else would dare create another!' Since his appearance in Dover One (1964), the chief inspector has seemed to be the antithesis of a Scotland Yard man: fat, dishonest, lazy and inefficient, concentrating his energies (such as they are) on eating and sleeping, and leaving his put-upon assistant, Sergeant MacGregor, to investigate the crimes for which, if successfully resolved, he will usually take credit. That he should have progressed so high in the force is a constant puzzle, although it has been suggested he was 'kicked upstairs' – though for quite what reason, good or bad, remains unresolved. Joyce Porter (1924–), Dover's creator, is nothing whatsoever like her character, having served with distinction as an officer in the Women's Royal Air Force until her retirement when she took up writing. The unique figure of Dover and Miss Porter's ability to combine humour with ingenious plotting have made her a favourite with readers of crime fiction, and she has now written almost a dozen novels about the Inspector as well as a small group of short stories.

When Dover made his debut on BBC TV in Detective, one at least of the nation's newspaper television critics thought it wise to warn viewers what to expect. 'Any similarity between Chief Inspector Dover of Scotland Yard and any other famous detective of fact or *fiction noted by viewers must be entirely imagined,' said Philip Phillips in the Sun. 'He is officially described as middle aged, fat, dyspeptic, lazy and frankly unintelligent. To put it mildly, his promotion seems to have been haphazard – as are his methods of detection.' Cast with the daunting task of bringing 'the unspeakable Dover' to the screen was the rotund character actor Paul Dawkins who made the inspector a mixture of the vulgar and the sly – but certainly a policeman no one could ignore. 'He did the character very proud,' saluted Stewart Lake of the Morning Star, adding, 'and James Cosmo as Sergeant MacGregor made an excellent foil.' Philip Phillips also had praise for James Cosmo's scene-stealing performance as 'a keen and ambitious officer almost perpetually embarrassed by his chief.' It was certainly a real regret to these two columnists – as well as a great many viewers – that Dover did not reappear for a second season. As a reminder, here is a typical story of the outrageous anti-hero detective investigating a case which all begins when he is supposed to be on holiday . . .*

'YOU'RE SUPPOSED TO be a detective, aren't you?'

Chief Inspector Dover – unwashed, unshaved, still in his dressing gown and more than half asleep – stared sullenly across the kitchen table at his wife. The great man was not feeling at his best. 'I'm on leave,' he pointed out resentfully as he spooned a half pound of sugar into his tea. 'Supposed to be having a rest.'

'All right for some,' muttered Mrs Dover crossly. She slapped down a plate of bacon, eggs, tomatoes, mushrooms, sausages and fried bread in front of her husband.

Dover had been sitting with his knife and fork at the ready but now he poked disconsolately among the goodies. 'No kidney?'

'You want it with jam on, you do!'

Dover responded to this disappointment with a grunt. 'Besides,' he said a few minutes later when he was wiping the egg yolk off his chin with the back of his hand, 'I'm Murder Squad. You can't expect me to go messing around with piddling things like somebody nicking your garden tools. Ring up the local coppers if something's gone missing.'

'And a fine fool I'd look, wouldn't I?' Mrs Dover sat down and poured out her own cup of tea. 'My husband a Chief Inspector at

Scotland Yard and me phoning the local police station for help! And I
told you, Wilf – nobody stole anything. They just broke in.'

Dover considerately remembered his wife's oft-reiterated injunc-
tions and licked the knife clean of marmalade before sticking it in the
butter. Well, it didn't do to push the old girl too far. 'It's like asking
Picasso to decorate the back bedroom for you, you see,' he explained
amid a spray of toast crumbs. 'And if there's nothing that's actually
missing . . .'

'Two can play at that game, you know.' Mrs Dover sounded
ominously like a woman who had got all four aces up her sleeve.

A frown of sudden anxiety creased Dover's hitherto untroubled
brow. 'Wadderyemean?' he asked nervously.

Mrs Dover ignored the question. 'Have another piece of toast,' she
invited with grim humour. 'Help yourself. Enjoy your breakfast. Make
the most of it while it's here!'

'Oh, 'strewth!' groaned Dover, knowing only too well what was
coming.

Mrs Dover patted her hair into place. 'If you can't do a bit of
something for me, Wilf,' she said with feigned reasonableness, 'you
may wake up one of these fine days and find that I can't do something
for you. Like standing over a hot stove all the live-long day!'

'But that's your job,' protested Dover. 'Wives are supposed to look
after their husbands' comfort. It's the law!'

But Mrs Dover wasn't listening. 'I wasn't brought up just to be your
head cook and bottle washer,' she claimed dreamily. 'My parents had
better things in mind for me than finishing up as your unpaid skivvy.
Why' – she soared off misty-eyed into the realms of pure fantasy – 'I
might have been a concert pianist or a lady judge or a TV personality,
if I hadn't met you.'

'And pigs might fly,' sniggered Dover, being careful to restrict his
comment to the range of his own ears. 'Well,' he said aloud and
making the promise, perhaps a mite too glibly, 'I'll have a look at the
shed for you. Later on. When the sun's had chance to take the chill off
things a bit.'

Mrs Dover was too battle-scarred a veteran of matrimony to be
caught like that. 'Suit yourself, Wilf,' she said equably. 'Your lunch
will be ready and waiting for you . . . just as soon as you come up with
the answer.' She began to gather up the dirty crockery. 'And not
before,' she added thoughtfully.

'So that,' snarled Dover, 'is what I'm doing here! Since you were so
gracious as to ask!'

Detective Sergeant MacGregor could only stand and stare. Almost any comment, he felt, was going to be open to misinterpretation.

But even a tactful silence gave no guarantee of immunity from Dover's quivering indignation. 'Cat got your tongue now, laddie?'

MacGregor suppressed a sigh. He didn't usually come calling when his boss was on leave, having more than enough of the old fool when they were at work in the normal way; but he needed a counter-signature for his Expenses Claim Form and, since most of the money had been dispensed on Dover's behalf, it was only fitting that his uncouth signature should grace the document.

So when, at eleven o'clock, the sergeant had called at the Dovers' semi-detached suburban residence, he had been quite prepared to find that His Nibs was still, on a cold and foggy December morning, abed. What he had not expected was Mrs Dover's tight-lipped announcement that her better half was to be found in the tool shed at the bottom of the garden. It had seemed a highly improbable state of affairs but, as MacGregor was now seeing for himself, it was true.

Dover, arrayed as for a funeral in his shabby black overcoat and his even shabbier bowler hat, was sunk dejectedly in a deck chair. He glared up at his sergeant. 'Well, don't just stand there like a stick of Blackpool rock, you moron! Come inside and shut that damn door!'

Even with the door closed the tool shed was hardly a cosy spot, and MacGregor was gratified to notice that Dover's nose was already turning quite a pronounced blue. 'Er – what exactly is the trouble, sir? Mrs Dover wasn't actually very clear about why you were out here.'

Dover cut the cackle with the ruthlessness of desperation. 'She's got this idea in her stupid head that somebody bust their way into this shed during the past week and borrowed a spade. Silly cow!'

'I see,' said MacGregor politely.

'I doubt it,' sniffed Dover. 'Seeing as how you're not married.'

'A stolen spade, eh, sir?' For the first time MacGregor turned his attention to his surroundings and discovered to his amazement that he was standing in the middle of a vast collection of implements which, if hygiene and perfect order were anything to go by, wouldn't have looked out of place in a hospital operating theatre. As MacGregor's gaze ran along the serried ranks of apparently brand-new tools he wondered what on earth they were used for. Surely not for the care and maintenance of that miserable strip of barren, cat-infested clay which lay outside between the shed and the house? Good heavens, they must have bought the things wholesale!

The walls were covered with hoes and rakes and forks and spades and trowels, all hung on special hooks and racks. A couple of shelves groaned under a load of secateurs, garden shears, seed trays, and a set of flower pots arranged in descending order of size, while the floor was almost totally occupied by wheelbarrows, watering cans, and a well-oiled cylinder lawn mower. MacGregor only tore his mind away from his inventory of sacks of peat and fertiliser when he realised that the oracle had said something. 'I beg your pardon, sir?'

'I said it wasn't stolen,' snapped Dover. 'It was only borrowed.' The lack of comprehension on MacGregor's face appeared to infuriate the Chief Inspector. 'That one, you idiot!'

MacGregor followed the direction of Dover's thumb which was indicating the larger of two stainless steel spades. He leaned forward to examine the mirror-like blade more closely. 'Er – how does Mrs Dover know it was – er – borrowed, sir?'

Dover blew wearily down his nose. 'Why don't you use your bloomin' eyes?' he asked. 'Look at it all!' He flapped a cold-looking hand at the tools on the wall. 'They're all hanging on their own hooks, aren't they? Right! Well, every bloody Tuesday morning without fail Mrs Dover comes down here and turns 'em all round. Get it? Regular as ruddy clockwork. One week all these spades and trowels and things have got their backs facing the wall and then, the next week, they've got the backs of their blades facing out to the middle of the shed. Follow me?'

'I understand perfectly, thank you, sir,' said MacGregor stiffly.

Dover scowled. 'Then you're lucky,' he growled, 'because it's more than I do. She reckons it evens out the wear, you know. Silly cow! Anyhow!' – he heaved himself up in his deck chair again and jerked his thumb at the spade – 'that thing is hanging the wrong way round. Savvy? So that means somebody moved it and that means, since this shed is kept locked up tighter than the Bank of England, that somebody must have broken in to do it.'

He sank back and the deck chair groaned and creaked in under-standable protest. 'Mrs Dover's developed into a very nervous sort of woman over the years.'

MacGregor's agile mind had already solved the problem. 'But, if you'll forgive me saying so, sir, the spade *isn't* the wrong way round.' He moved across to the appropriate wall so as to be able to demonstrate his thesis in a way that even a muttonhead like Dover could understand. 'All the tools are currently hanging with their backs turned towards the shed wall, aren't they? With the prongs and the – er – sharp edges pointing outward towards us. Right? Well, the spade in question is hanging on the wall in just the same way as all the other tools, isn't it? So, it's *not* hanging the wrong way round, unless of course – he ventured on a rather patronising little chuckle – 'Mrs Dover has got a special routine for that particular spade.'

Dover didn't bother opening his eyes. It would be a bad day, he reflected, when he couldn't outsmart young MacGregor with both hands tied behind his back. 'She killed a spider with it last week,' he explained sleepily. 'When she was in doing a security check. God knows what a spider was doing in this place, apart from starving to death, but there it was. On the floor. Mrs Dover's allergic to spiders, so she grabbed that spade and flattened the brute.'

'I see, sir,' said MacGregor who had not, hitherto, suspected that Mrs Dover was a woman of violence.

'Then,' said Dover, pulling his overcoat collar up closer round his ears, 'the spade had to be washed, didn't it? And disinfected, too, I shouldn't wonder.' He tried to rub some warmth back into his frozen fingers. 'Well, nobody in their right senses, it seems, would dream of hanging a newly washed spade with its back up against a shed wall. In case of rust. So Mrs Dover broke the habit of a lifetime and replaced the spade the wrong way round so that the air could circulate freely about it.'

'I see,' said MacGregor for the second time in as many minutes. 'Our mysterious borrower, when he returned the spade, then understandably hung it back on its hook in the same way that all the other implements were hung – with their backs to the wall. Yes' – he nodded his head – 'a perfectly natural mistake to make.'

' 'Strewth, don't you start!'

'Sir?'

Dover wriggled impatiently in his deck chair. 'Talking as though this joker really exists. He damn well doesn't!'

'Then how do you explain the fact that the spade is hanging the wrong way round, sir?'

'I don't!' howled Dover. 'I wouldn't be sitting here freezing to death if I could, would I, dumbbell?'

There was a moment's pause after this outburst. By rights MacGregor should have emulated Mrs Dover's way of dealing with pests by seizing hold of the nearest sufficiently heavy instrument and laying Dover's skull open with it; but the Metropolitan Police do too good a job on their young recruits. MacGregor swallowed all his finer impulses and concentrated hard on trying to be a detective. 'Are there any signs of breaking in, sir?'

There was a surly grunt from the deck chair. 'Search me!'

MacGregor crossed the shed and opened the door to examine the large padlock which had been left hooked carelessly in the staple. It looked as though it had recently been ravaged by some sharp-toothed carnivore.

Dover had got up to stretch his legs. He squinted over MacGregor's shoulder. 'I had a job getting the damn thing open.'

Oh, well, it wasn't the first time that Dover had ridden roughshod over what might have been a vital clue, and it wouldn't be the last. Just for the hell of it, MacGregor gave Dame Fortune's wheel a half-hearted whirl. 'I suppose you didn't happen to notice when you unlocked the padlock, sir, if –'

Dover was not the man to waste time nurturing slender hopes. 'No,' he said, 'I didn't.'

MacGregor closed the door. 'Well, presumably our chappie knows how to pick a lock. That's some sort of lead.'

'Garn,' scoffed Dover, 'they learn that with their mother's milk these days.' He began to waddle back to his deck chair. 'Got any smokes on you, laddie?' he asked. 'I'm dying for a puff.'

MacGregor often used to bewail the fact that he couldn't include all the cigarettes he provided for Dover on his swindle sheet but, as usual, he handed his packet over with a fairly good grace. He waited patiently until Dover's clumsy fingers had extracted a crumpled coffin nail and then gave him a light.

'Fetch us one of those plant pots,' ordered Dover. 'A little one.'

A look of horror flashed across MacGregor's face. A plant pot? Surely Dover wasn't actually going to –

'For an ashtray, you bloody fool!' snarled Dover. 'Mrs Dover'll do her nut if she finds we've made a mess all over her floor.'

MacGregor felt quite weak with the relief. 'I've been thinking, sir,' he said.

'The age of miracles is not yet past,' snickered Dover.

MacGregor turned the other cheek with a practised hand. 'We can deduce quite a bit about our Mr Borrower.'

'Such as what?' Dover leered up suspiciously at his sergeant.

MacGregor ticked the points off on well-manicured fingers. 'The spade must have been purloined for some illicit purpose.' He saw from the vacant look on Dover's face that he'd better watch his language. 'If the fellow just wanted a spade for digging potatoes or what-have-you, sir, he'd have just asked for it, wouldn't he? Taking a spade without permission and picking a padlock to get at it must add up to some criminal activity being concerned, don't you agree, sir?'

Dover nodded cautiously, unwilling to commit himself too far at this stage. 'You reckon he nicked the spade to dig something up?' he asked, eyes bulging greedily. 'Like buried treasure?'

'I was thinking more along the lines of him wanting to hide something, actually, sir. By concealing it in the ground. He returned the spade to the shed, you see. Surely, if he was merely digging up buried treasure, he wouldn't have gone to the trouble of putting the spade back carefully in its place?'

'*Burying* buried treasure?' Dover, dribbling ash down the front of his overcoat, tried this idea on for size.

'Or a dead body, sir,' said MacGregor. 'That strikes me as a more likely explanation.'

Dover's heavy jowls settled sullenly over where his shirt collar would have been if he'd been wearing one. For a member (however unwanted) of Scotland Yard's Murder Squad, dead bodies were in his mind inextricably connected with work, and work always tended to bring Dover out in a cold sweat. He tried to concentrate on an occupation more to his taste: nit-picking. 'How do you know it's a "he"?' he demanded truculently. 'It could just as well be a woman.'

MacGregor was so anxious to display his superior powers of reasoning and deduction that he, perhaps, showed insufficient regard for Dover's slower wits. 'Oh, I doubt that, sir! I don't know whether you've noticed, but Mrs Dover had two spades hanging on the wall. The one that was "borrowed" and a smaller one which is called, I believe, a border spade. You see? Now, surely if our intruder were a woman, she would have taken the lighter, more manageable border spade?'

Dover's initial scowl of fury was gradually replaced by a rather constipated expression, a sure indication that his thought processes were beginning to swing into action.

MacGregor waited anxiously.

'A *young* man!' said Dover at last.

'Sir?'

'You'd hardly find an old-age pensioner nipping over garden fences and picking locks and digging bloomin' great holes big enough to take a dead body, would you? 'Strewth, what you know about the real world, laddie, wouldn't cover a pinhead. We've had a frost out here for weeks! The ground's as hard as iron.'

MacGregor's unabashed astonishment at this feat of unsolicited reasoning was not exactly flattering, but Dover, the bit now firmly between his National Health teeth, didn't appear to notice.

'And I'll tell you something else, laddie,' he went on, 'if our joker borrowed my missus's spade to bury a dead body with, I'll lay you a pound to a penny that it's his wife!'

MacGregor perched himself gingerly on the edge of a wheelbarrow, having first inspected and then passed it for cleanliness. Mrs Dover certainly ran a tight garden shed. There was another deck chair stacked tidily in a corner but, since it was still in its plastic wrapper, MacGregor didn't feel he could really make use of it.

Having settled himself as comfortably as he could, MacGregor gave his full attention to putting the damper on Dover's enthusiasm. 'Oh, steady on, sir,' he advised.

'Steady on – nothing!' Dover had his fixations and he wasn't going to have any pipsqueak of a sergeant talking him out of them. In Dover's book, wives were always killed by their husbands. This was a simple rule of thumb which had more than a little basis in fact and saved a great deal of trouble all round – except for the odd innocent husband, of course, but no system is perfect. 'A strapping young man with a dead body to get rid of, nicking a neighbour's spade. Use your brains, laddie, who else could it be except his wife?'

MacGregor retaliated by taking a leaf out of Dover's book and, instead of dealing with the main issue, quibbled over a minor detail. 'A *neighbour's* spade, sir? I don't think we can go quite as far as –'

Dover went over his sergeant's objection like a steamroller over a cream puff. 'Well, he didn't bloomin' well come over by Tube from Balham, did he, you nitwit? Twice? Once to get the bloody spade and once to put it back? Of course he comes from somewhere round here. He wouldn't have known about our tool shed otherwise, would he?'

Without really thinking about it, MacGregor had pulled his notebook out. He looked up from an invitingly blank page that was just aching to be written on. 'Actually, sir, I have been wondering why anybody would pick on this particular tool shed to break into in the first place.'

Dover had no doubts. 'Spite!' he said.

'There must be dozens of garden sheds round here, sir. Why choose this one?'

Dover belched with touching lack of inhibition. His exile was playing havoc with his insides. 'Could be pure ruddy chance,' he grunted.

'He had to prize open a good-quality padlock to get in here, sir. There must be plenty of sheds that aren't even locked.'

Dover turned a lacklustre eye on his sergeant. 'All right, Mr Clever Boots, so what's the answer?'

'It's because Mrs Dover's tools are all kept so spotlessly clean, sir, and in such immaculate order. I'm sure our unwelcome visitor thought he'd be able to take the spade and return it without it ever being noticed that it had so much as been touched. You see, if the shed were dirty and dusty and untidy and covered, say, with cobwebs, it would be virtually impossible to borrow a tool and put it back without disturbing something. Do you follow me, sir? He'd be bound to leave a trail of clues behind him. But here' – MacGregor swept an admiring hand round the shed – 'our chap had every reason to believe that, as long as he cleaned the spade and replaced it neatly on the wall with all the others, no suspicions would ever be aroused.'

'He was reckoning without my old woman,' said Dover with a kind of gloomy pride. 'Like a bloodhound. More so, if anything.' He shook off his reminiscent mood. 'Anyhow, what you're saying just goes to show for sure that this joker is living somewhere round here. That's how he knows this is the cleanest garden shed in the country.'

He broke off to stare disgustedly around him. 'She got all this lot with trading stamps, you know. It's taken her years and years. Never asks me if there's anything *I* want, mind you,' he mused resentfully, 'though they've definitely got long woolly underpants because I've seen 'em in the damn catalogue.'

'I agree our chap probably does live near here, sir,' said MacGregor, who'd only been debating the point just to keep his end up. 'It's hard to see how he could have known about the tool shed or the tools otherwise. On the other hand, he must be something of a newcomer.'

Dover snapped his fat fingers for another cigarette and used the time it took to furnish him with one in trying to puzzle out what MacGregor was getting at. He was forced to concede defeat. 'Regular little Sherlock Holmes, aren't you?' he sneered.

Privately, MacGregor thought he was a jolly sight smarter than this supposed paragon, but he wasn't fool enough to confide such an opinion to Dover. 'Our Mr Borrower would hardly have come breaking into this particular tool shed, sir, if he'd known that you were a policeman. A Chief Inspector from New Scotland Yard, in fact.'

Dover, almost invisible in a cloud of tobacco smoke, mulled this over. He was rather taken with the idea that all the barons of the underworld might be going in fear and trepidation of him. 'He might be potty,' he observed generously. 'Otherwise he'd know he couldn't hope to pull the wool over the eyes of a highly trained observer like me.'

Another thought struck him and he flopped back in his deck chair, suffering from shock. 'Strewth,' he gasped, 'it's only a couple of hours since I first heard about this crime, and look at me now! I've solved it, near as damn it! All we've got to do is find a young, newly married villain who's recently moved into the district. And I'll lay odds he's living in that new block of flats they've built just across the way. They've got the dregs of society in that place.

'So, all we've got to do now is get on to the local cop shop and tell 'em to send a posse of coppers round to make a few inquiries. Soon as they find somebody who fits the bill, all they've got to do is ask him to produce his wife. If he can't – well, Bob's your uncle, eh? And that,' added Dover, seeing that MacGregor was dying to interrupt and being determined to thwart him, 'is why he had to borrow a spade in the first place! Because people who live in flats don't have gardens, and if they don't have gardens they don't have gardening tools, either!'

MacGregor put his notebook away and stood up. 'Oh, I don't think our man is living in a flat, do you, sir?'

Dover's eye immediately became glassy with suspicion, resentment, and chronic dyspepsia. 'Why not?'

'He'd have nowhere to bury the body, sir.'

Dover's scowl grew muddier. 'He could have shoved it in somebody else's garden, couldn't he?' he asked, reasonably enough.

MacGregor shook his head. 'Far too risky, sir. Digging a hole big enough to inter a body would take an hour or more, I should think. Now, it would be bad enough undertaking a job like that in one's own garden, but in somebody else's –' MacGregor pursed his lips in a silent whistle and shook his head again. 'No, I doubt it, sir, I really do. I think we must take it, as a working hypothesis, that –'

'He could have planted her in the garden of an empty house,' said Dover doggedly and, as a gesture of defiance against society, dropped his cigarette end into the empty watering can.

'Well, I suppose it's a possibility, sir,' said MacGregor with a sigh, 'and I agree that we ought to bear it in mind. The thing is, though, that you're hardly in the depths of the country out here, are you? I mean – well, everywhere round here does tend to be a bit visible, doesn't it?'

There are plenty of suburban mortgage holders who would have taken deep umbrage at such a damaging assessment of their property, but Dover was not cursed with that kind of pride. He simply reacted by nodding his head in sincere agreement. 'Too right, laddie!' he rumbled.

'There's another point that's been puzzling me, sir,' MacGregor said. 'Why did our chap go to all this trouble to *borrow* a spade? The way he broke into this shed may carry all the hallmarks of a professional job, but he was still running a terrible risk. Anybody might have seen him and blown the whistle on him.'

'He'd do it after dark,' said Dover, 'and, besides, you don't go in for murder if you aren't prepared to chance your arm a bit. And what choice did he have? With a dead body on his hands and no spade? He could hardly start digging his hole with a knife and fork.'

'He could have bought a spade, sir.'

'Eh?'

'He could have bought a spade,' repeated MacGregor, quite prepared for the look of horror that flashed across Dover's pasty face. The Chief Inspector regarded the actual purchasing of anything as a desperate step, only to be contemplated when all the avenues of begging, borrowing, and stealing had been exhaustively explored. 'It wouldn't have cost all that much, sir, and it would have been a much less hazardous operation.'

Dover wrinkled up his nose. 'The shops were shut?' he suggested. 'Or he didn't have any money?'

'A professional villain, sir? That doesn't sound very likely, does it? And if he's going to nick something, why not nick the money? A handful of cash wouldn't be as compromising, if something went wrong, as Mrs Dover's stainless steel spade would be.'

Dover shivered and shoved his hands as deep as they would go in his overcoat pockets. The shed wasn't built for sitting in and there was a howling gale blowing under the door. The sooner he got out of this dump and back into the warmth and comfort of his own home, the better. 'That's why he didn't buy a spade!'

'Sir?'

'Put yourself in the murderer's shoes, laddie. You've just knocked your missus off and you're proposing to get rid of the body by burying it in a hole. Sooner or later people are going to come around asking questions. Well, I'd have said the last thing you wanted was a bloomin' spade standing there and shouting the odds. No, borrowing the spade and putting it back again shows our chap has a bit of class about him. He's somebody who can see further than the end of his nose. An opponent,' added Dover with a smirk, 'worthy of my steel. Well' – he raised a pair of moth-eaten eyebrows at his sergeant – 'what are you waiting for? Christmas?'

'Sir?'

Dover sighed heavily and dramatically. 'It's no wonder you've never made Inspector,' he sneered. 'You're as thick as two planks. Look, laddie, what's a detective got to do if he wants to be everybody's little white-haired boy, eh?'

MacGregor wondered what on earth they were supposed to be talking about now. 'Well, I don't quite know, sir,' he said uncertainly. 'Er – solve his cases?'

''Strewth!' snarled Dover, giving vent to his opinion with unwonted energy. 'Look, you know what they're like, all these Commissioners and Commanders and what-have-you. They're forever yakking about a good detective being the one who goes out and finds his own cases, aren't they?'

'Oh, I see what you mean, sir.'

'Well, look at me!'

'Sir?'

'I'm on leave, aren't I?' asked Dover, warming gleefully to the task of blowing his own trumpet. 'But I don't go around sitting with my ruddy feet up! On the contrary, from the very faintest of hints – the sort any other jack would have brushed aside as not worth his attention – I've uncovered a dastardly murder that nobody else even knows has been committed.'

Too late MacGregor saw the danger signals. 'But, sir –'

'But, nothing!' snapped Dover. 'With the information I'm giving 'em, the local police'll have our laddie under lock and key before you can say Sir Robert Peel!'

'But we can't go to the local police, sir,' said MacGregor, breaking out in a sweat at the mere idea. 'After all, we've only been theorizing.'

Dover's face split into an evil grin. 'Of course *we* are not going to the local police, laddie,' he promised soothingly. 'Just you!' There was a brief interval while the old fool laughed himself nearly sick. 'Ask for Detective Superintendent Andy Andrews and mention my name – clearly! Tell him what we've come up with so far – that we're after a young, agile newly wed villain who's just moved into a house in this area. A specialist in picking locks.'

'Oh, sir!' wailed MacGregor.

'There can't be all that many jokers knocking around who'd fit that bill,' Dover went on. 'And, if there are, Andrews will soon spot our chap because he'll be the one with a newly turned patch of soil in his garden and no wife. Or girlfriend. You never know these days.'

MacGregor tried to believe that he was just having a nightmare. 'You're not serious, sir?'

'Never been more serious in my life,' growled Dover. 'And I've just thought of something else. If they're newcomers to the district, that's why nobody's reported the wife missing. She won't have had time to establish a routine yet or have made any close friends. Her husband will be able to give any rubbishy explanation for her absence.' He realised that MacGregor was still standing there. 'What's got into you, laddie? You're usually so damn keen they could use you for mustard!'

'It's just that I don't feel we're quite ready, sir.'

But Dover wasn't having any argument about it. He cut ruthlessly through his sergeant's feeble protests. 'And stick to old Andrews like a limpet, see? Don't move from his side till you've got the handcuffs on our chummie – I don't want Andrews stealing my thunder. I've solved this case and I'm going to get the glory for it. Well' – he glared up at a very shrinking violet – 'what are you waiting for now? A Number Nine bus?'

MacGregor answered out of a bone-dry throat. 'No, sir.'

'Leave us your cigarettes,' said Dover, not the man to get his priorities mixed. 'You'll not be having time to smoke.'

Reluctantly MacGregor handed over his pack of cigarettes and even found a spare packet of matches. When, however, he'd got his hand on the door handle he paused again. 'Er – you're staying here, are you, sir?'

In all the excitement Dover had not overlooked his own personal predicament. 'Call in at the house on your way out and tell Mrs Dover that I've solved the problem of her bloody spade and that you're off to arrest the bloke for murder. I'll give you five minutes' start, so she's got time to digest the good news, and then I'll follow you. And I don't mind telling you, laddie' – he surveyed the scene of his exile with a marked lack of enthusiasm – 'I'll be glad to get back to my own armchair by the fire.' He waggled his head in mild bewilderment. 'Do you know, she's never let me come in here on my own before. Funny, isn't it?'

Long before the allotted five minutes was up, however, Dover was infuriated to discover that Sergeant MacGregor was coming back down the garden path at the double. Extricating himself from his deck chair, he dragged the door open and voiced his feelings in a penetrating bellow of rage. 'That damn woman! Is she never satisfied?'

MacGregor glanced around nervously, although the silent, unseen watchers weren't his neighbours and he really didn't care what they thought about the Dovers. 'It's not that, actually, sir.'

'Then what is it, *actually*?' roared Dover, mimicking his sergeant's minor public-school accent.

'It's a message from Mrs Dover, sir.'

Dover knew when he was being softened up for the breaking of bad news. 'Spit it out, laddie,' he said bleakly.

MacGregor grinned foolishly out of sheer embarrassment. 'It's just that she's remembered she turned the spade round herself, sir. Mrs Dover, I mean. It had quite slipped her mind, she says, but she popped down to the shed before she went to church on Sunday morning to count how many tie-on labels she'd got and the spade being hung the wrong way round on the wall got on her nerves, she says. And since she reckoned it must have dried off after having been washed, she –'

'You can spare me the details,' said Dover as all his dreams of fame and glory crumbled to dust and ashes in his mouth.

'Mrs Dover was going to come down and tell you herself, sir, when she'd finished washing the leaves of the aspidistras.'

Dover seemed indifferent to such graciousness. 'You didn't get in touch with Superintendent Andrews, did you?'

MacGregor shook his head. 'There didn't seem much point, sir. As it was Mrs Dover who changed the spade back to its proper position, well' – he shrugged – 'that did rather seem to be that. Nobody broke into the shed to borrow the spade and, if nobody borrowed the spade, that means there was no dead body to be buried. And if there's no dead body to be buried, well that means that we haven't got a wife murderer and –'

But Dover had switched off. He had many faults, but crying over split milk wasn't one of them. He was already lumbering out through the shed door, his thoughts turning to the future. He tossed a final question back over his shoulder.

'Did she say what she was giving me for my dinner?'

The Man in the Lobby

BY RICHARD LEVINSON & WILLIAM LINK

The first new crimebuster of the seventies has since proved one of the most long-lasting. The cigar-smoking, shabby little cop Columbo has been called the most famous police officer ever created for television, and if ever there was an omen that he was going to be a success it is the fact that the very first episode, Ransom For A Dead Man, shown on 15 September 1971, was directed by a tyro in the business named Steven Spielberg. Interestingly, too, the homicide detective from the Los Angeles Police Department had actually made a sneak appearance on TV four years earlier, in 1967, in a rather traditional drama special, Prescription Murder, written by Richard Levinson and William Link, in which Peter Falk had tracked down and arrested a smooth-talking young doctor for murdering his wife. All that was really memorable as far as viewers were concerned, however, was Falk's understated performance as the cop and this Levinson and Link never forgot when Columbo was in development for NBC. The character was, quite simply, to be unprepossessing in appearance, inarticulate at times, but with an incredible eye for detail and an obsession with getting to the facts of a crime.

The master-minds of the series, Richard Levinson (1934–) and William Link (1937–) have been two of the most prolific and successful writer-producers for American TV and their credits include the private eye series Mannix, which starred Mike Connors (1967–75); McCloud, the New Mexican marshal played by Dennis Weaver (1970–7); the black sleuth Tenafly with James McEachin (1973–7); the Ellery Queen Mysteries starring Jim Hutton (1974–6); and Murder She Wrote (1984–) which has brought Angela Lansbury similar world-wide fame to that of Peter Falk. Much of the success of

Columbo has undoubtedly been due to its star's total dedication to the role, even to the point of wearing one of his own old raincoats. Falk believes that his character is not unlike Sherlock Holmes using brains instead of bullets and is blessed with an insatiable curiosity about people. Furthermore, Columbo has the ability to grind down those he thinks are guilty by lulling them into a false sense of superiority – usually inspired by his almost overweening politeness. Falk has admitted that there is a lot of himself in Columbo: he, too, is plagued by mannerisms, prefers to wear sloppy clothes and is happier driving old cars. He also has only one good eye, having lost the right one when he was just three years old. A rumour that Columbo's first name – which is never mentioned by him on screen – is actually Peter has been denied by the star: if he has a name at all, says Falk, it is Philip, which was the name used in the original story, Prescription Murder.

The success of Columbo *with its episodes ranging in length from ninety to a hundred and twenty minutes has attracted some major guest stars including Patrick McGoohan and William Shatner, both of whom played killers! Levinson and Link have continued as executive producers and recently revealed that their inspiration for the down-at-heel lieutenant had partly been the police inspector Porfiry Petrovich in Dostoevsky's classic novel,* Crime and Punishment, *and a cop named Wolfson who had appeared in a short story they wrote in the early sixties for* Alfred Hitchcock's Mystery Magazine. *Here is that landmark story in which the parallels with Columbo are not difficult to find . . .*

IT HAD BEEN a wasted morning for Wolfson. The captain had sent him over to the Golden Gate Hotel to check out a public nuisance complaint, but after a brief investigation he found that it was groundless – a few conventioneers had blundered into the wrong room after a night of carousing.

He left the elevator and glanced at the people coming in from Powell Street. It was not quite noon, but the hotel bar was already crowded with advertising men from the cluster of office buildings a few blocks away. All riding the expense account, he imagined. What would it take to pull them away from their martinis and black Russians? A stock market crash, probably. Either that or another earthquake.

Well, it was time to report back. As he started across the busy lobby he brushed by a man at the check-in desk. The face hung for an instant in his mind, then he dismissed it. At the street door he hesitated and turned back. The man at the desk was in his early fifties, meek and rumpled, with the slightly dazed expression of someone who had spent his life in front of a blackboard or an adding machine. He wore a cheap summer suit and a frayed blue shirt.

Wolfson strolled back to the counter and tried to get a better look.

'Anything on the twelfth floor?' the man was saying.

'Room 1205 is available,' said the desk clerk. 'Nice and spacious.' He slipped a registration card into a leather holder and pushed it across the counter. 'There's a lovely view of the pagodas on Grant Street.'

The man mumbled something, then signed the card and started for the elevators. Wolfson, no more than a casual foot away, instantly made the connection He took his wallet from his back pocket and crossed to the man, tapping him on the shoulder. 'San Francisco police,' he said, showing his badge. 'Sorry to bother you, sir, but would you mind telling me your name?'

The little man blinked at him from waltery eyes. 'Miller,' he said in a fuzzy, classroom voice. 'Charles Miller.'

'Mind waiting here just a minute, Mr Miller?'

Wolfson went to the desk and opened his wallet again. 'I'd like to see this gentleman's registration card, please.'

The clerk produced the information. 'Charles Miller, 10337 Lombard Street, San Francisco.'

Wolfson copied down the address and returned the card. When he swung back to Miller, the little man was staring vaguely up at the hotel clock, idly juggling the room key.

'You live here in San Francisco, don't you, Mr Miller?'

'Yes.' The voice seemed on the verge of disappearing.

'Then why are you checking into a hotel?'

Miller shrugged. 'Business.'

'What kind of business?'

Miller looked up again at the clock, as if he were a small boy waiting impatiently for a recess.

'What kind of business, Mr Miller?'

'I have to meet a few people. Salesmen, mostly.'

Wolfson glanced at the carpet. 'And no luggage?'

'Just overnight.'

Wolfson studied his face closely. Could he be mistaken? Was there a chance that this was a look-alike, a near-perfect double? There was a tiny white scar just below Miller's left eye that seemed to underscore the man's essential blankness. That scar and the rest of the description could be checked by teletype this afternoon.

'I'm afraid I'm going to have to ask you for some identification.'

After a slight pause the man patted most of his pockets and finally fished an old wallet from somewhere inside his jacket. He held it out.

'No, you go through it. Social security card, driver's licence. Anything.'

The man thumbed through a small packet of cards and handed him a licence. It was State of California issue and the name was Charles Miller.

As Wolfson studied it a group of bystanders had begun to gather, trying to edge closer.

'Sorry to trouble you like this, Mr Miller, but I'd like you to come with me. It shouldn't take more than a half-hour or so.'

The little man looked wistfully at the elevators. 'But I thought I could . . .' His voice threatened to disappear again. 'Is it important?' he asked.

'I've got a car outside. It'll be as quick as I can make it.'

'Well . . . I suppose so.' He looked down at the key in his white, plump hand. 'What should I do?'

Wolfson began to feel a little sorry for him. 'You've already registered. They'll hold the room for you.' He guided the man towards the door. 'You'll be back in plenty of time to keep your appointments.'

Outside in the bright, almost holiday air, Miller seemed dazed and lost. A cable car jangled, and he stiffened upright with the sound. Wolfson took his arm and led him up the hill, watching him carefully. The man was blinking hard in the glittering sunlight, but he looked more bewildered than trapped.

When they reached the automobile Wolfson held open the door, then got in and started the engine, throwing his companion a quick, assessing glance. The man was staring down at his hands, still toying with the key.

'Mr Miller,' Wolfson said, driving towards Market, 'there's something that bothers me. You haven't once asked why I'm taking you in.'

Miller shrugged listlessly. They were passing Union Square and a pigeon sprang grey and frightened across the windshield.

'Why aren't you interested?'

'I imagine I'll find out.'

'I imagine you will.' It would take only a short time to verify. And he was pretty sure that Miller wouldn't be returning to his hotel.

He parked the car a block off Market and walked the little man up the steps of the station house. There was no one in the squad room, just a few stale newspapers and the smell of new paint. He left Miller alone in the interrogation room and went down the corridor to Sy Pagano's office.

Pagano was leaning on the window-sill, looking up at the sky. 'I haven't seen a gull in weeks,' he said. 'You think it's the fall-out or something?'

Wolfson didn't bother closing the door. 'Got something, Sy.'

'Yeah?'

'Brought in a man by the name of Charles Miller. I think it's an alias.'

Pagano was looking up at the sky again. 'Who do you think he is?'

'Frederick Lerner. The schoolteacher from Santa Barbara who killed those two women last week.'

Pagano turned abruptly from the window. 'Are you sure it's him?'

'The description fits. LA sent a wire-photo up yesterday. They mentioned he might have headed for San Francisco.'

'Where'd you spot him?'

'The Golden Gate Hotel. He was checking in without luggage.'

Pagano picked up the phone and punched a button. 'I'll call LA, get more information. Where've you got him?'

'Interrogation.' Wolfson went out and walked back to the other office. Miller was sitting in a chair, looking at the wall. His eyes squinted slightly in the bright rush of light from the window. Wolfson drew the shade and sat down with him. He took his time lighting a cigarette. 'Sorry. You want one?'

'I don't smoke.'

'How long have you lived in San Francisco, Mr Miller?'

The little man rubbed his eyes. 'Only a few weeks.'

'Where did you live before that?'

'New York. My company sent me out here.'

Wolfson got up, went back to the window. There was no one in the street beneath the half-lowered shade. A church clock chimed the hour and he checked it with his watch. 'What line of work are you in, Mr Miller?'

'Heavy goods jobbing.'

'Married?'

There was a pause while the chimes succeeded each other like ripples in water. 'Yes, I'm married.'

'Happen to have a picture of your wife?'

'Is it important?'

Wolfson came back to him. The man's face was in half-shadow, but blinked up at the detective.

'It's important, Mr Miller. Do you have one?'

The old wallet came out again. The man fumbled through the celluloid card folder, then held up a photograph. Wolfson took it over to the light. It was a crisp new picture of an attractive blonde, considerably younger than her husband. There was an interesting pout to the mouth. 'Married long?' he asked.

'Few weeks.'

The door opened and Pagano came in, carrying a file folder. 'This is my partner, Mr Miller, Lieutenant Pagano. You make that call, Sy?'

'Tried. The lines are tied up.'

Wolfson took the photograph over to him. 'This is Mr Miller's wife.'

Pagano studied it expressionlessly. He opened the file folder and removed two photos, tilting them so that only his partner could see. 'The victims,' he said.

Wolfson touched the photos, moving them to catch the light. They both showed middle-aged women with vacant, trusting faces. Neither resembled the blonde.

'Your wife at home, Mr Miller?' Pagano asked suddenly. It was his first acknowledgment of the man's presence.

'Yes.'

Wolfson picked up the phone. 'What's the number?'

Miller swung around quickly in the chair. 'No – she's not at home. I made a mistake.'

Wolfson met Pagano's eyes. 'Oh? Where is she, then?'

'She – left for Nevada this morning. Visiting some friends.'

'I see. Has she got a phone number there?'

'No.'

Pagano came around the side of the desk. 'Stand up, Miller.'

Miller got awkwardly to his feet.

'See that blackboard on the far wall? Why don't you go over there and pick up that piece of chalk.'

Miller did as he was told.

'Fine,' said Pagano, glancing at Wolfson again. 'Now write something on the blackboard.'

The little man seemed ready to cry. 'What should I write?'

'Anything. I don't care.'

Miller was motionless for a moment, then his hand glided up and he wrote 'Charles Miller' in a graceful, sweeping line. He started to turn around but Pagano called, 'No, stay there. Write your name again.'

While Miller wrote, Pagano took the wallet from the desk and dug out the driver's licence. *Nice*, Wolfson thought. *Very nice*. Over

Pagano's shoulder, he compared the signature on the card with the writing on the board. They matched.

'You're pretty good at that blackboard,' Pagano observed. 'Some guys would have that chalk squeaking like a mouse. But not you. You sure you're not a schoolteacher or something?'

'Well . . . I've had some experience with blackboards,' the little man said. He still faced away from them.

'Really?' Pagano said.

'Yes. Before my company sent me out here I was teaching some of the younger men, the sales trainees.'

'But you never did any teaching at a school?'

'No.'

Wolfson walked to the blackboard. 'Here's another name. I want you to write "Frederick Lerner". Would you do that for me?'

The hand swung up without hesitation. It wrote the name in the same sure, graceful way.

'Uh-huh,' Wolfson said. He went back to Pagano and gestured at the folder. Pagano opened it, and Wolfson removed another photo. He set it face up on the desk under the unlit lamp. 'You can come back now, Mr Miller. Have a seat.'

The little man returned to the desk, blinking in confusion at them. He sat down wearily.

Wolfson pointed at the lamp. 'Mind turning on the light? I want to show you something.'

Miller snapped on the switch and then started, his hands gripping the arms of the chair. He was staring down at the photograph, a slow flush staining his face. 'Where did you get that?' he asked.

'From our files,' said Wolfson. He and Pagano edged closer to the desk. 'It's a picture of a man named Frederick Lerner. He killed two women in Santa Barbara last week.'

'But – but that's a picture of me,' Miller protested. He picked it up and stared. 'That's *me*.'

Pagano took the photo out of his hands. 'The Los Angeles police got it from the year-book of that private school where you used to teach.'

Miller shook his head. 'That's impossible. I was never in Santa Barbara in my life. Anybody can tell you that, anybody!'

'Can they?' Pagano said. 'How about your new wife? Can she tell us that?'

Miller turned pale, almost the colour of the photograph. He lowered his eyes and brought a cupped hand to his forehead. 'There's been a mistake,' he mumbled. 'You've got me mixed up with someone else.'

Pagano dropped down in the chair beside him. 'Where'd you get that wallet, Lerner? Who is Charles Miller?'

'*I'm* Charles Miller!' The little man seemed close to tears. 'You can ask my friends, my business associates. They can tell you.'

Pagano leaned closer. 'I think you're a liar. You killed those two women, and you came up here to hide. Look at me!'

'It's all a mistake! Can't you see that?'

Pagano's voice grew louder, more insistent. 'I think you should make a statement. I think you should tell us about those two women.'

'I don't know what you're talking about!'

Wolfson interceded. 'Take it easy, Sy. We still don't have a positive identification.'

'This guy is Frederick Lerner. The photo matches, he lied about having a wife, and he used that blackboard like a pro. I say book him.'

Wolfson thought it over. For a moment he wished he had never recognised the man, had walked right by him.

'What do we do?' Pagano pressed. 'Lock him up or let him run? Come on, buddy, make up your mind.'

Wolfson looked down at the little man. He was holding the photograph of Lerner again, studying it with dull incomprehension.

'Okay, we book him. I'm still not as sure as you are, but we can't take a chance.'

'Take my word,' Pagano said. 'Everything checks.'

'Let's go, Mr Miller.' Wolfson touched him gently on the shoulder. 'First stop is Fingerprints.'

Miller nodded. He stood up and groped his way towards the door.

Pagano leaned against the window-sill, slapping the file angrily against his hip. 'When you're finished,' he said, 'bring him back. I'm going to try LA again.'

He was beginning to dial the phone when Wolfson closed the door.

In the fingerprint office Miller was uninterested as they rolled his fingers on the inked glass. Wolfson sat in a corner, smoking a cigarette and thinking. Something was wrong; Charles Miller – or whatever his name was – was too mild, too apathetic for a murderer.

A minute later there was a soft knocking at the door and Pagano looked in. 'Wolfson? Could I see you?'

Wolfson followed him out, stamping his cigarette into the scarred floor. 'You reach LA?'

'Yeah.' Pagano didn't look at him directly. 'They picked up Frederick Lerner last night.'

'What!'

'Caught him hiding out in a friend's place near the UCLA campus. It's him, no chance of error.'

Wolfson tried not to show his relief. 'How do you like that!' he said. 'The guy looks just like him. The two could be twins.'

Pagano sighed and held up his hands. 'We goofed. We've done it before, we'll do it again. Look, you want to explain things to our friend in there? I'm not good on apologies. Tell him we're sorry, we made a mistake, the works.' He grinned sourly. 'You were always the diplomat. And give him a lift back to the hotel. He looks like he's gonna collapse any minute.'

It was a silent drive to the Golden Gate. Miller sat brooding in the front seat, completely withdrawn. He had taken Wolfson's apology blankly, once or twice looking at the smudge marks on his fingers.

'Tell you what,' Wolfson said, trying to brighten the atmosphere. 'We'll have a drink at the hotel. On me.'

Miller shook his head. 'No, thanks. You don't have to do that.'

'All right, but don't worry about anything. Nobody will ever know it happened. We didn't put you on the blotter so there's no record.'

In the lobby of the Golden Gate Wolfson managed an awkward goodbye and sent the little man towards the bank of elevators. When the doors slid closed he breathed a sigh of relief. The next time he would think twice before taking someone in for questioning.

He was about to leave when he heard his name being paged. There was a telephone call for him at the main desk.

Pagano was on the line. 'Thought I could catch you there. On a hunch, I called Miller's place on Lombard. His wife answered.'

Wolfson frowned. 'I thought he said she was in Nevada.'

'He lied. She's going to Nevada all right, but not to visit any friends. Reno, Nevada.'

'She's divorcing him?'

'That's right. You should have heard her on the phone. Sounds like a real swinger. She says it broke him up pretty bad but she doesn't care. Guess it was one of those May and December things.'

'The poor guy,' Wolfson said. 'And we didn't make matters any easier for him.'

'Yeah. Well, I thought you'd be interested. That'll be the last you'll ever hear of Mr Charles Miller.'

'Okay, Sy. Thanks.'

He hung up and walked across the lobby to the doors on Powell Street. Well, it all figured. That's why Miller had seemed so indifferent and apathetic, even before he was asked to go downtown.

Outside, all along the kerb, a crowd was beginning to gather. Cars had stopped and people were running up from the shops on Geary. Curious, Wolfson pushed through the door and looked up the steep stone slope of the hotel building. Miller stood on a ledge high up near the top, looking down at the crowd.

Now he knew why the little man had wanted a room on the twelfth floor.

The Man in the Inverness Cape

BY BARONESS ORCZY

Although women in crime series are now comparatively commonplace – vide Jessica Fletcher *of* Murder, She Wrote; *Agatha Christie's Miss Marple; Jemima Shore, Antonia Fraser's TV investigator; Liza Cody's workaholic detective Anna Lee; and the formidable Detective Chief Inspector Jane Tennison – the female crimebuster did not make her debut on the small screen until* 1971. *Here, once again, the choice of lady sleuth was an unusual one: Lady Molly of Scotland Yard who had been created over half a century earlier by Baroness Orczy, better known for her brave and resourceful (not to mention much-filmed) Scarlet Pimpernel. Lady Molly is, though, a genuinely original figure, a woman who, according to one of her cases, 'The Frewin Miniatures', uses 'methods that were not altogether approved of at Scotland Yard, yet nevertheless her shrewdness and ingenuity were so undoubted that they earned for her a reputation and placed her in the foremost rank of the force.' That she was an early feminist was also self-evident by another remark in the story of Sir Jeremiah's Will: 'When Lady Molly joined Scotland Yard she managed to keep her position in Society whilst exercising a profession which usually does not make for high social standing.' If any of her colleagues at the Yard might have been offended by such a remark, the beautiful, clever and resourceful woman expected no special favours because of her background as Lady Molly Robertson-Kirk, the daughter of the Earl of Flintshire.*

Lady Molly was launched on Thames Television in September 1971 *as a female rival of Sherlock Holmes, operating in the same London as the great Detective of Baker Street. The actress to achieve the distinction of being the first woman TV sleuth was the attractive part-Norwegian, Elvi Hale, who had been discovered by Laurence Olivier and hailed in the press as 'the new Joan Greenwood'. Before taking on the role of Lady Molly she had appeared in several successful movies including* True As A Turtle *(1957) and* The Navy Lark *(1959). It was a role she embraced enthusiastically as · she later told the press, describing Lady Molly as the most unlikely detective who had ever worked for Scotland Yard. 'I was astonished to discover that she really existed,' said Elvi. 'Off duty, she was a Suffragette, I believe.' The series itself was full of corpses, poisons, robbery and slow-thinking policemen who were no match for the aristocratic sleuth. Mary Malone of the* Daily Mirror *was just one of several critics who enthused on 30 January 1971: 'There was enough so you could lick your lips for a week and look forward to more.'*

Baroness Emmuska Orczy (1865–1947), Lady Molly's creator, had been born in Hungary, the daughter of a well-known composer, and moved to London where she proved herself a distinguished artist (several of her pictures were hung in the Royal Academy) as well as a writer of popular fiction. Apart from The Scarlet Pimpernel *(1905) and its sequels, Baroness Orczy wrote a number of crime novels including* The Old Man In The Corner *(1901) who solves mysteries without leaving his room;* The Man in Grey *(1910) about a secret agent in the Napoleonic era; and* Skin O' My Tooth *(1928) the nickname of an unscrupulous lawyer-detective whose real name was Patrick Mulligan. The stories of Lady Molly the head of the 'Female Department of Scotland Yard' – as she was described – first appeared in the popular monthly magazine,* Pearson's, *at the same time as the later cases of Sherlock Holmes were being published in the* Strand Magazine. *The sales of both were said to have been remarkable. Sadly, though, Lady Molly was given no second series, although Elvi Hale was convinced the female detective was here to stay on television. 'I think there is a good case for more women detectives,' she told the* Sun *in December 1971. 'Feminine intuition would be a very useful asset to a detective.' Time has proved her words not only very perceptive, but prophetic, too . . .*

I HAVE HEARD many people say – people, too, mind you, who read their daily paper regularly – that it is quite impossible for anyone to 'disappear' within the confines of the British Isles. At the same time these wise people invariably admit one great exception to their otherwise unimpeachable theory, and that is the case of Mr Leonard Marvell, who, as you know, walked out one afternoon from the Scotia Hotel in Cromwell Road and has never been seen or heard of since.

Information had originally been given to the police by Mr Marvell's sister Olive, a Scotchwoman of the usually accepted type: tall, bony, with sandy-coloured hair, and a somewhat melancholy expression in her blue-grey eyes.

Her brother, she said, had gone out on a rather foggy afternoon. I think it was the 3rd of February, just about a year ago. His intention had been to go and consult a solicitor in the City – whose address had been given him recently by a friend – about some private business of his own.

Mr Marvell had told his sister that he would get a train at South Kensington Station to Moorgate Street, and walk thence to Finsbury Square. She was to expect him home by dinner-time.

As he was, however, very irregular in his habits, being fond of spending his evenings at restaurants and music-halls, the sister did not feel the least anxious when he did not return home at the appointed time. She had her dinner in the *table d'hôte* room, and went to bed soon after ten.

She and her brother occupied two bedrooms and a sitting-room on the second floor of the little private hotel. Miss Marvell, moreover, had a maid always with her, as she was somewhat of an invalid. This girl, Rosie Campbell, a nice-looking Scotch lassie, slept on the top floor.

It was only on the following morning, when Mr Leonard did not put in an appearance at breakfast, that Miss Marvell began to feel anxious. According to her own account, she sent Rosie in to see if anything was the matter, and the girl, wide-eyed and not a little frightened, came back with the news that Mr Marvell was not in his room, and that his bed had not been slept in that night.

With characteristic Scottish reserve, Miss Olive said nothing about the matter at the time to anyone, nor did she give information to the police until two days later, when she herself had exhausted every means in her power to discover her brother's whereabouts.

She had seen the lawyer to whose office Leonard Marvell had intended going that afternoon, but Mr Statham, the solicitor in question, had seen nothing of the missing man.

With great adroitness Rosie, the maid, had made inquiries at South Kensington and Moorgate Street stations. At the former, the booking clerk, who knew Mr Marvell by sight, distinctly remembered selling him a first-class ticket to one of the City stations in the early part of the afternoon; but at Moorgate Street, which is a very busy station, no one recollected seeing a tall, red-haired Scotchman in an Inverness cape – such was the description given of the missing man. By that time the fog had become very thick in the City; traffic was disorganised, and everyone felt fussy, ill-tempered, and self-centred.

These, in substance, were the details which Miss Marvell gave to the police on the subject of her brother's strange disappearance.

At first she did not appear very anxious; she seemed to have great faith in Mr Marvell's power to look after himself; moreover, she declared positively that her brother had neither valuables nor money about his person when he went out that afternoon.

But as day succeeded day and no trace of the missing man had yet been found, matters became more serious, and the search instituted by our fellows at the Yard waxed more keen.

A description of Mr Leonard Marvell was published in the leading London and provincial dailies. Unfortunately, there was no good photograph of him extant, and descriptions are apt to prove vague.

Very little was known about the man beyond his disappearance, which had rendered him famous. He and his sister had arrived at the Scotia Hotel about a month previously, and subsequently they were joined by the maid Campbell.

Scotch people are far too reserved ever to speak of themselves or their affairs to strangers. Brother and sister spoke very little to anyone at the hotel. They had their meals in their sitting room, waited on by the maid, who messed with the staff. But, in face of the present terrible calamity, Miss Marvell's frigidity relaxed before the police inspector, to whom she gave what information she could about her brother.

'He was like a son to me,' she explained with scarcely restrained tears, 'for we lost our parents early in life, and as we were left very, very badly off, our relations took but little notice of us. My brother was years younger than I am – and though he was a little wild and fond of pleasure, he was as good as gold to me, and has supported us both for years by journalistic work. We came to London from Glasgow about a month ago, because Leonard got a very good appointment on the staff of the *Daily Post*.'

All this, of course, was soon proved to be true; and although, on minute inquiries being instituted in Glasgow, but little seemed to be known about Mr Leonard Marvell in that city, there seemed no doubt that he had done some reporting for the *Courier*, and that latterly, in response to an advertisement, he had applied for and obtained regular employment on the *Daily Post*.

The latter enterprising halfpenny journal, with characteristic mag-
nanimity, made an offer of £50 reward to any of its subscribers who
gave information which would lead to the discovery of the where-
abouts of Mr Leonard Marvell.

But time went by, and that £50 remained unclaimed.

2

Lady Molly had not seemed as interested as she usually was in cases of
this sort. With strange flippancy – wholly unlike herself – she
remarked that one Scotch journalist more or less in London did not
vastly matter.

I was much amused, therefore, one morning about three weeks after
the mysterious disappearance of Mr Leonard Marvell, when Jane, our
little parlour-maid, brought in a card accompanied by a letter.

The card bore the name 'Miss Olive Marvell'. The letter was the
usual formula from the chief, asking Lady Molly to have a talk with
the lady in question, and to come and see him on the subject after the
interview.

With a smothered yawn my dear lady told Jane to show in Miss
Marvell.

'There are two of them, my lady,' said Jane, as she prepared to obey.

'Two what?' asked Lady Molly with a laugh.

'Two ladies, I mean,' explained Jane.

'Well! Show them both into the drawing room,' said Lady Molly,
impatiently.

Then, as Jane went off on this errand, a very funny thing happened;
funny, because during the entire course of my intimate association
with my dear lady, I had never known her act with such marked
indifference in the face of an obviously interesting case. She turned to
me and said:

'Mary, you had better see these two women, whoever they may be; I
feel that they would bore me to distraction. Take note of what they
say, and let me know. Now, don't argue,' she added with a laugh,
which peremptorily put a stop to my rising protest, 'but go and
interview Miss Marvell and Co.'

Needless to say, I promptly did as I was told, and the next few
seconds saw me installed in our little drawing room, saying polite
preliminaries to the two ladies who sat opposite to me.

I had no need to ask which of them was Miss Marvell. Tall, ill-
dressed in deep black, with a heavy crape veil over her face, and black

cotton gloves, she looked the uncompromising Scotchwoman to the life. In strange contrast to her depressing appearance, there sat beside her an over-dressed, much behatted, peroxided young woman, who bore the stamp of *the* profession all over her pretty, painted face.

Miss Marvell, I was glad to note, was not long in plunging into the subject which had brought her here.

'I saw a gentleman at Scotland Yard,' she explained, after a short preamble, 'because Miss – er – Lulu Fay came to me at the hotel this very morning with a story which, in my opinion, should have been told to the police directly my brother's disappearance became known, and not three weeks later.'

The emphasis which she laid on the last few words, and the stern look with which she regarded the golden-haired young woman beside her, showed the disapproval with which the rigid Scotchwoman viewed any connection which her brother might have had with the lady, whose very name seemed unpleasant to her lips.

Miss – er – Lulu Fay blushed even through her rouge, and turned a pair of large, liquid eyes imploringly upon me.

'I – I didn't know. I was frightened,' she stammered.

'There's no occasion to be frightened now,' retorted Miss Marvell, 'and the sooner you try and be truthful about the whole matter, the better it will be for all of us.'

And the stern woman's lips closed with a snap, as she deliberately turned her back on Miss Fay and began turning over the leaves of a magazine which happened to be on a table close to her hand.

I muttered a few words of encouragement, for the little actress looked ready to cry. I spoke as kindly as I could, telling her that if indeed she could throw some light on Mr Marvell's present where-abouts it was her duty to be quite frank on the subject.

She 'hem'-ed and 'ha'-ed for a while, and her simpering ways were just beginning to tell on my nerves, when she suddenly started talking very fast.

'I am principal boy at the Grand,' she explained with great volubility; 'and I knew Mr Leonard Marvell well – in fact – er – he paid me a good deal of attention and –'

'Yes – and –?' I queried, for the girl was obviously nervous.

There was a pause. Miss Fay began to cry.

'And it seems that my brother took this young – er – lady to supper on the night of February 3rd, after which no one has ever seen or heard of him again,' here interposed Miss Marvell, quietly.

'Is that so?' I asked.

Lulu Fay nodded, whilst heavy tears fell upon her clasped hands.

'But why did you not tell this to the police three weeks ago?' I ejaculated, with all the sternness at my command.

'I – I was frightened,' she stammered.

'Frightened? Of what?'

'I am engaged to Lord Mountnewte and –'

'And you did not wish him to know that you were accepting the attentions of Mr Leonard Marvell – was that it? Well,' I added, with involuntary impatience, 'what happened after you had supper with Mr Marvell?'

'Oh! I hope – I hope that nothing happened,' she said through more tears; 'we had supper at the Trocadero, and he saw me into my brougham. Suddenly, just as I was driving away, I saw Lord Mountnewte standing quite close to us in the crowd.'

'Did the two men know one another?' I asked.

'No,' replied Miss Fay; 'at least, I didn't think so, but when I looked back through the window of my carriage I saw them standing on the kerb talking to each other for a moment, and then walk off together towards Piccadilly Circus. That is the last I have seen of either of them,' continued the little actress with a fresh flood of tears. 'Lord Mountnewte hasn't spoken to me since, and Mr Marvell has disappeared with my money and my diamonds.'

'Your money and your diamonds?' I gasped in amazement.

'Yes; he told me he was a jeweller, and that my diamonds wanted resetting. He took them with him that evening, for he said that London jewellers were clumsy thieves, and that he would love to do the work for me himself. I also gave him two hundred pounds, which he said he would want for buying the gold and platinum required for the settings. And now he has disappeared – and my diamonds – and my money! Oh! I have been very – very foolish – and –'

Her voice broke down completely. Of course, one often hears of the idiocy of girls giving money and jewels unquestioningly to clever adventurers who know how to trade upon their inordinate vanity. There was, therefore, nothing very out of the way in the story just told me by Miss – er – Lulu Fay, until the moment when Miss Marvell's quiet voice, with its marked Scotch burr, broke in upon the short silence which had followed the actress's narrative.

'As I explained to the chief detective inspector at Scotland Yard,' she said calmly, 'the story which this young – er – lady tells is only partly true. She may have had supper with Mr Leonard Marvell on the night of February 3rd, and he may have paid her certain attentions; but he never deceived her by telling her that he was a jeweller, nor did he obtain possession of her diamonds and her money through false statements. My brother was the soul of honour and loyalty. If, for some reason which Miss – er – Lulu Fay chooses to keep secret, he had her jewels and money in his possession on the fatal February 3rd, then I think his disappearance is accounted for. He has been robbed and perhaps murdered.'

Like a true Scotchwoman she did not give way to tears, but even her harsh voice trembled slightly when she thus bore witness to her brother's honesty, and expressed the fears which assailed her as to his fate.

Imagine my plight! I could ill forgive my dear lady for leaving me in this unpleasant position – a sort of peacemaker between two women who evidently hated one another, and each of whom was trying her best to give the other 'the lie direct'.

I ventured to ring for our faithful Jane and to send her with an imploring message to Lady Molly, begging her to come and disentangle the threads of this muddled skein with her clever fingers; but Jane returned with a curt note from my dear lady, telling me not to worry about such a silly case, and to bow the two women out of the flat as soon as possible and then come for a nice walk.

I wore my official manner as well as I could, trying not to betray the 'prentice hand. Of course, the interview lasted a great deal longer, and there was considerably more talk than I can tell you of in a brief narrative. But the gist of it all was just as I have said. Miss Lulu Fay stuck to every point of the story which she had originally told Miss Marvell. It was the latter uncompromising lady who had immediately marched the younger woman off to Scotland Yard in order that she might repeat her tale to the police. I did not wonder that the chief promptly referred them both to Lady Molly.

Anyway, I made excellent shorthand notes of the conflicting stories which I heard; and I finally saw, with real relief, the two women walk out of our little front door.

3

Miss – er – Lulu Fay, mind you, never contradicted in any one particular the original story which she had told me, about going out to supper with Leonard Marvell, entrusting him with £200 and the diamonds, which he said he would have reset for her, and seeing him finally in close conversation with her recognised *fiancé*, Lord Mountnewte. Miss Marvell, on the other hand, very commendably refused to admit that her brother acted dishonestly towards the girl. If he had her jewels and money in his possession at the time of his disappearance, then he had undoubtedly been robbed, or perhaps murdered, on his way back to the hotel, and if Lord Mountnewte had been the last to speak to him on that fatal night, then Lord Mountnewte must be able to throw some light on the mysterious occurrence.

Our fellows at the Yard were abnormally active. It seemed, on the face of it, impossible that a man, healthy, vigorous, and admittedly sober, should vanish in London between Piccadilly Circus and Cromwell Road without leaving the slightest trace of himself or of the valuables said to have been in his possession.

Of course, Lord Mountnewte was closely questioned. He was a young Guardsman of the usual pattern, and, after a great deal of vapid talk which irritated Detective Inspector Saunders not a little, he made the following statement:

'I certainly am acquainted with Miss Lulu Fay. On the night in question I was standing outside the Troc, when I saw this young lady at her own carriage window talking to a tall man in an Inverness cape. She had, earlier in the day, refused my invitation to supper, saying that she was not feeling very well, and would go home directly after the theatre; therefore I felt, naturally, a little vexed. I was just about to hail a taxi, meaning to go on to the club, when, to my intense astonishment, the man in the Inverness cape came up to me and asked me if I could tell him the best way to get back to Cromwell Road.'

'And what did you do?' asked Saunders.

'I walked a few steps with him and put him on his way,' replied Lord Mountnewte, blandly.

In Saunders' own expressive words, he thought that story 'fishy'. He could not imagine the arm of coincidence being quite so long as to cause these two men – who presumably were both in love with the same girl, and who had just met at a moment when one of them was obviously suffering pangs of jealousy – to hold merely a topographical conversation with one another. But it was equally difficult to suppose that the eldest son and heir of the Marquis of Loam should murder a successful rival and then rob him in the streets of London.

Moreover, here came the eternal and unanswerable questions: if Lord Mountnewte had murdered Leonard Marvell, where and how had he done it, and what had he done with the body?

I dare say you are wondering by this time why I have said nothing about the maid, Rosie Campbell.

Well, plenty of very clever people (I mean those who write letters to the papers and give suggestions to every official department in the kingdom) thought that the police ought to keep a very strict eye upon that pretty Scotch lassie. For she was very pretty, and had quaint, demure ways which rendered her singularly attractive, in spite of the fact that, for most masculine tastes, she would have been considered too tall. Of course, Saunders and Danvers kept an eye on her – you may be sure of that – and got a good deal of information about her from the people at the hotel. Most of it, unfortunately, was irrelevant to the case. She was maid-attendant to Miss Marvell, who was feeble in health, and who went out but little. Rosie waited on her master and mistress upstairs, carrying their meals to their private room, and doing their bedrooms. The rest of the day she was fairly free, and was quite sociable downstairs with the hotel staff.

With regard to her movements and actions on that memorable 3rd of February, Saunders – though he worked very hard – could glean but little useful information. You see, in an hotel of that kind, with an average of thirty to forty guests at one time, it is extremely difficult to state positively what any one person did or did not do on that particular day.

Most people at the Scotia remembered that Miss Marvell dined in the *table d'hôte* room on that 3rd of February; this she did about once a fortnight, when her maid had an evening 'out'.

The hotel staff also recollected fairly distinctly that Miss Rosie Campbell was not in the steward's room at supper-time that evening, but no one could remember definitely when she came in.

One of the chambermaids who occupied the bedroom adjoining hers, said that she heard her moving about soon after midnight; the hall porter declared that he saw her come in just before half-past twelve when he closed the doors for the night.

But one of the ground-floor valets said that, on the morning of the 4th, he saw Miss Marvell's maid, in hat and coat, slip into the house and upstairs, very quickly and quietly, soon after the front doors were opened, namely, about 7 a.m.

Here, of course, was a direct contradiction between the chambermaid and hall porter on the one side, and the valet on the other, whilst Miss Marvell said that Campbell came into her room and made her some tea long before seven o'clock every morning, including that of the 4th.

I assure you our fellows at the Yard were ready to tear their hair out by the roots, from sheer aggravation at this maze of contradictions which met them at every turn.

The whole thing seemed so simple. There was nothing 'to it' as it were, and but very little real suggestion of foul play, and yet Mr

Leonard Marvell had disappeared, and no trace of him could be found.

Everyone now talked freely of murder. London is a big town, and this would not have been the first instance of a stranger – for Mr Leonard Marvell was practically a stranger in London – being enticed to a lonely part of the city on a foggy night, and there done away with and robbed, and the body hidden in an out-of-the-way cellar, where it might not be discovered for months to come.

But the newspaper-reading public is notably fickle, and Mr Leonard Marvell was soon forgotten by everyone save the chief and the batch of our fellows who had charge of the case.

Thus I heard through Danvers one day that Rosie Campbell had left Miss Marvell's employ, and was living in rooms in Findlater Terrace, near Walham Green.

I was alone in our Maida Vale flat at the time, my dear lady having gone to spend the week-end with the Dowager Lady Loam, who was an old friend of hers; nor, when she returned, did she seem any more interested in Rosie Campbell's movements than she had been hitherto.

Yet another month went by, and I for one had absolutely ceased to think of the man in the Inverness cape, who had so mysteriously and so completely vanished in the very midst of busy London, when one morning early in January, Lady Molly made her appearance in my room, looking more like the landlady of a disreputable gambling-house than anything else I could imagine.

'What in the world –?' I began.

'Yes! I think I look the part,' she replied, surveying with obvious complacency the extraordinary figure which confronted her in the glass.

My dear lady had on a purple cloth coat and skirt of a peculiarly vivid hue, and of a singular cut, which made her matchless figure look like a sack of potatoes. Her soft brown hair was quite hidden beneath a 'transformation', of that yellow-reddish tint only to be met with in very cheap dyes.

As for her hat! I won't attempt to describe it. It towered above and around her face, which was plentifully covered with brick-red and with that kind of powder which causes the cheeks to look a deep mauve.

My dear lady looked, indeed, a perfect picture of appalling vulgarity.

'Where are you going in this elegant attire?' I asked in amazement.

'I have taken rooms in Findlater Terrace,' she replied lightly. 'I feel that the air of Walham Green will do us both good. Our amiable, if somewhat slatternly, landlady expects us in time for luncheon. You will have to keep rigidly in the background, Mary, all the while we are there. I said that I was bringing an invalid niece with me, and, as a preliminary, you may as well tie two or three thick veils over your face. I think I may safely promise that you won't be dull.'

And we certainly were not dull during our brief stay at 34, Findlater Terrace, Walham Green. Fully equipped, and arrayed in our extraordinary garments, we duly arrived there, in a rickety four-wheeler, on the top of which were perched two seedy-looking boxes.

The landlady was a toothless old creature, who apparently thought washing a quite unnecessary proceeding. In this she was evidently at one with every one of her neighbours. Findlater Terrace looked unspeakably squalid; groups of dirty children congregated in the gutters and gave forth discordant shrieks as our cab drove up.

Through my thick veils I thought that, some distance down the road, I spied a horsy-looking man in ill-fitting riding-breeches and gaiters, who vaguely reminded me of Danvers.

Within half an hour of our installation, and whilst we were eating a tough steak over a doubtful tablecloth, my dear lady told me that she had been waiting a full month, until rooms in this particular house happened to be vacant. Fortunately the population in Findlater Terrace is always a shifting one, and Lady Molly had kept a sharp eye on No. 34, where, on the floor above, lived Miss Rosie Campbell. Directly the last set of lodgers walked out of the ground-floor rooms, we were ready to walk in.

My dear lady's manners and customs, whilst living at the above aristocratic address, were fully in keeping with her appearance. The shrill, rasping voice which she assumed echoed from attic to cellar.

One day I heard her giving vague hints to the landlady that her husband, Mr Marcus Stein, had had a little trouble with the police about a small hotel which he had kept somewhere near Fitzroy Square, and where 'young gentlemen used to come and play cards of a night'. The landlady was also made to understand that the worthy Mr Stein was now living temporarily at His Majesty's expense, whilst Mrs Stein had to live a somewhat secluded life, away from her fashionable friends.

The misfortunes of the pseudo Mrs Stein in no way marred the amiability of Mrs Tredwen, our landlady. The inhabitants of Findlater Terrace care very little about the antecedents of their lodgers, so long as they pay their week's rent in advance, and settle their 'extras' without much murmur.

This Lady Molly did, with a generosity characteristic of an ex-lady of means. She never grumbled at the quantity of jam and marmalade which we were supposed to have consumed every week, and which anon reached titanic proportions. She tolerated Mrs Tredwen's cat, tipped Ermyntrude – the tousled lodging-house slavey – lavishly, and lent the upstairs lodger her spirit-lamp and curling-tongs when Miss Rosie Campbell's got out of order.

A certain degree of intimacy followed the loan of those curling-tongs. Miss Campbell, reserved and demure, greatly sympathised with the lady who was not on the best of terms with the police. I kept steadily in the background. The two ladies did not visit each other's rooms, but they held long and confidential conversations on the landings, and I gathered, presently, that the pseudo Mrs Stein had succeeded in persuading Rosie Campbell that, if the police were watching No. 34, Findlater Terrace, at all, it was undoubtedly on account of the unfortunate Mr Stein's faithful wife.

I found it a little difficult to fathom Lady Molly's intentions. We had been in the house over three weeks, and nothing whatever had happened. Once I ventured on a discreet query as to whether we were to expect the sudden reappearance of Mr Leonard Marvell.

'For if that's all about it,' I argued, 'then surely the men from the Yard could have kept the house in view, without all this inconvenience and masquerading on our part.'

But to this tirade my dear lady vouchsafed no reply.

She and her newly acquired friend were, about this time, deeply interested in the case known as the 'West End Shop Robberies,' which no doubt you recollect, since they occurred such a very little while ago. Ladies who were shopping in the large drapers' emporiums during the crowded and busy sale time, lost reticules, purses, and valuable parcels, without any trace of the clever thief being found.

The drapers, during sale-time, invariably employ detectives in plain clothes to look after their goods, but in this case it was the customers who were robbed, and the detectives, attentive to every attempt at 'shop-lifting,' had had no eyes for the more subtle thief.

I had already noticed Miss Rosie Campbell's keen look of excitement whenever the pseudo Mrs Stein discussed these cases with her. I was not a bit surprised, therefore, when, one afternoon at about tea time, my dear lady came home from her habitual walk, and, at the top of her shrill voice, called out to me from the hall:

'Mary! Mary! they've got the man of the shop robberies. He's given the silly police the slip this time, but they know who he is now, and I suppose they'll get him presently. 'Tisn't anybody I know,' she added, with that harsh, common laugh which she had adopted for her part.

I had come out of the room in response to her call, and was standing just outside our own sitting room door. Mrs Tredwen, too, bedraggled and unkempt, as usual, had sneaked up the area steps, closely followed by Ermyntrude.

But on the half-landing just above us the trembling figure of Rosie Campbell, with scared white face and dilated eyes, looked on the verge of a sudden fall.

Still talking shrilly and volubly, Lady Molly ran up to her, but Campbell met her halfway, and the pseudo Mrs Stein, taking vigorous hold of her wrist, dragged her into our own sitting room.

'Pull yourself together, now,' she said with rough kindness; 'that owl Tredwen is listening, and you needn't let her know too much. Shut the door, Mary. Lor' bless you, m'dear, I've gone through worse scares than these. There! you just lie down on this sofa a bit. My niece'll make you a cup o' tea; and I'll go and get an evening paper, and see what's going on. I suppose you are very interested in the shop robbery man, or you wouldn't have took on so.'

Without waiting for Campbell's contradiction to this statement, Lady Molly flounced out of the house.

Miss Campbell hardly spoke during the next ten minutes that she and I were left alone together. She lay on the sofa with eyes wide open, staring up at the ceiling, evidently still in a great state of fear.

I had just got tea ready when Lady Molly came back. She had an evening paper in her hand, but threw this down on the table directly she came in.

'I could only get an early edition,' she said breathlessly, 'and the silly thing hasn't got anything in it about the matter.'

She drew near to the sofa, and, subduing the shrillness of her voice, she whispered rapidly, bending down towards Campbell:

'There's a man hanging about at the corner down there. No, no; it's not the police,' she added quickly, in response to the girl's sudden start of alarm. 'Trust me, my dear, for knowing a 'tec when I see one! Why, I'd smell one half a mile off. No; my opinion is that it's your man, my dear, and that he's in a devil of a hole.'

'Oh! he oughtn't to come here,' ejaculated Campbell in great alarm. 'He'll get me into trouble and do himself no good. He's been a fool!' she added, with a fierceness wholly unlike her usual demure placidity, 'getting himself caught like that. Now I suppose we shall have to hook it – if there's time.'

'Can I do anything to help you?' asked the pseudo Mrs Stein. 'You know I've been through all this myself, when they was after Mr Stein. Or perhaps Mary could do something.'

'Well, yes,' said the girl, after a slight pause, during which she seemed to be gathering her wits together; 'I'll write a note, and you shall take it, if you will, to a friend of mine – a lady who lives in the Cromwell Road. But if you still see a man lurking about at the corner of the street, then, just as you pass him, say the word 'Campbell', and if he replies 'Rosie,' then give *him* the note. Will you do that?'

'Of course I will, my dear. Just you leave it all to me.'

And the pseudo Mrs Stein brought ink and paper and placed them on the table. Rosie Campbell wrote a brief note, and then fastened it down with a bit of sealing-wax before she handed it over to Lady Molly. The note was addressed to Miss Marvell, Scotia Hotel, Cromwell Road.

'You understand?' she said eagerly. 'Don't give the note to the man unless he says "Rosie" in reply to the word "Campbell."'

'All right – all right!' said Lady Molly, slipping the note into her reticule. 'And you go up to your room, Miss Campbell; it's no good giving that old fool Tredwen too much to gossip about.'

Rosie Campbell went upstairs, and presently my dear lady and I were walking rapidly down the badly lighted street.

'Where is the man?' I whispered eagerly as soon as we were out of earshot of No 34.

'There is no man,' replied Lady Molly, quickly.

'But the West End shop thief?' I asked.

'He hasn't been caught yet, and won't be either, for he is far too clever a scoundrel to fall into an ordinary trap.'

She did not give me time to ask further questions, for presently, when we had reached Reporton Square, my dear lady handed me the note written by Campbell, and said:

'Go straight on to the Scotia Hotel, and ask for Miss Marvell; send up the note to her, but don't let her see you, as she knows you by sight. I must see the chief first, and will be with you as soon as possible. Having delivered the note, you must hang about outside as long as you can. Use your wits; she must not leave the hotel before I see her.'

There was no hansom to be got in this elegant quarter of the town, so, having parted from my dear lady, I made for the nearest Underground station, and took a train for South Kensington.

Thus it was nearly seven o'clock before I reached the Scotia. In answer to my inquiries for Miss Marvell, I was told that she was ill in bed and could see no one. I replied that I had only brought a note for her, and would wait for a reply.

Acting on my dear lady's instructions, I was as slow in my

movements as ever I could be, and was some time in finding the note and handing it to a waiter, who then took it upstairs.

Presently he returned with the message: 'Miss Marvell says there is no answer.'

Whereupon I asked for pen and paper at the office, and wrote the following brief note on my own responsibility, using my wits as my dear lady had bidden me to do.

'Please, madam,' I wrote, 'will you send just a line to Miss Rosie Campbell? She seems very upset and frightened at some news she has had.'

Once more the waiter ran upstairs, and returned with a sealed envelope, which I slipped into my reticule.

Time was slipping by very slowly. I did not know how long I should have to wait about outside in the cold, when, to my horror, I heard a hard voice, with a marked Scotch accent, saying:

'I am going out, waiter, and shan't be back to dinner. Tell them to lay a little cold supper upstairs in my room.'

The next moment Miss Marvell, with coat, hat, and veil, was descending the stairs.

My plight was awkward. I certainly did not think it safe to present myself before the lady; she would undoubtedly recollect my face. Yet I had orders to detain her until the appearance of Lady Molly.

Miss Marvell seemed in no hurry. She was putting on her gloves as she came downstairs. In the hall she gave a few more instructions to the porter, whilst I, in a dark corner in the background, was vaguely planning an assault or an alarm of fire.

Suddenly, at the hotel entrance, where the porter was obsequiously holding open the door for Miss Marvell to pass through, I saw the latter's figure stiffen; she took one step back as if involuntarily, then, equally quickly, attempted to dart across the threshold, on which a group – composed of my dear lady, of Saunders, and of two or three people scarcely distinguishable in the gloom beyond – had suddenly made its appearance.

Miss Marvell was forced to retreat into the hall; already I had heard Saunders's hurriedly whispered words:

'Try and not make a fuss in this place, now. Everything can go off quietly, you know.'

Danvers and Cotton, whom I knew well, were already standing one each side of Miss Marvell, whilst suddenly amongst this group I recognised Fanny, the wife of Danvers, who is one of our female searchers at the Yard.

'Shall we go up to your own room?' suggested Saunders.

'I think that is quite unnecessary,' interposed Lady Molly. 'I feel convinced that Mr Leonard Marvell will yield to the inevitable quietly, and follow you without giving any trouble.'

Marvell, however, did make a bold dash for liberty. As Lady Molly had said previously, he was far too clever to allow himself to be captured easily. But my dear lady had been cleverer. As she told me subsequently, she had from the first suspected that the trio who lodged at the Scotia Hotel were really only a duo – namely, Leonard Marvell and his wife. The latter impersonated a maid most of the time; but among these two clever people the three characters were interchangeable. Of course, there was no Miss Marvell at all. Leonard was alternately dressed up as man or woman, according to the requirements of his villainies.

'As soon as I heard that Miss Marvell was very tall and bony,' said Lady Molly, 'I thought that there might be a possibility of her being merely a man in disguise. Then there was the fact – but little dwelt on by either the police or public – that no one seems ever to have seen brother and sister together, nor was the entire trio ever seen at one and the same time.

'On that 3rd of February Leonard Marvell went out. No doubt he changed his attire in a lady's waiting room at one of the railway stations; subsequently he came home, now dressed as Miss Marvell, and had dinner in the *table d'hôte* room so as to set up a fairly plausible alibi. But ultimately it was his wife, the pseudo Rosie Campbell, who stayed indoors that night, whilst he, Leonard Marvell, when going out after dinner, impersonated the maid until he was clear of the hotel; then he reassumed his male clothes once more, no doubt in the deserted waiting room of some railway station, and met Miss Lulu Fay at supper, subsequently returning to the hotel in the guise of the maid.

'You see the game of crisscross, don't you? This interchanging of characters was bound to baffle everyone. Many clever scoundrels have assumed disguises, sometimes personating members of the opposite sex to their own, but never before have I known two people play the part of three. Thus, endless contradictions followed as to the hour when Campbell the maid went out and when she came in, for at one time it was she herself who was seen by the valet, and at another it was Leonard Marvell dressed in her clothes.'

He was also clever enough to accost Lord Mountnewte in the open street, thus bringing further complications into this strange case.

After the successful robbery of Miss Fay's diamonds, Leonard Marvell and his wife parted for a while. They were waiting for an opportunity to get across the Channel and there turn their booty into solid cash. Whilst Mrs Marvell, *alias* Rosie Campbell, led a retired life in Findlater Terrace, Leonard kept his hand in with West End shop robberies.

Then Lady Molly entered the lists. As usual, her scheme was bold and daring; she trusted her own intuition and acted accordingly.

When she brought home the false news that the author of the shop robberies had been spotted by the police, Rosie Campbell's obvious terror confirmed her suspicions. The note written by the latter to the so-called Miss Marvell, though it contained nothing in any way incriminating, was the crowning certitude that my dear lady was right, as usual, in all her surmises.

And now Mr Leonard Marvell will be living for a couple of years at the tax-payers' expense; he has 'disappeared' temporarily from the public eye.

Rosie Campbell – *i.e.* Mrs Marvell – has gone to Glasgow. I feel convinced that two years hence we shall hear of the worthy couple again.

Hildegarde Withers is Back

BY STUART PALMER

Within a year of Lady Molly's debut on British television, American viewers had their first lady sleuth when the spinster, former school-teacher Hildegarde Withers who had been a favourite in novels and a series of movies from RKO for almost forty years, was featured on NBC in September 1972. Despite her impressive track record in the other mediums, the angular and waspish lady detective was a strange choice for producer Edward J. Montague to launch on television, though in Eve Arden he found a versatile actress who made the character a little younger, a bit more emancipated and even a little more charming than her predecessors. As the crotchety and rather unrefined Inspector Oscar Piper of the New York City Police Department whom Miss Withers helps to solve murder cases, the series cast the character actor James Gregory, who proved adept at playing the verbal exchanges and suggestions of a relationship that extends a little deeper than mere friendship which had provided the printed stories with much of their charm and originality. If the resulting production was not quite as successful as everyone hoped, this was doubtless due to the image of Miss Withers which had been so well established in the very popular novels and short stories, not forgetting the six films in which the angular, rather horse-faced Edna May Oliver had become everybody's idea of the lady sleuth — rather as Margaret Rutherford had been Miss Marple before Joan Hickson. There had even been two other actresses who had played Miss Withers on the cinema screen in the interim: Helen Broderick in Murder on a Bridle Path *(1936) and the former silent movie star, Zasu Pitts, in* The Plot Thickens *(1938). Viewed today, it is evident that NBC's Hildegarde Withers was ahead of its time, for many of the elements that have*

subsequently made other series with an older lady detective so successful – Murder, She Wrote being a prime example – are all there.

Stuart Palmer (1905–68), who was born in Wisconsin and was descended from some of the earliest English colonists, had held a variety of jobs including seaman, apple picker, taxi-driver and newspaper reporter before turning to fiction and creating Hildegarde Withers in The Penguin Pool *(1931). The model for the unusual sleuth had been his High School teacher, a Miss Fern Hakett, he later admitted. When* The Penguin Pool *was filmed the following year and proved a box office hit, Palmer expanded his work into script-writing and later wrote for a number of the other popular 'series' crime movies including* The Lone Wolf, The Falcon *and* Bulldog Drummond. *The success of his first novel also inspired Palmer to collect pictures and statues of penguins and he even devised a personal trademark featuring one of these birds. For those who still miss the irrepressible spinster sleuth,* Hildegarde Withers Is Back *offers a welcome reunion, made all the more fascinating by being set in the world of films and television that Stuart Palmer knew so well and of which the lady herself was one of the stars . . .*

A MUFFLED DIN sounded in the anteroom, and then the door banged open and an unexpected guest backed her way into the inspector's office, fending off the uniformed guardian of the gates with handbag and umbrella. 'Oscar! Do something!' she cried.

'Hildegarde Withers, as I live and breathe!' gasped the grizzled skipper of Homicide, managing to get out of his swivel chair and restore some semblance of order. 'Don't mind the sergeant, he's a new man and didn't know you from Adam – I mean, Eve. If you'd let me know you were coming to town I'd have had the welcome mat out. But I thought you were safely retired, and busy with your African daisies out in California.'

'African *violets*, Oscar.' The schoolteacher was preening her feathers like a ruffled Buff Orpington. 'And if you dare to add insult to injury by making one of your characteristic snide remarks about my new hat –'

'That's a *hat*? I thought it was a fallen soufflé!'

'This is hardly the time for persiflage. Not when I've just flown all the way across the country to come to your aid on the Barth case.'

'By broomstick? Well, dear lady, we've been getting along pretty well here at Centre Street without any amateur help since you quit being self-appointed gadfly to the Police Department –' Here Inspector Oscar Piper broke into a slow double-take. 'The *what* case?'

'Barth, Cecily Barth. You do recall the name?'

'It may ring a bell somewhere, but just now –'

'Oscar, I sometimes think that you are being intentionally dense! Cecily Barth happens to have been one of Hollywood's most famous stars in her day. You yourself must have been just about the right age to have had a schoolboy crush on her, back when she was the Love Goddess of the Silver Screen, unquote.'

'I used to be a Tom Mix fan, myself,' he said almost apologetically.

'But even you must have seen some of the recent newspaper publicity about how the great independent television producer Mr Boris Abbas is producing the life story of Cecily Barth as a special on filmed TV, bringing a famous Hollywood writer here to do the script in collaboration with Cecily herself, testing dozens of young sexpot actresses to play the leading role, and so on and so forth?'

The inspector carefully relighted his cigar. 'Oh, *that* one! I've got the flimsies here somewhere. Yeah, right here. You call it the Barth case, but it was some scenario writer name of Gary Twill who did the Dutch Act out of his hotel window late yesterday afternoon. According to all reports, it was a simple case of suicide.'

'Suicide is never simple! Oscar, most criminologists agree that falls from high windows, like drownings from canoes, are automatically suspect. Perfect murders, perhaps. I am quite aware of the fact that you police don't believe there is any such thing as the perfect murder, but remember, if it were perfect, you wouldn't know of it! And Gary Twill's death was no suicide, I'll wager a pretty penny. I feel it in my bones.'

'Of which you have a complete set,' Oscar Piper put in unkindly but accurately, softening the wisecrack with a Hibernian-type grin. 'Look, Hildegarde old girl, I'm personally delighted to have you back in town and tonight will joyfully buy you a spaghetti dinner at any place you name. I think I know just how bad you're itching to make like the old firehorse at the sound of the siren, but believe me, this case just *ain't* it!'

'*Isn't* it,' she corrected automatically.

'Okay, *isn't*. This Hollywood writer, the guy named Twill, had been out of work a while and he got this plush assignment to come to New York and do a TV script, with free hotel room and everything – and then it all went blooie. He had a thing going with the boss's playgirl-type secretary and he had a contract and he lost them both at the same time, the girl *and* the job. So he did the Dutch Act, like I said. What more do you want, chimes?'

'A suicide note or an eyewitness would help. Oscar, there is more here than meets the eye. I have known some screenwriters in my time – Los Angeles is crawling with them. They don't take their lives when they lose a girl, or a job either; they feel sure that another one, girl or job, will be along in a minute. Meanwhile, like Miniver Cheevy, they keep on drinking.'

'Miniver *who?*'

'A character in an almost forgotten poem by an almost forgotten poet named Edwin Arlington Robinson. No matter. I became interested in this case because of a certain letter which was shown to me over a week ago by a neighbour of mine out in Santa Monica, a Mrs Marcia Connell, whose three children are usually trampling down my flowerbeds. She happens to be the niece and presumably the only blood relation of the once glamorous Cecily Barth.

'I've caught glimpses of the old lady arriving on Christmas and birthdays, in an ancient Cadillac with equally ancient chauffeur, to deliver presents to her grandniece and grandnephews. Lady Bountiful – but she *never* has helped when Marcia needed a new washer and dryer or the children's teeth needed straightening. And I've seen Cecily mentioned in the newspapers; she's a fanatic anti-vivisectionist, makes speeches for the SPCA and Humane Society drives, and once – before arthritis totally crippled her below the belt and confined her to a wheelchair – she even tried to lead a protest march against the Chicago stockyards because of what she considered cruelty in slaughtering methods. Quite a personality, Oscar. Would you care to read the letter she wrote to her niece, a week or more ago?'

'Yes, but not very much,' said Oscar Piper. Nevertheless he meekly accepted the note, neatly typed on Hotel Harlow Towers stationery, and read:

Darling,
    Rain rain rain here in New York, and I wish I was home in my own house in Coldwater Canyon where I belong. I hope Jack is still working at Douglas and bringing home his paycheque intact. And darling Loramae and Timmy and Ricky! I hope to be back home for Christmas, but if I am still tied up here I have just oodles of goodies I've collected in these wonderful toy stores like Schwartz's, all wrapped and ready.
    The script goes well, except that Gary Twill, the writer – who is right handy in the room next to my suite – is sometimes a bit

stubborn and wants documentation for things that happened instead of trusting my memory, which as you know is perfect. I usually get my way, however. He does the structure and first draft of the scenes and then we hash them over and finally I type up the finished version and correct the dialogue and so forth. We are now on the final scenes.

I confess I'll be glad when it's over. The weather has been so nasty that I don't have Felicio, the most obliging Puerto Rican bellboy, push my wheelchair out on any more shopping trips. I don't feel so safe in this big town, either. Somebody doesn't want this film released – I've had some threatening phone calls and so has Mr Abbas and Gary Twill.

And I tell you, dear, I can almost smell Death around this hotel – close to me and coming closer. When I tell my fortune with the cards, I get the Queen of Spades or some other dismal symbol almost every time – and you know what that means!

I rescued a lost forlorn black kitten in an alleyway and sneaked it into the hotel – you know black cats are lucky! I named him Asmodeus, and I intend to bring him back with me and present him to our darlings.

If I ever come back! Marcia, I have a terrible presentiment that Death hovers over this old hotel – I mean it! Just as soon as the TV script is finished and approved by Mr Abbas – a very strange man but you know producers, almost always the enemies of talent – and as soon as the picture is completely cast and costumes picked, I am getting out of here. Maybe I'll come back when they actually start shooting and maybe I won't. This Lilith Lawrence who is to play me looks the part all right – she is beautiful enough – but she underacts terribly. I hate to say it about anybody but I fear she's a Method actress!

Must close now – room service will be bringing up my dinner and I have to lock Asmodeus in the closet as the little black devil will dash out through any open door and then I have to chase him, in my wheelchair, yet – unless Felicio or Gary Twill is around to help.

Don't worry about what I said – at my age Death is only a heartbeat away anyhow. And I know how to protect myself. I have a very authentic-looking pistol that shoots ammonia, plus some other precautions, like a chain on the door.

Kiss the dear kiddies for me. Your affectionate
Auntie Cecily

The inspector handed back the letter and shrugged. 'Sounds like some kind of a nut,' he observed. 'And I thought black cats were supposed to be *un*lucky.'

'I am not interested in primitive superstitions, Oscar. During the Dark Ages in Europe – and even in England during the witchcraft hunts – hundreds of thousands of cats were tortured and killed because they were thought to be witches' familiars, and rats and mice overran the land. How any cats survived I'll never know, but I prefer dogs myself, particularly big Standard poodles like my dear old Talley, who is languishing in a boarding kennel at the moment.'

The inspector looked at his watch pointedly.

'Very well, Oscar we'll get down to cases. Perhaps Cecily is a bit of a psychic, or has some ESP precognition power. Coming events do cast their shadows before: Abraham Lincoln foresaw his own death in a dream, and the day before President Kennedy was assassinated a clairvoyant ran all over Washington trying to get to somebody and warn him not to go to Dallas.'

'Coincidence,' said Oscar Piper.

'Perhaps. But suppose somebody actually *doesn't* want Cecily's life story to come out – somebody who knew her 'way back when and has since, shall we say, reformed and hoped that the wild oats would stay buried?'

'Come off it! The old dame is strictly a has-been! Who cares about scandals that happened more than forty years ago? It's ancient history. And how would knocking off the writer – or Cecily either – prevent Mr Abbas from making the picture anyway?'

'I don't know – yet! But I have all the newspaper clippings here in my handbag. There is something rotten, and I don't mean in Denmark. I'm not just working on a hunch, or on my so-called feminine intuition either. Oscar, how deeply have you looked into this Gary Twill death?'

'Things have changed in the Police Department, Hildegarde. I'm strictly administrative now, and other men on precinct level do the legwork. I'm supposed to be an inspector.'

'Well, then – *inspect!*'

'Hildy, why are you getting the wind up and making all these waves?'

'I'll tell you exactly why. I only got into town this morning – I tried to phone you from the airport and got a fast brushoff from that uniformed ape in your outer office. He told me you were in conference!' She sniffed. 'You were not to be disturbed!'

'That's right, I was down having a look at the morning lineup.'

'I got another brushoff at the Hotel Harlow Towers, where Cecily Barth is incommunicado and Mr Abbas is too tied up to see anybody, and so on. But I had noticed that Gary Twill, the man you say committed suicide, was reported by hotel employees to have gone out on a brief errand shortly before he died. He returned with a paper bag which he took up to his room. Right?'

'According to these reports, right. But it all fits. He thought he needed some Dutch courage –'

'I do wish, Oscar, you would stop insulting the people of Holland. And why should Gary Twill go out in the rain? Why buy liquor himself when he could have called room service and had drinks sent up from the bar and charged to Mr Abbas? Or at least sent a bellboy out on his errand? It just doesn't fit! So having nothing better to do I provided myself with a newspaper photograph of Twill – who, I must say, was a distinctive-looking man well over six feet, with prematurely white hair, and I went out cruising the neighbourhood shops to see if I could discover the *real* purpose of his last errand.' She paused dramatically.

'And so what?'

'So *this*! He not only bought a bottle of champagne at a package store on Sixth Avenue, but he also stopped in at a travel agency on Fifth and purchased a first-class airplane ticket to Los Angeles on the 11 p.m. flight! Now, don't tell me that a man who intends to die the hard way would go out and spend almost $200 on a plane ticket that he didn't intend to use!'

The inspector frowned. 'Then something must have happened to push him over the edge –'

'Exactly! Something – or someone.

'I mean, to make him change his mind.' But Oscar Piper was not quite as sure as he had been a few moments before.

'These are deep waters, Oscar. And getting deeper. If we could only look back in Time, and see Yesterday . . .'

It was late morning on a rainy Wednesday. Or a rainy morning on a late Wednesday. Gary Twill wasn't quite sure and didn't care which. He opened his bloodshot eyes somewhat gingerly, to survey the ceiling of his hotel room, wishing fervently that he were far, far away from this dingy pad, far from the darling if slightly demented old bat of a Cecily – he sometimes thought of her as 'Nightmare Alice' – in the next suite, far from Boris Abbas in his office up in the penthouse furnished in silver and black upholstery, and most particularly far from Janey Roberts, Valkyrie-cum-vixen.

Far from Manhattan. The big city, to a native Californian, always seemed dirty, raw, and cold – when it wasn't dirty, hot, and humid. Twill had worked almost all night on the final sequence of *The*

Thousand and One Loves of Cecily Barth – a title he loathed, but maybe he could talk Abbas into changing it later. He had turned the final ten pages over to Cecily for her to read and approve and type up the final version with two carbons; it kept her feeling that she was a part of it all to bang it out on her portable electric typewriter, and she could do nice clean copy. She was to take it up to Abbas, or at least leave it with Janey for the great man to read later. Anyway, the damn thing was done, finis, complete.

What a wild assignment! What a wild collaboration, with this crazy old relic who fancied herself as a writer because she'd taken some correspondence course in screen-writing and had turned out a dozen or so dramas that never even got to first base with movie or TV story editors! But today not even a former Oscar winner could pick and choose his assignments; there was eighty per cent unemployment in the Writers Guild West.

The big man sat up in his tangled blankets and sighed, ruffling his almost white but still very curly locks. Then he fumbled for the phone and called down to room service for breakfast – not that his stomach was really awake yet.

After a while the ubiquitous Felicio rolled in a cart bearing a pot of coffee, orange juice, some cold toast and obviously colder eggs. Felicio also wore his hopeful Puerto Rican smile, beneath the nose which had been flattened during some earlier attempts to become the terror of the welterweights – but you had to give the guy credit for trying.

Sometimes he was very trying, like now. For he had another manuscript with him; Twill could see it sticking out of a pocket. The Great American short story again. 'Oh, God!' moaned the man in the bed. 'Not today!'

'But you have feenish the job. You will go back soon to Hollywood. You take my manuscript and show it to Mr Goldwyn like you promise?'

'Yes, yes. Just leave it on the bureau.'

Gary Twill might just as well have said 'wastebasket' – and the hypersensitive Felicio sensed it immediately. He withdrew into his Latin sheath, with injured dignity. 'I guess it was all just kidding, no?' There was a sentence or two in mumbled Spanish, too fast for Gary Twill to catch – except for one or two words, and those not customarily found in Spanish-English tourist dictionaries. The door closed behind Felicio, and none too gently.

Twill sighed and shrugged. These would-be authors! He really should not have jollied Felicio along – now he'd probably made another enemy in this God-forsaken place. Twill drank the orange juice and a few sips of the cold coffee, then went back to a troubled sleep, from which he was rudely awakened around 2 p.m. by the sound of a key in the door and the entrance of a somewhat oversize but very blonde and very curvaceous young woman whose secret Mona Lisa smile boded no particular good.

She had been here many times before, under happier circumstances. It was obvious that at this moment she was not on loving dalliance bent, to put it mildly. 'You could have knocked, Janey dear,' he said, as he drew a sheet over the bare and exposed portions of his muscular figure.

'I could have knocked with a hammer on your thick skull, buster,' said Jane. 'With joy and gusto. But as it happens I just dropped by to return your room key, and to be the first to bring you some good news. Good from my point of view at least. Not from yours.'

'Don't be unkind when I have a king-size hangover. What happened? Didn't Cecily approve the script? She's already okayed all but the last ten pages.'

'Oh, she typed up the last scene real neat, and she said she approved the whole thing. She'd do anything for you, Lover Boy, like most women. But when His Nibs read your hunk of tripe –'

'Rewrite required?' asked Gary Twill, moaning.

'Rewrite my sainted painted toenails! Mr Abbas read it and then he blew up and he said – and I quote – that it is the most misbegotten, unshootable, useless one hundred and eighty pages of junk that he has ever seen, even in a lifetime involved with writers who can't write, and that it turns out to be sophomoric fantasy instead of the objective semi-documentary biography he hired you to do, and that if he could he'd hold up your cheque and that he fervently wished someone would restrain him from coming down here and strangling you with his bare hands for wasting over four grand of his hard-earned money and then delivering a package of pure garbage!'

Jane was enjoying this, Gary Twill suddenly discovered. She was trying to get a bit of her own back, as our British cousins say. But he was now fairly wide-awake. 'Come now; what was so wrong with the damn script?'

'You ought to know! You fictionised the whole thing!'

'Suddenly I feel confused – I didn't think it was fiction. But dear sweet love, knock it off! So what if Abbas puts another writer on the final, shooting version of the script? Forgive and forget; come back to Hollywood with me and live it up a little! We fit together so good – you make me happy!'

'Slap-happy,' said Jane. 'Mister Twill, I wouldn't go to Hollywood with you if by any chance I wanted to go to Hollywood and you were the accredited, uniformed driver of a brand-new Greyhound bus! I don't mess around with a guy who's already had three wives!'

'Two, and both legally divorced. I only pay token alimony.' He sighed, the handsome if slightly raddled face looking hurt. 'You shouldn't insist on taking it so seriously. I should have told you in the beginning, I know. But please, baby – I got a headache. I worked all night. Everybody hates me. Cecily thinks I didn't do her amours full justice, now you say Abbas isn't satisfied with the script, and Felicio hates me because I don't flip over his short stories cribbed from O. Henry –'

'And don't forget Lilith Lawrence, buster!'

'Lilith? Hell, she got the part, didn't she? She's set to play Cecily, thanks to me.'

'And you soft-talked her into testing for the role on the Beautyrest, which got her into trouble with her agent who happens also to be her boyfriend, a guy even bigger than you are and considerably stronger if not meaner, by the name of Hymie Rose. Keep out of dark alleys, darling, while you're still in Manhattan.'

'You *do* give a damn, then, Janey, darling!' Gary Twill said hopefully.

'Not for you, for Hymie. He might just possibly get caught, though it would be justifiable homicide in my book, you – you rat-fink!' Jane went out, slamming the door behind her.

Twill winced and then slid out of bed, stark naked. He paused to take a medicinal gulp from the almost empty bottle of whisky on the bureau and then – when the warm glow had hit his insides to a satisfactory degree – set about showering, shaving, and putting on some clothes. He'd phone Abbas pretty soon and find out how much Janey, in her vicious, holier-than-thou mood, had exaggerated the foul-up with the script. Probably she had exaggerated quite a lot, because while it wasn't going to be nominated for an Emmy it was still a damn good piece of work, considering what there had been to work with. Cecily's life story almost outstripped *Fanny Hill* and *Forever Amber* combined.

When Gary Twill was half-dressed he stopped short, sniffing. There was a strange smell in the air. It wasn't Janey's too liberal sprinkling of 'My Sin,' or the breakfast eggs, or Cecily's damn cat that had its litter box in the otherwise unused connecting bathroom; it was something else – something Gary couldn't identify.

'New York just smells, I guess,' he said to himself. 'Too many people too close together.' Being an essentially factual and objective man, he did not once consider the odour to be the smell of death, nor did he – for all his sensitivity – hear the beating of dark, invisible wings overhead.

'Here goes,' he said aloud, and finished the bottle. Then he mentally girded his loins, put on his armour, and went down the hall and up the elevator to the penthouse. Abbas had both his offices and his living quarters here, plus a tiny and somewhat bedraggled patio and garden outside, forty stories above the street.

Miss Bixby, the built-in receptionist, was a dour old doll, a sort of birdlike old biddy from whom he had never even been able to win a smile. Not at least until this afternoon, when she told Gary Twill that the great man was much too busy to see him, and that his severance cheque would be mailed to his agent. Gary Twill ruefully chalked up another sworn enemy, but he headed for the inner door.

It was locked. 'He's got Miss Lawrence and her agent in there now,' proffered Miss Bixby. 'And I don't think waiting around will do you any good, frankly. Jane distinctly said that I was to tell you not to wait.'

But Gary Twill waited anyway, reading an old magazine from the coffee table without actually seeing it. After a while the inner door opened and Lilith Lawrence – the spitting image of Cecily Barth at 25, even to the dark sleek hair and the billowy hips – emerged, closely followed by her agent. Hymie was a robust, sharply dressed man with close-shaved but darkish-blue chin and cheeks, who looked straight through Gary Twill and headed for the exit. Lilith Lawrence (born Mae Klotz) hesitated for a moment, giving the writer her sweetest smile.

'So sorry, Gary darling,' she trilled. 'But that's the way the ball bounces, isn't it? I only –' Hymie Rose grasped her by the elbow and propelled her hastily out of the place.

'So now can I see Abbas?' Twill demanded of the woman at the desk.

She shrugged and picked up the phone. After a moment she put it down and said, 'Mr Abbas says to tell you that he's very busy and that your room rent is paid up only through today and that if you keep hanging around and bothering him I am to call Mr Durkin, who as you know is the house detective, and have you forcibly eee-jected!'

'I get the message,' said Gary Twill. 'Have a good time at the next Coven.' He departed, with whatever dignity was left to him. Which was not too much.

As he rode down in the elevator he decided to travel westward under the alias of George Spelvin or something; no use letting everybody in the trade who read *Daily Variety* and its 'NY to LA and LA to NY' column know that screen-writer Gary Twill had flopped in the big city and was returning ahead of time with his tail between his legs . . .

In Inspector Piper's office Miss Hildegarde Withers was holding forth. 'But don't you see, Oscar, this man Twill was out of his element here in New York. He was surrounded by people he didn't understand and who didn't understand him. This independent producer, Mr Abbas, is reputed throughout show business to be a man of violent temper. According to the newspaper accounts, in his earlier days he was a professional wrestler in Hungary and a protégé of Sandor Szabo, whoever that was –'

'Just one of the greatest mat men in history,' said Piper, brightening.

'You see? If he became enraged at his writer –?'

'Hildegarde, you're tilting at windstorms.'

'It's *windmills*, if you insist on quoting from books you've never read! Abbas is a possibility, anyway. He had the physical ability to throw anybody through a window or over a parapet. And then there is this Jane Roberts person, the blonde Amazon type. With whom Gary Twill was for a time intimate, to put it politely. A woman scorned, Oscar – you know how dangerous they are.'

'Dream on, dream on. In this day and age women don't kill for that, not good-looking ones anyway.'

The spinster schoolteacher was consulting her sheaf of newspaper clippings. 'Then what about Lilith Lawrence, the girl chosen to play the part of the young Cecily in the TV film? Here's a night-club photo of her and Gary Twill, holding hands at some place called El Morocco and looking very fatuously at one another. A girl as physically equipped as Lilith must have plenty of boyfriends, some of whom might have resented a Hollywood writer getting into the act, as the phrase goes. An obvious jealousy motive. And there is also the unpleasant Mr Durkin, the house detective, who was very nasty to me this morning when I tried to see Cecily. According to the newspaper stories he had had several altercations with Twill over noise and high jinks in the hotel room. He's a suspect to be reckoned with.'

'He's also an ex-cop,' Piper said. 'I remember vaguely that there was some beef connected with his leaving the Force. That I will look into, if you insist. But don't let me stop you – go on with your brainwashing.'

'I think you mean brainstorming, but no matter. You're a real Mr Malaprop, Oscar. There is also this bellboy named Felicio

Bonaventura, who keeps cropping up in the affair and who seems to have told each reporter a different story. Anyway, not one of these people has an airtight alibi for the time of the murder – if it was, as I believe, an actual murder.'

'But do they *need* alibis? And while you're making up your list, better put down dear old Cecily Barth too. I don't see any motive for her – but you never know. And the wheelchair can be only a prop, and she can really walk as good as anybody else –'

'As *well*, Oscar! And I think you have been watching too many old movies on the Late Late Show. Even if it weren't for her crippling arthritis, even if she could get out of the wheelchair and walk, how on earth could she – a frail woman weighing less than a hundred pounds –throw a big man out of a window?'

'It's your frammis,' said Oscar Piper. 'Personally, I think it was the butler. Only I guess there really isn't any butler in our cast of characters, is there?'

'You're not being very funny. And you haven't explained the bottle of champagne or the airline ticket. I think the ticket alone proves that my worst suspicions are justified.'

'Do you ever have any *best* suspicions?' He grinned, and chose a fresh cigar. 'Hildegarde, I'm very fond of you, but sometimes you're nuttier than a fruit cake.'

'In case you don't know it, there are some new recipes for fruit cake. Remember, Oscar, that Cecily Barth did step on a lot of toes in her heyday, and no doubt she made a lot of enemies. In her time as a movie queen she was, according to legend, no better she should be, leading men on and then throwing them aside –'

'Like a wornout glove?'

'– and wrecking many a marriage and many a career. Her life story, if presented on television, might just possibly ruin certain people who have since grown mature and respectable. Suppose for a moment that she, and not Gary Twill at all, was the intended victim? Remember Cecily's letter to her niece? Suppose Gary Twill had been trying to protect her, and somehow got too close to the truth?'

'My supposer isn't quite that active nowadays, Hildegarde. But let's look at this thing seriously for a moment. It just *has* to be suicide. Twill was a big powerful, athletic-type man and nobody could have thrown or pushed him out of a hotel window, not without a hell of a lot of commotion anyway.'

'Unless he was knocked unconscious first, perhaps?'

'You're *reaching*, Hildegarde. No, I have a hunch he took the easy way out.'

'Suicide is "easy"?' she snapped. 'That could only be suggested by someone who has never experienced it. Oh, you know what I mean! And my dear Oscar, time was when if I came into your office with a bee in my bonnet, you'd have come instantly alive, grabbed your hat and a handful of those dreadful stogies, and we'd have taken off on the chase.'

'Time *was*,' admitted the Inspector soberly. 'I'm strictly desk level now; I don't actually go out on cases and try to do the work of the precinct men. And remember, neither of us is as young as we used to be.'

'Speak for yourself, Oscar!' And Miss Withers gathered herself and her belongings together and made an abrupt exit, slamming the door so hard that, out in the anteroom, the sergeant swallowed his gum.

Thirty seconds later the sergeant had another shock, as he saw the skipper erupt from the inner office, hat and topcoat and cigars in hand. 'Closed for the day,' Inspector Oscar Piper barked in passing. 'Hold the fort. I got to take off and try to keep my best friend from becoming her own worst enemy.' He hurried out into the main hallway – where he found Miss Hildegarde Withers leaning against the bulletin board with a patient yet cryptic smile on her somewhat equine visage.

'So here we go again,' she said. 'Better late than never.'

A little later the two oddly assorted sleuths climbed out of a taxi at the Hotel Harlow Towers, that once plush and now slightly run-down hostelry on Central Park South. They stood on the sidewalk, a chill autumnal wind whipping about their ankles, at presumably the same spot where Gary Twill had come plummeting down out of nowhere to splash his brains out on the cement. Just before 6 p.m. would have been a very busy hour at this location, as they both knew.

'It was only by the grace of God that the fool didn't take some innocent passerby with him on his trip to the Hereafter,' observed Oscar Piper. 'As it was – according to the reports – three people were knocked down, and one woman had to be hospitalised.'

'Another argument against suicide,' pointed out the retired schoolteacher. 'Unless Gary Twill had no compassion.'

Unfortunately there had been no actual eyewitnesses. If Twill had stood for a few moments in the window, or had hesitated on the narrow ledge outside while he screwed up his courage, nobody had seen him. It had all happened during one of Manhattan's sudden, blustering rainstorms. With no buildings across the street, nothing there except the reaches of a practically deserted Central Park, no one had been in position to catch an accidental glimpse of the beginning of the high dive – if indeed it had been a voluntary dive. Naturally, all the people in the street below were either shielded by umbrellas or by folded newspapers held over their heads; no eyes had been turned up against the slashing, icy rain.

'The first cruise car got here just two minutes after six,' Oscar Piper was patiently explaining. 'The officers took statements from several persons, including one newsboy –'

'Who very probably might be that little man in the kiosk over there,' Miss Withers interrupted impatiently. 'I wonder!'

For once she wondered correctly. Mr Herman Gittel, age 56, professional newsvendor, proved reasonably amenable to conversation after Miss Withers had purchased one copy of each of his evening newspapers, noting with sadness that the *Herald Tribune* was gone.

'Sure, I seen it,' said Mr Gittel. 'And I heard him yelling all the way down. He sounded real weird, like he was nuts or something. Stuff musta blown out of his pockets, because the air was like a snow-storm with bits of paper.'

'I really wish I knew exactly what bits of paper,' remarked the schoolteacher wistfully. 'But I suppose the street cleaners have done their work.' She surveyed the gutter, poking into a storm drain with her umbrella.

'I kept me one sheet as sort of a souvenir,' offered Mr Gittel. And from his well-worn leather jacket he produced a wrinkled, rain-stained piece of manuscript paper – which proved to be Page 172 of what seemed to be a teleplay script. Miss Withers and the Inspector read:

SCENE 88 – EXT COLDWATER CANYON HOUSE – MED CLOSE SHOT – DAY Cecily and Norman, she in daring and revealing swimsuit, he in smart yachting costume of the time. They are seated on a stone bench with profusion of flowers in B.G. He is concealing displeasure. Cecily is, however, mistress of the situation.

CECILY (moving closer)

Don't be difficult, Normie-pie. Isn't it enough to be my lover – do you have to be my leading man too? It really isn't your type of role anyway, Mr Lasky says. And when The Hunchback of Notre Dame is released, you can write your own ticket at Essanay or anywhere.
NORMAN

It isn't just that, beautiful. You're a lovely cheat. We were supposed to have a date to go down to Ensenada and gamble a little over the weekend – you broke it because you had to stay home and read the script of Passion's Pawn or something, and then you were seen dancing at the Miramar with somebody whose name I intentionally don't remember.

CECILY

Don't be difficult, darling. You have your career and I have mine. Let's leave it that way.

The rest was indecipherable. Which, Miss Withers thought, might be all for the best. 'Oscar,' she said on impulse, 'will you buy this for me?'

Somewhat reluctantly, the Inspector invested two dollars for the tattered souvenir.

'So the guy took his rejected manuscript with him,' he said. 'You getting morbid or something, collecting mementoes yet?'

'One never knows,' the schoolteacher pronounced mysteriously.

'Anyway,' Oscar Piper pointed out impatiently, 'whatever personal stuff blew out of his pockets on the way down, his billfold was there and he was immediately identified.'

'Did the airline ticket show up?'

'Not according to the report. Somebody probably found it and cashed it in. But he had a California driver's licence, membership cards in the Writers Guild West, Greater Los Angeles Press Club, Ace Hudkins Health Club and Gym, Civil Liberties Union, the NAACP and CORE, and the usual jumble of credit cards. There was also over $300 in currency, and his room key tagged Hotel Harlow Towers 2466. Our men went right in and upstairs and reported that 2466, a single, was something of a shambles. Bed unmade, a litter of coffee cups and empty liquor bottles, and manuscript pages scattered all over the floor. The room was sealed off, but if, you insist on taking a gander at it – '

Miss Withers had been vainly trying to count up to the windows of the 24th floor, but had only managed to get a crick in her neck. 'If you count the lobby and presumably the mezzanine, and skip the thirteenth floor which no hotel ever has, then –' She sighed, and gave it up.

'It was the twenty-fourth all right,' put in the cooperative Mr Gittel. 'I seen the open windows.'

'*Saw*,' corrected the schoolteacher absently. 'But are you sure?'

'The hotel is forty stories, and I counted down to where I saw the open windows –'

'Windows? *Plural?*'

'Well, the one on the left was wide open, curtains flying, and the second over to the right was just a little open. Before the cops got here it was closed.'

'Very interesting,' said the schoolteacher.

Inspector Oscar Piper found it less so. 'Well,' he grumbled, 'there doesn't seem to be any question about the guy going out the window of his own room. I suppose you're hell-bent to go up to the pad and have a look for clues; but Hildegarde, I warn you, those were trained investigators who handled this case, working on modern scientific lines.'

'And using computers, no doubt!' she said scornfully.

'Computers don't guess, like you do! Well, do we go upstairs?'

Miss Withers was deep in thought. 'I suppose so. But I am more interested in *people* than in the scene of the crime. I want to see Cecily Barth and make sure that the poor crippled old woman isn't the victim of another 'accidental' suicide or something, and I want to meet the various people who had reasons, large or small, for disliking Gary Twill.'

'Okay,' said the inspector resignedly. 'Let's go.'

They entered the ornate but somewhat musty lobby of the old hotel, almost but not quite a relic of the Gaslight Era, and immediately learned from a supercilious desk clerk that Miss Barth wasn't seeing anybody or taking any phone calls, and furthermore –'

'Who's your house dick?' demanded Oscar Piper.

'Why – our security officer is Mr Durkin, but –'

'Get him here, fast.' For once the schoolteacher had to admit the usefulness of a shiny gold badge (denoting over thirty years with the Department) which the inspector flashed briefly. Because wheels turned, and Mr Durkin (who had given her a sort of bum's rush earlier in the day) made an instant appearance from the restaurant-bar, where he must have been enjoying a very late lunch or a very early dinner for he was sucking his teeth and chewing chlorophyll mints.

'Was there something, Inspector?'

'There was and is.'

The stubby, choleric house detective lost no time getting into the record that he was very shocked that a thing like this should have occurred at a quiet, respectable hotel like the Harlow Towers but what can you do? A suicide is a suicide, and the least said about it, the better. And after all, this Twill twerp wasn't the sort of guest who would have been made welcome at the hotel, only he was working for Mr Abbas, a long-time resident of the penthouse and anything Mr Abbas asks for –

'Okay. Abbas took a room here for his imported Hollywood writer, and a suite next door for Cecily Barth – is that right?' The Inspector was getting more than a little impatient, perhaps because he had had a light lunch and was thinking of dinner. 'Anybody else?'

'Just Miss Lawrence, the star. She's in 2634. There's a reservation for the director when they pick one, and for the casting director and costumer. Mr Abbas likes to have all his staff right on hand. Only his secretary, Jane Roberts, lives home – I think in Brooklyn Heights. And Miss Bixby, the receptionist, who doesn't really count. I'll be glad to take you upstairs – '

'You better be,' said the Inspector. 'You know, Mr Durkin, I seem to remember something. You were a sergeant, working out in Queens or Staten Island or somewhere. There was a mishmash, and you were allowed to resign rather than stand charges. So you went out to California and didn't make out and then you came back to Manhattan and got this job.'

They were going up in a rocky old elevator. 'Can you cool it, Inspector?' Durkin was sweating. 'I need this job, and what's past is past. You know how it is, Inspector.'

'Maybe,' said Oscar Piper. 'We'll see how it plays. Where's the room the guy jumped out the window of?'

Durkin led the way down a long hall and then to the right, past a door which he pointed out as Miss Barth's. Then they came to Gary Twill's door. 'It's been sealed,' said the house detective.

'Then I'll just unseal it,' said Oscar Piper.

They went into the room, Miss Withers entering with some trepidation for the place was – from her point of view – in a mess. The bed looked as if some insomniac hippopotamus had been in it, the desk and surrounding territory were littered with pages of crumpled manuscript, the bureau bore an empty whisky bottle, and clothes were strewn everywhere.

'Yet he seems to have died,' the schoolteacher pointed out, 'rather nattily dressed in tweed jacket and slacks, including a necktie. Suicides usually don't care how they look. I think I have 'cased the joint,' as you would say. Let us go.'

'Okay, okay,' said the weary inspector as he resealed the door. 'So now you're satisfied?'

'Not at all! There were no signs of a fight or struggle, no broken furniture or other indications of combat. Yet still –'

'So it was suicide!'

'With the airline ticket?' The schoolteacher shook her head. Then she turned suddenly on the house detective. 'Mr Durkin, just why did you intimate that Gary Twill wasn't the type of guest welcomed at the sacrosanct Harlow Towers?'

Durkin said uneasily, 'Well, he was a sort of Bohemian type – loud stereo music at all hours, hipped on the liberal bit and fraternising with the help and giving 'em ideas. He had Felicio all steamed up about becoming a writer. And he had all sorts of people visiting his room. We can't have that sort of thing.'

'Dear me, no! We must live in the last century, mustn't we?' Her glance was scathing.

'Okay, okay!' put in the inspector. 'Let's go see the movie queen.'

'Miss Barth isn't going to let us in,' predicted Durkin. 'Since this happened she's been locked in tight, and she won't hardly even let the maids in to do her rooms.'

'No room service? How does she eat?' asked Piper sensibly.

'Didn't you know? Miss Barth is a vegetarian, and lives mostly on wheat germ and crackers and stuff like that, all out of cans and boxes.' They were now standing outside the door of the suite, and Durkin knocked. He knocked again, and then called out in a wheedling tone. 'It's just Durkin, Miss Barth. Can we see you for a minute?'

There was not the slightest sound from within. Inspector Oscar Piper who was not the most patient man in the world, saw a bell and leaned on it. 'Open up, lady – this is the police!'

'Go away!' came a querulous voice from within. 'You're not fooling me with that old one!'

Oscar Piper sighed, and nodded at the house dick – who reluctantly produced his master key. It worked, at first. The door swung open and then held, caught by a heavy chain.

Miss Withers felt that this had been mismanaged enough, and spoke up. 'Cecily, will you please listen?' she said in her best classroom voice of authority. 'Mr Durkin and Inspector Piper of the New York Police Department are with me, but I started the whole thing. You may not know me but my name is Hildegarde Withers and I happen to live next door to Marcia, out in Santa Monica, and she showed me your letter –'

'Prove it!' The voice was still hostile.

'Well, Marcia is on a new diet and has lost three pounds. John is working the swing shift at Douglas. Loramae had summer flu but got over it and she and her brothers are now trampling my flowerbeds again. Is that enough?'

'All right, I guess,' came the disembodied voice. The door closed, a chain rattled free, and then they were permitted inside – all but Mr Durkin, who found his way blocked by the inspector's right arm.

'Look, I got my job to do,' complained Durkin. 'I got to tell her we got rules about not installing chains and keeping pets and –'

'Blow,' said Oscar Piper, with the disdain of an honest cop for one who had cheated. Mr Durkin blew.

And Miss Withers and the inspector were entering a big, dimly lighted drawing room that smelled of perfume and cat and cigarette smoke. The schoolteacher had eyes only for the woman in the lightweight wheelchair who faced them, sitting on it grandly as if it were some sort of throne. She wore a flowered housecoat as if it were ermine and velvet, and her chin was high and defiant.

What was left of Cecily Barth, presumably in her seventies, was mostly spirit and spunk, though there were traces of ruined beauty under the heavy makeup and in her deep dark eyes. And her hair was still as raven-black and as sleekly arranged as it had been back in the halcyon days when this woman had rivalled Theda Bara and Nita Naldi and Clara Kimball Young . . .

'It was so good of you to come,' Cecily was saying, holding out her hand. 'You must forgive my seeming rudeness at the door. But my nerves are in a dither. However, any friend of dear Marcia's –'

Her words were for Miss Withers, but her attention was turned to Oscar Piper; he was a man. For a few seconds she was a faint echo of the Screen Vamp, the Sex Goddess of the Silver Screen, unquote. Quite evidently she expected the inspector to kiss her hand, but he only held it for a second and then sheepishly dropped it.

Meanwhile Miss Withers was gathering impressions, as was her habit. This elderly, crippled old woman was in fear of her life; the schoolteacher could almost feel the fear, could almost smell it above Cecily's perfume.

'You must excuse the way the place looks,' Cecily was saying, waving her hand vaguely. Indeed, the room was a jumble of untidiness. The tables, chairs, and even the mantelpiece suggested Christmas Eve in the family of a dozen or more small children: everything was piled high with toys, plus rolls of fancy wrappings, balls of varicoloured string, and boxes of bright Santa Claus stickers. There was a stack of packages, wrapped and ready for mailing, in one corner.

'Christmas – in September?' said the Inspector, unbelieving.

'I'm afraid I went simply mad in your New York toy stores,' admitted Cecily as she made ineffectual efforts to find them a place to sit. 'I had such fun shopping before – before I got too scared to go out any more, even with dear Felicio pushing my wheelchair. But now, I really don't trust anybody!'

The inspector was seated uneasily on the edge of a sofa and had taken out a fresh cigar, while Miss Withers prowled the room, the packages, the typewriter table. There were many scrapbooks, many old newsclips and photos of an earlier era. But what she was interested in was *now*.

'About this suicide next door –' the inspector began.

'If indeed it *was* suicide,' said Cecily Barth meaningfully.

'You didn't hear any sounds of a struggle, any raised voices?'

'No,' admitted Cecily. 'But there is an unused bathroom between, where I keep my cat's litter box. Mr Twill and I were working very closely together on the script, and we never locked the connecting doors. That would have made a fine scandal once upon a time, wouldn't it? But I'm afraid I wasn't here to notice anything yesterday afternoon; my cat had got out and down the hall and I was looking for him, as I often have to do when I can't get anybody to do it for me.'

'Let's get down to cases,' the inspector went on firmly. 'When did you last see Gary Twill?'

'Well, he brought in the last sequence of the script early in the morning, around eight o'clock. He'd worked on it all night, poor dear boy. Like most writers, he hated to make carbons and he always made a lot of typographic errors, so I had to type the final version of everything.'

Cecily nodded toward the corner of the room, where there they saw a bridge table, a portable electric typewriter similar to the one used by Gary Twill, and several piles of white and yellow paper.

'It wasn't actually as intimate and deep a collaboration as I had hoped it would be, but I'm still going to try for co-screenplay credit. The lovely TV residuals, you know! That's the payment to writers for re-runs, and it can go on for years.' She beamed at them. 'A sensational life story like mine will be released and re-released over and over again.'

'You were satisfied with the script, then?' asked Miss Withers.

'More than satisfied! Gary had caught the spirit of the really great days of Hollywood. Such a dear brilliant man! I can't believe he took his own life.'

'Who could have done it, then?' demanded Oscar Piper.

'Really, my dear man!' Cecily made a dramatic gesture. 'How on earth should I know? I'm a stranger in town.'

' "I a stranger and afraid, in a world I never made," ' said Miss Withers softly. Cecily was obviously winding the inspector around her little finger, with a practised charm that dated back two generations. The schoolteacher was less easily impressed. 'You're quite sure you heard nothing in the next room yesterday afternoon, and that you were out chasing your kitten at the time Gary Twill died?'

'Quite sure.'

'And you received Twill's version of the last sequence of the script about eight yesterday morning, and retyped it with carbons and then took it up to Mr Abbas say around ten or ten thirty?'

'Exactly. Only I gave it to Jane, his confidential secretary. I can manage these automatic elevators very well, if I take my time. I told Jane that I was delighted with the script and that I would sign formal approval anytime – I have that right in my contract.'

'And did you hear anything from Mr Abbas yesterday?' the school-teacher pressed.

'Nothing directly. I phoned Jane Roberts sometime after lunch to learn what the great man's verdict was, and she said he was still studying the script but that storm warnings were out. That didn't worry me; he's the sort of producer who never likes anything on paper in the first reading.'

She broke off when there was a sudden interruption from the bedroom. What erupted was at first sight a rather furious battle between two small black kittens. The fracas moved into the drawing room – and then it turned out to be a mimic battle between one black kitten and one very naturalistic toy kitten, with the former naturally getting the upper hand – or upper paw. Then just as suddenly it was all over; the live kitten turned its back on the stuffed kitten-on-a-string, stalked over to Cecily, and leaped lightly into her lap.

'Asmodeus baby!' said Cecily Barth. She turned to her visitors. 'I almost named him Lucifer – only then his nickname would have been "Loose," and I couldn't have that, could I?'

'We'll wait and see the film,' said Miss Withers ironically, conscious that they weren't getting anywhere. 'Miss Barth, I moved heaven and earth to get the inspector to come up here with me and look into this affair, and all because of Marcia. But I don't think you're being altogether frank with us. We happen to know that you saw Gary Twill die. So you weren't chasing your kitten – you were looking out of your open window. A newsvendor in the street below looked up and saw two open windows – and then yours was swiftly closed. Right?'

If the sally was supposed to put Cecily into one of her dithers, it failed completely. 'I wasn't going to admit that,' the aged screen star said. 'I just wanted to keep out of it. Yes, I had recovered Asmodeus, and I was sitting here and I heard the commotion. I did rush to the window and it was raining so hard I had to raise it to see anything –and I wish I hadn't.'

She faced them defiantly, like an angry child caught with a hand in the cookie jar. But Miss Withers was thinking. This ridiculous old woman knew something which she was not prepared to disclose. It might be important, it might be minor. But it was something.

'What I am really interested in,' said the schoolteacher, 'is the bottle of champagne. The one Gary Twill went out to buy shortly before his death. But he didn't drink it as a sort of stirrup cup into Eternity, because the empty bottle wasn't found among the other empties. Can you help us there, Miss Barth?'

Cecily hesitated for a very long second, and then she smiled. 'I thought that some things could be kept private,' she said, as she put the black kitten gently down out of her lap. 'All right, since you press me, I'll tell you.'

She wheeled herself over to the hall closet and almost immediately reappeared with an unopened, gold-topped bottle of champagne in her hand. It was, Miss Withers noticed, of 1938 vintage – whether a good year or a bad year she didn't know. But that did not matter.

'A going-away present,' Cecily explained. 'Just like Gary.'

'But no note with it?' pressed Miss Withers. 'I know writers.'

Cecily hesitated. 'I don't know just when Gary left the bottle. It was in the connecting bathroom, just inside the door on my side. And since you make such a point of it – yes, there *was* a note.'

Wheeling herself with a certain calculated dexterity, Cecily went over to the typewriter table and came back with a sheet of manuscript paper, which the inspector and Miss Withers read as one.

'Cecily dear, the hell with everything. I am taking it on the lam (as we used to say in the old Cagney pictures) and getting outa here. Don't say it hasn't been fun, because it hasn't. Drink this in good health, and think of me as not one who is dead but just gone far away. (Quote from Elizabeth Barrett Browning, I think). Anyway, I have had it. Your affectionate collaborator, Gary.'

It was the inspector who spoke first. 'Well, Hildegarde? You said you would be happier with an eyewitness or a suicide note. You now have the latter. Okay? Let's go somewhere and have dinner.'

'Let's not,' said Miss Withers, who was in a state of confusion but who had a little red light flashing on and off in the back of her brain. She faced Cecily. 'You have, you know, been withholding evidence and in essence you have been resisting police officers in the performance of their duty and otherwise impeding justice. I am quite sure that Inspector Piper can find some grounds for having you held as a material witness in Women's Jail for a few days –'

'It might be a most interesting experience,' said Cecily Barth. 'But if he did something foolish like that to me – while Jane Roberts, who is the one person who actually might have had real animosity to Gary, goes free – well, inspectors have become sergeants overnight. Or even sent to a beat over in Canarsie?'

The dear old lady had claws, it appeared. Longer than those of Asmodeus (named after a minor demon), who now was purring contentedly in a chair. A live prop for an ageless actress who was determined always to be on stage ... Cats, Miss Withers had observed, always had means of taking care of themselves.

'I think –' began Miss Withers. And then the telephone rang.

'I'm not supposed to have any phone calls,' Cecily pouted. But she wheeled herself over to the instrument. 'Yes?' Her voice changed into a dulcet tone. 'Yes, Mr Abbas?'

The voice at the other end was loud and emphatic; it could be heard across the room. 'Cecily, mine darlink, ve got problem. Somebody making stink about that fool Twill. Some old dame who minds other people's business. So ve haf a conference here in de office at eight dis evening, right? All of us! So ve agree on our storie. Hokay?'

'I think I can arrange to be there,' said Cecily. She hung up and turned back to her guests. 'You perhaps heard,' she said. 'Mr Abbas is disturbed at this reopening of the case. So he is calling a conference –'

'We know,' said Miss Withers. 'Things get more complicated all the time. And my best advice to you is –'

Just then the doorbell rang. Cecily wheeled herself over, put on the chain, then opened. Both Miss Withers and the inspector caught a glimpse of a frightened girlish face through the crack.

'It's me – Lilith!' came the voice. 'Miss Barth, I have to tell you something, but the switchboard girl won't ring you.'

'Those were my personal instructions, dear. I – I'm not feeling well and I'm not seeing anybody or talking to –'

'But you don't understand!' the voice from the hall persisted. 'We're all in trouble and the picture is in trouble. This whole thing is going to hell in a handbasket. Somebody is trying to reopen the mess and make out like Gary didn't kill himself! There's some old biddy rampaging around – she has some sort of *in* with the fuzz – and she's here only to try to make trouble. And any more bad publicity might frighten away Mr Abbas' backers. So if anybody asks you, don't tell them about Gary and me – it was only a night or two anyway and all in the course of show business. Really, it doesn't count!'

'Yes, dearie,' said Cecily calmly. 'My lips are sealed.'

'And another thing,' said the voice through the crack in the door. 'His Nibs wants us all up in the penthouse at eight tonight, for a sort of council of war. It's an ultimatum. We have to get our stories all straight or this picture isn't ever going to get made!'

'Roger – out and over,' said Cecily. She closed the door and turned back to her uninvited guests. 'You see what I mean?' she demanded a bit plaintively. 'I just don't know how to cope with it all.'

'You don't have to cope with it all by yourself, not now,' said the schoolteacher. 'But these are deep waters, and I feel there is more here than meets the eye, unquote.' She gave the inspector a signal, and they made their departure – with Asmodeus the black kitten making a determined but vain effort to go out with them.

'Well, Hildegarde?' said Oscar Piper as they approached the elevator. 'Did you see anything I didn't see? I figure that was a genuine twenty-four carat suicide note, and –'

'And a genuine, twenty-four carat plane ticket, don't forget. Oscar, I'm afraid I can't take you up on that dinner invitation, I have other things to do. But I suggest that we both crash Mr Abbas' party at eight.'

'Well – if you say so. In for a nickel, in for a dime. Fine old dramatic tradition – to have all the suspects gathered together in one place, while the great Hawkshaw unravels the mystery. Only, in this case, I don't see any possible motive for murder.'

'So then it might be an *impossible* motive,' Hildegarde retorted. 'I am not trying to be cryptic, Oscar. But a little red light is flashing on and off in the back of my head, a warning that perhaps I have missed something. And besides, I have an errand to do – some shopping, as it were.'

'Not another hat – when I was just getting used to this one!'

'No, not a hat. Something more in the line of a toy, but a rather unusual toy.' She nodded. 'And now, if you will be kind enough to hail me a taxi, I'll be off. We'll meet here again in the lobby at eight o'clock, right?'

'Right or wrong, we'll meet,' said the inspector wearily.

The penthouse apartment-cum-office where the self-admittedly great Mr Abbas lived and had his being was originally a magnificent (if now a somewhat rundown) centre of operations. The drawing-room office, in which he was now having a supposedly secret conference with his employees, protégés, and disciples, was large enough for a tennis court or at least a badminton court; it had been furnished in

1932 Moderne – plenty of glass and everything in black and silver, with sharp angles.

The paintings were early imitations of Picasso, the books were sumptuously leather-bound copies of Mr Abbas' scripts, the lighting was soft and slightly off-green. Miss Bixby loved it; Jane Roberts wished she had kept her date to go bowling; Lilith Lawrence thought belatedly that she should have taken up some other line of work. Hymie Rose sat beside his client and was chewing on an enormous but unlighted cigar. 'He should get me out of here and find me some nightclub bookings,' Lilith was thinking.

But a TV picture was a TV picture, with audiences in the millions. One mustn't forget that. And it meant so much to dear old Cecily . . .

Abbas was speaking, as from the mountaintop. He was directing his diatribe at them all, but looking at Cecily in her wheelchair.

'Ve got troubles,' said Mr Abbas. 'Troubles vith script and troubles vith publicity. Everybody here, including me myself, has goofed. But ve don't got to go on goofing. Don't any of you talk to no more reporters, understand? So vat is it if a fool bellboy suggests that maybe I trun – I trew – Gary Twill over the parapet? The script vas bad, but not dat bad. He musta kill himself, de no-goodnik.'

Just then there was a shrill alarm from the doorbell, which Miss Bixby hastily arose to answer. And in came Felicio, smiling apologetically. 'Sorry. Mr Abbas – but he have badge and what am I to do?'

So Inspector Oscar Piper, followed closely by Miss Hildegarde Withers, joined the party, though very much uninvited. 'As you were!' commanded the inspector. 'At ease! This isn't a pinch, yet.' Again he flashed the persuasive gold badge.

But the situation was obviously strained, and Miss Withers was, so to speak, up in arms. 'We are gathered together,' she began, 'all of those who knew Gary Twill here in Manhattan, to try to find out how and why he died –'

'Everybody but Mr Durkin,' put in Cecily Barth softly. 'A very nasty man.'

'Thank you,' said the schoolteacher. 'Which gives me an idea.' She winked to the inspector, who frowned and then caught on. He stepped catlike to the door and threw it open, disclosing the house detective crouching outside.

'Come in and join the party,' said Miss Withers. 'I had a hunch you wouldn't want to miss this.'

'I was only keeping tabs –' began Durkin defensively. Then he came sheepishly in.

'I shall continue,' the schoolteacher said firmly. 'But this is not a simple matter.'

'Understatement of de year,' put in Boris Abbas. 'I resent —'

'Go ahead and resent,' said Oscar Piper. 'But shut up when the lady is talking.'

'We have the case,' continued Miss Withers as if in a classroom, 'of an athletic, two hundred-pound man, in full possession of his faculties, who went to his death out of a hotel window. I discount the theory advanced by Felicio in one press interview that Gary Twill was hurled over the parapet by Mr Abbas —'

'I do not really mean it — I am a writer of fiction!' cut in the bellboy hastily. 'I let the imaginations run wild.'

'Because that would have required premeditation and an accomplice down on the twenty-fourth floor to open Twill's window. So I eliminated Mr Abbas.'

The producer bowed.

'But may I see the script which you found so disappointing?' she went on. Abbas nodded to Jane, who got it from the files. As she continued, Miss Withers riffled through the neatly typed pages. 'I also had to eliminate Mr Hymie Rose, who though he possibly had motive, could hardly have thrown Gary Twill out of the window without creating a battlefield in the room.'

'But if poor dear Gary had been sandbagged and was therefore unconscious?' suggested Cecily helpfully.

'He wasn't unconscious — he screamed all the way down. And pages of a manuscript went flying with him. I have one page of that manuscript which was rescued from the gutter and is still legible, and I note that it doesn't match the corresponding page just handed to me. On page 172, in the version Gary Twill took with him to his death, Cecily is playing a love scene in a garden with another Hollywood star of the time, one Norman Kerry —'

'Dat vas in the original outline!' cut in Abbas.

'And in the final version just given to me the scene is played with the Prince of Wales, no less! And later Cecily romances with Jack Dempsey and Charles Lindbergh and heaven knows who else!'

'Vich is vat makes me so infurious!' yelled Abbas. 'How to get releases from such big names?'

'Let me explain,' Cecily cooed. 'I simply took a few liberties as I typed the final version and livened it up a bit. Who remembers dear Norman today? Now Edward, later King of England —'

'His intimates, I understand, always have called him by his real name, which is David,' said the schoolteacher pedantically.

'I met him once at a party,' Cecily said defensively. She looked like a child who had just been told there is no Santa Claus.

'To continue,' said Miss Withers. 'I once liked Mr Durkin for the killer. He had left the police force under a cloud, and lived for a while in Los Angeles until the heat was off and he could come back and get this sinecure of a job as hotel security officer. If Twill had known him out west and learned of the old scandal, and if Mr Durkin had been afraid that Twill would talk and cost him this job –'

'You're dreaming, Hildegarde,' said the inspector.

'I know. I was clutching at straws. But again we face the problem of why the window was open on a stormy, rainy day, and why there were no signs of a struggle. I had to come to the conclusion that this was not a strongarm job, to use the vernacular. Even though Jane Roberts here has obviously strong arms –'

'*And* the only real motive!' Cecily put in gleefully. 'You should have heard them quarrelling!'

'You bitch!' said sweet Jane, with feeling.

'I must confess that at one time I even considered Miss Barth herself as a suspect,' continued Miss Withers.

'I wouldn't want to be ignored!' the old lady said happily. 'This is the most exciting thing that's happened to me in years!' She was obviously enjoying every moment of it.

'But it's only in old B-movies that a supposed cripple suddenly arises from a wheelchair and performs deeds of mayhem and murder.'

'I really am crippled,' Cecily said sadly. 'Look at my legs, once the most famous in Hollywood!' She lifted her skirt and displayed pitifully atrophied legs, like pipestems. 'So if strong men couldn't have pushed poor dear Gary out of a window, how could poor little me?'

'Exactly. How could you?'

'So that seems to leave only me,' spoke up the fair Lilith with some spirit. 'But how on earth –'

'You could possibly have called his attention to something down in the street, and then –'

'But *why?* He played fair with me, I got the job. And since we are getting down to cases, I didn't just romance him for the job, I really went for him!' And Lilith gave Hymie Rose a defiant stare.

There was a silence. Then the inspector coughed and murmured, 'Well, Hildegarde? Having eliminated everybody, we come back to suicide.'

'Not quite, Oscar. Not with that plane ticket.' She turned back to Cecily Barth. 'Cecily, you took liberties with Twill's script. Didn't you know he'd scream with rage and insist that Mr Abbas read the correct version – if he was still around? And that your machinations would all go for nothing?'

Cecily was suddenly quiet.

'It may seem to some of you that this is an insufficient motive for taking a man's life. But the human ego is a strange thing – especially the Hollywood ego. Cecily, you convinced yourself that with Gary Twill out of the way you could talk Mr Abbas here into using the more sensational version of your life story. True or false?'

The people in the big room were hardly breathing; you could have heard a soap bubble explode.

'Utter nonsense,' said Cecily finally, in a small voice. 'Granting for a moment what you say about the script, how could I, a ninety-pound cripple, throw a big strong man out of a window?' She finished on a high squeak of triumph.

'To make a long story longer,' said Miss Withers almost sadly, 'I suggest to you, as they say in British trials, that you worked out a clever and devilish scheme – playing on Gary Twill's good-hearted willingness to help you search for your kitten who was always getting out. You bought a life-like stuffed black kitten, which could easily have been mistaken for the real thing in a rainstorm, and with a cane or some other implement shoved it out on the ledge that runs beneath your room, the bathroom, and Twill's room. Then you rushed to him and asked him to try to reach out of his window and rescue it.'

'Pure fantasy!' said Cecily. 'I suppose I was right behind him in my wheelchair and gave him a superhuman shove? What jury would believe that?'

'I'm not quite through,' Miss Withers said quietly. 'I remembered that for years you've been an ardent worker for the Humane Society and the SPCA and kindred organisations, and that once you tried to lead a protest march against the Chicago stockyards. You had seen how they force cattle into the chutes. So you got an inspiration and you bought this.'

From her capacious handbag the schoolma'am produced a Xmas-wrapped parcel, and slowly and dramatically unwrapped it. The article inside looked something like a large flashlight, with no bulb.

'What on earth is that?' demanded Oscar Piper.

'It's known as a Shock Rod. At the stockyards it's called a cattle goad. Oscar, I don't suppose you would let me demonstrate, with you as the subject? I guarantee that if this instrument is applied to your anatomy you will automatically and involuntarily jump farther than you have ever jumped before.'

'No, thanks,' said Oscar Piper grimly.

Miss Withers pressed the button, and the Shock Rod buzzed like an angry rattlesnake. 'Cecily, now we know why Gary Twill went out the window. And how can you explain why we found this nasty thing among the Christmas toys wrapped up for your grandnieces and grandnephews?'

'You didn't! You couldn't! I mailed it – ' Then the ex-movie star realised what she had said.

Miss Withers and the inspector had their spaghetti dinner after all, if a bit late. Over the zabaglione he suddenly frowned. 'One thing bothers me. Oh, it's not the old woman; she won't stand trial –'

'Psychiatric care?' asked the schoolteacher.

'Some private place, with bars. For the rest of her days. No, I'm wondering how you got into her suite and found the gadget.'

'But I didn't! I hunted all over town until I found a place where you can buy them, and I got some Christmas gift paper like Cecily's and wrapped it, figuring it would shock her into a confession. Shock treatment can work both ways, Oscar.'

He grinned, and lifted his glass of Chianti. 'To you, Hildegarde, Long may you wave!'

Poor, Poor Ophelia

BY CAROLYN WESTON

The Streets of San Francisco *not only became one of the best loved police series of the seventies but also 'an absolutely reliable action-packed crime entertainment', according to Leslie Halliwell. First broadcast by ABC in September 1972, it recounted the cases of a veteran cop, Detective Lieutenant Mike Stone and his young, college-educated partner, Detective Inspector Steve Keller, and was made unmissable by the brilliant performances of the movie veteran Karl Malden as Stone, and Michael Douglas, who was then just starting out on the career which has subsequently made him one of the biggest stars in Hollywood. Speaking later about the series, Michael Douglas reminisced, 'Stone and Keller were true partners in every sense of the word — they worked together as equals. Steve respected Mike's experience and Mike respected Steve's training.' The relationship was almost like that of a father and son, in fact, and widower Mike Stone's daughter, Jean (Darleen Carr) regularly provided some female interest in the stories. Another often unconsidered star was San Francisco itself, for many of the hundred and twenty hour-long episodes were filmed on location with frequent dramatic car chases up and down the familiar steep-sloped, picturesque streets of the city. Some scenes were also shot in the real San Francisco Police Department buildings, including the squad room, cells and morgue.*

The series had been developed by executive producer Quinn Martin from the bestselling book, Poor, Poor Ophelia by the novelist Carolyn Weston (1946-). Carolyn, a native of San Francisco who had served briefly in the local police force, based the leading characters on two men she had known, though she has never disclosed their identity. When the book was adapted by script-writer Edward Hume for the

TV pilot which would lead to the series, the location and plot-line remained the same, but the names of the two detectives, Detective Lieutenant Dan Krug and young Detective Inspector Casey Thornton Kellog, were changed to the familiar Stone and Keller, ostensibly for legal reasons. The Streets of San Francisco was still at the top of the ratings when Michael Douglas left to go to Hollywood and even greater things, and although Karl Malden was given a new partner, the athletic Detective Inspector Dan Robbins, the magic of the earlier pairing was not quite repeated and the series ended after a further season in June 1980. It had, though, virtually spanned a decade and left fond memories which have never been erased. Here is the opening episode from Poor, Poor Ophelia *which inspired yet another piece of crime-on-TV history.*

'WHY YOU CAN'T eat a decent breakfast like other men,' his mother's voice floated plangent and unceasing as a millrace from the kitchen.

Casey glanced at his watch. Five minutes to spare, he was cutting it pretty thin. But then, he always did.

Gulping down the last of his coffee, he jumped up, knocking the table, setting the centrepiece of half-blown roses and drying maidenhair fern to trembling. Four petals dropped silently on to the gleaming waxy table top. His own blurry reflection stared up at him briefly – a ghost submerged in a dark brown pond.

Casey rammed his arms into the sleeves of his new hacking-type Edwardian sports coat, hunching his shoulders to settle it. He surveyed himself in the mirror over the sideboard – medium-sized, medium good-looking, brown sunbleached hair, hazel eyes, lifelong tan, a few muscles still left from his surfing days – and thought, Not bad. But maybe Edwardian was too way-out for work? Side vents and back pleats hadn't arrived yet in the Detective Division of the Santa Monica City Police Department. Well, starting this morning, a new sartorial style will be set. And by none other than your well-dressed junior-grade detective-about-town, Casey Thornton Kellog.

'– And don't forget to gargle before you leave,' his mother was saying. 'Fog's coming in, I can smell it.'

Breezing into the kitchen, he kissed her sunburned cheek. 'See you when I see you.'

'Good Lord' – she gaped at him – 'if you don't look like one of those Canyon pansies. Honestly, Case, if you can't *look* serious, how can you expect anyone to *take* you seriously?'

Swallowing an argument, he grinned at her. Styles in seriousness had changed like everything else, but he'd never convince her, he knew that. Just as he'd never convince his father that police work wasn't the worst possible choice of livelihood for a university-educated man. They had the old values, both of them – a compound of decency, snobbery, and that sort of old-fashioned ambition which demands that life should proceed vertically, every son exceeding his father.

'Edwardian,' she was saying. 'As if a nice Ivy League jacket –'

She was still talking as he waved goodbye and slammed out the back door, jogging down the driveway to the garage, where his Mustang sheltered from the damp sea breeze off the Pacific.

'Gargle!' she shrieked as he shot by the kitchen window in reverse. 'Call if you're going to be –' then, blessedly, the sound track faded out.

Ah, Mama, Mama, you're too much, he thought, grinning as he turned and gunned toward the light at the end of their street – zero to forty in five seconds flat.

According to an old weather tradition in Santa Monica, California, the coastal fog begins at Fourteenth Street. But this morning the veil of grey had crept inland as far as Seventeenth, dimming then blotting out the morning sun as he drove westward, hanging like theatrical scrim over the new high-rises along Ocean Avenue. The foghorn at the end of Santa Monica Pier gave periodic howls – like something dying, Casey thought, far out at sea. Of the Pacific, he could see nothing. But picturing eight thousand miles of open ocean to the coast of China, he felt a gypsy stir, a moment's dissatisfaction with the crystallising pattern of his life.

Then the traffic light changed. Casey gunned the Mustang, and a minute later swung into the asphalt-surrounded snow-white civic complex, which included the City Hall, the Police Department, and – separated by half an acre of parking lot – the Santa Monica Civic Auditorium.

A few years ago, he remembered, the Academy Awards had been held here. A rookie fresh out of the Police Academy, he'd been detailed to emergency traffic control, waving all the movie nabobs into parking slots. Glamour comes to Santa Monica. Oscar Night.

'You're late,' Krug said as he pounded up the stairs, passed by Juvenile and slid into the second-floor squad room of the Detective Bureau just under the time wire.

'Uh-uh.' Casey pointed to the clock. 'Thirty seconds to go. Anything doing this bright and sunshiny morning?'

'What world are you living in? It's pea soup out there. I got water on the lungs just breathing.' To prove his point, Krug coughed juicily, swallowing a knot of phlegm with a gulp that turned Casey's stomach. 'Malibu Sheriff Station's got a bulletin out on the Sampson kid. Some hikers found a cowboy hat in the brush about a mile from where the body was found. Red, child-sized. The parents haven't identified it yet, but Malibu's pretty sure it's the one the kid was wearing when he was grabbed.' He coughed again, grimacing. 'One mile away, would you believe it? They should've spotted it the first sweep. Christ, the way I heard it, they had everybody but the League of Women Voters out combing those hills!'

'It's rough country in those canyons and washes, Al. Thick underbrush. Rock slides. Take it from an old local Boy Scout, you could hide an elephant if you really wanted to.'

'What a case. Three weeks now, every molester in three counties processed – still nothing, no leads, no suspects. Well, anyhow' – his reddish-brown weathered face creased momentarily – 'you're looking pretty sharp this morning, partner. Got something going for you around here I don't know about?'

'Not yet, but I like to be ready.'

'Get a wife,' Krug advised, as usual. 'Get married. Best way I know to keep your mind on your work.'

'Anybody complaining that I don't?'

'Our one and only intellectual marvel – who'd have the nerve?' His grin made it a joke, but Krug's resentment was still there, Casey knew, buried but still ticking, ready to explode at any time.

And not only Krug, Casey reminded himself. His fast advance through the grades from rookie patrolman to detective galled all the old-timers on the force – all the middle-aged career cops for whom plainclothes assignments were the reward for long and faithful uniformed service. 'The college boy cop,' they called him. UCLA's gift to police work. Sure, they agreed, the answer to the law-and-order problem wasn't more police, it was better policemen. But a good policeman didn't learn to be one from any stack of books. A good cop got that way by long, hard service.

The argument was a stalemate by now, an uneasy truce. But one mistake, Casey knew, and they'd be down on him like a pack of wolves.

'We got a new stiff,' Krug was saying. 'Girl about twenty. Suicide maybe. Commercial fishing boat spotted her at dawn out beyond the breakwater. Lifeguards picked her up and got her to the pier. They booked her into the morgue a little while ago.' He pulled a long brown property envelope out of his top desk drawer. 'Take a look at that.'

Expecting jewellery – a wedding ring, the usual sort of thing found on drowning victims – Casey tipped up the envelope, staring at the oblong piece of plastic hooked on to a chain which slid out on Krug's desk top. 'What's this, an ID?'

'Could be. Take a look.'

Cold as ice, the cheap link necklace swung around his fingers as Casey picked up the piece of plastic with something white sealed inside. He blinked as he turned it over. 'What the – it's a business card!'

'Yeah.'

' "Scobie, Stone and Levinson," ' Casey read. ' "Attorneys at Law. Beverly Hills." ' Dampness or perhaps faulty lamination had partially destroyed the bottom edge of the card. He could decipher only the first half of the name engraved in tiny letters. 'David J. – somebody.'

'Go have a look at her, then call the guy. With any luck, we'll get a quick identification.'

'Right,' said Casey briskly.

But once out of the office, he didn't hurry, for the idea of a trip to the morgue this early made him queasy. A dead girl. Maybe twenty years old. Drowned, he thought as he thumped down the shining-clean stairway. Shouldn't he be grateful it wouldn't be a child's body lying in there, putrefied and unrecognisable after thirteen days' exposure to the September heat of a Malibu hills canyon? No leads, no suspects. Molested, then murdered. As his inside quivered, he cursed his too-vivid imagination. And he wondered as usual if his stomach was too weak after all for this job.

But when he looked at the girl, all he felt was pity. Poor Ophelia, he caught himself thinking. They hadn't started the autopsy yet, and a sodden dark brown pants suit still clung to her slender body. He noticed that the belt was missing. Poor, poor, Ophelia. Had she drifted, singing, into her watery death? Kelpish tendrils of hair clung to marble cheeks. She looked less dead than unreal.

'No ME yet,' the morgue attendant was saying behind him. 'We got two ahead of her already – a guy got himself knifed, and a hit-and-run case.'

'Don't hurry on my account.'

'I'll tell the boss you said so.'

'She was pretty, wasn't she?'

'They're none of 'em pretty when they get here.' He fingered Casey's lapel. 'Very nice, the new threads. You bucking for best-dressed man in the Department?'

'Could be. What's the prize – a gold watch?'

'A patrolman's badge, I think maybe.'

Haha, they mouthed together, then Casey drifted out again, feeling grey as the fog pressing softly against the windows, mournful as the distant hooting of the foghorn at the end of the pier. Poor Ophelia, he kept thinking. Poor, poor, Ophelia.

The Way of a Cop

BY ABBY MANN

Another of America's major cities, New York, was a co-star in a second seventies cop programme which enjoyed enormous popularity and made its star a household name throughout the world. The locality of the seamier side of the Big Apple was perhaps rather different from the open spaces of San Francisco, but in the character of Lieutenant Theo Kojak was a figure of whom legends are made. Interestingly, Kojak had actually made his debut in a 1972 television special, The Marcus-Nelson Murders, *based on a real case from the New York ghettos, in which he had tried to help a black youth wrongly accused of the murder of two women. Although the story was unrelentingly grim, the impact of the bald, sartorially elegant police-man in his three-piece suit captivated audiences and led to CBS immediately commissioning a series. Once Kojak was on television each week, his catch-phrases, 'Who loves ya, baby?' and 'pussycat' were soon on every viewer's lips and became an added element in the hundred and fifteen hour-long episodes which ran for five years from October 1973 to August 1978.*

Kojak was, however, quite a change of role for Telly Savalas who had made a career in films out of playing villains. But he knew New York well, having lived in the city most of his life, and especially the 13th Precinct in Manhattan South where the series was based. The catch-phrases, he later confessed, were his own invention based on years of listening to street jargon. The bald head, which many women viewers considered very sexy, was a by-product of the 1962 film, Birdman of Alcatraz, *starring Burt Lancaster, in which he had his head shaved to play a prisoner. Savalas quickly came to realise the influence Kojak was having on younger viewers and refused to have him take*

part in excessive violence and would only use a gun as a last resort. He
was also quick to appreciate and acknowledge the importance of his
co-stars in the series: Dan Frazer who played his boss Frank McNeil;
Kevin Dobson as his assistant, Lieutenant Bobby Crocker; and his
own brother, George Savalas, the plant-loving Detective Stavros. At
the height of the series' success, Telly was even briefly a chart-topping
recording artist, and the fact remains he was firmly identified with the
part until the day of his death in January 1994.

Many different script-writers worked on Kojak *after the detective's*
initial creation in The Marcus-Nelson Murders, *which had been written*
by Abby Mann (1927–), a prolific writer-director who first came to
public attention with TV plays such as Judgement at Nuremberg, King
and This Man Stands Alone. *In the following episode, Kojak reminisces*
in his typically dry and street-wise manner about his life as a policeman
and some of the lessons he has learned about solving crime. No one who
ever saw his sleek bald head, dark glasses and lollipop stick protruding
between his lips on a television screen will have any difficulty picturing
the man who speaks in the next few pages . . .

I'M ENJOYING MYSELF. That's not to say I don't enjoy myself at other
times, because I suppose I do. But being the head of a detective
squad in a crime-riddled city like New York is not supposed to make a
person sing happy songs. Or tell a lot of jokes. I don't go around all the
time with a sour face; I go around all the time with the only face I've
got: rugged, with a mole that looks like a beauty mark, straight eyes, a
bald head that looks something like a pink grapefruit. I keep it warm
with an alpine-style hat, and I think I look pretty good.

Mostly, I'm enjoying myself because I'm teaching a course in
criminology at the John Jay School in New York City. An old sinful
friend of mine named Barney Posnick conned the school's administration into hiring me as a guest lecturer in criminology. I say conned
because everybody knows that my methods are unorthodox, and the
last thing they wanted was for me to train twenty imitators. I've got a
good reputation for making good collars, but in twenty years on the
force I've stepped on more toes than a cripple at Arthur Murray's.
Anyway, I got the job and I'm enjoying it. Gives me a chance to
prepare beginners for what really goes down in the real world.

The other reason I'm enjoying myself is that I've gone and done the thing a teacher should never do: gotten interested in one of my students. If anybody was cut out to be a teacher's pet, Delta Lamar is it. She's tall enough so I don't feel like the jolly flesh-coloured giant out in the pea patch with the little people. She's old enough so that I don't feel like Rudy Vallee chucking Shirley Temple's chin. And she's beautiful enough so that I just plain feel good every time I see her in my class. Her long hair is a light brown with enough red in it, I guess, to be called auburn. If I were her arresting officer, I'd have to say that her eyes were hazel. Except hazel wouldn't be enough – she's got little gold flecks and slivers in among the green that seem to go off like neon when she's happy. Her mouth is sort of a cupid's bow, but the most important thing about it is that it fits mine just fine.

Delta Lamar is a policewoman from High Point, North Carolina. Her department sent her North to the land of the Yankees, crime, and the John Jay College of Criminal Justice. One semester, and she's going to go back and tear up High Point like a tobacco barn fire. The course is half over. We had our first date, if you can call it that, right after the second class session. I went big and took her out for coffee at a greasy spoon down the street.

There were two customers in the place besides us, and it turned out to be one of those times in your life when everything seems to go right. I wanted to talk about what she wanted to talk about, and she wanted to talk about what I wanted to talk about. We stretched our cups of coffee and made them last forty-five minutes. I had to go back to Manhattan South, so I cursed my luck and stood up to pay for the coffees. That was when the two other customers decided it was shake-up time.

They handled their Saturday-night specials, cheap handguns, like they had St Vitus dance. The tall one with the matted, stringy black hair covered me and Delta while the short one, wearing a Levi's suit and a pinhead, began to pistol-whip the man behind the counter. I figured this was no time to show off in front of my new girlfriend, so I did just like I was told. I eased my wallet out of my right hip pocket and gave it to Delta.

'Now the broad brings it over here,' the taller one said. 'And she brings her pocketbook, too.' Out of my left ear I could hear the sounds the pin-headed one was making with his pistol butt against the head of the counterman. The counterman wasn't screaming or carrying on because he had been knocked unconscious with the first blow. All I could do was hope that that would take the fun out of it for the short one, and he could move on to bigger things, like looting the cash register.

If you knew what to look for, you would have known that Delta Lamar was a policewoman for ten years. She was cool and calm, but not so cool and calm as to enrage the black-haired stickup man. She had enough actress in her to make the creep think he was pulling all the strings.

'That's it, broad, nice and easy.'

When he stuck out his sweaty palm for the merchandise, he was looking the wrong way. Delta's knee hit the bull's-eye so fast that all he ever saw was stars. Before his friend read the news, I had my weapon out. The pistol-whipper got very agreeable when he saw the black hole of my .38 aimed at his gut. He threw away his Saturday-night special like it had leprosy on it. While I cuffed him, Delta checked on the condition of the counterman.

He was still breathing, but the left side of his skull had one of those sickening dents in it – the kind that tell the whole story: if he lives, he's a vegetable.

I don't call that a romance made in heaven, and it's not my idea of a cheap date. All I know is, after Delta and I booked the two creeps, our relationship was off and running. I decided not to pay any attention to the fact that she wasn't going to leave High Point and I wasn't going to leave New York City. If you ask me, I don't think cops are looking for permanence in life anyway. If they were, they'd be bank tellers or pump jockeys at a filling station. Their chances of lasting in anything else would be a lot longer. So, you end up by being grateful for whatever it is you get.

So, it's like I said. I'm enjoying myself and this is the sixth class in the ten-class series. Besides Delta there are nineteen other students, and they seem to like what's happening. My mother wanted me to be a teacher she liked the idea of a steady income. During the Depression, teachers made out like bandits. Which is to say they survived better than my father. Now I'm a teacher, only I don't remind myself of any teacher I ever had. I can't teach criminology out of a grey book that's seven hundred and twenty-one pages long and says things like, 'Criminology is the body of knowledge regarding crime as a social phenomenon.' That may be true, but I've seen too many human bodies cut up in pieces as big as stew meat to start thinking of criminology as something you get out of a textbook. They'll have to get other teachers for that: some psychologists or sociologists, and then somebody from the prison system, a parole officer, and a judge if they want to get the whole picture. I'm too busy catching bad guys and cuckoos to give enough thought to why people become bad guys and cuckoos. I try to lock them up even though I know, somewhere in the back of my head, that the jails are going to give them a better education in how to be a bad guy than a year on the street would. And I also know that nothing positive is happening in those prisons, which means I'll have to chase the same bad guys in five or ten years.

But I like talking about what I do.

The classroom is small, and it looks like a classroom. A blackboard for me to use for diagrams, a desk that I usually sit on top of, a bulletin board that nobody ever uses, and twenty of those chairs with the writing arms on them. We have to make our own atmosphere. It's eight-fifteen. The class has been going on for a quarter of an hour, and we're getting into it.

'Okay, take this one, then,' I say. 'A body, unidentifiable, is found cut up in sections and laced up in a bag. You have a suspect out of your own intuition, but you can't pin a thing on him. What do you start looking for?'

'I don't understand the question,' Caz says. Caz is twenty-three, and he's one of those students who make a job of keeping their teachers on their toes. He's smart, very smart, and very quick, but he has that arrogance you expect out of somebody who's never ever been tested. Cool. Black hair and good-looking.

I nod. 'Okay, Caz. I'm keeping it general on purpose. I just want to see how good you can be at deducing things.'

Delta raises her gorgeous hand and I nod to her. 'What kind of lacing?'

'Amateur. It's a messy job and whoever did it isn't a professional seamstress.' I nod to Ray, a young plainclothesman in the back.

'If you're gonna go around cutting up bodies, all I can say is you're gonna be spilling blood around somewhere. A whole lot of blood,' he says.

'Good. Where ya gonna look?'

'In the bathroom,' Caz answers.

'Good. That's the easiest place to clean up, and any killer worth an award would do his butchering in the bathtub. I'm looking around in the bathroom, but this is one clean suspect. Now what?'

'Is the whole house scrubbed clean?' Delta asks.

'Yes, ma'am.'

'Any area cleaner than the others?' Bob Duval asks.

'Living room.'

'What's the floor surface?' Caz asks.

'Wood planks,' I say.

'Have Forensics rip up the boards in case some blood seeped between the cracks into the area below,' Delta says.

'Good. Only I think I can save you some time and money,' I say. 'Get yourself a bowl of water and pour it over the area you are suspicious of. Then watch very carefully on the surface. The water will seep down into the false floor and, with a pencil, you can stir it up, and if there's any blood clotted below it will usually float to the surface. If you get a sign, then you can go ahead and have a wrecking company come in, for all I care. But your work is pretty much done.

'You all did very well on that one. As a matter of fact, that's a famous case from the nineteenth century. A dude named Macé was the head of the Sûreté and he wrapped up the Voirbo case exactly that way. I don't think the technique is all that important, because for the most part you've got Forensics on your side and they know exactly what to look for. What I want you to get from this course and from your own work is that quality that nobody can label. It's the deducing and the putting together and knowing what questions to ask yourself. And it's also knowing enough to throw out all of the evidence and start all over again if you have to.

'Let's switch gears. How about embezzlers?'

The idea lies in the air for about forty-five seconds before anybody picks it up. Duval raises his hand. I nod to him. 'Sutherland and Cressey call embezzlers immature criminals.'

'What's that supposed to mean?' Caz snaps back.

Duval leans forward in his chair and tries to stare Caz down. 'They say there's like a chronological thing with criminals. You start out doing the usual juvenile kinds of stuff; you don't plan things and you have no idea of what you'll do if you get caught,' he says.

'Then what happens?' I ask.

'Well,' Duval says, 'if you're going to continue to be a criminal, you start to grow up.'

'At what age?' I ask.

'There doesn't have to be any particular age,' he says. 'A real hard case could mature at eleven years old if he'd been at it long enough. But, it's like the embezzler isn't really a criminal.' The other nineteen members of the class laugh at the surprise.

'Give him a chance,' I say.

Duval continues. 'The embezzler thinks of himself as a real straight arrow. The odds are pretty good that he's been working at a place in a fairly responsible job for a long time. He has no plan to rob the company; it just happens.' Another laugh. 'No, I mean it. Most embezzlers start by taking out little amounts. They run into problems that they don't think they can talk about. So they start snitching a little bit here and there. But they still don't think that they are criminals.

And then it hits them – wham! They haven't been keeping track and all of a sudden they face up to the fact that they've lifted four hundred thousand dollars, say. Now they *know* they're criminals.'

'What happens then?' I ask. 'You've got it pretty good.'

'They haven't got too many options. Some of them kill themselves. Some others decide that they'll make one last gamble. They steal a little bit more money and put it down on a horse or on a football team. Some others end up by becoming *real* criminals. I guess they decide they're gonna go the whole way; they even get involved with pros.'

I slide off the front of the desk and stroll around the classroom, up and down the rows of desks. 'That's fine – as far as it goes. And you're right. There is no way any of us in this class tonight could really get inside or understand what goes on in the head of an embezzler. These guys may be the sorriest SOBs in the whole criminal business. They don't belong, and if they get caught and pull a sentence they are the unhappiest prisoners in the pen. If they're lucky, somebody assigns them to be the chaplain's assistant or the warden's office boy, or something like that. If they're unlucky, they get stomped.

'In 1969 the department was asked by First Security National to make a discreet investigation of their staff. It seems that somebody higher up had done some homework and found that a lot of green had fallen out of the bottom of the bag somewhere. I was part of the team asked to make the investigation. I knew nothing from banking, and I asked to be relieved of the detail. Captain McNeil decided it would be a good idea for me to learn. And that's not a bad lesson for you all. If there's something you don't like, balk once – you've been heard, and if you're overruled, you do what you have to. Don't complain twice.

'There were five possibles: middle management. Each had worked his way up from teller to a level where he had some kind of responsibility and could even use a secretary every once in a while. We wasted our time right off the bat by checking their bank balances. Anybody in the business knows that if he puts more into his savings account than he's making, the cops will be all over him like honey. So we checked the accounts of their wives and parents. Again, nothing. What next?'

I looked around the room at the twenty eager faces. They liked story-time, but I wasn't teaching this course just to become a storyteller. Like the lady in the basement of the library every Saturday morning.

'You grilled them; you gave them the third degree,' Caz says with a grin.

'That would have shortened the investigation,' I say, 'but the

Supreme Court frowns on it these days, and even in 1969 they wouldn't let me use my rubber hose. Where would you start next, Caz?'

Caz smirks. 'I'd look around to see what kind of purchases they'd made,' he says.

'A new swimming pool? Or something like that?' Delta says.

'Yeah,' Caz answers.

'Let me put your mind at ease,' I say. 'They were all checked out and nobody's lifestyle had taken any fancy turns.'

'How about sexual deviation?' another student asks.

I stop my paces. 'Good idea.'

'Yeah,' Caz says. 'I vote for blackmail.'

'That's probably the most frequent reason,' I say. 'So we started checking up. Guess what we found?'

'All five of them had secret honeys,' Caz says flippantly.

Like I said, Caz is quick.

'*Exactly* it,' I say.

'All *five* of them?' Delta asks with her beautiful mouth open in disbelief.

I nod. 'All five of these poor jerks had girlfriends back as far as a year or two years before the investigation,' I say.

'Jesus!' Delta whispers.

'Maybe it's an occupational hazard of banking,' Caz jokes.

'It was for these dudes,' I say.

'What did you do next?' Duval asks.

'Anybody else got any ideas?' I ask.

Twenty pairs of eyes stare at me with dumb expressions. I close my eyes and pretend to snort out loud. 'You tried to find out which mistress was living best,' Ellis Stern answers.

'None of these girls was kept,' I answer. 'They were love objects, but none of their boyfriends was shelling out any extra funds.'

Delta looks up in surprise. 'Then what's the percentage in being a mistress?' she asks. The rest of the class erupts in giggles and guffaws.

'Beats me,' I answer in my most professional tone. 'All I know is that it was the weirdest coincidence I'd ever seen. But you people still haven't answered my question. Where do you go next?'

'I'd put a tail on them for about a month,' Duval says.

I nod. 'Okay, Duval, and how many men will that take?'

Duval looks a little sheepish, because he knows that if we're going to stake out these five bozos we'd need a minimum of fifteen trained detectives. 'You make it sound simple,' Duval says.

'Good point,' I say, 'Every solution of every crime I've ever known about was simple. But the important thing is that the solution wasn't simple until *after* somebody else had thought it up. Solving crimes is not a complicated business; it's not complicated *afterward*. So, come on, what did we do?'

Once again I look around me and see twenty dull pairs of eyes. Delta shrugs at me, putting on an expression that says, 'Okay, I'm stupid, go ahead and tell me.'

'We put a tail on their supervisor,' I say.

'Because it was cheaper?' Caz asks.

I grin. 'No, because it was the solution.'

'But it was the supervisor who called you in in the first place,' Delta says in a voice that sounds like some kid at a magician's show.

'Sure, and that's one of the things you weren't listening for when we heard the description of embezzlers. What'd you say? Embezzlers aren't really criminals? And that's the point. All the rest of this garbage about middle management and mistresses and everything else was just a smokescreen. The important thing was that embezzlers, since they're not a hundred per cent professional criminals, have a thing called guilt. And that guilt makes them do strange things. Like having us in to investigate in the hopes that we'd catch the person who was really doing it. Namely the person who asked us in. Clear?'

'You mean the guy wanted to be nailed?' Caz asks.

'Part of him did,' I say. 'And you'll find that's the strangest part of your job as a policeman. When you start running into criminals who turn themselves in with hints, evidence, leads, and all that garbage. I don't mean the ones who call up and confess to every crime that hits the newspapers; I mean the ones who really are your perpetrators.' I search the faces in front of me. 'An embezzler is not going to behave the same way as a rapist, and a rapist is not going to behave the same way as a safeman, and a safeman is not going to behave the same way as an arsonist. You've got to begin to learn the patterns. You can't play Sherlock Holmes without a programme.

'Okay, let's take our break and be back here in ten minutes.'

I stroll back around behind my desk and try to figure out what my lesson plan is for the next half of the class. The usual chatter starts up – everything from precinct gossip to discussions about what's going on in the class. Caz strolls casually up to the corner of my desk, trying to look like he doesn't care. For his sake, I wish he could figure out why he's in my class. He's not even a policeman; he wants to take the exam and he says he'd like to be a cop. I can't see it. 'I don't believe all that stuff about people wanting to be caught,' he says. 'I think that's pure Agatha Christie stuff.'

'You're right, Caz. Except for the fact that it happens so often. I'll grant you it happens more often on television than it does in real life, but you still have to keep your radar tuned in just in case. Why go around beating your head against the wall when, if you play your cards right, you can put the pieces together?'

He nods with his usual smirk. In some ways it's like I'm his father and he's my adolescent son, and he doesn't trust a word out of my mouth. He's got to prove to me that he's a big boy.

'I'll believe it when I see it,' he says as he turns away to walk back out into the hall.

'Fair enough,' I mumble.

For the rest of the class, after the break, I spend thirty minutes trying to convince them that very few crimes are ever solved with fingerprints. They're not ready to believe that, either. So, who am I to take away the dreams and fantasies they've gotten from movies and television?

Regan and the Stripper

BY JOE BALHAM

A new era of realistic cop series began on British television in January 1975 when Ian Kennedy Martin – the younger brother of Z-Cars' creator, Troy – devised the format for The Sweeney which focused on the seamier and criminal side of London life. Like Kojak, an essential element of the episodes was their use of criminal argot ranging from the title – derived from Cockney rhyming slang 'Sweeney Todd' for Flying Squad – through to the conversations between officers of the law and criminals which were littered with terms like 'blag' (for armed robbery), 'readies' (money) and 'porridge' (prison). The series had evolved from a ninety-minute special, Regan, which Ian Kennedy Martin had written in 1974 about two members of the Flying Squad, Detective Inspector Jack Regan (played by John Thaw) and Detective Sergeant George Carter (Dennis Waterman), who broke all the rules in their hunt for the killer of a young policeman. The Guardian echoed viewers' admiration for the play. 'It has spanking direction and excellent deadpan acting' – all of which prompted Thames to commission a series based around the two characters. A former Flying Squad officer, Jack Quarrie, was hired to help with the authenticity of the plots, while Thaw and Waterman went to considerable pains to absorb the ways of the squad which specialises in combating armed robbers. (John Thaw had, in fact, already appeared in Z-Cars as a DCI, and would later enjoy enormous popularity as the introspective, music-loving Inspector Morse.)

The partnership of Regan and Carter ultimately extended to over fifty hour-long episodes which were sprinkled with strong language, action-packed drama and occasionally a little too much violence, prompting complaints from viewers as well as the police themselves.

(In 1976, for example, after an episode in which the pair used inducements to get a confession, were guilty of wrongful arrest and broke a number of rules of procedure, Leslie Knowles of the Police Federation complained, 'Under the old complaints procedure they would have lasted five minutes – under the new set-up they wouldn't last two!') The older man Regan, a dedicated if sometimes intolerant and frustrated policeman, was often responsible for the violent outbursts and had to be restrained by Carter, a Cockney who might easily have become one of the criminals his 'Guv' (as he called him) so disliked. The two men shared a liking for drink, an eye for the women and mutual resentment of their superior officer, Chief Inspector Frank Haskins (Garfield Morgan). Many of the episodes of The Sweeney put the two men into contact with all sorts of criminal low-life and brought Regan no fewer than eighteen commendations before he finally quit the Force after being falsely acused of taking bribes in the dramatic story of Jack or Knave transmitted as an audience-winner at Christmas 1978. The whole series has subsequently been transmitted in America and regularly re-shown on commercial and satellite TV in Britain, thereby further enhancing its landmark reputation.

Although Ian Kennedy Martin created The Sweeney, the demand for scripts was such that a whole team of writers had to be assembled to work on the programme. Among the most memorable of the episodes, however, was 'Regan and the Stripper', for which Martin was responsible. In this the detective inspector becomes enmeshed in the activities of a certain Arthur Keane and his 'League of Decency' who are apparently trying to close down London's top strip clubs with bomb threats. Helping him in this 'mission' are two villains the Flying Squad has encountered before: Charles Prescott and Willie Milner, better known as 'Willie the Flasher'. It is their association with Keane that makes Regan believe there is more to the campaign than meets the eye and plunges him into the world of sleazy London strip clubs in order to resolve the mystery. The following episode from the story was written by Joe Balham, a pseudonymn for a well-known author of crime thrillers, and was published shortly after the transmission in 1977.

REGAN WALKED ROUND Soho. His patch. His territory. His kind of noise and smell. Neon lights, cooking oil stinking from Greek restaurants. Cars being illegally parked in the same streets in which the heavy Mob were lifting them away. A fifteen-year-old boy thinking he was being furtive about trying car doors. A flock of Japanese with their yens showing. Flotsam and jetsam. Booze brings lust for the money a man carries in his wallet, the sex a woman carries in her pants. And both are interchangeable, or so the promise goes. It's the oldest, and least fulfilled, of all the promises.

The strip clubs were all busy. The surveillance teams all in position. The scare had been a five-minute sensation, nothing more. Whoever tried to close them up by frightening people showed a total lack of understanding. Tell people cigarettes will kill them, they'll smoke twice as many. Tell 'em butter gives you heart attacks – they'll gobble it up. Tell 'em alcoholism is reaching epidemic proportions, they'll rush into the pubs, take home the bottles of South African sherry, guzzle it down. It seems, sometimes, the best sales and promotion gimmick is to tell people, with scare headlines, that your product will kill them!

The barman at the Two Coronets was more respectful, and flashed a smile and his memory. 'Sherry, isn't it? A schooner of the amontillado?'

'A pint and a double Scotch.'

'I've called last orders – is it all right?'

'I didn't hear you. And I'm off-duty.'

'We have a back door if ever you're thirsty. It takes me an hour to clean up.'

'Now that *would* be breaking the law!'

He was halfway through his beer when he felt a light tap on his shoulder. 'Bet you thought I was dead?' a welcome voice said in his ear. It was a long time since he'd been so pleased to see somebody. 'Hello, Sally,' he said. 'Where did *you* spring from?'

'I've been working.'

'I thought you didn't do evenings?'

'I've been accepted for university. The money will come in handy. And so many clubs are quietly closing up, you know, they've got too many girls. It's either work all the time, or they get somebody who will! It's become a very competitive world!'

'I could have told you that, love.'

A schooner of sherry appeared by his hand, as if by magic. The barman's voice sounded over the throng. 'Now let me have all your empty glasses, persons, please!' He bent towards Regan. 'Would you believe it, the governor won't let us say Ladies and Gentlemen any more? He had an awful argument from a customer about that one night. A terrible cow she was. So now, I'm a barperson, if you please! Makes you sick, doesn't it? All my friends are furious – it's taken us all this time to change the law so that we can tell everyone we're gay, and now we have to say, we're *persons*!' He minced away down the bar.

'I think he fancies you!' Sally said. 'But you never can tell. I thought you fancied me, but I haven't heard a word from you!'

'I've been busy, love, honest!'

'When a man says "honest", you know he feels guilty! I wasn't going to come across and speak to you, but you looked so miserable sitting there. Not like yourself. Usually, you have eyes in the back of your head. Normally, I guess, you'd have spotted me the minute I walked in the door.'

'Anybody would, love, honest . . . Christ, I mustn't say that, must I? I *do* feel guilty, but that's the way life is with a copper.'

'All the time?'

'Most of the time.'

'Then I must want my head examining. Are you working now?'

'No, not actually on duty.'

'But you're working all the same. Even in the short time I've known you, I've come to recognise the signs.'

'You can't just switch it off. It's not nine-to-five, and sandwiches in the Park for lunch. Half the time, I wish it was.'

'And the other half?'

'It's a chance to do something that matters. The world will always have villains; it'll always need people to go chasing 'em. We can't just hand London over to them and say "there it is, get on with it". They've practically done that in some places, like New York, and look what's happened. And it could happen here overnight. At least, you can still get in a tube after dark, and take the short way home through the back streets. Villains don't work nine-to-five, do they? So neither can we!'

'Which makes it tough on anybody who fancies one of you.'

I guess it does.'

She was silent for a minute, biting her lip. He drank his beer down, chased it with the whisky, slid a pound note unobtrusively across the bar.

'The moment of truth?' she said. 'Decision time?'

'You're a big girl. In more ways than two!'

'Bastard. You could say you fancied me.'

'That would amount to persuasion.'

'I don't go for this your-place-or-mine bit. You remember?'

'I do remember.'

'Where do you live? A police hostel?'

'That would fit, wouldn't it? I have a flat in Hammersmith. I don't see enough of it to keep it smelling sweet and clean, to remember always to do my washing-up and make my bed. The underwear I've got on disgusts even me! Some bugger tried to kill me today. That makes my underwear not very important to me, if you see what I mean.'

'You could take a bath. I could do your washing-up while you're taking it, make the bed, put clean sheets on it . . .'

'If I've remembered to collect my laundry. Look, Sally, the domestic bit is a heavy scene for me, know what I mean? I'd look fucking awful in a plastic apron, me drying while you washed.'

'All I asked was, where do you live. That's not a proposal of marriage, you know.'

'Just so we both realise that!'

They went out together, walked down the street to where a black XJ6 was parked with a uniformed chauffeur behind the wheel. A female person. She could fire a Webley .38 better than any man on the Flying Squad, had qualified on the range to draw one from the stores when they had a Magistrates Order.

'See that taxi just turning out of the street?' Regan asked.

'Yes, Inspector. Matter of fact, Larry Price just got in it and asked for Knightsbridge. He's probably going to his other club, the respectable one.'

'He might just be going to Hammersmith . . .'

'Then we'd better get after him. Is this young lady assisting with your inquiries?'

'You could say that.'

'Then you'd both better get in. We don't want to hold up your examination of a suspect, do we?'

'Cheeky bugger!'

'You trained me, Inspector.'

On the way, they stopped outside a late-night Indian-run grocery and Regan staggered out with an enormous bag full.

When the driver dropped them outside his flat, she said, 'I'm not logging this journey, Inspector.'

'Then don't knock down any old lady. She just might be one of the few taxpayers we have left.'

'It'll cost you an hour off, next time I have a heavy date and want to get my hair done!'

'Nothing is for nothing, Policeperson Brown! Even I know that!'

*

The luminous hands of his watch said four o'clock. Sally's head was on his arm, his hand on her shoulder. He tried to reach his cigarettes without disturbing her but her quiet voice said in the dark, 'I'm not asleep.'

'Did I waken you?'

'You were making a noise. Sort of groaning, and grinding your teeth. You need a holiday.'

'Don't mention that word to me.' He lit his cigarette, saw her face looking up at him in the glow of the match.

'And you need a shave,' she said.

'At this time of the morning?'

'I feel as if I've been rubbed all over with fine sandpaper.'

'Sexy.'

'It's not unpleasant. We had a loofah once that made you tingle the same way.'

'Loofah! I haven't heard that word in ages. It takes you back, doesn't it. Houses with bathrooms, big blocks of soap, lashings of hot water. My gran had a place like that in Bexley. My Dad was a rebel, ran away and joined the police. This flat was the best home he ever knew. I was born in Hammersmith Hospital, brought up right here. This was my Mum's bed.'

'If she could see you now . . .'

'She'd die laughing. Full of life, she was. My Dad was killed with a pick-axe handle. She kept herself going for twenty years afterwards, bringing me up. She never minded when I joined the Met. But she died a year after. I think, now, she couldn't bear it all over again, waiting for me to come home each night, wondering if I'd make it or they'd bring me home like they brought home my Dad. I never thought. You don't, when you're young. She laughed all the time. And was full of life, fighting off the fellers. I never realised that seeing me put on the uniform was just too much for her – how could I? I was only a lad.'

'I'll bet she was proud of you, too.'

'If she was, she never said. She taught me to keep your own feelings to yourself.'

'Would you like a cup of tea?'

'It would go down nicely.'

'Stay there and I'll bring you one.'

He lay back, dragging deep. Tempting, wasn't it? Good-looking bird, smashing figure. Intelligent with it but not toffee-nosed about it. And they were well suited in bed. Cups of tea at four o'clock. What more could a man ask? Poor old Charlie Prescott, having his nuts pulled about by a slag, in it for the money. Arthur Keane, that big house, and no sign of a woman about. You could keep the cut-glass, the polished mahogany, in exchange for a good woman in bed beside you. And Willie the Flasher, what the hell did he get out of life?

She brought him a corned beef sandwich with the tea.

'Now you're really spoiling me,' he said.

'It's time somebody did, stop that groaning in the night!'

'That was only because I got cramp in my arm!'

'To quote one of your favourite words – bollocks, Inspector!'

He munched the corned beef sandwich. Drank his tea. Lit another cigarette. 'What was that you said earlier, about them closing the clubs and the competition getting heavy . . . ?'

'That's right. Six of them closed down this week. They reckon there'll be more next week.'

He pulled the phone off the side table, cradled it on his chest, and dialled a number.

'Damn it, you're working again.'

'Shan't be a minute. Honest!'

'There you go with that word again.'

Sergeant Millbrough,' he said, when the number answered. Millbrough came on the line immediately.

'It's all quiet, Inspector. Only four more clubs open, then we can all pack up for the night.'

'What about the ones that are closing down for good?'

'Yes, quite a lot of them.'

'And no report on my desk about it?'

There was a long silence. Regan could hear Sergeant Millbrough breathing, but said nothing.

'Well, Inspector, I didn't realise that was what interested you in this case. After all, nobody's going to be planting bombs in clubs that have been shut, are they?'

Millbrough was waiting for an explosion that never came. Regan was, for once, conscious of the girl lying in bed beside him, and considerate. 'Tell you what you do, Sergeant,' Regan said quietly. 'Find out who ran each of the clubs that's been closed, find out who owns the leases of each one, or who rents them, and who those leases or rentings have been sold to. Find the agents who handled all this and if Charles Prescott was in any way involved.'

'Right, Inspector, I'll make a memo of that for Sergeant Wood when he takes over in the morning and I go off duty.'

'No, Sergeant. You don't leave any memos. You don't wait for the morning.' Regan's voice was quiet still, but deadly. 'You do it now, you go on doing it until it's done, and until it's done, you don't go off-duty, understand?'

'Four o'clock in the morning, Inspector . . .?'

'I *know* it's four o'clock in the morning. But it wouldn't have been if the information had been where it should have been, on my desk last evening!'

He put down the phone and smiled, knowing the curses that would be echoing round the Incidents Room.

Sally shivered. 'When you were talking to whoever that was,' she said, 'I had the impression that if crocodiles could speak, that's how they'd sound!'

He put his arm round her shoulders. 'That's only because I smoke too many cigarettes,' he said, 'and I've still got all my teeth!'

At nine o'clock, Regan was in Rupert Street. He'd surprised himself, had taken a bath, wore clean underwear and a tie, and had shaved. 'Jimmy,' he said, 'nice place you've got here. Give us a cup of tea and make it nice and strong.'

Sergeant Carter had taken a bath, wore clean underwear and a tie, and had shaved, but somehow, it hadn't had the same effect on him it had had on the guvnor. 'If it's all the same to you,' he said, 'I'll have black coffee. That Anita came round again. I'm thinking of moving into the Police Hostel so I can get a bit of rest.'

'Anita, eh? That gives me another idea . . .'

'A man your age, guvnor? She'd kill you . . .'

'Cheeky bugger! That's not what I meant.'

'It's not my morning for the psychic bit, guvnor.'

'Listen, and maybe you'll get clairvoyant!'

Jimmy was hovering over them. 'Ain't got no tea nor coffee, Mr Regan,' he said. 'We're not open for business yet. Got this lot to fix up – left it in a right mess last people did.'

'Jimmy McBray, and you haven't got a kettle boiling somewhere? I don't believe it. They tell me you even had a brew-up going night and day in Parkhurst.'

'That's a dirty lie, Mr Regan,' Jimmy said. 'I was never in Parkhurst. I was never in nowhere, and you know it.'

'That's right, Jimmy. I must have been thinking in the future.'

'In the future, Mr Regan. I don't rightly get you . . .?'

'But I'll rightly get you, Jimmy. One of these days. Now, get that kettle cracking, and a cup of tea for me, not too sweet, and a black coffee for my sergeant.'

They walked round the basement room. It wasn't in bad shape.

Regan had seen a lot worse after some of these 'ethnic' restaurateurs had moved out. The room was about forty feet by thirty feet, with a ten-foot ceiling. At the foot of the stairs was a small lobby with a large cupboard which would doubtless be turned into a Cloaks. Jimmy McBray had been sweating on a licence to serve alcoholic refreshments. The previous restaurant owner had had one, God knows how, and Jimmy, was hoping to take it over and move up a notch from the tea-and-toast, two-poached-eggs 'caff' he'd been running in a side street off Tottenham Court Road. Jimmy the Caff was a long-time Soho character, always in the catering trade. He'd had his ups and downs, had gone from a barrow to a 'hole in the wall' to a caff, and back down again. Everybody was surprised when he bought what had been The Blue Paradise, and started attending the catering auctions in Dean Street, bidding for snow-white table cloths, linen napkins, good 'catering' table-ware. His chairs came from an old Mayfair hotel that had been pulled down to make room for a glass and concrete American-plan thirty-quid-a-night doss-house.

The walls had been covered with a fancy maroon and red-striped 'velvet' wall-paper. Regan ran his hand down it. 'That must cost a bob or two!' he said. The maroon 'hard wear' carpet was rolled against a wall while electricians put separate outlets all over the floor, presumably one for each table. 'This is going to look very nice,' Regan said. 'You'll have to bring me here for a meal when Anita gives you the evening off.'

Jimmy brought them the cups they'd asked for. Regan turned over a chair to sit down on. 'Not one of them, Mr Regan,' Jimmy pleaded, 'they're still making a hell of a lot too much dust in here. I've had to vacuum the wallpaper clean three times.'

'This is going to be very nice, Jimmy.'

'It's giving me ulcers,' Jimmy said. 'I've got my first booking tomorrow for lunch, and look at all this lot. We'll never be ready.'

'You're a pessimist, Jimmy,' Regan said. 'Think on the bright side. When you get it done, it's going to look very nice. It ought to, of course, with all the money you spent on it.'

The mention of the word 'money' brought Jimmy's eyes round. 'Look, Mr Regan, you and me has never had any business together. I mean, you've never fingered my collar for nothing. But I get around, and listen to the lads. You've not come here for a cup of tea and a preview look at my restaurant . . .'

'Restaurant, Jimmy? I thought you were opening a strip club. After all, you've got the premises, you've got a catering licence, an entertainment licence, a wine and spirits licence, what more could you need? Of course, you'll need to put in a bit of a stage across there, and a curtain and some spot-lights, but that won't be difficult. Sergeant Carter here will help and advise you – he's a bit of an authority on the subject.'

'Okay, Inspector. You've had your bit of fun. Now what's the game?' Jimmy looked round at the workmen. 'Billy,' he shouted, 'take 'em all across to Roper's and give 'em a breakfast. Tell Millie it's on me, and I'll be across later.'

The men downed tools in a flash and left Jimmy the Caff alone with the two Flying Squad officers.

'All right, Inspector, what's the game?'

'No game, Jimmy. You're opening tonight. Not tomorrow. And it's going to be a strip club, not a restaurant.'

Jimmy shuddered. 'You know what they're doing to the strip clubs?'

'Not all of 'em, Jimmy. Only some of 'em.'

Carter was watching both of them, his head moving as if he were at a table-tennis match, his sex hangover completely forgotten.

Jimmy got up, walked to the bar at one end of the room, lifted the dust sheet and took out an unopened bottle of brandy. He came back with three glasses, put them on the box around which they were sitting, and poured. The brandy had that beautifully mature odour. 'This was going to be to impress the customers who knew about such things,' Jimmy said.

Regan picked up his glass and sipped it. 'Jimmy, you know what you're talking about. That would have impressed Winston Churchill!'

'Right,' Jimmy said, fortified by the drink which he'd drained in one gulp. 'Like I said, I listen to the boys. You're usually reckoned to be bad news, Inspector, no offence meant. Why do you think I'm going to open tonight as a strip club? Not that such a thing is even remotely possible, with everything that has to be done here.'

'You'll do it, Jimmy. And you'll put a stage across that side, with a curtain. That Ladies lav can do as a dressing-room for your artistes, as I believe they're called in the trade. You can stack the tables, put the chairs out in rows, open up the bar. A couple of signs outside with some lights on 'em, a few dirty pictures behind glass, a name above the door, and you're in business. And, do you know why you'll do it? Because I know where you got the money you've been spending on this lovely velvet wall-paper. Jimmy the Caff, they call you, but they ought to have called you Jimmy the Lay-Off. Because that's what you've always been, isn't it? The bookies' and punters' middle-man. The lad they come to when they don't want one side to know what the other side is doing. When there's a fix at Newmarket, or on the dogs down at

Caterham, you're the lad in the middle. Now, Jimmy, I'll tell you something that not even your backers know. You've got sticky fingers. That's why you've been up and down more times than a yo-yo, because you've had to find money in a hurry when you've taken a flier that hasn't worked out. About three months ago, you took a real chance, didn't you? Tommy Baxter came in with three thousand quid. What was the horse? I remember. Blue Rag. Tommy believed it had been fixed. It hadn't, and you knew it hadn't, so you took Tommy's money and instead of spreading it around on Blue Rag, the way Tommy wanted, you put it out in your own name on the nag that really had been fixed – Tarzan's Leap. Tarzan's Leap romped home paying ten to one, and you used the money to buy this place.'

'If we knew all this . . .' Carter said, but Regan cut him off.

'If villains want to turn each other over – the more the merrier in my book,' he said. 'Tommy Baxter is as big a villain as Jimmy here.' He looked at Jimmy over the rim of his glass. 'I don't need to remind you, Jimmy, that we've had Tommy Baxter inside twice for GBH – and even you know that means Grievous Bodily Harm. If the last surgeon hadn't been good at jigsaws, the last time would have been murder, not GBH. Tommy Baxter is a very violent man, Jimmy, and I don't think he'd like it if I told him you withheld information from him, costing him three thousand and lining your own pocket. And I would tell him, you know, Jimmy, and he'd listen to me.'

Jimmy shrugged his shoulders. 'They all said you were a bastard, Regan,' he said, 'but they didn't know the half of it, did they?' He poured three more glasses. 'The fellows were right. You are bad news. The worst sort. We'd better finish this bottle. This stuff's too good to leave lying about in a bloody strip club!'

'You're doing *what*?' Maynon said. Regan thought he was going to explode, like an over-ripe blood orange.

'I'm opening a strip club!'

'I thought that was what you said the first time.' Maynon shook his head, looking at Jack Regan. 'This time,' he said, 'you've really flipped, haven't you? A case in which the Commissioner himself is taking a personal interest and you tell me you've opened a strip club! As part of your investigation!'

'The clubs are closing down. One by one they're being frightened out of business. I reckon it's time we had access to one that won't be frightened. That won't go out of business, unless they bomb him out.'

'Have you seen the papers? Do you know there are three Questions on the table in the House? If the press gets a hold of this . . . 'Police run Strip Club!' I shall have to tell the Commissioner, you realise that?'

'I hoped you would. Do you think he'd like a ticket for the opening?'

'Don't tell me it's going to be a gala, with free champagne?'

'Not quite . . .'

'When is it?'

'Tonight!'

The tables had all been stacked and put away. The chairs were arranged in neat rows facing the improvised curtain that blocked off the 'stage'. Only one problem. Word had gone round, somehow, in that curious way of the underworld, the bad word that is as severe, as strict, as unappealable, as the black ball in the most exalted club. 'Something not quite right' about Jimmy's Club. Nothing you could put your finger on, but something not kosher, not according to Hoyle. None of the strippers would work there, even though Jimmy cornered four of them in Nick the Greek's place and offered them whatever wages they wanted. 'Name it, kids. Five quid a day? Ten?' There were no takers.

Jimmy was almost in tears when Regan came in at five o'clock to see how the preparations were going. 'I know you'll think I've done it deliberate,' Jimmy said, 'but straight up, I can't get any of the girls to strip. I can't even get any of the tarts to fill in until we have somebody to take over. Somebody's put the word out. It's the first time that's ever happened to me. Me, Jimmy! With the word out against him!' It couldn't have been worse if he'd been the local bank manager asked to resign from the golf club!

'You'll have to get up there and do it yourself,' Regan said. 'Attract all the gays! Well, at least it'd be a new gimmick!'

Jimmy turned green at the thought. Carter, looking at Jimmy's podgy figure, and mentally visualising him cavorting about on the stage like Peter the pig, turned the same colour.

'That bird of yours,' Regan said to Carter. 'You told me her show's finished. She out of work? Jimmy's paying good wages.'

'Now steady on, guvnor . . .'

'What's the matter? Scared because she's going to show her tits to a few half-blind eunuchs . . .?'

'No, guv'. I'm thinking what she'd be like after she'd spent an hour or two stripping off. If she's a raver now, think what that would do to her? She'd eat me alive!'

Sally was waiting for Regan, as arranged, in the corner of the bar of the Two Coronets. 'I can't stay long, love,' he said. 'I'm working!'

'But at least you made the date,' she said, happily. 'You've kept it on time . . . That's all a girl wants, you know. Not to be possessive, but to be recognised. Incidentally, I'm thinking of giving up "dancing". I mean, when you've got something going, it's a bit demeaning. On the other party, know what I mean?' Her embarrassment was plain to see; she tried to hide it by turning her head, taking a gulp from the glass of sherry. Jack stretched out his hand, placed it on her arm, waiting until she turned her head back, and they were looking into each other's eyes. 'You're going to have to learn, love, to let me decide what "demeans" me, and what doesn't. I know why you're doing the dancing. I know what your reasons are. It's got nothing to do with me, one way or the other, how you work out what you do, what you want to do. People have to make up their own minds, have to decide for themselves what is right and wrong. The thing you have to watch is not to hurt anybody else unnecessarily . . . That's where the villains are wrong, because what they do hurts other, often innocent, people. I can't see that your dancing hurts anybody. If strip clubs exist, and I hate the whole idea of them, then they have to have people to "dance" in them. Though I laugh when I think what a lot of them call dancing!'

'I try my best to give them a bit of a performance . . .'

'I know you do, but believe me, you're the only one. You should see the way some of the others carry on – talk about bumps and grinds!'

'So you don't feel ashamed of me, because I'm a stripper?'

'Ashamed? Like I said, Sally, it's got nothing to do with me. It's not against the law . . .'

'Yes, but I mean . . .'

'You and your "I mean . . ." It's as bad as my "honest". Look, Sally, if you've got a conscience about being a stripper . . .'

'I didn't have, until I met you . . . Now, I'm not so sure.'

'Tell you what. How about being a stripper for me?'

'Ah, now that's different. I'd feel embarrassed . . . It's, well, it's provocation, isn't it? And the last thing you need is provoking . . .'

'I'm offering you a job. Star performer. A brand-new club. Carpet on the floor, posh seats to sit in . . .'

She frowned at him. 'You mean it, don't you?'

'Too damned right I mean it.'

'You want me to go on stripping . . .?'

'Jimmy McBray's new place. Opens tonight. He'll give you a hundred quid a week.'

'You some kind of agent then? Anyway, I've heard waves about that place. Wrong waves. Word gets around, you know.'

'Forget what you've heard. Will you do it? I should warn you, it might get heavy.'

'What do you mean, heavy?'

'Some people might object to Jimmy opening a strip club when so many are closing down. I want to find out who those people are.'

'It's a police job you're giving me, then? Undercover agent . . .'

'I won't crack the usual joke. But you could call it that. Unofficially. I could get an out-of-town police girl to do it, but it might look a bit odd. They know you, know you work the clubs. And, what's more, they know you're straight!'

'Have you been having me vetted? That *would* be heavy! Just because we've been to bed a couple of times . . .'

He knew he'd put his foot in it. 'No, Sally, I haven't been having you vetted. But you have to understand that half my life is spent listening to people, trying to pick up a whisper. And I hear things . . .'

'And they've given me a clean bill of health, is that it? She doesn't go upstairs with the customers, doesn't meet them outside after the act is over. Is that it?'

He could hear the anger in her voice at the thought that he'd spied on her. Nobody likes to feel they've been 'investigated' without their knowledge. 'Now don't go off at halfcock,' he said. 'I haven't made any specific inquiries about you, for any reason whatsoever. I hear ordinary gossip in the course of my job. Gossip about everybody around this patch. Mostly it's in one and out the other, since that's all it deserves. You're different. Everybody says you are. You talk different, you dance different, you are different. The kind of slag you see around this place is very class-conscious. You can't fool them that you belong. You don't belong. Other people wanting to earn a bit of money to do something positive with, they go and get jobs as waitresses. Not as strippers . . .'

'The money's good, that's why I do it.'

'I *know* that, Sally. You don't have to convince me. Like I said, you do what you want, as long as you're not breaking any law. This is still a land of freedom, you know, no matter what anybody may say about the fascist police state. Now, what about Jimmy McBray's? Will you do it?'

'You asking? Or telling.'

He put his arm round her. 'If you don't know the answer to that question, love . . .'

'But it could get heavy . . .?'

'I'll be there to look after you.'

'You'd better be. I'm not one of your heroes.'

Carter got on to the Porn Squad. 'Come on, you must have a few photos,' he said. 'Big knockers, smiling faces . . .'

'I know about the knockers, but we never have time to look at the faces. Anyway, what do you want them for?'

'To assist me in my inquiries. And I need them like an hour ago. Six of 'em.'

The sergeant reached in his desk. 'These seem to have escaped the Destruction Order,' he said. 'They any good?'

Carter looked at them and whistled. 'Dead right,' he said. 'Unbelievable, but dead right!'

'Wipe the drool off your face! And I'll want 'em back.'

He watched Carter shuffle through them. 'It's all done by injecting,' he said. 'Handful of polystyrene, that's all you'd get. Do you know how you can tell? They float in the bath!'

Regan watched Jimmy McBray pinning the photographs in the hastily improvised frame by the door of what had been his restaurant, and was now, to all appearances, his strip club. 'Where in God's name did you get that collection?' he asked.

Jimmy looked sourly at him. 'Don't ask me,' he said. 'Ask your sergeant. I think they're out of his family album!'

Regan walked past him and down into the club. Everything, amazingly, was ready, and the long low room looked as if it had been designed and furnished for the express purpose of running a strip club. Carter himself was pinning a pelmet across the wire that carried the curtain. 'No idea of class, these people,' he said. 'They were just going to leave it hanging with the rings showing. Dead crude.'

'I didn't know you were an interior decorator. How about that girl of yours? Is she on?'

Carter looked sheepish. 'Bloody-well jumped at it, didn't she? And not for the bread. I think she's looking forward to being a peeler! There'll be no holding her after this. You've probably ruined my sex life . . .'

'Put it on your expenses . . .'

Jimmy had come back down the stairs. 'Eight o'clock, eh? How do you know anybody's going to turn up?'

'They'll turn up. Don't forget, there are fewer and fewer places they can go to get an eyeful.'

'And your lot will be here?'

'They'll be here.' He looked at his watch. 'You get that ad in the paper?'

'I got it in. They missed the City edition, but it's in the rest, just like you said. My name is dirt from now on. In all my years in the catering trade . . .'

'Your name is dirt already, Jimmy, so don't give me a lot of lip. I don't have to be talking to you, don't forget that. I could be bending Tommy Baxter's ear.'

A constable came down the steps, made a twisting motion with his hand, then held it to his ear. Universal sign. 'You're wanted on the telephone'.

Regan left the club, walked to the corner where his car was unobtrusively parked. Len, at the wheel, grinned sheepishly at him. 'I thought I told you to go home and stay there, with that foot of yours,' Regan said as he picked up the microphone.

Control came on the line. 'Man in Vine Street, Inspector, asking for you.'

'What's his name?'

'Milner. Our old friend, Willie the Flasher.'

'What's he doing in Vine Street?'

'What do you think? He was up to his old games. Picked a Norwegian tourist. She looks like an all-in wrestler. Grabbed him and held on until a policeman got there.'

The cell in Vine Street was about fifteen feet long, divided into two rooms, one of which held a sit-down lavatory. The walls were painted cream, the bed covered in black vinyl over horse-hair. There was one blanket which Willie had draped round his lap. His left eye was a sorry-looking mess.

'Who hit him?' Regan asked the sergeant who showed him into the cell.

'The Norwegian woman.'

'Has she made a statement to that effect?'

'Yes, she says he tried to escape.'

'Did you try to escape, Willie?'

'You must be joking, Mr Regan. Have you seen her?'

'But do you admit she hit you?'

'Yes.'

'And not a member of the police force?'

'No, they never touched me.'

'Have you been asked if you wish to prefer charges against this Norwegian lady?'

'She's no lady, Mr Regan. Anyway, I don't want to take it any further. I want to talk to you.'

'Right, Willie. I'm here. Talk to me.'

'On your tod . . .'

Regan gestured to the sergeant, who went out. 'I've got to lock the door, Inspector,' he said.

'I know, sergeant. I'll knock when I'm through.'

Regan sat down on the wooden bench at the foot of the bed. 'Right, Willie,' he said, 'what do you want to talk about? I heard you'd given up flashing. They said you'd sewed your flies up.'

Willie had tears in his eyes. 'I did, Mr Regan. I had given it up, honest. But then I got this new suit.'

'Looks like a good suit. Where did you get it? You never bought a suit like that.'

'Buy it? Me? It's worth at least sixty quid. I've never owned a sixty-quid suit in my life. I wish I'd never seen this bugger, either.'

'Where did you get it, Willie?'

'A friend bought it for me.'

Just because a man in the cells says he wants to talk to you, it doesn't mean he knows how to get it out when the time comes. Regan was used to having to lead people, letting a cough take its time. He was damned sure Willie wanted to cough something to him. And the only thing they might have in common was the bomb business.

'That friend,' Regan said. 'Wouldn't happen to be a Mister Keane, would it?'

Willie's face was wide open with surprise. 'How the devil did you know that, Mr Regan?'

'You'd be surprised what I know, Willie. I've got eyes in the back of my arsehole when I need 'em. And ears . . .'

Any interrogation is successful only if the man asking the questions already knows some of the answers. Regan thought he knew one or two answers. 'You've been working for this Mr Keane, haven't you, Willie? You met him inside, last time. He offered you a job when you came out. Another man who met him inside was Charles Prescott. Mr Prescott has given you a flat, hasn't he, Willie?'

'I'm paying him rent . . .'

'Of course you are, Willie. All nice and legal. But what are you paying the rent with? Money you're earning by working for Mr Keane.'

'Can't tell you nothing, can I?'

'Oh yes, Willie, that's where you're wrong. You can tell me everything.'

Regan saw the crafty look that flicked across Willie's face. Bloody lags. Dead stupid. Here it comes. A deal.

'What's it worth, Mr Regan? Eh? What's it worth?'

'Depends what it is, Willie, and what you expect to get for it. A load of old cobblers isn't worth very much, is it? The real info, well, that would be different. You're coming up in the morning on a charge of Indecent Exposure. They'll either do you under the Vagrancy Act of 1824, or the Town Police Clauses Act of 1847. With that Norwegian lady giving evidence, they'll find you guilty, no doubt about it. And then they'll open up your past record. That'll be nasty, Willie, won't it?'

Willie buried his face in his hands. 'I'll kill myself if they put me back inside, Mr Regan. I swear I'll kill myself.'

'Then you'd better start talking, Willie, hadn't you? Because I wouldn't give even money on your chances, otherwise.'

Willie looked up at Regan through his fingers. He was a sorry sight. 'If it hadn't been for this new suit,' he said. 'I was all right so long as I had my flies sewn up. I notice you aren't saying anything about what's in it for me.'

Regan laughed. 'Willie,' he said, 'you're wasting my time. You're in no position to make a deal with me. Tomorrow you're going up before the beak. I can hold that up for you. I can apply for a remand in custody while we 'complete our inquiries'. I can even make sure we don't object to an application for bail. We can drag the case out. I don't suppose this Norwegian bird is going to be here too long. By the time we're ready to come to court, she can be safely back in Norway. The case can be closed for lack of evidence. But, Willie, you're asking a lot, a helluva lot. And so far, I haven't had a dickie bird out of you, have I?'

'What if I tell you I was leaving briefcases in clubs?'

'I know you were, Willie. It had to be you. The only lad who could get in and out without suspicion.'

'You *know*? Bloody hell!'

'What I don't know, Willie, was what went on when you had those meetings. Charles Prescott was there, I know that. Arthur Keane was there, I know that. But I don't have all the dialogue. I know some of it. I know, for example, you went in to see Charles Prescott because you were worried about – what was it you said? – *the ones that went off.* Come on, Willie. As the Yanks say, piss or get off the pot. I have other fish to fry. Who gave you the briefcases?'

'Nobody give 'em to me, Mr Regan. They was left in the Left Luggage office in Euston Station.'

'Bollocks, Willie.'

'It's true, Mr Regan. I'd get a ticket in the post at the flat. Go to Euston, hand over the ticket, pay whatever was necessary, and bring the briefcase away with me.'

'You expect me to believe that?'

'It's true, Mr Regan. God's honest truth.'

'We can check it, you know. The man up there is bound to be able to recognise you if you went there that often.'

'Course he'll recognise me. That's why I say it's true.'

'What did you think was in the cases, Willie?'

'I was told it was slush money.'

'Who told you?'

'The letter. The first letter I got. It said, "Do you want to do a job? You'll get a flat and be paid. Go see Charles Prescott." I went along there, out of curiosity. He told me some geezer wanted to give me a helping hand, and was going to give me a job. I asked Mr Prescott what the job was, and he said he didn't know, but there's the keys of this flat in Rupert Court, one room, kitchen, and bath . . .'

'A pity you didn't use the bath more often, Willie.'

'I don't like taking a bath. That's how you get pneumonia. Anyway, I moved in, didn't I?'

'I don't know, Willie. You're the one telling the story. And so far, it sounds like a load of rubbish to me.'

'It's not rubbish, Mr Regan. Then Mr Prescott asks me to go along to his office to meet this man, Mr Keane, who says he's the one providing the flat and I'll get the job later on, if I keep my nose clean and stop flashing. I tried, Mr Regan, honest I tried. Well, the money kept coming, regular as clockwork, every Friday in a registered envelope. A twenty-quid note. And then one day, I got a note saying, "Take this ticket to Euston, get out the briefcase, and take it to Milly's Club in Dean Street. Leave it under a chair. And leave." I did what I was told.'

'Who did you think sent that note?'

'I guessed it was Mr Keane, though there was nothing to show who sent it. There was a fiver in with it. Registered.'

'Did you keep any of these registered envelopes, Willie? They have the name and the address of the sender written on the back.'

'Yes, and that was kinda funny. That was written in as L of D, 274 Gerrard Street, London W1. And you know something else, Mr Regan . . .?'

'You looked, and there is no 274 Gerrard Street. Right?'

'Can't tell you nothing, can I? One thing I can tell you, though. One thing you don't know.'

'All right, Willie. I'm too old, too tired, too busy for guessing games.'

'Bombs in strip clubs that went off. The one under the bookie's. The one in the lavvie. I never planted them. None of the briefcases I ever planted went off . . . I didn't know they was bombs until I read it in the *Mirror*!'

Regan remembered what Major Rhodes had told him. Two bombs with a structure different from all the others. The two that went off. What Willie said could be true. None of the ones he'd planted had gone off. Were never meant to go off. 'Tell you what I'll do with you, Willie. You give me a list of every briefcase you planted, with the date you planted it, and I'll see you're remanded in custody for a month while we make "further inquiries". Is it a deal? And, if the information checks out, if what you've been telling me is the truth, you never know, somebody just might forget to take a written statement out of that Norwegian lady before she goes home. But I warn you, if you breathe a word of this outside this cell, I'll have your knackers, Willie, and feed 'em to the police dogs, on toast.'

'Oh, my God, Mr Regan. It's true, s'help me God, it's true.'

'Check the Post Office,' Regan said to Sergeant Millbrough. 'They keep lists of registered letters. I want a trace on all the ones sent to Willie's address, and a description of the man handing them in at the counter, wherever that may have been. And another team to Euston Station. Somebody has been handing briefcases to the Left Luggage office. I want a description.'

'What do you want done about Arthur Keane?'

'What can we do? An old lag, helping another old lag, giving him a flat and twenty quid a week, with a promise of a job some time in the future. If we connect Arthur Keane to the briefcases, I'll eat the charge book.'

'Where will you be?'

'I'm going to watch a strip show at Jimmy McBray's. I'd better be there early. I have a feeling it may not last for long.'

A black Bentley was parked outside the viewing-theatre Incidents Room when Regan came out. A heavy-built man with a hatchet face contrived, neatly, to block Regan's path. 'Would you care to get in the car, Inspector?' the man said, flashing a wallet.

Regan climbed in the back, the man went into the front next to the driver, and the car pulled away. Straight up the street, across Oxford Street, round to Berners Street. 'In the lounge, Inspector,' the man said.

Sir Ralph Wilson, the Police Commissioner, was sitting in a corner, wearing plain clothes. 'It's quiet in here, Inspector,' he said. 'We can talk. What will you have to drink.'

'A Scotch, sir.'

The waiter, obviously alerted, had been hovering. 'Two Scotches, and make them large ones.'

Regan looked around. Quiet atmosphere. Tourists of the richer kind. Businessmen and their clients. Berners Street forms one edge of the rag-trade district. Everyone up there is too busy making money to bother the police. It's a noisy bustling neighbourhood without much crime, unless you count the prices charged for some of the modern glad-rags. Sir Ralph watched Regan look around. 'There aren't many places I can still have a quiet drink,' he said. 'This is one of them. I hope you will respect that as a confidence.'

'I'm one of the original three monkeys,' Regan said.

'I hear you're thinking of going into the strip-club business; the original three monkeys were noted for wisdom.'

'And you don't think opening a new strip club is very wise?'

'If anyone else but you were doing it, I'd say it was downright foolish, but I imagine you have a reason. If you'd care to tell me, I'd like to hear that reason. I promised no interference and that still goes, but I might have to field some very pertinent and embarrassing questions if anything goes wrong. It would help me to know the motive, so that I can start rehearsing my ad-libs.'

'Strip clubs are closing down. I just thought it might be a good idea to swim against the stream and open one up and see what happens. I was in a position to influence a man who owns a licensed premises . . .'

The Commissioner interrupted, laughing.

'You mean, you knew you could put the arm on Jimmy McBray. What did you have on him, or shouldn't I ask? On second thoughts, don't tell me. I'm sure I ought not to know. Obviously, you're opening that club tonight because you expect something to happen?'

'Yes, I expect one of two things. Either somebody will plant a bomb, or a gang of heavies will move in. If it's a bomb, we'll try to follow whoever plants it. If it's the heavy mob, we'll thump 'em, arrest 'em, and one of them will sing his head off.'

'Either way, it seems to me that Jimmy McBray isn't going to come out of this too well. He either has his club destroyed by a bomb, or a gang of vandals.'

'I wouldn't recommend wasting a lot of time and thought on Jimmy McBray, sir. He's a villain even to the villains. One morning they'll be picking Jimmy out of the water at Wapping. And, incidentally, saving us the expense of taking him to trial.'

'You're a hard man, Regan. Don't worry. I like hard men on the Force. We have too few of them. But just remember one thing, will you? Even the hardest of us has to bend sometimes, has to learn how to give a little. Just let me give you one word of warning. If this caper of yours tonight goes badly wrong, and by that I mean innocent people killed or injured in a situation that was basically arranged by you, a lot of people will be after your blood. And mine. At least, I can now say I knew about it in advance. I can say you consulted me. The can is lighter, they say, if you have two people to carry it! One more thing. We've caught the chap giving out information. Nasty bit of work. I've had my eye on him for a long time. He was with the Obscene Publications Squad. They didn't find enough to can him, so he was shuffled out of the way into Communications to wait out his retirement.'

'What was he doing?'

'Telephoning an Essex number with information about police activities. That will be enough to can him this time. He thought he was being smart by using a coin box in the building. We recorded him, played the tapes to him.'

'I wish that hadn't been done, sir! Now he knows we know.'

'I'm afraid he does.'

'I hope he's either in custody or being watched day and night.'

'To see if he leads us anywhere . . .?'

'No, sir. To save his bloody life. There's no way we can charge a dead man!'

Regan was still cursing when he arrived at the strip club Jimmy McBray was opening against his will. The downstairs room was already packed out, though the 'show' was not due to start for ten minutes. Carter was serving behind the bar.

'Trust you to get the key spot,' Regan said. 'But keep your hands off the bottles, except for customers. And that doesn't count any of our lads.'

'How about you, guvnor?'

'Rank has got to have some bloody privileges. A large Scotch.' Regan ran his eye round the room identifying faces, types. All Sally's regulars were there, including the one who'd led Regan into the wet concrete. He turned round, saw Regan, started guiltily. Then, with a look of defiance, he sat and looked to the front.

Jimmy McBray came and stood beside Regan. 'One thing I've got to say for you,' he admitted grudgingly, 'you know a good prospect. If it keeps like this, I might not even bother with it as a restaurant.'

Nothing like the chink of money in a till to keep Jimmy McBray happy. 'Don't build any dreams on it, Jimmy,' Regan said. 'You've heard of "here today, gone tomorrow"? In your case it might turn out to be, "here today, gone tonight".'

Jimmy blanched. 'They seem such a nice orderly crowd.'

'They all do, until the aggro starts. See that lad in the front row? We call him Bermondsey Bill. Picked up a seventeen-stone copper once, and threw him through a plate-glass window. He did two years for that. I didn't know he was out again. Lad behind him comes from Clapham. I didn't know he worked this far north. He specialised at one time in opening safes. Know what he used to do? Carry them, on his back, up three flights of stairs, then drop them out of a window. They taught him weight-lifting in a Youth Club; nothing like learning a useful trade, I always say. I hope you managed to get yourself insured?'

'With all these bombings about? Nobody would touch it. I've got my own insurance.'

'If it's a shotgun, Jimmy, forget it. You fire a shotgun in here and I personally will wrap it round your balls. Both barrels.'

'A shotgun? Where would I get a shotgun licence? No, it's a little idea of my own. And don't lean on me, Jack Regan, because I'm going to keep it to myself unless I need to use it.'

Sally Evans came down the steps carrying her blue denim zipper bag.

'You all ready?' Regan asked.

'I'm a bit reluctant. It seems funny, now, with you here.'

'I've seen you do it, I've seen you peel 'em off.'

'Yes, but that was before . . .'

'I can't see that makes a difference.'

'Can't you? When I do it tonight, knowing you're watching, I'll be remembering, and knowing you'll be remembering, knowing you're looking at me and thinking about me in a certain way. It'll make me nervous.'

'God knows what it'll do to me! I might have to strap it down!'

'That's exactly what I mean.'

He looked at her; she really was naïve. No, that was the wrong word, he told himself. She was innocent. She hadn't realised that Regan wasn't the only man in the room who'd have to strap it down! And, though she might think, might believe, that because she was trying to give an artistic performance, she would be judged that way, there wasn't a single man in that room who wouldn't be thinking sexually about her while she danced, who wouldn't be having the dreams that for Regan had become a reality. 'Look, love,' he said, 'just this once. And then no more. I promise you.'

She caught something new in the tone of his voice. Though she hadn't known him for a long time, she'd realised that Jack Regan was a hard man, a man who despised sentimentality, was afraid of loving and of affection. And somehow, she realised, she'd got through to him in a new way that thrilled and excited her. She squeezed his hand. 'Okay, copper,' she said. 'For you. But it would help me if you were somewhere I couldn't see you.'

He stood part concealed behind a curtain, cigarette in his mouth, just another mick watching the show. Jimmy McBray put a cassette in the tape recorder that fed the four loudspeakers and switched it to 'play'. The music boomed out. There was no announcement. The curtains parted and there she was. Her 'regulars' applauded. The men in the back row whistled coarsely. The coppers in the audience, all Flying Squad, were silent, but appreciative. One of them bent and whispered to his mate. 'They say Regan's knocking her off . . .'

'Nice work if you can get it . . .'

'Perks of an Inspector . . .'

'Roll on promotion.'

A chorus of 'shssh!' silenced them. Sally went into her routine.

Regan watched her through the mirror behind the bar. Was it his imagination or were her movements more restrained, less abandoned? Was she holding something back, something special for him alone? He shrugged the thought away, but it didn't go easy. The last thing he wanted, he stubbornly told himself, was an involvement with a bird. Though, if it did come, he'd like it to be with somebody like Sally Evans.

Work to be done. No briefcases. That had been checked at the doorway by Mick, the bouncer Jimmy McBray had hired. With a copper watching discreetly. Pocket check, too, looking for bulk, and concealed weapons. Not just guns. Hammers, big spanners, pick-axe handles down trouser-legs. They were all clean. The air was hot with all that generated feeling the dance was drawing from the punters. Carter was watching from behind the bar, his mouth open, his eyes almost popping out.

Anita came down the steps, looked round the room, located Carter, followed the direction of his eyes, and stood by the bar. Carter's eyes didn't move. She reached out, poked her finger into his mouth, turned his head. He came back to the land of the living with a jerk.

'Me next,' she said. 'I've been rehearsing in front of a mirror!'

'The mind boggles . . .'

'You wouldn't like to come into the changing-room? Get me in the mood?'

He gulped. 'I'm working.'

'A quickie?'

'The guvnor would kill me!'

'All right, you miserable sod. But don't be working afterwards. I'll be dead hungry, then!'

Carter needn't have worried. Anita never got the chance to dance, and all that rehearsal was wasted.

When Sally finished amidst tumultuous applause, the curtain closed, the music was switched off and the lights over the bar were switched on. 'Last orders, gentlemen, please,' Carter called out. It was something to say.

A big man in the second row turned to a big man in the third row. 'Who're you pushing?' he asked belligerently.

'Shut your face, you ponce,' the man in the third row said, and started to get up. A big man in the fourth row pulled the chair, that priceless chair that was the joy of Jimmy McBray's eyes, out from under him. As he sprawled, his booted foot lashed out and kicked the chair over in front of him. Suddenly, as if by spontaneous combustion, the whole room became an explosion of pounding boots and fists, curses and shouts. Jimmy's precious chairs were picked up, smashed against the floor, to provide the weapons. The men holding the chair legs started swinging, smashing anybody within reach across the back, arms, legs, shoulders.

Regan rested his back against the wall.

Carter moved away from the bar with its vulnerable bottles and mirrors. 'Go on, lads, have a go,' he said.

Half the back of a chair came flying through the air, cleared a shelf of the bottles it carried, cracked the mirror from top to bottom. The next missile shattered the mirror into a thousand pieces.

'Aren't you going to do anything?' Jimmy yelled at Regan. 'They're breaking the place apart . . .'

'I know,' Regan said. 'Making a mess, aren't they?' He had to shout to make himself heard.

Jimmy reached into his trouser pocket, took out a canister the size of a large pepper pot and, before Regan could stop him, he yanked the green tab that ran along the side of it.

Nothing happened.

The lad from Bermondsey was standing in the centre of the room, the chair-leg in his hand swinging in a tidy arc. The light of battle shone from his eyes. 'Come on, you soft buggers,' he yelled. Two of the Sweeney lads jumped on his back and he swung them round like babies. Another kicked him with the side of his boot behind his knees.

The boy from Bermondsey dropped like a felled oak, his arms wildly waving branches that cleared everything in their descent. A boot came from nowhere, caught the side of his head. His eyes closed in blissful sleep, oblivious to the heavy bodies, the hob-nailed booted feet that trampled over him.

A man came staggering backwards out of the mêlée, his arms windmilling wildly. Regan put the sole of his Italian shoes into the small of the man's back, pushed, and sent the man back into the throng. Two men, fighting, staggered into the curtain which came down with a crash. Sally edged her way along the side of the wall opposite Regan. Carter and Anita were crouched between the door and the bottom of the bar. Anita's eyes were alight with pleasure as if she were in a ringside seat at the World Heavyweight championship where the contender was trying to last out the fifteen rounds.

One man came reeling out of the fight, hit the bar with his head, spun round with a silly grin on his face, and slid down until he was sitting on the floor next to Carter, who crossed his hands in his lap for him. The man opened one rapidly swelling eye. 'Thanks,' he said, then passed out.

Anita was holding her hands tightly clasped. 'Isn't it *super*?' she said to Carter.

'I've been in better. You don't think my nose was always shaped like this, do you?'

One of Sally's regulars was kneeling on the floor, his head a mass of blood; Regan dashed in, grabbed him by the trouser seat and the coat collar, picked him up like a sack of potatoes, and rushed him to the bottom of the stairs. The man went up them like a jack-rabbit coming out of a burrow. One by one, the 'regulars' were pulled from the mêlée like worms from a tin, and despatched outside. Then the heavies and the lads from the Sweeney settled down to a slugging match that left the inside of the room a total wreck. Jimmy was holding the canister from which he'd stripped the green tape. Nothing had happened. Finally, in disgust, he threw it away from him, and it went off in a cloud of thick, white, lung-rasping smoke. Regan and Carter belted up the stairs, coughing.

Jimmy followed them. 'Paid two quid for that tear-gas bomb,' he said bitterly, 'and the bloody thing didn't work!'

Two paddy-wagons blocked the street. As the lads came from the cellar, coughing their guts out, they were arm-locked and thrown inside the back of the wagons.

Regan counted twelve.

The ten Sweeney men who followed them out were coughing, and all were bloodied. One had a torn ear. Another held his arm at an odd angle. An ambulance was parked behind the paddy-wagons, with its back door open and a doctor standing waiting.

'Broken arm,' he said. 'Get inside. Take these pills. Bruised eye. It'll be all right in a day or two. Nasty cut that. Get inside and I'll stitch it.'

Everybody had something. 'I was getting married at the week-end,' one constable gasped, 'but there doesn't seem any point, now!'

'Get her to rub some cream into them. You'll do all right!'

Anita and Sally stood together against the wall, coughing, tears running down their faces. Luckily, neither wore make-up. Their eyes were as bloodshot as a meths drinker's. Sally was gulping air into her lungs. Regan came over. 'You all right, love?'

'You devil! We could have been poisoned.'

'I didn't know about the tear gas. That bugger Jimmy McBray trying a bit of private enterprise.'

The boy from Bermondsey had been the last out. Regan walked across to him. 'Enjoy yourself?' he said, quietly.

'Smashing evening, Mr Regan. They told me Soho had died the death. I'll have to come up west more often if this is the kind of show you put on.'

'Just out for an evening's entertainment, eh? Just you and the lads?'

'The lads? This lot of pooves? I never saw 'em before in my life. Night out on my own, wivout the missis, know what I mean? Change is as good as a rest. Where they taking us, Vine Street? Used to be a good nick, that one. Nice and clean. What do they do for breakfast these days? Used to be toast, sausage and beans. Cup of tea. Very *nice*. Better than that bloody Rowton House used to be. It'll be good to see the lads in Vine Street again. What's on the sheet? Disorderly conduct? Good job your lads wasn't in uniform or you could have charged me with all sorts of things, couldn't you? No, I'll go down quiet for disorderly, know what I mean? Plead guilty, pay my three quid, fiver in the Widders and Orphans . . .'

'You trying to bribe me?'

'Bribe you, Mr Regan? You're not a widder and orphan, are you?' He turned round to climb into the paddy-wagon, then turned back. 'By the way, met an old pal of yours the other day, Mr Regan. Told me to give you his regards next time I saw you . . .'

'And his name was . . .'

'Arthur Keane! Nice man, when you get to know him! A gent!'

The Commissioner came down to the Incidents Room in the viewing theatre. 'They wrecked your strip club,' he said.

'I guessed they would.'

'So what's next? Or was that the last act of some little private drama your suspect, Arthur Keane, has been scripting?'

'With me cast in the lead . . .? No, I don't think so. I think we're supposed to think it was the last act. But I think it's the last scene of the first act. Arthur Keane was just showing us he doesn't give a toss for the Met, the Porn Squad, the Sweeney. Now the real action starts!'

'And what do you think the real action might be?'

'My guess is a gambling club. I've been giving it a lot of thought. Arthur Keane is up to something here in the West End. He wants us to get our knickers in a twist, worrying about him and his League of Decency, his take-over of the strip joints, his bombs, none of which have gone off.'

'I read your report about the two that did explode, and the confession you got from that chap Willie.'

'There's always somebody waiting to jump on any band-wagon . . . Where's the largest concentration of money in the West End, now that the Arabs have hit town? The gambling clubs, on a Friday and Saturday night. The Stardust Club in Shaftesbury Avenue, the Las Vegas in Old Compton Street. It's the old conjuror's trick. Watch my left hand while my right hand goes in my pocket. We're so busy looking at the strip clubs . . .'

'They have good security in there . . .'

'Arthur Keane was inside, right? He had a "family" inside, like everybody does, except the perves and the child molesters. Charles Prescott was in that "family". So was Willie Milner. Four other lads were in that "family". The boy from Bermondsey, who went inside tonight and won't be out again for a bloody – sorry, a damned long time, if I have my way. A first-timer called Harris, works as a technician in a film processing lab in Wardour Street, done for GBH on his girlfriend's boyfriend, and two lads, McBride and Lavery, *both croupiers*. Started in Manchester before the Gaming Board days, transferred to London. McBride was a pit-boss, and worked out a fiddle with Lavery and a punter, name and present whereabouts unknown, who disappeared with the money. Dead simple. The punter cashed a hundred at the table. Given chips with a table mark on 'em value *one* pound, marked on the board as being value *five* pounds. The punter played a few, make it look real, cashed the rest in for five times what he paid for them. We've run a check on all these lads. Bermondsey was idling and turned up here tonight. Harris is working in the lab again, living the quiet life with another bird in Fulham. Lavery and McBride have gone to ground. My guess is, they've planned a caper, with Arthur Keane, on the last place they worked, the Stardust Club in Shaftesbury Avenue. There's a strip club, right next door, in the basement. One of the few that hasn't closed down. And, do you know who manages the property? Charles Prescott.'

'So you want to pull your lads, such of them as are fit for duty after tonight's punch-up, out of the strip clubs and into the casino, where they can walk about with a bundle of taxpayers' money in their hands?'

Regan laughed. 'That'd be nice, wouldn't it? And me signing the vouchers? I'd get writer's cramp – the DCI would have a baby – God knows what would happen to my superintendent! That's not my idea at all. If, as you say, sir, the casinos have good security, let them work for once in a while. Let them earn some of that money the Arabs are pouring down the drain. The super will kill me – last time we met in a casino he had a very nice tickle, very nice indeed!'

One of Those Days

BY WILLIAM BLINN

Set against the background of some of the roughest areas in Los Angeles and crowded with petty criminals, drug-pushers, pimps and prostitutes, the adventures of the two plain clothes mid-seventies cops, Starsky and Hutch, were perhaps most memorable for the young stars' casual dress style and their high-speed chases and gun battles in their highly tuned, red and white 1974 Ford Torino. They were very much crimebusters of their times and in the best television tradition had graduated into a series after the transmission of a very successful ABC pilot show of the same title in the spring of 1975. In it Starsky (whose full name was Detective David Starsky) and Hutch (aka Detective Ken Hutchinson) had been the subject of what was to prove the first of several murder threats and set out to find why. Once the series had begun, the close relationship between the two detectives became the core of the action, as they looked out for each other whenever things got tough and they seemed to carry out a seemingly endless number of last-minute rescues. The pair even spent time together when off duty, relentlessly pursuing a succession of leggy, usually blonde and sun-tanned Californian girls.

David Soul, who played Hutch, had been a singer before turning to acting and was later able to cash in on his television fame to make five very successful pop records. Paul Michael Glaser, as the street-wise Starsky, had worked in the theatre and a few films before getting his big break in the series. Both actors chose their own clothes – Hutch preferring check shirts, Starsky T-shirts – which were soon being imitated by young fans all over the world. The style infuriated some police chiefs in America and Britain who wanted to keep their undercover lawmen in suits and ties – but they were fighting a losing battle as is now very evident in contemporary crime series. Another feature of the show was the supporting performances of Bernie Hamilton as the young partner's boss, Captain Harold Dobey, forever trying to keep them under control; and Antonio Fargas as their jive-talking contact with the underworld, Huggy Bear. Starsky and Hutch *lasted for eighty-eight hour-long episodes and was finally concluded in a heart-tugging episode on 4 December 1981 when, after a gun-battle in which Starsky was shot, he died in hospital with his faithful partner at the bedside. Curiously, although David Soul has continued to appear on television and in films, Paul Michael Glaser has disappeared completely from show business: leaving the kind of mystery the two men would love to have investigated.*

William Blinn (1938–), the creator of the series, was a veteran Hollywood television producer, who worked for a number of years for Aaron Spelling, the mastermind behind several other equally successful TV shows including Burke's Law, Charlie's Angels *and* Dynasty. *Blinn wrote by far the largest number of scripts for the series, which is also remembered for its powerful theme tune by the talented Lalo Schifrin.* One of Those Days *is based on an episode from the first season of* Starsky and Hutch *in which the two friends are investigating the murders of several young people and find the threads of evidence leading them inexorably to someone who also works on the side of the law . . .*

A S STARSKY PULLED on to the Hall of Justice parking lot, he said, 'You know police headquarters used to be here, along with the courtrooms, and the morgue, and all the other stuff still here, before they built Parker Center?'

'Yeah, I know,' Hutch said. 'Must have been crowded.'

Starsky managed to find a parking place. They walked over to a side entrance and took the stairway to the basement. Spotting a drinking fountain, Starsky stopped, bent over it, and pressed the foot lever. It was one of those refrigerated fountains shaped like a large box standing on end. No water came out of the drinking spout, but Starsky felt it gush over his shoes.

Backing away, Starsky looked at the puddle on the floor. Hutch, not seeing what had happened and thinking Starsky had wanted only a sip, bent over the fountain.

Stepping back an instant later, he looked at the now wider puddle on the floor, then glared at Starsky. 'Thanks for the warning, buddy,' he said.

Starsky grinned innocently. 'I thought you wanted your feet washed.'

A man in coveralls came along at that moment and pasted a sticker on the front of the fountain reading OUT OF ORDER.

'Perfect timing,' Starsky said. 'I told you this morning I had a hunch it was going to be one of those days.'

They moved on to the morgue, identified themselves, and were allowed into the storage room. The attendant in charge was a wizened little man in his early sixties who resembled a gnome.

After showing their IDs, Starsky said, 'Couple of kids came in night before last. Killed by shotgun blasts while parked in a red and white Torino on a beach north of Santa Monica.' He turned to Hutch. 'I don't even know those kids' names. Shows how much attention any cops paid to them.'

'Stanley Cather and Patricia Talbot,' the attendant said. 'Names are fresh in my mind because they just came back.'

'Back?' Hutch said, staring at him. 'From where?'

'The PM. Post mortem.' He looked down at their shoes. 'Is it raining outside? Both of you got wet shoes.'

'No, it's not raining,' Hutch said.

'Ought to be careful, walking around with wet shoes. Catch your death of cold. Which you want to see first?'

'The boy, I guess,' Starsky said in a reluctant tone suggesting he'd really prefer to see neither.

Going over to a chart on the wall consisting of brass-edged slots into which removable cards were shoved, the attendant studied it. 'Fifteen and sixteen,' he said.

One entire wall contained metal drawers whose fronts were about two feet square. Going over to the one numbered 15, the little man slid it out.

Without much enthusiasm Starsky and Hutch looked into the drawer. The naked body of a young man was in it, unrecognisable from the chest up.

After quick glances, both detectives looked away. 'How'd they identify him?' Hutch asked.

'Fingerprints. He had a record.'

Starsky gestured for the attendant to slide the drawer back in. The man did, and slid out the one next to it. It contained the nude body of a young woman with a strawberry birthmark just below her navel. The upper part of her body was as mutilated as the young man's.

The attendant said, 'Trim little figure she had. Wonder what her face looked like.'

Starsky gestured for him to close the drawer. He asked, 'Identification verified through fingerprints, too?'

Sliding the drawer closed, the little man shook his head. 'Driver's licence in her purse told who she was. Positive identification made by her roommate. By that birthmark on her tummy you may have noticed.' He bent to peer at the label on the front of drawer 16. 'Nineteen years old. Female Caucasian. Used to call 'em white.'

Hutch asked, 'PM turn up anything?'

The little man peered up at him. With a touch of sarcasm he said, 'She was killed by a shotgun blast at close range.'

Hutch was examining him glumly, seemingly on the verge of telling him to shove it, when the attendant added casually, 'She was about two months pregnant. No wedding ring or engagement ring, either.'

Neither had any comment to make to that. Starsky asked, 'Can we see the girl's personal effects?'

'Don't think so. Her roommate was out there at the front desk picking them up when you two came in. Probably gone by now.'

After a quick glance at one another, Starsky and Hutch raced for the door. The attendant called after them, 'Careful! That tile's slippery if you got wet shoes!'

As they burst out of the storage room, they spotted a short, dumpy girl of about twenty at the far end of the corridor, heading for the exit. In her arms she carried a large paper bag. She turned when she heard pounding footsteps behind her, and backed against the wall with a frightened look in her eyes.

Hutch unnecessarily called, 'Hold it, please, miss!'

When the two detectives came to a halt, rather hemming her in, she looked at them from wide, apprehensive eyes. Both detectives showed their IDs.

'Police officers, miss,' Starsky said. 'Are you Patricia Talbot's roommate?'

The girl looked a little less frightened, but still wary. 'Yes.'

Nodding toward the paper bag she was clutching, Hutch asked, 'Are those her personal effects?'

'Yes,' the girl admitted.

Starsky said, 'We'd like to take a look at them, please.'

'Well, I'm not sure,' the girl said uncertainly. 'I mean, I signed a receipt for them back there.'

Starsky asked, 'What's your name, miss?'

'Knebel. Gretchen Knebel.'

'Well, Miss Knebel, we never knew Patricia Talbot, but we know she was murdered, and we'd like to find out who did it. I think that makes us her friends, too.'

'A lot of cops say things like that,' Gretchen said warily.

Starsky said, 'A lot of cops say, "Oh, what a beautiful morning," too, but you ought to be able to tell the difference between the ones who really know the melody, and the ones who are just saying the words. Besides, we don't want to keep the stuff. We just want to look at it.'

Relenting, Gretchen said, 'Well, all right. But how come the police didn't hang on to Patty's stuff?'

Hutch's and Starsky's eyes met. 'Interesting point,' Hutch said thoughtfully. 'Why *didn't* the department order them held?'

They both knew the answer. Someone with official clout had to authorise their release.

But before either had a chance to comment, the dumpy girl said, 'Look, the reason I wanted all this junk was so that I could go through it before her folks did.'

'Why?' Hutch asked.

'Because you know parents. Suppose they found a joint in her purse? Or suppose they found she was taking the pill? They're going to have it bad enough without anything like that.'

Starsky lifted the paper bag from the girl's unresisting arms, set it on a bench next to the wall, and took a purse out of it. He began taking items from it and laying them on the bench.

Hutch said dryly, 'If she was taking a pill, it was aspirin. She was pregnant.'

'Patty was?' Gretchen said in a surprised voice. Then, after a reflective pause, 'She was always kind of careless.'

His attention on the items Starsky was taking from the purse, Hutch asked, 'Any idea who the father could be?'

The dumpy girl shrugged. 'Some guy. Over fourteen, under fifty. I'd narrow it down that much, I guess.'

Starsky finished emptying the purse, set it down, and poked in the bag again. The only thing else in it was the clothing the girl had been wearing, most of it stiff with dried blood. After briefly examining it, he shoved it back into the bag.

'I got a notion,' Hutch said to his partner.

Glancing around at him, Starsky said, 'Tell me.'

'We've just been assuming the department ran makes on both kids, because the morgue attendant mentioned that Cather was identified by fingerprints. Maybe they didn't.'

'On my way,' Starsky said, immediately heading for the desk, where there was a phone.

'Check out Zale and Canelli, too,' Hutch called after him.

'*Sí*.'

The girl on duty at the desk looked up from the magazine she was reading as Starsky stopped in front of her and lifted the phone on the desk.

'Dial 8 for an outside line,' she said.

Starsky gave her a pained smile. He dialled 8, then the number of Parker Center.

Meantime Hutch was examining the items from the dead girl's purse that Starsky had laid out on the bench. There were the usual things: a wallet with a few dollars in it, a driver's licence and various cards, a comb, a small mirror, a lace handkerchief, keys, a lipstick, and a miscellaneous assortment of other items, including a number of papers.

As he started going through the papers, Hutch asked, 'You close friends with Miss Talbot?'

i   'Not really,' Gretchen said. 'They just assigned us. We didn't take the same courses or anything. I'm a phys ed major. She was taking pre-law.'

At the other end of the hallway Starsky was saying into the phone, 'A priority one make on the following individuals: Patricia Talbot, deceased.'

Hutch slipped a personal letter he had just read back into its envelope and laid it aside. He started thumbing through a small notebook which seemed to contain lecture notes.

'You said pre-*law*, is that correct?' he asked Gretchen.

The girl nodded. 'Not that she was a big book drudge, though. Because lawyers are rich and she always wanted a rich husband.'

'She said that?' he inquired.

'Often.'

At the other end of the hall Starsky was continuing on the phone: 'And Zale. Z as in Zebra, A as in Adam, L as in Lincoln, E as in Edgar. Should have a long run on both him and Canelli. Probably be in the red file.'

Hutch was still studying the notebook. 'They ever have guest instructors out at the university?' he asked.

'Hardly ever in phys ed.'

'How about pre-law?'

'I don't know,' Gretchen said. 'I take phys ed.'

Hutch set down the notebook and opened a folded sheet of paper. The sheet was divided into four columns. In the first column were listed class subjects. The second listed the days and times the classes met. The third showed buildings and room numbers. The fourth listed the instructors.

'What's this here?' Hutch said, really meaning it as an exclamation rather than as a question, since he already knew the answer.

Peering at it, Gretchen said, 'Looks like a class schedule.'

Hutch ran his finger down the list of subjects until he came to *Principles of Western Law*. In the next column was listed *Mon., Wed., Fri. – 10 a.m.* In the third column was *Adams Hall, Rm 5*. The last column listed the instructor as *Mark Henderson*. The 'o' in Henderson had been doodled in the shape of a heart.

Starsky came running along the hall toward them. 'It's Henderson!' he called in a jubilant voice when he was only halfway to them.

Hutch and Gretchen both turned in surprise to look at Starsky bearing down on them at a near-gallop.

When Starsky came to a panting halt, Hutch said, 'Yeah, it's Henderson, but how did you know?'

Starsky took a moment to recover his breath before saying, 'Well, I don't know how he got to the girl – '

'I do,' Hutch interrupted. 'He teaches a class she was in at the university.'

Starsky looked interested. 'Okay, that answers that. Love happens. She blooms. Won't go away, won't get rid of the kid. He's got a marriage coming up. The girl's got to go.'

'Fill me in,' Hutch said.

'Zale and Canelli. He had them up on murder two. Tight rap. Charges were dropped on the recommendation of Assistant District Attorney Henderson.'

Hutch asked, 'What about the driver, the kid who stole the Torino?'

'He was on probation for dealing pot when he got busted on two counts of grand theft, auto. Should have drawn at least two years, but he was on probation at the equest of Assistant District Attorney Henderson.'

Hutch, now speaking with rapid enthusiasm, said, 'He has the kid steal a car identical to yours. Has him take the girl out to the beach, where he's got Canelli and Zale waiting.' Suddenly his enthusiasm abated a little and he frowned. 'How'd he talk the kid into suicide?'

Starsky made an impatient gesture. 'Gave him some kind of snow job. Doesn't matter how he sold him, but you can bank on it the kid wasn't expecting a shotgun blast. Canelli and Zale blow the two kids apart, and Henderson gets everyone in the department thinking I was the intended victim and you were next in line so that we couldn't testify at the Tallman trial.'

They looked at each other for a long time, mentally replaying the mixture of evidence and assumptions one more time. Finally Hutch said in a tone of satisfaction, 'I think it holds.'

With a touch of excitement Starsky said, 'I heard that sound, Hutch. The ball's in the air.'

Together they headed for the door, taking long strides. Gretchen Knebel, who all during the rapid-fire conversation had been swivelling her head back and forth like a spectator at a tennis match, gazed after them until they disappeared through the door. Then she began to pick the items up off the bench and return them to the purse.

As they climbed into the Torino outside in the parking lot, Starsky said, 'You having the same thought I am about our next move?'

'If you're thinking about Fat Rolly,' Hutch said.

'I am,' Starsky said grimly. He backed up, swung toward the parking lot exit and drove off the lot. 'Rolly has to be the one who spread the phoney story about there being a contract on us. Probably Henderson used him as a go-between for Canelli and Zale, too. He probably wouldn't risk being seen with them himself.'

'Think we can get the tub of lard to talk?' Hutch asked.

'If we can't, we'll render him down to soap.'

Fat Rolly's Bargain Circus was in a large, ramshackle one-story building in the centre of the district. In the front part of the building was a secondhand store offering every type of used goods imaginable, from furniture to clothing. Behind it was a second store which the general public never saw. To get in you either had to be a preferred customer or bring an introduction from someone whose judgment Rolly trusted. The items in the rear store were also used, but they were as a rule newer, in top condition, and hot.

Starsky drove the Torino up the alley behind the Bargain Circus and on to the hard-packed dirt area behind the building. He parked next to a truck loading platform. The two detectives got out of the car and climbed the wooden steps at one end of the platform.

There was a sliding door through which larger pieces of merchandise could be passed in and out, closed and padlocked at the moment. Beyond it was an ordinary doorway with both a door and a screen door. As it was now midmorning, the sun was well up, and it was starting to get quite warm, but the screen door barred the way inside.

That is, the screen door was the only inanimate bar. There was also a large, bulky man with a pushed-in face, seated on a folding bridge chair, reading a comic book. The chair was tilted backward against the latch-side edge of the door, so that entry into the building was impossible unless he moved.

The man looked up from his comic book when the Torino pulled in and parked. His gaze fixed on the two detectives as they got out of the car, followed them as they climbed the steps and approached him, then deliberately returned to the comic book when they came to a halt before him.

'Hiya, Marty?' Hutch said genially. 'Open sesame and announce us to the merchant prince.'

Without looking up, Marty said, 'Get lost. Go on. Beat it, or I'll rip your chest off.'

Hutch and Starsky exchanged looks. 'How do you rip a chest off?' Starsky asked his partner curiously.

Shrugging, Hutch snaked out a toe, hooked it around one of the upraised front legs of the tilted chair, and jerked the chair out from under the bulky man. The chair skidded off the edge of the loading platform and tumbled to the ground below, and the comic book went flying. Marty landed with a thump on his buttocks.

'That's to get your attention,' Hutch said.

Springing to his feet with rather remarkable agility for such a large man, Marty whipped out a leather sap and swung it at Hutch. The blond man pulled back his head like a tortoise withdrawing into his shell, and the sap whistled harmlessly past his chin.

Hutch circled to place his back to the screen door as Marty bore in with the sap again raised. Starsky fingered the butt of his .38, but decided to let Hutch handle it.

As Marty swung the sap for a second time, Hutch ducked beneath it, slipped to one side, and grabbed the man's shirtfront with his left hand. He jerked him into a bent-over position, placed his right palm against his butt, and shoved. As Marty dived headfirst into the screen door, Hutch increased his momentum by giving him a tremendous kick in the rump.

Marty went inside, right through the screen door, leaving a large gap in it.

'That's to open the door,' Hutch said.

The hole in the door was large enough for the detectives to pass through, too, but only if they ducked down low. Hutch pulled it open to go in, and Starsky followed behind him.

Another large man, this one with a bulbous nose and elephant ears, was standing flat against the wall to the right of the door. As Hutch went by, he raised a baseball bat.

He kept it raised, frozen in position, when Starsky whipped out his gun and flicked off the safety. 'Bad, Leo,' Starsky said chidingly. 'That's bad.'

His gaze fixed on the gun, Leo slowly lowered the bat to his side and let it drop to the floor. Turning his back to Starsky, he put both hands behind him, familiar with the drill from long practice. Starsky pushed the safety back on, put the gun away, and snapped on cuffs.

As Marty climbed dazedly to his feet, Hutch picked up the dropped leather sap, walked over to within two feet of the bulky man, and began contemplatively slapping the sap lightly into his left palm. After gazing sourly at the rhythmic movement for a few seconds, Marty also turned his back and put his hands behind him. Tossing aside the sap, Hutch handcuffed him.

Both detectives then shook down their prisoners, but found no weapons other than the sap and baseball bat.

All this time Fat Rolly remained seated behind an old desk to one side of the room, his hands folded across his substantial belly and his expression resembling that of a disapproving schoolteacher watching horseplay among students. Today he wore a blue bandanna around his forehead, and his T-shirt bore the legend *Stud Service – By Appointment Only.*

Behind the desk, on both sides of it, and all around the walls were piled washing machines, dryers, TV sets, stereo outfits, bicycles, and assorted other items.

In a scathing tone the fence said, 'Marty, I like you because you're so fast on your feet. You too, Leo. You're an ace.'

Neither man said anything, merely gazed at the fat man sullenly.

There was a coffee machine against the wall directly opposite the desk. Going over to it, Starsky dropped in a dime. Over his shoulder he said, 'What's happening, Rolly?'

Rolly, a trifle pale, but trying to play it with nonchalance, leaned back in his swivel chair, swung his feet up on the desk, and crossed his ankles. 'Business ain't too good,' he said. 'But like it says in the papers, the Gross National Product should be up by year's end.'

Hutch said, 'You would know about anything gross, Rolly.'

Starsky was staring at the coffee machine in outrage. It had failed to drop a cup, and the coffee was squirting out into nothing and running down the drain.

Turning toward his partner, he said, 'You see that!'

The blond man said with sympathy, 'In a machine world, you have no mechanical touch, Starsk.'

Hutch seated himself on a corner of the desk. In a conversational tone he said, 'Did you know Manny Torro got scratched because of that story you spread around, Rolly? Gerry Tallman added two and two and got five. Poor Manny. And he hadn't done a damn thing.'

'I didn't hear nothing about that,' Rolly said warily. 'What story?'

The one about there being contract out on Starsky and me. You spread it too wide, Rolly. Tallman realised that if there really was a contract out on two cops, every two-bit punk on the street wouldn't know about it. So he rightly figured it was a planted story. Only he guessed wrong about who planted it. Since it was obvious to him he was being set up, he figured the only logical framer had to be the guy next in line to him. So good-bye, Manny.'

'That's too bad,' the fat man said. 'It's the risk those big-shot hoods take, though. Step out of line once, and it's curtains. I didn't spread that story. I just heard it, like everybody else.'

Starsky, still over by the coffee machine, said, 'Little shots like you take risks, too, Rolly, when you get involved with people like Zale and Canelli.'

Fat Rolly gave him a sharp look. 'Never heard of them.'

Hutch said, 'And run errands for a guy like Assistant District Attorney Mark Henderson.'

Rolly looked up at him with no change of expression, but a bead of perspiration suddenly ran down his cheek. 'Never heard of him either.'

Spinning around, Hutch kicked the fat man's feet off the desk, then swung to his own feet. Rolly's feet hit the floor with a jolt. He straightened in his chair and stared at the blond detective with a mixture of trepidation and indignation.

'Don't get physical,' he said.

'Yeah,' the bulbous-nosed Leo said. 'You guys got no right to push citizens around. That's police brutality.'

Starsky walked over to Leo and gazed up into the taller man's face. The man looked abashed, as though he wished he had kept his mouth shut. Starsky walked behind him, removed his cuffs, and put them away.

'Take a walk,' he said. 'Far.'

The man gave him an uncertain look, glanced at Fat Rolly, back at Starsky again, and decided he had better obey. He left rather hurriedly.

Hutch went over to Marty and uncuffed him. 'You walk with him. Just as far.'

Marty didn't even look at his employer. He just hurried after Leo.

'Why'd you do that?' Fat Rolly asked uneasily.

'Because we didn't want any witnesses,' Starsky told him.

Getting up from his chair, Fat Rolly sidled toward the curtained doorway leading into the legitimate secondhand store occupying the front of the building. Hutch took three long strides to block the way, and Starsky bore in on the fat man from the other side. Without touching him, merely moving toward him inexorably, the two detectives backed Rolly into a corner.

'You better not hit me,' Rolly said desperately, sweat now running down both cheeks. 'There's laws against that.'

'We're not going to hit you, Rolly,' Starsky said, giving him a malevolent smile. 'Why do you think we're going to hit you?'

Rolly's gaze jumped from one to the other. 'You're going to do something,' he said fearfully. 'Why you looking at me like that?'

'Yeah, we're going to do something to you,' Hutch agreed. 'But it isn't going to be physical. We're going to put you away in the joint for the rest of your goddamned life.'

'For what?' Rolly squealed. 'I ain't done nothing.'

'For accessory to murder one, Rolly,' Starsky told him. 'We've got you nailed to the wall.'

Jerking the blue bandanna from around his forehead in order to mop his drenched face, Rolly said on a high note, 'I got nothing to do with no murder. Whose murder?'

'Those two kids who were shotgun-blasted on the beach night before last,' Hutch said. 'Stanley Cather and Patricia Talbot. Twenty-two years old and nineteen years old, Rolly. Hardly even started out in life. Both good-looking kids, too. The jury's not gonna be happy with you, Rolly. There'll be no recommendation for leniency. You're going to get the book.'

'I had nothing to do with that,' the fat man said, terrified. 'You guys know I had nothing to do with that.'

'We can prove you were Henderson's go-between when he sicked Zale and Canelli on us,' Starsky shot at him. 'You think the jury's going to believe you weren't the go-between for the first job, too?'

'I had no part of that,' Rolly protested, frenziedly mopping his face again. 'I didn't even know about it. I mean, I heard it on the air next morning, and read about it in the newspaper, but I never knew it was going to happen. I never even heard of those kids until I turned on the radio next morning. You guys know I wouldn't get involved in no murder. The other thing was different. There was a guarantee nobody would really get —'

He came to a terrified halt, appalled at his slip. His eyes darted from Starsky to Hutch and back again, hoping without real hope that they hadn't caught it. Their uncompromising gazes bored into him.

Licking his lips, he whispered, 'Deal?'

The forbidding looks on the two detectives' faces instantly dissolved into bright, friendly smiles.

'Sure, Rolly,' Starsky said wholeheartedly. 'We don't really want to see you rot your life away in the joint. Just mean some other fence would open up in our district, and we'd have to break him in on what he could get away with, and what he'd get stepped on for. We kind of like the status quo. So we're going to get you off the hook entirely. We're not even going to bust you for all the hot merchandise in this place.'

This sudden affability frightened Rolly nearly as much as their previous forbidding manner. 'What do I have to do?' he asked warily.

Hutch said, 'Just set up Henderson and the shotgun twins for us.'

'Oh, my God!' Rolly said in abject terror. 'Zale and Canelli would kill me!'

Starsky gave his head a slow shake. 'Not where they're going, Rolly. If the jury would give you maximum for setting up those kids, how you suppose they're going to feel about the guys who actually pulled the triggers?'

Licking his lips again, Rolly's eyes moved back and forth from one to the other.

Hutch said, 'Course if you'd rather go into the joint with Zale and Canelli, that's all right, too. But don't count on your clamming up saving you from their revenge. Starsky and I are just mean enough to leak word into the prison grapevine that you snitched on them.'

Rolly's eyes grew enormous.

Starsky said, 'He's not going to cooperate, Hutch. Let's cut the gaff, take him in, and book him for accessory to murder one.'

Grabbing the fat man's shoulder, Starsky spun him around, jerked his arms behind his back, and clamped on the cuffs.

'I am too going to cooperate,' Rolly squealed.

Taking his shoulder, Hutch spun him around to face them again. 'I think you understand the charge, Rolly,' he said. 'You have the constitutional right to remain silent. If you do make a statement, it may be taken down and used against you in evidence. You are entitled to legal counsel at all stages of your arrest, arraignment, and trial procedure –.' At that point Hutch departed slightly from the standard warning to add, '– from the time we reach the booking desk in the Felony Section until they throw you in the slammer for life.' He concluded by reverting to the formula. 'If you are unable to afford a lawyer, one will be furnished you at public expense.'

'I said I'd cooperate,' Rolly said plaintively. 'Why are you guys doing this?'

As though they hadn't heard him, Starsky and Hutch each took one arm and marched him out the back door. They pushed him down the wooden steps and into the back seat of the Torino. Hutch got into the back seat with him, while Starsky slid under the steering wheel.

'Listen,' Rolly said. 'Will you guys listen to me?'

Starsky said, 'Hutch told you that you have the constitutional right to remain silent, so shut up.'

'But I want to talk,' Rolly insisted. 'I waive my right to remain silent. You're allowed to do that.'

Hutch said, 'You're too late, Rolly. You had your chance. We also have the constitutional right not to listen. So do like Starsky told you, and shut up.'

The fat man lapsed into miserable silence. They drove to Parker Center without further conversation.

As they pulled on to the lot, a shiny avocado-green Jaguar sports car nosed up out of the underground garage. Starsky said, 'Jiggers! There's Henderson!'

Hutch gripped the handcuffed man by the nape of the neck and hurled him face down on the floor of the back seat. As the Jaguar headed for the parking lot exit, one lane over, Henderson glanced over, spotted the Torino, smiled, and waved. Starsky and Hutch smiled and waved back.

Hutch lifted his foot from the middle of Rolly's back as they drove down the ramp into the garage. Pulling the fat man upright, he shoved him back into the seat. Rolly gaped at him without understanding.

Parking next to the dispatcher's cubicle and leaving the engine running, Starsky climbed from the car as Hutch hauled the prisoner from the back seat. 'Suspect for booking,' Starsky said. 'Park it where we can get at it fast, because we may have to leave in a hurry.'

'Sure,' the dispatcher said. 'There's an empty slot right by the exit ramp.'

They hustled the prisoner over to the elevator. En route Starsky glanced at his watch. 'Only a quarter to twelve. Henderson breaks for lunch early.'

'Maybe he'll come back early, then,' Hutch said hopefully.

'Dreamer,' Starsky said.

When they got on the elevator, Starsky punched the button for the third floor. Fat Rolly said, 'Felony Section's on first.'

'We're going to feed you lunch before we book you,' Hutch informed him. 'We have to eat, too, and we want your scintillating companionship.'

'Cafeteria's on eight,' Rolly said suspiciously.

'Our squad room's on three,' Starsky explained. 'We wash our hands before we go to lunch. You're going to wash both your hands and your face. You look like hell.'

When they reached the squad room, Captain Dobey stuck his head out of his office door just as Starsky was unlocking Fat Rolly's cuffs. He examined the inscription on the suspect's T-shirt curiously.

'What you got?' he asked.

'Just a luncheon guest, Captain,' Starsky said. 'We'll explain later.'

The captain said, 'Cafeteria food's not all that bad that you have to drag guests in handcuffed.'

'This is a special guest,' Starsky told him. 'After lunch he's going in the slammer.'

Captain Dobey gave the prisoner another quizzical look, shrugged, and went back into his office.

Lifting a phone from one of the long tables in the squad room, Starsky dialled three numbers. After two rings a feminine voice said, 'Traffic Bureau, Ruskin speaking.'

'Starsky, Anne,' Starsky said. 'Do me a favour?'

'Sure, love. Virtually anything.'

'Mark Henderson's office is right across the hall from you. He's out to lunch. Will you sort of keep watch and ring me at the squad room when he logs back in?'

'If it's before one, love. That's when I go to lunch myself.'

'He ought to be back by then, sweets. Thanks.'

Hanging up, he said to Fat Rolly, 'Okay, lard, we'll show you the washroom, so you can make yourself presentable.'

They were back down from the eighth-floor cafeteria by twelve-thirty. The three of them sat at one of the long tables, Starsky and Hutch idly conversing and ignoring Fat Rolly, until a phone call came for Starsky from the girl in the Traffic Bureau shortly after one o'clock.

'Henderson just walked into his office,' she said. 'I skipped five minutes of my lunch hour waiting for him, just as a special favour to you. Any reward?'

'You win my body,' Starsky told her. 'You can collect tonight.' Then he remembered he had a date with Cindy. 'No, tomorrow night. I forgot.'

'Forgot what?'

'Night duty.'

'Night duty, rats, you rat,' she said. 'You've got another date. Phone me in the morning and I'll let you know if I'm available tomorrow night.'

She hung up.

Starsky stood up. 'Okay, Rolly, let's get it over with.'

The two officers led him from the squad room to the elevator, not bothering to handcuff him again. When they got on, Hutch punched the first-floor button.

'You guys really going through with this?' Rolly asked. 'Even after I said I'd cooperate?'

Neither detective gave him any answer.

Downstairs at the jail, instead of leading the suspect directly to the Felony Section, they steered him over to the bank of phones on the shelf against the wall. Stopping in front of a free one, the eyes of both detectives bored into Rolly's.

'One last chance, Rolly,' Hutch said.

'Sure,' Rolly said eagerly. 'I been telling you all along I'll cooperate.'

Hutch said, 'Phone Henderson. Tell him Zale and Canelli want to see him right now. They're threatening to blow the whistle if he isn't there within the next hour.'

Fat Rolly licked his lips. 'What if he asks questions?'

'All you know is what you told him. Zale and Canelli didn't give you any explanation, and you're too afraid of them to ask what it was about. He'll buy that.'

Rolly nodded. 'It's the living truth. What if he asks why I'm phoning from the jail?'

'You don't tell him you're phoning from the jail, asshole,' Starsky said. 'If he asks, you're phoning from your place.'

Nodding, Fat Rolly picked up the phone and dialled three numbers. Starsky and Hutch bent their heads on either side of him to listen.

Henderson's voice answered on the other end, 'District Attorney's Liaison Office. Henderson.'

Fat Rolly relayed the message he had been instructed to give.

When he finished, Henderson said in a shaky voice, 'What's the matter with them? What do they want?'

'All they told me was that, sir,' Rolly said. 'You'll have to find out from them.'

'All right,' Henderson said tightly. 'Where are you calling from?'

'The Bargain Circus.'

'Okay. Thanks for calling.' Henderson hung up.

Fat Rolly hung up, too. Starsky and Hutch hustled him over to the Misdemeanor desk.

Hutch said to the booking sergeant, 'Stick this suspect in the can on suspicion of possession of stolen property. We'll make out the papers later, because we haven't time now.'

'You guys said I'd be off the hook,' the fat man protested. 'I cooperated.'

'Beautifully,' Starsky agreed. 'But if you think you're going to be running around loose to make phone calls before we wrap this up, you must be nuts.' He turned to the booking sergeant. 'No phone calls. He just had his one call.'

He and Hutch hurried to the elevator to take it down to the garage.

The Christmas Killer

BY DENNIS SPOONER

Explosive action, violence and murder were staple ingredients of The Professionals *which was launched by LWT on 30 December 1977. It was all about an elite squad of crimebusters known as CI5 (Criminal Intelligence 5) and made cult heroes of its two young stars, Lewis Collins playing William Bodie and Martin Shaw as Ray Doyle. Heroes with the viewing public that is, for although the show was to run successfully for six years and a total of fifty-seven one-hour episodes, both men became disillusioned with their roles as tough guys as well as the repeated attacks on the programme by newspapers and certain sections of society because of what they saw as its violence and bloodshed. Even the calming influence of Gordon Jackson as the boss of CI5, George Cowley (who was still familiar in many people's minds for his role as the punctilious butler, Hudson, in the long-running series* Upstairs, Downstairs *about life in a London house in the early years of the century which had only finished its run in 1975), could not assuage all the complaints. The task of the two 'professionals' was to combat terrorism, to catch assassins and generally carry out missions that were considered to be too dangerous for the ordinary police forces. In order to fulfil these orders, Bodie and Doyle were rarely out of someone's gunsight or more than a few yards away from an exploding bomb. But such was their popularity that young men everywhere imitated Martin Shaw's shock of permed curls (while girls collected pin-up photographs of him) or else took to wearing Lewis Collins' specially styled leather jackets.*

The Professionals *was created by Brian Clemens and Albert Fennell who had earlier worked together on* The Avengers. *Initially, the collaborators had two other actors in mind for the starring roles,*

Anthony Andrews and Jon Finch, but both turned the opportunity down. Clemens and Fennell then remembered a pair of actors who had worked together well in an episode of The Avengers *– Collins and Shaw – and offered them the parts instead. Though both later claimed the series actually hindered their careers, they are still working and Martin Shaw is, of course, now the star of the prestigious police series,* The Chief. *A team of script-writers contributed to* The Professionals, *perhaps most notably Dennis Spooner (1932–), another veteran of TV series work, whose previous credits had included* The Avengers, Department S, Randall and Hopkirk (Deceased) *and* The Champions. *At the height of the show's popularity – and appropriately for Christmas publication – Spooner wrote the following short story about Bodie and Doyle for the* Daily Mirror *of 24 December 1981. It is appearing here in book form for the first time.*

B ODIE AND DOYLE stood outside Harrods in Knightsbridge. Christmas was really in the air.

The windows were packed with decorations and lights shone out into the growing gloom of the afternoon.

It looked like it was going to snow again. Nice for the kids, but the adults – their clouded breath billowing on the cold air – had only one thing in mind, to complete their shopping and get back home.

Bodie and Doyle stood for a while before going into the store, their eyes examining the faces around them.

Although they had the photograph of Ramos etched into their brains they did not pretend to understand why.

What would a top international assassin like Ramos be doing at Harrods? His Christmas shopping?

Yet Cowley had been quite specific.

'We know he's in the country, and we've got a pretty good idea why,' Cowley had said. 'The biggest manhunt ever staged is going on, and every available C15 agent is on the case as of now!'

Then Cowley had taken them aside and given them their assignment, Harrods.

It didn't make sense to either Bodie or Doyle. But 'The Cow' hadn't said anything else, and when he didn't say – you didn't ask!

Ramos lay on the bed in the Knightsbridge apartment that had been found for him.

It was getting dark outside and as he stared at the window he realised it somehow made him feel safer.

He had got into the country easily enough, but he was pretty sure they knew he was here. It would make no difference to his plans.

He could hear sounds of a party from somewhere below. Probably some firm giving out Christmas drinks to the staff, celebrating early.

Ramos smiled to himself. He'd have something to celebrate soon, £50,000.

He looked again at the photograph of the man he had to kill. It was an impersonal look. Just another contract.

Ramos sighed and wished the phone would ring from his tip-off. Not that he was anxious, but he wanted to get the job over — he couldn't stand this English weather, coming as he did from a hot climate.

He turned the photograph over. The man's name was on the back, James Fielding.

The C15 men patrolling the 'safe' house in the inconspicuous back street had no idea that James Fielding was inside. It was, so far as they were concerned, just another guard duty.

Fielding was going over some documents. He lost concentration and glanced at his watch. He wondered when Cowley would phone. Soon, he hoped.

He would be glad when the investigation was over. Cooped up and watched, it was like being in prison himself.

He wished he hadn't got the information on the terrorist organisation, but it was too late for wishing. The group would try to kill him, he knew that, but maybe, after his debriefing with the judicial committee, he could disappear, go back to Canada with his daughter Deborah.

Since his wife died Debbie was all he had. Luckily, at eight years of age, she had no idea of what was going on.

Matheson, his assistant, opened the door and came in with the flies he had asked for. He caught a glimpse of Debbie in the next room playing with her dolls.

Doyle wandered around the packed department store, mingling with the shoppers, pushing his way through the crowds, all the time keeping a watchful eye.

Could Ramos possibly be coming here? Maybe Cowley was just giving him a soft touch. It's unlike him, Doyle thought, even though he wasn't one hundred per cent fit. His side still hurt from that oil rig business.

He thought of the hours he had spent in his skinsuit under the rig in the black, cold water of the North Sea and shivered. What kind of a job was this, anyway?

He comforted himself with the thought that Harrods was at least warm. Cowley could do him favours like this anytime. Except, of course, it couldn't be a favour. Otherwise, Bodie wouldn't be here.

Bodie perused the perfume display. Cowley hadn't said he couldn't do his Christmas shopping. If he took offence Bodie would say, in his most innocent voice, that he was melting into the crowd.

The tall, slim elegant blonde behind the counter smiled at him and he wondered just how long her legs were. He couldn't see for the counter.

She was being run off her feet and she still had time to smile. That was a come on if ever he saw one. Then he admitted to himself that he saw everything as a come-on – even the brush off!

He ordered twelve identical toiletry sets and saw the blonde raise and eyebrow. He would like to have told her he'd decided to buy all his girlfriends the same present.

It would stop a repeat of all the trouble of last year when he'd gone crazy trying to remember which girl he'd given what to. Maybe he should buy one for her? No – thirteen was unlucky.

James Fielding finally received his phone call from Cowley. He was asked to reconsider, but Fielding insisted on going through with it. He had promised Deborah, and it was the only request he had made.

Cowley drew a sharp breath, making his opinion clear, but he was in no position to argue. He asked to talk to Braben, the senior C15 man, and – as arrangements were finalised – Fielding went to fetch his daughter.

Debbie squealed her delight. 'Are we going? Are we going to see Father Christmas now, Daddy?'

Matheson watched the car containing Fielding Deborah, Braben, and two other C15 men, pull away. The moment it turned the corner he lifted the phone and dialled a number.

He spoke a password and replaced the receiver, so raw to the game that he never even suspected that the line was bugged and he would be arrested later. The Group had promised him money and rated him expendable.

After receiving the password from Matheson, Ramos took less than a minute to leave the apartment for the last time.

All he had to do was put on his coat and pick up a shoebox-sized parcel – gaily wrapped in Christmas paper – that contained the gun.

Ramos would slide his hand into the collapsible end flap and pull the trigger when the moment presented itself.

Bodie and Doyle met up in the store. Nothing had happened. Cowley must be slipping up in his old age. They had both noticed that he wasn't around.

Ramos entered the department store on the south side. He wore a soft hat pulled low and a scarf muffled most of his face. With his Christmas parcel clutched tight he was soon lost in the thronging mass of shoppers.

The car containing Fielding pulled to a halt in front of Harrods. Fielding and Deborah moved out, flanked by Braben and one of the C15 men, while the other man stayed behind the wheel of the car.

Bodie and Doyle had arrived in the security section. Without much hope, they watched the shoppers on the bank of television screens.

Then, to their surprise, they thought they saw Ramos. A needle in a haystack? Or a look-alike? Whatever the outcome, checking the man out would relieve the boredom.

Bodie and Doyle followed his progress on the screens, through several departments, until they were sure where he was heading. 'Toys and Games' and the grotto of Father Christmas.

Fielding and Deborah arrived in Reindeer Land and joined the queue to see Santa Claus.

Braben thought it was crazy, mixing in these sort of crowds. But maybe there was safety in numbers. Fielding's daughter was excited. What was worth spoiling a visit to Father Christmas anyway?

Braben and his colleague watched the doors, scrutinising every face closely. How were they to know that Ramos was already inside the area?

Fielding and Deborah had almost reached the red-robed, white-bearded figure. Not much of a job, thought Fielding. He wondered how they kept their temper with all the children.

Debbie was jumping up and down now, scarcely able to contain her excitement.

Ramos edged closer. The gun in the parcel he carried pointed towards Fielding. He should be able to escape in the panic that followed.

He had thoroughly cased the store and knew the back corridors and short cuts like the back of his hand.

Ramos waited for a clear shot. He would more than likely only get one chance, and the silencer should give him a head start before anyone realised what had happened.

Bodie and Doyle arrived together into the grotto. They saw Ramos – saw immediately that it was him – and although they couldn't see the gun they saw the way he was holding his parcel and it didn't take much imagination to realise what it was.

Both Bodie and Doyle shouted a warning – despite having no idea who the target was – and launched themselves towards Ramos.

Ramos was startled, and – although the bullet sped from the gun, it only shattered a coloured light on the Christmas tree.

Before Ramos could get off another shot Santa Claus, with an agility that belied his years, grabbed what looked like a toy gun beside him, and got off two shots.

Ramos, hit in the shoulder and leg, went down in a heap as Bodie and Doyle threw themselves on top of him.

Bodie grabbed the gun, and Doyle held on to Ramos although he obviously wasn't going to be any more trouble.

They looked up as Santa Claus stared down at them. 'Well done.'

The voice was unmistakable, even from behind the flowing white beard. 'But you could have been five seconds faster!'

Bodie and Doyle looked at each other and started to laugh. One thing you could always count on. Cowley – even dressed up as Father Christmas – was never satisfied!

One Good Turn

BY LEON GRIFFITHS

Arthur Daley, the roguish dealer in black-market mechandise forever looking for a 'nice little earner', is now a part of television and English folklore – the latest in a long tradition of spivs stretching back as far as Falstaff and kept alive by the comedian Arthur English as Flash Harry, Corporal Walker (James Beck) in Dad's Army, *and Del Boy (David Jason) the Peckham market trader in* Only Fools and Horses. *Surprisingly, though, the truth is that Daley, brilliantly portrayed by George Cole, was never intended to be the star of* Minder, *but only a client of a professional London bodyguard, Terry (Dennis Waterman), in a series of crime dramas in which he ran foul of the local police in the shape of Detective Sergeant Chisholm played by Patrick Malahide. For those who had watched the series from its beginnings in 1979, the appearances of Chisholm – 'Malahide's great comic creation,' according to* The Independent *– were always highlights of any episode because of the actor's wonderful parody of a tense, dark man who would have loved to be able to intimidate petty crooks but was somehow never quite able to manage it. When Chisholm finally left the police force he did not completely sever his connection with the series and has subsequently returned in a new job as a security officer. (The only other ever-present has been Dave, the ubiquitous owner of the Winchester Club, played by Glynn Edwards.)*

What cannot be denied, however, is that the longevity of Minder *– it recently passed its one hundreth episode – is very much due to George Cole who has, of course, not only recently taken on a new foil, Ray (Gary Webster), but enlarged the scope of his nefarious operations to even include two specials filmed Down Under. (In Australia, where the show has been transmitted for years, Cole was amused to find a* *number of car dealers calling themselves 'A. Daley', while in New Zealand there was even an 'Arthur Daley Rip-Off Store'!) This is all a long way from the series' modest beginnings on Thames Television in October 1979, although the indications it might be a 'runner' – to use another of Daley's cornucopia of slang expressions – was evident from the response of viewers and early reviews like that of Philip Purser: 'Funny about crime without making crime funny, and equipped with two dreadfully endearing characters, the series is in a class of its own.' That position has never been seriously challenged, as Peter Waymark of The Times was able to write when Episode One Hundred, 'All Things Brighton Beautiful', was shown on 20 January 1994. Waymark reported that the show was 'as resilient as ever' and he went on, 'After fifteen years there is nothing more to say about George Cole's performance except that it fits Arthur as closely as his trilby hat.'*

Certainly the creator of Minder, Leon Griffiths (1928–), the writer of a number critically acclaimed television plays and an occasional contributor to crimes series, never expected it to be still so popular after all this time. Indeed, he remains better known for the series than for his Writers' Guild Award in 1964 and BAFTA Writers Award twenty years later. But George Cole, with velvet-collared overcoat and fat cigar, has undeniably put the name Arthur Daley into the language once and for all as the archetypal dealer in shady goods, second-hand cars in particular. (His expression "Er indoors' has even entered the Oxford English Dictionary.*) And regular press speculation that 'Our Arfur' might be about to film his last* Minder *have invariably produced howls of protest from viewers and a resigned shrug of amusement from the actor himself. Leon Griffiths has gone on to other projects, but retains a great fondness for* Minder *which he emphasised by writing this unique short story at Christmas 1982. It is appearing in book form for the first time.*

ARTHUR DROPPED A Harrods carrier bag on the bar: 'A video Christmas to us all,' he said.

'Never mind your holly and your ivy, I've joined the electronic revolution.'

'Any threat of a drink out of it,' said Terry and pushed his empty glass to Dave, the owner of the Winchester Club which is smaller than the Savoy Grill, but handier for Craven Cottage. Arthur ignored the plea.

'I'm going to make you a rich man, Terence. Cop the contents of this simple carrier-bag,' said Arthur.

Terry opened the bag and said: 'Video tapes, so what?'

'Ah, but not ordinary tapes, my son. These are master tapes, originals of the ten best films ever, the ones that Barry Norman loves and cares for. In fact, I am about to be a movie mogul. Incidentally, where are the punters?' Arthur glanced around the empty club.

'Some of them are doing their last-minute Christmas shop-lifting,' muttered Terry, still waiting for his drink.

'And also there's a posse out,' said Dave. 'Slippery Charlie's on the missing list, he being the treasurer of the Christmas Loan Club. Duly elected and everything, a fully qualified accountant and mustard at figures.'

'Of course, he is,' said Arthur. 'That's why he got a five-stretch for fraud. I mean, six years on the trot and somebody's done a runner with the Loan Club funds.

'Don't you ever learn, you people. This is a bad environment, dishonesty is a way of life for the membership. Everybody knew that Charlie was a tea-leaf.'

'He was a good spender,' said Dave, staring at Arthur, who still hadn't put his hand in his pocket to pay for the drinks. 'I should have sussed it though when he told me that he was sending a card to old Biggsie in Rio de Janeiro. He'll have his turkey on a sun-drenched beach.'

'Who needs all that,' said Arthur. 'Christmas Day means family, goodwill, a star above Bethlehem, ageless values and . . .'

'And what?' asked Dave.

'Bing Crosby,' said Arthur. 'The late troubadour of the tonsils. Without old Bing singing 'White Christmas' it's like Whit Monday with rain.'

'Personally, I'm a Sinatra man,' said Dave. And Arthur looked at him as if he had blasphemed in front of the Pope.

''Er indoors worshipped old Bing,' said Arthur. It was a simple rebuke. 'And a nice golfer, an' all.'

Arthur had taken a ten-pound note from his pocket at last.

'Should I take that,' suggested Dave, 'before you wear out the Queen's picture on it?' Arthur reluctantly released the note.

'I've hit the market at the right time, y'know. When they get their redundancy money they all buy videos, don't they? I was talking to my contacts on the coast this morning . . .'

'Bognor?' asked Terry.

'You may scoff,' said Arthur with a tolerant smile. 'The West Coast. You know . . . LA. I was on the trumpet to all of the Warner brothers . . .'

'I didn't know you knew them,' said Terry.

'Of course I know 'em,' said Arthur, 'and their mum, an' all.'

In the street Arthur was still muttering about Dave. 'What's he got against the late Bing Crosby, eh?'

He took a card from the inside pocket of his camel-hair coat. 'Shoot down to this address and get the videos and tapes from Freddie Chambers' studio.'

'Old Freddie,' said Terry. 'He got caught with a fistful of credit cards last year – he's a bit warm.'

'Are you suggesting that he's a pedlar of porn?' said Arthur. 'If so, may I disabuse you of that notion. Freddie is a family man like meself. In our modern permissive society there is a place for more adult tastes as well as singing nuns.'

'I'm going,' said Terry, 'before we get a crowd.'

Freddie's 'studio' turned out to be a fourth floor council flat near Queen's Park Rangers' ground. On a clear day you could hear Terry Venables shouting at his players.

The living room was littered with obsolete video recorders, broken cassettes, dirty dishes and discarded clothes. Freddie apologised for the mess. He hadn't shaved for a week and his cardigan was due for a session at Sketchley's.

'That's what happens when you're a single parent family,' he said. 'She's gone. Had enough of films. Funnily enough, her mum was an usherette at the Hammersmith Odeon years ago. That's show business, eh?'

On a monitor set an Indian film looked as if it had been shot through a monsoon.

'My last rush job,' explained Freddie, 'I cater for a lot of minorities. I mean, I was well into them before Channel 4 started.'

'Then why are you selling out to Arthur?' asked Terry.

'Fresh pastures,' said Freddie. 'I'm going to live in Brazil. Incidentally, d'you wanna buy a nice council flat?'

By the time Arthur had got a couple of take-away kebabs Terry had set up the various recorders.

Arthur had said that it was a doddle. 'Bung a tape in the machine and push a button. You don't have to be one of the three wise men to do that,' he'd said.

Terry had tried – as a result 'White Christmas' was playing and fork lightning and white blobs were distorting the image.

'What's that?' said Arthur.

'I think it's old Bing in a snowstorm,' said Terry. 'But that's better than The Invisible Man . . .'

'A classic,' said Arthur. 'Claude Rains with bandages round his boat. You can't see him, see?'

'Well, in this one,' said Terry, 'you can't see *anybody*. Your pal Freddie is a dab hand at editing. All these tapes are 60-minute ones.

'He's lost five characters out of The Dirty Dozen, and Deep Throat is mixed up with Match of the Day. Kevin Keegan scored a cracker just when it was getting interesting.'

'I don't want this kebab,' said Arthur.

'It gets worse,' said Terry. 'Jaws looks just like a big kipper in Freddie's video. I think he's done the same to you.'

'Talking about film titles,' said Arthur, dropping his Panatella and loosening his collar,' I think I'm going to be a bit Moby Dick in a minute.'

They heard children singing carols as Arthur rang the bell at Freddie's flat.

'It's down to you,' he said to Terry. 'A quick smack in the teeth with plenty of claret as soon as he opens the door.'

'Not me,' said Terry. 'It's a business dispute and I'm carrying these videos.'

Arthur scowled. 'Goodwill within and betrayal without – that's charming, innit?'

Freddie opened the door and his beloved ones gathered around him. Mrs Chambers could have been a welterweight contender a few years ago; his muscular teenage son was practising martial arts movements and the two girls looked like double trouble.

'What can I say, Arthur,' said Freddie, buttoning up his new cashmere cardigan. 'I turned you over, no question about it. It was you or the blissful reconciliation of my loved ones. Don't my Tina look nice? Had her hair done in Sloane Square.'

Arthur clenched his teeth and his flats. His eyes were wild. 'Where's my dough?'

'Spent it,' said Freddie without a morsel of remorse. 'Bikes for the kids, new fridge, washing machine, hi-fi, two continental quilts, a family computer and a red setter puppy, which is being delivered tomorrow.'

Spittle sprayed from Arthur's lips. 'You're a thief.'

'I know,' said Freddie.

The roar was cataclysmic. 'Then rob banks!'

'It's too risky,' said Freddie. 'But I guarantee that you'll get your money back. I'm a grafter, Arthur. I'll take those videos and I'll sell them to somebody else.

'It's just a loan. But do you realise what you've done? None of the social workers couldn't do it but you, Arthur Daley, has reunited my family. Don't you feel nice inside?'

'I feel as if a rat was gnawing at my liver,' said Arthur.

Tina offered him a large glass of brandy. 'You must be a religious man,' she said as if she had witnessed a miracle.

'Not after tonight,' said Arthur as he took the triple brandy and gulped it in one.

Two hours later Terry helped Arthur to his car and the street lights seemed hazier than one of Freddie's video tapes.

'What am I?' sobbed Arthur. 'The Good Samaritan? Or a right wally?'

'I was proud of you,' said Terry.

'I'm worse than a Loan Club,' said Arthur. 'Don't you ever, ever say a word in the club. I mean, they'll all have a go. I may as well dress up like Santa Claus.'

'No,' said Terry, 'you should get the Nobel Prize for tonight.'

'Yeah,' said Arthur, as he collapsed into the passenger seat, 'how much is it?'

The John Detail

BY SERITA STEVENS

The year 1982 brought another major breakthrough in crime television with the transmission on CBS TV of Cagney and Lacey, *the first ever series about a pair of female police detectives. There had, of course, already been individual female crimebusters (vide* Lady Molly *and* Hildegarde Withers) *not to mention a trio of gorgeous undercover agents known as* Charlie's Angels, *but the new show was a landmark in that it presented its two central characters, Detective Mary Beth Lacey (played by Tyne Daly) and Detective Christine Cagney (Sharon Gless), as equals with the male members of their New York police squad. As Sharon Gless was later to aptly summarise the phenomenal success of the programme, 'Cagney and Lacey was a breakthrough series – we showed women doing a so-called man's job and without ever forgetting they were women.' Sharon was, of course, speaking at a time when the show was being transmitted all over the world, but it had, in fact, very nearly not been made at all . . .*

The idea of presenting a series about the public and private lives of a pair of female detectives had come from two New York script-writers, Barbara Avedon and Barbara Corday, who enlisted the aid of producer Barney Rosenzweig to try and interest the networks. Amazingly, in the light of what has subsequently transpired, all three major companies summarily dismissed the project. Still believing in their idea, though, the trio obtained funding and produced a ninety-minute special in which Cagney and Lacey *used all their skills to catch a vicious murderer. In this pilot Tyne Daly played Lacey, but her co-star was Loretta Swift, already famous for her role as Major 'Hotlips' Houlihan in* M*A*S*H. *However, even though the show received unexpectedly high ratings, the prospect of a series appeared to have* *been dashed when Loretta announced that her commitments to the Army medical series would preclude her from appearing. The first substitute to be found for her role, Meg Foster, was deemed unsuitable by CBS, and it was only when Sharon Gless was cast that the dream at last started to become a reality.*

Undoubtedly the combination of the resourceful, happily married Mary Beth and the attractive, extrovert Christine – who rapidly proved themselves to be an intelligent and formidable partnership who were very good at their job – was what won them favour with viewers of both sexes and all ages. The added dimension of insights into Lacey's home-life and Cagney's frequent sparring with predatory men were also important elements in ensuring the series' long run of one hundred and twenty-five hour-long episodes during which both girls won an Emmy award for their performance. Among the supporting male roles, Al Waxman was outstanding as the girl's uncompromising boss, Lieutenant Samuels; while Carl Lumbly played the serious-minded Detective Petrie and Martin Kove the womanising Detective Isbecki. John Karlen was Lacey's dependable husband, Harvey – a man who was quite often literally left holding their baby while Mary Beth was off solving yet another crime. If there were any complaints about the series, it was that none of the other police officers got their man – it was always Cagney and Lacey.

It can be seen in hindsight that the role of women in police series has never been quite the same since Cagney and Lacey, *and the durability of the programme (which ended in August 1988) has been proved by its regular reshowing on both commercial and satellite TV. As a reminder of how the saga of these two remarkable girl detectives began, here is an adaptation of an early episode scripted by Barbara Avedon and Barbara Corday which has been novelised by Serita Stevens. In it the girls find that their personal involvement in an operation to clamp down on prostitution not only puts them under threat of physical violence, but endangers their very status in the police force . . .*

IN THE LOCKER room, Mary Beth grimaced as she adjusted the jet-black wig. 'I thought you said *plain*clothes.'

'Well –' Christine zipped up the miniskirt and eyed the patterned hose.

'Harve rarely sees this much cleavage.' Mary Beth laughed, tugging at her sequined blouse.

Chris eyed the fringed top sceptically in the mirror. 'It's all rather degrading. I can't imagine them putting a man on this detail.'

Mary Beth sighed. 'We might as well go to the captain's office and get this over with.'

Within minutes they stood in front of Captain Wells' desk.

As if reading her mind, Wells began to placate Chris. 'The John detail is very important.'

'Captain –' Chris tried to be patient '– with all the heavy crime going on, we have to trap some horny bastards?'

Trying to soften Chris' remark, Mary Beth said, 'She means it's a victimless crime. Look, we're good cops –'

'I know.' Wells lowered his feet from the desk. 'Why do you think you got promoted? That was a terrific collar you kids made last month. Like real policemen.'

Mary Beth's voice was tight. 'We *are* real policemen, sir.'

'And we want off this cleavage detail,' Chris added.

'Look, I'm gonna run it down for you.' Captain Wells cleared his throat. 'The approach must be explicit. Know what I mean?'

Mary Beth and Chris exchanged an amused look. They had no choice but to play along. At least for now. 'Excuse me, sir, but maybe you should spell it out for us,' Mary Beth suggested sweetly.

'Yeah,' Chris chimed in. 'She's a mother and I'm not a married woman – yet.'

Wells flushed. 'The John *has* to be explicit for the team to make the bust.'

Christine batted her eyelashes and innocently asked, 'Can you give us an example?'

'Oh, yeah. Sure.' He walked around the desk. 'Well, you stand there looking real provocative.'

'Like this?' Chris struck a suggestive pose.

'Good. Yes. Like that. Well, then, so a John comes up to you and he'll say something like "Are you busy?" '

They nodded, listening with rapt attention, as if this was something they had never heard before.

'You say to him, 'What do you want?' And he says – he says –'

'And he says?' Mary Beth asked.

'He says,' the captain repeated, 'something – explicit. You'll know it when you hear it.' He cleared his throat. 'Come on, I'll take you to meet the others.' There was no choice except to follow.

*

They paused inside the doorway. The squad room was in worse shape than Captain Wells' office. Desks were piled high with file folders containing unsolved, yet-to-be-solved, and never-in-a-million-years-to-be-solved cases.

'Can't find anything around here,' an attractive young black detective complained as he searched through a pile of folders with mounting desperation.

'Men.' Wells cleared his throat. 'We've got two welcome new additions to the Fourteenth. This here is Lacey and Cagney.'

'*Detective* Cagney and *Detective* Lacey,' Chris corrected.

'Let me introduce you to the men.' Wells pointed toward a stocky man who had just gotten off the phone. 'Samuels.' Motioning toward a blond officer, Wells said, 'Isbecki.' He pointed toward the officer who had complained about the files. 'That's Petrie. You'll meet the rest of the gang later.'

'Which are our desks?' Chris asked, surveying the room.

Captain Wells smiled. 'Oh, we'll work out something, don't worry.'

'Over there would be nice.' Chris pointed to a corner, near the coffeepot.

'What?'

'She means our desks, sir,' Mary Beth explained.

'Oh, yeah. Desks. Don't worry. You'll get desks, phones, the works. We're a team here — we work close.'

Isbecki, his eye on Chris, said, 'Yeah, we work close.'

Chris froze him with an icy stare.

'I want to get something straight at the outset.' Wells' tone was sharp. 'We've all heard a lot about male chauvinism the last couple of years. Well, we're not gonna have any of that at the Fourteenth. Maybe there's been trouble in the other precincts, but around here they're gonna be treated like equals.' Wells slapped both women on their fannies. 'Go get 'em, girls.'

On Forty-seventh Street — in the diamond district — among the merchants going about their business, three prostitutes leaned against a building. Chris was one of them. A middle-aged man who had been eyeing her finally approached. 'Are you busy?' he asked apprehensively.

'No,' Chris responded.

'What is the, uh, tariff?'

'What do you want?'

The John looked puzzled. 'What do I want?'

'Yeah, what do you want?' Chris lowered her voice seductively. 'In detail.'

'It's my first time. I thought you'd know. Never mind,' he said. 'I'd better find somebody more experienced.'

In an ice-cream truck parked not far from where Chris was standing, Isbecki and Davidson heard the last of the John's conversation on the tape setup. 'Did you see the legs on her?' Davidson asked.

'You're talking about a fellow officer,' Isbecki said with a smile.

'I know. And I'm a married man. Gladys isn't too happy about having broads in the precinct.'

'Tell her she ought to be glad it ain't you out there in mesh stockings,' Isbecki retorted.

'You know the other one's married?'

'Yeah?' Davidson said, surprised. 'She doesn't look it.'

The subject of their conversation was standing in a doorway, doing her best to look like a prostitute. A few feet from her, wearing an abbreviated cowgirl outfit complete with rhinestone-studded vest, a black prostitute negotiating with a macho John told him to get lost and turned to another customer. Undaunted, he swaggered over to Mary Beth.

'How much?' he asked.

Assuming her best Mae West stance, Mary Beth countered with 'What do you want?'

'I want you to rub peanut butter all over me. I don't want you to miss a spot.'

Mary Beth tried to appear as if this was suggested to her every day. 'Could you be more explicit? Tell me exactly what you want me to do.' She thrust out her chest, supposedly seductively but really for him to talk into her hidden microphone.

'I want you to –'

Suddenly Mary Beth gasped. 'Hey! That's my car!' she shouted, recognising her station wagon that had been stolen a few days before. She left the John and dashed into the middle of the street. 'That's my car!' she shouted as the car turned the corner.

She ran over to the ice-cream truck parked discreetly up the street and, forgetting all her orders, she waved to the undercover detective inside. 'Follow that guy! The bum stole my car!'

Isbecki and Davidson looked at her in disbelief. 'You almost had the John cold,' Davidson said to her.

'Yeah,' Isbecki interjected. 'Now we'll never know if he wanted chunky or creamy.'

*

Trudging back to the precinct, Mary Beth and Chris were glad the day was over. They were tired and, in Chris's case, thoroughly disgusted. As they headed toward the squad room, Chris stopped short and grabbed Mary Beth's arm. A desk was standing in the hall. The phone, its cord extending from the detectives' room, perched precariously on the edge of the desk.

Mary Beth felt Chris's anger. 'Maybe it's not one of ours.'

'Right,' Chris said sarcastically. 'Ours are probably in the ladies' room.' She hurried into the squad room with Mary Beth right behind her.

Marcus Petrie was trying to find something in the stack of files under the window. Samuels was at his desk explaining things to Taylor and Haun. 'You can't tell me it's an outside job,' he was saying, 'that joint is a fortress.'

'A diamond broker kills another diamond broker – the ice doesn't hit the street,' Taylor added.

'Twice!' Petrie chimed in.

'Yeah,' said Taylor.

'So if it's not robbery, what is it?' Haun asked. He looked up as Chris and Mary Beth came toward them. 'Downstairs, girls.'

'Detectives Cagney and Lacey,' Petrie interjected. 'Meet Taylor and Haun.'

'Welcome to the Fourteenth.' The men smiled.

'Excuse me,' Chris said to anyone who would listen, 'we can't work in the hall.' She pointed toward the coffeepot. 'Why don't you put the desk over there?'

'Please.' Petrie touched her shoulder. 'I'm trying to organise this room. We can't move anything until all the files are organised. Then I'm sure we can arrange something.'

Chris glared at him.

Mary Beth asked, 'Which of you guys wore these frills before we came on the scene?'

The men exchanged looks.

'There wasn't a John detail before we came on, right?' Chris asked.

Samuels stood up and reached for his hat. 'Petrie, let's get out of here.'

'I can't until I finish –'

'Petrie, it's a murder. Let's get on it.'

'Sure thing.' Petrie closed the file drawer.

As Samuels went past her, Chris asked, 'Is it the same MO?'

Samuels stared at her as if not comprehending.

'Was the murder the same?' Chris repeated. 'You know, the

Friedlander case – that other diamond merchant. You never broke that case, did you?'

'It was the same MO.' Samuels bristled, looking her in the eye. 'Your mascara is running,' he said, and left.

Once in the locker room, Chris let loose. 'Damn, but he makes me angry!'

Knowing her partner, Mary Beth's tone was firm. 'Christine, let it be.'

'It's been eight months since that *first* guy was killed. Samuels doesn't have the brains he was born with!'

'You keep out of it, Chris. They'll put us on some real stuff after we've been here a while.'

'Okay. Okay.' Christine put on some fresh lipstick. 'Lighten up, Mary Beth. Say hi to Harvey.'

Mary Beth grinned. 'I'll give him your best.'

The lights in most of the station offices had been turned off. Day officers were leaving, night shift was coming on. One light remained in the detectives' offices. Sitting at one of the desks, Christine drank coffee as she absorbed the contents of the Friedlander file. Concentrating hard, she neither heard the footsteps nor saw Marcus Petrie come in with an armload of files. Only after she felt his eyes on her did she look up.

She forced a smile, closed the file, and grabbed her coat. 'Date cancelled out on me – had nothing else to do.'

Petrie said nothing.

Flushing, Chris rose and, with one last glance at him, hurried from the building.

Mary Beth aimed at the target and cursed. She hated firearms practice, especially when she had something on her mind. Glancing at her partner in the other booth, she said, 'You know, Chris, I wouldn't blame Petrie if he told on you. You had no business being there in the first place.'

Chris's back stiffened. 'What I do on my own time is my business.'

'Yeah, well, not when it makes the both of us look bad.' Looking at the target, Mary Beth saw she was way off. 'You'll only get their backs up and then where'll we be?'

'They won't give us a chance to prove we can do the job. We've got to show them or we'll be stuck on this damn John detail forever!' As if to punctuate her anger, she fired four times in succession, hitting the heart of the target each time.

Mary Beth sighed, upset at her own inability to shoot properly. 'They're only testing us. It's natural. We're the first women detectives in the precinct. Can you imagine what Petrie must have gone through?'

Chris's tone was acid. 'Well, it sure didn't raise his consciousness.' Once more she aimed and fired, hitting the centre dead-on.

'Chris, it's their case. They've been working at it for a year. They don't want to hear from you about it.'

'So I should just keep smiling and take it. Like you. I bet you even smile in your sleep.' Even as she said the words, Chris was sorry she'd said them.

Back on the street in their spiked heels, standing provocatively against the wall, Chris was bored. She glanced at the black prostitute in the cowgirl outfit and eyed the man coming up to her. The prostitute stepped in front of him. 'Black is beautiful, don't you know that, sweetie?' She smiled at the man.

Reacting to the invitation, he smiled uncomfortably at the prostitute. 'I'm sorry, I was going to talk to the blonde over there,' he said, indicating Chris.

'Whatsamatter? You got something against blacks?'

'Oh, I hope you don't think that was the reason. It wasn't at all. It was her legs. Not that yours aren't terrific.'

Chris moved closer to the John. 'Just tell me what you want.'

The prostitute sidled up to him. 'You don't have to tell *me* what you want, honey. I *know* what you want.'

'Bug off,' Chris said, elbowing the prostitute away.

'Uh, ladies, I'm on my lunch hour.' The nervous John shifted his feet.

'I'll have you back at your desk in twenty minutes – and you'll be *smiling*,' the prostitute claimed.

Pointing toward Chris, he said, 'It's the legs. Try to understand.'

As he took another step in Chris's direction, the prostitute became ugly. 'We don't like independent agents around here.' She grabbed Chris's hair. 'On this corner, you work for Sugar or you don't work.'

'Let go of me,' Chris demanded. Without using any of her martial arts, so that she wouldn't blow her cover, she tried to break the other woman's grip.

Scared, the John took off and left the two women fighting.

'Look,' said Chris, trying to keep her cool, 'what's your name, sister?'

'Name's Female – rhymes with tamale. Female Hudson.'

'How'd you get a name like Female?'

Female snorted. 'How'd you think I'd get a name like that? My mother had nine girls. When I came round, she ran out of names, so they took it off the birth certificate.'

Chris took a deep breath. 'Let's call it quits. I'm leaving.' She had to get off this detail, and soon.

Female nursed her sore wrist and glared as Chris strode away.

Back in street clothes, Chris reported to Captain Wells. Ineffectively, she tried to explain her position.

'Look,' Wells said, 'the name of the game is statistics. You make your collars, you get your promotion. It's as simple as that.'

Trying to quell her anger, Chris's voice was sharp. 'Those streets are full of *real* crime.'

'And there aren't enough policemen to solve one tenth of them. The commissioner wants those women off the street. You're a cop, you do your job.'

Returning to her desk, Chris sat down hard. Then, hearing conversation coming from the office, she was glad the desk was out in the hall where she could eavesdrop without appearing to.

'Sitting *shivah*!' Samuels bellowed. 'We've got a murder to solve and she's sitting shivah! Who sits shivah any more?'

'No one on a Hundred and thirty-fifth,' Petrie said.

Samuels was surprised. 'You know what it is?'

'If he's an Orthodox Jew, it's seven days.'

Sitting at her desk, Chris listened to the conversation. As Samuels started out of the office, Chris took out her mirror and pretended to be fixing her lipstick. As soon as he had gone, she went into the squad room. 'Uh, I never thanked you for covering for me that day,' she told Petrie.

Marcus glanced at her. 'You're welcome.'

Chris sat down on his desk, crossing her legs. 'You know, you're really a fountain of information.'

'I know.' Marcus narrowed his eyes. 'What information do you want?'

'Whatever gave you the idea I wanted something from you?' Chris went wide-eyed. If these fools thought all she was good for was dressing up, she was going to play their game.

Marcus laughed. 'I may be a man, Detective Cagney, but that doesn't mean I'm stupid.'

Chris gave him a smile. 'No. I don't think you're stupid, Petrie.'

'So what do you want?'

'Tell me about this shivah. I mean, what would I need to know if I went up to see Mrs Goldman?'

Petrie whistled. 'You're going to play for the big stakes, huh? You realise Samuels will have your badge if he ever finds out.'

Christine nodded. 'But he hasn't solved the crime yet. He should give others a chance.'

'Others meaning you.'

Chris stood, her anger rising. 'Are you going to tell me what I need to know or do I just go there on my own?'

Marcus pulled out a chair and sank down into it. 'I'll tell you, if you promise it stays between us.'

Putting her hand up as if in court, Chris nodded. 'I promise.'

Moments later, Christine hurried to the locker room, whistling, and found Mary Beth was there changing back into her hooker clothes. 'I'm going to a meeting,' Mary Beth told her, adjusting her patterned hose.

'What type of meeting? PTA?'

Frustrated, Mary Beth retorted, 'You wouldn't be interested.'

'Try me.' Chris put her hand on the locker as Mary Beth started to close it.

'Some of the women are trying to form a union.'

'What women? *Those* women? A union?' Chris laughed.

'It's not funny. They get pushed in every direction.' Mary Beth put the zebra coat over her shoulders and fixed the wig.

'Who'll be there?' Chris asked.

'All of them – Shanghai, Honey, the rest.'

Christine turned toward her locker. 'And what are you going to do about it?'

'What do you care? You don't even want to come. Those women are so scared, Christine.'

'Well, they should be.' Chris tied the belt of her trenchcoat. 'Those pimps are bad news.' She sighed. 'Where's it going to be?'

A smile came to Mary Beth's eyes. 'I got the address here.'

'Write it down for me.'

'Why?' Mary Beth said suspiciously.

'I got an errand to run.'

'Where?' Mary Beth eyed her partner. 'What are you up to?'

Chris smiled her elusive smile and shrugged. 'Something. See you later.'

She hurried out of the station before Mary Beth could question her more.

The home of the murdered man was a penthouse on the Upper West

Side. The Goldman living room was furnished in expensive new 'antiques,' with cabriole legs, damask covers, and shepherdess bisque lamps.

Chris stood at the entrance, seeing the women seated about the room. All were tastefully dressed, but each had a piece of cloth torn in a symbol of mourning. Trays of food, cakes, and drinks were on the table, but no one was eating or drinking. All the mirrors and pictures had been covered by sheets – another symbol of mourning.

Chris could hear the men gathered in the other room, praying. Taking off her shoes, she entered the room.

She felt all eyes on her as she moved toward where the widow was seated. With reverence, she approached the woman who was pointed out as the widow. 'Excuse me – Mrs Goldman?' Chris sat down on the sofa.

The teary-eyed woman glanced up at her. 'You knew my husband? How?'

Chris blushed slightly. 'No, actually I didn't know him. I'm from the police.' She showed her badge.

'Please.' Mrs Goldman pulled out a handkerchief and wiped her eyes. 'Please – go. It will do no good to talk now.'

Desperate for a lead that would give her the edge, that would make Samuels take notice of her, Chris pleaded, 'Mrs Goldman, I understand your grief – really I do. But we're only trying to help.'

'Help? What help? My husband, rest his soul, is in the grave. How will you help?' She used the handkerchief again to blow her nose. Chris could only stare at the numbers the Nazis had tattooed on the woman's arm.

'Please. Go. Have some respect for the dead.'

The raised voice of the widow brought a halt to the prayers. One of the black-coated Hasidim came out of the other room and stared at Chris.

'I'm just trying to do my job,' she told him. 'We can't let a murderer get away.'

'What job?' the Hasid said.

'I'm a police officer,' Chris responded, showing them her badge.

None of them looked at her identification. They didn't seem to believe her.

Mrs Goldman took a tissue from a nearby box. 'I don't know what you want, but please go. Have respect for the dead.'

With a heavy heart, Christine stood. 'All right. I'll go. I'm sorry to have bothered you.'

*

Leaning against the door, Mary Beth listened as the other women talked about their grievances. She wanted to help, but all she could do was be another voice.

'We have to legalise,' Honey stated. 'We don't need more laws. They just give the cops more to hassle us with.'

'Yeah,' Mary Beth started to say. Then she realised all eyes had turned toward her and she felt herself blush. What the hell was she going to say? Here she was a cop and if these women found out, she would be the one being hassled. 'You're perfectly right,' she managed to add.

'If my dude so much as knew I was here, he'd neutralise my natural,' said Terry.

Honey grabbed a candy from the tray. 'Sugar's my man,' she said, trying to make a joke as she held up the sweet. 'As the government report says, sugar can kill you.'

'Well, I've been talkin', like you said. Only, as much as I rev 'em up, Female knocks 'em down,' Gloria reported.

'Keep talkin',' Terry said.

'I do. I do.' Gloria paused as they all heard the knock on the door. Mary Beth could sense their fear, each girl worried it was her pimp. She opened the door.

'So?' Christine asked, coming in and lighting a cigarette. 'What's been happening? Sorry I'm late. I had a live one.'

Walking away from the meeting nearly an hour later, Chris and Mary Beth were on either side of Honey as a white Cadillac Seville pulled up to the kerb. 'My God,' Honey cried, 'it's Sugar!' Within seconds she had run down an alley. Mary Beth and Chris began to follow as two thugs raced out of the car behind them.

There was no mistaking Sugar. Wearing velvet jeans and a two-hundred-dollar silk shirt, he was the meanest-looking pimp either woman had ever seen. With a right jab, Chris slugged one of the men and Mary Beth kicked another as a third pulled on her zebra coat, yanking her back to the car and inside.

Horrified, Chris began to run after the car as it pulled away. What the hell was she going to do? If she pulled her gun, it would blow their cover. On the other hand, she couldn't let anything happen to Mary Beth. There was no choice. She reached into her purse, but before she could do anything the car screeched to a halt and Mary Beth was thrown violently from the Cadillac. As it sped off, Chris ran to her. 'You okay?'

'Yeah.' Mary Beth sighed, getting painfully to her feet. 'I think so. Sugar obviously wanted Honey, not me.'

*

With ice over her eye, Mary Beth winced as Harvey looked over her bruises. 'I'm okay, Harve. Really I am.'

'All the same,' he said, 'we're going to the hospital tomorrow to check you out.'

The door to Michael's room opened and he came out, rubbing his eyes. He ran to his mother. 'Mommy, you're hurt.'

'No, sweetie, I'm all right.' Mary Beth hugged her son to her.

Chris stared a moment at the family scene. 'I'll see you tomorrow, Mary Beth, okay?'

'Not tomorrow!' Harvey's voice was hot.

Mary Beth glanced at her husband a moment and then nodded at Christine. 'Wednesday,' she said . . .

In a way, Chris thought, although she didn't want her partner hurt, this was probably the best thing that could have happened. If Wells thought there was real danger involved, he'd have to pull them off.

As Chris began to tell the captain what had happened, the phone rang.

'No, damn it! I don't have any statement.' He slammed the phne down. He looked up at Cagney. 'Go on.'

'She's okay. It was just a fluke they got her. It was Sugar. He was after one of his girls.'

The phone rang again.

Frowning, the captain thundered, 'I don't want to talk to him!' He listened a moment. 'All right, all right, put him through.' As he lifted the red phone, Chris noticed an immediate change in his manner. 'Your Honour, how good of you to call.' He paused, listening. 'I know you are, sir. We are, too. Very concerned. I have my best men on the case. We'll have a report to you within the week.' Wincing at the click at the other end, he put down the receiver.

'Excuse me, sir,' Chris said, 'I've been doing a little legwork in my spare time –'

Wells wasn't listening to her. 'It's the convention. He wants all those broads off the street, everything solved nice and tidy. You do your job and let Samuels and Petrie do theirs.'

'You may not have to worry about the "broads". The pimps will take them off the street for you,' Chris protested.

'Good.'

'No, not good. They're human beings – they need protection.'

Wells seemed surprised at her reaction. 'You gonna be emotional –or you gonna be a good cop?'

His words stopped Chris short. There was no response she could give to that.

'Why don't you take the day off, Cagney.' It wasn't a question but a command. Her only response was to leave the room, shutting the door firmly behind her.

Isbecki stopped her on the stairs. 'Hey, Cagney, you like Polish food?'

'Is that a joke?'

'No joke,' Isbecki said. 'I'm a good cook.'

Chris looked at him. 'Your place?'

'Yeah.' He grinned.

Turning abruptly, Chris responded, 'That's a joke.' She left him standing on the stairs and hurried down to the squad room.

Petrie was alone in the office. 'It was like you said,' Chris told him.

'You got in?' Petrie was amazed.

Chris nodded. 'But I didn't learn much. How do *you* know so much about Jewish customs?'

'I read it somewhere. I'm blessed with total recall.'

'You didn't tell Samuels where I was going?'

'I forgot,' Petrie said as Samuels came into the office.

'What did you forget, Marcus?' Samuels asked.

Petrie told him.

Even Chris, who could cuss and swear like a trucker, didn't believe the words Samuels yelled. She stared at Petrie, who took it all stoically.

'Are you done, sir?' Marcus asked.

Samuels merely glared at him as Petrie grabbed his coat and gave Chris hers.

She followed him out and down the street to Casey's bar.

After they ordered beers, Chris said, 'I'm sorry, Petrie.'

'Sticks and stones. He'll cool off.'

'Well, it was nice of you to try.'

'No favour. Sometimes you get a fresh eye on a case, and God knows you've got some fresh eye.'

Chris gave a laugh. 'It comes with the mouth. I don't know how *you* take it. It's the same package, racism and sexism.'

'Dinosaurs fighting extinction.' Petrie shrugged and took a long drink on his beer. 'You get anything from Goldman's widow?'

Chris shook her head. 'She was in a camp, too. I saw the tattoo.'

'It's not much of a clue,' Petrie told her. 'Ninety-eight per cent of the diamond industry is Jewish. A lot of the old ones went through that.'

'What about the other guy – Friedlander.'

'Auschwitz. Same as Goldman.'

'You think it might have been revenge?'

Petrie shook his head.

Looking down into her drink, Chris hesitated. 'There were some who collaborated with the Nazis – to save their kids.'

'The Kapos. We looked into it. Neither Goldman nor Friedlander.'

Chris sipped her beer. 'I'm glad I'm wrong on that, but I don't get it.'

'Welcome to the club.' Petrie gave her a smile.

'What about Friedlander? He has a widow, too, doesn't he?'

Laughing, Marcus put his hand on her shoulder. 'You'll have an even harder time getting in to see her.'

Chris grinned up at him. 'How much do you want to bet?'

At one that afternoon, Christine left the subway at Forty-seventh Street and walked to the National Jewelry Exchange. The guard at the first floor stopped her as four Hasidic Jews – brokers – filed past. Smiling her prettiest, Christ whipped out her badge. The guard nodded and she climbed the stairs to the second floor.

Opposite the steel door marked FRIEDLANDER – DIAMONDS WHOLESALE AND RETAIL, Chris was stopped by a second guard. Waiting until she was given the nod, she reached for the doorknob – only to find it locked. Seeing a TV monitor, she buzzed and held up her identification. 'Detective Cagney, Fourteenth Precinct,' she said. The buzzer released the lock. As she stepped into the office, she said, 'I want to see Mrs Friedlander.'

'You have an appointment?' The secretary spoke to her through a glass pane and bars.

'It's police business. About Mr Friedlander.'

'Sorry, if you don't have an appointment –' The receptionist turned away from Chris and picked up the phone. A few seconds later, Chris heard the admitting buzz once more. The receptionist indicated that Chris was to go in.

Mrs Friedlander was a tiny woman with wavy reddish hair. She seemed lost behind the mounds of papers on her desk and yet she seemed to be efficiently taking care of them. It was impossible not to notice the picture of her husband prominently on the wall. The office was masculine right down to the cigar humidor on the desk.

Wearing a black suit with a tasteful diamond brooch and combined wedding and engagement rings, Mrs Friedlander looked the proper businesswoman as she came around to the other side of the desk and offered Chris a seat.

'What can I do for you?' she asked. 'What can I tell you that I haven't already told the police?'

'I don't know.' Chris shrugged. 'But maybe I'll hear it differently.'

Mrs Friedlander assessed Chris. 'Maybe you will.' Picking up the phone, she instructed the receptionist to hold all calls.

'You worked with your husband?'

Sighing, Mrs Friedlander shook her head. 'No, I stepped in and took over. Someone had to. My daughter's married. My son is married, too. *She* has to live in Phoenix. There's no one else to work the business.'

'I bet you've learned a lot this past year.'

The widow stared at her a moment. 'You wouldn't believe what I've learned.'

Chris gave a bitter laugh. 'Oh, I believe it. I work in a world full of men, too.'

The atmosphere relaxed. 'What else do you want to know?'

Chris came to the point. 'Did your husband have any enemies?'

'My dear, he was a Jew. Jews always have enemies.'

Chris shook her head. 'I mean of a personal nature.'

Tears came to the widow's eyes. 'My Joey would have given you the shirt off his back – monogrammed. No, he had no enemies. Besides, who would have gotten in? You see our security.'

Chris nodded. 'Then it had to have been someone he knew. Trusted. Another Jew? Someone from the camps in Germany?'

A pained expression crossed Mrs Friedlander's face. 'It's possible. I saw –' She closed her eyes. 'God in heaven, what I saw. People. They do terrible things. Terrible.'

'He was under pressure, your husband?'

'Who isn't?' Mrs Friedlander toyed with some paper clips on the desk.

'But I mean some exceptional pressure,' Chris continued to press.

The widow sighed. 'He was. I tried not to see it, but I would wake in the night and see him awake. He was worried, but he didn't want me to worry. 'Be pretty,' he would tell me.' She shrugged. 'What could I do? He would have worried more if he knew I was worried.'

'You have no ideas?'

Once more Mrs Friedlander shrugged. 'He was a Jew in the diamond business. You can put a million dollars' worth of diamonds in your pocket. I think that's why so many Jews are in the business.' She forced a smile. 'A country decides it doesn't want you, you have to leave quickly. Sometimes with no luggage.' She stared at Chris.

'So he carried the stones. Was he insured for those stolen?'

'Who said stolen? That's what they told you?' She paused. 'So if they were stolen, where are they? If they were stolen, they would have been sold.' Mrs Friedlander went back behind the desk, took some sheets of paper from one of the piles, and handed them to Chris. 'Not in Belgium, Africa, Buenos Aires. Not even behind the Iron Curtain. Nowhere.'

Chris's eyes widened. 'But how?' She scanned the papers. 'How can you be so sure?'

Mrs Friedlander smiled slightly. 'A CIA we're not. But we do have the Diamond Market Association. Every stone ever cut is listed. They can't refuse to talk to a cop – even if you *are* a woman.'

Cagney stood as Mrs Friedlander began writing out the address for her. Then, standing, the widow crumpled the paper in her hands. 'Wait. I'll go with you. There are things I want to know, too. Maybe it's about time.'

At the Diamond Market, Chris shook hands with a jovial man wearing a monocle. But even as they talked, it appeared Manny Silverman didn't know anything more than Mrs Friedlander had. But he was, at least, able to relieve the widow's worry. There had been no other woman in the murdered man's life. But unfortunately, although Manny said he loved Joseph Friedlander like a brother and would have killed for him if necessary, the dead man hadn't trusted his friend with the secret of his worry.

'All he used to say was "An eye for an eye, a tooth for a tooth." '

Thanking Mr Silverman for his help, Chris stood. She had a lead, but where was it going to take her?

Female was talking with Coleman, the desk sergeant, when Mary Beth and Chris arrived at the precinct the next day. He was razzing her about her pimp beating her up, and Female was trying to explain about her ten-year-old son who had saved her life.

Mary Beth stared at the girl's swollen left eye and her lips, which had been cut, and held her breath. If she and Chris turned away quickly, the hooker wouldn't see them. But it was too late. In the midst of her complaint, which Coleman didn't seem to be taking too seriously, Female spotted both women.

Rushing toward them in anger, she said, 'I might have known you two were trouble!' She brushed past them out the door without giving them a chance to talk.

'Well, that does it,' Chris said, all too pleased. 'I'm going to talk to Wells and get us off this assignment.'

Horrified, Mary Beth glared at her. 'No! Don't you dare!' She started for the door.

'Where you going?'

'To talk to her!'

Outside, Mary Beth intercepted Female. 'Please – wait!'

'Why should I?' The prostitute was angry. 'You're a cop!'

'Look, it's a job. My husband's out of work,' Mary Beth said, trying to win the woman's trust.

'Otherwise you'd be home baking cookies, right?'

Mary Beth took a deep breath. 'No.'

The acid was clear in Female's tone. 'Well, maybe I would. Only I didn't have no choice.' Her voice was hoarse, obviously a result of her injury.

'Sugar did that to you, didn't he?'

Female stared coldly at Mary Beth. 'What do you care?'

'I care. Look –' Mary Beth put her hand on the girl's arm '– we can help you. Really we can.'

There was no response from the hooker.

'You got kids?' Mary Beth said, refusing to give up. 'I got two.'

'I got me one,' Female said grudgingly. 'It was him who saved me. He slashed that dude with our bread knife.'

'Please. Let us help.'

Female looked at Mary Beth and walked away.

There was nothing Mary Beth could do but wait and hope to win the woman's trust. She only hoped Female wouldn't tell the others. Their cover couldn't be blown. Not now.

A few hours later, Christine decided to try her luck with Samuels. He was on the phone when she walked in, apparently trying to mollify someone who wanted to know why he hadn't done anything about some case.

When he hung up, she approached him. 'Sir, I've got some leads on the Friedlander case. I know you questioned the widow, but –'

Samuels wagged a finger at her. 'I want you to keep your nose out of my case. If you don't, I'll get you transferred. Is that clear?'

Chris met his gaze. 'Transparent.'

Samuels narrowed his eyes. 'What's that supposed to mean?'

'It means you don't want to have this case solved. Not by Petrie or me. I know you've got him on some nothing detail for having talked to me.' She paused and tried another tactic. 'Look, I only want to help.'

'Yeah?' His voice was doubtful.

'Yes!'

'Then get out of my light,' Samuels growled. 'I've got work to do.'

Without another word, Chris slammed out of the office.

Mary Beth had been about to enter.

'Where are you going?' Mary Beth asked as they collided.

'Out. I need a drink.'

'Good. I know just the place.'

The bar was nearly ten blocks away.

'I really think I've got a lead on that damn case,' Chris complained as she drank her wine. 'Samuels wouldn't even listen to me.'

'No kidding.'

Chris glared at her. '*You're* not listening to me, either.'

Mary Beth glanced at her watch. 'Okay. So tell me about it.'

'Friedlander had an enemy.'

'I'll say.' Mary Beth drained her glass and glanced about.

'Now, if Goldman had the same enemy that would be really heavy.'

'Christine,' Mary Beth warned, 'I think you better stay out of this. Samuels is a good cop.'

'I don't want his shield.'

'Don't you?'

'No.' Chris poured more wine from the decanter between them. 'I want my own.' She paused. 'So why did we come here? We could have gone to Casey's.'

'You didn't want to be overheard, did you?'

Chris studied her partner's face. She knew Mary Beth almost as well as Mary Beth knew her. 'What's the real story?'

Mary Beth sighed. 'We're meeting some people.'

Chris felt her back stiffen. 'Who?'

'The women.'

'You're kidding.'

'Christine, they really want this union.' She paused, seeing her friend's disbelief. 'Promise me you won't tell Wells about the cover being blown.'

Chris sighed. 'I promise.' She looked up as the waiter came over and handed them a piece of paper.

'We don't want —' Mary Beth began, and then she saw it wasn't the check. The note said: *Betsy's place.*

'Come on,' she said to Chris. 'We've got a meeting to attend.'

The meeting wasn't the success Mary Beth had hoped it would be. She was shocked at some of the stories the girls told. They wanted the union all right, but they were scared. Sugar already suspected something and had beaten Honey up. 'Where did he get you?' Chris asked.

'Where he always get me,' Honey replied.

The other prostitutes laughed sourly.

'He beat you in your bedroom?' Mary Beth was aghast.

'Sugar is a natural man,' Terry said as the door opened and Female walked in.

'You keep Sugar out of your mouth,' Female said. 'Sittin' here conversin' with cops.'

Honey went up to Female. 'Hey Female – join us.'

'A whore needs a pimp,' Female said, wrenching away from her. 'You're a whore, just like me.'

'I'm a working woman,' Honey defended herself.

'You're a piece of meat, baby. Ain't nothin' gonna change that.' Without another word, Female walked out. Honey started after her.

'You're wasting your breath,' Gloria told her.

Terry was clearly frightened. 'She'll head straight for Sugar, tell him everything. Where we're meeting, who was here.' She stood as if to leave.

Betsy, the youngest of the group, looked around at each of them. 'Who could be a cop?' she said fearfully.

Each of the girls sized up the others suspiciously.

'What do *you* shoot up, sweetheart?' Terry asked Chris.

Chris smiled. 'Mother's chicken soup.'

Mary Beth stepped into the centre of things. 'So what are you going to do? Just forget it? You think it was ever easy for working people to organise?'

'Can the speeches,' Chris told her. 'What's your idea?'

Mary Beth looked around the room and then turned to her partner. 'We go. You and me. And we talk to her until she hears us. Somewhere, she knows what side she's on.'

In a scared voice, Terry said, 'She's on Sugar's side. That honcho's got her so tied she takin' tricks at home. Moonlightin'.'

Chris put on her coat. 'Hey, if anyone can talk to her, Mary Beth can, right?'

As they reached street level, Mary Beth said, 'I just hope we get to her before she talks to anyone else. It's not going to do these women any good if they know we're cops.'

'Yeah,' Chris said, 'but it might do us some good . . .'

They reached the run-down neighbourhood in Harlem where Female lived with her little boy. It was impossible not to be horrified by the broken windows and the poor condition of the streets as the kids played near an open fire hydrant. Passing an Ace Cleaner's truck, they parked the car.

As they climbed the stairs, Christine was instinctively on the alert. Female was standing at the entrance to the apartment, wearing a glittery rhinestone outfit.

Wordlessly, she motioned them up.

'What's wrong?' Chris asked her.

Female shook her head, still unable to speak. Drawing her gun, Chris entered the apartment. As she followed Mary Beth inside, Female's voice was dull. 'I didn't do it.'

'Sugar?' Mary Beth asked, seeing the body on the bed.

Female nodded and turned away from the sight of the blood.

'No one in here,' Chris said. She crossed the room to the phone and began reading Female her rights according to the Miranda law. 'You have the right to remain silent –'

'Wait a minute,' Mary Beth interrupted her. 'She said she didn't do it. You can wait two minutes, can't you?'

Chris put her finger on the phone button, but didn't put the receiver down. 'You got something to say?' She looked at the prostitute.

'Nothin',' Female said.

Turning, Chris began to dial.

Mary Beth reached over and cut her off. 'Give her a chance.'

With the receiver still in her hand, Chris said, 'Go on, then.'

'I found him like – that.'

'Chris, she couldn't have done it. She was at Betsy's. There wasn't time.'

Christine couldn't believe what she was hearing. 'We're her alibi, you mean?'

'It's true.'

'A definite maybe.' Chris paused. 'But she *could've* gotten here – that kind of knife job doesn't take long.'

With a defiant air, Female said, '*Call*'em. I don't give a damn. They wanna hang it on me, they'll hang it on me.'

Mary Beth had given Christine something to think about. She turned to the prostitute again. 'Who was here?'

'Nobody. A trick. An old man.'

'What's his name?' Mary Beth asked, trying to be gentle.

'No name.'

Chris found that hard to believe. 'You don't know anything about him?'

Female shrugged. 'What I do know ain't for no court and don't do no good. An old man – an old Jew. One of them religious kinds.'

'And he came to you?' Mary Beth asked.

'You'd be surprised who come to us.'

Chris put down the receiver. 'How do you know he's religious?'

'You know them dudes – long black coats, beards, funny hats – Hey, come on, he didn't do *that*.' She looked down at Sugar's body and quickly back to Chris. 'You think he did that? No way.'

'Female, if you didn't, we've got to find him.'

Female sat down on a chair and shook her head. 'Comes here every Thursday like clockwork.' Her voice took on its habitual irony. 'Maid's day off. Not mine.'

'But today's Friday,' Chris was quick to point out.

'Yeah. His hat wasn't ready yesterday. I was fixin' it for him. Big holiday or somethin'. Good-lookin' fur hat.'

Chris and Mary Beth were all attention now. 'Did he get the hat?' Chris's nerves prickled.

'What? You think I'm gonna leave a fur hat sittin' in the middle of my livin' room on *this* block?' Going to the closet, she took out the flat dark hat belonging to the Bubov sect of the Hasidim. Chris examined it carefully, but there was no name in it, nothing that could identify the man.

'Ain't that a winner? I told him when he give me this skirt, "You get tired of it, baby, I'll take it off your hands." '

Chris stared at Female's vest, and then at her skirt, her excitement rising. Those were diamonds, not rhinestones! 'He gave you that outfit?'

'Yeah.'

'When?'

'I don't know.' The hooker was startled.

'Last month? Last year?'

Female thought a moment. 'Last year. Right about this time.'

'I thought so. Get out of the vest and the skirt and give them to me,' Chris ordered, helping Female out of the clothes. The prostitute cooperated, but she was totally confused – as was Mary Beth.

'Call the precinct and report the murder,' Chris told her.

'Where you going?' Mary Beth demanded as Chris headed out the door with the clothes.

'I'll be right back. Put the hat in the closet.'

Chris's footsteps echoed on the stairs as Mary Beth picked up the phone and called the Fourteenth.

Downstairs, Chris looked about. She had to hide the outfit someplace, but where? The old man would be coming back for it soon. Spying the Ace Cleaner's truck they had passed on the way in, she ran over to it.

'Hey!' She stopped the driver just as he was about to pull away. 'I want these cleaned.' She handed him the vest and skirt.

The boy whistled. 'Wow!' He examined the leather and the intricate weaving of the studs.

'Yeah,' Chris agreed.

'I don't know how much it will be, but it's gonna cost you a bundle, especially because of these.' He indicated what he believed to be rhinestones.

'I don't care,' Chris said hurriedly. 'Name's Cagney.'

The boy shrugged. Writing out a receipt and handing it to her, he put the garment in back and drove off.

It didn't take long for the homicide team to arrive. Mary Beth kept close to Female, reassuring her that everything was going to be all right. Chris kept looking about, trying to see if there were any clues she had missed. 'You'll take care of my boy?' Female asked Mary Beth, astonished a cop would do that.

'Like he was my own.' Mary Beth raised her hand, Girl Scout style.

Female sighed. 'Guess I was wrong about you.' She kissed her son.

Mary Beth forced a smile, and gave the ten-year-old Randy instructions about what to pack. While the boy was busy, she moved over to Chris. 'So? You want to tell me about that vest and skirt?'

Chris glanced at the homicide people. 'Later,' she said.

When they were finally alone in the apartment, except for Randy packing a suitcase in the other room, Mary Beth asked again, 'So?'

Chris flipped open her notebook. 'Okay, listen to this. Two Hasidic diamond merchants are killed – probably by a fellow Jew. The diamonds don't appear anywhere on the international market. Now a pimp is killed by a Hasidic Jew who has given the pimp's best lady a vest and a skirt covered with rhinestones.'

'You can't be saying he gave Female diamonds?'

'Why not?' Christine said. 'What better way to hide them than in plain sight? Sugar sees him, sees the diamonds, puts two and two together, and *whammo!*'

Mary Beth's eyes widened. 'Could it have been?'

'If we don't find him, Female's had it. I can't imagine the good old liberal public defender shedding many tears at a pimp being killed by a prostitute. It would be open-and-shut.'

Mary Beth sighed. 'But what about the vest and skirt?'

'They're safe.' Christine gave one of her mysterious smiles.

Mary Beth stood. 'You know, I sometimes have the feeling you don't trust even me. I think we ought to go back to the station and tell Samuels about those clothes.'

Christine's back went ramrod. 'I am not telling Samuels anything! You think I want to end up on some dirt detail like Petrie?'

'Petrie broke the rules.'

'Well, I'm going to break a few rules, too.'

Mary Beth stared at her. She couldn't believe this was the same Christine who was a stickler for doing everything by the book. 'Listen, I know you're trying to be tough, but you're not going to break them by showing how macho you are.'

Chris shrugged and started for the door.

'Where ya *going*?' Mary Beth demanded.

Chris smiled at her. 'Oh, I thought I'd have my hair done and get a manicure, and perhaps have some of those dainty tea sandwiches at the ladies' auxiliary.'

Mary Beth stared at her. 'I'm going to tell Samuels.'

'You do that,' Chris said as her parting shot. 'Or maybe you have to ask Harve's permission first.' She ran down the steps before her partner could answer.

Mary Beth shook her head and waited for Randy. When he came out of his room carrying a suitcase, she took his hand. 'Come on, sweetie.' Leading him to the door, she suppressed a smile as he reached behind the couch for his Snoopy doll.

In the lockup, Christine paced as Female sat on the narrow cot, her head in her hands. Her dinner tray was on the table, untouched. 'I'm trying to help,' Christine said through clenched teeth.

'I know all about the good cop and the bad cop. Your partner would have been more convincing.'

Christine stared at her. 'We all make career choices.'

Female stood and began to pace the cell with Chris. 'I had two hot choices – to clean other women's houses or mess with their husbands.'

With a chill, Chris realised Female was probably right. 'Well, you got a choice now. Look, I *am* a good cop, but right now they've got me on a crud detail. But I've got this lead and I want to prove I'm good for more. I can't do it without your help.' Chris sat on the bed. 'Please. Tell me anything you remember.'

'I told you I don't *know* anything more.'

'You've got to remember,' Chris insisted. 'I can't help you unless you do.'

Female sighed. She sat beside Christine and closed her eyes as she tried to recall. 'He didn't talk much, just gave orders.'

'Orders?'

'Do this, do that. His way. I didn't care. They were his bucks.'

Chris hesitated. 'Was he – mean?'

'No.' Female shook her head. 'But I'm sure he could be. Those eyes.' She shivered.

'Did he have an accent?'

'They all do, them folks. Look alike and sound alike. From Europe someplace, I guess.'

'A Jew from the diamond merchants'?'

'Diamonds?' Female's voice went hoarse.

'You didn't know?' Chris stared at her. 'I thought you knew when I took the vest and skirt.'

'Diamonds,' Female repeated to herself in a daze as she stared at the bars to her cell. 'Diamonds. Me and my boy and my man could have been long gone. *Diamonds?*' She turned to Chris again.

Christine nodded. 'Tell me when he gave you the vest and the skirt.'

Female shook her head as she tried to think. 'The vest a few weeks ago maybe. But I had the skirt at least a year.'

'When is important,' Chris told her. 'Look, a year ago a diamond merchant was killed. Two weeks ago another one was stabbed, too.'

Female took in a fearful breath. '*He* did that?'

Christine nodded. 'I think so. But we have to find him to prove it.'

Shaking her head as if to stimulate her thought, Female said, 'You know, I didn't think nothin' of it. I mean, some dudes have their own things, you know. I figured he just wanted me to dress up.'

'Did he ever mention being in the camps during the war?' Chris felt her blood buzzing. She was close, so very close.

'Yeah, he mentioned it. Auschwitz, I think it was.'

Christine felt her heart beat faster. She swallowed hard. 'What was his tattoo number? Do you remember?'

Female gave her a strange look. 'Tattoo? That dude didn't have no tattoo. Less it was under his beard.'

'He had to have,' Chris insisted. 'On his arm.'

'That dude didn't have no tattoo,' Female insisted. 'Who would know better?'

'Okay.' Chris sighed. 'If you recall anything more, let me know. I'll be by tomorrow.' She stood.

'Wait, I just remembered somethin' funny.'

'What?'

'It was his cock.'

'His what?' For all her sophistication, Chris felt herself flushing. 'What do you mean?'

Female grinned at Chris's discomfort. 'It weren't like the other Jew boys I been with. They're all –' She waved her hand as if searching for the word.

'Circumcised?'

'Yeah, they ain't got no foreskin.' Female stood. 'But *he* did.'

Christine stared at her. Jews had to be circumcised. Even those that didn't practise the religion had it done, didn't they? She would have to ask Petrie. He would know.

In a rare show of emotion, she touched the prostitute's hand. 'Thanks. What you've remembered is a big help.' Turning, she called out, 'Guard, I'm ready.'

The uniformed man swaggered over. 'Yeah, what are you ready for, blondie?'

Chris glared at him and flashed her shield. 'Detective Cagney. Fourteenth.'

'Pardon me, sir. I just came on duty.' The guard quickly undid the lock.

'Not *sir – ma'am*,' Chris corrected him as she left the cell.

'Hey, Cagney –' Female called out.

Chris looked back.

It was difficult for Female to say thank you, especially to a white cop. 'See you later.'

There was only one person who could answer Chris's questions. Quickly, she hurried to the National Jewelry Exchange. She found Mrs Friedlander just about to leave.

'Please,' Chris said. 'I must talk to you. It won't take long.'

'It's my night to see my grandson. I must get there quickly before they put him to bed.'

'It won't take long, I promise.' Christine hurried along the street with Mrs Friedlander as the woman kept up a brisk pace. 'Tell me, would it be possible to be in the camps and not have a number?'

'Maybe when they were busy at the end, I don't know. Maybe plastic surgery.'

'No, no – that doesn't make sense. This suspect isn't someone trying to pass. He's a Jew. A religious man. Who else was in the camps?'

'Nazis.'

'Nazis.' Christine let the idea run through her brain.

Mrs Friedlander snorted. 'What? You're so young? They don't teach in school? There were Nazis, nuns, priests, and anyone else who dared to go against the butchers.'

Chris stopped suddenly and gazed at the woman. 'Wait. If a Nazi wanted to get out, to escape before the war-crimes trials, could he dress like a Jew – act like a Jew?'

Mrs Friedlander halted, catching her breath. 'There was one who did that.' Chris could hear the hatred in her voice. 'May he rot in hell. He even spoke our language. A spy. He would ask about our families. They would go out and get them. We didn't know.' Tears were in her eyes. 'We didn't know. Schirmer.' She shook her head. 'Schirmer!'

Her eyes seemed to widen. 'My God! Schirmer is here! Schirmer killed my Yosel. A hundred years later it seems. Schirmer. Oh, my God!'

'Schirmer?' Chris put her hands on the woman's shoulders. 'Where would he be?'

The widow closed her eyes, cursing and crying. 'I saw it. I saw it in Yosel's writing. He wrote the name over and over. I thought he was just recalling the past.'

'How can I find him?'

Mrs Friedlander shook her head. 'Don't find him. Don't let him find you! You don't know what he is. Maybe no one else will recognise him. Maybe it's over.'

'You know better than that.' Chris took her hand.

Yaffa Friedlander shook her head. 'I'm afraid.'

'Where do I go?' Chris insisted. 'He's posing as a Hasid. How do I start?'

It was overwhelming. 'So many sects. So many types. Different neighbourhoods. The Hasids have their own splits. This one thinks this, this one thinks that. The only ones who might talk to you are over there.' Yaffa pointed toward the Lubavitch Sukkah Mobile.

Nodding, Chris ran over to the wagon. 'May I speak to you a moment?'

'Can we help you?' A young boy with long curls down his cheeks and the traditional head covering looked at her. He handed her a lulab and ethrog, the ornaments of the Sukkoth holiday. 'Would you like some literature?'

'I'm the police. Detective Cagney. Fourteenth.'

The boy stepped back. 'We have a permit.'

Chris shook her head. 'No. That's not what I want. I need to find someone. A man named Schirmer. You ever hear of him?'

The boy shook his head. 'Maybe we can talk some other time.'

Refusing to be put off, Chris continued, 'He was in Auschwitz, posing as a Jew. He got information and passed it on. You've never heard the name? Schirmer?'

'No,' the boy said.

'Schirmer?' A second Hasidic boy came over to them and spat on the ground.

Chris felt a glimmer of hope. 'You know him? You've heard of him?'

'I've heard of him.'

'Then I must talk to you.'

'Does it have to be now? It's nearly a holiday.'

'This man's a murderer. I must find him. Now.'

The boys opened the door to the trailer – the 'Sukkoth on Wheels.' 'Come,' the second one said, 'we'll talk.'

At the table inside, the three sat. 'All I know is he's a Hasid,' Cagney said.

'That's a lot of territory. What did he look like?'

'Like you.'

'A *little like us*? A *lot* like us? There's a difference. There are those from Crown Heights and those from Borough Park. We all dress different. 'Do you know his clothes? His fringes?'

Chris shook her head, feeling helpless. Was it all going to end here?

'No, not his fringes,' the second boy said, 'it's his hat. That will be the giveaway.'

'Hat!' Chris's face lit up. 'I know his hat. It was fur.'

'And you're a detective,' the boy sneered. 'Describe it.'

'Dark fur. Not mink.'

The boys shook their heads. 'Round? Short? Flat?'

Excited, Chris took out paper. 'Here, let me draw it.'

It took several drawings before she got it right. The Lubavitcher determined Schirmer was among the group from Borough Park.

Chris hailed a taxi. She told herself she would get that bastard, and get him tonight. Then Samuels would have to admit she was good.

Once in Borough Park, though, things didn't prove as easy as she had hoped. She talked to one storekeeper and then another. She went into clothing stores and talked to women on the street.

Finally, she stopped at a greengrocer's.

'You looking for someone?' the owner asked. He pushed at the skullcap on his head.

'Yes, I am. Do you live in the area?' Chris showed him her shield.

'What is it? Drugs?'

She shook her head. 'Murder.'

'Murder? Here?'

Chris nodded.

'You're wrong. Not in our area.'

Chris sighed. 'You've lived here a long time?'

'Who can afford to move?'

Chris nodded. 'This man, his name is Schirmer. He would have only recently moved here. Maybe a year or so ago. He wears the Bubar dress.'

The owner shook his head. 'A religious man? How could he face God?'

'He won't have the chance to. He'll be with all the rest of the master race. I'll be back in case you think of anything.' Hurrying out, she continued asking questions.

Finally, thirst overcame her and she stopped at a diner.

'You want something more than coffee? Eggs?'

Chris shook her head. 'I don't want anything more. I just want to find a man named Schirmer. Look, Miss –'

'Ruby. My sister's Pearl. Would you believe it? My father wasn't even in the business –'

'The man is a murderer. I have to find him.'

'So,' Ruby said, 'tonight, if he's in Borough Park, where would he be?'

Chris drummed her fingers on the countertop. 'That's what I want to know.'

'I forgot,' Ruby said, 'you're an outsider. Tonight on Hoshanna Rabbah, the seventh day of the holiday, the Torahs are brought to the bimah.'

'What?'

Ruby smiled. 'The reading desk of the synagogue.'

'And everyone goes there?'

'Anita Bryant will probably stay home in Florida.'

Chris stood abruptly. Throwing money on the counter, she said, 'Your folks were right. You are a jewel.'

Going to the phone, she dialled Mary Beth's phone number.

At the Lacey apartment, Michael Harvey, Jr., and Randy were staring at their dinner. No one was eating.

'Great stew, Harve,' Mary Beth said.

'Yeah,' Harvey muttered.

'Mom, can I go? I can't stand squishy peas,' Michael said.

Mary Beth nodded.

Michael threw down his napkin and left the room. His brother followed, taking Female's son with him.

'I had a real bad day today,' Mary Beth said.

There was no response from Harvey.

'I guess you did, too,' Mary Beth said lamely. She attempted to touch her husband and he pulled away.

'I got up today.'

'Oh.' Mary Beth paused. 'Chris and I had words.'

'No kidding. I thought you only had deeds.'

'Harve, she's my best friend.'

'Well, good.' He stood and started to clear the table. 'I hope you'll both be very happy.'

Tucking the kids in, she stood for a moment and stared out the window at the coming darkness. Hearing Harvey go into the bedroom, her heart was heavy. Maybe, if they could talk. She went to the bedroom door and knocked. 'Can I come in?'

Harvey was sitting on the bed. 'You pay the rent.'

His words were a barb but she ignored them and sat down on the bed. 'I'm worried about Christine. It's been tough for her. Those guys treat us like lepers.'

'So?' Harvey refused to look at her. 'I really don't care.'

Mary Beth felt hot tears come to her eyes. Quickly she brushed them away. Harvey turned toward her. 'I'm sorry, I didn't mean that. I do care about *you. She's* probably driving them up the wall.'

'In a Sherman tank.' Mary Beth gave a laugh.

'I knew it.'

Mary Beth stood. 'She's liable to do something foolish.'

'So what else is new?'

There was no talking with this man. Mary Beth grabbed her shoes and coat.

'Where do you think you're going?'

'To look for my partner.'

Harvey stood. 'You're not going out of this house tonight.'

Mary Beth's mouth dropped open. 'I don't even talk to the kids like that.'

'Maybe they don't need it.'

Tears came again to her eyes. 'Maybe I don't need it, either! Maybe I need some loving and comfort – some support!'

'I know. Have you hugged your cop today?'

'Harvey Lacey,' she said, 'I was a cop before we were married. We talked about this from the beginning.'

'If your job is so important –'

Her temper was up now. The dam that had held everything in suddenly burst. 'And I *do* pay the rent! And I'm sick and tired of all this.' Her voice caught with the tears. 'I hate looking in the mirror and wondering why I'm so unattractive, why my husband won't make love to me.' She couldn't help the tears now.

'I'm sorry.' Harvey started to come forward.

'Don't sorry me – I'm not sad, I'm mad.'

He came closer.

'Don't you touch me, Harvey Lacey!' She turned to leave. 'I'm going to find my partner.'

'Well, how the hell do you think that makes me feel? Your partner! I mean, knowing I can't support my family.'

Mary Beth came forward now. The anger was still in her. 'If you're having a problem, quit hanging around here for a construction job. There are other things you can do.'

'What the hell – you want me to get a job as a dishwasher?'

She glared at him. 'You've had enough experience now, haven't you?'

Harvey's eyes showed his hurt, but he forced a laugh.

There was a long silence before Mary Beth got hold of her emotions. 'Honey, I know you feel like a real man when you're up on those girders, swearing with the guys, wearing your hard hat, but you've always been a man to me.'

Harvey turned and stared at her. 'How would you feel if I took over the super's job? I mean, now that he's moving to Florida.'

Mary Beth held her breath. 'Super.'

'You mean it?'

She nodded as Harvey put his arms on her shoulders and looked into her eyes. Leaning down, he kissed her. Mary Beth responded, kissing him with all the pent-up passion she had missed the whole past year. Kissing him again, she dropped her shoes and her coat.

He kissed her nose. 'We gotta make up for lost time,' he said.

'We will,' she laughed. 'We will.'

Back in the Borough Park phone booth, Chris waited anxiously. Finally, on the sixth ring, her partner answered. 'Look, I got him. I'm sure I've got him. I'm in Borough Park. He's going to be in one of the synagogues. He has to be. I'm going to try and get him to Ace Cleaners, where I have Female's outfit.'

'Wait a minute. Explain it to me.'

Partway into her explanation, the operator broke in. 'Your time is up.'

'No – no, wait! Mary Beth, tell –'

The call was cut.

'Damn!' Chris cursed. She found more change in her pocket. 'Thank you, God.' Redialling, she spoke quickly as soon as Harvey picked up. 'Listen, tell Mary Beth to get the troops. Petrie's on some stupid detail in the Forty-ninth. Tell her to get him. I'll see you.'

'Find out where she is,' Mary Beth instructed Harvey as she slipped into a sweater and pulled on her jeans.

Harvey held the receiver so Mary Beth could hear the disconnection. 'She wants you to get the troops. Where did she tell you she is?'

'Borough Park.'

Harvey jumped out of the bed. 'I'll drive you.'

'Who's going to watch the boys?'

'You're dealing with a killer –'

'I'll get Petrie to take me.' She hugged Harvey and put on her gun. Giving him another fast peck on the cheek, she left.

Randy came to the doorway.

'I think you got monsters in this here apartment,' the boy said. 'I can't sleep.'

Harvey smiled. Indicating the bed, he said, 'Be my guest.'

Bravely, Randy marched into the room, hugging his Snoopy doll.

In Borough Park, Chris was having a more difficult time than she thought. None of the men would talk to her – they even went to the other side of the street to avoid her.

Going up to some of the women, she held out her shield. 'I'm looking for a murderer.'

Several of the women spoke in Hebrew, but none spoke to her. 'Please, two women are widowed because of him. He's just murdered a third time to protect the diamonds he stole. I have those diamonds. Help me smoke him out. He must be here tonight. You have to help me – please, we're sisters.'

The women continued on toward the synagogue, not talking to her.

At the station, Samuels reacted just as Mary Beth had expected.

'All right,' he said, 'run it by me one more time.'

There was fury in Mary Beth's voice. 'If something happens to her because you're too pigheaded to listen –'

Samuels interrupted. 'I just want to know what she's doing out there.'

Once more, Mary Beth repeated, 'She thinks she's found the murderer, the one you've – your case, you know?'

'My case.' He began putting talcum powder into his shoes.

'Look, she could be in terrible trouble while we're sitting here arguing! Please!'

Samuels made no comment. Furious, Mary Beth dialled the Forty-ninth station. 'I tell you, if anything happens to her, I'll hold you personally responsible.' She spoke into the phone. 'Detective Lacey, Fourteenth. Is Petrie there?' She listened a moment. 'Damn! He's not back yet.' She hung up the phone just as Isbecki and Davidson walked in. 'You gotta listen – Chris is in trouble.'

Getting no reaction from them, she backed away in disgust. 'Forget it! I'll go myself!'

As Mary Beth put on her coat, Isbecki melted. 'I'll drive with you,' he told her. He turned toward Samuels. 'What the hell, I got a sweet little redhead out in Bensonhurst.'

Slowly, Samuels stood. 'I'm going. I just want to know where.'

'I told you,' Mary Beth said. 'Borough Park. The synagogue there someplace.' She started out the door.

'Tell me again,' Samuels said.

Fighting hysteria, Mary Beth repeated, 'She said she was going to smoke him out with the skirt and the vest – at the cleaners'.' Suddenly, she understood what Samuels wanted. 'The cleaners up in Harlem. One of those A's – Acme? Ace?' She paused. 'Yes, it's Ace. I'm sure.'

'Good,' Samuels said, grabbing his coat and the phonebook. 'Let's go.'

Christine continued to walk the streets. Her sixth sense told her that Schirmer knew she was around and that she was looking for him. He would probably try to get to her. If only she could convince him she knew about the diamonds.

He needed the vest and the skirt. They were crucial.

She wandered past the sukkahs with their grass roofs and decorative trimmings.

Her presence was all around. She stepped into an alley, her hand on her gun. But she was purposely putting herself in his path.

The yowl of a cat made her jump. Her heart raced. It was nothing. She continued walking, knowing she had to find him soon. Then, stopping for a moment, she explored one of the harvest houses – and let her guard down.

Swiftly, Schirmer came upon her. His hand clasped over her mouth, and with his other arm he lifted her off the ground, dragging her with him toward his car. Christine looked up into the cold grey eyes and knew Female had been right. There was no question. He had murdered all three.

In the moonlight, his knife glinted near her throat. He motioned her into the driver's seat as he continued to press the knife on her.

As she began driving toward Harlem and the cleaners, Christine started to chatter. 'Ironic, isn't it, a Nazi killing to retain his identity as a Jew? How many more are you going to kill because they recognise you? What happened? You get hooked on the chicken soup?'

He said nothing, but Chris could feel the coldness of the metal on her neck. She prayed Mary Beth had gotten hold of Petrie. Someone had to come help her . . .

Still holding the knife on her, Schirmer and Chris left the car. He broke the window of the cleaning plant and forced her inside. 'Show me,' he ordered, dragging her along the racks as he searched for the clothes, the knife still at her throat. She had to think of something.

'Upstairs.' Her voice was tight as she led the way to the elevator. Christine had never been to a cleaning plant at night, but she could only guess and play for time. Pressing the fourth-floor button, she continued to pray.

The choice had been a correct one – at least Schirmer didn't suspect her ruse yet.

'*Where?*' She glanced about. Someone had left a window open. The rows upon rows of plastic garment bags and gleaming metal rods were moving like ghosts walking. Christine shivered.

'*Where?*' he repeated.

Chris pointed toward the centre of the room and suddenly she saw her chance. Kicking the switch with her foot, she started the wheels in motion and the clothes racks started to spin. Startled, Schirmer let her go and she dived for cover under the plastic bags.

Her gun. Where were her gun and her purse? Then she saw her purse several feet away, by Schirmer's feet. She must have dropped it when she scrambled away from him.

She heard Schirmer's heavy breathing as he moved through the clothes and plastic trying to find her. Could *he* hear *her*? Where were the others? How long could she hold him off?

She inched forward. There was no way to get to her gun. Grabbing a piece of plastic, she twisted it into a rope. Too late, she realised that he had the same plan. The plastic bag on her face was suffocating her.

She fought desperately to be free of his hands around her neck. She didn't know how much longer she could hold out. He was stronger than she. If there was a God in heaven, he had to help her now.

'Chris! Christine!' Mary Beth yelled. 'Where are you?'

Even through the plastic and the veil of haziness descending over her vision, Christine could see the terror in Schirmer's eyes.

'Hold it! Hold it!' Mary Beth cried as she burst through the door, with Samuels following.

The surprise was enough to gain Christine time. Tearing the plastic off her face, she gulped in air. Reaching to the floor, she grabbed for her purse and the gun.

Too late, Schirmer realised his captive was free.

Chris stared in horror as he lunged at her. She hadn't killed anyone yet and she didn't want to now. She could feel the air from the open window behind her. As he lunged at her, she did the natural thing. She ducked.

The next few moments were a blur as the huge, bull-like figure of the Nazi sailed over her and crashed through the fourth-floor window. The glass flew everywhere, hitting Chris, hitting the floor, scattering on the street as Schirmer's body thudded on the ground below.

A stunned Chris went to the window and stared down. It was over. He was dead.

'You okay?' Mary Beth came over to her partner.

Chris nodded. She touched Mary Beth's arm. 'Thanks. I knew you'd come.'

Samuels grunted, and for the first time Christine realised he was there, too.

'Good work, Cagney,' he said. He glanced about the place. 'I'd like to see this fabulous outfit.'

'Yes, sir.' Christine brushed the glass off her and, spinning the clothes rack, watched for the plastic bag through which diamonds would show – glimmering in the moonlight. It didn't take long.

The next day, the whole crew did a massive clean-up job, and before the end of the shift Lacey and Cagney's desk was moved from the booking area outside to the area where Chris had first suggested – near the coffeepot.

'Well, we're off the John detail, at least.'

Samuels came up to them. 'You may be off John detail, but you've got other work to do now.'

He handed them a folder.

Christine picked it up and read the cover page. 'You've got to be kidding – investigation of a weight-loss-clinic scam?'

Samuels nodded. 'It's all in a day's work, ladies. By the way –' He handed Cagney a small plant for her desk. 'Thanks to you, it's Lieutenant Samuels now.'

Cagney looked up at him and smiled. But he had already turned to his desk – too busy, or perhaps too embarrassed, to smile back.

Taggart and a Bit of Skulduggery

BY PETER CAVE

Detective Chief Inspector Jim Taggart of the Northern Division of the Glasgow City Police was the first of a new breed of unashamedly tough and cynical cops on the box who emerged in the eighties and have now become an integral part of contemporary television crime series. Introduced in September 1983 in an STV three-episode story entitled Killer, *the solemn, obsessive policeman played by Mark McManus has subsequently earned numerous accolades, including that of being 'the toughest man on television', while the series itself has fans all over the world, not to mention in the most unlikely circles as* The Times. *Peter Waymark revealed in January 1994 while the twenty-eighth case was being shown: 'Over the years, audience ratings for the show have risen along with production values – even the Queen Mother is said to be a fan. Grittier and gorier than other police procedurals, it is often spiked with a winning gallows humour.' It might also be added that the other elements in its success have been consistently excellent plots, taut script-writing and the use of authentic Scottish locations.*

Taggart *was created by Scottish script-writer Glen Chandler and his immediate impact in* Killer *undoubtedly owed a great deal to the inspired casting of Mark McManus, a miner's son and former professional boxer, in the role of the uncompromising DCI. As a native Glaswegian, Mark already had a good idea about the life of a policeman amongst the crime and violence of the city, but he also took a lot of trouble to make the part authentic by spending time touring Glasgow at night and using two hard-bitten detectives for role models. As added dimensions to the story, Taggart has a wheelchair-bound wife, Jean (Harriet Buchan) and had (for the first four years of the*

*series) a university-trained assistant, Detective Sergeant Peter
Livingstone (Neil Duncan) with whom he was clearly ill at ease and
frequently clashed. When Duncan left the series in 1987, he was
replaced by James Macpherson as Detective Sergeant Mike Jardine, a
self-professed Christian who suffers from the worst sin of all in
Taggart's book – he is a teetotaller. Their equally uneasy alliance has,
in its turn, given an additional edge to the stories. (Peter Livingstone
has, of course, subsequently reappeared in the series, and is now
apparently the comfortably-off head of a successful Edinburgh
Security Firm – a red rag to both Taggart and Jardine.) Increasing
prominence has also been given to a female member of Taggart's
squad, Detective Constable Jackie Reid, played by Blythe Duff.*

*The successful transmission of that first story Killer – and the quite
evident fact that it was Taggart who had grabbed the audiences – was
what prompted the producer Robert Love to give the star his own
series, and subsequent stories have varied in length from three-part
episodes of sixty minutes to single ninety-minute specials. The DCI
has appeared in a total of over sixty episodes. In* Taggart and a Bit of
Skulduggery *by Peter Cave, based on the story, 'Nest of Vipers', the
DCI is investigating the discovery of two skulls that may belong to
murder victims who disappeared some years earlier. Once again
Jardine is in danger of falling foul of his boss, while the episode also
provides another insight into Taggart's home life . . .*

MIKE JARDINE TURNED in to the City Arms and headed for the bar,
nodding at several colleagues along the way. The place had
become more or less the unofficial social club for Maryhill Police
Station over the past couple of months.

Dr Andrews, the City Pathologist, sidled up to him as he prepared to
order his drink.

'How would you like to impress your superiors?' he asked with a
knowing grin. Andrews was well aware of the ongoing duel between
the young DS and Taggart, and right now he was in a position to turn it
to his advantage. He drained his whisky glass and set it down on the
counter under Jardine's nose. 'Large whisky, please.'

Jardine smiled ruefully and dug in his pocket.

'Well?' he asked eventually, when they had both been served.

'There's an old university chum of mine. Professor Peter Hutton. Widely acknowledged as one of the greatest experts in the technique of reconstructing faces on skulls. He's scored some amazing successes, I understand.'

Jardine nodded. 'Yes, I've heard of the technique. Based on the relationship between the face and the contours of the skull, I believe. But I thought most of that sort of work had been carried out in America?'

'Ah – that's where the good bit comes in,' Andrews said, tapping the side of his nose. 'He's right here in Glasgow at the moment. Oddly enough they brought him over to put faces to those two Roman skulls.'

Jardine was hooked. 'Where could I find him?'

Andrews drained his glass again and waited for Jardine to pay for another refill before continuing. 'Department of Anatomy at Glasgow University. You should be able to catch him in the morning.'

Jardine was feeling pleased with himself as he crossed the university campus on his way to the Department of Anatomy. It felt good to be one jump ahead of Taggart for a change.

There were two men in the room as he entered. One of them, scruffily dressed and in his middle fifties, was puffing at a cigarette with the nervous compulsion of the confirmed chain-smoker. An unprepossessing figure, he hardly looked the type to be a leading expert at anything.

Jardine addressed himself to the younger, smarter man.

'Excuse me, but I was looking for Professor Peter Hutton. Any idea where I might find him?'

Surprisingly, it was the older man who answered, somewhat brusquely. 'I'm Hutton. What do you want? I'm due at a press conference.'

Jardine produced his ID card. 'Detective Sergeant Michael Jardine, Maryhill Station. I need a few words. It should only take a couple of minutes.'

Hutton turned to his companion. 'Carl, could you go ahead to the lecture room and tell them I'm on my way?'

As Carl Young left the room, Hutton lit another cigarette from the burning stub between his fingers and regarded Jardine over a cloud of blue smoke.

'What's all this about?'

'An old colleague of yours, Dr Stephen Andrews, said you might be able to help us,' Jardine told him.

'Ah, Stephen,' Hutton mused. 'Has he still got that ridiculous beard?' Without waiting for an answer, he made a move towards the door. 'Look, can we discuss this on the way to the lecture hall? I'm running late as it is.'

Jardine followed the man back outside. There were several people loitering and strolling around the campus. Jardine failed to spot Mike Gallagher, a reporter from the *Evening Times* who had tailed him all the way from Maryhill Station. Gallagher fell into step slightly behind them, his ears pricked.

'There would have to be a fee, of course,' Hutton said when Jardine had explained the position. 'For the department, of course – you understand?'

'I can't authorise that off my own back,' Jardine told him. 'But I'm sure something can be arranged.'

It seemed to satisfy Hutton. 'How much do you know about my work?'

Jardine shrugged. 'Very little,' he admitted. 'The point is, do you think you can help us?'

'Oh, I should think so.' Hutton sounded very confident. 'I did a similar job for the police in Chicago not so long ago. They had three skulls in a trunk and no bodies. I put faces on all three, and they positively identified two of them. What do you know about yours so far?'

'Only that they are both young females. That's about it.'

'Hair samples?'

'Blonde, in both cases.'

Hutton seemed to be weighing things up in his mind. 'Well, it sounds like I should be able to help you. Dependent on the fee, of course. The Americans are most generous in these matters, I seem to recall.'

They had reached the entrance to the lecture hall.

'Look – this is not official yet, so I'd be obliged if you didn't say anything,' Jardine said.

Hutton didn't seem to be listening any more. He strode up the steps of the lecture hall, pausing only to light up yet another cigarette. He was closely followed by Gallagher.

Jardine walked back to his car, congratulating himself on a good morning's work. There was the problem of the fee, of course, but he was certain Taggart could make sure that some funds were made available.

Inside the lecture hall, Hutton took his place on the rostrum. Carl

Young had laid out everything neatly for him in readiness: his notes, and plaster casts of the two Roman skulls.

Hutton picked one of them up and addressed his small audience, launching into his prepared speech. 'Good morning, ladies and gentlemen. I'd like you to meet Flavius Hierombalus and his auxiliary here. I invented Flavius because it was a common first name at the time.'

Gallagher climbed to his feet, interrupting Hutton in full flow. 'Professor Hutton – can you tell us any more about the work you are doing on the two murder victims' skulls found yesterday?'

Hutton was completely thrown off guard. 'I haven't started yet.'

'But you have helped police forces before with this sort of thing?'

'Well, yes,' Hutton admitted.

Gallagher smiled with satisfaction, having obtained an official confirmation. 'And you will be able to reconstruct their faces just as you could on these Roman ones?' he prompted.

'Yes, the principle is exactly the same,' Hutton agreed.

Gallagher sat down again, more than pleased with himself.

The story made the midday edition. It also made Taggart's office.

Scowling furiously, Taggart waved the newspaper under Jardine's nose.

'What are you – a one-man band?' he demanded angrily.

Jardine cowered slightly under the attack. 'I told him not to say anything,' he muttered defensively. 'I thought I was using my initiative.'

Taggart took a few seconds off to read the newspaper story fully, calming down as he realised that his young colleague had, actually, made a significant breakthrough. 'I've got nothing against you using your initiative,' he said finally, in a less aggressive tone. 'Just as long as you keep me informed.' Taggart pointed to the photograph of Hutton. 'What is this guy? Some kind of witch-doctor?'

Jardine relaxed, knowing that Taggart's anger had dissipated. 'Why don't we go and find out?' he suggested.

Taggart's suspicions of witch-doctory were confirmed by his first sight of Hutton's work lab. Rows of human skulls and various pieces of bone littered the shelves and work-tops. A human skeleton in one corner of the room had been pressed into service as a coat rack and the man had even found a use for one piece of skull as an ashtray, into which he ritually tapped the ash from his ubiquitous cigarette.

Jardine placed the large cardboard box he had been carrying upon the nearest work-top. Opening it, he gently lifted out the two skulls.

Hutton weighed them both in his hands as though he were testing two melons for ripeness. 'And one of these you believe to be the skull of Janet Gilmour?' he asked.

Taggart nodded. 'That's right. We're going on estimated age alone – so we figure skull number two. They're both tabbed.'

Hutton selected the correct skull and examined it carefully. 'The teeth and jawbone might be a bit of a problem, but I can probably build it up reasonably accurately. Have you brought the hair samples?'

Jardine produced two plastic bags, also tagged and numbered. 'Do you need a photograph of Janet?'

Hutton shook his head. 'I don't want to know what she looked like. It might affect my reconstruction. I'm a scientist, not a sculptor.'

'How long will it take?' Taggart wanted to know.

Hutton considered for a moment. 'Well, I should do a bit more work on the Roman skulls. There's an exhibition next week.'

'They'll have to wait,' Taggart snapped testily. He was still slightly miffed about the size of Hutton's fee. 'They've been around for two thousand years. I'm sure they'll wait a bit longer.'

Hutton shrugged carelessly. 'I'll start on them as soon as I can. I'll be in touch when I have something to show you.'

He was obviously unwilling to be more specific. Taggart decided that he wasn't going to achieve much by pressing the man. Besides, the ghoulish lab unnerved him slightly, and he couldn't wait to be out of it. 'Right, then – we'll leave you to it,' he muttered, turning to leave.

Jardine followed him rather reluctantly. He had found the place totally fascinating.

Taggart came down for breakfast to find Jean seated in her wheelchair cuddling a large ginger cat. He groaned aloud. 'Aw, Jean – you know I can't stand cats.'

His wife was instantly on the defensive. 'He'll keep me company during the day. And most of the evenings, seeing as you're hardly ever here.'

Taggart accepted the implied rebuke without comment. 'Where did it come from, anyway?'

'Mrs MacPherson asked me to have it. They're moving to a new flat and they're not allowed to keep pets.'

'Did she not have a dog?' Taggart asked. 'At least you can talk to a dog.'

'And who would walk it?' Jean countered. 'You'd never find the time.'

Taggart could sense that his wife was warming to her old, familiar theme. He decided to skip breakfast. Putting on his tie, he prepared to leave.

'You will make an effort to be home for our Burns Supper on Friday?' Jean queried. 'You'll remember I mentioned it to you last week. I've invited Margaret MacKenzie and her family, and we're having a disabled piper.'

Taggart groaned again. He had vague memories about the supper, but the disabled piper was something new. 'You're not seriously having bagpipes in this house?' he said, as though it had been some kind of a joke.

'And why not?' Jean demanded. She had thought it was a rather good idea.

Her husband managed a faint smile. 'Well, all I can say is, he really will be disabled if the neighbours come round.'

The telephone started to ring. Taggart moved to answer it.

'You will try to get home in time, won't you?' Jean stressed, anxious to pin him down to some sort of commitment before his mind was taken up with other things.

'You know me, Jean. I always try,' Taggart answered, picking up the phone.

It was Mike Jardine. He sounded depressed. 'Sir – Hutton's lab was broken into last night. Someone stole the skulls.'

'What!' Taggart shouted, hardly able to believe his ears. 'Was there no damned security there at all?'

'I doubt if it would have made much difference, sir,' Jardine told him. 'The thief was pretty determined. He smashed open two doors and forced the outside lock as it was.'

'Meet me there in ten minutes,' Taggart snapped. He tugged his tie into position and reached for his coat. He left without remembering to say goodbye to his wife.

Although, as Jardine had explained, there was a lot of external damage caused by the break-in, there was virtually no disruption to the lab itself. To Taggart, it was patently obvious that the thief had known exactly what he was looking for.

Hutton was distraught. 'They're utterly irreplaceable. Priceless,' he complained bitterly, sucking at his cigarette angrily.

Taggart did a double-take. 'Wait a minute. Priceless, did you say? What skulls are we talking about here?'

Hutton looked at him as though he were a simpleton. 'Why, the Roman skulls of course. Why do you think I'm so upset?'

'You mean – *our* skulls weren't taken?' Taggart asked, hardly able to believe his luck.

'Of course they didn't take *your* skulls,' Hutton said peevishly. 'They're quite safe in the bottom of the cupboard over there.' He indicated a wall cupboard across the room.

Jardine beat Taggart to the cupboard by a clear couple of feet. Reaching in, he drew out a small, plain cardboard box and carried it back over to the work-top.

'Now let's get this clear,' Taggart said, trying to make sense of the whole business. 'How many skulls are we actually talking about?'

'Two, of course,' Hutton said. 'They've stolen the two Roman skulls and all the plaster casts I had made of them.'

'And none of the skulls are ours?' Taggart double-checked.

'Only the plaster casts, apparently,' Jardine put in. 'But they can always be made again.' He stared closely at the box he had just carried from the cupboard. 'Wait a minute – this isn't the box I brought the skulls in. Ours had "Strathclyde Police" clearly stamped on it. This one is completely plain.'

Hutton regarded him as though he was mad. 'Someone has stolen two of the most important archaeological finds in years – and you're worried about a *box*?' he said, as though he couldn't quite believe it.

But Jardine wasn't really listening. 'Our box – where is it?' he demanded.

Hutton glowered at him. 'How the devil should I know? I'm a professor of anatomy, not cardboard boxes.'

Taggart, who had only just realised the full significance of what Jardine was saying, jumped to his colleague's assistance. He turned on Hutton angrily. 'This is your lab, and you're responsible for the things in it. That box was entrusted to your care. Now where is it?'

Hutton's incredulity turned to fury. The whole business of the box seemed like the worst possible case of petty bureaucracy bordering on the obsessional. 'I am not responsible for the security of this university. Nor do I spend my nights with my work.'

The lab door opened at that moment, and Carl Young walked in. He looked surprised at the unusual activity. 'What's going on?'

'Someone broke in last night. They've stolen the two Hamian skulls and all the plaster casts we made of them. It's all gone – everything –and all the damned police seem to be worried about is a blasted cardboard box.'

'We've every right to be,' Jardine pointed out, pointing to the plain box on the work-top. 'That is not the box we brought our skulls in.'

Carl Young stepped over to the cupboard and peered inside.

Returning, he too looked at the box on the lab table. 'I cleared up last night. I must have put the skulls back into different boxes. Why, does it matter much?'

'Of course it matters,' Taggart said, explaining as if to a child. 'It means that whoever stole those skulls thought he was stealing ours. He wasn't after your Roman skulls at all.' He turned back to Hutton. 'I'll have to have this lab closed off for a few hours,' he informed the man. 'In the meantime, I don't want anything touched until the fingerprint boys have finished their work. Is that clear?'

Hutton nodded wordlessly.

'Right – everybody out,' Taggart said, ushering them all towards the door.

Outside, in the university grounds, Taggart chose a position from which he could view the Department of Anatomy building as a whole.

'I want twenty-four-hour security on this place from now on,' he told Jardine. 'They might as well have put out welcome notices for the thief. Hutton's name was on the door and there are no checks at all on who goes in or out of the building. All our man had to do was to hide somewhere inside until everyone had gone home for the night.'

'Is it our murderer, do you think, sir? Or just some sort of ghoul?' Jardine mused.

'A ghoul would have found plenty in there without ransacking cupboards,' Taggart observed. He paused, thoughtfully. 'On the other hand – why would our murderer fear his victim being identified?'

Jardine followed the line of reasoning to its logical conclusion. 'Unless he was directly connected to them in some way,' he finished off.

Taggart nodded. 'Right.'

All A Matter of Balance

BY JIMMY NAIL

The surly and enigmatic Tyneside cop Freddie Spender has been called 'Gateshead's answer to Dirty Harry', and less flatteringly, 'A yuppie detective set against the exotic landscape of downtown Newcastle.' The man himself is over six foot tall, broad-shouldered and with a broken nose that immediately marks him out as the kind of person not to mess with when he is working undercover on one of the cases that have proved too difficult for the local police. Spender is, in fact, a cop who likes flying in the face of convention and has a reputation for being rather introverted as well as using unorthodox methods to get results – as his alter ego, Jimmy Nail (1954–) explained recently: 'He's actually a bit of a misery, but I think his rules are OK. He might do the right thing the wrong way, but his intentions are good.' The Newcastle-born actor created Spender *for the BBC in 1991, drawing on his own background as a notorious tearaway which earned him a four-month prison sentence for GBH before he unexpectedly discovered his talent as an actor and became a cult hero as Oz, the slob brickie in the series,* Auf Wiedersehen, Pet *(1984). During the five years he worked on the programme Jimmy became very friendly with the script-writer, Ian La Frenais, who encouraged him to write and ultimately became his collaborator on* Spender.*

In the first series, Spender *was working as a detective sergeant in London, but because of his frequent run-ins with authority had to accept a transfer back to his native Newcastle. Since his return to the North, he has tackled cases of robbery, arson, drug running and the illegal trade in rare birds – as well as being sent to Marseilles to collect a wanted man – all with varying degrees of help from his boss, the frequently exasperated Superintendent Yelland (Paul Greenwood);*

his occasional colleague, Detective Sergeant Dan Boyd (Berwick
Kaler); an apparently reformed thief and reluctant accomplice named
Stick (Sammy Johnson); and Keith Moreland (Tony McAnaney) a
crippled rock musician who runs a music shop which is the detective's
point of contact. (As a matter of interest, Jimmy Nail himself for a time
fronted a rock group, the King Crabs, in which he apparently wore a
pair of Doc Marten's boots and a frock!)

A trademark of the series has been Spender's blue Ford Scorpio RS
Cosworth; while among the hallmarks are the frequent injections of
humour by Nail and Ian La Frenais such as this comment by
Superintendent Yelland about the detective and his 'team': 'We have a
man in a wheelchair strumming a banjo, an officer of the law who
looks like he belongs with destitute winos, and a convicted felon —
what kind of outfit is this?' The relationship between these three has,
in fact, provided some of the best moments in the series and is also the
theme of the following story about a valuable stamp collection that
Stick has 'appropriated'. Apart from the black humour and Spender's
ability to step across the line between crime and expediency to solve a
problem, it also offers an interesting insight into his personal
philosophy towards crime . . .

S PENDER FOUND STICK and Keith facing each other across the table
in the kitchen at the flat. He looked at them, reading their glum
expressions, imagining them communicating wordlessly with some
miserable angel hovering just above the table.

'I'll make us some coffee,' Stick said.

'No, I'll do it.' Spender went to the draining-board. 'It'll be one for
each of you, I'm not having any. My stomach's a bit dicky. I just
popped back here for a quick word with a pal of mine that likes
dropping me in the shit.'

Stick pretended not to guess who Spender meant.

'Did you hear about the lads from Jude's People?' he said. 'They got
back in one piece, but pretty badly shook up, according to one of the
girls at the Happy Carrot.'

'I heard,' Spender said. 'In a round-about way.'

He had called at Jeremy's house and had spoken to Ralph, who appeared to trust him enough to outline what had happened. Jeremy was in bed by that time, sedated with Valium.

Some time earlier Alfie MacIntyre, catching up with Spender in the cattle-dressing bay at the abattoir, had been pleased to tell him that the visitors hadn't seemed to enjoy the guided tour he and his brother had laid on for them. Alfie added that he thought Spender was looking kind of peaky himself.

'What happened to the lads, exactly?' Keith asked. 'Dory couldn't get anything out of either of them.'

'They were brain-battered,' Spender said. 'It'll be all the rage one of these days.'

He finished making the coffee and brought the mugs to the table. He sat down, looking at Stick.

'You don't mind me mentioning a certain legacy of yours in front of Keith, do you?'

Stick shook his head firmly. 'No sweat. Talk away.'

'I've had the item looked at. It's worth a few quid.'

'That's what I thought.'

'A few *thousand* quid, in fact.' Spender put his elbows on the table and leaned very close to Stick. 'Whose is it?'

'I told you –

'Bugger what you told me.'

Stick looked at Keith, who was shaking his head already.

'I might not have explained too clearly about ownership . . .' Stick looked at the table. He made a finger-pattern in a coffee puddle beside his mug. 'Listen, now.' He looked up at Spender. 'Nobody knows about it. I mean it's not something that's likely to be missed from anywhere, not that I'm saying it came from anywhere where it would be –'

'Be quiet and let me explain something to you,' Spender said. 'In the course of time, the true owner of that collection is bound to notice it's missing. When he does, he'll call the police. When they arrive, they'll all sit down together and go over the owner's videotape records – any bets he's got videotape records, eh? – and they'll look at a few mugshot albums, too. Now then, what's the odds that between recorded tape and prompted memory, a certain browsing punter is suddenly going to stand out with the clarity of a big sore thumb?'

Stick sipped his coffee sullenly.

'So.' Spender sat back in his chair. 'I've had a bloody awful day, one of my worst, and I'm in no mood for being pissed about. Just give me a name, Stick, and we'll get on with talking about something else. Like how you two are coming unstuck from your girlfriends.'

'And what makes you think that?' Keith demanded.
'I know commiseration when I walk in on it,' Spender said.

'The hobby used to be less specialised than it is now,' Mr Thurston was telling a lady customer. 'Booty's and Gray's catalogues a century ago listed two thousand four hundred varieties, but that included what we call nowadays postal stationery – envelopes, wrappers and letter sheets – as well as a lot of local stamp issues.' He pointed to the stack of thick volumes on the counter beside him. 'The standard modern catalogues like Yvert and Tellier in France, Michel's in Germany, Minkus in America and, of course, Gibbons' in Britain, they exclude all that extraneous stuff, but even so the total listings, if you include the minor varieties, come to more than a hundred thousand.'

You learn something every day, Spender thought. He moved slowly across the opulent little shop, adopting the gaze of the curious expert, rather than the gawp of the outright novice. The whole shop exuded the notion of costliness. From the rich red-and-blue Indian carpet to the mahogany showcases and miniature gilded chandeliers, this was a place for enthusiasts who had real money to put into their hobby.

Spender stopped by a showcase and examined two stamps mounted side by side on black card, sharing the soft beam from a polished, brass picture light. The label beneath the one on the right said: CANADA: 1852–7 10d DULL BLUE ON THIN HANDMADE WOVE PAPER, LARGE MARGINS AND EXCEPTIONALLY LIGHT CANCELLING. HIGHLY ATTRACTIVE AND RARE; £800. The one on the left had a more detailed label: CAPE OF GOOD HOPE: 1861 'WOODBLOCK' 1d BRICK RED, VERY LIGHTLY CANCELLED WITH GOOD MARGINS AND EXCEPTIONAL FRESH DEEP COLOUR. TINY NATURAL PAPER FAULT AT APEX, WELL CLEAR OF DESIGN. A BEAUTIFUL RARITY; £1800.

The album tucked under Spender's coat began to feel hot. Bringing it back in when the shop was open had seemed like the best proposition, though now he was here he couldn't imagine where he would plant it. Apart from catalogues, nothing was lying around. All horizontal surfaces were clear and uncluttered. In a place where prices could run into hundreds and even thousands for tiny rectangular pieces of paper, that was a wise precaution, but it was a bad situation for anyone wanting to do a reverse-klepto act.

'Can I be of help at all, sir?'

The young assistant folded one hand over the other as he spoke. He ventured a tiny polite smile as Spender turned, realising he had been addressed.

'Uh, no, not right at the moment, thanks. I'm just looking, if that's all right.'

'Of course, sir.' The assistant turned away and lost interest at once.

Having moved close to the counter, Spender could see into a small anteroom beyond the spot where Mr Thurston, the owner, stood talking to his female customer. There was a safe (the make and type registered automatically: John Tann, key and combination, fire-resistant, four-corner bent-banded construction) and its door was half open. On the top shelf Spender saw perhaps twelve or fifteen little albums exactly like the one under his coat. Mr Thurston obviously believed in having his nest-eggs by the clutch.

For a moment Spender fantasised strangling Stick. He had done it before, at moments like this when facts didn't line up with information supplied. Stick had said nothing about a safe, or that it was out of reach in a little room behind the counter. He said he just lifted the book when the moment was right. He was curiously modest about his ferret-like abilities, his talent for dodging in, lifting, then dodging out again without anyone being aware he had moved. It was superstition again, Spender reminded himself: Stick, like others with his skills and inclinations, felt it would shrink his luck if he boasted about his talent, or even discussed it in any detail.

There were four members of the public in the shop and three of them, including Spender, were browsing. Behind the counter were Mr Thurston, a portly woman Spender took to be Mrs Thurston, a hook-nosed elderly man who appeared to be visiting and who watched the browsers suspiciously, and the young assistant. Trade just wasn't brisk enough for any funny business.

Spender began a third circuit of the shop, pausing even longer by the cases this time, racking his brain. If he didn't get the plant made today it would be on his mind like a lump of lead, an unwanted job waiting to be carried out. He was determined it would be done and off his plate before he left the place. Somehow. He wondered how long he could hang about browsing before the management got shirty.

Then providence marched into the shop in the shape of a sallow-skinned, half-toothless old woman with a battered brown stamp album under her arm. She marched straight to the counter and waved the young assistant forward.

'I want this lot valued,' she said, slapping the album on the counter.

People were watching. The woman's style was loud and un-consciously comic. At a street stall she wouldn't have rated a second look, but in here she was an event. Spender edged towards the counter.

'They've been in the family a lot of years,' she said, echoing Stick's heart-clutching little story. 'I don't want to part with them, but if I'm offered even half what I know they're worth, I won't say no.'

'And what do you believe they're worth, madam?' The assistant was turning the pages with the very tips of his fingers, as if there might be a risk of contamination.

'Ah, well now, I don't know if I should be talking about that.' The woman looked about her uncertainly. 'I mean, it's a very private matter. Best if you make me an offer and let me decide if it's fair.'

'We don't normally buy collections like this,' the assistant said stiffly.

'What do you mean?' Sharp indignation had entered the woman's tone. 'It's a good and valuable collection, lovingly put together, too, I might tell you.' She stepped back from the counter and pointedly looked up and down the shop. 'Is there anybody older I could talk to? Somebody that knows more about these things?'

Mr Thurston asked his customer to excuse him. He moved along the counter to deal with the small scene that was developing.

'How can I help you, madam?'

Spender slid into the space between Thurston's customer and the end of the counter. In straight-line terms he was six feet from the open safe door. He eased the book from under his coat and held it just out of sight, waiting for things to warm up. When the lady customer glanced at him he smiled eagerly at her, which made her turn away.

So far so good.

'Your assistant tells me you don't buy collections like this,' the little woman said, her voice now dripping disbelief. 'I explained to him it's got considerable value, and not just sentimental, neither . . .'

Everybody was watching. Mr Thurston cleared his throat carefully, turning the pages of the tatty album exactly the way his assistant had done, with the merest tips of two fingers.

'Well, I'm afraid Mr Simpson was correct, madam.' He closed the album and pushed it back towards her. 'This is not, strictly speaking, a proper stamp collection. Not by philatelic standards, you understand.'

'So what is it, then?'

'It's what I would personally describe as an agglomeration . . .' Thurston smirked to the shop at large, making Spender suddenly dislike him. 'Or, indeed, I might even say a gallimaufry.'

All eyes were on the little woman. Spender lifted the album to chest height, leaned forward across the counter and spun the volume like a Frisbee towards the gap in the safe door. He was standing upright again and peering through the glass top of the counter at an expensive Great Britain set before the book landed. When it did there was the merest *pop*, a sound without character or force. In the tension of the confrontation between Mr Thurston and the little woman, nobody noticed a thing.

'I don't know about any gally-whatever-it-is,' the woman said haughtily, sticking the album under her arm again. She strode to the door with all the dignity she could muster, and paused momentarily. 'I'll tell you this much, though,' she said, 'you lot in here just talk out the back of your arses.'

She left and the tension dropped. Thurston, pink-cheeked, apologised without directly looking at anyone. He went back to his customer. As he reached her he glanced aside, frowned, and ducked into the anteroom. Spender watched him pick up the album and put it with the others in the safe. He came out again, smiling politely, ready to resume business. The tiny matter of the album mysteriously finding its way to the floor had been forgotten.

A short time later Spender sat enjoying a cup of tea and a biscuit in a café round the corner from Thurston's. Thinking back over the last twenty minutes, he silently revived the exhilaration of what he had done.

'Great,' he whispered.

In order to reverse a crime he had actually gone through the motions of committing one. That was where the buzz came from. Breaking the rules and getting away with it produced a thrill that was completely divorced from the motive. Every civilised strand in Spender was aligned with law and order, and he would risk his own safety to uphold the law. That much being asserted, he still knew that at the centre of himself there was a wild character built for adventure and the sheer kick of flouting the rules.

More than that though, he thought.

What sometimes worried him was that he saw the opportunities villains saw, and worked out perfect ways to take advantage of them. Often, he stood in court and inwardly sided with men and women who committed acts that breached the law. The sense of being two people –two kinds of person – was not always pleasant. There was, too, the worry that one day the balance in his nature would shift, and the law-abider in him would have to take second place.

Thoughts of crime and its link with adventure stayed in his mind as he got in the Cosworth and headed out for the suburbs. At his destination one more wrong waited to be put right, and he wasn't going to kid himself – the means he planned to use could easily be interpreted as criminal.

I Can Find My Way Out

BY NGAIO MARSH

Amongst all the new crimebusters who have been especially developed for television in recent years, several old literary favourites have continued to exercise their timeless appeal on viewers: Sherlock Holmes, Hercule Poirot, Miss Marple, Inspector Maigret, and, most recently, Chief Inspector Roderick Alleyn, the 'upper-crust' Scotland Yard detective created in the thirties by Dame Ngaio Marsh. Just as all the other TV detectives seem at last to have found a definitive characterisation, so Patrick Malahide has risen to the challenge of Alleyn – a challenge made all the more interesting after his years of association with Minder. *'Alleyn's as different as he could possibly be, both professionally and personally, from Chisholm,' Patrick said recently. 'I enjoy playing him because he's a very sympathetic character. He's referred to as 'that thoroughly nice man, Alleyn'. He's extremely intelligent, very mercurial, with an intuitive grasp of things. He is also very old-fashioned with a great sense of duty and he turned his back on the aristrocracy to go into the police.' The Inspector is, in truth, something of a toff and his cases tend to take him into aristocratic circles, though his unfailing good manners mask a penetrating mind and an ability to unnerve anyone suspected of a crime into making a confession.*

Although the opening story in the BBC series, A Man Lay Dead, *based on Ngaio Marsh's very first novel, was announced as the detective's debut on the small screen, Alleyn had, in fact, already appeared three times: twice in the UK and once in New Zealand. The first of these was in the BBC's anthology series,* Detective, *in June 1964, when* Death In Ecstasy *(1936) was adapted with Michael Allison as Alleyn. New Zealand TV followed this in 1976 with four adaptations starring George Baker, the British actor who would later became a household name as Chief Inspector Wexford in the series of Ruth Rendell Mysteries. Finally, in 1990, Simon Williams donned his mantle for the BBC again in an adaptation of* Artists in Crime *(1938). In this last production, Alleyn's assistant, Inspector Fox, was played by William Simons; and his wife, the famous painter Agatha Troy, by Belinda Lang, both of whom have repeated their roles in the new series. Viewers and critics alike have enjoyed the stories, Simon London in* Today *declaring, 'It's watchable and entertaining . . . there should be few complaints from devoted fans of the Sunday night whodunnit.' And George Perry in the* Sunday Times *predicted a long run, adding that the series, 'gives Alleyn a chance to demonstrate his professional skills: polite, Poirot-type interviews and Holmesian summings-up, with helpful visual flashbacks'.*

Dame Ngaio Marsh (1899–1982), the creator of Alleyn, was born in Christchurch, New Zealand, the direct descendant of one of the country's early English settlers, and divided much of her later life between the two countries. Intriguingly, the main preoccupations of her life are all reflected in the novels about the aristocratic sleuth: painting (her original choice of career), the theatre (she was an actress for two years before writing a number of plays and then directing a large number of productions) plus tales of murder and mystery. She apparently named her gentlemanly sleuth after Edward Alleyn, the actor who founded Dulwich College which her father attended, and whose famous ex-pupils include P.G. Wodehouse, Raymond Chandler and the playwright Simon Brett. The Alleyn cases were an immediate success with readers and critics, while the character himself was something of a phenomenon in thirties crime fiction as a detective who had entered the profession from the aristocracy. In all, Dame Ngaio wrote thirty books about him between 1934 and 1974 and in 1966 she was honoured as a Dame of the British Empire for her work. Her readers were, though, sometimes split in their appreciation of Agatha Troy's involvement in the cases, though never the loyal Inspector Fox, whom Alleyn had a curious habit of referring to as either 'Br'er Fox' or 'Foxkin'!

Yet despite the regard in which Chief Inspector Alleyn has long been held by crime aficianados, it has been a source of mystery to them that he has received nothing like the attention from films or television that Holmes, Poriot, Maigret et al have enjoyed. Patrick Malahide, it is earnestly hoped by the most viciferous, could well change all that! I Can Find My Way Out is one of the very few short stories featuring 'the handsome detective' (as he is referred to by the popular press in

the books) and it is all the more welcome in this collection because it is
set in Dame Ngaio's favourite locality – a theatre.

AT HALF-PAST SIX on the night in question, Anthony Gill, unable to
eat, keep still, think, speak or act coherently, walked from his
rooms to the Jupiter Theatre. He knew that there would be nobody
backstage, that there was nothing for him to do in the theatre, that he
ought to stay quietly in his rooms and presently dress, dine and arrive
at, say, a quarter to eight. But it was as if something shoved him into
his clothes, thrust him into the street and compelled him to hurry
through the West End to the Jupiter. His mind was overlaid with a thin
film of inertia. Odd lines from the play occurred to him, but without
any particular significance. He found himself busily reiterating a
completely irrelevant sentence: 'She has a way of laughing that would
make a man's heart turn over.'

Piccadilly, Shaftesbury Avenue. 'Here I go,' he thought, turning into
Hawke Street, 'towards my play. It's one hour and twenty-nine
minutes away. A step a second. It's rushing towards me. Tony's first
play. Poor young Tony Gill. Never mind. Try again.'

The Jupiter. Neon lights: I CAN fiND MY WAY OUT – *by Anthony Gill.*
And in the entrance the bills and photographs. *Coralie Bourne with H.*
J. Bannington, Barry George and Canning Cumberland.

Canning Cumberland. The film across his mind split and there was
the Thing itself and he would have to think about it. How bad would
Canning Cumberland be if he came down drunk? Brilliantly bad, they
said. He would bring out all the tricks. Clever actor stuff, scoring off
everybody, making a fool of the dramatic balance. 'In Mr Canning
Cumberland's hands indifferent dialogue and unconvincing situations
seemed almost real.' What can you do with a drunken actor?

He stood in the entrance feeling his heart pound and his inside
deflate and sicken.

Because, of course, it was a bad play. He was at this moment and for
the first time really convinced of it. It was terrible. Only one virtue in it
and that was not his doing. It had been suggested to him by Coralie
Bourne: 'I don't think the play you have sent me will do as it is, but it
has occurred to me –' It was a brilliant idea. He had rewritten the play
round it and almost immediately and quite innocently he had begun to

think of it as his own although he had said shyly to Coralie Bourne: 'You should appear as joint author.' She had quickly, over-emphatically, refused. 'It was nothing at all,' she said. 'If you're to become a dramatist you will learn to get ideas from everywhere. A single situation is nothing. Think of Shakespeare,' she added lightly. 'Entire plots! Don't be silly.' She had said later, and still with the same hurried nervous air: 'Don't go talking to everyone about it. They will think there is more, instead of less, than meets the eye in my small suggestion. Please promise.' He promised, thinking he'd made an error in taste when he suggested that Coralie Bourne, so famous an actress, should appear as joint author with an unknown youth. And how right she was, he thought, because, of course, it's going to be a ghastly flop. She'll be sorry she consented to play in it.

Standing in front of the theatre he contemplated nightmare possibilities. What did audiences do when a first play flopped? Did they clap a little, enough to let the curtain rise and quickly fall again on a discomfited group of players? How scanty must the applause be for them to let him off his own appearance? And they were to go on to the Chelsea Arts Ball. A hideous prospect. Thinking he would give anything in the world if he could stop his play, he turned into the foyer. There were lights in the offices and he paused, irresolute, before a board of photographs. Among them, much smaller than the leading players, was Dendra Gay with the eyes looking straight into his. *She had a way of laughing that would make a man's heart turn over.* 'Well,' he thought, 'so I'm in love with her.' He turned away from the photograph. A man came out of the office. 'Mr Gill? Telegrams for you.'

Anthony took them and as he went out he heard the man call after him: 'Very good luck for tonight, sir.'

There were queues of people waiting in the side street for the early doors.

At 6.30 Coralie Bourne dialled Canning Cumberland's number and waited.

She heard his voice. 'It's me,' she said.

'O, God! darling, I've been thinking about you.' He spoke rapidly, too loudly. 'Coral, I've been thinking about Ben. You oughtn't to have given that situation to the boy.'

'We've been over it a dozen times, Cann. Why not give it to Tony? Ben will never know.' She waited and then said nervously, 'Ben's gone, Cann. We'll never see him again.'

'I've got a "Thing" about it. After all he's your husband.'

'No. Cann, no.'

'Suppose he turns up. It'd be like him to turn up.'

'He won't turn up.'

She heard him laugh. 'I'm sick of all this,' she thought suddenly. 'I've had it once too often. I can't stand any more . . .' 'Cann,' she said into the telephone. But he had hung up.

At twenty to seven, Barry George looked at himself in his bathroom mirror. 'I've got a better appearance,' he thought, 'than Cann Cumberland. My head's a good shape, my eyes are bigger and my jaw line's cleaner. I never let a show down. I don't drink. I'm a better actor.' He turned his head a little, slewing his eyes to watch the effect. 'In the big scene,' he thought, 'I'm the star. He's the feed. That's the way it's been produced and that's what the author wants. I ought to get the notices.'

Past notices came up in his memory. He saw the print, the size of the paragraphs; a long paragraph about Canning Cumberland, a line tacked on the end of it. 'Is it unkind to add that Mr Barry George trotted in the wake of Mr Cumberland's virtuosity with an air of breathless dependability?' And again: 'It is a little hard on Mr Barry George that he should be obliged to act as foil to this brilliant performance.' Worst of all: 'Mr Barry George succeeded in looking tolerably unlike a stooge, an achievement that evidently exhausted his resources.'

'Monstrous!' he said loudly to his own image, watching the fine glow of indignation in the eyes. Alcohol, he told himself, did two things to Cann Cumberland. He raised his finger. Nice, expressive hand. An actor's hand. Alcohol destroyed Cumberland's artistic integrity. It also invested him with devilish cunning. Drunk, he would burst the seams of a play, destroy its balance, ruin its form and himself emerge blazing with a showmanship that the audience mistook for genius. 'While I,' he said aloud, 'merely pay my author the compliment of faithful interpretation. Pshaw!'

He returned to his bedroom, completed his dressing and pulled his hat to the right angle. Once more he thrust his face close to the mirror and looked searchingly at its image. 'By God!' he told himself, 'he's done it once too often, old boy. Tonight we'll even the score, won't we? By God, we will.'

Partly satisfied, and partly ashamed, for the scene, after all, had smacked a little of ham, he took his stick in one hand and a case holding his costume for the Arts Ball in the other, and went down to the theatre.

*

At ten minutes to seven, H.J. Bannington passed through the gallery queue on his way to the stage door alley, raising his hat and saying: 'Thanks so much,' to the gratified ladies who let him through. He heard them murmur his name. He walked briskly along the alley, greeted the stage-door-keeper, passed under a dingy lamp, through an entry and so to the stage. Only working lights were up. The walls of an interior set rose dimly into shadow. Bob Reynolds, the stage manager, came out through the prompt-entrance. 'Hello, old boy,' he said, 'I've changed the dressing rooms. You're third on the right: they've moved your things in. Suit you?'

'Better, at least, than a blackhole the size of a w.c. but without its appointments,' H.J. said acidly. 'I suppose the great Mr Cumberland still has the star-room?'

'Well, yes, old boy.'

'And who pray, is next to him? In the room with the other gas fire?'

'We've put Barry George there, old boy. You know what he's like.'

'Only too well, old boy, and the public, I fear, is beginning to find out.' H.J. turned into the dressing-room passage. The stage manager returned to the set where he encountered his assistant. 'What's biting *him*?' asked the assistant. 'He wanted a dressing room with a fire.' 'Only natural,' said the ASM nastily. 'He started life reading gas meters.'

On the right and left of the passage, nearest the stage end, were two doors, each with its star in tarnished paint. The door on the left was open. H.J. looked in and was greeted with the smell of grease paint, powder, wet-white, and flowers. A gas fire droned comfortably. Coralie Bourne's dresser was spreading out towels. 'Good evening, Katie, my jewel,' said H.J. 'La Belle not down yet?'

'We're on our way,' she said.

H.J. hummed stylishly, '*Bella figlia del amore*,' and returned to the passage. The star-room on the right was closed, but he could hear Cumberland's dresser moving about inside. He went on to the next door, paused, read the card, 'Mr Barry George,' warbled a high, derisive note, turned in at the third door and switched on the light.

Definitely not a second lead's room. No fire. A wash-basin, however, and opposite mirrors. A stack of telegrams had been placed on the dressing-table. Still singing, he reached for them, disclosing a number of bills that had been tactfully laid underneath and a letter, addressed in a flamboyant script.

His voice might have been mechanically produced and arbitrarily switched off, so abruptly did his song end in the middle of a roulade.

He let the telegrams fall on the table, took up the letter and tore it open. His face, wretchedly pale, was reflected and endlessly re-reflected in the mirrors.

At nine o'clock the telephone rang. Roderick Alleyn answered it. 'This is Sloane 84405. No, you're on the wrong number. *No.*' He hung up and returned to his wife and guest. 'That's the fifth time in two hours.'

'Do let's ask for a new number.'

'We might get next-door to something worse.'

The telephone rang again. 'This is not 84406,' Alleyn warned it. 'No, I cannot take three large trunks to Victoria Station. No, I am not the Instant All Night Delivery. No.'

'They're 84406,' Mrs Alleyn explained to Lord Michael Lamprey. 'I suppose it's just faulty dialling, but you can't imagine how angry everyone gets. Why do you want to be a policeman?'

'It's a dull hard job, you know –' Alleyn began.

'Oh,' Lord Mike said, stretching his legs and looking critically at his shoes, 'I don't for a moment imagine I'll leap immediately into false whiskers and plain clothes. No, no. But I'm revoltingly healthy, sir. Strong as a horse. And I don't think I'm as stupid as you might feel inclined to imagine –'

The telephone rang.

'I say, do let me answer it,' Mike suggested and did so.

'Hullo?' he said winningly. He listened, smiling at his hostess. 'I'm afraid –' he began. 'Here, wait a bit – Yes, but –' His expression became blank and complacent. 'May I,' he said presently, 'repeat your order, sir? Can't be too sure, can we? Call at 11 Harrow Gardens, Sloane Square, for one suitcase to be delivered immediately at the Jupiter Theatre to Mr Anthony Gill. Very good, sir. Thank you, sir. Collect. Quite.'

He replaced the receiver and beamed at the Alleyns.

'What the devil have you been up to?' Alleyn said.

'He just simply wouldn't listen to reason. I tried to tell him.'

'But it may be urgent,' Mrs Alleyn ejaculated.

'It couldn't be more urgent, really. It's a suitcase for Tony Gill at the Jupiter.'

'Well, then –'

'I was at Eton with the chap,' said Mike reminiscently. 'He's four years older than I am, so of course he was madly important while I was less than the dust. This'll larn him.'

'I think you'd better put that order through at once,' said Alleyn firmly.

'I rather thought of executing it myself, do you know, sir. It'd be a frightfully neat way of gate-crashing the show, wouldn't it? I did try to get a ticket, but the house was sold out.'

'If you're going to deliver this case you'd better get a bend on.'

'It's clearly an occasion for dressing up, though, isn't it? I say,' said Mike modestly, 'would you think it most frightful cheek if I – well I'd promise to come back and return everything. I mean –'

'Are you suggesting that my clothes look more like a vanman's than yours?'

'I thought you'd have things –'

'For Heaven's sake, Rory,' said Mrs Alleyn, 'dress him up and let him go. The great thing is to get that wretched man's suitcase to him.'

'I know,' said Mike earnestly. 'It's most frightfully sweet of you. That's how I feel about it.'

Alleyn took him away and shoved him into an old and begrimed raincoat, a cloth cap and a muffler. 'You wouldn't deceive a village idiot in a total eclipse,' he said, 'but out you go.'

He watched Mike drive away and returned to his wife.

'What'll happen?' she asked.

'Knowing Mike, I should say he will end up in the front stalls and go on to supper with the leading lady. She, by the way, is Coralie Bourne. Very lovely and twenty years his senior, so he'll probably fall in love with her.' Alleyn reached for his tobacco jar and paused. 'I wonder what's happened to her husband,' he said.

'Who was he?'

'An extraordinary chap. Benjamin Vlasnoff. Had a violent temper. Looked like a bandit. Wrote two very good plays and got run in three times for common assault. She tried to divorce him, but it didn't go through. I think he afterwards lit off to Russia.' Alleyn yawned. 'I believe she had a hell of a time with him,' he added.

'All Night Delivery,' said Mike in a hoarse voice, touching his cap. 'Suitcase. One.'

'Here you are,' said the woman who had answered the door. 'Carry it carefully, now, it's not locked and the catch springs out.'

'Fanks,' said Mike. 'Much obliged. Chilly, ain't it?'

He took the suitcase out to the car.

It was a fresh spring night. Sloane Square was threaded with mist and all the lamps had halos round them. It was the kind of night when individual sounds separate themselves from the conglomerate voice of London; hollow sirens spoke imperatively down on the river and a bugle rang out over in Chelsea Barracks; a night, Mike thought, for adventure.

He opened the rear door of the car and heaved the case in. The catch flew open, the lid dropped back and the contents fell out. 'Damn!' said Mike and switched on the inside light.

Lying on the floor of the car was a false beard.

It was flaming red and bushy and was mounted on a chin piece. With it was incorporated a stiffened moustache. There were wire hooks to attach the whole thing behind the ears. Mike laid it carefully on the seat. Next he picked up a wide black hat, then a vast overcoat with a fur collar, finally a pair of black gloves.

Mike whistled meditatively and thrust his hands into the pockets of Alleyn's mackintosh. His right-hand fingers closed on a card. He pulled it out. 'Chief Detective Inspector Alleyn,' he read, 'CID New Scotland Yard.'

'Honestly,' thought Mike exultantly, 'this is a gift.'

Ten minutes later a car pulled in to the kerb at the nearest parking place to the Jupiter Theatre. From it emerged a figure carrying a suitcase. It strode rapidly along Hawke Street and turned into the stage-door alley. As it passed under the dirty lamp it paused, and thus murkily lit, resembled an illustration from some Edwardian spy story. The face was completely shadowed, a black cavern from which there projected a square of scarlet beard, which was the only note of colour.

The doorkeeper, who was taking the air with a member of the stage staff, moved forward, peering at the stranger.

'Was you wanting something?'

'I'm taking this case in for Mr Gill.'

'He's in front. You can leave it with me.'

'I'm so sorry,' said the voice behind the beard, 'but I promised I'd leave it backstage myself.'

'So you will be leaving it. Sorry, sir, but no one's admitted be'ind without a card.'

'A card? Very well. Here is a card.'

He held it out in his black-gloved hand. The stage-door-keeper, unwillingly removing his gaze from the beard, took the card and examined it under the light. 'Coo!' he said, 'what's up, governor?'

'No matter. Say nothing of this.'

The figure waved its hand and passed through the door.

''Ere!' said the doorkeeper excitedly to the stage-hand, 'take a slant at this. That's a plain-clothes flattie, that was.'

'*Plain* clothes!' said the stage-hand. 'Them!'

''E's disguised,' said the doorkeeper. 'That's what it is. 'E's disguised 'isself.'

''E's bloody well lorst 'isself be'ind them whiskers if you arst me.'

Out on the stage someone was saying in a pitched and beautifully articulate voice: '*I've always loathed the view from these windows. However, if that's the sort of thing you admire. Turn off the lights, damn you. Look at it.*'

'Watch it, now, watch it,' whispered a voice so close to Mike that he jumped. 'OK,' said a second voice somewhere above his head. The lights on the set turned blue. 'Kill that working light.'

'Working light gone.'

Curtains in the set were wrenched aside and a window flung open. An actor appeared, leaning out quite close to Mike, seeming to look into his face and saying very distinctly: 'God: it's frightful!' Mike backed away towards a passage, lit only from an open door. A great volume of sound broke out beyond the stage. 'House lights,' said the sharp voice. Mike turned into the passage. As he did so, someone came through the door. He found himself face to face with Coralie Bourne, beautifully dressed and heavily painted.

For a moment she stood quite still; then she made a curious gesture with her right hand, gave a small breathy sound and fell forward at his feet.

Anthony was tearing his programme into long strips and dropping them on the floor of the OP box. On his right hand, above and below, was the audience; sometimes laughing, sometimes still, sometimes as one corporate being, raising its hands and striking them together. As now; when down on the stage, Canning Cumberland, using a strange voice, and inspired by some inward devil, flung back the window and said: 'God: it's frightful!'

'Wrong! Wrong!' Anthony cried inwardly, hating Cumberland, hating Barry George because he let one speech of three words override him, hating the audience because they liked it. The curtain descended with a long sigh on the second act and a sound like heavy rain filled the theatre, swelled prodigiously and continued after the house lights welled up.

'They seem,' said a voice behind him, 'to be liking your play.'

It was Gosset, who owned the Jupiter and had backed the show. Anthony turned on him stammering: 'He's destroying it. It should be the other man's scene. He's stealing.'

'My boy,' said Gosset, 'he's an actor.'

'He's drunk. It's intolerable.'

He felt Gosset's hand on his shoulder.

'People are watching us. You're on show. This is a big thing for you; a first play, and going enormously. Come and have a drink, old boy. I want to introduce you –'

Anthony got up and Gosset, with his arm across his shoulders, flashing smiles, patting him, led him to the back of the box.

'I'm sorry,' Anthony said, 'I can't. Please let me off. I'm going backstage.'

'Much better not, old son.' The hand tightened on his shoulder. 'Listen, old son –' But Anthony had freed himself and slipped through the pass door from the box to the stage.

At the foot of the breakneck stairs Dendra Gay stood waiting. 'I thought you'd come,' she said.

Anthony said: 'He's drunk. He's murdering the play.'

'It's only one scene, Tony. He finishes early in the next act. It's going colossally.'

'But don't you understand –'

'I do. You *know* I do. But your success, Tony darling! You can hear it and smell it and feel it in your bones.'

'Dendra –' he said uncertainly.

Someone came up and shook his hand and went on shaking it. Flats were being laced together with a slap of rope on canvas. A chandelier ascended into darkness. 'Lights,' said the stage manager, and the set was flooded with them. A distant voice began chanting. 'Last act, please. Last act.'

'Miss Bourne all right?' the stage manager suddenly demanded.

'She'll be all right. She's not on for ten minutes,' said a woman's voice.

'What's the matter with Miss Bourne?' Anthony asked.

'Tony, I must go and so must you. Tony, it's going to be grand. *Please* think so. *Please.*'

'Dendra –' Tony began, but she had gone.

Beyond the curtain, horns and flutes announced the last act.

'Clear, please.'

The stage hands came off.

'House lights.'

'House lights gone.'

'Stand by.'

And while Anthony still hesitated in the OP corner, the curtain rose. Canning Cumberland and H. J. Bannington opened the last act.

As Mike knelt by Coralie Bourne he heard someone enter the passage behind him. He turned and saw, silhouetted against the lighted stage, the actor who had looked at him through a window in the set. The silhouette seemed to repeat the gesture Coralie Bourne had used, and to flatten itself against the wall.

A woman in an apron came out of the open door.

'I say – here!' Mike said.

Three things happened almost simultaneously. The woman cried out and knelt beside him. The man disappeared through a door on the right.

The woman, holding Coralie Bourne in her arms, said violently: 'Why have you come back?' Then the passage lights came on. Mike said: 'Look here, I'm most frightfully sorry,' and took off the broad black hat. The dresser gaped at him, Coralie Bourne made a crescendo sound in her throat and opened her eyes. 'Katie?' she said.

'It's all right, my lamb. It's not him, dear. You're all right.' The dresser jerked her head at Mike: 'Get out of it,' she said.

'Yes, of course, I'm most frightfully –' He backed out of the passage, colliding with a youth who said: 'Five minutes, please.' The dresser called out: 'Tell them she's not well. Tell them to hold the curtain.'

'No,' said Coralie Bourne strongly. 'I'm all right, Katie. Don't say anything. Katie, what was it?'

They disappeared into the room on the left.

Mike stood in the shadow of a stack of scenic flats by the entry into the passage. There was great activity on the stage. A chandelier ascended into darkness. He caught a glimpse of Anthony Gill on the far side talking to a girl. The callboy was speaking to the stage manager who now shouted into space: 'Miss Bourne all right?' The dresser came into the passage and called: 'She'll be all right. She's not on for ten minutes.' The youth began chanting: 'Last act, please.' The stage manager gave a series of orders. A man with an eyeglass and a florid beard came from further down the passage and stood outside the set, bracing his figure and giving little tweaks to his clothes. There was a sound of horns and flutes. Canning Cumberland emerged from the room on the right and on his way to the stage, passed close to Mike, leaving a strong smell of alcohol behind him. The curtain rose.

Behind his shelter, Mike stealthily removed his beard and stuffed it into the pocket of his overcoat. A group of stage-hands stood nearby. One of them said in a hoarse whisper:

''E's squiffy.'

'Garn, 'e's going good.'

'So 'e may be going good. And for why? *Becos* 'e's squiffy.'

Ten minutes passed. Mike thought: 'This affair has definitely not gone according to plan.' He listened. Some kind of tension seemed to be building up on the stage. Canning Cumberland's voice rose on a loud but blurred note. A door in the set opened. 'Don't bother to come,' Cumberland said. 'Goodbye. I can find my way out.' The door slammed. Cumberland was standing near Mike. Then, very close, there was a loud explosion. The scenic flats vibrated, Mike's flesh leapt on his bones and Cumberland went into his dressing room. Mike heard the key turn in the door. The smell of alcohol mingled with the smell of gunpowder. A stagehand moved to a trestle table and laid a pistol on it. The actor with the eyeglass made an exit. He spoke for a moment to the stage manager, passed Mike and disappeared in the passage.

Smells. There were all sorts of smells. Subconsciously, still listening to the play, he began to sort them out. Glue. Canvas. Grease paint. The callboy tapped on doors. 'Mr George, please.' 'Miss Bourne, please.' They came out, Coralie Bourne with her dresser. Mike heard her turn a door handle and say something. An indistinguishable voice answered her. Then she and her dresser passed him. The others spoke to her and she nodded and then seemed to withdraw into herself, waiting with her head bent, ready to make her entrance. Presently she drew back, walked swiftly to the door in the set, flung it open and swept on, followed a minute later by Barry George.

Smells. Dust, stale paint, cloth. Gas. Increasingly, the smell of gas.

The group of stagehands moved away behind the set to the side of the stage. Mike edged out of cover. He could see the prompt corner. The stage manager stood there will folded arms, watching the action. Behind him were grouped the players who were not on. Two dressers stood apart, watching. The light from the set caught their faces. Coralie Bourne's voice sent phrases flying like birds into the auditorium.

Mike began peering at the floor. Had he kicked some gas fitting adrift? The callboy passed him, stared at him over his shoulder and went down the passage, tapping. 'Five minutes to the curtain, please. Five minutes.' The actor with the elderly make-up followed the call-boy out. 'God, what a stink of gas,' he whispered. 'Chronic, ain't it?' said the callboy. They stared at Mike and then crossed to the waiting group. The man said something to the stage manager, who tipped his head up, sniffing. He made an impatient gesture and turned back to the prompt box, reaching over the prompter's head. A bell rang somewhere up in the flies and Mike saw a stagehand climb to the curtain platform.

The little group near the prompt corner was agitated. They looked back towards the passage entrance. The callboy nodded and came running back. He knocked on the first door on the right. '*Mr Cumberland! Mr Cumberland!* You're on for the call.' He rattled the door handle. '*Mr Cumberland! You're on.*'

Mike ran into the passage. The callboy coughed retchingly and jerked his hand at the door. 'Gas!' he said. 'Gas!'

'Break it in.'

'I'll get Mr Reynolds.'

He was gone. It was a narrow passage. From halfway across the opposite room Mike took a run, head down, shoulder forward, at the door. It gave a little and a sickening increase in the smell caught him in the lungs. A vast storm of noise had broken out and as he took another run he thought: 'It's hailing outside.'

'Just a minute if *you* please, sir.'

It was a stagehand. He'd got a hammer and screwdriver. He wedged the point of the screwdriver between the lock and the doorpost, drove it home and wrenched. The screws squeaked, the wood splintered and gas poured into the passage. 'No winders,' coughed the stagehand.

Mike wound Alleyn's scarf over his mouth and nose. Half-forgotten instructions from anti-gas drill occurred to him. The room looked queer but he could see the man slumped down in the chair quite clearly. He stooped low and ran in.

He was knocking against things as he backed out, lugging the dead weight. His arms tingled. A high insistent voice hummed in his brain. He floated a short distance and came to earth on a concrete floor among several pairs of legs. A long way off, someone said loudly: 'I can only thank you for being so kind to what I know, too well, is a very imperfect play.' Then the sound of hail began again. There was a heavenly stream of clear air flowing into his mouth and nostrils. 'I could eat it,' he thought and sat up.

The telephone rang. 'Suppose,' Mrs Alleyn suggested, 'that this time you ignore it.'

'It might be the Yard,' Alleyn said, and answered it.

'Is that Chief Detective-Inspector Alleyn's flat? I'm speaking from the Jupiter Theatre. I've rung up to say that the Chief Inspector is here and that he's had a slight mishap. He's all right, but I think it might be as well for someone to drive him home. No need to worry.'

'What sort of mishap?' Alleyn asked.

'Er – well – er, he's been a bit gassed.'

'*Gassed*! All right. Thanks, I'll come.'

'*What* a bore for you, darling,' said Mrs Alleyn. 'What sort of case is it? Suicide?'

'Masquerading within the meaning of the act, by the sound of it. Mike's in trouble.'

'What trouble, for Heaven's sake?'

'Got himself gassed. He's all right. Good night, darling. Don't wait up.'

When he reached the theatre, the front of the house was in darkness. He made his way down the side alley to the stage door where he was held up.

'Yard,' he said, and produced his official card.

''Ere,' said the stage-doorkeeper. ''Ow many more of you?'

'The man inside was working for me,' said Alleyn and walked in. The doorkeeper followed, protesting.

To the right of the entrance was a large scenic dock from which the double doors had been rolled back. Here Mike was sitting in an armchair, very white about the lips. Three men and two women, all with painted faces, stood near him and behind them a group of stagehands with Reynolds, the stage manager, and, apart from these, three men in evening dress. The men looked woodenly shocked. The women had been weeping.

'I'm most frightfully sorry, sir,' Mike said. 'I've tried to explain. This,' he added generally, 'is Inspector Alleyn.'

'I can't understand all this,' said the oldest of the men in evening dress irritably. He turned on the doorkeeper. 'You said –'

'I seen 'is card –'

'I know,' said Mike, 'but you see –'

'This is Lord Michael Lamprey,' Alleyn said. 'A recruit to the Police Department. What's happened here?'

'Dr Rankin, would you –?'

The second of the men in evening dress came forward. 'All right, Gosset. It's a bad business, Inspector. I've just been saying the police would have to be informed. If you'll come with me –'

Alleyn followed him through a door on to the stage proper. It was dimly lit. A trestle table had been set up in the centre and on it, covered with a sheet, was an unmistakable shape. The smell of gas, strong everywhere, hung heavily about the table.

'Who is it?'

'Canning Cumberland. He'd locked the door of his dressing room. There's a gas fire. Your young friend dragged him out, very pluckily, but it was no go. I was in front. Gosset, the manager, had asked me to supper. It's a perfectly clear case of suicide, as you'll see.'

'I'd better look at the room. Anybody been in?'

'God, no. It was a job to clear it. They turned the gas off at the main. There's no window. They had to open the double doors at the back of the stage and a small outside door at the end of the passage. It may be possible to get in now.'

He led the way to the dressing room passage. 'Pretty thick, still,' he said. 'It's the first room on the right. They burst the lock. You'd better keep down near the floor.'

The powerful lights over the mirror were on and the room still had its look of occupancy. The gas fire was against the left-hand wall. Alleyn squatted down by it. The tap was still turned on, its face lying parallel with the floor. The top of the heater, the tap itself, and the carpet near it, were covered with a creamish powder. On the end of the dressing-table shelf nearest to the stove was a box of this powder. Further along the shelf, grease paints were set out in a row beneath the mirror. Then came a wash-basin and in front of this an overturned chair. Alleyn could see the track of heels, across the pile of the carpet, to the door immediately opposite. Beside the wash basin was a quart bottle of whisky, three-parts empty, and a tumbler. Alleyn had had about enough and returned to the passage.

'Perfectly clear,' the hovering doctor said again, 'isn't it?'

'I'll see the other rooms, I think.'

The one next to Cumberland's was like his in reverse, but smaller. The heater was back to back with Cumberland's. The dressing shelf was set out with much the same assortment of grease paints. The tap of this heater, too, was turned on. It was of precisely the same make as the other and Alleyn, less embarrassed here by fumes, was able to make a longer examination. It was a common enough type of gas fire. The lead-in was from a pipe through a flexible metallic tube with a rubber connection. There were two taps, one in the pipe and one at the junction of the tube with the heater itself. Alleyn disconnected the tube and examined the connection. It was perfectly sound, a close fit and stained red at the end. Alleyn noticed a wiry thread of some reddish stuff resembling packing that still clung to it. The nozzle and tap were brass, the tap pulling over when it was turned on, to lie in a parallel plane with the floor. No powder had been scattered about here.

He glanced round the room, returned to the door and read the card: 'Mr Barry George.'

The doctor followed him into the rooms opposite these, on the left-hand side of the passage. They were a repetition in design of the two he had already seen but were hung with women's clothes and had a more elaborate assortment of grease paint and cosmetics.

There was a mass of flowers in the star room. Alleyn read the cards. One in particular caught his eye: 'From Anthony Gill, to say a most inadequate 'Thank you' for the great idea.' A vase of red roses stood before the mirror: 'To your greatest triumph, Coralie darling.

C.C.' In Miss Gay's room there were only two bouquets, one from the management and one 'From Anthony, with love.'

Again in each room he pulled off the lead-in to the heater and looked at the connection.

'All right, aren't they?' said the doctor.

'Quite all right. Tight fit. Good solid grey rubber.'

'Well then –'

Next on the left was an unused room, and opposite it, 'Mr H.J. Bannington.' Neither of these rooms had a gas fire. Mr Bannington's dressing table was littered with the usual array of grease paint, the materials for his beard, a number of telegrams and letters, and several bills.

'About the body,' the doctor began.

'We'll get a mortuary van from the Yard.'

'But – Surely in a case of suicide –'

'I don't think this is suicide.'

'But, good God! D'you mean there's been an accident?'

'No accident,' said Alleyn.

At midnight, the dressing room lights in the Jupiter Theatre were brilliant, and men were busy there with the tools of their trade. A constable stood at the stage door and a van waited in the yard. The front of the house was dimly lit and there, among the shrouded stalls, sat Coralie Bourne, Basil Gosset, H.J. Bannington, Dendra Gay, Anthony Gill, Reynolds, Katie the dresser, and the callboy. A constable sat behind them and another stood by the doors into the foyer. They stared across the backs of seats at the fire curtain. Spirals of smoke rose from their cigarettes and about their feet were discarded programmes. 'Basil Gosset presents I CAN FIND MY WAY OUT, by Anthony Gill.'

In the manager's office Alleyn said: 'You're sure of your facts, Mike?'

'Yes, sir. Honestly. I was right up against the entrance into the passage. They didn't see me because I was in the shadow. It was very dark off stage.'

'You'll have to swear to it.'

'I know.'

'Good. All right, Thompson. Miss Gay and Mr Gosset may go home. Ask Miss Bourne to come in.'

When Sergeant Thompson had gone Mike said: 'I haven't had a chance to say I know I've made a perfect fool of myself. Using your card and everything.'

'Irresponsible gaiety doesn't go down very well in the service, Mike. You behaved like a clown.'

'I *am* a fool,' said Mike wretchedly.

The red beard was lying in front of Alleyn on Gosset's desk. He picked it up and held it out. 'Put it on,' he said.

'She might do another faint.'

'I think not. Now the hat: yes – yes, I see. Come in.'

Sergeant Thompson showed Coralie Bourne in and then sat at the end of the desk with his notebook.

Tears had traced their course through the powder on her face, carrying black cosmetic with them and leaving the grease paint shining like snail-tracks. She stood near the doorway looking dully at Michael. 'Is he back in England?' she said. 'Did he tell you to do this?' She made an impatient movement. 'Do take it off,' she said. 'It's a very bad beard. If Cann had only looked –' Her lips trembled. 'Who told you to do it?'

'Nobody,' Mike stammered, pocketing the beard. 'I mean – As a matter of fact, Tony Gill –'

'*Tony?* But *he* didn't know. Tony wouldn't do it. Unless –'

'Unless?' Alleyn said.

She said frowning: 'Tony didn't want Cann to play the part that way. He was furious.'

'He says it was his dress for the Chelsea Arts Ball,' Mike mumbled. 'I brought it here. I just thought I'd put it on – it was idiotic, I know – for fun. I'd no idea you and Mr Cumberland would mind.'

'Ask Mr Gill to come in,' Alleyn said.

Anthony was white and seemed bewildered and helpless. 'I've told Mike,' he said. 'It was my dress for the ball. They sent it round from the costume-hiring place this afternoon, but I forgot it. Dendra reminded me and rang up the Delivery people – or Mike, as it turns out – in the interval.'

'Why,' Alleyn asked, 'did you choose that particular disguise?'

'I didn't. I didn't know what to wear and I was too rattled to think. They said they were hiring things for themselves and would get something for me. They said we'd all be characters out of a Russian melodrama.'

'Who said this?'

'Well – well, it was Barry George, actually.'

'*Barry*,' Coralie Bourne said. '*It was Barry*.'

'I don't understand,' Anthony said. 'Why should a fancy dress upset everybody?'

'It happened,' Alleyn said, 'to be a replica of the dress usually worn by Miss Bourne's husband, who also had a red beard. That was it, wasn't it, Miss Bourne? I remember seeing him –'

'Oh, yes,' she said, 'you would. He was known to the police.' Suddenly she broke down completely. She was in an armchair near the desk, but out of the range of its shaded lamp. She twisted and writhed, beating her hand against the padded arm of the chair. Sergeant Thompson sat with his head bent and his hand over his notes. Mike, after an agonised glance at Alleyn, turned his back. Anthony Gill leaned over her: 'Don't,' he said violently. 'Don't! For God's sake, stop.'

She twisted away from him and, gripping the edge of the desk, began to speak to Alleyn; little by little gaining mastery of herself. 'I want to tell you. I want you to understand. Listen.' Her husband had been fantastically cruel, she said. 'It was a kind of slavery.' But when she sued for divorce he brought evidence of adultery with Cumberland. They had thought he knew nothing. 'There was an abominable scene. He told us he was going away. He said he'd keep track of us and if I tried again for divorce, he'd come home. He was very friendly with Barry in those days.' He had left behind him the first draft of a play he had meant to write for her and Cumberland. It had a wonderful scene for them. 'And now you will never have it,' he had said, 'because there is no other playwright who could make this play for you but I.' He was, she said, a melodramatic man, but he was never ridiculous. He returned to the Ukraine, where he was born, and they had heard no more of him. In a little while she would have been able to presume death. But years of waiting did not agree with Canning Cumberland. He drank consistently and at his worst used to imagine her husband was about to return. 'He was really terrified of Ben,' she said. 'He seemed like a creature in a nightmare.'

Anthony Gill said: 'This play – was it –?'

'Yes. There was an extraordinary similarity between your play and his. I saw at once that Ben's central scene would enormously strengthen your piece. Cann didn't want me to give it to you. Barry knew. He said: Why not? He wanted Cann's part and was furious when he didn't get it. So you see, when he suggested you should dress and make up like Ben –' She turned to Alleyn. 'You see?'

'What did Cumberland do when he saw you?' Alleyn asked Mike.

'He made a queer movement with his hands as if – well, as if he expected me to go for him. Then he just bolted into his room.'

'He thought Ben had come back,' she said.

'Were you alone at any time after you fainted?' Alleyn asked.

'I? No. No. I wasn't. Katie took me into my dressing room and stayed with me until I went on for the last scene.'

'One other question. Can you, by any chance, remember if the heater in your room behaved at all oddly?'

She looked wearily at him. 'Yes, it did give a sort of plop, I think. It made me jump. I was nervy.'

'You went straight from your room to the stage?'

'Yes. With Katie. I wanted to go to Cann. I tried the door when we came out. It was locked. He said: 'Don't come in.' I said: 'It's all right. It wasn't Ben,' and went on to the stage.'

'I heard Miss Bourne,' Mike said.

'He must have made up his mind by then. He was terribly drunk when he played his last scene.' She pushed her hair back from her forehead. 'May I go?' she asked Alleyn.

'I've sent for a taxi. Mr Gill, will you see if it's there? In the meantime, Miss Bourne, would you like to wait in the foyer?'

'May I take Katie home with me?'

'Certainly. Thompson will find her. Is there anyone else we can get?'

'No, thank you. Just old Katie.'

Alleyn opened the door for her and watched her walk into the foyer. 'Check up with the dresser, Thompson,' he murmured, 'and get Mr H.J. Bannington.'

He saw Coralie Bourne sit on the lower step of the dress-circle stairway and lean her head against the wall. Nearby, on a gilt easel, a huge photograph of Canning Cumberland smiled handsomely at her.

H.J. Bannington looked pretty ghastly. He had rubbed his hand across his face and smeared his make-up. Florid red paint from his lips had stained the crêpe hair that had been gummed on and shaped into a beard. His monocle was still in his left eye and gave him an extraordinarily rakish look. 'See here,' he complained, 'I've about *had* this party. When do we go home?'

Alleyn uttered placatory phrases and got him to sit down. He checked over H.J's movements after Cumberland left the stage and found that his account tallied with Mike's. He asked if H.J. had visited any of the other dressing rooms and was told acidly that H.J. knew his place in the company. 'I remained in my unheated and squalid kennel, thank you very much.'

'Do you know if Mr Barry George followed your example?'

'Couldn't say, old boy. He didn't come near *me*.'

'Have you any theories at all about this unhappy business, Mr Bannington?'

'Do you mean, why did Cann do it? Well, speak no ill of the dead, but I'd have thought it was pretty obvious he was morbid-drunk. Tight as an owl when we finished the second act. Ask the great Mr Barry

George. Cann took the big scene away from Barry with both hands and left him looking pathetic. All wrong artistically, but that's how Cann was in his cups.' H.J.'s wicked little eyes narrowed. 'The great Mr George,' he said, 'must be feeling very unpleasant by now. You might say he'd got a suicide on his mind, mightn't you? Or don't you know about that?'

'It was not suicide.'

The glass dropped from H.J.'s eye. 'God!' he said. 'God, I told Bob Reynolds! I told him the whole plant wanted overhauling.'

'The gas plant, you mean?'

'Certainly. I was in the gas business years ago. Might say I'm in it still with a difference, ha-ha!'

'Ha-ha!' Alleyn agreed politely. He leaned forward. 'Look here,' he said: 'We can't dig up a gas man at this time of night and we may very likely need an expert opinion. You can help us.'

'Well, old boy, I was rather pining for a spot of shut-eye. But of course –'

'I shan't keep you very long.'

'God, I hope not!' said H.J. earnestly.

Barry George had been made up pale for the last act. Colourless lips and shadows under his cheekbones and eyes had skilfully underlined his character as a repatriated but broken prisoner-of-war. Now, in the glare of the office lamp, he looked like a grossly exaggerated figure of mourning. He began at once to tell Alleyn how grieved and horrified he was. Everybody, he said, had their faults, and poor old Cann was no exception, but wasn't it terrible to think what could happen to a man who let himself go downhill? He, Barry George, was abnormally sensitive and he didn't think he'd ever really get over the awful shock this had been to him. What, he wondered, could be at the bottom of it? Why had poor old Cann decided to end it all?

'Miss Bourne's theory –' Alleyn began.

Mr George laughed. 'Coralie?' he said. 'So she's got a theory! Oh, well. Never mind.'

'Her theory is this. Cumberland saw a man whom he mistook for her husband and, having a morbid dread of his return, drank the greater part of a bottle of whisky and gassed himself. The clothes and beard that deceived him had, I understand, been ordered by you for Mr Anthony Gill.'

This statement produced startling results. Barry George broke into a spate of expostulation and apology. There had been no thought in his mind of resurrecting poor old Ben, who was no doubt dead, but had been, mind you, in many ways, one of the best. They were all to go to the Ball as exaggerated characters from melodrama. Not for the world – He gesticulated and protested. A line of sweat broke out along the margin of his hair. 'I don't know what you're getting at,' he shouted. 'What are you suggesting?'

'I'm suggesting, among other things, that Cumberland was murdered.'

'You're mad! He'd locked himself in. They had to break down the door. There's no window. You're crazy!'

'Don't,' Alleyn said wearily, 'let us have any nonsense about sealed rooms. Now, Mr George, you knew Benjamin Vlasnoff pretty well. Are you going to tell us that when you suggested Mr Gill should wear a coat with a fur collar, a black sombrero, black gloves and a red beard, it never occurred to you that his appearance might be a shock to Miss Bourne and to Cumberland?'

'I wasn't the only one,' he blustered. 'H.J. knew. And if it had scared him off, *she* wouldn't have been so sorry. She'd had about enough of him. Anyway, if this is murder, the costume's got nothing to do with it.'

'That,' said Alleyn, getting up, 'is what we hope to find out.'

In Barry George's room, Detective Sergeant Bailey, a fingerprint expert, stood by the gas heater. Sergeant Gibson, a police photographer, and a uniformed constable were near the door. In the centre of the room stood Barry George, looking from one man to another and picking at his lips.

'I don't know why he wants me to watch all this,' he said. 'I'm exhausted. I'm emotionally used up. What's he doing? Where is he?'

Alleyn was next door in Cumberland's dressing room, with H.J., Mike and Sergeant Thompson. It was pretty clear now of fumes and the gas fire was burning comfortably. Sergeant Thompson sprawled in the armchair near the heater, his head sunk and his eyes shut.

'This is the theory, Mr Bannington,' Alleyn said. 'You and Cumberland have made your final exits; Miss Bourne and Mr George and Miss Gay are all on the stage. Lord Michael is standing just outside the entrance to the passage. The dressers and stage staff are watching the play from the side. Cumberland has locked himself in this room. There he is, dead drunk and sound asleep. The gas fire is burning, full pressure. Earlier in the evening he powdered himself and a thick layer of the powder lies undisturbed on the tap. Now.'

He tapped on the wall.

The fire blew out with a sharp explosion. This was followed by the hiss of escaping gas, as Alleyn turned the taps off. 'You see,' he said, 'I've left an excellent print on the powdered surface. Now, come next door.'

Next door, Barry George appealed to him stammering: 'But I didn't know. I don't know anything about it. I don't *know*.'

'Just show Mr Bannington, will you, Bailey?'

Bailey knelt down. The lead-in was disconnected from the tap on the heater. He turned on the tap in the pipe and blew down the tube.

'An air lock, you see. It works perfectly.'

H.J. was staring at Barry George. 'But I don't know about gas, H.J. H.J., tell them –'

'One moment.' Alleyn removed the towels that had been spread over the dressing shelf, revealing a sheet of clean paper on which lay the rubber push-on connection.

'Will you take this lens, Bannington, and look at it. You'll see that it's stained a florid red. It's a very slight stain but it's unmistakably grease paint. And just above the stain you'll see a wiry hair. Rather like some sort of packing material, but it's not that. It's crêpe hair, isn't it?'

The lens wavered above the paper.

'Let me hold it for you,' Alleyn said. He put his hand over H.J.'s shoulder and, with a swift movement, plucked a tuft from his false moustache and dropped it on the paper. 'Identical, you see. Ginger. It seems to be stuck to the connection with spirit-gum.'

The lens fell. H.J. twisted round, faced Alleyn for a second, and then struck him full in the face. He was a small man but it took three of them to hold him.

'In a way, sir, it's handy when they have a smack at you,' said Detective Sergeant Thompson half an hour later. 'You can pull them in nice and straightforward without any 'Will you come to the station and make a statement' business.'

'Quite,' said Alleyn, nursing his jaw.

Mike said: 'He must have gone to the room after Barry George and Miss Bourne were called.'

'That's it. He had to be quick. The callboy would be round in a minute and he had to be back in his own room.'

'But look here – what about motive?'

'That, my good Mike, is precisely why, at half-past one in the morning, we're still in this miserable theatre. You're getting a view of the duller aspect of homicide. Want to go home?'

'No. Give me another job.'

'Very well. About ten feet from the prompt entrance, there's a sort of garbage tin. Go through it.'

At seventeen minutes to two, when the dressing rooms and passage had been combed clean and Alleyn had called a spell, Mike came to him with filthy hands. '*Eureka*,' he said, 'I hope.'

They all went into Bannington's room. Alleyn spread out on the dressing table the fragments of paper that Mike had given him.

'They'd been pushed down to the bottom of the tin,' Mike said.

Alleyn moved the fragments about. Thompson whistled through his teeth. Bailey and Gibson mumbled together.

'There you are,' Alleyn said at last.

They collected round him. The letter that H.J. Bannington had opened at this same table six hours and forty-five minutes earlier, was pieced together like a jigsaw puzzle.

'Dear H.J., – Having seen the monthly statement of my account, I called at my bank this morning and was shown a cheque that is undoubtedly a forgery. Your histrionic versatility, my dear H.J., is only equalled by your audacity as a calligraphist. But fame has its disadvantages. The teller recognised you. I propose to take action.'

'Unsigned,' said Bailey.

'Look at the card on the red roses in Miss Bourne's room, signed C.C. It's a very distinctive hand.' Alleyn turned to Mike. 'Do you still want to be a policeman?'

'Yes.'

'Lord help you. Come and talk to me at the office tomorrow.'

'Thank you, sir.'

They went out, leaving a constable on duty. It was a cold morning. Mike looked up at the façade of the Jupiter. He could just make out the shape of the neon sign: I CAN FIND MY WAY OUT, *by Anthony Gill*.

The Keeper of Souls

BY LYNDA LA PLANTE

Crime on television took on yet another new dimension in 1991 when Detective Chief Inspector Jane Tennison, a hard-nosed career police-woman, was introduced in the first of the series, Prime Suspect, *written by Lynda La Plante. Tennison, who is memorably played by Helen Mirren, controls her feelings and her squad with equal rigour, and was described by Hilary Kingsley in* The Times *as, 'the most important female character television has brought us all year – a continuing inspiration to any woman trying to work well while all around her pull on different ropes'. The series has already won a total of sixteen awards in Britain and abroad, making it a triumph for Granada TV to match their great success with Sherlock Holmes. Helen Mirren herself has also won several awards for her performance, including BAFTA Best Television Actress two years running as well as the Broadcasting Press Guild and the Royal Television Society awards. Even the rival BBC's* Radio Times *has acknowledged that Helen has helped make* Prime Suspect, *'one of the most irresistible forces in television drama.' And talking herself about the role of DCI Tennison, she said recently, 'I'm very comfortable with the character – it's a relief that she doesn't have to be glamorous and she can have dislikable qualities, even be a bully.'*

In Prime Suspect I, *which was primarily about a serial killer, Tennison was seen wrestling with her conscience about the conflicts between her marriage and her job. She settled for her work. In the second series, which focused on tensions in a racially mixed community, she had a short-lived relationship with a black police officer.* Prime Suspect III *saw her transferred to the Soho Vice Squad to lead 'Operation Contract', an attempted large-scale clean-up of the evil of rent-boys, and put to work to solve the murder of one of the youngsters whose body had been found at the scene of a fire. Her investigations into the seedy underworld of homeless children, male prostitution, paedophilia and pornography also brought her into dangerous conflict with the higher echelons of power in the police force itself. Helen Mirren's performance has undoubtedly been strengthened by the expert guidance of a real-life DCI Jackie Malton of the Metropolitan Police Force who has acted as a consultant on the series since its inception. An added element of* frisson *has also been provided by the lizard-eyed Detective Sergeant Otley, played by Tom Bell, who is forever trying to undermine Tennison's authority and get a laugh with the other male policemen at her expense.*

The author of Prime Suspect, *Lynda La Plante (1946–), has enjoyed a meteoric rise to fame in TV drama. Born in Liverpool, she actually trained to be an actress at RADA and worked at the National Theatre and the Royal Shakespeare Company as well as in cabaret, musicals, films and on television before turning to writing. Her TV series such as* Widows, Civvies *and* Framed *have been internationally acclaimed, while her four novels,* The Legacy, The Talisman, Bella Mafia *and* Entwined *have all been bestsellers. In Jane Tennison, however, she has undeniably created a memorable female character trying to make it in what is still a man's world; a woman whose edgy sexuality has also become as important an element as her police work in all of the stories. The following extract from* Prime Suspect III *finds the DCI and a member of her team, Detective Inspector Brian Dalton (Andrew Woodall), interviewing a victim of a paedophile named Edward Parker and beginning to realise the implications of where her investigations are leading. The millions of admirers of this latest example of the enduring appeal of cops on the box will hope that it is not too long before Jane Tennison is back on TV again.*

T HE GIRL WHO let them in – not more than eighteen – had a baby in a vest but no nappy balanced on her hip, and she was about seven months pregnant with the next one. She had a hollow-chested wasted look and lacklustre eyes. She led them through the tiny hallway, where they had to squeeze past a pram, into the living room. It was oppressively hot, with the close dank smell that comes from clothes drying in a sealed room. The source was woollen baby clothes steaming gently on a wooden frame in front of a gas fire going full blast. Fluffy toys and plastic building bricks were strewn everywhere, along with empty beer cans and dirty cups and plates, strategically located to make it odds on that you'd step on or into something. The few sticks of furniture looked like the remnants of a car boot sale on a bad day.

Jason came in from the kitchen. He was tall and very thin, with straggling hippie-length hair, and he was exceptionally good-looking. Over ragged blue jeans he wore a striped pyjama top. The buttons were missing, showing his ribs and flat, fish-white belly. He was barefoot, the nails long and curved, grime between his toes.

'She's no need to be in on this.'

'Not unless you want her to be,' Tennison agreed.

Jason jerked his head. 'Go on.'

The girl went out with the baby. Jason heeled the door shut.

'I'm Jane Tennison, and this is Brian Dalton. Can we sit down?'

'Sure. Sorry about the mess.' He pushed both hands up into his hair and flung his head back.

Tennison sat down in the lumpy armchair, shifting to avoid the spring. Dalton chose a hard-backed chair, well away from the fire. Jason semi-reclined on the arm of the settee, one knee pulled up to his chin. 'You want tea or . . .?'

'No thanks,' Tennison said politely. That was the second surprise. He had a lazy, low-pitched voice, easy to listen to. What had she been expecting? she asked herself. Grunts and slobbering growls? She glanced at Dalton, making sure he was taking notes, and smiled at Jason. 'So, where do you want to begin?' He was studying his thumbnail.

'You're from Liverpool originally, aren't you? How old were you when you went into the home?'

'Which one?'

'The home run by Mr Edward Parker.'

'Ten.' Jason flicked away something he'd found under his thumbnail. 'I was sent there from a foster home. I got into a bit of thieving, so they got shot of me.'

'Would you be prepared to act as a witness for the prosecution?'

'Sure.' Jason twitched his thin shoulders in a listless shrug.

'Would you tell me when the sexual abuse started?'

His eyes flicked towards her, and quickly away. He had thick, dark lashes any woman would have been proud of. And any woman would have fallen for the full-lipped mouth with a slightly sullen droop to it.

'Second or third day I was there, Parker just called me into his office and that was it. Started then. And you couldn't say anything, or do anything about it – like he was a law unto himself. And it wasn't just me, he was having us all. He'd give you a certain amount of fags, like five say, for a blow job. Always knew when one of the kids had gone the whole way with him, they were flush with fags. Have you got one, by the way?'

Tennison reached into her briefcase. 'I have, as a matter of fact. Here, keep the packet, I've given up.'

Jason uncoiled from the arm of the settee and knelt down to get a light from the gas fire. Tennison rummaged for matches, but he was already lit up. He stayed where he was, long legs stretched out on the tatty hearthrug. The pose was overtly sexual, the pyjama top falling open, the tight jeans displaying the bulge at his crotch. It made Tennison unsure whether he was behaving naturally, unself-consciously, or trying it on, deriving some secret amusement from the situation. He was a very disconcerting young man.

'I'm grateful that you're being so frank with us,' Tennison said. The heat of the closed room was making her sweat, and she was sorry she hadn't taken off her raincoat when she came in. Now didn't seem the right time.

'No other way to be, really, is there?' he said, dribbling tiny puffs of smoke from his mouth.

'What made you report him?'

'He shortchanged me on some fags, so I thought: screw him. So I went to the probation officer. Stupid bitch, I think she fancied him – he used to get it off with women, too. Anyway,' Jason said in a long sigh, 'she went on and on at me, did I know what I was saying, what it meant? I said, "Oh yeah, you know what it fuckin' means to me?" ' I said, "If you don't do something, I'll go to the cops." '

'And how old were you?'

'Twelve or thirteen.'

'And did you go to the cops?'

'Yeah . . .' Jason rolled on to his stomach, flicking ash on the carpet. 'Well, he wouldn't leave me alone, and she wasn't doing anything about it. So I went to the police station, made a statement, and then – sort of everybody run around like, asking me all these questions. Then a doctor examined me, and . . .' He dragged deeply, letting the smoke trickle out. 'Oh yeah. This copper. He gets me into his office.'

'And?' Tennison leaned forward. 'What happened then, Jason?'

'He said that if I said I was lying, he would make sure I had it cushy – you know, money, cigarettes. Things like that. And that they'd move me . . . somewhere nice.' He shook his hair back and looked up at her. He had beautiful eyes, but their expression was opaque, a deadness deep down.

'Do you remember this police officer's name?' Tennison asked quietly. 'Was he wearing uniform?'

'Na! He was a friend of Parker's. They worked it between them.' His tone was dismissive. That's how the world operated. Those with power and influence dumped on the great unwashed below. Fact of life. 'So they sent me back,' he went on, and laughed without humour. 'They never got round to moving me, and I became a very heavy smoker.'

Jason took a last drag and stubbed out the cigarette on the tiled hearth. He sat up and favoured Tennison with a sunny, beaming smile.

'That's it.'

Tennison nodded. 'Do you remember the name of the doctor? The one who examined you?'

'Be no help if I did. He died of cancer, nice guy. Think his name was something Ellis.'

Dalton made a note.

Tennison said, 'Was it all the boys, Jason? Or specifically the very young ones?'

'The little 'uns, he liked the little ones.'

'Do you have a job?'

'Nope. No qualifications. A five-year-old kid reads better than me. I do odd jobs around the place, fix up cars.' He smiled in a simple, childlike way. 'I get drunk, and sometimes I get angry.'

'And then you get into trouble?' Tennison hesitated. 'Have you ever told somebody about your past, Jason?'

'There's no point.' Again the off-hand dismissal. 'I just have to live with it.'

Tennison fastened her briefcase and sat with it across her knees, her hands gripping the sides. She said softly, 'I will do everything possible to put this man away. I promise you.'

Jason stared at her, as if she might possibly mean it, and then he laughed harshly. 'You haven't even got him, have you?'

She couldn't find it in her heart to lie to him. She shook her head, and Jason laughed again, harsh and angry.

He led them out, past the pram in the hallway, and stood on the concrete balcony in his bare feet. A short flight of steps led down to the walkway, littered with broken bottles and crushed beer cans. The breeze ruffled Jason's pyjama top. A change had come over him. He followed after them, speaking in a mechanical monotone, telling them a tale, his breathing rapid.

'One night at the home we was watching a documentary, Nazi thing. This guy ran a concentration camp, you know what they are?'

Tennison and Dalton had paused to listen. They both nodded.

Jason leaned back, his shoulder blades pressed against the concrete wall. 'Yeah, well, this guy was called the "Angel of Death", right? And after the war, he escaped, right? He was never hanged, nobody arrested him, nobody brought him to trial . . .' He gave a peculiar croaking giggle. 'Just like Parker. He did me for eight years, he did every boy in his care. You know what we used to call him? We called him "The Keeper of Souls".' He grinned down at them.

Tennison put her hand out. 'Go back up the stairs, Jason. There's glass on the stairs, you'll hurt yourself . . .'

Jason's fingers tore at the pyjama top. He ripped it off and flung it down the stairs. 'You want to see what the "Keeper" did to me?'

He staggered down the steps towards Tennison. Dalton tensed, about to dive up, thinking he was about to attack her. But Jason turned around, showing the pale scars on his skinny back. Tennison touched his shoulder, and moved her hand gently down the hard ridges of puckered flesh. 'I will make him pay, Jason, I promise you . . .'

Jason slowly turned, and Tennison could barely tolerate the desolate anguish in his eyes. The buried pain, the torment of those years, was even worse than the horrible scars. His lips trembled, but he couldn't speak. He bowed his head and nodded mutely, his hair hanging down over his bare white shoulders.

Tennison went down. Hunched inside, her throat dry and tight, she heard his agonised whisper, swirled by the breeze down the concrete stairwell. '*Keeper of Souls . . . Keeper of Souls*'.

Bronwen stood by the car, the rear door open. 'We'll only just make your train.'

Drained of all energy, Tennison tossed her briefcase inside. She turned, holding the door, taking one last look back at the godforsaken place. She clutched her throat. Jason was balanced on the edge of the balcony, his arms spread wide, exposing his ribcage, the narrow chest. He swayed forward.

'Jason! No!' Tennison's cry was shrill, almost a screech. 'No!'

He fell, a pale blur, turning over in the air, and they heard his body hit the ground, a soft moist sound, hidden behind a concrete parapet. Dalton raced across the scrubby patch of mud and scrambled over the wall. Tennison, in her heeled boots, struggled up the slope. She gripped the wall and craned to see over. Dalton was kneeling by the crumpled body, feeling for his pulse. He lifted the eyelids, searching for a reflex. Very gently he cupped Jason's head in his hands, and looked towards Tennison

Badly hurt, but he wasn't dead. Tennison knew that because the boy was weeping; she could see the tears streaming down his cheeks from his closed eyes.

She closed her own eyes and rested her forehead against the rough grey concrete. Tears smarted her eyes, but she wouldn't cry. She refused to cry. She held on to the emotion, hoarding it, needing it like a fix, feeding her the strength for what she had to do.

Acknowledgements

The Editor is grateful to the following authors, publishers and agents for permission to include the copyright stories in this collection: Watkins/Loomis Agency Inc for 'A Man Called Falcon' by Michael Arlen; Davis Publications Inc for 'The Man Who Swallowed A Horse' by Craig Rice, 'Dover Does Some Spadework' by Joyce Porter, and 'Hildegarde Withers is Back' by Stuart Palmer; Pocket Books Inc for 'The Stranger in Church' by Jack Webb; The Naldrett Press for 'The Traffic in Damnation' by Robert Fabian; BBC Enterprises for 'PC Crawford's First Pinch' by Ted Willis; H.S.D. Publications Inc for 'A Little Push From Cappy Fleers' by Gilbert Ralston, and 'The Man in the Lobby' by Richard Levinson & William Link; Bailey Brothers & Swinfen Ltd for 'The Flushing of Al Capone' by Eliot Ness; Harper's Magazine for 'Dressing Up' by W.R. Burnett; Random Publishing Group for 'Mobile Commandos' by Troy Kennedy Martin; Atlas Publications for 'What's A Ghoul Like You Doing In A Place Like This?' by Peter Leslie; John Farquharson Ltd for 'Sadie When She Died' by Ed McBain; Ziff-Davis Publishing Company for 'Man in the Dark' by Roy Huggins; The Estate of Jeffrey Farnol for 'Footprints' by Jeffrey Farnol; Cassell plc for 'The Man in the Inverness Cape' by Baroness Orczy; Random House for 'Poor, Poor Ophelia' by Carolyn Weston, and 'One of Those Days' by William Blinn; MCA Publishing for 'The Way of a Cop' by Abby Mann; Weidenfeld & Nicolson for 'Regan and the Stripper' by Joe Balham; Mirror Group Newspapers for 'The Christmas Killer' by Dennis Spooner and 'One Good Turn' by Leon Griffiths; Creative Licensing Corporation for 'The John Detail' by Serita Stevens; Mainstream Publishing for 'Taggart and a Bit of Skulduggery' by Peter Cave; Bantam Books for 'All A Matter of

Balance' by Jimmy Nail; Victor Gollancz Ltd for 'I Can Find My Way Out' by Ngaio Marsh; Reed Consumer Books for 'The Keeper of Souls' by Lynda La Plante. While every effort has been made to contact the copyright holders of the stories in this book, in the case of any accidental infringement, concerned parties are asked to contact the Editor in care of the publishers.